WORLD
MARKET
SHARE
REPORTER

ISSN 1078-6783

WORLD MARKET SHARE REPORTER

A Compilation of Reported World Market Share Data and Rankings on Companies, Products, and Services

2001-2002

Robert S. Lazich

GALE GROUP

THOMSON LEARNING

Detroit • New York • San Diego • San Francisco
Boston • New Haven, Conn. • Waterville, Maine
London • Munich

Robert S. Lazich, *Editor*

Editorial Code & Data, Inc. Staff

Susan Turner, *Associate Editor*
Joyce Piwowarski, *Programmer/Analyst*

Gale Group Staff

Eric Hoss, *Coordinating Editor*

Dorothy Maki, *Manufacturing Manager*
Nekita McKee, *Buyer*

Kenn Zorn, *Product Design Manager*
Mike Logusz, *Graphic Artist*

TABLE OF CONTENTS

TABLE OF TOPICS

The *Table of Topics* lists all topics used in *World Market Share Reporter* in alphabetical order. One or more page references follow each topic; the page references identify the starting point where the topic is shown. The same topic name may be used under different SICs; therefore, in some cases, more than one page reference is provided.

INTRODUCTION

World Market Share Reporter (WMSR) is a compilation of global market share data from periodical literature. *WMSR* is modeled after the popular Gale business title, *Market Share Reporter*. As shown by reviews of previous editions of *MSR*, plus correspondence and telephone contact with many users, this is a unique resource for competitive analysis, diversification planning, marketing research, and other forms of economic and policy analysis.

Features of the fifth edition of *WMSR* include:

- Over 1,600 entries.
- Coverage of the period 1995 through 2000.
- More than 210 geographic locations the world over, including countries, regions, and cities.
- SIC classification, with entries arranged under 433 SIC codes.
- International SIC (ISIC) and Harmonized Code classifications of many entries.
- Corporate, brand, product, service, and commodity market shares.
- Coverage of private and public sector activities.
- Comprehensive indexes, including products, companies, brands, places, sources, and SICs.
- Table of Topics showing topical subdivisions of chapters with page references.
- Graphics.

WMSR is a one-of-a-kind resource for ready reference, marketing research, economic analysis, planning, and a host of other disciplines.

Categories of Market Shares

Entries in *World Market Share Reporter* fall into four broad categories. Items were included if they showed the relative strengths of participants in a market or provided subdivisions of economic activity in some manner that could assist the analyst.

- **Corporate market shares** show the names of companies that participate in an industry, produce a product, or provide a service. Each company's market share is shown as a percent of total industry or product sales for a defined period, usually a year. In some cases, the company's share represents the share of the sales of the companies shown (group total)—because shares of the total market were not cited in the source or were not relevant. The shares of not-for-profit organizations in some economic or service functions also fall under this heading. In some corporate share tables, brand information appears behind company names in parentheses. In these cases, the tables can be located using either the company or the brand index.

- **Institutional shares** are like corporate shares but show the shares of other kinds of organizations. The most common institutional entries in *WMSR* display the shares of states, provinces, or regions in an activity.

- **Brand market shares** are similar to corporate shares with the difference that brand names are shown. Brand names include equivalent categories such as the names of television programs, magazines, publishers' imprints, etc. In some cases, the names of corporations appear in parentheses behind the brand name; in these cases, tables can be located using either the brand or the company index.

- **Product, commodity, service, and facility shares** feature a broad category (e.g., household appliances) and show how the category is subdivided into components (e.g., refrigerators, ranges, washing machines, dryers, and dishwashers). Entries under this category cover products (autos, lawnmowers, polyethylene, etc.), commodities (cattle, grains, crops), services (telephone, health care), and facilities (port berths, hotels, etc.). Subdivisions may be products, categories of services (long-distance telephone, residential phone service), types of commodities (varieties of grain), size categories (e.g., horsepower ranges), modes (rail, air, barge), types of facilities (categories of hospitals, ports, and the like), or other subdivisions.

- **Other shares**. *WMSR* includes a number of entries that show subdivisions, breakdowns, and shares that do not fit neatly into the above categorizations but properly belong in such a book because they shed light on public policy, foreign trade, and other subjects of general interest. These items include subdivisions of governmental expenditures, environmental issues, and the like.

Coverage

The fifth edition of *World Market Share Reporter* covers the entire range of economic activities on a global basis.

Geographic Coverage. *WMSR's* geographic coverage is the world outside North America. North American market shares (Canada, United States, and Mexico) will be found in Market Share Reporter.

Industrial Coverage. Material in *WMSR* includes items within the full range of Standard Industrial Classifications (SICs). In addition items of general interest difficult to classify by SIC code are also included (e.g., foreign trade and consumer spending).

WMSR reports on *published* market shares rather than attempting exhaustive coverage of all markets, products, or commodities. Despite this limitation, *WMSR* holds share information on more than 3,500 companies, 900 brands, and 1,270 product, commodity, service, and facility categories. Several entries are usually available for each industry group in the SIC classification.

WMSR reflects the current concerns of the business press. In addition to being a source of market share data, it mirrors journalistic preoccupations, issues in the business community, and events abroad. Important and controversial industries and activities command the most attention. Heavy coverage is provided in those areas that are—

- large, important, basic (autos, chemicals)
- on the leading edge of technological change (computers, electronics, software)
- frequently traded commodities (minerals, grain)
- in the media because of new product introductions, mergers and acquisitions, lawsuits, foreign trade importance, and for other newsworthy reasons
- popular issues (environment, crime)
- extensive coverage in the trade press

In many cases, several entries are provided on a subject each citing the same companies. No attempt was made to eliminate such seeming duplication if the publishing and/or original sources were different and the market shares were not identical. Those who work with such data know that market share reports are often little more than the "best guesses" of knowledgeable observers rather than precise measurements. To the planner or analyst, variant reports about an industry's market shares are useful for interpreting the data.

Publications appearing in the June 1998 to June 2001 period were used in preparing *WMSR*. As a rule, material on market share data for 2000 were used by preference; in response to reader requests, we have included historical data when available. In some instances, information for earlier years was included if the category was unique or if the earlier year was necessary for context. In a few other cases, projections for 2001 and later years were also included.

Organization of Chapters

World Market Share Reporter is organized into chapters by 2-digit SIC categories (industry groups). The exception is the first chapter, entitled *General Interest and Broad Topics*; this chapter holds all entries that bridge two or more 2-digit SIC industry codes (e.g., packaging, media firms, and luxury goods, etc.) and cannot, therefore, be classified using the SIC system without distortion. Please note, however, that a topic in this chapter will often have one or more additional entries later—where the table could be assigned to a detailed industry. Thus, in addition to a tabls on food packaging in the first chapter, numerous tables appear later on glass containers, metal cans, etc.

Within each chapter, entries are shown by 4-digit SIC (industry level). Within blocks of 4-digit SIC entries, entries are sorted alphabetically by topic, then alphabetically by title.

SICs and Topics

WMSR's SIC classifications are based on the coding as defined in the *Standard Industrial Classification Manual* for 1987, issued by the Bureau of the Census, Department of Commerce. This 1987 classification system introduced significant revisions to the 1972 classification (as slightly modified in 1977).

The closest appropriate 4-digit SIC was assigned to each table. In many cases, a 3-digit SIC had to be used because the substance of the table was broader than the nearest 4-digit SIC category. Such SICs always end with a zero. In other cases, the closest classification possible was at the 2-digit level; these SICs terminate with double-zero. If the content of the table did not fit the 2-digit level, it was assigned to the first chapter of *WMSR* and classified by topic only.

Topic assignments are based on terminology for commodities, products, industries, and services in the *SIC Manual*; however, in many cases phrasing has been simplified, shortened, or updated; in general, journalistically succinct rather than bureaucratically exhaustive phraseology was used throughout.

International Industrial Classification

Where applicable, *World Market Share Reporter* entries are supplied with 4-digit classification codes from the International Industrial Standard Classification (ISIC) coding system, developed by the United Nations. The codes were assigned from *Series M, No. 4, Rev. 3*.

Where applicable, 2-digit chapter codes were assigned to the entries from the Harmonized Commodity Description and Coding System of the Customs Co-Operation Council in Brussels. Because the coding rules do not allow for assigning a general classification as does the U.S. Standard Industrial Classification (for instance SIC 2000 includes both meat and cereal products), entries were coded consistently at the 2-digit level, wherever possible. Because the Harmonized system is used for the classification of commodities, codes will be missing for areas such as transportation, services, and civic affairs.

Coverage of industrial classifications for each of the international coding systems is provided in separate appendices at the back of the book.

Organization of Entries

Entries are organized in a uniform manner. A sample entry is provided in the next column. Explanations for each part of an entry, shown in boxes, are provided below and on the facing page.

1   *Entry Number.* A numeral between star symbols. Used for locating an entry from the index.

2   *Topic.* Second line, small type. Gives the broad or general product or service category of the entry.

3   *Industrial Codes.* Third line, small type, follows the topic. This line consists of a Standard Industrial Classification (SIC) code, followed where applicable by an International Standard Industrial Classification (ISIC) code, followed where applicable by a Harmonized Commodity (HC) code.

General entries in the first chapter do not have any industrial codes.

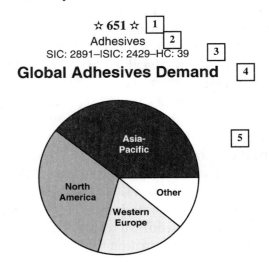

★ 651 ★ **1**

Adhesives **2**

SIC: 2891–ISIC: 2429–HC: 39 **3**

Global Adhesives Demand **4**

5

Demand is shown in millions of dollars. **6**

	1999	2004	Share **7**
Asia-Pacific	$ 4,886	$ 6,500	39.16%
North America	4,535	5,210	31.39
Western Europe	2,644	3,030	18.25 **8**
Other	1,450	1,860	11.20

Source: *Research Studies*, January 8, 2001, p. 1, from Freedonia Group. **9**

4   *Title.* Third line, large type. Describes the entry with a headline.

5   *Graphic.* When a graphic is present, it follows the title. Some entries will be illustrated with a pie or bar chart. The information used to create the graphic is always shown below the pie or bar chart.

6   *Note Block.* When present, follows the title and is in italic type. The note provides contextual information about the entry to make the data more understandable. Special notes about the data, information about time periods covered, market totals, and other comments are provided. Self-explanatory entries do not have a note block.

7 | *Column Headers*. Follow the note block. Some entries have more than one column or the single column requires a header. In these cases, column headers are used to describe information covered in the column. In most cases, column headers are years (1999) or indicators of type and magnitude ($ mil.). Column headers are shown only when necessary for clarity of presentation.

8 | *Body*. Follows the note block or the column header and shows the actual data in two or more columns. In most cases, individual rows of data in the body are arranged in descending order, with the largest market share holder heading the list. Collective shares, usually labelled "Others" are placed last.

9 | *Source*. Follows the body. All entries cite the source of the table, the date of publication, and the page number (if given). In many cases, the publisher obtained the information from another source (original source); in all such cases, the original source is also shown.

Continued Entries. Entries that extend over two adjacent columns on the same page are not marked to indicate continuation but continue in the second column. Entries that extend over two pages are marked *Continued on the next page*. Entries carried over from the previous page repeat the entry number, topic (followed by the word *continued*), in-

dustrial codes, title, and column header (if any).

Use of Names

The editors reproduced company names as they appeared in the source unless it was clearly evident from the name and the context that a name had been misspelled in the original. Large companies, of course, tend to appear in a large number of entries and in variant renditions. General Electric Corporation may appear as GE, General Electric, General Electric Corp., GE Corp., and other variants. No attempt was made to enforce a uniform rendition of names in the entries. In the Company Index, variant renditions were reduced to a single version or cross-referenced.

Use of Numbers

Throughout *WMSR*, tables showing percentage breakdowns may add to less than 100 or fractionally more than 100 due to rounding. In those cases where only a few leading participants in a market are shown, the total of the shares may be substantially less than 100.

Numbers in the note block showing the total size of the market are provided with as many significant digits as possible in order to permit the user to calculate the sales of a particular company by multiplying the market total by the market share.

In a relatively small number of entries, actual unit or dollar information is provided rather than share information in percent. In such cases, the denomination of the unit (tons, gallons, $) and its magnitude (000 indicates multiply by 1,000; mil., multiply by 1,000,000) are mentioned in the note block or shown in the column header.

Data in some entries are based on different kinds of currencies and different weight and liquid measures. Where necessary, the unit is identified in the note block or in the column header. Examples are long tons, short tons, metric tons or Canadian dollars, etc.

Graphics

Pie and bar charts are used to illustrate some of the entries. The graphics show the names of companies, products, and services when they fit on the charts. When room is insufficient to accommodate the label, the first word of a full name is used followed by three periods (...) to indicate omission of the rest of the label.

In the case of bar charts, the largest share is always the width of the column, and smaller shares are drawn in proportion. Two bar charts, consequently, should not be compared to one another.

Sources

The majority of entries were extracted from newspapers and from general purpose, trade, and technical periodicals normally available in larger public, special, or university libraries. All told, 1112 sources were used; of these, 656 were primary print sources. Many more were reviewed but lacked coverage of the subject. These primary sources, in turn, used 466 original sources.

In many cases, the primary source in which the entry was published cites another source for the data, the original source. Original sources include other publications, brokerage houses, consultancies and research organizations, associations, government agencies, special surveys, and the like.

Many sources have also been used from the World Wide Web. The citation includes the Web address, the date the article was retrieved, and, if possible, the title of the article or report. In many cases Web pages have no title or author name. As well, it is not uncommon for Web pages to be moved or temporarily out of operation.

Since many primary sources appear as original sources elsewhere, and vice-versa, primary and original sources are shown in a single Source Index under two headings. Primary sources included in *WMSR* almost always used the market share data as illustrative material for narratives covering many aspects of the subject. We hope that this book will also serve as a guide to those articles.

Indexes

World Market Share Reporter features five indexes and a two appendices.

- **Source Index**. This index holds 1112 references in two groupings. *Primary sources* (656) are publications where the data were found. *Original sources* (466) are sources cited in the primary sources. Each item in the index is followed by one or more entry numbers arranged sequentially, beginning with the first mention of the source.

- **Place Names Index**. This index provides references to 210 countries, regions, and cities, the world over. References are to entry numbers.

- **Products, Services, and Issues Index**. This index holds more than 1,260 references to products and services in alphabetical order. The index also lists subject categories that do not fit the definition of a product or service but properly belong in the index. Examples include *budgets, conglomerates, crime, defense spending, economies, lotteries*, and the like. Some listings are abbreviations for chemical substances, computer software, etc. which may not be meaningful to those unfamiliar with the industries. Wherever possible, the full name is also provided for abbreviations commonly in use. Each listing is followed by one or more references to entry numbers.

- **Company Index**. This index shows references to more than 3,500 company names by entry number. Companies are arranged in alphabetical order. In some cases, the market share table from which the company name was derived showed the share for a combination of two or more companies; these combinations are reproduced in the index.

- **Brand Index**. This index shows references to more than 900 brands by entry number. The arrangement is alphabetical. Brands include names of publications, computer software, operating systems, etc., as well as the more conventional brand names (e.g. Coca Cola and Persil).

Appendix I

- **SIC Coverage**. The first appendix shows SICs covered by *World Market Share Reporter*. The listing shows major SIC groupings at the 2-digit level as bold-face headings followed by 4-digit SIC numbers, the names of the SIC, and a *page* reference (rather than a reference to an entry number, as in the indexes). The page shows the first occurrence of the SIC in the book. *WMSR*'s SIC coverage is quite comprehensive, as shown in the appendix. However, many 4-digit SIC categories are further divided into major product

groupings. Not all of these have corresponding entries in the book.

- **ISIC Coverage**. This section of the appendix provides a listing of the International Standard Industrial Classification (ISIC) codes that appear in *World Market Share Reporter*. The listing shows ISIC groupings at the 4-digit level along with the names of the industries. Page numbers of first instances are not shown for international classifications because entries in *WMSR* are arranged by SIC and there is no one-to-one correspondence between the codes. Thus, an ISIC may occur variably, rather than in a consecutive number of entries.

- **HC Coverage**. This section provides a listing of the Harmonized Commodity classifications that appear in *WMSR*. The listing shows industrial groupings at the 2-digit, or chapter, level along with the names of the industries. Page numbers of first instances are not shown for international classifications because entries in *WMSR* are arranged by SIC and there is no one-to-one correspondence between the codes. Thus a Harmonized Code may occur variably, rather than in a consecutive number of entries.

Appendix II

- **Annotated Source List**. This second appendix provides a list of publishers' names, addresses, telephone and fax numbers and publication frequency of primary sources in *World Market Share Reporter,* 5th Edition.

Acknowledgements

World Market Share Reporter is something of a collective enterprise that involves not only the editorial team but also many users who share comments, criticisms, and suggestions over the telephone. Their help and encouragement are very much appreciated. *WMSR* could not have been produced without the help of many people in and outside of Gale Group. The editors would like to express their special appreciation to Mr. Eric Hoss (Coordinating Editor, Gale Group) and to the staff of Editorial Code and Data, Inc.

Comments and Suggestions

Comments on *WMSR* or suggestions for improvement of its usefulness, format, and coverage are always welcome. Although every effort is made to maintain accuracy, errors may occasionally occur; the editors will be grateful if these are called to their attention. Please contact:

Editors
World Market Share Reporter
The Gale Group
27500 Drake Rd.
Farmington Hills, MI 48331-3535
Phone: (248) 699-GALE or (800) 347-GALE
Fax: (248) 699-8069

General Interest and Broad Topics

★ 1 ★
Contraception

Contraception Use Worldwide

Only 1% in the United States use intrauterine devices.

Female sterilization 32.0%
Intrauterine devices 22.0
Oral contraceptives 14.0
Condoms 7.0
Male sterilization 7.0
Injectable 3.0
Other 15.0

Source: *Med Ad News*, March 2001, p. 36, from Ortho-McNeil Pharmaceutical.

★ 2 ★
Duty-Free Industry

Duty-Free Industry Leaders

Market shares are shown in percent. Cigarettes are the leader in a $20 billion industry.

DFS Group 6.8%
Nuance Global Traders 6.5
Gebr. Heinemann 5.5
World Duty Free PLC 5.5
Weitnauer Trading Co. 4.4
Other 71.3

Source: *International Herald Tribune*, November 13, 2000, p. 21.

★ 3 ★
Duty-Free Industry

Duty-Free Industry Worldwide

Market shares are shown in percent.

	2000	2010
Luxury goods	40.3%	49.3%
Perfumes & cosmetics	23.8	22.1
Wines & spirits	18.5	13.7
Tobacco goods	9.7	7.7
Confectionery & fine foods	7.7	7.2

Source: *Travel Retailer International*, October 2000, p. 139.

★ 4 ★
Flooring

Largest Flooring Makers, 1998

Companies are ranked by sales in millions of dollars.

Shaw Industries . . . . $ 3,542
Mohawk 2,639
Armstrong 2,075
Tarkett Sommer 1,528
Beaulieu of America 1,500

Continued on next page.

★ 4 ★
[Continued]
Flooring

Largest Flooring Makers, 1998

Companies are ranked by sales in millions of dollars.

Interface . . . . $ 780
Forbo 735
Oriental Weavers 600
Collins & Aikman 574
Burlington 490

Source: *Floor Focus*, August-September 1999, p. 1.

★ 5 ★
Gardening

Gardening Products Sector in Japan

Market sizes are shown in billions of yen. Domestic products have the largest share of the market here. Import leaders are watering cans, pruning shears and shovels.

	(bil.)	Share
Garden care	133.0	35.0%
Garden decoration	106.4	28.0
Garden maintenance	49.4	13.0
Garden plants	49.4	13.0
Electric power tools	19.0	5.0
Garden furniture	19.0	5.0
Other	3.8	1.0

Source: *Jetro Japanese Market Report*, March 1999, p. 5.

★ 6 ★
Luxury Goods

Luxury Goods Sales, 2005

Total sales reached $120 billion.

Health care and prescriptions 28.0%
Groceries and supplies 24.0
Beauty 21.0
Gourmet food and wine 18.0
Pet supplies 9.0

Source: *PC Magazine*, March 7, 2000, p. 81, from ActivMedia Research.

★ 7 ★
Media

Largest Media/Entertainment Firms

Firms are ranked by revenues for the four quarters ended June 2000.

AOL/Time Warner . . . . $ 41.0
Disney 24.8
Vivendi/Seagram 16.6
Bertelsmann 14.8
Viacom 14.8
News Corp. 14.1
Sony 10.8

Source: *New York Times*, November 13, 2000, p. C19, from Bloomberg Financial Markets.

★ 8 ★
Packaging

Top Packagers in the Slovak Republic

Firms are ranked by 1998 income in millions of tolars.

Valkarton D.D. Logatec	5.5
Plutal Ljubljana	3.2
Tespack D.O.O. Brestanica	3.0
Saturnus Embalaza D.D. Ljubljana	2.2
Tuba Ljubljana	1.5
Makoter D.O.O. Cven	1.3
Plastik Kanal Ob Soci	1.1
Gep Kartonaza Embalaza D.O.O.	1.0
KTL Navita Embalaza D.O.O. Ljubljana	1.0
Valkarton Potiskana Embalaza D.O.O.	1.0

Source: *Slovenian Business Report*, Summer 1999, p. 51.

★ 9 ★
Pets

Pet Population in Italy

Data show population. The Italian pet products market is the fastest growing in Europe, and is the fourth largest overall. One quarter of families own at least one dog or cat.

	(mil.)	Share
Ornamental fish	28.0	49.7%
Birds	13.0	23.1
Cats	7.0	12.4
Dogs	6.2	11.1
Rodents	1.2	2.1
Reptiles	0.9	1.6

Source: *Market Europe*, July 2000, p. 6, from U.S. Commercial Service Report.

★ 10 ★
Research

Largest R&D Spenders

Total investments are shown in billions of dollars for 1999.

United States	$ 247.2
Japan	92.4
Germany	43.2
France	27.8
United Kingdom	23.5
Korea	16.9
Italy	13.2
Canada	12.7
Netherlands	7.3
Sweden	6.8

Source: *Industry Standard*, November 13, 2000, p. 179, from OECD Science.

★ 11 ★
Sex

Global Sex Industry, 1998

The table shows a rough estimate of the legal sex business. While illegal prostitution is not included, statistics on the industry are now being included in European Union Statistics. Illegal prostitution is a 2 billion British pound a year business in Britain. Sex clubs generally refer to the 2,500 strip clubs in the U.S. Cable, satellite and pay-per-view refer to Adam & Eve, The Spice Channel and hotel channels. Illicit markets are not included.

	Sales ($ bil.)	Share
Adult videos	$ 20.0	35.71%
Escort services	11.0	19.64
Magazines	7.5	13.39
Sex clubs	5.0	8.93
Phone sex	4.5	8.04
Cable/satellite/pay-per-view TV	2.5	4.46
CD-ROM/DVD-ROM	1.5	2.68
Internet (sales and memberships)	1.5	2.68
Novelties	1.0	1.79
Other	1.5	2.68

Source: *Forbes*, June 14, 1999, p. 218, from Private Media Group Inc.

★ 12 ★
Siding

Siding Materials Market in Turkey

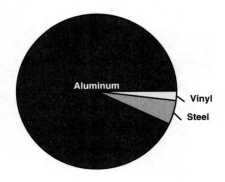

The construction sector ranks third in the Turkish economy.

	($ mil.)	Share
Aluminum	$ 268	93.0%
Steel	14	5.0
Vinyl	5	2.0

Source: "Turkey: Roofing and Siding Materials."
Retrieved September 19, 2000 from the World Wide Web:
http://www.tradeport.org.

SIC 01 - Agricultural Production - Crops

★ 13 ★
Produce
SIC: 0100–ISIC: 0111–HC: 012

Largest Produce Firms in the U.K.

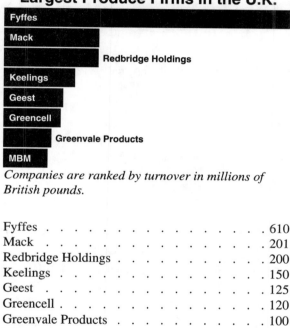

Companies are ranked by turnover in millions of British pounds.

Fyffes	610
Mack	201
Redbridge Holdings	200
Keelings	150
Geest	125
Greencell	120
Greenvale Products	100
MBM	92

Source: ''Fruit and Vegetables Industry.'' Retrieved November 9, 1999 from the World Wide Web: http://www.just-food.com.

★ 14 ★
Grain
SIC: 0110–ISIC: 0111–HC: 12

Leading Cereal Grain Producers

Production of wheat, barley and oats are shown in thousands of tons.

	Tons	Share
China	119,050	16.12%
India	72,246	9.78
United States	70,920	9.60
Canada	43,688	5.92
Australia	27,132	3.67
United Kingdom	21,920	2.97
Ukraine	20,618	2.79
Argentina	15,285	2.07
Poland	13,899	1.88
Other	333,717	45.19

Source: *Forest Products Journal*, January 2001, p. 16, from FAO.

★ 15 ★
Rice
SIC: 0112–ISIC: 1320–HC: 26

Top Rice Producers

Data are in millions of tons.

China	192.9
India	122.2
Indonesia	46.2
Bangladesh	28.2
Vietnam	27.6

Continued on next page.

★ 15 ★

[Continued]
Rice
SIC: 0112–ISIC: 1320–HC: 26

Top Rice Producers

Data are in millions of tons.

Thailand	23.2
Myanmar	16.6
Japan	12.5
Philippines	10.0

Source: *The Unesco Courier*, June 1999, p. 48, from FAOSTAT Database.

★ 16 ★

Corn
SIC: 0115–ISIC: 0111–HC: 12

Largest Corn Consumers

Nearly 24 million bushels were produced worldwide. Figures are in millions of bushels.

United States	7.70
China	4.70
European Union	1.60
Brazil	1.40
Mexico	0.95

Source: *USA TODAY*, May 31, 2000, p. A1, from U.S. Agricultural Department, Foreign Agricultural Service.

★ 17 ★

Corn
SIC: 0115–ISIC: 0111–HC: 12

Maize Seed Market in Argentina

Market shares are shown in percent.

Cargill	45.0%
Novartis	34.0
Pioneer	17.0
Dow	2.0
Other	2.0

Source: *El Cronista*, August 7, 2000, p. 1.

★ 18 ★

Corn
SIC: 0115–ISIC: 0111–HC: 12

Top Corn Seed Producers in Brazil

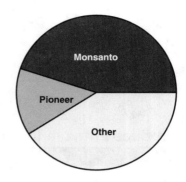

Market shares are shown in percent.

Monsanto	45.0%
Pioneer	14.0
Other	41.0

Source: *Valor Economico*, August 1, 2000, p. B12.

★ 19 ★

Soybeans
SIC: 0116–ISIC: 0111–HC: 12

Largest Soybean Producers, 1998

Data are in metric tons.

	mt	Share
United States	75.030	47.4%
Brazil	31.360	19.8
Argentina	18.720	11.8
Parana	7.130	4.5
Rio Grande do Sul	6.662	4.2
Other	33.220	21.0

Source: *Soybean Digest*, August 1999, p. 37, from FAO CONAB.

★ 20 ★
Soybeans
SIC: 0116–ISIC: 0111–HC: 12

Largest Soybean Producers in South America

Production is shown in millions of bushels.

	(mil.)	Share
Brazil	1,099.98	59.35%
Argentina	648.99	35.01
Paraguay	104.50	5.64

Source: *Soybean Digest*, January 2000, p. 70, from NorthStar.

★ 21 ★
Soybeans
SIC: 0116–ISIC: 0111–HC: 12

Soya Seed Market in Argentina

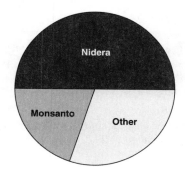

Market shares are shown in percent.

Nidera	50.0%
Monsanto	20.0
Other	30.0

Source: *El Cronista*, August 7, 2000, p. 1.

★ 22 ★
Crops
SIC: 0130–ISIC: 0111–HC: 12

Transgenic Crop Production Worldwide

Crops are ranked by millions of acres under cultivation. The United States is the leading producer, with 70.9 million acres under cultivation, followed by Argentina with 16.5 million and Canada with 9.9 million.

	1998	1999
Soybeans	35.8	53.4
Corn	20.5	27.4
Cotton	6.2	9.1
Canola	5.9	8.4
Potatoes	0.3	0.3

Source: *Wired*, March 2000, p. 130, from International Service for the Acquisition of Agri-biotech Applications.

★ 23 ★
Seeds
SIC: 0130–ISIC: 0111–HC: 12

Largest Seed Making Firms

Firms are ranked by 1998 seed sales in billions of dollars.

DuPont	$ 1.85
Monsanto	1.25
Syngenta	1.00
Limagrain	0.79
Seminis	0.43
Advanta	0.41
KWS	0.38
Dow	0.22

Source: *Financial Times*, December 3, 1999, p. 13, from Primark Datastream and Wood Mackenzie.

★ 24 ★
Cotton
SIC: 0131–ISIC: 0111–HC: 12

Largest Cotton Producers

Data are in millions of 480-lb bales for 1999-2000.

China	19.0
United States	18.3
India	12.7
Pakistan	7.0
Uzbekistan	5.0
African Zone	4.3
Turkey	3.8
Australia	3.2
Brazil	2.1

Source: *Textile Asia*, October 1999, p. 131, from United States Department of Agriculture.

★ 25 ★
Potatos
SIC: 0134–ISIC: 0111–HC: 07

Largest Potato Producers, 1998

Potatos are the main source of food, second only to wheat. More than 1 billion people eat potatos worldwide. Data are in millions of tons.

China	47.8
Russia	31.3
Poland	25.9
United States	21.3
India	19.2
Ukraine	17.5
Germany	12.1
Belarus	10.0
Netherlands	7.7
United Kingdom	6.5

Source: "Canadian Potato Crop." retrieved June 14, 1999 from the World Wide Web: http://www.agr/ca/misb/hort/potato.html, from FAO of the United States.

★ 26 ★
Fruit
SIC: 0170–ISIC: 0113–HC: 08

Largest Fruit Crops Worldwide, 1997

Oranges
Bananas
Grapes
Apples
Watermelons
Coconuts
Plantains
Mangoes
Clementines, tangerines, satsumas
Pears

Production is shown in millions of tons.

Oranges	66.4
Bananas	63.8
Grapes	63.1
Apples	60.3
Watermelons	51.2
Coconuts	50.7
Plantains	32.7
Mangoes	24.2
Clementines, tangerines, satsumas	17.1
Pears	14.4

Source: *Christian Science Monitor*, April 29, 1999, p. 24, from *Top 10 of Everything 1999*.

★ 27 ★
Apples
SIC: 0175–ISIC: 0113–HC: 08

Leading Apple Producers, 1997

Countries are ranked by production in billions of pounds.

China	37.7
United States	10.2
Turkey	5.2
France	4.2
Iran	4.2

Source: *Detroit News*, April 4, 1999, p. C1.

★ 28 ★
Bananas
SIC: 0175–ISIC: 0113–HC: 08

Banana Industry in Europe

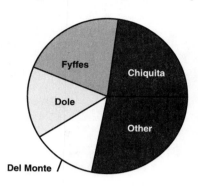

A total of 4.3 million tons were imported into Europe in 2000. There has been a trade war brewing recently, with Europe maintaining import quotas to protect the small nations (and former colonies, often) where the fruit is grown. The United States wants unrestricted trade.

Chiquita	23.0%
Fyffes	21.0
Dole	15.0
Del Monte	13.0
Other	28.0

Source: *New York Times*, February 7, 2001, p. W1, from Goodbody Stockbrokers.

★ 29 ★
Bananas
SIC: 0175–ISIC: 0113–HC: 08

Banana Sales in the U.K., 2000

Sales are for the year ended May 2, 2000. Tesco claims 22.5% share of the banana retail market.

	(mil.)	Share
Loose	381.84	87.35%
Prepackaged	55.30	12.65

Source: *The Grocer*, July 8, 2000, p. 1, from Taylor Nelson Sofres Superpanel.

★ 30 ★
Bananas
SIC: 0175–ISIC: 0113–HC: 08

Largest Banana Consumers in Europe

Consumption is shown in thousands of tons.

Germany	1,114
United Kingdom	675
Italy	460
France	450
Spain	450
Portugal	162
Sweden	142
Netherlands	130
Austria	120
Belgium	94

Source: *Financial Times*, April 8, 1999, p. 4, from European Commission.

★ 31 ★
Fruit
SIC: 0175–ISIC: 0113–HC: 08

Saudi Arabia's Mango Market

Data show the source of the country's mangos.

Yemen	30.0%
Pakistan	20.0
India/Sudan	15.0
South Africa	5.0
Other	30.0

Source: *IPR Strategic Business Information Database*, May 10, 2001, p. NA, from *Al-Bayan*.

★ 32 ★
Prunes
SIC: 0175–ISIC: 0113–HC: 08

Prune Industry Worldwide

The fruit is losing market share each year with annual sales about $100 million.

Prune Board 70.0%
Other 30.0

Source: *Marketing*, September 25, 2000, p. 5.

★ 33 ★
Mushrooms
SIC: 0182–ISIC: 0112–HC: 07

Mushroom Consumption in Japan

Data are in tons.

Fresh shiitake 105,613
Bunashimeji 78,655
Maitake 36,850
Dried shittake 14,386
Matsutake 3,495

Source: ''Market Overview.'' Retrieved September 19, 2000 from the World Wide Web: http://www.jetro.go.jp.

SIC 02 - Agricultural Production - Livestock

Largest Broiler Firms in Turkey

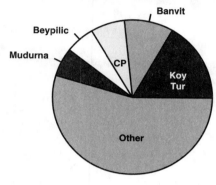

The industry has experienced enormous growth over the last ten years, with a 7% growth in 1999 and a 20% growth in white meat production. Market shares are shown in percent.

Koy Tur	17.0%
Banvit	10.0
CP	6.5
Beypilic	6.0
Mudurna	6.0
Other	54.5

Source: *World Poultry*, no. 3, 2001, p. 12.

Largest Chicken Processors in Europe, 1998

Market shares are shown based on production.

Doux	8.0%
Grampian	6.0
Bourgoin	5.0
AIA Verona	3.0
Hillsdown	3.0
Pingo/Sada	3.0
Agrovic Tecna	2.0
Lohmann-Wesjohann	2.0
Scandinavian Poultry	2.0
Storteboom	2.0
Other	64.0

Source: *World Poultry*, no. 4, 1999, p. 31.

Largest Broiler Producing Countries

Production is shown in metric tons.

	(000)	Share
United States	13,367	32.9%
Brazil	5,526	13.6
China	5,500	13.6
Mexico	1,784	4.4
France	1,180	2.9
Other	13,235	32.6

Source: *World Poultry*, no. 2, 2001, p. 11, from United States Department of Agriculture.

★ 37 ★
Eggs
SIC: 0252–ISIC: 0122–HC: 04

Largest Hen Egg Producers

Countries are ranked by production in thousands of metric tons. The number of layers in the world is estimated to be 4.65 billion, with total egg production falling just short of 48 million metric tons (including hatching eggs).

	(000)	Share
China	17,814	37.13%
United States	4,724	9.85
Japan	2,580	5.38
Russian Federation	1,700	3.54
India	1,611	3.36
Mexico	1,422	2.96
Brazil	1,415	2.95
France	954	1.99
Germany	847	1.77
Other	14,913	31.08

Source: *Egg Industry*, July 1999, p. 4.

★ 38 ★
Poultry
SIC: 0253–ISIC: 0122–HC: 04

Largest Turkey Processors in Europe, 1998

Market shares are shown based on production.

AIA Verona	9.0%
Doux	8.0
Bernard Matthews	7.0
Bourgoin	5.0
Hillsdown	5.0
Nolke	5.0
Even	4.0
Sun Valley	3.0
Unicopa	3.0
Ronsard	2.0
Other	49.0

Source: *World Poultry*, no. 4, 1999, p. 31.

★ 39 ★
Farming
SIC: 0291–ISIC: 0130–HC: 03

Biotech Crops Worldwide

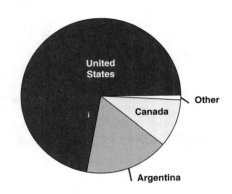

Data show where most crops were planted. Total biotech crop acreage was 98.6 million.

United States	72.0%
Argentina	17.0
Canada	10.0
Other	1.0

Source: *C&EN*, October 2, 2000, p. 25, from Intenational Service for the Acquisition of Agri-Biotech Applications.

★ **40** ★
Timber
SIC: 0811–ISIC: 0200–HC: 06

Largest Timber Tract Holders in Indonesia, 1998

The country has 64 million hectares of production forests and 51.4 million hectares which are divided into 421 concessions (HPHs). The HPHs include 326 held by private companies, 86 units held by joint ventures and 9 by state owned companies. The value of Indonesia's export of forest products is to reach $8.5 billion. The table lists the largest HPH holders, in millions of hectares.

Barito Pacific	3.01
Kayu Lapis Indonesia	2.73
Kalimanis	1.86
Alas Kusuma	1.54
Korindo	1.18
Bhudi Nusa	1.13
Djajanti Djaya	1.11
Probu	1.08
Waponga	1.03

Source: STAT-USA, *National Trade Data Bank*, February 2001, p. NA, from Department of Forestry and Plantations.

SIC 09 - Fishing, Hunting, and Trapping

★ 41 ★
Fish Farming
SIC: 0921–ISIC: 0122–HC: 03
Ornamental Fish Market, 2000

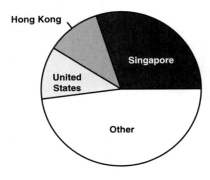

Market shares are shown in percent. Singapore exported $76 million in ornamental fish.

Singapore	30.0%
Hong Kong	11.0
United States	11.0
Other	48.0

Source: *Straits Times*, June 1, 2001, p. 12, from Agri-food and Veterinary Authority.

★ 42 ★
Fishing
SIC: 0971–ISIC: 0150–HC: 01
Largest Salmon Exporters in Chile

Shares are shown for the first quarter of the year.

Salmones Unimarc	7.1%
Salmones Tecmar	6.0
Salmones Multiexport	5.9
Other	81.0

Source: *Estrategia*, May 10, 2000, p. 1.

SIC 10 - Metal Mining

★ 43 ★
Iron
SIC: 1011–ISIC: 1310–HC: 26

Largest Iron Ore Producers

Shares are shown based on total production.

China	. 20.6%
Brazil	. 19.1
Australia	. 15.0
China	. 7.3
United States	. 6.2
Other	. 31.8

Source: "Summary of Mining Statistics." Retrieved June 18, 2001 from the World Wide Web: http://www.nma.org.

★ 44 ★
Copper
SIC: 1021–ISIC: 1320–HC: 26

Largest Copper Producers

Shares are shown based on total production.

Chile	. 30.6%
United States	. 15.2
Chile	. 6.4
Canada	. 5.8
Australia	. 5.0
Other	. 37.3

Source: "Summary of Mining Statistics." Retrieved June 18, 2001 from the World Wide Web: http://www.nma.org.

★ 45 ★
Zinc
SIC: 1031–ISIC: 1320–HC: 26

Largest Zinc Producing Mines, 1998

The top mines in the Western world are ranked by output in kiltons. The top 10 firms handle 49% of the western world's production.

Cominco	. 661,569
Noranda	. 367,958
Pasminco	. 302,345
MIM	. 248,577
Western Metals	. 225,679
Centromin	. 210,000
Hindustan Zinc	. 189,462
Grupo Mexico	. 180,218
Boliden	. 178,800
Outokumpu	. 172,800

Source: *Mining Engineering*, November 1999, p. 9.

★ 46 ★
Zinc
SIC: 1031–ISIC: 1320–HC: 26
Leading Zinc Producers

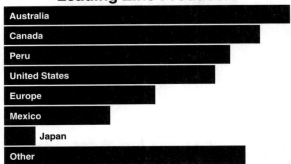

Data are in metric tons.

	mt	Share
Australia	1,110	19.06%
Canada	1,010	17.34
Peru	900	15.45
United States	815	13.99
Europe	590	10.13
Mexico	390	6.70
Japan	90	1.55
Other	920	15.79

Source: *Engineering & Mining Journal*, April 2000, p. 38, from ILZSG.

★ 47 ★
Gold
SIC: 1041–ISIC: 1320–HC: 26
Largest Gold Manufacturers

Firms are ranked by output in millions of troy ounces. Data are current as of December 1999.

AngloGold	6.92
Newmont Mining	4.18
Gold Fields	3.82
Barrick Gold	3.66
Placer Dome	3.10
Rio Tinto	2.98

Freeport McMoran	2.38
Homestake Mining	2.37
Normandy Mining	1.87
Ashanti	1.49

Source: *Financial Times*, June 14, 2000, p. 25, from Primark Datastream and World Gold Analyst.

★ 48 ★
Gold
SIC: 1041–ISIC: 1320–HC: 26
Largest Gold Producers

Shares are shown based on total production.

South Africa	18.9%
United States	14.9
Australia	12.7
China	7.2
Canada	6.7
Other	39.6

Source: "Summary of Mining Statistics." Retrieved June 18, 2001 from the World Wide Web: http://www.nma.org.

★ 49 ★
Silver
SIC: 1044–ISIC: 1320–HC: 26
Largest Silver Producers

Data are in tons.

	Tons	Share
Mexico	2,877	16.95%
Peru	2,024	11.93
United States	1,954	11.52
Australia	1,469	8.66
Chile	1,344	7.92
Soviet Union/CIS	1,302	7.67
China	1,190	7.01
Canada	1,125	6.63
Poland	1,119	6.59
Bolivia	406	2.39
Other	2,159	12.72

Source: *Mining Journal*, May 28, 1999, p. 26.

★ 50 ★
Silver
SIC: 1044–ISIC: 1320–HC: 26

Largest Silver Producing Firms, 2000

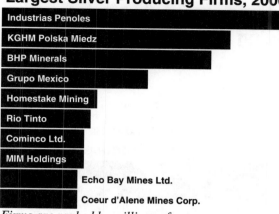

Firms are ranked by millions of ounces.

Industrias Penoles	44.7
KGHM Polska Miedz	36.0
BHP Minerals	32.5
Grupo Mexico	23.2
Homestake Mining	14.7
Rio Tinto	14.4
Cominco Ltd.	13.3
MIM Holdings	12.7
Echo Bay Mines Ltd.	12.3
Coeur d'Alene Mines Corp.	11.7

Source: ''Production.'' Retrieved June 18, 2001 from the World Wide Web: http://www.silverinstitute.org.

★ 51 ★
Cobalt
SIC: 1061–ISIC: 1310–HC: 26

Largest Cobalt Producers

Figures are in metric tons.

OMG	7,600
Gecamines	3,800
Falconbridge	3,400
Zambia	3,100

ICCI	2,920
INCO	1,650
QNI	1,440
Union Miniere	1,200

Source: *Engineering & Mining Journal*, March 2001, p. 45.

★ 52 ★
Palladium
SIC: 1099–ISIC: 1320–HC: 26

World Palladium Demand

Demand is shown in thousands of ounces.

	1998	2000	Share
Autocatalysts	4,715	6,254	65.53%
Electrical	2,075	1,700	17.81
Dental	1,230	1,000	10.48
Jewelry	235	250	2.62
Chemicals	230	240	2.51
Other	115	100	1.05

Source: *American Metal Market*, July 6, 2000, p. 10A, from Salomon Smith Barney.

★ 53 ★
Platinum
SIC: 1099–ISIC: 1320–HC: 26

Leading Platinum Suppliers

Data are in thousands of ounces.

	1999	2000	Share
South Africa	3,900	3,920	72.46%
Russia	540	1,100	20.33
North America	270	285	5.27
Other	160	105	1.94

Source: *Financial Times*, November 15, 2000, p. 32, from Johnson Matthey.

SIC 12 - Coal Mining

★ 54 ★

Coal

SIC: 1220–ISIC: 1000–HC: 27

Largest Coal Consumers, 1998

Data are in metric ton equivalent.

	M.t.	Share
China	619.8	29.11%
United States	533.7	25.06
India	153.6	7.21
Russia	102.8	4.83
South Africa	88.9	4.17
Japan	88.8	4.17
Germany	84.7	3.98
Poland	60.9	2.86
Australia	45.8	2.15
Untied Kingdom	40.7	1.91
Other	309.7	14.54

Source: *Mining Magazine*, September 1999, p. 181, from BP Statistical Review of World Energy.

★ 55 ★

Coal

SIC: 1220–ISIC: 1000–HC: 27

Largest Coal Producers

Shares are shown based on total production.

China	26.6%
United States	22.1
India	7.1
Russia	5.4
Australia	4.8
Other	34.0

Source: "Summary of Mining Statistics." Retrieved June 18, 2001 from the World Wide Web: http://www.nma.org.

★ 56 ★
Coal
SIC: 1220–ISIC: 1000–HC: 27

Leading Coal Producers

Market shares are shown in percent.

Peabody 13.0%
Arch Coal 10.0
Kennecott Energy & Coal 10.0
Consol 6.0
RAG American Coal 6.0
AEI Resources 5.0
Other 50.0

Source: *Financial Times*, May 21, 2001, p. 18, from RDI
Consulting.

SIC 13 - Oil and Gas Extraction

★ 57 ★
Oil
SIC: 1311–ISIC: 1110–HC: 27

Largest Oil Reserves

Saudi Arabia	
Iraq	
United Arab Emirates	
Kuwait	
Iran	
Venezuela	
	Russian Federation
Libya	
	United States

Proven reserves are shown in billions of barrels.

Saudi Arabia	263.5
Iraq	112.5
United Arab Emirates	97.8
Kuwait	96.5
Iran	89.7
Venezuela	72.6
Russian Federation	48.6
Libya	29.5
United States	28.6

Source: *Wall Street Journal*, March 14, 2001, p. A14, from U.S. Department of Energy.

★ 58 ★
Oil
SIC: 1311–ISIC: 1110–HC: 27

Largest Oil Processors in the Philippines

Market shares are shown in percent.

Petron	35.3%
Pilipinas Shell	33.2
Other	31.5

Source: *BusinessWorld (Philippines)*, December 7, 2000, p. 1.

★ 59 ★
Oil
SIC: 1311–ISIC: 1110–HC: 27

Oil Market in Pakistan

Market shares are shown in percent.

National Refining	45.0%
Pakistan Refining	36.7
Attock Refining	17.0
Other	1.3

Source: *Today's Refinery*, February 2000, p. 12.

★ 60 ★
Liquid Petroleum Gas
SIC: 1321–ISIC: 1110–HC: 27

Liquid Petroleum Gas Market in Europe, 1998

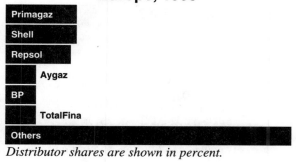

Distributor shares are shown in percent.

Primagaz	12.4%
Shell	12.2
Repsol	10.9
Aygaz	5.4
BP	5.0
TotalFina	4.7
Others	49.3

Source: "Press Releases." Retrieved February 17, 2000 from the World Wide Web: http://www.datamonitor.com, from Datamonitor.

★ 61 ★
Oil Wells
SIC: 1381–ISIC: 1120

Offshore Fabrication Market

The industry continues to make rapid technological advances. The source estimates that in another 15 years there will not be a single part of the seabed the industry cannot reach. Data are in millions of dollars.

	1999	2001	2003
Northwest Europe	$ 2,304	$ 1,174	$ 1,083
Far East	2,074	1,462	3,619
Latin America	1,707	1,027	529
North America	1,468	1,467	1,386
West Africa	951	1,615	1,018
FSU	848	1,547	681
Middle East	294	491	112
Mediterrenean	58	41	183

Source: *Hart's E&P*, January 2000, p. 65, from Norland Consultants.

★ 62 ★
Oil
SIC: 1389–ISIC: 1120

Top Oil and Exploration Firms

Companies are ranked by revenues in billions of dollars.

Unocal	$ 5.5
Kerr-McGee	2.1
Union Pacific Resources	1.8
Burlington Resources	1.6
Apache	0.9
Vastar Resources	0.9
Enron Oil & Gas	0.8
Pioneer Natural Resources	0.7

Source: *Wall Street Journal*, August 16, 1999, p. B4, from Bear, Stearns & Co. and Arthur Andersen.

SIC 14 - Nonmetallic Minerals, Except Fuels

★ 63 ★

Mining

SIC: 1400–ISIC: 1429–HC: 25

Nonferrous Mining Exploration

Spending is shown by region. Total spending peaked at $5.2 billion in 1997.

	($ mil.)	Share
Latin America	$ 661.9	28.3%
Australia	404.8	17.3
Canada	348.0	14.9
Africa	293.1	12.6
United States	234.5	10.0
Pacific/SE Asia	199.2	8.5
Rest of world	196.7	8.4

Source: *Engineering & Mining Journal*, January 2001, p. 9.

★ 64 ★

Mining

SIC: 1400–ISIC: 1429–HC: 25

Top Western World Mining Companies, 1998

Shares are for nonfuel mineral production.

Anglo American Corp.	7.1%
Rio Tinto	5.5
BHP	3.9
CVRD	3.8
Codelco	2.2
Freeport McMoRan Copper & Gold	1.9
Noranda	1.3
Phelps Dodge	1.2
Newmont	1.1
Placer Dome	1.1
Other	70.9

Source: *E&MJ*, October 1999, p. 37.

★ 65 ★

Diamonds

SIC: 1499–ISIC: 1429–HC: 25

Largest Diamond Producers

The industry is valued at $7 billion, $56 billion at the retail jewelry level. Value is shown in millions of dollars.

Botswana	$ 1,782
Russia	1,625
South Africa	776
Angola	618
Namibia	430
Canada	405
Congo, Democratic Rep. Of	396
Australia	367
Venezuela	120

Source: *Wall Street Journal*, July 20, 2000, p. A21, from De Beers.

★ 66 ★
Diamonds
SIC: 1499–ISIC: 1429–HC: 25

Largest Polished Diamond Consumers

The market is valued at $13.5 billion. Of the $7.5 billion rough diamond trade, Botswana commands 27% of the market, followed by Russia with a 23% share.

United States 48.0%
Japan 14.0
Europe 13.0
Asia-Arabia 10.0
Asia-Pacific 10.0
Other 5.0

Source: *Financial Times*, March 19, 2001, p. 2, from De Beers.

★ 67 ★
Rare Earths
SIC: 1499–ISIC: 1429–HC: 25

Rare Earth Sales

Rare earths are a group of 17 elements with unique physical and chemical properties. Sales are shown in millions of dollars.

	1999	2004	Share
Magnets, metallurgical, nuclear	$ 1,267	$ 1,787	69.89%
Glass, ceramics, lighting, lasers, superconductors . .	3,350	648	25.34
Hydrogen storage/ separation, catalysts, chemicals	108	122	4.77

Source: ''Rare Earths.'' Retrieved August 29, 2000 from the World Wide Web: http://www.buscom.com, from Business Communications Co.

SIC 15 - General Building Contractors

★ 68 ★

Residential Construction
SIC: 1521–ISIC: 4520

Prefabricated Housing Construction in Japan

The prefab sector is shown by type of framing. Total construction reached 227,863 units.

Steel	73.0%
Wood	18.0
Reinforced concrete	9.0

Source: ''Japan: Solid Wood Products.'' Retrieved September 1, 2000 from the World Wide Web: http://ffas.usda.gov, from Japan Prefabricated Construction Supplies & Manufacturers Association.

SIC 16 - Heavy Construction, Except Building

★ 69 ★
Construction
SIC: 1600–ISIC: 4520

Top Construction Markets, 2000

Construction spending is shown in millions of dollars.

United States	$ 819,300.00
Japan	617,909.12
Germany	252,681.54
China	181,323.45
United Kingdom	109,223.95
Brazil	109,124.74
France	106,666.96
Italy	95,779.83
Spain	86,389.84
Korea, Rep.	68,183.50

Source: *ENR*, December 4, 2000, p. 30.

SIC 17 - Special Trade Contractors

★ 70 ★
Framing Materials
SIC: 1751–ISIC: 4540

Window And Facade Industry in Europe

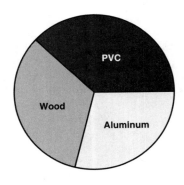

Share of framing materials is shown by use.

PVC	. 37.8%
Wood	. 32.8
Aluminum	. 29.3

Source: Retrieved June 6, 2000 from the World Wide Web: http://www.window.de/pr003_3.htm.

★ 71 ★
Windows
SIC: 1751–ISIC: 4540

Germany's Window Market

Production is shown in millions of units.

	1999 (mil.)	2001 (mil.)	Share
Plastic	12.1	10.0	55.56%
Wood	5.4	4.0	22.22
Aluminum	3.5	3.2	17.78
Aluminum + wood	0.8	0.8	4.44

Source: "Solid Wood Products." Retrieved January 1, 2001 from the World Wide Web: http://www.ffas.usda.gov, from German Windows Manufacturers Association.

★ 72 ★
Swimming Pools
SIC: 1799–ISIC: 4530

Swimming Pool Market in Egypt

The private sector's share of the pool construction market is 90%, with the balance held by the Egyptian Army. The residential market is controlled by summer resorts with a 40% share; the commercial market is controlled by hotels with a 45% share.

Hayward Pools	. 19.0%
Astral	. 17.0
Sta-Rite	. 11.0
Jaccuzi	. 10.0
American Products	. 6.0
Kripsol	. 6.0
Aqua-Tech	. 5.0
Back Fab	. 5.0
Culligan Filter	. 5.0
Miami Tank	. 5.0
Other	. 11.0

Source: "Swimming Pools." by STAT-USA, National Trade Data Bank, December 1999.

SIC 20 - Food and Kindred Products

★ 73 ★
Food
SIC: 2000–ISIC: 1500
Functional Food Sales

Sales are in millions of dollars.

	1995	1999	Share
United States	$ 26.3	$ 42.2	49.01%
Japan	22.4	23.4	27.18
Germany	2.5	2.4	2.79
Brazil	2.4	2.7	3.14
France	1.8	2.0	2.32
United Kingdom	1.8	3.1	3.60
Canada	1.2	1.6	1.86
China	1.1	2.0	2.32
Australia	1.0	1.2	1.39
Mexico	0.5	1.2	1.39
Other	3.9	4.3	4.99

Source: *Brand Strategy*, February 2001, p. 22.

★ 74 ★
Food
SIC: 2000–ISIC: 1500
Largest Packaged Food Companies

Companies are ranked by food sales in billions of dollars.

Nestle	$ 34.9
Unilever/Bestfoods	32.4
Philip Morris	27.8
PepsiCo.	11.6
Group Danone	9.8
H.J. Heinz	9.3

Nabisco Holdings	.$ 8.4
Kellogg	7.7
General Mills	6.7
Campbell's	6.2

Source: *New York Times*, June 7, 2000, p. C1.

★ 75 ★
Food
SIC: 2000–ISIC: 1500
Organic Food Market in Europe, 1998

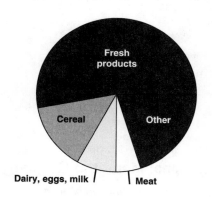

Market shares are shown in percent.

Fresh products	53.0%
Cereal	14.0
Dairy, eggs, milk	8.0
Meat	5.0
Other	20.0

Source: *Checkout*, September 1, 1999, p. 1, from European Market for Organic Foods.

★ 76 ★
Food
SIC: 2000–ISIC: 1500

Organic Food Market in France

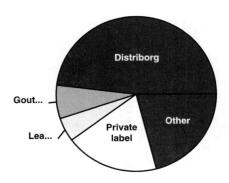

The market is active with sales up 20% in supermarkets and hypermarkets. Price remains an obstacle.

Distriborg	48.0%
Gout de la Vie	7.0
Lea Vitel	5.4
Private label	19.0
Other	20.6

Source: *LSA*, February 17, 2000, p. 1.

★ 77 ★
Food
SIC: 2000–ISIC: 1500

Prepared Meal Market in Germany

The market has been in decline lately, with the exception of the pizza category.

Bestfoods Markenartikel GmbH	57.0%
Dr. Oetker	22.0
Other	21.0

Source: *Lebensmittel Zeitung*, June 2, 2000, p. 1, from A.C. Nielsen.

★ 78 ★
Food
SIC: 2000–ISIC: 1500

Top Food and Drink Firms Worldwide

Companies are ranked by food and beverage sales in millions of dollars. Data do not include U.S. and Canada companies.

Nestle	$ 49,730
Unilever	22,864
Diageo	19,540
Danone	14,170
Snow Brand Milk Products	9,870
Suntory	9,600
Eridania Beghin-Say	9,010
Asahi Breweries	8,630
Kirin	7,740
Heineken	7,360

Source: *Prepared Foods*, July 2000, p. 20, from Elsevier Food International and Alimentos Procesados.

★ 79 ★
Food
SIC: 2000–ISIC: 1500

Top Pre-Cooked Food Makers in Japan

Market shares are shown as of October 1998. Data refer to pre-cooked for microwave ovens.

S&B Foods	19.2%
Sato Shokuhin Kogyo	18.8
Otsuka Foods	18.5
Ktokichi	12.7
House Foods	8.5
Maruha	8.1
Other	14.2

Source: "DVL Market Share Library." Retrieved April 3, 2001 from the World Wide Web: http://dvl/daiwa.co.jp, from DVL Market Share Library and Marketing Data Bank.

★ 80 ★
Beef
SIC: 2010–ISIC: 1511–HC: 02

Largest Beef Producers in Great Britain

Firms are ranked by throughput.

	Throughput	Share
Anglo Beef Producers	186,000	10.2%
Dawn Meats	122,000	6.6
St. Merryn Meat	103,000	5.5
Midland Meat Packers	102,000	5.4
McIntosh Donald	69,000	3.7

Source: *The Grocer*, June 17, 2000, p. 20, from National Beef Association.

★ 81 ★
Beef
SIC: 2010–ISIC: 1511–HC: 02

Largest Beef/Veal Producers

Production is shown in thousands of metric tons.

United States	12,023
Brazil	6,300
China	5,400
Former U.S.S.R.	2,870
Argentina	2,800
Mexico	1,900
Australia	1,870
Insia	1,700
France	1,590
Germany	1,342

Source: *Wall Street Journal*, January 19, 2001, p. A11, from Argentine Secretariat of Agriculture and U.S. Department of Agriculture.

★ 82 ★
Meat
SIC: 2010–ISIC: 1511–HC: 02

Global Meat Consumption

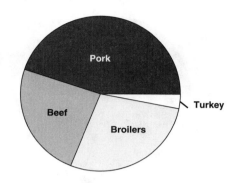

Beef is expected to lose more ground to chicken. Poultry, however, remains the dominant meat. American exports have jumped 400% since 1990, and they are expected to dominate the market.

	1997	2007
Pork	46.0%	45.0%
Beef	28.0	24.0
Broilers	23.0	28.0
Turkey	3.0	3.0

Source: *Feedstuffs*, June 7, 1999, p. 32, from Sparks Companies Inc.

★ 83 ★
Meat Processing
SIC: 2011–ISIC: 1511–HC: 02

Meat Processing Industry in Poland

Market shares are shown in percent.

Sokolow	20.0%
Animex	12.0
Other	68.0

Source: *Business Central Europe*, July/August 2000, p. 22.

★ 84 ★

Meat Processing
SIC: 2011–ISIC: 1511–HC: 02

Top Meat Processors in Brazil

Market includes sausage and cold cuts.

Sadia 43.9%
Perdigo 29.2
Seara 6.8
Other 20.1

Source: "Food Processing and Packaging Machinery."
Retrieved October 19, 2000 from the World Wide Web:
http://www.tradeport.org.

★ 85 ★

Bacon
SIC: 2013–ISIC: 1511–HC: 02

Top Bacon Makers in Japan, 1998

Market shares are shown as of October 1998.

Nippon Meat Packers 18.0%
Ito Ham Foods 10.3
Prima Meat Packers 9.0
Marudai Food 8.5
Snow Brand Food 5.0
Other 49.2

Source: "DVL Market Share Library." Retrieved April 3,
2001 from the World Wide Web: http://dvl/daiwa.co.jp,
from DVL Market Share Library and Marketing Data
Bank.

★ 86 ★

Poultry
SIC: 2013–ISIC: 1511–HC: 02

Poultry Ham Processors in France, 1998

Poultry ham has 56.1% of the poultry processing segment.

Fleury Michon 47.4%
Gaulois 5.3
Private label 31.9
Other 15.4

Source: *Points de Vente*, March 3, 1999, p. 1.

★ 87 ★

Poultry
SIC: 2015–ISIC: 1511–HC: 02

Poultry Market in Brazil

Market shares are shown in percent.

Sadia 12.44%
Perdig 7.69
Seara 5.60
Frangosul 4.84
Avipal 4.55
Penabranca 3.69
De Granja 3.30
Aurora 2.35
Sertanejo 1.48
Others 54.06

Source: *Valor Economico*, July 17, 2000, p. B12, from
South American Business Information and Agfa.

★ 88 ★
Dairy Foods
SIC: 2020–ISIC: 1520–HC: 04

Largest Dairy Firms in Europe, 1999

Companies are ranked by sales in millions of dollars.

	($ mil.)	% of Group
Nestle	$ 11.85	24.62%
Danone	5.91	12.28
Parmalat	5.20	10.80
Unilever	5.00	10.39
Lactails (Besnier)	4.54	9.43
Friesland Coberco	3.62	7.52
Campina Melkunie	3.30	6.86
Bongrain	3.27	6.79
MD Foods	2.80	5.82
Unigate	2.64	5.49

Source: *Dairy Foods*, July 2000, p. 18, from Seymour-Cooke Associates.

★ 89 ★
Dairy Foods
SIC: 2020–ISIC: 1520–HC: 04

Top Dairy Firms in Argentina

Market shares are shown in percent.

SanCor Cooperativas	23.0%
Milkaut	7.0
Other	70.0

Source: *EFE World News Service*, May 12, 2001, p. NA.

★ 90 ★
Butter
SIC: 2021–ISIC: 1520–HC: 04

Top Butter Brands in France, 1999

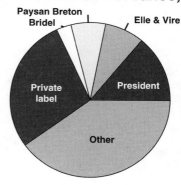

Total production reached 175,000 tons.

President	13.7%
Elle & Vire	7.7
Paysan Breton	6.9
Bridel	3.4
Private label	27.9
Other	40.4

Source: *Points de Vente*, February 23, 2000, p. 1.

★ 91 ★
Butter
SIC: 2021–ISIC: 1520–HC: 04

Top Butter Brands in the U.K., 1999

Shares are shown based on dollar sales for the year ended December 1999.

Anchor Butter	18.5%
Lurpak Spreadable	15.7
Lurpak Butter	15.3
Country English Butter	6.8
Anchor Spreadable	5.5
Kerrygold Butter	4.9
Harmonie Organic Butter	0.6
Other	32.7

Source: *Super Marketing*, February 25, 2000, p. 24, from A.C. Nielsen.

★ 92 ★
Butter
SIC: 2021–ISIC: 1520–HC: 04

Top Butter Makers in Japan

Market shares are shown as of October 1998.

Snow Brand Milk Products	35.5%
Yotsuba Nyugyo	27.0
Meiji Milk Product	13.0
Morinaga Milk Industry	11.5
Zenrakuren	7.0
Other	6.0

Source: "DVL Market Share Library." Retrieved April 3, 2001 from the World Wide Web: http://dvl/daiwa.co.jp, from DVL Market Share Library and Marketing Data Bank.

★ 93 ★
Cheese
SIC: 2022–ISIC: 1520–HC: 04

Cheese Sales in France, 1999

Sales are shown by type.

Roquefort	31.8%
French blue-type cheese	19.2
Bleu d'Auvergne	14.4
Foreign blue cheese	12.1
Bleu des Causses	5.4
Other	17.1

Source: *LSA*, September 2000, p. 120, from A.C. Nielsen and Information Resources Inc. Secodip.

★ 94 ★
Cheese
SIC: 2022–ISIC: 1520–HC: 04

Natural Cheese Market in the U.K., 1999

Market shares are shown based on value. Hard cheese had a 54.9% share, followed by curd cheese with a 12.4% share.

Dairy Crest	22.8%
Glanbia	20.8
St. Ivel UK	15.8
Irish Dairy Board	7.6
New Zealand Dairy Baord	7.6
Bois Wessanen	2.9
Other	22.5

Source: "UK Natural Cheese." Retrieved January 12, 2001 from the World Wide Web: http://www.clearlybusiness.com, from Datamonitor.

★ 95 ★
Cheese
SIC: 2022–ISIC: 1520–HC: 04

Top Fresh Cheese Makers in France

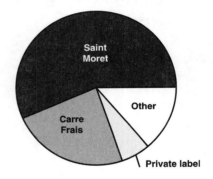

Market shares are shown in percent.

Saint Moret	56.5%
Carre Frais	23.5
Private label	6.1
Other	13.9

Source: *Points de Vente*, May 24, 2000, p. 50.

★ 96 ★
Frozen Desserts
SIC: 2024–ISIC: 1520–HC: 21

Chilled Dessert Market in Europe, 1999

Market shares are shown in percent.

Germany	33.0%
France	22.0
Spain	10.0
Netherlands	9.0
United Kingdom	8.0
Italy	5.0
Other	13.0

Source: ''Chilled Desserts in Europe.'' Retrieved February 5, 2001 from the World Wide Web: http://www.lfra.co.uk/lfra/press786.html.

★ 97 ★
Frozen Desserts
SIC: 2024–ISIC: 1520–HC: 21

Dessert Market in Brazil

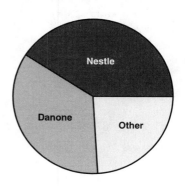

Market shares are shown in percent.

Nestle	41.0%
Danone	35.0
Other	24.0

Source: *Valor Economico*, October 19, 2000, p. B3, from A.C. Nielsen.

★ 98 ★
Frozen Desserts
SIC: 2024–ISIC: 1520–HC: 21

Frozen Dessert Market in the U.K., 1998

Market shares are shown in percent.

Retailer brands	45.2%
Sara Lee	22.9
UB	2.4
Birds Eye Wall	1.4
Other	28.1

Source: ''Frozen Food Outperforms the Overall Food Market in 1998.'' Retrieved September 1, 2000 from the World Wide Web: http://www.bfff.co.uk.

★ 99 ★
Frozen Desserts
SIC: 2024–ISIC: 1520–HC: 21

Frozen Dessert Sales in Western Europe, 1999

Sales are shown in millions of dollars. Top brands are Algida, Magnum and Motta.

Ice cream	$ 17,413.5
Ice cream, impulse	9,039.4
Ice cream, dairy based impulse	7,831.0
Ice cream, artisanal	4,585.0
Ice cream/desserts, take-home	3,767.9
Ice cream/desserts, dairy-based takehome	3,486.1
Ice cream, water-based impulse	1,208.4
Desserts, dairy based	903.3
Ice cream/desserts, water-based take-home	281.9
Frozen yogurt	21.0

Source: *Brand Strategy*, September 2000, p. 23.

★ 100 ★
Ice Cream
SIC: 2024–ISIC: 1520–HC: 21

Ice Cream Market in Hong Kong

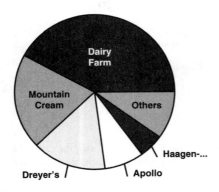

Market shares are shown in percent.

Dairy Farm	42.0%
Mountain Cream	20.0
Dreyer's	15.0
Apollo	8.0
Haagen-Dazs	5.0
Others	10.0

Source: "Hong Kong Frozen Desserts Product Brief."
Retrieved September 1, 2000 from the World Wide Web:
http://ffas.usda.gov, from Foreign Agricultural Service,
United States Department of Agriculture, and Eastern
Strategic Consulting Limited.

★ 101 ★
Ice Cream
SIC: 2024–ISIC: 1520–HC: 21

Ice Cream Market in India

Hindustan Lever
Amul
Other

The Rs 450 crore market is shown in percent.

Hindustan Lever	50.0%
Amul	35.0
Other	15.0

Source: *Economic Times*, May 29, 2000, p. 1.

★ 102 ★
Ice Cream
SIC: 2024–ISIC: 1520–HC: 21

Ice Cream Market in New Zealand, 2000

Market shares are shown in percent as of November 5, 2000. Figures are for the low fat segment.

Talley's Guilt Free ice cream	36.8%
Tip Top Lite n Creamy	28.2
Weight Watchers	15.3
Other	19.7

Source: "Dairy Good." Retrieved April 11, 2001 from the
World Wide Web: http://www.grocersreview.co.nz, from
A.C. Nielsen.

★ 103 ★
Ice Cream
SIC: 2024–ISIC: 1520–HC: 21

Ice Cream Market in Poland

Algida's share is estimated at 23-25% while Scholler runs from 15-17% share. On average, Americans eat about 22 liters a year, while Europeans eat about 6 liters and Poles average about 3 liters.

Algida	25.0%
Scholler	17.0
Koral	15.0
Zielona Budka	15.0
Other	17.2

Source: *Warsaw Business Journal*, August 28, 2000, p. 1.

★ 104 ★
Ice Cream
SIC: 2024–ISIC: 1520–HC: 21

Premium Ice Cream Market in France

Market shares are shown in percent.

Unilever	38.0%
Nestle	16.0
Other	46.0

Source: *Ice Cream Reporter*, June 20, 2000, p. 1.

★ 105 ★
Ice Cream
SIC: 2024–ISIC: 1520–HC: 21

Premium Ice Cream Market in Thailand

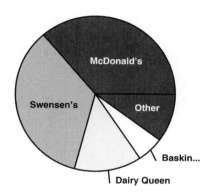

Market shares are shown in percent.

McDonald's 40.0%
Swensen's 38.0
Dairy Queen 15.0
Baskin Robbins 6.0
Other 11.0

Source: *Bangkok Post*, December 28, 2000, p. B8.

★ 106 ★
Ice Cream
SIC: 2024–ISIC: 1520–HC: 21

Top Ice Cream Firms in Japan, 1999

Shares are shown based on domestic sales.

Meiji Milk Products Co. 13.8%
Morinaga Milk Industry Co. 13.2
Ezaki Glico Co. 11.9
Lotte Co. 10.4
Haagen Dazs Japan Inc. 9.5
Other 41.2

Source: *Nikkei Weekly*, August 21, 2000, p. 9, from Nihon Keizai Shimbun.

★ 107 ★
Cream
SIC: 2026–ISIC: 1520–HC: 04

Top Fresh Cream Makers in Japan

Market shares are shown as of October 1998.

Snow Brand Milk Products 39.0%
Nagoya Seiraku 22.4
Toraku 9.6
Morinaga Milk Industry 6.4
Meiji Milk Product 5.0
Nakazawa Nyugyo 4.1
Other 13.5

Source: "DVL Market Share Library." Retrieved April 3, 2001 from the World Wide Web: http://dvl/daiwa.co.jp, from DVL Market Share Library and Marketing Data Bank.

★ 108 ★
Milk
SIC: 2026–ISIC: 1520–HC: 04

Largest Milk Producers in Saudi Arabia

About 60% of all milk produced is fermented into a product called laban, similar to natural drinking yogurt.

Al-Marai 24.0%
Sadafco 19.6
Al-Safi 18.0
Other 38.4

Source: "Saudia Arabia Dairy Industry." Retrieved September 8, 2000 from the World Wide Web: http://www.tradeport.org.

★ 109 ★
Milk
SIC: 2026–ISIC: 1520–HC: 04
Leading Milk Producers in the U.K.

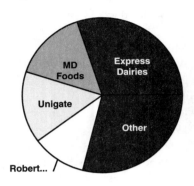

Market shares are shown in percent.

Express Dairies	30.0%
MD Foods	15.0
Unigate	15.0
Robert Wiseman	11.0
Other	29.0

Source: ''Dairy Crest Milks Top Brands.'' Retrieved November 2, 1999 from the World Wide Web: http://www.marketingclick.com.

★ 110 ★
Milk
SIC: 2026–ISIC: 1520–HC: 04
Milk Market in Belgium

Market shares are shown in percent.

Semi-skimmed	55.0%
Whole milk	20.0
Skimmed milk	9.0
AA	5.0
Chocolate milk	3.0
Fermented milk	3.0
Milk shake	2.0

Source: *Dairy Markets Weekly*, June 1, 2000, p. 9.

★ 111 ★
Milk
SIC: 2026–ISIC: 1520–HC: 04
Top Milk Producers in France

Market shares are shown is percent. The market in declining in volume but raising in value. The market has been stimulated by special milks and users' preference for new brick cartons with pour spouts.

Candia/Nactalis	28.0%
Lactel	14.7
Private label	26.4
Other	30.9

Source: *Points de Vente*, January 31, 2001, p. 44, from IriSecodip.

★ 112 ★
Milk
SIC: 2026–ISIC: 1520–HC: 04
Top Milk Producers in Japan, 1998

Japan produced 4.79 million tons of milk for drinking.

Snow Brand Milk Products	19.1%
Meiji Milk Products	14.0
Morinaga Milk Industry	8.3
Other	58.6

Source: *Japanscan Food Industry Bulletin*, October 1, 1999, p. 1.

★ 113 ★
Milk
SIC: 2026–ISIC: 1520–HC: 04
Top UHT Milk Producers in Thailand

UHT stands for ultra-heat treated.

Foremost	42.0%
Nong Pho	17.0
(Thai Danish) Dairy Farming Promotion	15.0
(Mali) Thai Dairy Milk Industries	9.0
Other	17.0

Source: *Bangkok Post*, February 28, 2001, p. NA.

★ 114 ★
Yogurt
SIC: 2026–ISIC: 1520–HC: 04

Organic Yogurt Sales in the U.K.

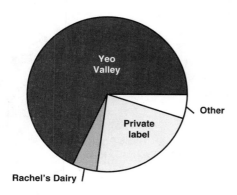

Market shares are shown in percent.

Yeo Valley	68.0%
Rachel's Dairy	5.0
Private label	22.0
Other	5.0

Source: *Super Marketing*, June 23, 2000, p. 5, from A.C. Nielsen.

★ 115 ★
Yogurt
SIC: 2026–ISIC: 1520–HC: 04

Top Yogurt Brands in Portugal, 1999

Market shares are shown in percent.

Danone	34.0%
Nestle	25.0
Yoplait	12.0
Other	19.0

Source: *MOCI*, March 23, 2000, p. 1.

★ 116 ★
Yogurt
SIC: 2026–ISIC: 1520–HC: 04

Top Yogurt Makers in Brazil

Market shares are shown in percent.

Danone	22.8%
Nestle	22.7
Parmalat	11.0
Paulista	9.7
Batavo	8.9
Other	24.9

Source: *Gazeta Mercantil*, January 25, 1999, p. 1.

★ 117 ★
Baby Food
SIC: 2032–ISIC: 1540–HC: 20

Baby Food Market Worldwide

The market was valued at $14 billion in 1997.

United States	27.0%
China	21.0
France	8.0
Japan	8.0
Germany	5.0
Italy	4.0
United Kingdom	4.0
Spain	3.0
Others	20.0

Source: ''Baby Food - the Majors and Minors Battle it Out.'' Retrieved October 2, 2000 from the World Wide Web: http://www.just-food.com.

★ 118 ★

Baby Food
SIC: 2032–ISIC: 1540–HC: 20

Baby Food Market in China

Market shares are shown in percent.

Nestle	21.0%
Wei Chuan	16.0
Heinz	11.0
Heilongjiang	9.0
Hangzhou Foodstuffs	7.0
Others	36.0

Source: "Baby Food - the Majors and Minors Battle it Out." Retrieved October 2, 2000 from the World Wide Web: http://www.just-food.com, from Access Asia.

★ 119 ★

Baby Food
SIC: 2032–ISIC: 1540–HC: 20

Baby Food Market in France

Sales at super/hypermarkets are for the year ended December 1, 1999.

Milk formula and growing milks	35.5%
Baby food in jars and plates	35.0
Cereals and breakfast foods	10.0
UHT (ultra high temp)	5.0
Chilled baby food	4.0
Juices and drinks	4.0
Other	6.5

Source: *Point de Vente*, January 5, 2000, p. 1.

★ 120 ★

Baby Food
SIC: 2032–ISIC: 1540–HC: 20

Baby Food Market in Middle East/ North Africa, 1998

The market was roughly valued at $356 million, although the source also places the figure as low as $330 million.

Nestle	33.3%
Numico	13.6

Abbott	11.1%
Novartis	10.4
Wyeth	7.8
Remedia	6.3
Maabarot	5.2
Rid	1.7
Other	10.5

Source: *Eurofood*, May 1999, p. 2, from ERC Group.

★ 121 ★

Baby Food
SIC: 2032–ISIC: 1540–HC: 20

Baby Milk Market in the U.K.

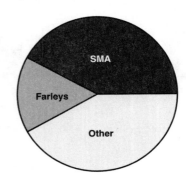

The 164 million British pounds market is shown in percent.

SMA	42.0%
Farleys	16.0
Other	42.0

Source: *The Observer*, August 22, 1999, p. 1.

★ 122 ★
Baby Food
SIC: 2032–ISIC: 1540–HC: 20

Top Baby Food Makers in France, 2000

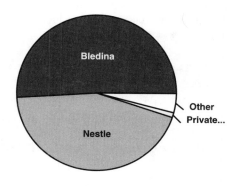

Shares are for the year ended March 31, 2000.

Bledina	50.7%
Nestle	44.4
Private label	1.2
Other	3.7

Source: *LSA*, January 18, 2001, p. 78.

★ 123 ★
Canned Food
SIC: 2032–ISIC: 1540–HC: 20

Baked Beans Market in Australia, 1998

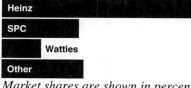

Market shares are shown in percent.

Heinz	59.6%
SPC	15.7
Watties	8.1
Other	16.6

Source: ''Australia: Food Processing Sector.'' Retrieved September 1, 2000 from the World Wide Web: http:// ffas.usda.gov, from A.C. Nielsen.

★ 124 ★
Canned Food
SIC: 2032–ISIC: 1540–HC: 20

Best-Selling Canned Goods in the U.K., 2000

Sales are shown in thousands of British pounds for the year ended October 8, 2000.

	(mil.)	Share
Heinz (baked beans)	79,642	5.94%
John West (tuna)	32,614	2.43
Princes (tuna)	30,230	2.26
John West (salmon)	24,035	1.79
Princes (corned beef)	18,937	1.41
Princes (salmon)	16,605	1.24
Heinz (baked beans/sausages) . .	15,295	1.14
Heinz (spaghetti)	14,272	1.07
Fray Bentos (pies)	13,759	1.03
Green Giant Niblets (sweet corn)	12,300	0.92
Other	1,082,008	80.77

Source: *The Grocer*, December 16, 2000, p. 43, from Information Resources Inc.

★ 125 ★
Canned Food
SIC: 2032–ISIC: 1540–HC: 20

Canned Food Sales by Country, 1999

Figures are for selected markets. Sales are in thousands of tons. Vegetables command the largest share of the canned food market in most countries. In Spain, fish was the largest sector.

United States	3,780
France	1,419
United Kingdom	1,391
Germany	1,255
Japan	669
Italy	488
Spain	446

Source: Retrieved July 6, 2000 from the World Wide Web: http://www.just-food.com, from Euromonitor.

★ 126 ★
Canned Food
SIC: 2032–ISIC: 1540–HC: 20

Canned Meat Market in Hong Kong

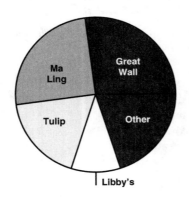

Market shares are shown in percent.

Great Wall	27.0%
Ma Ling	25.0
Tulip	18.0
Libby's	10.0
Other	20.0

Source: ''Hong Kong Canned Food Market Brief.'' Retrieved September 1, 2000 from the World Wide Web: http://ffas.usda.gov, from Foreign Agricultural Service and United States Department of Agriculture.

★ 127 ★
Canned Food
SIC: 2032–ISIC: 1540–HC: 20

Canned Vegetable Market in Hong Kong

Market shares are shown in percent.

Del Monte	25.0%
Park'N Shop	15.0
S&W	10.0
Heinz	8.0

Hyde Park	7.0%
Campbell's	5.0
No Frills	5.0
Other	25.0

Source: ''Hong Kong Canned Food Market Brief.'' Retrieved September 1, 2000 from the World Wide Web: http://ffas.usda.gov, from Foreign Agricultural Service and United States Department of Agriculture.

★ 128 ★
Infant Formula
SIC: 2032–ISIC: 1540–HC: 20

Top Infant Formula Brands in France, 1999

Market shares are shown in percent.

Guigoz	27.7%
Alma	18.9
Bledilait	13.4
Nidai	10.7
Other	29.3

Source: *Points de Vente*, January 5, 2000, p. 1.

★ 129 ★
Canned Fruit
SIC: 2033–ISIC: 1549–HC: 20

Canned Fruit Market in Australia, 1998

Shares are shown based on A$161 million market. Canned peaches had 35.7% share of the market.

Ardmona	42.9%
SPC	34.4
Generic	11.0
Berri	5.0
Housebrands	2.4
Golden Circle	1.9
Cottee's	1.0
Other	1.4

Source: ''Australia Canned Fruit.'' Retrieved October 1, 2000 from the World Wide Web: http://www.usda.gov.

★ 130 ★
Canned Fruit
SIC: 2033–ISIC: 1549–HC: 20

Canned Fruit Market in Hong Kong

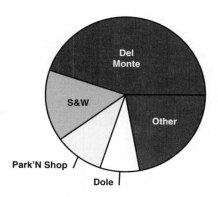

Market shares are shown in percent.

Del Monte	45.0%
S&W	15.0
Park'N Shop	10.0
Dole	8.0
Other	22.0

Source: ''Hong Kong Canned Food Market Brief.''
Retrieved September 1, 2000 from the World Wide Web:
http://ffas.usda.gov, from Foreign Agricultural Service and
United States Department of Agriculture.

★ 131 ★
Canned Fruit
SIC: 2033–ISIC: 1549–HC: 20

Top Canned Fruit Makers in the U.K., 1999

Market shares are shown based on value.

Del Monte	22.7%
John West	4.5
Australian Gold	1.4
Dole	1.2
Private label	52.0
Other	18.2

Source: ''UK Bread and Rolls.'' Retrieved January 11,
2001 from the World Wide Web: http://
www.clearlybusiness.com, from Datamonitor.

★ 132 ★
Jams
SIC: 2033–ISIC: 1549–HC: 20

Best-Selling Jam Brands in the U.K.

*Sales are in millions of British pounds for the year
ended November 1998.*

	(mil.)	Share
Robertson's standard	10.4	4.16%
Robertson's Golden Shred Fine . . .	9.7	3.88
Hartley's standard	9.3	3.72
Sun-Pat peanut butter	7.4	2.96
Lyle's Golden syrup	5.2	2.08
Nutella chocolate spread	5.2	2.08
Gales pure honey	4.8	1.92
Bonne Maman extra fruit	4.2	1.68
Streamline reduced sugar	4.1	1.64
St. Dalfour extra fruit	3.2	1.28
Other	186.5	74.60

Source: *The Grocer*, January 16, 1999, p. 39.

★ 133 ★
Jams
SIC: 2033–ISIC: 1549–HC: 20

Best-Selling Jams in Poland

*The top marmalades are made by Agros Bialystock
(22.9% share) and Miedzychod (5.4% share).*

Materne	46.0%
Stovit	19.2
Agros	11.1
Other	23.7

Source: *Eurofood*, November 18, 1999, p. 5, from GfK
Polonia.

★ 134 ★
Jams
SIC: 2033–ISIC: 1549–HC: 20

Top Jelly Makers in Japan

Market shares are shown as of October 1998.

Morinaga Milk Industry	29.9%
Glico Kyodo Nyugyo	15.8
Snow Brand Milk Products	15.1
Meiji Milk Product	10.2
Zenrakuren	3.5
Other	25.5

Source: "DVL Market Share Library." Retrieved April 3, 2001 from the World Wide Web: http://dvl.daiwa.co.jp, from DVL Market Share Library and Marketing Data Bank.

★ 135 ★
Juices
SIC: 2033–ISIC: 1549–HC: 20

Juice Market in Moscow, Russia

Market shares are shown in percent.

Wimm-Bill-Dann	70.0%
Other	30.0

Source: *Moskovskie Novosti*, January 9, 2001, p. 21, from COMCON.

★ 136 ★
Juices
SIC: 2033–ISIC: 1549–HC: 20

Juice Market in the Czech Republic, 1999

Market shares are shown in percent.

Toma	28.0%
Linea Nivice	21.0
Walmark	20.0
Fruiko	5.0
Limova	4.0
Other	22.0

Source: "Czech Republic: Fruit Juice and Fruit Nectar Report." Retrieved September 1, 2000 from the World Wide Web: http://ffas.usda.gov, from Foreign Agricultural Service and United States Department of Agriculture.

★ 137 ★
Juices
SIC: 2033–ISIC: 1549–HC: 20

Top Juice Drinks in the U.K., 1997

A total of 435 million liters were sold in 1997, 47% were small cartons and 23% were liter cartons.

Ribena	23.0%
Robinson's	14.0
Capri-Sun	8.0
Five Alive	7.0

Continued on next page.

★ 137 ★
[Continued]
Juices
SIC: 2033–ISIC: 1549–HC: 20

Top Juice Drinks in the U.K., 1997

A total of 435 million liters were sold in 1997, 47% were small cartons and 23% were liter cartons.

Del Monte	3.0%
Libby's	3.0
Private label	14.0
Other	28.0

Source: ''Soft Drink Alert.'' Retrieved April 14, 2000 from the World Wide Web: http://www.just-drinks.com.

★ 138 ★
Ketchup
SIC: 2033–ISIC: 1549–HC: 20

Ketchup Market in India

The Rs 109 crore market has grown 27% over the last two years (by value) and still has room to expand. The two leading companies are looking to expand into the semi-urban and rural markets, where ketchup goes up against things like spicy home-made chutneys.

Maggi Ketchup	29.2%
Kissan Ketchup	22.0
Maggi Hot & Sweet	13.2
Kissan Sauce	9.2
Kissan Tom-Chi	6.6
Other	19.8

Source: *Business Today*, July 22, 1999, p. 30, from ORG-MARC.

★ 139 ★
Ketchup
SIC: 2033–ISIC: 1549–HC: 20

Ketchup Market in Poland

Market shares are shown in percent.

Tortex	22.8%
Pudliszki	15.1
Miwex	12.6
Kotlin	12.4
Roleski	11.6
Heinz	4.4
Billy	3.7
Other	17.5

Source: *Eurofood*, August 26, 1999, p. 6, from Puls Biznesu.

★ 140 ★
Ketchup
SIC: 2033–ISIC: 1549–HC: 20

Top Tomato Catsup Makers in Japan

Market shares are shown as of October 1998.

Kagome	56.3%
Dellmonte Japan	22.8
Heinz Japan	4.7
Nagano Tomato	4.1
Other	12.1

Source: ''DVL Market Share Library.'' Retrieved April 3, 2001 from the World Wide Web: http://dvl/daiwa.co.jp, from DVL Market Share Library and Marketing Data Bank.

★ 141 ★
Coffee Creamer
SIC: 2034–ISIC: 1549–HC: 21

Top Coffee Creamer Brands in Japan, 1998

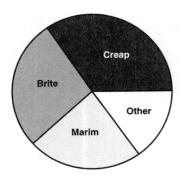

Nagoya Seiraku leads the market for creamer in portion packs.

Creap (Morinaga Milk Industry)	34.2%
Brite (Nestle Japan)	27.4
Marim(AGF)	23.3
Other	15.1

Source: *Japanscan Food Industry Bulletin*, November 1999, p. 32.

★ 142 ★
Soup
SIC: 2034–ISIC: 1549–HC: 21

Instant Noodle Market in Thailand

Ma Ma
Wai Wai
Quick!
Other

Market shares are shown in percent.

Ma Ma	61.0%
Wai Wai	14.0
Quick!	6.0
Other	19.0

Source: *Bangkok Post*, September 18, 2000, p. 8.

★ 143 ★
Soup
SIC: 2034–ISIC: 1549–HC: 21

Top Soup Makers in Japan, 1999

Market shares are estimated based on 71.3 billion yen in 1999.

	(mil.)	Share
Ajinomoto	34,990	32.79%
Nagoya Seiraku	4,700	4.40
Kyowa Hakko	4,350	4.08
Pokka	3,560	3.34
Nestle Japan	2,800	2.62
Campbell	1,700	1.59
Nihon Nosan	1,250	1.17
Other	53,350	50.00

Source: "Retail Soups Market in Japan." Retrieved September 28, 2000 from the World Wide Web: http://www.japanscan.com, from *Shurui Shokuhin Tokei Geppo*.

★ 144 ★
Soup
SIC: 2034–ISIC: 1549–HC: 21

U.K. Soup Sales, 1999

Tinned
Instant
Fresh chilled
Dry packet bowl

Soup enjoys a high level of household penetration, with over 84% of homes serving tinned soup. Volume sales have been declining, however. Total sales reached 376 million British pounds in 1999.

Tinned	60.0%
Instant	19.0
Fresh chilled	15.0
Dry packet bowl	6.0

Source: *The Grocer*, February 17, 2001, p. 58, from Mintel.

★ 145 ★
Culinary Products
SIC: 2035–ISIC: 1549–HC: 21

Retail Culinary Sales in Western Europe

Culinary products include fermented sauces, ketchup, mayonnaise, mustard, salad dressings and pickles. The growth in volume is in part the result of the growth of the ethnic foods category. Data are in tons.

	1999	2004
Germany	317,976	342,145
United Kingdom	203,230	229,910
France	149,284	153,744
Spain	114,009	126,694
Sweden	99,788	101,617
Turkey	63,612	89,682
Netherlands	74,334	77,019
Italy	65,220	75,668
Belgium	52,436	55,203
Austria	39,966	44,928

Source: "Ketchup Catches up with the Latest Food Trends." Retrieved August 21, 2000 from the World Wide Web: http://www.just-food.com, from Euromonitor.

★ 146 ★
Honey
SIC: 2035–ISIC: 1549–HC: 21

Top Honey Brands in the U.K., 2000

Total sales reached 13.3 million British pounds for the year ended November 4, 2000.

Nutella	43.9%
Own label	28.3
Cadbury	8.8
Mars	8.5
Scotts	5.7
Penotti	0.6
Other	3.9

Source: *The Grocer*, January 13, 2001, p. 35, from A.C. Nielsen.

★ 147 ★
Mayonnaise
SIC: 2035–ISIC: 1549–HC: 21

Mayonnaise Market in Austria, 1999

Total mayonnaise sales were valued at 197 million Austrian schillings. Mayonnaise is consumed most often in October and December, accounting for 37% of sales.

Kuner	77.0%
Supermarket labels	13.0
Thomy of Nestle	4.0
Kronen-Mayonnaise	1.0
Other	5.0

Source: "Austria Product Brief Mayonnaise." Retrieved October 1, 2000 from the World Wide Web: http://ffas.usda.gov.

★ 148 ★
Mayonnaise
SIC: 2035–ISIC: 1549–HC: 21

Top Mayonnaise Firms in Chile, 1999

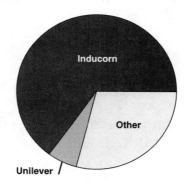

Shares are shown in percent. Inducorn's share was 66.6% in 1997.

Inducorn	64.9%
Unilever	5.7
Other	29.4

Source: "Chile: Watts and Inducorn Lead Olive Oil and Mayonnaise Markets." Retrieved July 10, 2000 from the World Wide Web: http://wwww.prnewswire.com, from South American Business Information and A.C. Nielsen.

★ 149 ★
Salad Dressings
SIC: 2035–ISIC: 1549–HC: 21

Salad Dressing Market in Australia, 1998

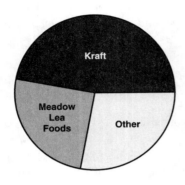

Market shares are shown in percent.

Kraft 46.9%
Meadow Lea Foods 25.3
Other 27.8

Source: "Australia: Food Processing Sector." Retrieved September 1, 2000 from the World Wide Web: http://ffas.usda.gov, from A.C. Nielsen.

★ 150 ★
Sauces
SIC: 2035–ISIC: 1549–HC: 21

Best-Selling Sauce Brands in the U.K., 2000

Sales are shown in thousands of British pounds for the year ended October 8, 2000.

Dolmio (pasta) 48,564
Chicken Tonight 42,643
Homepride 41,346
Ragu 26,351
Uncle Ben's 23,706
Dolmio (stir in) 14,866
Homepride (pasta) 12,233
Patak's (cook in) 12,204
Saucia (pesto) 12,047
Sharwood's (stir fry) 9,587

Source: The Grocer, December 16, 2000, p. 43, from Information Resources Inc.

★ 151 ★
Sauces
SIC: 2035–ISIC: 1549–HC: 21

Sauces & Condiment Sales in the U.K., 2000

Sales are shown in millions of British pounds for the year ended August 12, 2000.

	(mil.)	Share
Tomato ketchup	82,706	16.36%
Pickled vegetable	80,262	15.88
Condiment sauces	77,702	15.37
Mayonnaise	69,511	13.75
Sweet pickle & chutney	61,624	12.19
Salad cream	41,154	8.14
Brown/fruity sauce	39,251	7.76
Salad dressing	36,869	7.29
Other thick sauces	16,497	3.26

Source: The Grocer, October 7, 2000, p. 57, from A.C. Nielsen.

★ 152 ★
Sauces
SIC: 2035–ISIC: 1549–HC: 21

Top Sauce Producers in Hong Kong, 1997

Market shares are shown in percent.

Amoy Foods 35.0%
Pearl River Bridge 30.0
Lee Kum Kee 15.0
Kikkoman 3.0
Kim lan 3.0
Others 14.0

Source: "Hong Kong Sauces, Relishes and Condiments Brief." Retrieved September 1, 2000 from the World Wide Web: http://ffas.usda.gov, from Foreign Agricultural Service and United States Department of Agriculture.

★ 153 ★
Sauces
SIC: 2035–ISIC: 1549–HC: 21

Top Worcestershire Sauce Makers in Japan

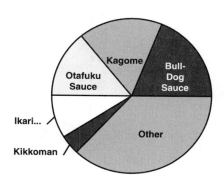

Market shares are shown as of October 1998.

Bull-Dog Sauce 19.0%
Kagome 16.8
Otafuku Sauce 14.2
Ikari Sauce 8.9
Kikkoman 4.0
Other 37.1

Source: "DVL Market Share Library." Retrieved April 3, 2001 from the World Wide Web: http://dvl/daiwa.co.jp, from DVL Market Share Library and Marketing Data Bank.

★ 154 ★
Frozen Vegetables
SIC: 2037–ISIC: 1549–HC: 16

Prepared Vegetable Sales in the U.K., 1998

Market shares are shown in percent.

UB 30.6%
Birds Eye Wall 8.3
Other 50.7

Source: "Frozen Food Outperforms the Overall Food Market in 1998." Retrieved September 1, 2000 from the World Wide Web: http://www.bfff.co.uk.

★ 155 ★
Frozen Foods
SIC: 2038–ISIC: 1549–HC: 16

Frozen Hamburger Market in Argentina

Market shares are shown in percent.

Quickfood 45.0%
Goodmark 17.0
Granja del Sol 9.0
Other 29.0

Source: *El Cronista*, July 5, 2000, p. 24.

★ 156 ★
Frozen Foods
SIC: 2038–ISIC: 1549–HC: 16

Frozen Pizza Market by Sector in the U.K., 1998

The 270 million British pound market is shown in percent. Goodfellas led with sales of 27.9 million, followed by Schwans Chicago Town with 23.2 million, followed by San Marco with 18.4 million.

	(mil.)	Share
Main meal pizzas	175.8	65.1%
Extra-large main meal pizzas	27.5	10.2
Individual pizzas	27.3	10.1
Pizza grills	20.8	7.7
French bread pizzas	10.0	3.7
Pizza slices	7.0	2.6
Snack pizzas	1.6	0.6

Source: "Pizza." Retrieved December 7, 1999 from the World Wide Web: http://www.just-food.com, from *The Grocer*, Information Resources Inc., and Key Note.

★ 157 ★
Frozen Foods
SIC: 2038–ISIC: 1549–HC: 16

Frozen Pizza Market in the U.K., 1998

Market shares are shown in percent.

Retail own brand 42.3%
UB 16.4
Nestle 4.2
McCain 4.0
Other 33.1

Source: "Frozen Food Outperforms the Overall Food Market in 1998." Retrieved September 1, 2000 from the World Wide Web: http://www.bfff.co.uk.

★ 158 ★
Frozen Foods
SIC: 2038–ISIC: 1549–HC: 16

Frozen Pizza Sales in Western Europe

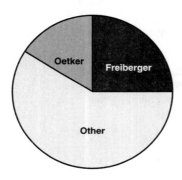

Shares are shown based on volume. Germany is the largest national market with about 400 million units sold.

Freiberger 25.0%
Oetker 16.0
Other 59.0

Source: *Lebensmittel Zeitung*, September 22, 2000, p. 16.

★ 159 ★
Frozen Foods
SIC: 2038–ISIC: 1549–HC: 16

Top Frozen Food Firms in Japan, 1999

Shares are shown based on domestic shipments.

Nichirei Corp. 18.6%
Katokichi Co. 12.8
Ajinomoto Co. 9.7
Nippon Suisan Kaisha Ltd. 8.4
Nichiro Corp. 6.9
Other 43.6

Source: *Nikkei Weekly*, August 21, 2000, p. 9, from Nihon Keizai Shimbun.

★ 160 ★
Frozen Foods
SIC: 2038–ISIC: 1549–HC: 16

Top Frozen Food Makers in Spain

The market is dominated by multinational companies; Pescanova is the largest domestic producer.

Danone 21.8%
Own-label 21.4
Unilever 13.5
Other 43.3

Source: "Euro Ready Meals Mkt Spain." Retrieved November 16, 1999 from the World Wide Web: http://www.northernlight.com, from Leatherhead Food Research and MarkIntel.

★ 161 ★
Frozen Foods
SIC: 2038–ISIC: 1549–HC: 16

Top Frozen Meatball Makers in Japan

Market shares are shown as of October 1998.

Unichika Sanko	28.3%
Nichirei	18.5
Ajinomoto	16.2
Nippon Suisan Kaisha	12.3
Asahi Foods	10.1
Other	14.6

Source: ''DVL Market Share Library.'' Retrieved April 3, 2001 from the World Wide Web: http://dvl/daiwa.co.jp, from DVL Market Share Library and Marketing Data Bank.

★ 162 ★
Frozen Foods
SIC: 2038–ISIC: 1549–HC: 16

Vegetarian Food Market in the U.K., 1998

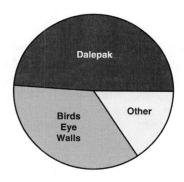

Market shares are shown in percent.

Dalepak	46.5%
Birds Eye Walls	33.7
Other	14.9

Source: ''Frozen Food Outperforms the Overall Food Market in 1998.'' Retrieved September 1, 2000 from the World Wide Web: http://www.bfff.co.uk.

★ 163 ★
Flour
SIC: 2041–ISIC: 1531–HC: 19

Top Flour Makers in Brazil

Market shares are shown in percent.

Nisshin Flour Milling	37.0%
Nippon Flour Mills	21.0
Other	42.0

Source: ''Market Leaders in Japan.'' Retrieved March 20, 2000 from the World Wide Web: http://www.just-food.com.

★ 164 ★
Flour
SIC: 2041–ISIC: 1531–HC: 19

Top Flour Makers in Ireland

Market shares are shown in percent.

Odlums	50.0%
Bolands	25.0
Other	25.0

Source: ''Cereal, Grains.'' Retrieved April 11, 2001 from the World Wide Web: http://www.irc.ie.com.

★ 165 ★
Flour
SIC: 2041–ISIC: 1531–HC: 19

Top Wheat Flour Makers in Indonesia, 1999

The import duty was abolished in 1998, affecting the local market. Imports were 1% of the market in 1997 and jumped to 14.4% in 1999.

Bogasari	64.6%
Imports	14.4
Berdikari	9.8
Sriboga	5.7
Panganmas	5.6

Source: *Indonesian Commercial Newsletter*, December 5, 2000, p. 7, from Aptindo.

★ 166 ★
Flour
SIC: 2041–ISIC: 1549–HC: 09

Top Flour Makers in Australia, 1998

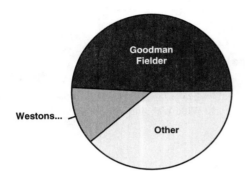

Market shares are shown in percent.

Goodman Fielder	49.0%
Westons Tip Top	12.4
Other	38.6

Source: ''Australia: Food Processing Sector.'' Retrieved September 1, 2000 from the World Wide Web: http://ffas.usda.gov, from A.C. Nielsen.

★ 167 ★
Cereal
SIC: 2043–ISIC: 1531–HC: 19

Ready-to-Eat Cereal Market in Europe, 1999

Sales are in millions of dollars. Figures are for children, adults, and family. European countries are buying more cereal for convenience, health and pleasure.

United Kingdom	$ 1,884.2
Germany	846.2
France	653.9
Sweden	150.9
Italy	142.8
Spain	74.7
Netherlands	58.0

Source: *Food Ingredients and Analysis International*, November-December 1999, p. 50, from Datamonitor.

★ 168 ★
Cereal
SIC: 2043–ISIC: 1531–HC: 19

Top Cereal Firms in Western Europe, 1998

Market shares are shown in percent.

Kellogg Co.	41.2%
Cereal Partners Worldwide	12.4
Weetabix Ltd.	8.4
Quaker Oats Co.	3.1
Private label	13.9
Other	21.0

Source: ''Private Labels Undermine Big Breakfast Brands.'' Retrieved June 1, 2001 from the World Wide Web: http://www.euromonitor.com.

★ 169 ★
Cereal
SIC: 2043–ISIC: 1531–HC: 19

Top Cereal Makers in Australia, 1998

Market shares are shown in percent.

Kelloggs	52.5%
Uncle Tobys	20.7
Sanitarium	17.5
Other	9.3

Source: ''Australia: Food Processing Sector.'' Retrieved September 1, 2000 from the World Wide Web: http://ffas.usda.gov, from A.C. Nielsen.

★ 170 ★
Cereal
SIC: 2043–ISIC: 1531–HC: 19

Top Cereal Makers in France, 2000

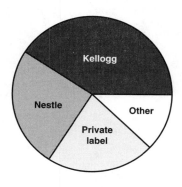

The market was worth 3.47 billion French francs for the year ended March 2000. Children's cereal has 53.2% of volume sales.

Kellogg 40.7%
Nestle 24.6
Private label 22.4
Other 12.3

Source: *Points de Vente*, May 10, 2000, p. 1.

★ 171 ★
Cereal
SIC: 2043–ISIC: 1531–HC: 19

Top Cereal Makers in Germany

Market shares are shown in percent.

Kellogg Co. 41.2%
Cereal Partners Worldwide 12.4
Weetabix Ltd. 8.4
Quaker Oats Co. 3.1
Private label 13.9
Other 21.0

Source: "Press Release." Retrieved May 9, 2000 from the World Wide Web: http://www.euromonitor.com, from Euromonitor.

★ 172 ★
Cereal
SIC: 2043–ISIC: 1531–HC: 19

Top Cereal Makers in India, 1999

Shares are shown for the first six months of the year.

Kellogg 76.1%
Mohan Meakin 17.2
Other 6.7

Source: *Business India*, September 22, 1999, p. 28.

★ 173 ★
Cereal
SIC: 2043–ISIC: 1531–HC: 19

Top Cereal Makers in New Zealand

Market shares are shown in percent. By volume, the numbers change significantly: Sanitarium has 47.1% and Kellogg 20.4% of the market.

Sanitarium 39.6%
Kellogg 30.6
Other 29.8

Source: *Eurofood*, December 2, 1999, p. 6, from A.C. Nielsen.

★ 174 ★
Rice
SIC: 2044–ISIC: 1531–HC: 19

Plain Rice Sales in the U.K.

Plain rice has a 75.9% share of the 107.2 million British pound market. In the plain rice segment, own label leads over branded with a 72.5% share. In the overall rice market, own label leads over branded with a 66.5% share. For the year ended June 25, 2000, the top dried rice brands were Tesco, Sainsbury and Uncle Ben's.

White 53.7%
Basmati 29.4
Brown 7.7
Arborio/risotto 3.2
Pilau 2.5

Continued on next page.

★ 174 ★
[Continued]
Rice
SIC: 2044–ISIC: 1531–HC: 19
Plain Rice Sales in the U.K.

Plain rice has a 75.9% share of the 107.2 million British pound market. In the plain rice segment, own label leads over branded with a 72.5% share. In the overall rice market, own label leads over branded with a 66.5% share. For the year ended June 25, 2000, the top dried rice brands were Tesco, Sainsbury and Uncle Ben's.

Wild	1.5%
Thai	1.2
Paella	0.3
Red	0.3

Source: *The Grocer*, August 19, 2000, p. 55, from Taylor Nelson Sofres Superpanel.

★ 175 ★
Cake Mixes
SIC: 2045–ISIC: 1531–HC: 19
Cake Mix Market in Australia, 1998

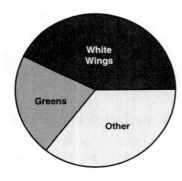

Market shares are shown in percent.

White Wings	42.5%
Greens	21.5
Other	36.0

Source: "Australia: Food Processing Sector." Retrieved September 1, 2000 from the World Wide Web: http://ffas.usda.gov, from A.C. Nielsen.

★ 176 ★
Dessert Mixes
SIC: 2045–ISIC: 1531–HC: 19
Dessert Mix Market in France, 1998

The market reached sales of 373 million French francs.

Alsa	44.4%
Francorusse	15.2
Ancel	14.9
Other	25.5

Source: *Points de Vente*, April 7, 1999, p. 1.

★ 177 ★
Pet Food
SIC: 2047–ISIC: 1533–HC: 23
Cat Food Market in the U.K., 1998

Market shares are shown in percent.

Unisabi	42.9%
Nestle	38.6
Other	18.5

Source: *Points de Vente*, November 25, 1999, p. 1.

★ 178 ★
Pet Food
SIC: 2047–ISIC: 1533–HC: 23
Pet Food Market in Europe, 1998

Market shares are shown in percent.

Mars	48.0%
Nestle	21.0
Private label	14.0
Other	17.0

Source: "Press Releases." Retrieved February 17, 2000 from the World Wide Web: http://www.datamonitor.com, from Datamonitor.

★ 179 ★
Pet Food
SIC: 2047–ISIC: 1533–HC: 23

Pet Food Market in Hong Kong

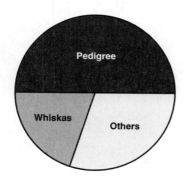

Market shares are shown in percent.

Pedigree 50.0%
Whiskas 20.0
Others 30.0

Source: "Hong Hong Pet Food Market Brief." Retrieved November 1, 2000 from the World Wide Web: http://www.ffas.usda.gov.

★ 180 ★
Pet Food
SIC: 2047–ISIC: 1533–HC: 23

Pet Food Market in Poland

Master Foods

Nestle

Other

Market shares are shown in percent. The market is growing 20% annually.

Master Foods 80.0%
Nestle 7.0
Other 13.0

Source: *Warsaw Business Journal*, May 15, 2000, p. 1.

★ 181 ★
Pet Food
SIC: 2047–ISIC: 1533–HC: 23

Pet Food Sales in the U.K., 2000

Sales are shown in millions of British pounds for the year ended January 9, 2000.

	(mil.)	Share
Cat food, wet	461.09	45.4%
Dog food, wet	336.91	33.2
Biscuits	225.10	2.5
Cat food, dried	76.46	7.5
Completes	64.12	6.3
Mixes	34.16	3.4

Source: *The Grocer*, February 26, 2000, p. 1, from Taylor Nelson Sofres Superpanel.

★ 182 ★
Pet Food
SIC: 2047–ISIC: 1533–HC: 23

Premium Pet Food Market

The premium nutrition market is the fastest growing segement of the $25 billion market.

Hill's 33.0%
Iams 27.0
Ralston 15.0
Other 25.0

Source: *Wall Street Journal*, August 12, 1999, p. B1.

★ 183 ★
Pet Food
SIC: 2047–ISIC: 1533–HC: 23

Top Cat Food Makers in Japan, 1997

Market shares are shown based on shipments.

Friskies 18.6%
Masterfoods 18.2
Maruha Petfood 9.4
Nisshin Petdoof 9.0
Petline 7.0
Nihon Petfood 4.6

Continued on next page.

★ 183 ★
[Continued]
Pet Food
SIC: 2047–ISIC: 1533–HC: 23

Top Cat Food Makers in Japan, 1997

Market shares are shown based on shipments.

Purina Japan	4.4%
Other	28.8

Source: "DVL Market Share Library." Retrieved April 3, 2001 from the World Wide Web: http://dvl/daiwa.co.jp, from DVL Market Share Library and Marketing Data Bank.

★ 184 ★
Pet Food
SIC: 2047–ISIC: 1533–HC: 23

Top Dog Food Makers in Japan

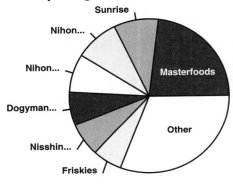

Market shares are shown as of September 1998.

Masterfoods	23.2%
Sunrise	9.0
Nihon Petfood	8.6
Nihon Hills Corgate	7.6
Dogyman Hyashi	7.0
Nisshin Petdoof	6.8
Friskies	6.4
Other	31.4

Source: "DVL Market Share Library." Retrieved April 3, 2001 from the World Wide Web: http://dvl/daiwa.co.jp, from DVL Market Share Library and Marketing Data Bank.

★ 185 ★
Pet Food
SIC: 2047–ISIC: 1533–HC: 23

Top Dog Food Makers in the U.K., 1999

Market shares are estimated based on value. Mars leads the wet dog food sector wth a 54% share, ties wirth Harrison & Crossfield in the dry dog food sector with a 13.0% share.

Mars	35.5%
Nestle	17.6
Own label	13.8
Harrison & Crossfield	5.4
The Baker Group	5.2
Other	22.5

Source: "UK Dog Food." Retrieved January 11, 2001 from the World Wide Web: http://www.clearlybusiness.com, from Datamonitor.

★ 186 ★
Pet Food
SIC: 2047–ISIC: 1533–HC: 23

Top Fish Food Makers in Japan

Market shares are shown as of September 1998.

Kyorin	40.6%
Easter	29.8
Yoshida Shiryo	17.4
Smac	8.8
Other	3.4

Source: "DVL Market Share Library." Retrieved April 3, 2001 from the World Wide Web: http://dvl/daiwa.co.jp, from DVL Market Share Library and Marketing Data Bank.

★ 187 ★
Pet Food
SIC: 2047–ISIC: 1533–HC: 23

Top Pet Food Producers in Thailand

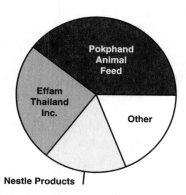

Market shares are shown in percent.

Pokphand Animal Feed 40.0%
Effam Thailand Inc. Ltd. 25.0
Nestle Products (Thailand) Inc. Ltd. 17.0
Other 19.0

Source: ''Pet Food Industry.'' Retrieved April 24, 2001
from the World Wide Web: http://www.bbl.co.th/mreview/
200010_pet1.htm.

★ 188 ★
Bakery Products
SIC: 2050–ISIC: 1541–HC: 19

Global Bakery Product Sales

Sales are shown in thousands of tons. In 1997, West-ern Europe had the highest sales, followed by Africa and the Middle East.

	1993	1997	Share
Bread	84,789	88,328	81.72%
Cakes and pastries . . .	8,984	10,008	9.26
Morning goods	8,252	9,745	9.02

Source: *Quick Frozen Foods International*, September
1999, p. 216, from Euromonitor.

★ 189 ★
Bakery Products
SIC: 2050–ISIC: 1541–HC: 19

Top Cake Makers in Poland

Market shares are shown in percent.

Wedel 28.0%
United Biscuits 19.0
Bahlsen-Skawina 14.0
Kaliszanka 9.0
Nestle-Goplana 6.4
Olza-Jacobs-Suchard 4.8
Other 18.8

Source: *Eurofood*, March 16, 2000, p. 22.

★ 190 ★
Bakery Products
SIC: 2051–ISIC: 1541–HC: 19

Packaged Cake Market in France

The majority of cakes sold in France are unwrapped and produced by artisan operations.

Brossard 12.9%
Own-label 12.6
Vandamme 12.6
Gaillard 5.7
Kinder Delice 3.6
Others 52.6

Source: ''Cakes.'' Retrieved January 26, 2000 from the
World Wide Web: http://www.amerconsult.com/f_ext.htm.

★ 191 ★
Bakery Products
SIC: 2051–ISIC: 1541–HC: 19

Top Cake Producers in Hong Kong

Market shares are shown in percent.

Garden	35.0%
Dan Cake	20.0
Maxim's	17.0
Tai pan	13.0
Other	15.0

Source: "Hong Kong Cakes, Cookies and Crackers Market Brief." Retrieved September 1, 2000 from the World Wide Web: http://ffas.usda.gov, from Foreign Agricultural Service and United States Department of Agriculture.

★ 192 ★
Bakery Products
SIC: 2051–ISIC: 1541–HC: 19

Top Morning Goods/Bagel Brands in the U.K., 2000

Sales are shown in millions of British pounds for the year ended October 8, 2000. Figures are for multiple grocers. Morning goods sales reached 497,106 million pounds, bagels reached 13,640 million pounds.

Warburton Rolls	15,235
Kingsmill Rolls	11,150
Soreen Fruit malt	9,504
New York Bagels	9,282
Hovis Rolls	3,979

Source: *The Grocer*, December 16, 2000, p. 43, from Information Resources Inc.

★ 193 ★
Bakery Products
SIC: 2051–ISIC: 1541–HC: 19

Viennese Pastry Industry in France

The market reached sales of 592 million euros for the year ended November 19, 2000. Sales are for supermarkets and hypermarkets. The principal brands are Brioche Pasquier with a 37% share, Harry's with a 18% share and Boulangere with an 8% share.

Brioches	58.0%
Soft rolls	23.0
Pastry with chocolate filling	10.2
Croissants	7.4
Other	0.8

Source: *LSA*, January 11, 2001, p. 82, from A.C. Nielsen.

★ 194 ★
Bread
SIC: 2051–ISIC: 1541–HC: 19

Top Bread Brands in Brazil

The industry has sales of $550 million.

Santista Alimentos	18.0%
Seven Boys	12.6
Other	69.4

Source: *Gazeta Mercantil*, May 8, 2000, p. C1.

★ 195 ★
Bread
SIC: 2051–ISIC: 1541–HC: 19

Top Bread/Roll Makers in the U.K., 1999

Market shares are shown based on value.

Allied Bakeries	16.1%
British Bakeries	15.1
Artisanal	9.0
Warbuton's	5.4
Private label	35.3
Other	19.1

Source: "UK Bread and Rolls." Retrieved January 11, 2001 from the World Wide Web: http://www.clearlybusiness.com.

★ 196 ★
Bread
SIC: 2051–ISIC: 1541–HC: 19

Unpackaged/Artisanal Bread Market in Western Europe

Sales are shown in billions of dollars.

	1994	1998
Germany	$ 8.87	$ 8.82
Italy	5.66	5.18
France	4.94	4.65
Spain	3.31	3.10
United Kingdom	0.83	0.88

Source: "Industrial Bakers Copy Traditional Styles." Retrieved August 10, 2000 from the World Wide Web: http://www.just-foods.com, from Euromonitor.

★ 197 ★
Cookies
SIC: 2052–ISIC: 1541–HC: 19

Sweet Biscuit Market in France

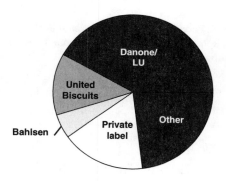

Sweet biscuit sales reached 7.3 billion French francs during the year.

Danone/LU	42.1%
United Biscuits	13.1
Bahlsen	4.9
Private label	16.6
Other	23.3

Source: *Points de Vente*, March 10, 1999, p. 1.

★ 198 ★
Cookies
SIC: 2052–ISIC: 1541–HC: 19

Top Cookie Producers in India

Market shares are shown in percent. The Rs 2,5000 crore organized biscuit market. The unorganized sector is half of the 450,000 ton sector.

Britannia	40.0%
Parle	35.0
Bakeman	10.0
Other	15.0

Source: *Business Today*, September 21, 2000, p. 48, from ORG and NCEAR.

★ 199 ★
Cookies and Crackers
SIC: 2052–ISIC: 1541–HC: 19

Top Cookie and Cracker Brands in Brazil

Market shares are shown in percent.

Danone	12.1%
Nestle	10.2
Tostines	5.0
Other	71.7

Source: *South American Business Information*, April 27, 2001, p. NA.

★ 200 ★
Cookies and Crackers
SIC: 2052–ISIC: 1541–HC: 19

Top Cookie/Crackers Producers in Hong Kong

Market shares are shown in percent.

Garden	33.0%
Arnott's	10.0
McVities	10.0
Dynasty	6.0
Keebler Pacific	5.0
Kjeldsen	5.0
Other	31.0

Source: ''Hong Kong Cakes, Cookies and Crackers Market Brief.'' Retrieved September 1, 2000 from the World Wide Web: http://ffas.usda.gov, from Foreign Agricultural Service and United States Department of Agriculture.

★ 201 ★
Frozen Bakery Products
SIC: 2053–ISIC: 1541–HC: 19

Savory Bakery Market in the U.K., 1998

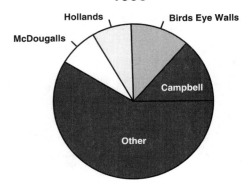

Market shares are shown in percent.

Campbell	10.3%
Birds Eye Walls	9.3
Hollands	6.1
McDougalls	5.8
Other	43.5

Source: ''Frozen Food Outperforms the Overall Food Market in 1998.'' Retrieved September 1, 2000 from the World Wide Web: http://www.bfff.co.uk.

★ 202 ★
Sugar
SIC: 2060–ISIC: 1542–HC: 17

Largest Sugar Markets, 2005

Figures are in billions of dollars.

	($ bil.)	Share
Asia	$ 19.77	31.19%
Europe	17.46	27.54
Middle East	11.25	17.76

Source: ''The 2000-2005 World Outlook for Sugar.'' Retrieved June 1, 2001 from the World Wide Web: http://www.just-food.com.

★ 203 ★
Sugar
SIC: 2060–ISIC: 1542–HC: 17

Sugar Market in France, 1999

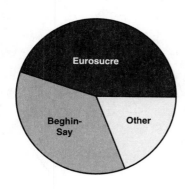

Shares are for the year ended October 1999.

Eurosucre 45.4%
Beghin-Say 36.0
Other 18.6
Source: *Points de Vente*, December 8, 1999, p. 1.

★ 204 ★
Sugar
SIC: 2062–ISIC: 1542–HC: 17

Sugar Market in the Czech Republic, 1998

Market shares are shown in percent.

Cukrovary SDA 39.6%
Cukrspol Praha 17.8
Cukrovar Hrusovan 15.8
Other 26.8
Source: *Ekonomicke Zpravodajstvi*, January 21, 1999, p. 1.

★ 205 ★
Sweeteners
SIC: 2062–ISIC: 1542–HC: 17

Sweetener Market in France, 1998

The 425 million French franc market has reached maturity, growing only 1.9% a year.

Canderel 65.0%
Hermesetas 10.0
Carte Blanch 8.7
Source: *Points de Vente*, December 8, 1999, p. 1.

★ 206 ★
Sweeteners
SIC: 2062–ISIC: 1542–HC: 17

Table Sweetener Market in Israel

Market shares are shown in percent.

Biscol 75.0%
Other 25.0
Source: "About Us." Retrieved April 5, 2001 from the World Wide Web: http://www.biscol.com/about.

★ 207 ★
Cereal Bars
SIC: 2064–ISIC: 1543–HC: 17

Top Cereal Bar Brands in Argentina

Market shares are shown in percent.

Cereal Fort of Felfort 28.6%
Chewy of Quacker 23.1
Cereal Mix 21.0
Other 27.3
Source: "Argentina: Sales of Cereal Bars Increases." Retrieved April 10, 2001 from the World Wide Web: http://library.northernlight.com, from South American Business Information.

★ 208 ★
Confectionery Products
SIC: 2064–ISIC: 1543–HC: 17

Largest Candy Producers

Firms are ranked by net sales in millions of dollars. This is a $100 billion industry.

Nestle	$ 9,257
Kraft Food International	9,251
Mars Inc.	9,250
Ferrrero SpA	4,730
Hershey Foods Corporation	4,000
Cadbury Schweppes	3,350
Adams, a div. of Pfizer	3,000
Meiji Seika Kaisha	2,976
B. Sprengel GmbH & Co.	2,100
William Wrigley Jr.	2,061

Source: *Candy Industry*, October 2000, p. 32.

★ 209 ★
Confectionery Products
SIC: 2064–ISIC: 1543–HC: 17

Top Confectionery Makers in Australia

Market shares are shown in percent.

Nestle	38.0%
Cadbury	10.0
Housebrands/generics	9.0
Kenman	8.0
Ferrero	2.0
Mars	2.0
Other	31.0

Source: *The Manufacturing Confectioner*, May 1999, p. 48.

★ 210 ★
Confectionery Products
SIC: 2064–ISIC: 1543–HC: 17

Top Confectionery Makers in Chile, 2000

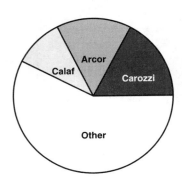

Market shares are shown in percent.

Carozzi	17.4%
Arcor	15.2
Calaf	10.0
Other	57.4

Source: "Calaf Increases Market Share." Retrieved February 5, 2001 from the World Wide Web: http://www.northernlight.com, from South American Business Information.

★ 211 ★
Confectionery Products
SIC: 2064–ISIC: 1543–HC: 17

Top Confectionery Makers in the Ukraine

Market shares are shown in percent. Imports make up 3-10% of the market.

"Svitoch" Lviv Confectionery	32.0%
Karl Marx Confectioners	31.0
Kraft Jacobs Suchard Ukraine	12.0
A.V.K.	10.0
Kharkiv Confectioners	8.0
Other	7.0

Source: "Ukraine Confections Sector." Retrieved November 3, 2000 from the World Wide Web: http://www.usatrade.gov, from *Food Products*.

★ 212 ★
Confectionery Products
SIC: 2064–ISIC: 1543–HC: 17

Top Sugar Confectionery Markets

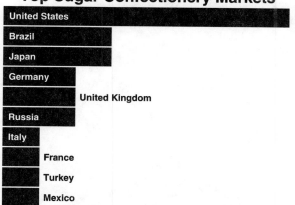

Retail sales are shown in billions of dollars.

	1996	1999
United States	$ 7.10	$ 7.90
Brazil	3.20	2.60
Japan	2.70	2.50
Germany	1.90	1.70
United Kingdom	1.80	2.30
Russia	1.40	2.20
Italy	1.20	1.10
France	0.89	0.84
Turkey	0.77	1.00
Mexico	0.58	0.73

Source: *The Manufacturing Confectioner*, September 2000, p. 21, from Euromonitor.

★ 213 ★
Chocolate
SIC: 2066–ISIC: 1543–HC: 18

Chocolate Market Worldwide

Total annual sales reach $60 billion.

	($ bil.)	Share
United States	$ 16.6	27.67%
United Kingdom	6.5	10.83
Germany	5.1	8.50
Russia	4.9	8.17
Japan	3.2	5.33
France	2.1	3.50

	($ bil.)	Share
Brazil	$ 2.0	3.33%
Other	19.6	32.67

Source: *USA TODAY*, February 14, 2000, p. B1, from Euromonitor.

★ 214 ★
Chocolate
SIC: 2066–ISIC: 1543–HC: 18

Chocolate Market in Germany, 2000

Sales are shown in deutschmarks for the first 31 weeks of the year.

Bars	1,056.6
Pralines	948.9
Solid chocolates	850.4
Chocolate bars	672.1
Solid chocolate 100g	665.7
Praline-like articles	522.2
Praline mixture	216.4
Chocolate snacks	162.3
Muesli bars	75.9

Source: *The Manufacturing Confectioner*, November 2000, p. 23, from A.C. Nielsen.

★ 215 ★
Chocolate
SIC: 2066–ISIC: 1543–HC: 18

Top Chocolate Brands in New Zealand

Market shares are shown in percent.

Cadbury Dairy Milk	4.2%
Cadbury Roses	3.9
Cadbury Moho	2.4
Cadbury Crunchie	2.3
Nestle Milk Bar	2.1
Cadbury Continental	1.9
Other	83.2

Source: Retrieved September 16, 1999 from the World Wide Web: http://www.cadburynz.co.nz/yearbook99/market.html.

★ 216 ★
Chocolate
SIC: 2066–ISIC: 1543–HC: 18

Top Chocolate Brands in the U.K.

Nestle Kit Kat	
Mars Bar	
Cadbury's Dairy Milk	
Mars Twix	
Mars Maltesers	
Cadbury's Roses	
Mars Celebrations	
Mars Snickers	
Nestle Aero	
Nestle Quality Street	
Other	

Total market sales reached 3.4 billion British pounds. Figures refer to grocery and impulse sales.

	(mil.)	Share
Nestle Kit Kat	143.1	4.21%
Mars Bar	123.5	3.63
Cadbury's Dairy Milk	92.8	2.73
Mars Twix	88.0	2.59
Mars Maltesers	87.7	2.58
Cadbury's Roses	83.3	2.45
Mars Celebrations	77.3	2.27
Mars Snickers	72.1	2.12
Nestle Aero	63.5	1.87
Nestle Quality Street	60.5	1.78
Other	2,508.2	73.77

Source: *The Manufacturing Confectioner*, March 2000, p. 22.

★ 217 ★
Chocolate
SIC: 2066–ISIC: 1543–HC: 18

Top Chocolate Candy Brands in Russia, 1998

Shares are shown based on value. Udarnica is the leader with 7.8% share, followed by Rot Front Joint Stock Co. with a 6.7% share.

Alpen Gold	5.2%
Mars	2.9

Snickers	2.5%
Kinder Surprise	1.4
Twix	1.4
Skazki Pushkina	1.2
Sh OK	1.1
Cadbury's Fruit & Nut	1.0
Cadbury's Wispa	0.9
Other	82.5

Source: *The Manufacturing Confectioner*, April 2000, p. 32, from Euromonitor.

★ 218 ★
Chocolate
SIC: 2066–ISIC: 1543–HC: 18

Top Chocolate Makers in Australia

Market shares are shown in percent. Retail sales of confectionery hit almost $2.4 billion in 1998, a seven percent jump over the previous year. Major segments are chocolate bars with 42%, block with 26% and boxed with 10% of the market.

Cadbury	46.0%
Nestle	24.0
Mars	18.0
Ferrero	2.0
House, generics	1.0
Other	9.0

Source: *The Manufacturing Confectioner*, September 1999, p. 32, from Retail Sales Value.

★ 219 ★
Chocolate
SIC: 2066–ISIC: 1543–HC: 18

Top Chocolate Makers in Japan

Market shares are shown in percent.

Meiji	24.0%
Lotte	20.0
Glico	13.0
Morinaga	12.0
Other	31.0

Source: *The Manufacturing Confectioner*, September 1999, p. 32, from Retail Sales Value.

★ 220 ★
Chocolate
SIC: 2066–ISIC: 1543–HC: 18

Top Chocolate Markets

Retail sales of chocolate confectionery are shown in billions of dollars.

	1996	1999
United States	$ 16.30	$ 17.0
Germany	6.00	5.2
United Kingdom	5.40	6.1
Japan	4.10	3.7
Italy	2.30	2.2
Brazil	2.10	1.5
France	2.10	2.0
Russia	1.70	2.1
Poland	0.90	1.2
Turkey	0.67	1.0

Source: *The Manufacturing Confectioner*, September 2000, p. 21, from Euromonitor.

★ 221 ★
Cocoa
SIC: 2066–ISIC: 1543–HC: 18

Largest Cocoa Producers

Market shares are shown in percent.

Cote d'Ivoire	42.0%
Ghana	14.0
Indonesia	14.0
Nigeria	7.0
Brazil	5.0
Cameroon	4.0
Malaysia	3.0
Other	8.0

Source: *Candy Industry*, June 2000, p. 15.

★ 222 ★
Cough Drops
SIC: 2066–ISIC: 1543–HC: 18

Best-Selling Medicated Confectionery Brands in the U.K.

Sales are shown in millions of British pounds for the year ended October 8, 2000.

Strepsils	12.67
Halls	4.02
Dequacaine	2.04
Tyrozets	1.73
Potters Traditional	1.66

Source: *Chemist & Druggist*, December 30, 2000, p. 14, from Information Resources Inc.

★ 223 ★
Gum
SIC: 2067–ISIC: 1543–HC: 17

Chewing Gum Market in Argentina

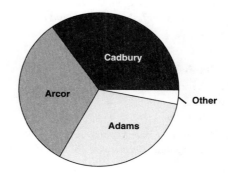

Market shares are shown in percent.

Cadbury	35.0%
Arcor	32.0
Adams	30.0
Other	3.0

Source: *South American Business Information*, February 19, 2001, p. NA.

★ 224 ★
Nuts
SIC: 2068–ISIC: 1549–HC: 20

Snack Nut Market in the U.K., 1999

Market shares are estimated based on value.

KP 47.2%
Walkers Smiths 0.6
Planters 0.4
Golden Wonder 0.2
Private label 49.3
Other 2.3

Source: "UK Snack Nuts." Retrieved January 12, 2001 from the World Wide Web: http://www.clearlybusiness.com, from Datamonitor.

★ 225 ★
Fish Oil
SIC: 2077–ISIC: 1514–HC: 15

How Fish Oil is Used

The market is in a downward turn right now, in part from restrictions on fishing worldwide and animal fats in Europe.

Aquaculture 61.0%
Edible 30.0
Industrial 7.0
Pharmaceuticals 2.0

Source: *Chemical Market Reporter*, February 26, 2001, p. 12, from International Fishmeal & Oil Manufacturers.

★ 226 ★
Fats and Oils
SIC: 2079–ISIC: 1514–HC: 15

Domestic Oil Sales in Peru

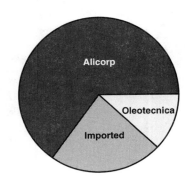

The Peruvian oils market generates sales between $250 - $300 million.

Alicorp 65.0%
Imported 23.0
Oleotecnica 12.0

Source: *Gestion*, December 20, 2000, p. 6.

★ 227 ★
Fats and Oils
SIC: 2079–ISIC: 1514–HC: 15

Largest Cooking Oil Makers in Japan

Market shares are shown in percent.

Cheil Jedang 42.0%
Shindongbang 38.0
Other 20.0

Source: *AsiaPulse News*, March 27, 2001, p. NA.

★ 228 ★
Fats and Oils
SIC: 2079–ISIC: 1514–HC: 15

U.K. Yellow Fat Sales, 2000

Sales are shown in tons for the year ended April 30, 2000.

	Tons	Share
Pufa/Mufa margarine spread	93,390	25.18%
Total butter	88,047	23.74
Dairy spreads	78,539	21.18
Low fat spread	53,272	14.36
Packet margarine	9,150	2.47
Other	48,464	13.07

Source: *The Grocer*, July 1, 2000, p. 1, from Taylor Nelson Sofres Superpanel.

★ 229 ★
Olive Oil
SIC: 2079–ISIC: 1514–HC: 15

Top Olive Oil Brands in Chile, 1999

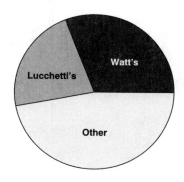

Market shares are shown in percent.

Watt's	30.6%
Lucchetti's	22.1
Other	47.3

Source: *Estrategia*, June 21, 2000, p. 6, from South American Business Information.

★ 230 ★
Olive Oil
SIC: 2079–ISIC: 1514–HC: 15

Top Packed Olive Oil Makers in Greece

Market shares are shown in percent.

Elais	37.0%
Minerva	21.0
Elaiourgiki	10.0
Other	27.0

Source: *Eurofood*, August 12, 1999, p. 8.

★ 231 ★
Beverages
SIC: 2080–ISIC: 1550–HC: 22

Beverage Market in Europe, 2000

According to the source, Greater Europe has seen average consumption of all beverages reach the halfway point of the theoretical saturation level of 730 liters per head per year. Soft drinks continue to have growth, cutting deeper into the total beverage category. In Western Europe, soft drinks had the largest share of throat with 38% and in Eastern Europe, hot drinks had 41% share.

Soft drinks	33.0%
Hot drinks	30.0
Alcoholic drinks	21.0
Milk/milk drinks	16.0

Source: ''Beverage Trends.'' Retrieved May 4, 2001 from the World Wide Web: http://www.just-drinks.com, from Canadean.

★ 232 ★
Beverages
SIC: 2080–ISIC: 1550–HC: 22

Europe's Top Beverages

In the last ten years soft drink's share of throat has increased from 29% to 37%; carbonates dropped 4% to 34%; bottled water increased 4% to 42%.

Bottled water	42.0%
Carbonates	34.0
Jucie & nectars	11.0
Syrups	7.0
Stil drinks	3.0
Iced tea	2.0
Sports & energy	1.0

Source: "UK: Europe Loses its Fizz." Retrieved October 23, 2000 from the World Wide Web: http://www.just-drinks.com, from Canadean.

★ 233 ★
Beverages
SIC: 2080–ISIC: 1550–HC: 22

Health Beverage Market in India

Horlicks	54.0%
Bournvita	13.0
Complan	12.0
Boost	10.0
Maltova & Viva	8.0
Milo	3.0

Source: *Business Today*, January 22, 2000, p. 35.

★ 234 ★
Beverages
SIC: 2080–ISIC: 1550–HC: 22

Hot Drinks Market

Coffee has roughly 70% of the market, helped along by Starbucks. Its goal is to grow from 3,817 outlets worldwide to 10,000 by 2005. Sales are shown in billions of dollars.

	1993	1997	2001
Coffee	$ 29	$ 37	$ 42
Tea	9	11	12
Fruit drinks/other	5	6	6

Source: *Investor's Business Daily*, January 24, 2001, p. 1, from Merrill Lynch, Euromonitor, and U.S. Bancorp. Piper Jafrray.

★ 235 ★
Beverages
SIC: 2080–ISIC: 1550–HC: 22

Largest Beverage Firms

Firms are ranked by worldwide net sales in billions of dollars.

Coca-Cola Co.	$ 19.8
Nestle SA	12.0
Anheuser-Busch	11.7
Diageo	11.1
PepsiCo Inc.	7.0
The Seagram Co.	5.0
Miller Brewing Co.	4.3
Pernod-Ricard	3.6
Danone Group	3.5
Cadbury Schweppes	3.0

Source: *Beverage Industry*, June 2000, p. 32.

★ 236 ★
Beer
SIC: 2082–ISIC: 1553–HC: 22

Beer Market in Brazil

Market shares are shown in percent.

Skol	28.0%
Brahma	21.5
Kaiser	14.0
Antarctica	12.2
Schincariol	9.0
Bavaria	4.3
Other	11.0

Source: *Gazeta Mercantil*, June 12, 2000, p. C7, from South American Business Information.

★ 237 ★
Beer
SIC: 2082–ISIC: 1553–HC: 22

Beer Market in Israel

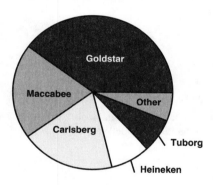

Market shares are shown in percent.

Goldstar	40.0%
Maccabee	20.0
Carlsberg	19.0
Heineken	8.0
Tuborg	7.0
Other	6.0

Source: STAT-USA, *National Trade Data Bank*, April 5, 1999, p. 1, from U.S. Department of Commerce.

★ 238 ★
Beer
SIC: 2082–ISIC: 1553–HC: 22

Beer Market in Italy, 1998

Market shares are shown in percent.

Heineken	36.0%
Peroni	28.0
Carlsberg	10.0
Bira Forst	4.0
Other	22.0

Source: "Italy Beer Market Brief." Retrieved September 1, 2000 from the World Wide Web: http://ffas.usda.gov.

★ 239 ★
Beer
SIC: 2082–ISIC: 1553–HC: 22

Beer Market in Sweden

Market shares are shown in percent.

Pripps	33.0%
Falcon	25.9
Spendrups	22.5
Other	18.6

Source: "Falcon Gains Market Share in Sweden." Retrieved June 29, 2000 from the World Wide Web: http://www.northernlight.com.

★ 240 ★
Beer
SIC: 2082–ISIC: 1553–HC: 22

Beer Market in Taiwan

Market shares are shown in percent.

Chang	49.0%
Shangha	39.0
Other	12.0

Source: *Bangkok Post*, October 4, 1999, p. 8.

★ 241 ★
Beer
SIC: 2082–ISIC: 1553–HC: 22
Global Beer Market by Segment

Sales are shown in millions of dollars.

	1994	1998	Share
Lager	$ 114,590.7	$ 113,769.8	48.47%
Standard lager . . .	82,812.0	82,819.9	35.29
Premium lager . . .	31,778.7	30,949.9	13.19
Dark beer	4,791.0	5,076.9	2.16
Non/low-alcohol beer	2,221.2	2,085.1	0.89

Source: *Brand Stratgey*, August 2000, p. 26.

★ 242 ★
Beer
SIC: 2082–ISIC: 1553–HC: 22
Global Beer Producers, 1999

Market shares are shown in percent.

Anheuser-Busch	11.8%
Interbrew	6.5
Heineken	5.6
AmBev	4.5
SAB	4.2
Carlsberg	4.0
Miller	3.9
Kirin	3.0
Scottish & Newcastle	2.5
Other	54.0

Source: *Wall Street Journal*, August 25, 2000, p. A12, from Merrill Lynch.

★ 243 ★
Beer
SIC: 2082–ISIC: 1553–HC: 22
Global Beer Producers, 2000

Firms are ranked by forecast volume in millions of hectoliters.

Anheuser-Busch	155
Heineken	71
Interbrew	66
Miller	54
SAB	48
Brahma	40
Asahi	33
Kirin	33
Carlsberg	32
Danone	32

Source: "Global Brewer Handbook." Retrieved January 9, 2001 from the World Wide Web: http://www.just-drinks.com.

★ 244 ★
Beer
SIC: 2082–ISIC: 1553–HC: 22
Global Beer Sales

Sales are shown in millions of hectoliters.

Budweiser	50.1
Bud Light	27.3
Brahma Chopp	21.9
Asahi Super Dry	21.7
Corona Extra	9.5
Skol	9.4
Antarctica	9.2

Continued on next page.

★ 244 ★
[Continued]
Beer
SIC: 2082–ISIC: 1553–HC: 22

Global Beer Sales

Sales are shown in millions of hectoliters.

Miller Lite	9.2
Heineken	8.8
Coors Light	7.6

Source: *L'Express*, April 13, 2000, p. 75, from Impact Databank.

★ 245 ★
Beer
SIC: 2082–ISIC: 1553–HC: 22

Top Beer Brands Worldwide, 1999

- Budweiser
- Bud Light
- Asahi Super Dry
- Skol
- Corona Extra
- Heineken
- Brahma Chopp
- Coors Light
- Miller Lite
- Polar
- Other

Market shares are shown in percent.

Budweiser	3.6%
Bud Light	2.6
Asahi Super Dry	1.8
Skol	1.8
Corona Extra	1.7
Heineken	1.6
Brahma Chopp	1.5
Coors Light	1.4
Miller Lite	1.4
Polar	1.1
Other	81.5

Source: *The Economist*, January 20, 2001, p. 64, from Impact Databank.

★ 246 ★
Beer
SIC: 2082–ISIC: 1553–HC: 22

Top Beer/Low-Malt Beer Firms in Japan, 1999

Shares are shown based on domestic shipments.

Kirin Brewery Co.	39.8%
Asahi Breweries Ltd.	35.2
Sapporo Breweries Ltd.	15.1
Suntory Ltd.	9.1
Orion Brewery Ltd.	0.8

Source: *Nikkei Weekly*, August 21, 2000, p. 9, from Nihon Keizai Shimbun.

★ 247 ★
Beer
SIC: 2082–ISIC: 1553–HC: 22

Top Beer Makers in Argentina

The market has become more competitive with the stabilization of the peso. Market shares are shown in percent.

Quilmes	63.4%
Brahma	14.7
CCU	9.5
Isenback	8.7
Other	3.7

Source: *Beverage World International*, July/August 2000, p. 34, from CCR and Information Resources Inc.

★ 248 ★
Beer
SIC: 2082–ISIC: 1553–HC: 22

Top Beer Makers in Australia

Market shares are shown in percent.

Foster's Brewing Group	55.0%
Lion Nathan	41.9
Other	3.1

Source: *Australian Financial Review*, October 17, 2000, p. 3.

★ 249 ★
Beer
SIC: 2082–ISIC: 1553–HC: 22

Top Beer Makers in Europe, 1998

Firms are ranked by production in millions of hectoliters.

Heineken	37.5
Carlsberg	26.0
Danone	24.6
Bass	18.9
Interbrew	17.3
Scottish & Newcastle	16.7
Guinness	15.2
Oetker (Binding Brauerel)	10.7
South African Breweries	9.5
BBAG	9.2

Source: *Financial Times*, March 21, 2000, p. 20, from Candean New Perspectives in Europe: *The Europe Beer Report.*

★ 250 ★
Beer
SIC: 2082–ISIC: 1553–HC: 22

Top Beer Makers in France

Market shares are shown in percent.

Scottish & Newcastle	45.0%
Heineken	31.0
Interbrew	9.0
Others	15.0

Source: *L'Express*, April 13, 2000, p. 75, from Impact Databank.

★ 251 ★
Beer
SIC: 2082–ISIC: 1553–HC: 22

Top Beer Makers in India

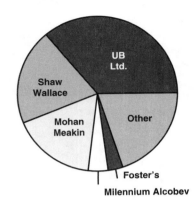

Market shares are shown based on 600 lakh cases.

UB Ltd.	36.0%
Shaw Wallace	20.0
Mohan Meakin	17.0
Milennium Alcobev (UB Group)	4.0
Foster's	3.0
Other	20.0

Source: *Business Today*, December 6, 2000, p. 39.

★ 252 ★
Beer
SIC: 2082–ISIC: 1553–HC: 22

Top Beer Makers in Spain

Cruzcampo-El Aguila
Mahou
Damm
Other

Market shares are shown in percent.

Cruzcampo-El Aguila (Heineken)	40.2%
Mahou	32.9
Damm	16.3
Other	10.6

Source: *Pais*, March 21, 2000, p. 66.

★ 253 ★
Beer
SIC: 2082–ISIC: 1553–HC: 22

Top Beer Markets in Western Europe

Sales are shown in millions of dollars.

	1994	1998
Germany	$ 6,540	$ 6,278
United Kingdom	2,241	2,642
France	1,465	1,523
Netherlands	866	879
Italy	841	904
Spain	809	989
Austria	592	544
Sweden	468	450
Belgium	384	392
Turkey	268	426
Other	1,505	1,407

Source: *Beverage Industry*, November 1999, p. 94, from
Euromonitor.

★ 254 ★
Beer
SIC: 2082–ISIC: 1553–HC: 22

Top Beer Producers in the U.K., 1999

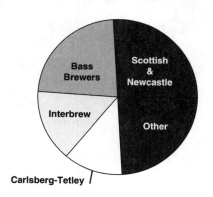

Market shares are shown in percent.

Scottish & Newcastle	26.0%
Bass Brewers	23.4
Interbrew	14.5
Carlsberg-Tetley	11.8
Other	24.3

Source: *Financial Times*, January 4, 2001, p. 20, from
Thomson Financial Datastream.

★ 255 ★
Beer
SIC: 2082–ISIC: 1553–HC: 22

Top Take-Home Brewers in the U.K., 1998

Market shares refer to the take-home segment.

Scottish & Newcastle	22.0%
Whitbread	20.0
Bass	17.0
Carlsberg-Tetley	9.0
Others	32.0

Source: *Financial Times*, December 7, 1999, p. 28, from
DKBR estimates.

★ 256 ★
Wine
SIC: 2084–ISIC: 1552–HC: 22

Best-Selling Wines in Germany, 1999

*Brands are ranked by sales in millions of .75 liter
bottles sold by food retailers.*

Amselkeller	11.85
Langguth Erben	10.12
Himml. Troepfchen	7.47
Blanchet	6.97
Maedchentraube	6.11
E. Maestro	5.95
JP Chenet	5.68
Gallo Range	5.61
Viala	5.50
Bongeronde	5.00

Source: *Lebensmittel Zeitung*, March 17, 2000, p. 1, from
GfK.

★ 257 ★
Wine
SIC: 2084–ISIC: 1552–HC: 22

Best-Selling Wines in the U.K., 2000

Retail sales are shown in millions of British pounds.

Jacob's Creek	71.4
E&J Gallo	69.0
Hardy's Stamp/Nottage Hill	62.6
Stowell's of Chelsea	41.0
Rosemount	37.5
Lindemans	34.1
Penfolds	25.6
Le Plat d'Or	23.5
Blossom Hill	20.1
Banrock Station	15.9

Source: *Financial Times*, February 8, 2001, p. 24, from UK Wines and Spirits Association.

★ 258 ★
Wine
SIC: 2084–ISIC: 1552–HC: 22

Largest Wine Producers, 1999

Market shares are shown in percent.

France	23.0%
Italy	22.0
Spain	14.0
Argentina/Chile	8.0
United States	8.0
Australia/New Zealand	3.0
South Africa	2.0
Other	21.0

Source: *Financial Times*, May 5, 2001, p. 9, from Morgan Stanley Dean Witter.

★ 259 ★
Liquor
SIC: 2085–ISIC: 1551–HC: 22

Alcoholic Beverage Market in Poland

Market shares are shown in percent.

Vodka	53.1%
Beer	36.8
Wine	7.3
Whiskey	1.0
Brandy	0.9
Liquor	0.6
Gin	0.3

Source: "Grape Wine Market." Retrieved April 3, 2001 from the World Wide Web: http://www.usatrade.gov.

★ 260 ★
Liquor
SIC: 2085–ISIC: 1551–HC: 22

Alcoholic Fruit Beverage Market in South Africa

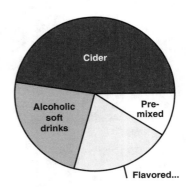

Market shares are shown in percent.

Cider	47.0%
Alcoholic soft drinks	23.0
Flavored grape based coolers	20.0
Pre-mixed	9.0

Source: "AFBs are the Flavor of the Month." Retrieved December 5, 2000 from the World Wide Web: http://www.just-drinks.com, from Stellenbosch Farmers Winery.

★ 261 ★
Liquor
SIC: 2085–ISIC: 1551–HC: 22

Cognac Market in Germany

Market shares are shown in percent.

Remy Martin	19.0%
Hennessey	17.0
Comte Joseph	13.0
Martell	12.0
Chantre	7.0
Biscuit	3.0
Courvoisier	1.0
Other	28.0

Source: *Wirtschaftswoche*, February 3, 2000, p. 76, from Bureau National Interprofessional du Cognac.

★ 262 ★
Liquor
SIC: 2085–ISIC: 1551–HC: 22

Local Champagne Sales in Argentina

Market shares are shown in percent.

Chandon	72.0%
Other	28.0

Source: *South American Business Information*, April 16, 2001, p. NA.

★ 263 ★
Liquor
SIC: 2085–ISIC: 1551–HC: 22

Top Champagne Brands in the U.K.

Shares are shown based on supermarket sales.

Own label	31.3%
Moet & Chandon	15.2
Lanson Black Label	7.3
Piper Heidsieck	5.1
Heidsieck Monopole	4.9
Veuve Cliquot	4.0
Perrier Jouet	2.4
Bollinger	2.0

Laurent Perrier	2.0%
Mercier	1.7

Source: ''Champagne.'' Retrieved January 2, 2001 from the World Wide Web: http://www.just-drinks.com, from A.C. Nielsen.

★ 264 ★
Liquor
SIC: 2085–ISIC: 1551–HC: 22

Top Cognac Brands in Hong Kong

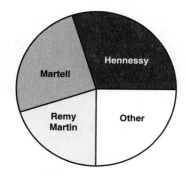

Market shares are shown in percent.

Hennessy	30.0%
Martell	25.0
Remy Martin	20.0
Other	25.0

Source: ''Hong Kong Bourbon and Liquor Product Brief.'' Retrieved October 1, 2000 from the World Wide Web: http://ffas.usda.gov, from Eastern Strategic Consulting Ltd.

★ 265 ★
Liquor
SIC: 2085–ISIC: 1551–HC: 22

Top Distilled Spirit Brands

Brands are ranked by retail value in billions of dollars.

Stolichnaya	$ 1.98
Bacardi	1.88
Smirnoff	1.86

Continued on next page.

★ 265 ★
[Continued]
Liquor
SIC: 2085–ISIC: 1551–HC: 22

Top Distilled Spirit Brands

Brands are ranked by retail value in billions of dollars.

Hennessey	$ 1.67
Johnnie Walker Red	1.30
Jinro	1.27
Absolut	1.25
Jack Daniel's	1.23
J&B	1.12
Ballantine's	1.10

Source: *Financial Times*, August 24, 2000, p. 13, from Impact Databank.

★ 266 ★
Liquor
SIC: 2085–ISIC: 1551–HC: 22

Top Liquor Brands in Brazil

Market shares are shown in percent.

Dreher	36.1%
Old Eight	32.7
Drury's	14.0
Other	17.2

Source: *Gazeta Mercantil*, May 4, 2000, p. C8, from A.C. Nielsen.

★ 267 ★
Liquor
SIC: 2085–ISIC: 1551–HC: 22

Top Sake Makers in Japan

Market shares are shown as of September 1998.

Gekkeikan	6.5%
Hakutsuru Shuzo	6.0
Nishinomiya Shuzo	4.8
Oozeki	4.8
Takara Shuzo	4.2
Kikumasamune Shuzo	4.0
Other	69.7

Source: "DVL Market Share Library." Retrieved April 3, 2001 from the World Wide Web: http://dvl/daiwa.co.jp, from DVL Market Share Library and Marketing Data Bank.

★ 268 ★
Liquor
SIC: 2085–ISIC: 1551–HC: 22

Top Scotch Whisky Brands

Brands are ranked by sales of 9-liter cases.

Johnnie Walker Red	7.4
J&B Rare	6.2
Ballantine's	5.0
Grant's	4.0
Chivas Regal	3.2
Johnnie Walker Black	3.0
Bell's	2.7
Dewar's	2.6
The Famous Grouse	2.2
Cutty Sark	1.9

Source: "100 Million Tonic for Scotch Whiskey." Retrieved March 3, 2000 from the World Wide Web: http://www.just-drinks.com, from UDV.

★ 269 ★
Liquor
SIC: 2085–ISIC: 1551–HC: 22

Top Spirits and Liquor Brands in the U.K., 1999

Sales are shown in millions of British pounds.

Bell's	112.7
Famous Grouse	91.0
Smirnoff Red Label	91.0
Gordon's	82.4
Bacardi	61.3
Teacher's	61.3
Bailey's Irish Cream	46.1
J Grant's Vodka	32.5
William Grant's	31.0
Martel VS	28.7

Source: *Checkout*, July 1, 2000, p. 1, from A.C. Nielsen.

★ 270 ★
Liquor
SIC: 2085–ISIC: 1551–HC: 22

Top Vodka Brands Worldwide, 1999

Brands are ranked by non-liter case depletions.

Stolichnaya	55.0
Moskovskaya	33.0
Russkaya	17.0
Smirnoff	16.3
Wyborowa	7.0

Source: *Financial Times*, September 11, 2000, p. 9, from Impact Databank.

★ 271 ★
Liquor
SIC: 2085–ISIC: 1551–HC: 22

Top Whiskey Brands in Hong Kong, 1997

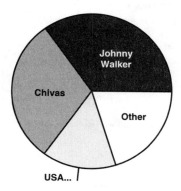

Market shares are shown in percent.

Johnny Walker	35.0%
Chivas	30.0
USA bourbon and whisky	15.0
Other	20.0

Source: "Hong Kong Bourbon and Liquor Product Brief." Retrieved October 1, 2000 from the World Wide Web: http://ffas.usda.gov, from Eastern Strategic Consulting Ltd.

★ 272 ★
Liquor
SIC: 2085–ISIC: 1551–HC: 22

Top Whiskey Producers in Korea, 2000

Market shares are shown based on case sales. A total of 2.56 million boxes of whiskey were sold.

Doosan Seagram	37.5%
Jinro Ballantine's	30.3
Hiscot	27.2
Other	5.0

Source: *Korea Herald*, January 15, 2001, p. K, from Korea Alcohol & Liquor Industry.

★ 273 ★
Bottled Water
SIC: 2086–ISIC: 1554–HC: 22

Bottled Water Sales by Packaging

The market continues to be driven by the quality of tap water and the quest for healthier lifestyles. Distribution is shown in selected countries.

	France	Germany	U.K.
Plastic	91.8%	8.9%	74.7%
Glass	8.1	89.4	24.8
Can	0.1	0.1	0.5

Source: *Brand Strategy*, March 2001, p. 24.

★ 274 ★
Bottled Water
SIC: 2086–ISIC: 1554–HC: 22

Bottled Water Market in Germany

Market shares are shown in percent.

Gerolsteiner	9.6%
Volvic (Danone)	3.7
Apollinaris	3.5
Vilsa	3.1
Furtst Bismarck	2.8
Other	77.3

Source: *Lebensmittel Zeitung*, April 20, 2001, p. 16, from Gfk.

★ 275 ★
Bottled Water
SIC: 2086–ISIC: 1554–HC: 22

Bottled Water Market in India

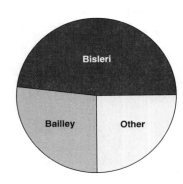

The Rs 500 crore bottled water industry is seeing a large number of new players entering the market. It is the only segment of the consumer goods sector to see growth of over 50 percent in one year. The growth comes from the fact that the bottled water segment has always been underdeveloped and now soft drinks have become very expensive. Market shares are shown in percent.

Bisleri	48.0%
Bailley	27.0
Other	25.0

Source: *Hindu*, February 18, 2001, p. NA, from Samsika Marketing Consultants.

★ 276 ★
Bottled Water
SIC: 2086–ISIC: 1554–HC: 22

Bottled Water Market in Spain, 1998

Market shares are shown in percent.

Grupo Danone	16.3%
Grupo Vichy Catalan	8.6
Grupo Pascual	5.2
Other	69.9

Source: ''Spain: Bottled Water Report.'' Retrieved September 1, 2000 from the World Wide Web: http://ffas.usda.gov, from Foreign Agricultural Service and United States Department of Agriculture.

★ 277 ★
Bottled Water
SIC: 2086–ISIC: 1554–HC: 22

Top Bottled Water Brands in Indonesia

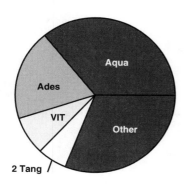

Market shares are shown in percent.

Aqua	36.0%
Ades	19.0
VIT	8.0
2 Tang	6.0
Other	31.0

Source: *Jakarta Post*, March 21, 2001, p. NA, from Ministry of Trade and Industry and Directorate General of Food and Medicine Control.

★ 278 ★
Bottled Water
SIC: 2086–ISIC: 1554–HC: 22

Water-Cooler Rental Market in Australia

Market shares are shown in percent.

Neverfail	65.0%
Other	35.0

Source: *Australian Financial Review*, February 23, 2001, p. NA.

★ 279 ★
Soft Drinks
SIC: 2086–ISIC: 1554–HC: 22

Carbonated Beverage Market in China

Data are for the top 30 cities.

Coke	33.0%
Pepsi	13.0
Other	54.0

Source: *Advertising Age International*, October 2000, p. 6, from A.C. Nielsen.

★ 280 ★
Soft Drinks
SIC: 2086–ISIC: 1554–HC: 22

Energy Drink Market in New Zealand, 2000

Market shares are shown in percent.

Frucor's	56.8%
Other	43.2

Source: ''Beverage Companies Drink to Good Health and Style.'' Retrieved April 11, 2001 from the World Wide Web: http://www.grocersreview.co.nz, from A.C. Nielsen.

★ 281 ★
Soft Drinks
SIC: 2086–ISIC: 1554–HC: 22

Global Energy Drink Market, 1999

Market shares are shown in percent.

Red Bull	60.0%
Other	40.0

Source: *Nutraceuticals International*, September 2000, p. NA.

★ 282 ★
Soft Drinks
SIC: 2086–ISIC: 1554–HC: 22

Global Soft Drink Market

Colas are the most important flavor segment, the industry experienced the most growth in the non-cola segment. Sprite and Mountain Dew had growth rates of 9.4% and 10.9% respectively. Data are in millions of 192-oz cases.

	1998	2003	Share
North America	13,355.6	15,638.6	42.59%
Europe	6,538.9	7,689.3	20.94
South America	4,021.8	5,242.5	14.28
Asia	3,879.6	5,186.4	14.12
Middle East	981.3	1,286.1	3.50
Africa	951.3	1,150.4	3.13
Oceania	449.2	528.7	1.44

Source: "World Soft Drink Market." Retrieved Apriul 26, 2000 from the World Wide Web: http://www.just-drinks.com, from Beverage Marketing Corp.

★ 283 ★
Soft Drinks
SIC: 2086–ISIC: 1554–HC: 22

Power Drink Market in Brazil

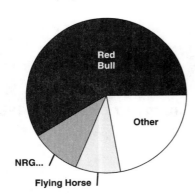

Market shares are shown in percent.

Red Bull	58.1%
NRG Trading	10.2
Flying Horse	9.4
Other	22.3

Source: *South American Business Information*, May 11, 2001, p. NA, from A.C. Nielsen.

★ 284 ★
Soft Drinks
SIC: 2086–ISIC: 1554–HC: 22

Soft Drink Market in Brazil

Market shares are shown in percent.

Coke	49.9%
Antarctica	9.4
Pepsi	3.9
Brahma	3.7
Others	33.1

Source: *Wall Street Journal*, March 6, 2000, p. A17, from A.C. Nielsen.

★ 285 ★
Soft Drinks
SIC: 2086–ISIC: 1554–HC: 22

Soft Drink Market in Denmark

Market shares are shown in percent.

Coke	46.8%
Pepsi	7.5
Other	45.7

Source: *Wall Street Journal*, May 19, 2000, p. A3, from *Beverage Digest*.

★ 286 ★
Soft Drinks
SIC: 2086–ISIC: 1554–HC: 22

Soft Drink Market in France

Market refers to cola sales.

Coke	80.0%
Pepsi	7.0
Other	13.0

Source: *USA TODAY*, September 29, 1999, p. 5B.

★ 287 ★
Soft Drinks
SIC: 2086–ISIC: 1554–HC: 22

Soft Drink Market in Germany

The market for carbonated soft drinks had a volume of 3.04 billion.

Sodas and sparkling drinks	39.0%
Colas	37.0
Diet cola	9.0
Cola-mix drinks	6.0
Bitter drinks	2.0
Other	7.0

Source: *Lebensmittel Zeitung*, April 20, 2001, p. 46.

★ 288 ★
Soft Drinks
SIC: 2086–ISIC: 1554–HC: 22

Soft Drink Market in India

The table compares the difference in share between urban and rural areas.

	Rural	Urban
Coke	29.0%	54.0%
Pepsi	22.0	41.0
Other	49.0	54.0

Source: ''India Soft Drinks Come Of Age.'' Retrieved October 23, 2000 from the World Wide Web: http://www.just-drinks.com.

★ 289 ★
Soft Drinks
SIC: 2086–ISIC: 1554–HC: 22

Soft Drink Market in Italy

Market shares are shown in percent.

Coca-Cola Co.	44.9%
PepsiCo.	6.2
Cadbury Schweppes	1.0
Other	47.9

Source: *Wall Street Journal*, August 13, 1999, p. 3, from *Beverage Digest*.

★ 290 ★
Soft Drinks
SIC: 2086–ISIC: 1554–HC: 22

Soft Drink Market in Spain, 1998

Market shares are shown in percent.

Coca-Cola	56.9%
Pepsi-Cola	13.7
La Casera	10.3
Private label	17.2
Other	1.8

Source: ''Spain: Soft Drinks Report.'' Retrieved September 1, 2000 from the World Wide Web: http://ffas.usda.gov, from Foreign Agricultural Service and United States Department of Agriculture.

★ 291 ★
Soft Drinks
SIC: 2086–ISIC: 1554–HC: 22

Top Soft Drink Firms in Finland

Shares are shown for the first four months of the year.

Hartwell	43.5%
PepsiCo.	19.9
Other	36.6

Source: ''Hartwell Upcider is the Success Story.'' Retrieved May 30, 2000 from the World Wide Web: http://WWW.BUSINESSWIRE.COM.

★ 292 ★

Soft Drinks

SIC: 2086–ISIC: 1554–HC: 22

Top Soft Drink Firms in Japan, 1999

Shares are shown based on domestic shipments.

Coca-Cola	29.5%
Suntory Ltd.	14.6
Kirin Beverage Corp.	7.8
Asahi Soft Drinks Co.	7.7
Otsuka Pharmaceuticals Co.	7.4
Other	33.0

Source: *Nikkei Weekly*, August 21, 2000, p. 9, from Nihon Keizai Shimbun.

★ 293 ★

Soft Drinks

SIC: 2086–ISIC: 1554–HC: 22

Top Soft Drink Firms in the U.K., 1998

Market shares are shown in percent.

Coca-Cola Schweppes	26.5%
Britvic	14.1
Princes	9.8
Cott	9.3
Gerber	5.0
Other	25.3

Source: "Britvic Aims to Add Fizz to Soft Drink Market." Retrieved May 11, 1999 from the World Wide Web: http://www.just-drinks.com.

★ 294 ★

Soft Drinks

SIC: 2086–ISIC: 1554–HC: 22

Top Soft Drink Makers in the Czech Republic, 1999

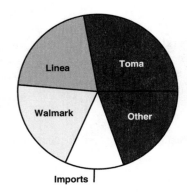

Market shares are shown based on sales.

Toma	28.0%
Linea	20.8
Walmark	19.5
Imports	11.7
Other	20.0

Source: *Ekonom*, February 24, 2000, p. 1.

★ 295 ★

Soft Drinks

SIC: 2086–ISIC: 1554–HC: 22

Top Soft Drink Producers in Africa & the Middle East, 1998

Market shares are shown in percent.

Coca-Cola Co.	40.3%
PepsiCo Inc.	16.0
Cadbury Schweppes	3.8
Quality Beverages	1.0
Appletiser South Africa	0.9

Source: *Beverage Industry*, March 2000, p. 36, from Euromonitor International.

★ 296 ★
Soft Drinks
SIC: 2086–ISIC: 1554–HC: 22

Top Soft Drink Producers in Greece

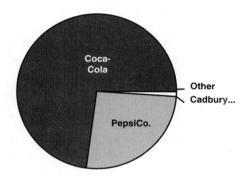

Market shares are shown in percent.

Coca-Cola	72.7%
PepsiCo.	25.9
Cadbury Schweppes	0.1
Other	1.3

Source: *Financial Times*, July 22, 1999, p. 2, from *Beverage Digest*.

★ 297 ★
Soft Drinks
SIC: 2086–ISIC: 1554–HC: 22

Top Soft Drink Producers in Ireland

Market shares are shown in percent.

Coca-Cola	36.8%
PepsiCo.	20.0
Cadbury Schweppes	1.8
Other	41.4

Source: *Financial Times*, July 22, 1999, p. 2, from *Beverage Digest*.

★ 298 ★
Soft Drinks
SIC: 2086–ISIC: 1554–HC: 22

Top Soft Drink Producers in the Asia/ Pacific Region, 1998

Market shares are shown in percent.

Coca-Cola Co.	46.7%
PepsiCo. Inc.	18.8
Cadbury Schweppes	3.0
Asahi Breweries	2.3
Cosmos Bottling Corp.	2.0

Source: *Beverage Industry*, March 2000, p. 36, from Euromonitor International.

★ 299 ★
Soft Drinks
SIC: 2086–ISIC: 1554–HC: 22

Top Soft Drink Producers in Western Europe, 1998

Market shares are shown in percent.

Coca-Cola Co.	47.1%
PepsiCo. Inc.	10.8
Cadbury Schweppes	5.3
Iberian Beverage Group SA	1.5
Pernod Ricard Groups	1.1
Nestle SA	0.9

Source: *Beverage Industry*, March 2000, p. 36, from Euromonitor International.

★ 300 ★
Soft Drinks
SIC: 2086–ISIC: 1554–HC: 22

Top Soft Drink Producers Worldwide, 1998

Coca-Cola Co.

PepsiCo. Inc.

Cadbury Schweppes

Companhia Antarctica Paulista Industria Brasilieria

National Beverage Corp.

Panamerican Beverages

Triarc Cos. Inc.

Market shares are shown in percent.

Coca-Cola Co.	46.1%
PepsiCo. Inc.	21.1
Cadbury Schweppes	6.9
Companhia Antarctica Paulista Industria Brasilieria	0.9
National Beverage Corp.	0.8
Panamerican Beverages	0.6
Triarc Cos. Inc.	0.6

Source: *Beverage Industry*, March 2000, p. 36, from Euromonitor International.

★ 301 ★
Sports Drinks
SIC: 2086–ISIC: 1554–HC: 22

Best-Selling Sports/Energy Drinks in the U.K., 1999

Sales are shown in millions of British pounds.

Luzozade	88.5
Red Bull	30.9
Lucozade Sport	20.9
Lucozade Low Calorie	5.5
Lucozade Solstis	2.5
Purdey's	2.3
Indigo	1.8
Oasis	1.8
Lucozade NRG	1.4

Source: *The Grocer*, February 19, 2000, p. S6, from A.C. Nielsen.

★ 302 ★
Sports Drinks
SIC: 2086–ISIC: 1554–HC: 22

Sports Drink Market in South Africa

Market shares are shown in percent.

Energade	55.0%
Powerade	30.0
Game's	4.0
Lucozade	1.0
Other	10.0

Source: "Bromor Gets Fo-Ahead for Game Merger." Retrieved April 24, 2000 from the World Wide Web: http://www.northernlight.com, from Africa News Service.

★ 303 ★
Seafood
SIC: 2091–ISIC: 1512–HC: 03

Canned Fish Market in Hong Kong

Market shares are shown in percent.

Pearl River	15.0%
Del Monte	12.0
John West	10.0
No Frills	10.0
Red Marubean	8.0
Sea Pearl	7.0
Hyde Park	5.0
Other	33.0

Source: "Hong Kong Canned Food Market Brief." Retrieved September 1, 2000 from the World Wide Web: http://ffas.usda.gov, from Foreign Agricultural Service and United States Department of Agriculture.

★ 304 ★
Seafood
SIC: 2091–ISIC: 1512–HC: 03

Top Tuna Makers in the U.K.

Market shares are shown in percent.

John West 24.0%
Princes 20.0
Other 56.0

Source: *The Grocer*, January 20, 2001, p. 23.

★ 305 ★
Seafood
SIC: 2091–ISIC: 1512–HC: 03

Vacuum-Packed Seafood Category in New Zealand, 2000

Market shares are shown in percent. The market is worth $6.7 million in supermarket sales and has grown 20.1% over the previous year.

Smoked salmon 86.2%
Smoked mussels 8.4
Smoked eel 1.2
Other 4.2

Source: "Foodtown's Instore Revolution." Retrieved April 11, 2001 from the World Wide Web: http://www.grocersreview.co.nz, from A.C. Nielsen.

★ 306 ★
Seafood
SIC: 2092–ISIC: 1549–HC: 16

Coated Fish Market in the U.K., 1998

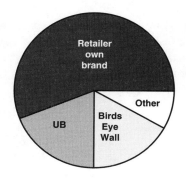

Market shares are shown in percent.

Retailer own brand 56.1%
UB 19.3
Birds Eye Wall 17.1
Other 7.5

Source: "Frozen Food Outperforms the Overall Food Market in 1998." Retrieved September 1, 2000 from the World Wide Web: http://www.bfff.co.uk.

★ 307 ★
Seafood
SIC: 2092–ISIC: 1549–HC: 16

Frozen Fish Market in the U.K., 1998

Retail own brand
Birds Eye Wall
UB
Other

Market shares are shown in percent.

Retail own brand 49.0%
Birds Eye Wall 23.2
UB 19.3
Other 8.5

Source: "Frozen Food Outperforms the Overall Food Market in 1998." Retrieved September 1, 2000 from the World Wide Web: http://www.bfff.co.uk.

★ 308 ★
Coffee
SIC: 2095–ISIC: 1549–HC: 09

Best-Selling Instant Coffee Brands in New Zealand

Instant coffee represents 73% of total coffee sales. Standard and premium are the two main categories. Premium has a 23% growth rate over the previous year. Sales are shown in New Zealand dollars for the year ended August 13, 2000.

	Sales	Share
T. Nescafe	3,256,704	44.27%
T. Moccona	3,193,530	43.41
T. Robert Larris	906,444	12.32

Source: "Premium Brands Boost Instant Coffee Market." Retrieved April 11, 2001 from the World Wide Web: http://www.grocersreview.co.nz, from A.C. Nielsen.

★ 309 ★
Coffee
SIC: 2095–ISIC: 1549–HC: 09

Coffee Market in Ireland

Market shares are shown in percent.

Nescafe	50.0%
Maxwell House	25.0
Other	25.0

Source: "Experts Overview of Hot Market." Retrieved May 11, 1999 from the World Wide Web: http://www.just-drinks.com.

★ 310 ★
Coffee
SIC: 2095–ISIC: 1549–HC: 09

Instant Coffee Market in Australia, 1998

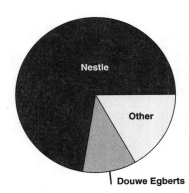

Market shares are shown in percent.

Nestle	72.6%
Douwe Egberts	10.9
Other	16.5

Source: "Australia: Food Processing Sector." Retrieved September 1, 2000 from the World Wide Web: http://ffas.usda.gov, from A.C. Nielsen.

★ 311 ★
Coffee
SIC: 2095–ISIC: 1549–HC: 09

Instant Coffee Market in Germany

| Nestle Nescafe |
| Kraft Jacobs Suchard |
| Deutsche Extrakt Kaffee |
| Other |

Germans drank 7.5 billion cups of instant coffee in 1999. Ground coffee is still the preference, but the iced segment has been growing thanks to iced coffees and cappuccinos.

Nestle Nescafe	34.0%
Kraft Jacobs Suchard	29.0
Deutsche Extrakt Kaffee	27.0
Other	10.0

Source: *Eurofood*, May 25, 2000, p. 19.

★ 312 ★
Coffee
SIC: 2095–ISIC: 1549–HC: 09

Largest Coffee Consumers

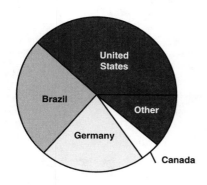

Data are in millions of 60 kg bags.

	(mil.)	Share
United States	18.0	38.14%
Brazil	12.0	25.42
Germany	10.0	21.19
Canada	2.1	4.45
Other	5.1	10.81

Source: *Globe and Mail*, October 28, 1999, p. C4.

★ 313 ★
Coffee
SIC: 2095–ISIC: 1549–HC: 09

Largest Coffee Growers

Data are in millions of bags for 1998-99.

Brazil	26.5
Colombia	12.7
Indonesia	7.2
Vietnam	7.0
Mexico	5.2
Cote d'Ivoire	5.0
India	4.5
Guatemala	3.3

Source: *New York Times*, September 25, 2000, p. B1, from U.S. Department of Agriculture.

★ 314 ★
Coffee
SIC: 2095–ISIC: 1549–HC: 09

Top Coffee Brands in Brazil

Market shares are shown in percent.

Café Pilao	14.0%
Café do Ponto	4.5
Merlitta	4.5
Other	77.0

Source: *Gazeta Mercantil*, May 16, 2000, p. B20, from South American Business Information and *Gazeta Mercantil*.

★ 315 ★
Coffee
SIC: 2095–ISIC: 1549–HC: 09

Top Coffee Brands in Spain, 1998

Market shares are shown in percent. The country is the fourth largest coffee consumer in Europe.

Nescafe	51.0%
Marcilla	8.0
Saimaza	3.6
La Estrella	3.5
Café 143	1.1
Mokanor	0.7
Other	8.9

Source: *Tea & Coffee Trade Journal*, December 1999, p. 33.

★ 316 ★
Snacks
SIC: 2096–ISIC: 1532–HC: 20
Extruded Snack Market in France, 1999

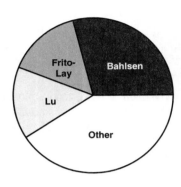

Savory appetizer sales reached 83,880 tons for the year ended August 31, 1999.

Bahlsen	28.6%
Frito-Lay	15.4
Lu	14.8
Other	41.2

Source: *Points de Vente*, October 20, 1999, p. 1.

★ 317 ★
Snacks
SIC: 2096–ISIC: 1532–HC: 20
Largest Snack Producers, 1998

The largest bakery product and snack makers are ranked by turnover in sales in millions of dollars.

Frito-Lay	$ 10,975
George Weston	9,529
Nabisco	8,734
General Mills	7,100
Yamazaki Baking	4,926

Source: "Press Release." Retrieved January 1, 2000 from the World Wide Web: http://www.lfra.com, from Leatherhead Food.

★ 318 ★
Snacks
SIC: 2096–ISIC: 1532–HC: 20
Leading Snack Markets

Market shares are shown in percent.

	1996	2000
North America	34.6%	37.4%
Asia-Pacific	24.7	20.3
Western Europe	23.7	22.9
Eastern Europe	16.0	2.3
Latin America	9.3	11.4
Africa and the Middle East	3.9	3.6
Australasia	2.1	2.1

Source: *Brand Strategy*, April 2001, p. 22.

★ 319 ★
Snacks
SIC: 2096–ISIC: 1532–HC: 20
Popcorn Market in the U.K., 1999

Market shares are estimated based on value. Ready-to-eat had 63% of the market, microwavable had 32% and unpopped had 5%.

Trebor	42.3%
ConAgra	11.2
Others	46.5

Source: "UK Snack Nuts." Retrieved January 12, 2001 from the World Wide Web: http://www.clearlybusiness.com, from Datamonitor.

★ 320 ★
Snacks
SIC: 2096–ISIC: 1532–HC: 20
Salty Snack Market in Egypt

Market shares are shown in percent.

PepsiCo	60.0%
Other	40.0

Source: *Food Institute Report*, January 15, 2001, p. 5.

★ 321 ★
Snacks
SIC: 2096–ISIC: 1532–HC: 20
Savory Snacks Market Worldwide

Sales are in billions of dollars.

	1996	2001	Share
United States	$ 14.3	$ 17.3	35.8%
Japan	7.7	6.9	14.2
United Kingdom	3.8	4.5	9.3
Germany	1.9	1.8	3.7
Mexico	1.7	2.4	4.9
Brazil	1.0	1.2	2.5
Australia	0.8	0.9	1.8
Canada	0.8	0.8	1.6
China	0.8	0.9	1.9
France	0.8	0.7	1.5

Source: "Savory Snacks Get A Change." Retrieved March 22, 2001 from the World Wide Web: http://www.euromonitor.com.

★ 322 ★
Snacks
SIC: 2096–ISIC: 1532–HC: 20
Top Popcorn Makers in Argentina

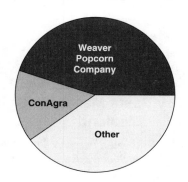

Market shares are shown in percent.

Weaver Popcorn Company	45.0%
ConAgra	15.0
Other	40.0

Source: "Popcorn." Retrieved November 1, 2000 from the World Wide Web: http://www.usatrade.gov.

★ 323 ★
Snacks
SIC: 2096–ISIC: 1532–HC: 20
Top Potato Chip Makers in Thailand

The 3.8 billion baht market is shown in percent.

Frito Lay	50.0%
Tasto	14.0
Other	36.0

Source: *Bangkok Post*, March 16, 2001, p. NA.

★ 324 ★
Snacks
SIC: 2096–ISIC: 1532–HC: 20
Top Potato Chip Producers in Hong Kong, 1997

Market shares are shown in percent.

Calbee Foods	50.0%
Frito-Lay	15.0
Pringles	15.0
Jen-Jen	10.0
Others	10.0

Source: "Hong Kong Snack Food Brief." Retrieved September 1, 2000 from the World Wide Web: http://ffas.usda.gov, from Foreign Agricultural Service and United States Department of Agriculture.

★ 325 ★
Snacks
SIC: 2096–ISIC: 1532–HC: 20

Top Potato Crisp Makers in Germany

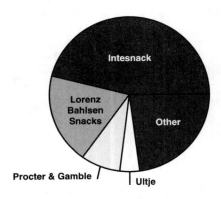

Market shares are shown in percent. Intesnack makes Funny Fish and Procter & Gamble makes Pringles.

Intesnack 46.0%
Lorenz Bahlsen Snacks GmbH & Co KG . . . 19.0
Procter & Gamble 8.0
Ultje 4.0
Other 23.0

Source: *Lebensmittel Zeitung*, February 11, 2000, p. 14.

★ 326 ★
Pasta
SIC: 2098–ISIC: 1544–HC: 19

Leading Pasta Markets

Data show sales in selected markets in thousands of tons. Dried held the largest segment in the big markets with 80% in the U.K. and 98% in Spain and the U.S.

Italy 1,329.31
United States 1,029.89
Japan 968.96
Germany 361.41
Spain 160.16
United Kingdom 126.17

Source: *Brand Strategy*, May 31, 2000, p. 22.

★ 327 ★
Pasta
SIC: 2098–ISIC: 1544–HC: 19

Top Chilled Pasta Brands in France

Shares are for 1997.

Lustucru 25.5%
Panzani 16.4
Roberto 4.7
Other 53.4

Source: *Food Manufacture*, February 2000, p. 36, from Leatherhead Food Research.

★ 328 ★
Pasta
SIC: 2098–ISIC: 1544–HC: 19

Top Dry Pasta Brands in Argentina

Market shares are shown in percent.

Matarazzo 19.0%
Luchetti 8.0
Other 73.0

Source: *South American Business Information*, February 19, 2001, p. NA.

★ 329 ★
Pasta
SIC: 2098–ISIC: 1544–HC: 19

Top Dry Pasta Makers in New Zealand

Market shares are shown in percent. Dry pasta is a more mature category than fresh pasta, so it has a higher household penetration. Fresh pasta is roughly eaten three times a month in New Zealand homes. Frescarini was the leader in the fresh pasta segment with a 42% share.

Diamond 38.3%
San Remo 33.5
Other 28.2

Source: "Spaghetti Westerners." Retrieved April 11, 2001 from the World Wide Web: http://www.grocersreview.co.nz, from A.C. Nielsen.

★ 330 ★
Pasta
SIC: 2098–ISIC: 1544–HC: 19

Top Fresh Pasta Makers in Denmark

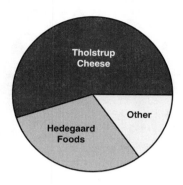

Market shares are shown in percent.

Tholstrup Cheese 55.0%
Hedegaard Foods 30.0
Other 15.0

Source: *Boersen*, December 16, 1999, p. 1.

★ 331 ★
Pasta
SIC: 2098–ISIC: 1544–HC: 19

Top Pasta Makers in Germany

Shares are shown based on value.

Birkel/3 Glocken 23.5%
Buitoni (Nestle) 11.5
Barilla 7.5
Private label 28.0
Other 29.5

Source: *Lebensmittel Zeitung*, March 2, 2001, p. 56.

★ 332 ★
Pasta
SIC: 2098–ISIC: 1544–HC: 19

Top Pasta Makers in Japan

Market shares are shown as of October 1998.

Nisshin Flour Milling 35.0%
Nippon Flour Mills 28.0
Showa Sangyo 11.0
Nestle Japan 7.0
Other 19.0

Source: "DVL Market Share Library." Retrieved April 3, 2001 from the World Wide Web: http://dvl/daiwa.co.jp, from DVL Market Share Library and Marketing Data Bank.

★ 333 ★
Bacon Bits
SIC: 2099–ISIC: 1549–HC: 09

Top Bacon Bit Brands in France, 1999

A total of 3,300 tons of bacon bits, valued at 1.45 billion French francs were sold in supermarkets. Shares are shown based on value.

Herta 27.4%
Fleury Michon 7.5
Other 65.1

Source: *LSA*, January 20, 2000, p. 1, from A.C. Nielsen.

★ 334 ★
Baking Powder
SIC: 2099–ISIC: 1549–HC: 09

Top Baking Powder Makers in Brazil

The industry generates sales of R$170 million a year.

Santista 37.9%
Vilma .15.1
J. Macedo 12.7
Oetker 11.0
Other 23.3

Source: *South American Business Information*, June 21, 2000, p. NA, from A.C. Nielsen.

★ 335 ★
Food Supplements
SIC: 2099–ISIC: 1549–HC: 09

Health Food Supplement Market in Korea

Sales are shown in millions of dollars.

	($ mil.)	Share
Chitosan processed food	$ 157.0	19.77%
Calcium-containing food	123.0	15.49
Aloe food products	116.0	14.61
Purified fish oil food	53.2	6.70
Yeast products	46.1	5.81
Pollen processed food	42.2	5.31
Squalene food	41.5	5.23
Enzyme food	30.5	3.84
Lactobacillus food	25.5	3.21
Other	159.0	20.03

Source: ''Health Food Supplements.'' Retrieved November 3, 2000 from the World Wide Web: http://www.usatrade.gov.

★ 336 ★
Iced Tea
SIC: 2099–ISIC: 1549–HC: 09

Iced Tea Market in France

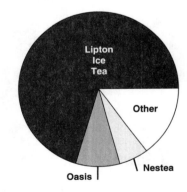

Market shares are shown in percent.

Lipton Ice Tea	71.0%
Oasis	8.8
Nestea	5.7
Other	14.5

Source: *LSA*, March 16, 2000, p. 1.

★ 337 ★
Salad
SIC: 2099–ISIC: 1549–HC: 09

Chilled Salad Market in France, 1999

Value shares are for the year ended February 2000.

Martinet	32.2%
Bonduelle	16.6
Michel Caugant	15.5
Other	35.7

Source: *Points de Vente*, April 14, 2000, p. 1.

★ 338 ★
Seasonings
SIC: 2099–ISIC: 1549–HC: 09

Seasonings Market in the U.K., 1998

Market shares are shown in percent.

Dried herbs, spices, seasonings	43.0%
Salt	23.8
Ground pepper	13.5
Fresh herbs	11.1
Fresh herbs and spices in oil	4.6
Curry powder	4.0

Source: ''Executive Summary.'' Retrieved February 8, 2000 from the World Wide Web: http://www.the-list.co.uk, from Key Note.

★ 339 ★
Spices
SIC: 2099–ISIC: 1549–HC: 09

Top Spice Brands in Brazil, 2000

Market shares are shown in percent.

Ajinomoto	27.0%
Unilever	27.0
Other	26.0

Source: *South American Business Information*, March 16, 200, p. NA, from A.C. Nielsen.

★ 340 ★
Syrup
SIC: 2099–ISIC: 1549–HC: 09

Global Maple Syrup Industry, 1999

Market shares are shown in percent.

Quebec	82.0%
United States	13.0
Ontario/New Brunswick	5.0

Source: *Marketing Magazine*, October 23, 2000, p. 15, from Bell-Garde.

★ 341 ★
Tea
SIC: 2099–ISIC: 1549–HC: 09

Largest Tea Producers

Data are in tons.

India	805,612
China	675,871
Sri Lanka	283,761
Kenya	248,818
Indonesia	165,371
Argentina	50,000
Vietnam	46,000
Bangladesh	44,200
Malawai	38,090

Source: *Financial Times*, March 27, 2001, p. 26, from J. Thomas.

★ 342 ★
Tea
SIC: 2099–ISIC: 1549–HC: 09

Tea Market in Chile

Chilean tea consumption is estimated at 10,000 tons per year.

Unilever	53.0%
Cambiaso Hermanos	37.0
Other	10.0

Source: *South American Business Information*, February 22, 2001, p. NA.

★ 343 ★
Tea
SIC: 2099–ISIC: 1549–HC: 09

Tea Market in Germany

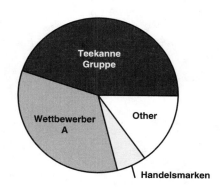

Market shares are shown in percent.

Teekanne Gruppe	45.0%
Wettbewerber A	34.0
Handelsmarken	6.0
Other	15.0

Source: "Market Share." Retrieved June 9, 2000 from the World Wide Web: http://www.teekanne.de/teewett2.htm.

★ 344 ★
Tea
SIC: 2099–ISIC: 1549–HC: 09

Tea Market in India

Market shares are shown in percent.

Hindustan Lever	41.0%
Tata Tea	20.0
Other	39.0

Source: *Business India*, June 26, 2000, p. 72.

★ 345 ★
Tea Bags
SIC: 2099–ISIC: 1549–HC: 09

Tea Bag Sales in the U.K., 1999

Shares are shown based on sales volume for the year ended June 12, 1999. Tea has a 56.1% share of beverage consumption, followed by carbonated drinks with a 21.8% share.

Tetley	20.3%
PG Tips	19.5
Typhoo	9.8
Private label	34.9
Other	15.5

Source: *Financial Times*, July 26, 1999, p. 14, from Datamonitor and A.C. Nielsen.

★ 346 ★
Vinegar
SIC: 2099–ISIC: 1549–HC: 09

Top Vinegar Makers in Italy

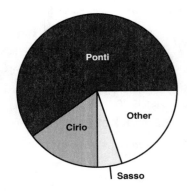

Market shares are shown in percent.

Ponti	60.0%
Cirio	15.0
Sasso	5.0
Other	20.0

Source: *Liquid Foods International*, March 1998, p. 1.

SIC 21 - Tobacco Products

★ 347 ★
Cigarettes
SIC: 2111–ISIC: 1600–HC: 24
Tobacco Industry in Russia, 2000

Shares are for the second quarter.

Philip Morris	17.0%
Japan Tobacco International	16.0
British-American Tobacco	12.0
Ligett-Dukat	10.0
Donskoi Tabak	9.0
Balkanskaya Zvezda	7.0
Other	29.0

Source: *Business in Russia*, January/February 2001, p. 84, from Tabakprom.

★ 349 ★
Cigarettes
SIC: 2111–ISIC: 1600–HC: 24
Top Cigarette Brands in Japan

Foreign brands had 25% for the first half of FY 2000. Sales were 166.2 billion units sold during this period.

Mild Seven Super Light	9.6%
Mild Seven Light	9.4
Mild Seven	8.6
Other	72.4

Source: "Foreign-brand Cigarettes Account for 25% Market Share." Retrieved October 26, 2000 from the World Wide Web: http:/www.office.com.

★ 348 ★
Cigarettes
SIC: 2111–ISIC: 1600–HC: 24
Top Cigarette Brands in Australia

The tobacco market was valued at A$6.5 billion, led by Philip Morris with 39.9% share. The market had decreased in unit sales but increased in value. Sales in grocery stores have increased at the expense of other outlets.

Longbeach 25s/40s	20.6%
Horizon 50s	17.1
Peter Jackson 20s/30s	14.0
Winfield 25s	13.4
Holiday 50s	9.7
Benson & Hedges 20s/25s	7.4
Alphine 25s	3.2
Stradbroke 40s	3.0
Other	11.6

Source: "Australia Tobacco Report." Retrieved October 1, 2000 from the World Wide Web: http://ffas.usda.gov.

★ 350 ★
Cigarettes
SIC: 2111–ISIC: 1600–HC: 24

Top Cigarette Brands in Norway

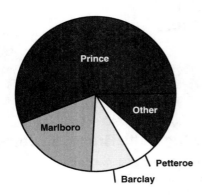

Shares are shown in percent. Tiedemanns Tobaksfabrik has an 82% of the tobacco market.

Prince	55.9%
Marlboro	18.3
Barclay	8.7
Petteroe	5.3
Other	11.8

Source: *Dagens Naeringsliv*, January 18, 1999, p. 1.

★ 351 ★
Cigarettes
SIC: 2111–ISIC: 1600–HC: 24

Top Cigarette Brands in the Netherlands, 1999

Market shares are shown in percent.

Marlboro	22.7%
Marlboro lights	9.9
Carmel filter	7.8
Barclay	5.8
Caballero filter	5.8
Peter Stuyvesant	5.0
Caballero plain	3.8

Pall Mall export filter	3.2%
Marlboro medium	2.2
Camel medium	2.1
Other	31.7

Source: "Tobacco Report." Retrieved December 1, 2000 from the World Wide Web: http://ffas.usda.gov, from Association of the Cigarette Industry.

★ 352 ★
Cigarettes
SIC: 2111–ISIC: 1600–HC: 24

Top Cigarette Brands in the U.K., 1999

Market shares are shown in percent.

Lambert & Butler	11.8%
Benson & Hedges	9.9
Mayfair	5.8
Superkings	5.5
Silk Cut	4.8
Regal	4.4
Rothmans Royals	4.3
Embassy No 1	3.4
Soverign	3.4
Other	46.7

Source: *Checkout*, June 1, 2000, p. 1, from RAL.

★ 353 ★
Cigarettes
SIC: 2111–ISIC: 1600–HC: 24

Top Cigarette Firms, 1997

Market shares are shown in percent.

China National Tobacco Corp.	24.6%
Philip Morris	13.7
British American Tobacco	10.3
R.J. Reynolds	4.6
Japan Tobacco	4.2
Others	42.6

Source: *USA TODAY*, November 30, 1999, p. A1, from *World Tobacco File, 1998-2000*.

★ 354 ★
Cigarettes
SIC: 2111–ISIC: 1600–HC: 24

Top Cigarette Firms in France, 1998

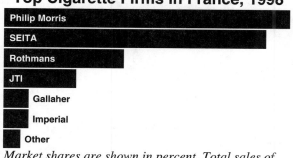

Market shares are shown in percent. Total sales of tobacco products reached $13.4 billion, with cigarettes taking the lion's share (92.5%) of the market. Smoking and cut tobacco followed with 4.2% of the market. The value of sales has increased over the last few years, largely because of price increases.

Philip Morris	35.9%
SEITA	33.1
Rothmans	14.6
JTI	8.8
Gallaher	3.2
Imperial	2.9
Other	1.5

Source: "Greece Tobacco Annual Report." Retrieved October 1, 2000 from the World Wide Web: http://ffas.usda.gov, from United States Department of Agriculture.

★ 355 ★
Cigarettes
SIC: 2111–ISIC: 1600–HC: 24

Top Cigarette Firms in Germany

Market shares are shown in percent.

Philip Morris	38.8%
Reemtsa	23.4
BAT	23.1
Handelsmarken	9.9
JTI (Reynolds)	3.9
Other	0.9

Source: "Marktanteile der Zigarettenhersteler." Retrieved March 12, 2001 from the World Wide Web: http://www.horizon.net, from Deutsche Zigarettenindustrie.

★ 356 ★
Cigarettes
SIC: 2111–ISIC: 1600–HC: 24

Top Cigarette Firms in Greece, 1998

Consumption had been increasing from 1996-98. Roughly 65% of cigarettes consumed are domestically produced. Market shares are shown in percent.

Philip Morris	22.5%
Papastratos	14.5
Rothmans	14.4
Reynolds	10.5
Sekap & Karella	10.4
Gallaher	3.9
Reemtsa	3.6
Keramis	2.7
Other	17.5

Source: "Greece Tobacco Annual Report." Retrieved October 1, 2000 from the World Wide Web: http://ffas.usda.gov, from United States Department of Agriculture.

★ 357 ★
Cigarettes
SIC: 2111–ISIC: 1600–HC: 24

Top Cigarette Firms in Poland

Market shares are shown in percent.

	1998	1999
Philip Morris	34.0%	31.9%
Reemtsma	24.4	22.6
Seita	15.5	13.4
BAT	11.5	10.3
House of Prince	8.7	14.1
Other	6.1	7.7

Source: "Poland Tobacco and Products Annual." Retrieved November 1, 2000 from the World Wide Web: http://ffas.usda.gov.

★ 358 ★
Cigarettes
SIC: 2111–ISIC: 1600–HC: 24

Top Cigarette Firms in Switzerland, 1999

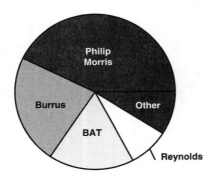

Market shares are shown in percent.

Philip Morris 47.14%
Burrus 24.85
BAT 18.67
Reynolds 9.34
Other 10.00

Source: *Neue Zuercher Zeitung*, February 25, 2000, p. 10.

★ 359 ★
Cigarettes
SIC: 2111–ISIC: 1600–HC: 24

Top Cigarette Firms in Western Europe, 1999

Market shares are shown in percent.

Philip Morris 36.0%
BAT 14.0
Altadis 13.0
Others 37.0

Source: *Financial Times*, December 21, 2000, p. 16, from Altadis.

★ 360 ★
Cigars
SIC: 2121–ISIC: 1600–HC: 24

Top Global Cigar Firms, 1999

Market shares are shown in percent.

Altadis 27.0%
Swisher Intl. 14.0
Swedish Match 12.0
Others 47.0

Source: *Financial Times*, December 21, 2000, p. 16, from Altadis.

★ 361 ★
Tobacco Products
SIC: 2131–ISIC: 1600–HC: 24

Top Rolling Tobacco Brands in the U.K., 1999

Market shares are shown in percent.

Golden Virginia 51.3%
Old Holborn 25.6
Amber Leaf 8.0
Cutters Choice 5.9
Drum 2.9
Other 6.3

Source: *Checkout*, June 1, 2000, p. 1, from Imperial Tobacco.

★ 362 ★
Tobacco Products
SIC: 2131–ISIC: 1600–HC: 24

Top Suppliers of Roll-Your-Own Tobacco in Germany

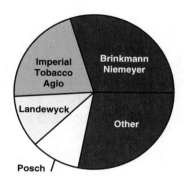

Market shares are shown in percent.

Brinkmann Niemeyer 30.0%
Imperial Tobacco Agio 21.0
Landewyck 11.0
Posch 10.0
Other 28.0

Source: ''Cigarettes and Tobacco.'' Retrieved February 6, 2001 from the World Wide Web: http://www.cior.com.

SIC 22 - Textile Mill Products

★ 363 ★
Textiles
SIC: 2200–ISIC: 1700

Largest Nonwoven Fabric Makers

Firms are ranked by sales in millions of dollars.

Freudenberg	$ 1,250
DuPont	1,180
BBA	844
PGI	801
Kimberly-Clark	694
Johns Manville	500
Ahlstrom/Dexter	296
Japan Vilene	219
Buckeye Technologies	217
Colbond	203

Source: *Nonwovens Industry*, September 2000, p. 47.

★ 364 ★
Textiles
SIC: 2200–ISIC: 1700

Largest Textile Exporters in Peru

Market shares are shown in percent.

Michell & Compania	45.0%
Grupo Inca	23.0
Sarfaty	15.0
San Miguel	2.8
Other	14.1

Source: *South American Business Information*, April 23, 2001, p. NA.

★ 365 ★
Textiles
SIC: 2200–ISIC: 1700

Textile Contract Finishing Market, 1999

The market is shown in millions of deutschmarks.

Czech Republic	414
Poland	389
Hungary	280
Romania	132
Slovakia	128
Morocco	112
Portugal	112
Netherlands	103
France	90
Slovenia	90

Source: *Textil-Wirtschaft*, August 10, 2000, p. 1, from Corporate Solution.

★ 366 ★
Textiles
SIC: 2221–ISIC: 1711–HC: 50
Worldwide Spandex Market

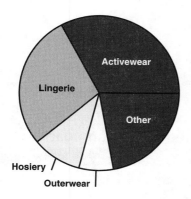

Spandex fibers were introduced in the late 1950s, and it would be 30 years before industry consumption would exceed 50 million pounds, large enough for the source to be considered a business. Dupont, at that time, owned 80% of spandex distribution. Since then, the industry continues to redefine itself as style and comfort continue to influence the apparel business. Shipments are shown in millions of pounds.

	2000	2005	Share
Activewear	69.5	94.0	33.36%
Lingerie	61.5	79.5	28.21
Hosiery	26.9	27.8	9.87
Outerwear	11.5	18.5	6.56
Other	42.5	62.0	22.00

Source: *Textile Industries*, May 2001, p. 65, from Freedonia Group and Fiber Economics Bureau.

★ 367 ★
Hosiery
SIC: 2250–ISIC: 1723–HC: 61
Stockings Market in Brazil

Meias Scalina's share is 55-60% share. Trifil and Lolypop are the top brands.

Meias Scalina	60.0%
Malharia Nossa Senhora da Conceicao	27.0
Other	13.0

Source: *Gazeta Mercantil*, April 6, 2000, p. C8.

★ 368 ★
Textiles
SIC: 2253–ISIC: 1730–HC: 61
Knitted Technical Textile Markets

Technical textile market is currently growing globally at the rate of 2.4% annually. Figures are in billions of dollars.

	($ bil.)	Share
Asia	$ 20.6	34.33%
North America	17.0	28.33
Western Europe	13.7	22.83
Other	8.7	14.50

Source: *Textile World*, December 2000, p. 82, from David Rigby Associates.

★ 369 ★
Carpets
SIC: 2273–ISIC: 1722–HC: 57
Contract Carpet Market in the U.K.

The contract flooring market is set to grow overall. The contract carpet market is a relatively stable market, with automotive being the largest segment, followed by offices and leisure.

Automotive	31.0%
Offices	26.0
Leisure	21.0
Retail	11.0
Public sector	9.0
Other	2.0

Source: *Carpets & Floorcoverings Review*, March 9, 2001, p. 16.

SIC 23 - Apparel and Other Textile Products

★ 370 ★

Apparel

SIC: 2300–ISIC: 1800–HC: 62

Largest Clothing Markets in Europe, 1998

Market sizes are shown in billions of British pounds.

	(bil.)	Share
Germany	48.0	20.9%
United Kingdom	40.1	17.5
Italy	35.6	15.5
France	31.9	13.9
Spain	17.1	7.5
Netherlands	8.6	3.7
Belgium	7.9	3.4
Switzerland	5.2	2.3
Austria	5.1	2.2
Poland	4.9	2.1

Source: "Halcyon Days Are Over for M&S." Retrieved October 17, 2000 from the World Wide Web: http://www.cior.com, from Retail Intelligence.

★ 371 ★

Apparel

SIC: 2300–ISIC: 1800–HC: 62

Men's Fashion Leaders

Companies are ranked by estimated menswear revenues in millions of dollars. Men's clothing is worth $180 billion at retail worldwide.

Hugo Boss	$ 800
Armani	450
Zegna	330
Brioni	150
Paul Smith's	125
Gucci	75
Burberry	35

Source: *Forbes*, September 18, 2000, p. I40.

★ 372 ★
Apparel
SIC: 2300–ISIC: 1800–HC: 62

Sportswear Market in China

Market shares are shown for the first six months of the year.

Li-Ning	50.0%
Nike	30.0
Adidas	10.0
Other	10.0

Source: "No Longer a Shoe-In in Chinese Market." Retrieved October 16, 2000 from the World Wide Web: http://www.chinaonline.com.

★ 373 ★
Apparel
SIC: 2300–ISIC: 1800–HC: 62

Top Children's Apparel Makers in Japan

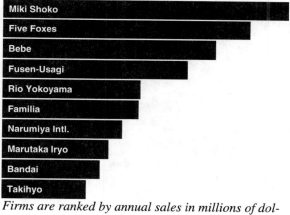

- Miki Shoko
- Five Foxes
- Bebe
- Fusen-Usagi
- Rio Yokoyama
- Familia
- Narumiya Intl.
- Marutaka Iryo
- Bandai
- Takihyo

Firms are ranked by annual sales in millions of dollars.

Miki Shoko	$ 332.7
Five Foxes	287.5
Bebe	248.3
Fusen-Usagi	215.0
Rio Yokoyama	159.8
Familia	157.9

Narumiya Intl.	$ 139.2
Marutaka Iryo	123.0
Bandai	113.4
Takihyo	97.3

Source: "Children's Wear Market." Retrieved November 22, 2000 from the World Wide Web: http://www.csjapan.doc.gov.

★ 374 ★
Apparel
SIC: 2300–ISIC: 1800–HC: 62

Top Tennis Apparel Makers in Japan, 1997

Market shares are shown based on shipments.

Goldwin MODA	23.0%
Descente	11.0
Yonex	9.5
Other	56.5

Source: "DVL Market Share Library." Retrieved April 3, 2001 from the World Wide Web: http://dvl/daiwa.co.jp, from DVL Market Share Library and Marketing Data Bank.

★ 375 ★
Apparel
SIC: 2311–ISIC: 1810–HC: 62

Top Men's Suit Makers in Japan, 1997

Market shares are shown based on shipments.

Onward Kashiyama	4.5%
Durban	3.8
Sanyo Shokai	3.5
F-One	2.8
Oga	2.6
Other	82.8

Source: "DVL Market Share Library." Retrieved April 3, 2001 from the World Wide Web: http://dvl/daiwa.co.jp, from DVL Market Share Library and Marketing Data Bank.

★ 376 ★
Apparel
SIC: 2323–ISIC: 1810–HC: 62

Top Necktie Makers in Japan, 1997

Market shares are shown based on shipments.

Asakura Shoji	7.8%
Ara Shoji	7.0
Tanaka Eikodo	4.2
Mimatsu Shoji	3.6
Ohki Jitsugyo	3.0
Other	74.4

Source: "DVL Market Share Library." Retrieved April 3, 2001 from the World Wide Web: http://dvl/daiwa.co.jp, from DVL Market Share Library and Marketing Data Bank.

★ 377 ★
Apparel
SIC: 2337–ISIC: 1810–HC: 62

Top Women's Suit Makers in Japan, 1997

Market shares are shown based on shipments.

Onward Kashiyama	4.1%
Renown	4.0
Sanyo Shokai	3.5
World	3.2
Renown Look	2.8
Tokyo Style	2.7
Other	79.7

Source: "DVL Market Share Library." Retrieved April 3, 2001 from the World Wide Web: http://dvl/daiwa.co.jp, from DVL Market Share Library and Marketing Data Bank.

★ 378 ★
Homefurnishings
SIC: 2392–ISIC: 1729–HC: 63

Homefurnishing Market Worldwide

Spending is shown in millions of dollars.

	($ mil.)	Share
Asia	$ 74,662	29.9%
North America	73,431	29.4
Western Europe	68,876	27.6
Africa	8,496	3.4
Latin America	8,159	3.3
Eastern Europe	6,476	2.6
Middle East	6,150	2.5
Australia, New Zealand	3,563	1.4

Source: *Modern Plastics*, January 2001, p. 50, from *2000 Global State of Industry Report*.

★ 379 ★
Homefurnishings
SIC: 2392–ISIC: 1729–HC: 63

Household Textiles Market in the U.K.

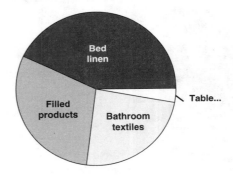

The bed linen sector was worth about 425 million. Duvet covers had a 46% share, followed by sheets with 31%. Filled products was worth about 297 million, with duvets having a 43% share, followed by cushions with 42% share.

Bed linen	43.0%
Filled products	30.0
Bathroom textiles	24.0
Table linen	3.0

Source: *Cabinet Maker*, February 23, 2001, p. 4, from AMA Research.

★ 380 ★
Homefurnishings
SIC: 2392–ISIC: 1729–HC: 63

Housewares Market in Europe

The market is shown for selected countries.

	France	Germany	Spain
Glassware	33.2%	29.9%	38.2%
China & porcelain . . .	18.3	14.5	14.4
Cutlery	16.6	11.3	10.9
Metal housewares . . .	16.2	20.5	10.7
Ceramics	6.7	11.2	13.5
Plastic housewares . . .	6.4	10.7	10.1
Other	2.5	1.9	2.3

Source: *Industrial Ceramics*, September 2000, p. 138, from Euromonitor.

SIC 24 - Lumber and Wood Products

★ 381 ★
Lumber
SIC: 2411–ISIC: 0200–HC: 44
Lumber Industry in South Africa

Market shares are shown in percent.

Mondi	30.0%
Sappi	21.0
Hans Merensky	17.0
Safcol	9.0
Yorkor	6.0
Other	17.0

Source: *National Trade Data Bank*, February 26, 1999, p. NA, from South African Lumber Millers Association.

★ 382 ★
Lumber
SIC: 2421–ISIC: 2010–HC: 44
Global Lumber Market

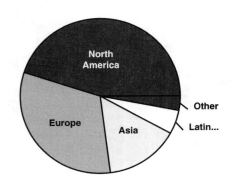

Market shares are shown in percent.

North America	45.0%
Europe	32.0
Asia	15.0
Latin America	5.0
Other	3.0

Source: ''Market Size.'' Retrieved July 28, 2000 from the World Wide Web: http://www.invision-intech.com.

★ 383 ★
Shutters
SIC: 2431–ISIC: 2022–HC: 44

Top Shutters Makers in Japan, 1997

Market shares are shown based on shipments.

Sanwa Shutter	33.0%
Banka Shutter	24.3
Toyo Shutter	11.0
Suzuki Shutter Kogyo	5.6
Other	26.1

Source: "DVL Market Share Library." Retrieved April 3, 2001 from the World Wide Web: http://dvl/daiwa.co.jp, from DVL Market Share Library and Marketing Data Bank.

★ 384 ★
Softwood
SIC: 2436–ISIC: 2021–HC: 44

Largest Softwood Lumber Producers

Firms are ranked by capacity in millions of board beet.

Weyerhaeuser	5,600
UPM-Kymmene/Champion/Weldwood . . .	2,700
Stora Enso	2,675
Georgia-Pacific	2,650
Canfor	2,550
International Paper	2,550
Abitibi-Consolidated/Donohue	2,175
West Fraser	1,650
Louisiana Pacific	1,550
Slocan	1,475

Source: "The Billion Board Foot Club." Retrieved June 12, 2001 from the World Wide Web: http://www.woodmarkets.com, from company reports and International Wood Markets Research Inc.

★ 385 ★
Prefabricated Buildings
SIC: 2452–ISIC: 2022–HC: 94

Top Prefabricated Building Makers in Japan, 1999

Shares are shown based on domestic pre-fab housing starts.

Sekisui Homes Ltd.	21.1%
Daiwa House Industry Co.	13.8
Misawa Homes Co.	12.4
Sekisui Chemical Co.	8.7
National House Industrial Co.	6.8
Other	37.2

Source: *Nikkei Weekly*, August 21, 2000, p. 9, from Nihon Keizai Shimbun.

★ 386 ★
Saunas
SIC: 2452–ISIC: 2022–HC: 94

Top Home Sauna Makers in Japan, 1997

Market shares are shown based on shipments.

Fuji Iryoki	23.1%
Noritz	17.5
Sunipet	14.6
Matsushita Electric Works	6.2
Nakayama Sangyo	4.8
Toto	4.7
Other	29.1

Source: "DVL Market Share Library." Retrieved April 3, 2001 from the World Wide Web: http://dvl/daiwa.co.jp, from DVL Market Share Library and Marketing Data Bank.

★ 387 ★
Woodenware
SIC: 2499–ISIC: 2029–HC: 44

Woodenware Market in the U.K.

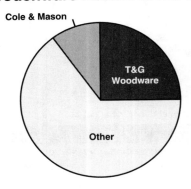

Market shares are shown in percent.

T&G Woodware 24.9%
Cole & Mason 10.2
Other 64.9

Source: *Housewares*, September 1995, p. 30.

SIC 25 - Furniture and Fixtures

★ 388 ★
Furniture
SIC: 2500–ISIC: 2029–HC: 94

Largest Furniture Makers in Russia

Market shares are shown in percent.

Imports	38.0%
Shatura Company	12.0
ElektrogorskMebel	6.0
Interior Company	4.0
Skhodnya Plant	4.0
IvanovoMebel Plant	3.0
MiasNebel Plant	3.0
Other	30.0

Source: "Furniture Market Growing." Retrieved May 8, 2001 from the World Wide Web: http://www.usatrade.gov.

★ 390 ★
Furniture
SIC: 2510–ISIC: 3610–HC: 94

Bedroom Furniture Market in the U.K., 1999

Market shares are shown in percent. Bedroom furniture has 33.1% of the furniture market, followed by living rooms with 32.6% and kitchen with 29.5%.

MFI	13.5%
Sharps	6.4
Silentnight	5.3
Other	74.8

Source: "UK Furniture." Retrieved January 12, 2001 from the World Wide Web: http://www.clearlybusiness.com, from Datamonitor.

★ 389 ★
Furniture
SIC: 2500–ISIC: 2029–HC: 94

Top Furniture Makers in Japan

Firms are ranked by sales in millions of yen. Japan has about 12,000 wooden and metal furniture makers with an estimated production of 2,296 billion yen.

Kokuyo	323.2
Okamura	187.8
Uchida Yoko	164.1
Itoki	124.9
France Bed	77.6
Itoki Crebio	53.1
Karimoku	51.0
Paramount Bed	49.1
Kariya Mokuzai	37.0
Kurogane	32.6

Source: STAT-USA, *National Trade Data Bank*, March 1999, from *AIK/Home Living* and IDAFIJ.

★ 391 ★
Furniture
SIC: 2511–ISIC: 3610–HC: 94

Kitchen Furniture Industry in the U.K., 1999

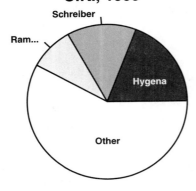

Market shares are estimated based on value. The market reached 1.2 billion British pounds, with kitchen specialists carving out the lead share of the market.

Hygena	18.9%
Schreiber	14.3
Ram Kitchens	9.2
Other	57.6

Source: ''UK Kitchen Furniture.'' Retrieved January 11, 2001 from the World Wide Web: http:// www.clearlybusiness.com, from Datamonitor.

★ 392 ★
Furniture
SIC: 2511–ISIC: 3610–HC: 94

Wardrobe Market in France

Market shares are shown in percent.

Celio	70.0%
Other	30.0

Source: *Les Echos*, January 13, 2000, p. 17.

★ 393 ★
Mattresses
SIC: 2515–ISIC: 3610–HC: 94

Largest Mattress Producers in Brazil

Brazil is home to about 300 flexible foam producers, and a number of rigid foam producers. The polyurethane industry has recovered here as well. Sealy and Serta have built plants in Brazil, giving Ortobom some competition. Market shares are shown in percent.

Ortobom	60.0%
Other	40.0

Source: *Rubber & Plastics News*, April 16, 2001, p. 12.

★ 394 ★
Furniture
SIC: 2519–ISIC: 3610–HC: 94

Garden Furniture Industry in the U.K., 1999

Market shares are estimated based on value.

Halls	62.4%
Alton Silvermist	10.5
Juliana	9.3
Other	17.8

Source: ''UK Kitchen Furniture.'' Retrieved January 11, 2001 from the World Wide Web: http:// www.clearlybusiness.com, from Datamonitor.

★ 395 ★
Office Furniture
SIC: 2520–ISIC: 3600–HC: 94

Largest Office Furniture Firms in Japan

Japan has about 1,200 office furniture manufacturing plants, producing $2.5 trillion worth of products in 1998 (the market translated to $2.9 billion). Firms are ranked by sales in millions of dollars.

Kokuyo	$ 2,338.2
Okamura	1,439.7
Uchida Yoko	1,139.7
Itoki	838.2
Plus	577.9
France Bed	544.3
Lion	471.0
ITO	447.3

Continued on next page.

★ 395 ★
[Continued]
Office Furniture
SIC: 2520–ISIC: 3600–HC: 94

Largest Office Furniture Firms in Japan

Japan has about 1,200 office furniture manufacturing plants, producing $2.5 trillion worth of products in 1998 (the market translated to $2.9 billion). Firms are ranked by sales in millions of dollars.

Paramount . . . . $ 360.3
Itoki Crebio 342.7

Source: "Office Furniture." Retrieved November 30, 2000 from the World Wide Web: http://www.csjapan.doc.gov, from *AIK/Home Living* and Japan Office and Institutional Furniture Manufacturers Association.

★ 396 ★
Blinds
SIC: 2591–ISIC: 3610–HC: 44

Top Blinds Makers in Japan, 1997

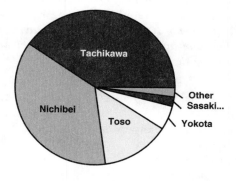

Market shares are shown based on shipments.

Tachikawa 41.0%
Nichibei 37.2
Toso 13.5
Yokota 4.8
Sasaki Blind Kogyo 1.9
Other 1.6

Source: "DVL Market Share Library." Retrieved April 3, 2001 from the World Wide Web: http://dvl/daiwa.co.jp, from DVL Market Share Library and Marketing Data Bank.

SIC 26 - Paper and Allied Products

★ 397 ★
Paper
SIC: 2600–ISIC: 2010–HC: 48

Largest Paper and Board Producers Worldwide

Firms are ranked by production in millions of tons.

International Paper + Champion International	16.9
Stora Enso + Consolidated Papers	15.0
Georgia Pacific + Fort James	10.5
UPM Kymmene + Changsu Mill + Repap	9.3
Smurfit Stone Container + St. Laurent	8.9
Abitibi Consolidated + Donohue	7.7
Metsa-Serla Group + Modo Paper	6.5
Oji Paper	6.2
Norse Skog + Fletcher Challenge Paper	5.9
Asia Pulp & Paper	5.7

Source: *Paperboard Packaging*, October 2000, p. 28, from Paperinfo.

★ 398 ★
Paper
SIC: 2600–ISIC: 2010–HC: 48

Largest Paper and Board Producers in Western Europe

Firms are ranked by production in millions of tons.

Stora Enso	12.6
UPM + Kymmene	8.1
Metsa-Serla Group + Modo Paper	6.5
SCA + Metsa Tissue	5.6
Jefferson Smurfit Group	2.9

Norske Skog	2.8
Haindl	2.7
AssiDomain	2.3
Sappi Fine Paper Europe	2.3

Source: *Paperboard Packaging*, October 2000, p. 28, from Paperinfo.

★ 399 ★
Paper
SIC: 2600–ISIC: 2010–HC: 48

Leading Paper/Paperboard Producers

Consolidation continues in the industry. The top 10 companies in North America have 52% of the market in 2000, the top 10 in Western Europe have 55% and the top 10 in Japan have 78% of the market. Market shares are shown in percent.

International Paper	4.9%
Stora Enso	4.3
Jefferson Smurfit Group	3.8
Georgia-Pacific	3.1
UPM-Kymmene	2.8
Weyerhaeuser	2.5
Abitibi-Consolidated	2.1
Metsa-Serla	1.8
Norske Skog	1.8
Oji Paper	1.8
Other	71.1

Source: *PIMA's North American Papermaker*, April 2001, p. 29, from Salomon Smith Barney.

★ 400 ★
Paper
SIC: 2621–ISIC: 2101–HC: 48

Top Newsprint Producers

Shares are shown based on tons manufactured.

Abitibi Donohue 19.0%
Norske Skog 13.0
Stora Enso 9.0
Bowater 7.0
Champion 5.0
Other 47.0

Source: *Financial Times*, April 4, 2000, p. 20, from Norske
Skog.

★ 401 ★
Paper Containers
SIC: 2650–ISIC: 2102–HC: 48

Paper Container Industry in Brazil

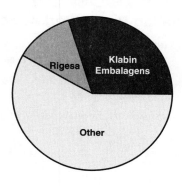

Market shares are shown in percent.

Klabin Embalagens 30.0%
Rigesa 12.0
Other 58.0

Source: *South American Business Information*, May 30,
2001, p. NA.

★ 402 ★
Boxes
SIC: 2652–ISIC: 2102–HC: 48

Largest Cardboard Box Makers in Australia

*Shares are estimated for the $2 billion Australian
dollar sector.*

Amcor 46.0%
Visy 46.0
Other 8.0

Source: *Australian Financial Review*, November 17, 1999,
p. 1.

★ 403 ★
Boxes
SIC: 2652–ISIC: 2102–HC: 48

Top Box Makers in Argentina

Market shares are shown in percent.

Cartocor 22.3%
Zucamor 16.3
FACCA 5.6
Smurfit 5.6
Stone 5.4
Uruguay 4.2
Other 40.6

Source: *Paperboard Packaging*, August 1999, p. 30, from
Zucamor and Paperboard Packaging Worldwide.

★ 404 ★
Boxes
SIC: 2652–ISIC: 2102–HC: 48

Top Box Makers in Chile

Market shares are shown in percent.

Envases Impresos 39.0%
IP 13.0
Dole 12.0
Inland Paperboard 8.0
Imports 7.0
Smurfit-Stone 7.0
Other 14.0

Source: *Paperboard Packaging*, August 1999, p. 30, from Zucamor and Paperboard Packaging Worldwide.

★ 405 ★
Boxes
SIC: 2653–ISIC: 2102–HC: 48

Corrugated Box Shipments

The market is expected to grow four percent a year through 2003 to reach 152 billion square meters. Demand will be influenced by reduction of trade barriers and the rise of Internet shopping. Shipments are shown in billions of square meters.

	1998	2003	Share
United States	$ 36.7	$ 41.8	27.57%
Western Europe	30.6	35.7	23.55
Other Asia	15.1	20.9	13.79
Other world	14.2	19.1	12.60
Japan	13.0	14.1	9.30
China	9.0	13.8	9.10
Canada & Mexico	4.9	6.2	4.09

Source: *Research Studies*, March 16, 2000, p. 3, from Freedonia Group.

★ 406 ★
Cartons
SIC: 2657–ISIC: 2102–HC: 48

Largest Carton Convertors in Europe

Firms are ranked by estimated turnover in millions of dollars.

A&R Carton . . . . $ 665
MM Karton 400
Chesapeake 375
Van Genechten 300
Bonar/MCA 270
Amcor-Rentsh 180
Mead 170
Riverwood 100

Source: *Paperboard Packaging*, March 2000, p. 18.

★ 407 ★
Paper Products
SIC: 2670–ISIC: 2109–HC: 48

Insulating Paper Worldwide

Market shares are shown in percent.

Nippon Kodoshi 70.0%
Other 30.0

Source: *Nonwovens Industry*, December 2000, p. 16.

★ 408 ★
Tape
SIC: 2672–ISIC: 2109–HC: 48

Pressure Sensitive Tape Sales

The market is expected to hit $20.5 billion by 2004. Demand is shown in millions of square meters.

	1999	2004	Share
United States	5,060	6,346	25.75%
Western Europe	4,112	4,886	19.83
China	2,490	4,384	17.79
Other world	2,239	3,192	12.95
Other Asia	2,153	3,038	12.33
Japan	1,489	1,739	7.06
Canada & Mexico	768	1,059	4.30

Source: *Research Studies*, July 28, 2000, p. 3, from Freedonia Group.

★ 409 ★
Diapers
SIC: 2676–ISIC: 2109–HC: 48

Incontinence Product Sales in Europe

Sales are shown in millions of dollars.

	1998	2003
Germany	$ 188.9	$ 241.1
France	73.1	115.6
Italy	56.5	70.2
United Kingdom	18.6	32.6
Spain	5.6	8.4

Source: *Market Europe*, February 2000, p. 1, from Euromonitor.

★ 410 ★
Diapers
SIC: 2676–ISIC: 2109–HC: 48

Top Diaper Makers in Brazil

Data are for March and April 2000.

Kimberly Clark	24.0%
Procter & Gamble	14.4
Other	61.6

Source: *Gazeta Mercantil*, May 26, 2000, p. C7, from A.C. Nielsen.

★ 411 ★
Diapers
SIC: 2676–ISIC: 2109–HC: 48

Top Diaper Makers in Chile

Market shares are shown in percent. Top brands include Pampers and Huggies.

Procter & Gamble	45.0%
Kimberly-Clark	25.0
Other	30.0

Source: *El Diario*, October 4, 2000, p. 6.

★ 412 ★
Diapers
SIC: 2676–ISIC: 2109–HC: 48

Top Diaper Makers in France

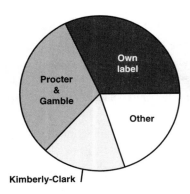

Market shares are shown in percent.

Own label	32.2%
Procter & Gamble	30.7
Kimberly-Clark	17.0
Other	20.1

Source: *Points de Vente*, September 20, 2000, p. 78.

★ 413 ★
Diapers
SIC: 2676–ISIC: 2109–HC: 48

Top Diaper Makers in Japan

Market shares are shown in percent.

Uni-Charm	47.4%
Kao	27.3
P&G Far East	11.6
Dai Paper	9.0
Other	4.7

Source: *Nonwovens Industry*, August 2000, p. 14.

★ 414 ★
Diapers
SIC: 2676–ISIC: 2109–HC: 48

Top Diaper Makers in Poland

630 million diapers were sold in the country.

Procter & Gamble	58.0%
SCA	19.0
Tzmo	11.0
Kimberly-Clark	5.0
Euro Cristal	2.0
Other	5.0

Source: *Nonwovens Industry*, October 2000, p. 70.

★ 415 ★
Diapers
SIC: 2676–ISIC: 2109–HC: 48

Top Diaper Makers in the Czech Republic

66.6 million diapers were sold in the country.

Pampers	37.0%
K-C	20.0
SCA	10.0
Hartmann	9.0
Ontex	6.0
Other	18.0

Source: *Nonwovens Industry*, October 2000, p. 70.

★ 416 ★
Feminine Hygiene Products
SIC: 2676–ISIC: 2109–HC: 48

Best-Selling Feminine Protection Brands in the U.K., 2000

Sales are shown in thousands of British pounds for the year ended October 8, 2000.

	(mil.)	Share
Always	72,636	24.04%
Tampax	61,193	20.25
Lil Lets	31,219	10.33
Bodyform	20,962	6.94
Kotex	19,388	6.42
Other	96,729	32.02

Source: *The Grocer*, December 16, 2000, p. 43, from Information Resources Inc.

★ 417 ★
Feminine Hygiene Products
SIC: 2676–ISIC: 2109–HC: 48

Feminine Hygiene Leaders in India, 1999

Market shares are shown in percent.

Johnson & Johnson	53.3%
Procter & Gamble	40.0
Others	6.7

Source: *Business Today*, April 7, 2000, p. 39.

★ 418 ★
Feminine Hygiene Products
SIC: 2676–ISIC: 2109–HC: 48

Feminine Hygiene Market in Brazil

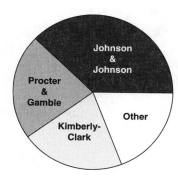

The estimated market size reached 3.1 billion units in 1999. Market shares are shown in percent.

Johnson & Johnson	38.0%
Procter & Gamble	22.0
Kimberly-Clark	21.0
Other	19.0

Source: *Nonwovens Industry*, March 2000, p. 34.

★ 419 ★
Feminine Hygiene Products
SIC: 2676–ISIC: 2109–HC: 48

Sanitary Pad Leaders in Thailand

| Laurier |
| Sofy |
| Modess |
| Whisper |
| Other |

December to January sales reached 185 million pads.

Laurier	34.8
Sofy	27.7
Modess	22.4
Whisper	11.1
Other	11.0

Source: *Bangkok Post*, February 28, 2001, p. NA, from A.C. Nielsen.

★ 420 ★
Feminine Hygiene Products
SIC: 2676–ISIC: 2109–HC: 48

Top Pantyliner Brands in Germany

The market was valued at $140 million.

Carefree	36.0%
Alldays	33.0
Kotex Brevia	7.0
Other	24.0

Source: *Euromarketing via E-mail*, July 14, 2000, p. 1.

★ 421 ★
Sanitary Paper Products
SIC: 2676–ISIC: 2109–HC: 48

Best-Selling Bathroom Tissue Brands in the U.K., 2000

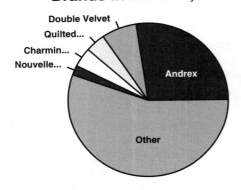

Double Velvet
Quilted...
Charmin...
Nouvelle...
Andrex
Other

Sales are shown in thousands of British pounds for the year ended October 8, 2000.

	(mil.)	Share
Andrex	174,174	26.75%
Double Velvet	48,762	7.49
Quilted Velvet	27,978	4.30
Charmin Ultra	27,292	4.19
Nouvelle Quilted	14,531	2.23
Other	358,297	55.04

Source: *The Grocer*, December 16, 2000, p. 43, from Information Resources Inc.

★ 422 ★
Sanitary Paper Products
SIC: 2676–ISIC: 2109–HC: 48

Best-Selling Facial Tissue Brands in the U.K., 2000

Sales are shown in thousands of British pounds for the year ended October 8, 2000.

	(mil.)	Share
Kleenex For Men	23,961	13.23%
Kleenex Balsam	18,199	10.05
Kleenex Ultra Soft	12,877	7.11
Kleenex for Family	11,042	6.10
Tempo Plus	6,876	3.80
Other	108,128	59.71

Source: *The Grocer*, December 16, 2000, p. 43, from Information Resources Inc.

★ 423 ★
Sanitary Paper Products
SIC: 2676–ISIC: 2109–HC: 48

Best-Selling Kitchen Towel Brands in the U.K., 2000

Sales are shown in thousands of British pounds for the year ended October 8, 2000.

	(mil.)	Share
Bounty	26,872	14.32%
Kittensoft	10,947	5.84
Gulp	9,074	4.84
Wipe & Clean	6,914	3.69
Fiesta	5,753	3.07
Other	128,048	68.25

Source: *The Grocer*, December 16, 2000, p. 43, from Information Resources Inc.

★ 424 ★
Sanitary Paper Products
SIC: 2676–ISIC: 2109–HC: 48

Paper Product Market in Europe

The market is shown in selected countries.

	France	Spain	Italy
Personal	55.2%	50.8%	48.3%
Tissue	31.5	34.6	33.8
Household	13.3	14.6	17.9

Source: *Brand Strategy*, January 1998, p. 1, from Euromonitor Market Decisions.

★ 425 ★
Sanitary Paper Products
SIC: 2676–ISIC: 2109–HC: 48

Top Paper Towel Makers in Japan, 1997

Market shares are shown based on shipments.

Lion	24.3%
Cresia	19.0
Nepia	15.0
Daio Paper	11.0
Other	30.7

Source: ''DVL Market Share Library.'' Retrieved April 3, 2001 from the World Wide Web: http://dvl/daiwa.co.jp, from DVL Market Share Library and Marketing Data Bank.

★ 426 ★
Sanitary Paper Products
SIC: 2676–ISIC: 2109–HC: 48

Top Tissue Makers in Japan, 1997

Market shares are shown based on shipments.

Cresia	25.5%
Daio Paper	22.0
Nepia	18.5
Kami Shoji	6.1
Hoxi	5.9
Nisshinbo Industries	4.8
Other	17.2

Source: ''DVL Market Share Library.'' Retrieved April 3, 2001 from the World Wide Web: http://dvl/daiwa.co.jp, from DVL Market Share Library and Marketing Data Bank.

★ 427 ★
Sanitary Paper Products
SIC: 2676–ISIC: 2109–HC: 48

Top Toilet Paper Makers in France

Market shares are shown in percent.

Own label	50.3%
Fort James	34.9
Kimberly-Clark	8.3
Other	6.5

Source: *Points de Vente*, October 25, 2000, p. 78.

★ 428 ★
Stationery
SIC: 2678–ISIC: 2109–HC: 48

Corporate Stationery Industry in Australia

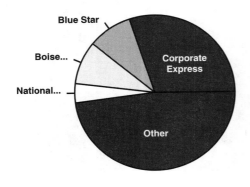

The $1.5 billion market is shown in percent.

Corporate Express	30.0%
Blue Star	9.0
Boise Cascade	9.0
National 1	4.0
Other	48.0

Source: "National 1." Retrieved May 16, 2001 from the World Wide Web: http://www.personalinvestor.au.

SIC 27 - Printing and Publishing

★ 429 ★
Publishing
SIC: 2700–ISIC: 2210–HC: 49

Reference Information Publishing Market

Reference portion of the information content industry is roughly $2.9 billion.

	Rev. ($ mil.)	Share
Thomson-Reference	$ 327	12.0%
Encyclopedia Britannica	279	10.0
Macmillan Publishers Ltd.	228	8.0

Source: "Outsell Releases Landmark Report." Retrieved November 1, 2000 from the World Wide Web: http://www.outsellinc.com, from Outsell Inc.

★ 430 ★
Publishing
SIC: 2700–ISIC: 2210–HC: 49

Research Information Market

There are 300 companies in this segment, which consists of syndicated and custom research and databases. The top 10 firms have 50% of the market.

	Rev. ($ mil.)	Share
A.C. Nielsen Corp.	$ 1,500	10.0%
IMS Health	1,400	9.0
Gartner Group	734	5.0

Source: "Outsell Releases Landmark Report." Retrieved November 1, 2000 from the World Wide Web: http://www.outsellinc.com, from Outsell Inc.

★ 431 ★
Publishing
SIC: 2700–ISIC: 2210–HC: 49

Science, Technical & Medical Information Publishing

Outsell identified 132 companies in the $9.5 billion market and classified them in this way: commercial publishers have 56% of the market, Primary nonprofit and membership publishers with 26% of the market; STM Aggregators have 18% of the market.

	($ mil.)	Share
Elsevier Science Inc. and Elsevier Medical Inc.	$ 1,100	12.0%
Harcourt General Inc. WW STM . .	698	7.0
Thomson Scientific & Healthcare .	607	6.0

Source: "Outsell Releases Landmark Report." Retrieved November 1, 2000 from the World Wide Web: http://www.outsellinc.com, from Outsell Inc.

★ 432 ★
Publishing
SIC: 2700–ISIC: 2210–HC: 49

Top Publishers in Germany, 1999

Publishers are ranked by number of issues.

Heinrich Bauer	20.86
ADAC	13.10
Axel Springer	12.75
Burda	10.36
Gruner & Jahr	8.72
Dt Supplement	8.07
Prisma	4.70
Michstrasse	3.97
Gong-Gruppe	3.33
WAZ	3.27

Source: *Horizont*, February 10, 2000, p. 1, from VDZ.

★ 433 ★
Publishing
SIC: 2700–ISIC: 2210–HC: 49

Top Publishing Firms in Japan, 1999

Market shares are shown based on domestic sales of 2.0 trillion yen.

Recruit Co.	11.1%
Kodansha Ltd.	9.4
Shogakukan Inc.	8.0
Shueisha Inc.	7.4
Kadokawa Shoten Publishing Co.	4.3
Other	59.8

Source: *Nikkei Weekly*, July 31, 2000, p. 8, from Nihon Keizai Shimbun.

★ 434 ★
Newspapers
SIC: 2711–ISIC: 2212–HC: 49

Newspaper Market in Turkey

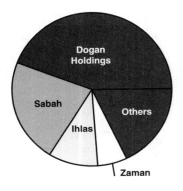

Shares are shown based on circulation in the first quarter of 1999. Dogan Holdings also has 38% of ad revenues.

Dogan Holdings	44.0%
Sabah	22.0
Ihlas	10.0
Zaman	6.0
Others	18.0

Source: *Financial Times*, September 6, 1999, p. 17, from Ata Invest and Yaysat.

★ 435 ★
Newspapers
SIC: 2711–ISIC: 2212–HC: 49

Press Advertising in Poland

Press advertising was worth about 2 billion PLN in 1999, which is about 37% of the entire ad market. In most European countries press advertising has about 40% of the market (Czech Republic has 42.8%, France has 42.7%, Hungary has 43.4%).The nationaldaily press are ranked by ad revenues for the first six months of the year.

Dziennik Zachodni	9.4
Przeglad Sportowy	5.5
Parkiet	2.5
Prawo I Gospodarka	2.5
Puls Biznesu	1.2

Source: "Poland: Press Advertising." Retrieved October 27, 2000 from the World Wide Web: http://www.mac.doc.gov, from Boss Economic Information.

★ 436 ★
Newspapers
SIC: 2711–ISIC: 2212–HC: 49

Top Daily Newspapers in Europe, 1999

Circulation is shown in millions.

Bild	4.41
The Sun	3.61
Daily Mail	2.30
The Mirror	2.29
Komsomolskaya	1.40
CAN Abendzeitungen	1.16
Zeitungsgruppe WAZ	1.14
The Express	1.10
The Daily Telegraph	1.03
Trud	1.01

Source: *Campaign*, November 12, 1999, p. 1, from Zenith Media and World Association of Newspapers.

★ 437 ★
Magazines
SIC: 2721–ISIC: 2211–HC: 49

Leading Magazine Publishers, 1998

Time Warner

Bertelsmann

United News and Media

Hachette Filipacchi

Heinrich Bauer

Companies are ranked by revenues in billions of dollars.

Time Warner	$ 3.07
Bertelsmann	2.91
United News and Media	2.74
Hachette Filipacchi	2.01
Heinrich Bauer	1.66

Source: *New York Times*, January 30, 2000, p. 14, from International Federation of the Periodical Press.

★ 438 ★
Magazines
SIC: 2721–ISIC: 2212–HC: 49

Leading Custom Magazines in the U.K.

Magazines are ranked by circulation. Custom publishing is more develoepd in Europe then the United States, particularly in the U.K. Custom publishing for the Brits is expected to hit $471 million by 2004.

AA Magazine	4.37
Sky Customer Magazine	2.64
Boots Health & Beauty	1.98
Safeway Magazine	1.77
Skyview	1.42
Asda Magazine	1.38
O Magazine - consumer edition	1.37
The Somerfield Magazine	1.35
Voila Magazine	1.20
Spirit of Superdrug	0.98

Source: *Advertising Age Global*, February 2001, p. 32.

★ 439 ★
Magazines
SIC: 2721–ISIC: 2212–HC: 49

Major Women's Magazines in the Gulf

The market is booming right now as advertisers recognize women's spending power in the region. Weeklies are ranked by circulation.

Sayidaty	142,157
Kolennas (Egyptian)	109,934
Al Yakaza (Kuwait)	97,605
Zaharat Al Khaleej	86,760
Sayidaty Saadati	75,600
Hia	43,921
Jamalouki	35,000
Osrati	32,640
Arabian Woman	30,500

Source: *Advertising Age International*, December 2000, p. 19.

★ 440 ★
Magazines
SIC: 2721–ISIC: 2212–HC: 49

Top Comics and Teenage Periodicals in the U.K., 2000

Data are as of June 2000.

JazzyBooks (group)	1,194,100
JazzyBooks (secondary)	794,825
Sugar	415,973
Top of the Pops	389,245
It's Bliss	287,897
Smash Hits	250,388
TV Hits	204,805
J-17	200,030
Mizz	162,195
Live & Kicking	140,168

Source: *Marketing*, August 2000, p. 24, from Audit Bureau of Circulations.

★ 441 ★
Magazines
SIC: 2721–ISIC: 2212–HC: 49

Top Home Interest Magazines in the U.K., 2000

Data show circulation for the first six months of the year.

Ideal Home	255,058
House Beautiful	210,034
Homes & Antiques	185,185
Your Home	172,565
Homes & Gardens	165,033
Country Living	163,553
Home & Garden	150,045
Good Homes	145,723
Real Homes	133,004

Source: *Campaign*, August 25, 2000, p. 8, from Audit Bureau of Circulation.

★ 442 ★
Magazines
SIC: 2721–ISIC: 2212–HC: 49

U.K. Video Games and Home Computing Magazines

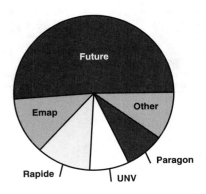

Market shares are shown in percent.

Future	51.0%
Emap	12.0
Rapide	11.0
UNV	8.0
Paragon	8.0
Other	10.0

Source: *Financial Times*, August 9, 1999, p. 14, from Audit Bureau of Circulations, Merrill Lynch, and Datastream.

★ 443 ★
Books
SIC: 2731–ISIC: 2211–HC: 49

Best-Selling Books Worldwide

Data show millions of books.

The Bible	2,000
Questions from the Works of Mao Tse-Tung .	800
American Spelling Book by Noah Webster . .	100
The Guinness Book of Records	81
The McGuffey Readers	60

Source: *USA TODAY*, December 29, 1999, p. D1, from *The Top Ten of Everything, 2000.*

★ 444 ★
Books
SIC: 2731–ISIC: 2211–HC: 49

Book Industry in Taiwan, 1999

Book publishing is more competitive here than anywhere else in the Pacific region. It is a $1 billion market with 28,500 titles in the year 2000. 12% were translations of bestsellers.

	1997	1999
Religion/philosophy	16.7%	14.8%
Textbook/reference	14.6	12.5
Lifestyle/travel/hobby	13.8	15.6
Literature	11.3	11.9
Children's	9.5	10.9
Business/economic	8.7	11.5
History/geography	4.6	2.4
Computer	4.2	3.2
Pure science	1.5	1.8
Comic books	1.2	1.2
Dictionary	0.9	1.9
Other	11.1	11.3

Source: "Books & Periodicals." Retrieved January 19, 2001 from the World Wide Web: http://www.usatrade.gov.

★ 445 ★
Books
SIC: 2731–ISIC: 2211–HC: 49

Leading Book Publishers, 1999

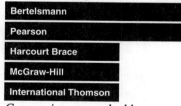

Companies are ranked by revenues in billions of dollars.

Bertelsmann	$ 4.70
Pearson	3.55
Harcourt Brace	1.86
McGraw-Hill	1.65
International Thomson	1.54

Source: *New York Times*, January 30, 2000, p. 14, from Subtext.

★ 446 ★
Books
SIC: 2731–ISIC: 2211–HC: 49

Scientific/Technical Publishing Industry

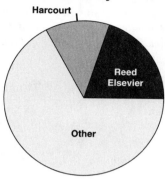

Reed Elsevier is planning to acquire Harcourt General. The merger will give Reed a lead in educational publishing in the English speaking world. Market shares are shown in percent.

Reed Elsevier	20.3%
Harcourt	13.1
Other	66.6

Source: *Mergers & Acquisitions*, January 2001, p. 21, from ARL.

★ 447 ★
Books
SIC: 2731–ISIC: 2211–HC: 49

Top Book Publishers in France

The top 68 groups and major stand-alone imprints reached sales of roughly $4.9 billion in 1998. According to the source, it is a stable but not stagnant market.

Havas	21.0%
Hachette	17.0
Albin Michel	4.5
Gallimard	4.1
Flammarion	3.8
Seuil	2.8
Other	46.8

Source: *Publishers Weekly*, November 1999, p. 15, from *Livres Hebdo*.

★ 448 ★

Textbooks

SIC: 2731–ISIC: 2211–HC: 49

Top Markets for U.S. Textbooks, 2000

While dollar sales of U.S. exports abroad rose only slightly, Asia experienced significant growth. The table shows the top markets in millions of dollars. The top 10 accounted for sales of $281.9 million, or 86.2% of the entire market.

	($ mil.)	Share
United Kingdom	$ 93.3	28.54%
Canada	67.5	20.65
Japan	25.3	7.74
Other	140.8	43.07

Source: *Educational Marketer*, April 9, 2001, p. NA.

★ 449 ★

Labels

SIC: 2761–ISIC: 2221–HC: 49

Who Purchased Pressure Sensitive Labels in Europe

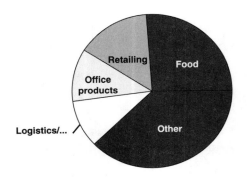

The top industries are shown. Pressure sensitive labels command 58% of the European label market.

Food	26.0%
Retailing	15.0
Office products	11.0
Logistics/transport	10.0
Other	38.0

Source: *Converting*, August 2000, p. 20.

SIC 28 - Chemicals and Allied Products

★ 450 ★
Chemicals
SIC: 2800–ISIC: 2429

Fine Chemicals Industry, 1999

Sales are shown in billions of dollars.

	($ bil.)	Share
DSM	$ 1,300	3.66%
Clariant	845	2.38
Degussa-Huls	733	2.07
Bayer	725	2.04
Rhodia	709	2.00
Lonza	633	1.78
Laporte	506	1.43
BASF	350	0.99
Eastman Chemical	342	0.96
Reilly Industries	250	0.70
Other	29,100	81.99

Source: *C&EN*, December 4, 2000, p. 35, from Jan Ramakers Fine Chemical Consulting Group.

★ 451 ★
Chemicals
SIC: 2800–ISIC: 2429

Global Chemicals Market, 2010

Distribution is shown by region.

Western Europe	24.0%
North America	22.6
Japan	10.7
C&S America	7.4
C&E Europe	4.1
Indian SC	3.8
Other	27.4

Source: *Chemistry & Industry*, March 1, 1999, p. 169.

★ 452 ★
Chemicals
SIC: 2800–ISIC: 2429

Largest Flurocarbon Makers in Western Europe

Shares are shown based on capacity.

ATOFINA	31.0%
Solvay	20.0
Ausimont	16.0
Other	33.0

Source: *Chemical Market Reporter*, May 21, 2001, p. 17.

★ 453 ★
Chemicals
SIC: 2800–ISIC: 2429
Liquid Chemical Market, 1999

Shares are shown based on a market of $673 million.

Ashland	26.0%
Kanto Chemical	26.0
Arch Chemical	10.0
Merck KGaA	10.0
Wako Pure Chemical	9.0
Sumitomo Chemical	7.0
Mallinckrodt Baker	5.0
General Chemical	4.0
Others	3.0

Source: *Chemical Week*, June 28, 2000, p. 35, from The Information Network.

★ 454 ★
Chemicals
SIC: 2800–ISIC: 2429
Top Chemical Firms, 1999

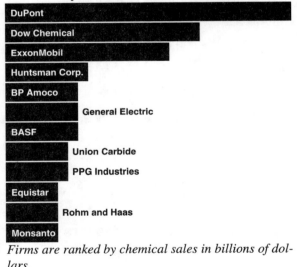

Firms are ranked by chemical sales in billions of dollars.

DuPont	$ 27.6
Dow Chemical	18.6
ExxonMobil	15.9
Huntsman Corp.	8.0
BP Amoco	7.1

General Electric	$ 6.9
BASF	6.7
Union Carbide	5.8
PPG Industries	5.5
Equistar	5.4
Rohm and Haas	5.3
Monsanto	5.1

Source: *C&EN*, May 1, 2000, p. 22.

★ 455 ★
Chemicals
SIC: 2800–ISIC: 2429
Top Chemical Firms in Asia

Firms are ranked by chemical sales in billions of dollars.

Sumitomo Chemical	$ 8.9
Dainippon Ink and Chemicals	8.8
Mitsubishi Chemical	8.3
Mitsui Chemicals	8.3
Kao	7.9
Toray Industries	7.9
Asahi Chemical	7.6
Formosa Group	6.2
Shin-Etsu	5.4
Reliance Industries	4.8

Source: *Chemical Week*, December 6, 2000, p. 43.

★ 456 ★
Chemicals
SIC: 2800–ISIC: 2429
Top Chemical Firms in Europe

Firms are ranked by chemical sales in billions of dollars.

BASF	$ 22.5
Unilever	19.8
TotalFina	17.5
Bayer	16.1
E.On	14.6
Royal Dutch Shell	12.8
ICI	12.1
Akzo Nobel	11.6

Continued on next page.

★ 456 ★
[Continued]
Chemicals
SIC: 2800–ISIC: 2429

Top Chemical Firms in Europe

Firms are ranked by chemical sales in billions of dollars.

Henkel	$ 11.4
BP	9.3

Source: *Chemical Week*, December 6, 2000, p. 43.

★ 457 ★
Chemicals
SIC: 2800–ISIC: 2429

Top Process Chemical Producers

Ashland Specialty Chemical Co.
Kanto Chemical
Arch Chemicals Inc.
Wako Pure Chemicals
Sumitomo Chemical
Mallinckrodt Baker
Other

Market shares are shown in percent.

Ashland Specialty Chemical Co.	26.0%
Kanto Chemical	26.0
Arch Chemicals Inc.	10.0
Wako Pure Chemicals	10.0
Sumitomo Chemical	7.0
Mallinckrodt Baker	4.0
Other	17.0

Source: *Solid State Technology*, December 1999, p. 28, from Rose Associates.

★ 458 ★
Chemicals
SIC: 2800–ISIC: 2429

Wet Process Chemicals Market

The market is valued at $240-275 million. Some have placed the market at $690-693 million.

Etchants	27.0%
Hydrogen peroxide	25.0
Sulfuric acid	25.0
Solvents	11.0
Ammonium hydroxide	9.0
Hydrochloric acid	7.0
Other	5.0

Source: *CMR Focus*, May 15, 2000, p. 16, from industry estimates.

★ 459 ★
Alkalies and Chlorine
SIC: 2812–ISIC: 2411–HC: 28

Chlorine Production in Western Europe

Market shares are shown in percent.

Mercury process	64.0%
Diaphragm	24.0
Membrane	11.0
Other	1.0

Source: *Chemical Week*, March 14, 2001, p. 41, from Euro-Chlor.

★ 460 ★
Industrial Gases
SIC: 2813–ISIC: 2411–HC: 27

Industrial Gas Market Shares, 2000

The $34 billion market is shown in percent.

Air Liquide	17.1%
BOC	14.1
Praxair	13.0
Air Products	10.1
Linde-AGA	10.1

Continued on next page.

★ 460 ★

[Continued]
Industrial Gases
SIC: 2813–ISIC: 2411–HC: 27

Industrial Gas Market Shares, 2000

The $34 billion market is shown in percent.

Nippon Sanso	6.1%
Messer	4.6
Other	24.6

Source: *Chemical Week*, February 28, 2001, p. 25, from
J.R. Campbell & Associates.

★ 461 ★

Industrial Gases
SIC: 2813–ISIC: 2411–HC: 27

World Oxygen Market, 2000

Market shares are shown in percent.

Air Liquide	13.0%
Praxair	9.0
Air Products	7.0
BOC	6.0
Linde	4.0
Messer	4.0
NSC	3.0
Other	55.0

Source: *Chemical Week*, August 23, 2000, p. 43, from
CryoGas Consulting.

★ 462 ★

Inorganic Chemicals
SIC: 2816–ISIC: 2411–HC: 28

Largest Titanium Dioxide Makers

*Market shares are shown in percent. The major end
use is in coatings.*

DuPont	23.0%
Millennium	16.0
Huntsman Tioxide	13.0
Kerr-McGee	13.0
Kronos	10.0
ISK	4.0
Kemira	3.0
Other	18.0

Source: *Chemical Week*, December 13, 2000, p. 30, from
Huntsman Tioxide and International Business Managmenet
Association.

★ 463 ★

Plastics
SIC: 2821–ISIC: 2413–HC: 39

Largest Nylon Makers

Market shares are shown in percent.

DuPont	24.4%
BASF	13.8
GE/Honeywell	12.5
Rhodia	9.1
Other	40.2

Source: *Modern Plastics*, March 2001, p. 62, from IBM
Chem Systems.

★ 464 ★
Plastics
SIC: 2821–ISIC: 2413–HC: 39

Largest Polyvinyl Alcohol Producers

Total capacity reached 790,000 metric tons.

Kurray	16.0%
Celanese	11.0
Nippon Goshel	10.0
Chang Chung	9.0
DuPont	7.0
Sichuan Vinylon	6.0
Clariant	5.0
Other	36.0

Source: *C&EN*, September 11, 2000, p. 7.

★ 465 ★
Plastics
SIC: 2821–ISIC: 2413–HC: 39

Polybutylene Terephthalate Industry, 2000

Market shares are shown based on capacity.

GE Plastics	31.0%
DuPont	13.0
BASF	7.6
DSM	5.6
Ticona	5.6
Bayer	4.6
Mitsubishi Engineering Plastics	4.5
Other	28.0

Source: *Chemical Week*, October 18, 2000, p. 9, from Chem Systems.

★ 466 ★
Plastics
SIC: 2821–ISIC: 2413–HC: 39

Polyurethane Demand Worldwide

Demand is shown in kilotons.

	1999	2004	Share
North America	2,237	2,725	35.86%
Western Europe	1,899	2,315	30.46
Asia/Pacific	1,018	1,365	17.96
Eastern Europe	694	865	11.38
Latin America	146	175	2.30
Africa/Middle East	129	155	2.04

Source: *Urethanes Technology*, August 2000, p. 50, from Freedonia Group.

★ 467 ★
Plastics
SIC: 2821–ISIC: 2413–HC: 39

Top Polystyrene Makers in Brazil

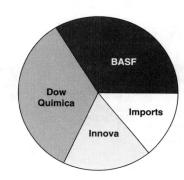

Market shares are shown in percent.

BASF	34.0%
Dow Quimica	34.0
Innova	18.0
Imports	14.0

Source: *South American Business Information*, March 11, 2000, p. NA.

★ 468 ★
Rubber
SIC: 2822–ISIC: 2413–HC: 40

Largest Non-Tire Rubber Producers, 1999

Firms are ranked by estimated non-tire rubber sales in billions of dollars.

Bridgestone Corp.	$ 2.19
Hutchinson S.A.	2.07
Freudenberg Group	2.02
Tomkins P.L.C.	2.00
Mark IV Industries Inc.	1.49
Continental A.G.	1.40
Goodyear Tire & Rubber Co.	1.21
Dana Corp.	1.10
Federal-Mogul Corp.	1.10
Parker Hannifin Corp.	1.10

Source: *Rubber & Plastics News*, July 10, 2000, p. 14.

★ 469 ★
Rubber
SIC: 2822–ISIC: 2413–HC: 40

Largest Rubber Producers, 1999

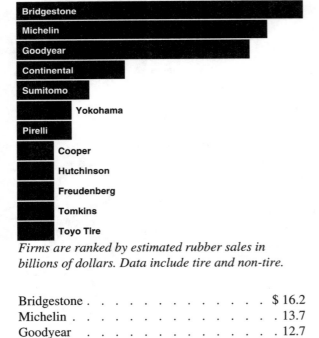

Firms are ranked by estimated rubber sales in billions of dollars. Data include tire and non-tire.

Bridgestone	$ 16.2
Michelin	13.7
Goodyear	12.7
Continental	6.2

Sumitomo	$ 4.2
Yokohama	3.2
Pirelli	2.8
Cooper	2.1
Hutchinson	2.1
Freudenberg	2.0
Tomkins	2.0
Toyo Tire	2.0

Source: *European Rubber Journal*, September 2000, p. 6.

★ 470 ★
Rubber
SIC: 2822–ISIC: 2413–HC: 40

Rubber Market Worldwide

World rubber consumption will grow almost three percent a year to reach 19.5 million tons by 2004. Demand for non-tire rubbber is expected to grow faster than demand for tire rubber as a result of the growing industrial rubber segment.

	1999	2004	Share
North America	$ 4,099	$ 4,525	23.17%
Other Asia	3,308	4,200	21.51
Western Europe	3,233	3,445	17.64
China	2,112	2,600	13.31
Japan	1,867	2,020	10.34
Other	2,309	2,740	14.03

Source: *European Rubber Journal*, December 2000, p. 34.

★ 471 ★
Fibers
SIC: 2823–ISIC: 2430–HC: 39

World Fiber Production, 2000

Total production is expected to reach 30 million metric tons.

Polyester	62.0%
Nylon	12.0
Acrylic	9.0
Cellulose	9.0
Other	9.0

Source: *C&EN*, May 15, 2000, p. 25, from Accordis.

★ 472 ★
Supplements
SIC: 2833–ISIC: 2423–HC: 30

Best-Selling Supplements in the U.K., 1998

The U.K. is the fourth largest supplements market in the world. The market has benefited from the growth in the over 50 market (a key segment) and the trend in healthier lifestyles. Market shares are shown in percent.

	($ mil.)	Share
Seven Seas	$ 127	23.0%
Other own label	126	23.0
Boots	121	22.0
Roche	71	13.0
Efamol	27	5.0
Peter Black	19	4.0
Other	56	10.0

Source: "Nutritional Supplements." Retrieved November 8, 2000 from the World Wide Web: http://www.usatrade.gov, from *Chemist & Druggist* and Mintel.

★ 473 ★
Supplements
SIC: 2833–ISIC: 2423–HC: 30

Top Supplement Makers in Australia, 1998

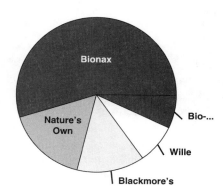

Market shares are in pharmacies. Complimentary medicine includes vitamin, mineral herbal or homeopathic supplements. The typical user is female, 30-50 years old and has a college education.

Bionax	40.4%
Nature's Own	11.9
Blackmore's	10.3
Wille	5.5
Bio-Organics	5.4

Source: *National Trade Data Bank*, November 1, 1999, p. NA, from *Pharmacy Trade Report, 1999.*

★ 474 ★
Vitamins
SIC: 2833–ISIC: 2423–HC: 30

Global Vitamin Market

Total sales reached $3.3 billion in 1998.

Roche	40.0%
BASF	20.0
Rhone-Poulenc	15.0
Lonza	7.5
Others	17.5

Source: *Chemical Week*, June 2, 1999, p. 9.

★ 475 ★
Vitamins
SIC: 2833–ISIC: 2423–HC: 30
Top Vitamin Makers in Australia, 1998

Market shares are in pharmacies.

Roche	24.6%
Blackmore	18.2
Nature's Own	10.1
Whitehall	7.9
British Medical Laboratories	6.8
Other	32.4

Source: *National Trade Data Bank*, November 1, 1999, p. NA, from *Pharmacy Trade Report, 19999*.

★ 476 ★
Vitamins
SIC: 2833–ISIC: 2423–HC: 30
Vitamin Market in Israel

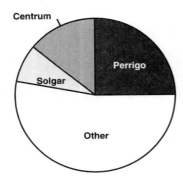

Data show the share of the $25 million market by U.S. companies. Perrigo makes a private label brand.

Perrigo (private label)	25.0%
Centrum	14.0
Solgar	8.0
Other	53.0

Source: "Vitamins Market." Retrieved April 3, 2001 from the World Wide Web: http://www.usatrade.gov.

★ 477 ★
Analgesics
SIC: 2834–ISIC: 2423–HC: 30
Best-Selling Cold/Flu Decongestants in the U.K.

Sales are shown in millions of British pounds for the year ended October 8, 2000.

Night Nurse	37.75
Lemsip	16.95
Beechams	12.24
Vicks	8.00
Sudafed	7.90

Source: *Chemist & Druggist*, December 30, 2000, p. 14, from Information Resources Inc.

★ 478 ★
Analgesics
SIC: 2834–ISIC: 2423–HC: 30
Best-Selling Indigestion Remedies in the U.K.

Sales are shown in millions of British pounds for the year ended October 8, 2000.

Gaviscon	14.23
Rennie	9.98
Zantac 75	5.18
Bisodol	2.89
Milk of Magnesia	2.10

Source: *Chemist & Druggist*, December 30, 2000, p. 14, from Information Resources Inc.

★ 479 ★
Analgesics
SIC: 2834–ISIC: 2423–HC: 30

Health Care Market Worldwide, 1999

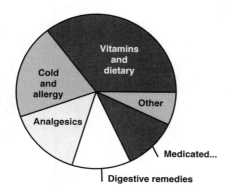

The $82.5 billion market is shown in percent.

Vitamins and dietary supplements	36.3%
Cold and allergy remedies	19.8
Analgesics	15.1
Digestive remedies	11.5
Medicated skin care	10.6
Other	6.7

Source: *The Economist*, June 3, 2000, p. 106.

★ 480 ★
Analgesics
SIC: 2834–ISIC: 2423–HC: 30

Leading Analgesic Firms in France, 1999

Market shares are shown in percent.

Aspro Range	20.0%
Prontalgine	16.0
Asprine du Rhone	14.0
Asprine Vitamin C	11.0
Migralgine	9.0
Nurofen	3.0
Other	27.0

Source: *Snapshots Industry Profile*, Annual 2000, p. NA.

★ 481 ★
Analgesics
SIC: 2834–ISIC: 2423–HC: 30

Leading Rubs/Balms in India

Market shares are shown in percent.

Vicks	55.0%
Amrutanjan	20.0
Zandu Balm	20.0
Other	5.0

Source: *Business Today*, June 7, 1999, p. 100.

★ 482 ★
Analgesics
SIC: 2834–ISIC: 2423–HC: 30

Over-the-Counter Medicine Market in the U.K., 1999

Sales are shown in millions of British pounds.

Cough/cold/sore throat	337.4
Vitamins & minerals	310.0
Analgesics, adult oral	277.3
Skin treatments	240.7
Gastro-intestinal	177.7
Cold flu decongestants	154.9
Cough liquids	94.0
Indigestion remedies	88.5
Medicated confectionery	88.5
Multivitamins (total)	75.7
Fish oils	65.8
Medicated skin care	61.4
Hayfever remedies	49.8

Source: *Chemist & Druggist*, July 8, 2000, p. 33, from Information Resources Inc.

★ 483 ★
Drugs
SIC: 2834–ISIC: 2423–HC: 30
AIDS Drug Sales, 2000

The first antiretroviral drug was introduced in 1987. With the introduction of protease inhibitors, a wide range of drugs hit the 1990s.

	($ bil.)	Share
North America	$ 2.64	70.21%
Europe	0.95	25.27
Africa/Asia/Australia	0.11	2.93
Latin America	0.06	1.60

Source: *Wall Street Journal*, May 30, 2001, p. B4.

★ 484 ★
Drugs
SIC: 2834–ISIC: 2423–HC: 30
Antidepressant Market Shares

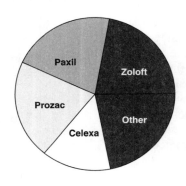

Market shares are shown in percent.

Zoloft	21.8%
Paxil	21.4
Prozac	20.8
Celexa	14.2
Other	21.8

Source: *Investor's Business Daily*, January 8, 2001, p. A10, from company reports, Banc of America Securities, and First Call.

★ 485 ★
Drugs
SIC: 2834–ISIC: 2423–HC: 30
Contraception Market in Brazil

Market shares are shown in percent.

Schering	48.0%
Wyeth	26.2
Mircovalar	17.7
Akzo	8.7
Boerhinger Ingelheim	5.1

Source: *South American Business Information*, May 7, 2001, p. NA, from Instituto IMS.

★ 486 ★
Drugs
SIC: 2834–ISIC: 2423–HC: 30
Generic Drug Market in France

Market shares are shown in percent.

Biogalen	14.3%
Merck Generics	8.0
Bayer Classic	5.0
Other	72.7

Source: *Les Echos*, March 28, 2000, p. 1.

★ 487 ★
Drugs
SIC: 2834–ISIC: 2423–HC: 30
Global Pharmaceutical Market, 1999

Total sales reached $338 billion.

United States	40.0%
Japan	13.0
Latin America	8.0
France	6.0
Germany	6.0

Continued on next page.

★ 487 ★
[Continued]
Drugs
SIC: 2834–ISIC: 2423–HC: 30

Global Pharmaceutical Market, 1999

Total sales reached $338 billion.

Italy	4.0%
United Kingdom	3.0
Spain	2.0
Other	18.0

Source: *Financial Times*, April 6, 2000, p. 2, from HSBC.

★ 488 ★
Drugs
SIC: 2834–ISIC: 2423–HC: 30

Largest Drug Firms, 2000

Glaxo SmithKline
Pfizer
Astra Zeneca
Aventis
Merck
BMS
Novartis
J&J
Roche
Lilly
Other

Market shares are shown in percent.

Glaxo SmithKline	7.0%
Pfizer	6.7
Astra Zeneca	4.6
Aventis	4.4
Merck	4.4
BMS	4.1
Novartis	4.1
J&J	3.6
Roche	3.2
Lilly	3.1
Other	54.8

Source: *Financial Times*, December 27, 2000, p. 15.

★ 489 ★
Drugs
SIC: 2834–ISIC: 2423–HC: 30

Leading Schizophrenic Drug Makers, 2000

Market shares are shown in percent.

	($ mil.)	Share
Eli Lilly	$ 2,400	46.51%
Johnson & Johnson	1,600	31.01
AstraZeneca	420	8.14
Novartis	340	6.59
Other	400	7.75

Source: *Financial Times*, May 9, 2001, p. 19, from Lehman Brothers.

★ 490 ★
Drugs
SIC: 2834–ISIC: 2423–HC: 30

Pharmaceutical Outsourcing Market, 1999

Shares are shown based on $250 million.

ChiRex	11.0%
Albany Molecular	8.0
MediChem	7.0
Pharm-Eco	7.0
Oxford Asymmetry	6.0
Other	61.0

Source: *C&EN*, March 12, 2001, p. 28, from Rhodia ChiRex.

★ 491 ★
Drugs
SIC: 2834–ISIC: 2423–HC: 30

Pharmaceutical Outsourcing Market by Segment

Market shares are shown in percent.

Advanced pharmaceutical intemediates . . . 38.0%
Custom synthesis 25.0
Dose form 22.0
Intermediates 15.0

Source: *Chemical Week*, February 16, 2000, p. 32, from A.D. Little.

★ 492 ★
Drugs
SIC: 2834–ISIC: 2423–HC: 30

Top Antiasthmatic Drugs in Moscow, 2000

Shares are shown for the first quarter of the year. Total retail sales reached $6.03 million in 1999. The market was represented by 56 brands. Berotec was the top brand.

Glaxo-Wellcome 39.5%
Boehringer Ingelheim 20.7
Rhone-Poulenc Rorer 9.6
Moskhim farm preparatary 6.3
Nycomed 3.6
Schering-Plough 2.8
Lek 2.6
Servier Lab. 1.9
Other 13.0

Source: *AIPM-RMBC Market Bulletin*, May 5, 2000, p. 1.

★ 493 ★
Drugs
SIC: 2834–ISIC: 2423–HC: 30

Top Drug Firms in Brazil, 1999

The industry is expected to recover slightly in 2000 after dropping 20% in the past year. The market fell to $7.6 billion in 1999 from $10.3 billion in 1998. However, prices are up, capacity is being improved and more investments are coming.

	Sales ($ mil.)	Share
Ache Labs	$ 481.1	9.2%
Novartis	350.8	6.7
Hoechst	264.6	5.0
Bristol-Myers Squibb	246.1	4.7
Hoffmann-La Roche	217.2	4.1
American Home Products . . .	210.2	4.0
Johnson & Johnson	184.3	3.5
Boehringer Ingelheim	158.7	3.0

Source: *CMR Focus*, March 20, 2000, p. 14, from IMS Health.

★ 494 ★
Drugs
SIC: 2834–ISIC: 2423–HC: 30

Top Drug Firms in Chile, 1999

Market shares are shown in percent.

Laboratorios Chile 12.8%
Recalcine 8.1
Saval 5.3
Other 73.8

Source: *Estrategia*, March 9, 2000, p. 1.

★ 495 ★
Drugs
SIC: 2834–ISIC: 2423–HC: 30

Top Drug Firms in Hungary, 2000

Shares are as of May 2000.

Richter Gedeon	9.3%
Egis	7.8
Chinoin-Sanofi Winthrop	6.1
Novartis	5.0
AstraZeneca	4.1
Merck Sharp & Dohme	4.1
Biogal	3.9
Pfizer	3.5
Roche	3.5
Other	53.7

Source: *Marketletter*, August 21, 2000, p. 1, from Credit Suisse First Boston.

★ 496 ★
Drugs
SIC: 2834–ISIC: 2423–HC: 30

Top Drug Groups in Sweden, 2000

Firms are ranked by sales in millions of dollars. Losec, Zocord and Cipramil are the top 3 drugs.

Astra Zeneca	$ 297.5
Pharmacia	226.8
Glaxo Wellcome	131.6
MSD	128.1
Pfizer	109.4
Roche	79.9
Novo Nordisk	58.4
Oripharm	56.3
Wyeth Lederle	56.1

Source: "Pharmaceutical Market." Retrieved April 3, 2001 from the World Wide Web: http://www.usatrade.gov.

★ 497 ★
Drugs
SIC: 2834–ISIC: 2423–HC: 30

Veterinary Drug Market in Brazil

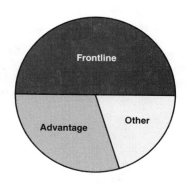

The pet segment moved $80 million in 2000, or 10% of the veterinary drug sector's entire turnover. Market shares are shown in percent.

Frontline	50.0%
Advantage	30.0
Other	20.0

Source: *Valor Economica*, December 28, 2000, p. B8, from Sindan.

★ 498 ★
Diagnostics
SIC: 2836–ISIC: 2423–HC: 30

Diagnostics Market in Germany

Industry sales reached 3.05 billion deutschmarks.

Roche	28.0%
Abbot	12.0
Dade-Behring	9.0
Bayer-Chiron	8.0
Ortho	5.0
Others	38.0

Source: *Frankfurter Allgemeine*, February 9, 2000, p. 1, from Roche.

★ 499 ★
Diagnostics
SIC: 2836–ISIC: 2423–HC: 30

Top Pregnancy Test Makers in Japan, 1997

Market shares are shown based on shipments.

Rohto Pharmaceutical	30.4%
Araks	19.8
Lion	11.4
Omron	10.4
Terumo	10.4
Taisho Pharmaceutical	6.6
Other	11.0

Source: "DVL Market Share Library." Retrieved April 3, 2001 from the World Wide Web: http://dvl/daiwa.co.jp, from DVL Market Share Library and Marketing Data Bank.

★ 500 ★
Detergents
SIC: 2841–ISIC: 2424–HC: 34

Dishwashing Product Industry in the U.K., 1999

Market shares are estimated based on value.

Handwash	60.3%
Automatic	35.4
Rinsing agents	4.3

Source: "UK Dishwashing Product." Retrieved January 11, 2001 from the World Wide Web: http://www.clearlybusiness.com, from Datamonitor.

★ 501 ★
Detergents
SIC: 2841–ISIC: 2424–HC: 34

Largest Textile Washing Product Makers in France, 1999

Market shares are shown in percent.

Unilever	22.4%
Procter & Gamble	19.9

Henkel	19.4%
Colgate-Palmolive	11.3
Reckitt Benckiser	6.9
SC Johnson & Son	1.2
Private label	5.9
Other	13.0

Source: *Soap & Cosmetics*, January 2001, p. 19, from Euromonitor.

★ 502 ★
Detergents
SIC: 2841–ISIC: 2424–HC: 34

Largest Textile Washing Product Makers in Germany, 1999

Market shares are shown in percent.

Henkel	35.8%
Procter & Gamble	27.5
Unilever	11.5
Reckitt Benckiser	4.6
Colgate-Palmolive	2.1
Private label	6.3
Other	12.2

Source: *Soap & Cosmetics*, January 2001, p. 19, from Euromonitor.

★ 503 ★
Detergents
SIC: 2841–ISIC: 2424–HC: 34

Largest Textile Washing Product Makers in Italy, 1999

Market shares are shown in percent.

Procter & Gamble	23.6%
Henkel	19.4
Reckitt Benckiser	14.7
Unilever	8.6
Colgate-Palmolive	3.6
SC Johnson & Son	1.1
Private label	10.8
Other	18.2

Source: *Soap & Cosmetics*, January 2001, p. 19, from Euromonitor.

★ 504 ★
Detergents
SIC: 2841–ISIC: 2424–HC: 34

Largest Textile Washing Product Makers in Spain, 1999

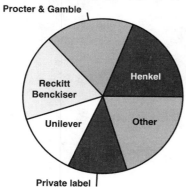

Market shares are shown in percent.

Henkel	19.4%
Procter & Gamble	17.9
Reckitt Benckiser	17.9
Unilever	12.5
Private label	12.0
Other	20.3

Source: *Soap & Cosmetics*, January 2001, p. 19, from Euromonitor.

★ 505 ★
Detergents
SIC: 2841–ISIC: 2424–HC: 34

Laundry Soap Market in Argentina

Market shares are shown in percent.

Unilever	70.0%
Procter & Gamble	16.0
Other	14.0

Source: "Argentina Frozen Food Market." Retrieved September 8, 2000 from the World Wide Web: http://www.tradeport.org, from *Clarin*.

★ 506 ★
Detergents
SIC: 2841–ISIC: 2424–HC: 34

Leading Laundry Detergent Brands in the U.K.

Market shares are shown in percent.

Persil Powder	11.5%
Bold Powder	10.9
Ariel Powder	6.0
Daz Powder	5.2
Surf Powder	3.6
Other	62.9

Source: "Product Ranges." Retrieved May 17, 2001 from the World Wide Web: http://www.corerange.com.

★ 507 ★
Detergents
SIC: 2841–ISIC: 2424–HC: 34

Specialty Detergent Industry in Germany

Market shares are shown in percent.

Calgonit	40.0%
Somat	35.0
Fairy	5.0
Other	20.0

Source: *Frankfurter Allgemeine*, December 7, 2000, p. 28.

★ 508 ★
Detergents
SIC: 2841–ISIC: 2424–HC: 34

Top Detergent Brands in Chile, 1999

Market shares are shown in percent.

Omo	36.5%
Drive	34.1
Ariel	8.4
Rinso	7.0
Skip	5.5
Bold 3	2.1
Brisa 3	0.9
Kel	0.7
Other	4.8

Source: *El Diario*, January 19, 2000, p. 5, from South African Business Information.

★ 509 ★
Detergents
SIC: 2841–ISIC: 2424–HC: 34

Top Detergent Brands in the U.K., 1999

Market shares are shown in percent.

Persil	26.0%
Ariel	20.0
Other	54.0

Source: *Super Marketing*, January 28, 2000, p. 1, from *Lever Brothers 1999 U.K. Laundry Report*.

★ 510 ★
Detergents
SIC: 2841–ISIC: 2424–HC: 34

Top Laundry Detergent Makers in Japan, 1999

Market shares are shown based on 201.2 billion yen.

Kao	43.5%
Lion	33.0
P&G	18.0
Nippon Lever	3.0
Other	2.5

Source: *Nikkei Weekly*, February 5, 2001, p. 1, from Mandom Corp. and Ministry of Economy, Trade and Industry.

★ 511 ★
Soaps
SIC: 2841–ISIC: 2424–HC: 34

Powdered Soap Market in Brazil

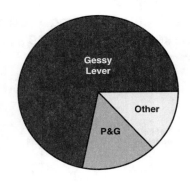

Market shares are shown in percent.

Gessy Lever	71.4%
P&G	15.2
Other	13.4

Source: *O Estado de Sao Paulo*, December 31, 2000, p. B5.

★ 512 ★
Soaps
SIC: 2841–ISIC: 2424–HC: 34

Soap and Detergent Market in Japan, 1999

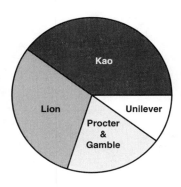

The 8.5 trillion yen market is estimated in percent.

Kao	40.0%
Lion	30.0
Procter & Gamble	20.0
Unilever	10.0

Source: *Chemical Week*, January 26, 2000, p. 36.

★ 513 ★
Soaps
SIC: 2841–ISIC: 2424–HC: 34

Top Bar Soap Brands in the U.K.

Sales are for the year ended August 2000.

Dove	21.5%
Imperial Leather	18.5
Simple	6.0
Palmolive	4.5
Pearl	4.5
Mild Cream	4.0
Fairy	3.0
Pears	3.0
Lux	2.5
Shield	2.5
Other	30.0

Source: *European Cosmetic Markets*, January 2001, p. 13, from Taylor Nelson Sofres European Toiletries and Cosmetics Database.

★ 514 ★
Soaps
SIC: 2841–ISIC: 2424–HC: 34

Top Bath Products in Italy, 1999

Volume shares are shown in percent. Bathroom products have a 99.7% penetration rate in Italy.

Felce Azzurra	6.0%
Neutro Roberts	5.0
Nivea	5.0
Infansil	3.5
Other	80.5

Source: *European Cosmetic Markets*, January 2000, p. 19, from UNIPRO.

★ 515 ★
Soaps
SIC: 2841–ISIC: 2424–HC: 34

Top Bath Soap Makers in Japan, 1997

Market shares are shown based on shipments.

Shiseido	24.6%
Kao	23.4
Gyunyu Sekken	14.5
Kenabo	9.9
Nippon Lever	9.7
Lion	8.2
Other	9.7

Source: "DVL Market Share Library." Retrieved April 3, 2001 from the World Wide Web: http://dvl/daiwa.co.jp, from DVL Market Share Library and Marketing Data Bank.

★ 516 ★
Soaps
SIC: 2841–ISIC: 2424–HC: 34

Top Bathroom Product Brands in Germany

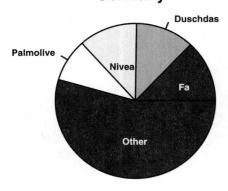

Sales are for the year ended October 2000.

Fa	12.5%
Duschdas	12.0
Nivea	12.0
Palmolive	8.5
Other	55.0

Source: *European Cosmetic Markets*, January 2001, p. 13, from Taylor Nelson Sofres European Toiletries and Cosmetics Database.

★ 517 ★
Soaps
SIC: 2841–ISIC: 2424–HC: 34

Top Dish Soap Makers in Japan, 1999

Market shares are shown based on 65.5 billion yen.

P&G	32.0%
Kao	30.0
Lion	26.0
Other	12.0

Source: *Nikkei Weekly*, February 5, 2001, p. 1, from Mandom Corp. and Ministry of Economy, Trade and Industry.

★ 518 ★
Soaps
SIC: 2841–ISIC: 2424–HC: 34

Top Disinfectants Worldwide, 1999

Market shares are shown in percent.

Lysol	16.2%
Pine Sol	10.2
Dettox	6.4
Pinho Sol	5.7
Other	61.5

Source: *Soap & Cosmetics*, December 2000, p. 35, from Euromonitor.

★ 519 ★
Soaps
SIC: 2841–ISIC: 2424–HC: 34

Top Liquid Soap Brands in Italy, 2000

Sales are for the year ended August 2000.

Neutro Roberts	9.0%
Badedas	8.5
Fresh & Clean	7.5
Felce Azzurra	7.0
Douss Douss	6.5
Other	61.5

Source: *European Cosmetic Markets*, January 2001, p. 13, from Taylor Nelson Sofres European Toiletries and Cosmetics Database.

★ 520 ★
Soaps
SIC: 2841–ISIC: 2424–HC: 34

Top Liquid Soaps in Italy, 1999

Volume shares are shown in percent.

Supersoap	11.0%
Neutro Roberts	8.0
Douss Douss	7.5
Felce Azzurra	6.0
Infansil	3.5
Other	64.0

Source: *European Cosmetic Markets*, January 2000, p. 19, from UNIPRO.

★ 521 ★
Soaps
SIC: 2841–ISIC: 2424–HC: 34

Top Shower Gel Brands in the U.K.

Sales are for the year ended August 2000.

Imperial Leather	14.0%
Radox	10.5
Olay	10.0
Palmolive	8.0
Dove	6.5
Lynx	6.5
Johnson's	5.5
Other	39.0

Source: *European Cosmetic Markets*, January 2001, p. 13, from Taylor Nelson Sofres European Toiletries and Cosmetics Database.

★ 522 ★
Soaps
SIC: 2841–ISIC: 2424–HC: 34

Top Shower Product Brands in Spain

Sales are for the year ended August 2000.

Sanex	13.5%
Hidrogenesse	6.5
Avena Kinesia	5.5
Neutro-Balance	5.5

Fa	4.5%
Lactovit	4.5
Magno	4.5
Natural Honey	2.5
Other	53.0

Source: *European Cosmetic Markets*, January 2001, p. 13, from Taylor Nelson Sofres European Toiletries and Cosmetics Database.

★ 523 ★
Soaps
SIC: 2841–ISIC: 2424–HC: 34

Top Shower Product Makers in France, 2000

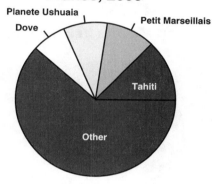

Sales are for the year ended October 2000.

Tahiti	12.5%
Petit Marseillais	10.0
Planete Ushuaia	9.0
Dove	7.0
Other	61.5

Source: *European Cosmetic Markets*, January 2001, p. 13, from Taylor Nelson Sofres European Toiletries and Cosmetics Database.

★ 524 ★
Soaps
SIC: 2841–ISIC: 2424–HC: 34

Top Soap Brands in Brazil

Market shares are shown in percent.

Rexona	24.0%
Axe	16.0
Nivea	8.0
Other	52.0

Source: *O Estado de Sao Paulo*, January 16, 2001, p. B9.

★ 525 ★
Soaps
SIC: 2841–ISIC: 2424–HC: 34

Top Soap Makers in Brazil, 2000

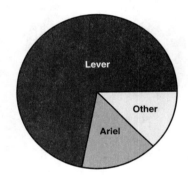

Market shares are shown in percent.

Lever	79.1%
Ariel	16.5
Other	13.6

Source: *South American Business Information*, February 22, 2001, p. NA.

★ 526 ★
Bleach
SIC: 2842–ISIC: 2424–HC: 34

Top Chlorine Bleach Brands Worldwide, 1999

Market shares are shown in percent.

Clorox	19.1%
Ace	5.8
Domestos	5.3
Cloralex	4.2
Purex	3.3
Other	62.3

Source: *Soap & Cosmetics*, December 2000, p. 35, from Euromonitor.

★ 527 ★
Cleaning Preparations
SIC: 2842–ISIC: 2424–HC: 34

Best-Selling Household Cleaners in the U.K., 2000

Sales are shown in thousands of British pounds for the year ended October 8, 2000.

	(mil.)	Share
Domestos Bleach	33,777	8.95%
Flash Excel	23,664	6.27
Jif Cream	16,729	4.44
Ambi Pur Liquifresh Rim Block	11,843	3.14
Mr. Muscle Kitchen	9,193	2.44
Flash Wipes	8,873	2.35
Jif Mousse Bathroom	8,834	2.34
Jeyes Bloo Cistern Block	7,303	1.94
Dettox Kitchen	7,124	1.89
Flash Spray with Bleach	7,123	1.89
Other	242,731	64.35

Source: *The Grocer*, December 16, 2000, p. 43, from Information Resources Inc.

★ 528 ★
Cleaning Preparations
SIC: 2842–ISIC: 2424–HC: 34

Cleaning Products Market in Western Europe

Sales are shown in millions of dollars.

	1995	1999	Share
Textile washing products	$ 12,848.0	$ 12,206.5	53.86%
Dishwashing products	3,167.7	3,194.9	14.10
Surface cleaners	3,178.1	3,164.0	13.96
Air fresheners	816.5	1,010.4	4.46
Toilet care products	837.7	962.0	4.24
Chlorine bleach	861.9	787.0	3.47
Polishes	857.9	743.9	3.28
Insecticides	635.8	596.4	2.63

Source: *Brand Strategy*, October 2000, p. 26, from Euromonitor.

★ 529 ★
Cleaning Preparations
SIC: 2842–ISIC: 2424–HC: 34

Leading Bathroom Cleaners in the U.K.

Market shares are shown in percent.

Domestos Bleach	9.1%
Parazone Bleach	2.4
Domestos Toilet Block	2.1
Harpic Lav Cleaners	2.0
Domestos Active Toilet Gel	1.6
Other	83.8

Source: "Product Ranges." Retrieved May 17, 2001 from the World Wide Web: http://www.corerange.com.

★ 530 ★
Cleaning Preparations
SIC: 2842–ISIC: 2424–HC: 34

Leading Fabric Conditioner Makers in the U.K.

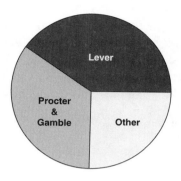

Market shares are shown in percent.

Lever	40.05%
Procter & Gamble	34.04
Other	24.57

Source: "Product Ranges." Retrieved May 17, 2001 from the World Wide Web: http://www.corerange.com.

★ 531 ★
Cleaning Preparations
SIC: 2842–ISIC: 2424–HC: 34

Leading Household Cleaner Makers in the U.K.

Market shares are shown in percent.

Lever	26.6%
P&G	15.2
Reckitt & Colman	7.9
SC Johnson Wax	6.9
Private label	33.0
Other	11.4

Source: "Product Ranges." Retrieved May 17, 2001 from the World Wide Web: http://www.corerange.com.

★ 532 ★
Cleaning Preparations
SIC: 2842–ISIC: 2424–HC: 34

Specialty Cleaners Market in Germany, 1998

Market shares are shown in percent.

Thompson	29.2%
Lueth	12.1
Werner & Mertz	9.9
Lever	9.0
Colgate & Palmolive	5.4
Reckitt & Colman	4.3
Procter & Gamble	3.1
Jeyes/Globol	2.7
Benckiser	1.9
Melitta	1.3
Other	21.1

Source: *Lebensmittel Zeitung*, April 9, 1999, p. 1, from Lebensmittelzeitung.

★ 533 ★
Floor Waxes
SIC: 2842–ISIC: 2424–HC: 34

Floor Wax Market in Brazil, 1999

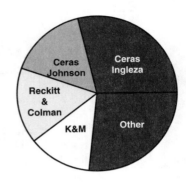

Grand Prix is the top brand with a 52% share, followed by Carnu with a 17.5% share.

Ceras Ingleza	28.6%
Ceras Johnson	15.8
Reckitt & Colman	15.7
K&M	13.1
Other	26.8

Source: *Gazeta Mercantil*, January 10, 2000, p. C2, from South American Business Information.

★ 534 ★
Floor Waxes
SIC: 2842–ISIC: 2424–HC: 34

Floor Wax Market in Peru

Market shares are shown in percent.

Clorox Peru	60.0%
Other	40.0

Source: *South American Business Information*, February 16, 2001, p. NA.

★ 535 ★
Furniture Polish
SIC: 2842–ISIC: 2424–HC: 34

Furniture Polish in the U.K., 1999

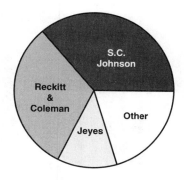

Market shares are estimated based on value.

S.C. Johnson 36.2%
Reckitt & Coleman 31.4
Jeyes 11.5
Other 20.0

Source: ''UK Furniture Polish.'' Retrieved January 11, 2001 from the World Wide Web: http://www.clearlybusiness.com, from Datamonitor.

★ 536 ★
Scouring Products
SIC: 2843–ISIC: 2424–HC: 34

Leading Scouring Product Makers in the U.K., 1999

Market shares are estimated based on value.

Unilever 43.4%
Colgate Palmolive 15.3
Procter & Gamble 13.8
Jeyes 10.3
Other 17.2

Source: ''UK Scouring Products.'' Retrieved January 11, 2001 from the World Wide Web: http://www.clearlybusiness.com, from Datamonitor.

★ 537 ★
Baby Care
SIC: 2844–ISIC: 2424–HC: 34

Baby Care Market in Europe, 1999

The baby care market in Europe is still highly concentrated and dominated by several major companies. Johnson & Johnson remains the top firm in the United Kingdom and Germany. Market shares are shown in percent.

	France	Germany	Italy
Wipes	26.1%	42.4%	52.3%
Hair care	23.5	5.3	21.4
Bath products	14.5	15.6	15.6
Lotions	21.3	24.0	6.5
Sun care	5.9	13.0	2.9
Fragrances	8.8	0.0	1.3

Source: *European Cosmetic Markets*, March 2001, p. 113, from Euromonitor.

★ 538 ★
Baby Care
SIC: 2844–ISIC: 2424–HC: 34

Best-Selling Baby Care Brands in the U.K.

Sales are shown in millions of British pounds for the year ended February 1, 2000.

Pampers Baby Dry disposable nappies . . . 174.2
Kleenex Huggies disposable nappies 93.1
Heinz baby food 55.0
Pampers Premium Extra Comfort disposable
  nappies 47.9
Johnsons Baby Skincare Wipes 24.0
Cow & Gate Premium 21.8
SMA Gold Infant Milk 19.3
SMA White Infant milk 17.5

Source: *Checkout*, April 1, 2000, p. 1, from Information Resources Inc.

★ 539 ★
Baby Care
SIC: 2844–ISIC: 2424–HC: 34

Top Baby Skin Care Product Makers in Japan, 1997

Market shares are shown based on shipments.

Johnson & Johnson	32.5%
Pigeon	20.8
Gyunyu Sekken	16.0
Tanhei Seiyaku	10.1
Wakado	6.8
Oshima Tsubaki	5.0
Other	8.8

Source: "DVL Market Share Library." Retrieved April 3, 2001 from the World Wide Web: http://dvl/daiwa.co.jp, from DVL Market Share Library and Marketing Data Bank.

★ 540 ★
Cosmetics
SIC: 2844–ISIC: 2424–HC: 34

Cosmetics Market in China

The market has been growing rapidly with foreign brands appealing to high-income urban women and domestic brands appealing to lower income urban/rural women. Sales reached $3.4 billion in 1999 and are expected to hit $4.1 billion in 2000. Market shares are shown in percent.

Guangzhou P&G	23.0%
Shanghai Jahwa	5.0
Shanghai Unilever	4.0
Other	68.0

Source: *China Chemical Industry News*, August 4, 2000, p. 1.

★ 541 ★
Cosmetics
SIC: 2844–ISIC: 2424–HC: 34

Cosmetics Market in Greece

Multinationals dominate the market, with six holding 40% of the market. Shares are shown in percent.

Hair care	39.0%
Skin care	35.0
Fragrances	15.0
Makeup	11.0

Source: *European Cosmetic Markets*, March 2001, p. 83.

★ 542 ★
Cosmetics
SIC: 2844–ISIC: 2424–HC: 34

Ethnic Cosmetics Sales

Sales are shown in millions of dollars.

	1996	1997	Share
Face makeup	$ 116	$ 120	57.42%
Lip makeup	54	56	26.79
Nail makeup	16	16	7.66
Eyeshadow	7	7	3.35
Eyeliner	6	6	2.87
Mascara	4	4	1.91

Source: *Global Cosmetic Industry*, September 1999, p. 36, from Datamonitor.

★ 543 ★
Cosmetics
SIC: 2844–ISIC: 2424–HC: 34
Global Cosmetics Sales

Sales are in millions of dollars.

	1995	1999	Share
Facial makeup	$ 7,817.0	$ 8,139.4	34.74%
Lip products	5,912.5	6,840.7	29.20
Eye makeup	4,760.2	5,608.7	23.94
Nail products	2,331.9	2,841.5	12.13

Source: *Soap Perfumery & Cosmetics*, January 2001, p. 18, from Euromonitor.

★ 544 ★
Cosmetics
SIC: 2844–ISIC: 2424–HC: 34
Lipstick Market in India, 1999

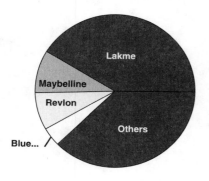

Urban shares are shown based on total market size reached Rs 105 crore.

Lakme	42.1%
Maybelline	8.5
Revlon	7.5
Blue Heaven	4.3
Others	37.6

Source: *Business Today*, September 21, 2000, p. 51, from ORG-MARG.

★ 545 ★
Cosmetics
SIC: 2844–ISIC: 2424–HC: 34
Top Cosmetics Brands in the Asia/ Pacific

Market shares are shown in percent.

Revue	3.2%
Pieds Nus	3.1
Amore	2.7
Proudia	2.3
Sofina	2.3
Reciente	2.1
Deux Seize	1.9
SK-II	1.8
T'Estimo	1.8
Raphale	1.7
Other	77.1

Source: *Soap & Cosmetics*, November 2000, p. 29, from Euromonitor.

★ 546 ★
Cosmetics
SIC: 2844–ISIC: 2424–HC: 34
Top Cosmetics Firms in Japan, 1999

Shares are shown based on domestic shipments

Shiseido	21.5%
Kao Corp.	14.5
Kanebo Ltd.	11.6
Kose Corp.	7.9
Pola Cosmetics	4.9
Other	39.6

Source: *Nikkei Weekly*, August 21, 2000, p. 9, from Nihon Keizai Shimbun.

★ 547 ★
Cosmetics
SIC: 2844–ISIC: 2424–HC: 34

Top Cosmetics Firms in South Africa

Market shares are shown in percent.

Lever Ponds	24.7%
Amka	9.5
Beige	7.5
Colgate Palmolive	7.1
Carson (L'Oreal)	6.4
Adcock Ingram	6.3
National Brands	4.0
Avroy Shlain	3.7
Le Sel	3.1
Other	27.7

Source: ''Cosmetics.'' Retrieved May 29, 2001 from the World Wide Web: http://www.usatrade.gov.

★ 548 ★
Cosmetics
SIC: 2844–ISIC: 2424–HC: 34

Top Cosmetics Firms Wordwide

Firms are ranked by sales in billions of dollars.

L'Oreal Group	$ 11.20
Procter & Gamble	7.50
Unilever	6.91
Shiseido Co.	4.90
Estee Lauder Companies Inc.	4.20
Johnson & Johnson	3.40
Avon Products Inc.	3.20
Kao Corp.	2.60
Beiersdorf	2.52
Wella Group	2.43

Source: *WWD*, September 15, 2000, p. 8S.

★ 549 ★
Cosmetics
SIC: 2844–ISIC: 2424–HC: 34

Top Eye Care Cream/Gel Producers in Poland

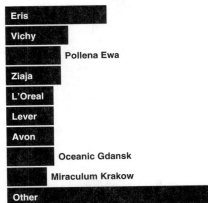

The skin care cosmetic market is estimated to be worth $170-180 million. There are about 300 suppliers in this segment. The entire cosmetics market is led by Beiersdorf-Lechia with a 28.5% share.

Eris	13.4%
Vichy	7.7
Pollena Ewa	6.7
Ziaja	6.7
L'Oreal	6.2
Lever	6.2
Avon	5.7
Oceanic Gdansk	5.7
Miraculum Krakow	5.2
Other	36.5

Source: ''Skin Care Cosmetics.'' Retrieved October 27, 2000 from the World Wide Web: http://www.mac.doc.gov, from GfK Polonia.

★ 550 ★
Cosmetics
SIC: 2844–ISIC: 2424–HC: 34

Top Face Makeup Brands in Germany, 2000

Market shares are shown in percent for the first six months of the year. Face makeup had 37.2% of the color cosmetics market, eye makeup had 26% share.

Jade	19.5%
Ellen Betix	10.0
Manhattan	9.5

Continued on next page.

★ 550 ★
[Continued]
Cosmetics
SIC: 2844–ISIC: 2424–HC: 34

Top Face Makeup Brands in Germany, 2000

Market shares are shown in percent for the first six months of the year. Face makeup had 37.2% of the color cosmetics market, eye makeup had 26% share.

L'Oreal Perfection	8.5%
Nivea Beaute	8.5
Margaret Astor	7.5
Lancome	6.0
Other	30.5

Source: *European Cosmetic Markets*, November 2000, p. 11, from Information Resources Inc. and GfK Retail Services.

★ 551 ★
Deodorants
SIC: 2844–ISIC: 2424–HC: 34

Deodorant Market in Germany, 1999

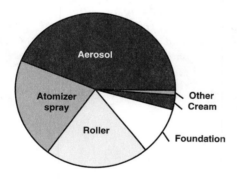

Market shares are shown in percent.

Aerosol	44.0%
Atomizer spray	21.0
Roller	21.0
Foundation	10.0
Cream	3.0
Other	1.0

Source: *Der Spiegel*, August 28, 2000, p. 236.

★ 552 ★
Deodorants
SIC: 2844–ISIC: 2424–HC: 34

Top Deodorant Brands for Men in France, 2000

Market shares are shown for the year ended March 2000.

Axo	18.0%
Brut	18.0
Mennen	13.5
Gillette	7.0
Narta	6.5
Scorrio	5.0
Nivea	4.5
Planete Ushalla	3.5
Others	24.0

Source: *European Cosmetic Markets*, July 2000, p. 267.

★ 553 ★
Deodorants
SIC: 2844–ISIC: 2424–HC: 34

Top Deodorant Brands in Germany

Beiersdorf
Rexona
Axe
Other

Market shares are shown in percent.

Beiersdorf	15.0%
Rexona	11.0
Axe	6.5
Other	67.5

Source: *Euromarketing via E-mail*, May 18, 2001, p. NA.

★ 554 ★
Deodorants
SIC: 2844–ISIC: 2424–HC: 34

Top Deodorant Brands in the U.K., 2000

Market shares are shown for the year ended March 2000. Aerosols had a 68.6% share, roll-ons had a 15.6% share and creams a 7.1% share.

Sure	27.0%
Right Guard	10.0
Soft & Gentle	9.0
Dove	7.0
Vasoline Intensive Care	6.0
Other	41.0

Source: *European Cosmetic Markets*, July 2000, p. 267.

★ 555 ★
Deodorants
SIC: 2844–ISIC: 2424–HC: 34

Top Roll-On Deodorant Brands in Spain, 2000

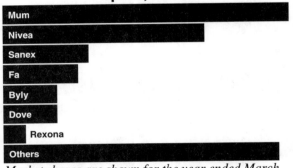

Mum
Nivea
Sanex
Fa
Byly
Dove
Rexona
Others

Market shares are shown for the year ended March 2000. About 79.5% of men and women 11-74 use a deodorant at least once in an average week.

Mum	27.0%
Nivea	19.0
Sanex	7.5
Fa	7.0
Byly	5.0
Dove	5.0
Rexona	1.5
Others	26.0

Source: *European Cosmetic Markets*, July 2000, p. 267, from ETCD.

★ 556 ★
Fragrances
SIC: 2844–ISIC: 2424–HC: 34

Fragrance Market in Latin America

Sales are shown in millions of dollars.

	2000	2005
Brazil	$ 790.8	$ 1,053.9
Mexico	392.3	581.7
Argentina	217.5	250.4
Venezuela	181.0	259.8
Peru	109.2	156.3
Chile	101.6	135.2

Source: *Global Cosmetic Industry*, January 2001, p. 56, from Datamonitor.

★ 557 ★
Fragrances
SIC: 2844–ISIC: 2424–HC: 34

Top Aftershaves in Spain, 1999

The men's fragrance market was valued at 30.3 billion pesetas for the year ended June 1999, with suggested growth of 20% annually. About 31% of men btween 11-74 used cologne during the year ended September 1999. This is the highest rate in the "big five" European countries. Volume shares are for the first four months.

La Toja	23.0%
Gillette	21.0
Williams	11.0
Nivea	8.0
Lea	7.0
Edge	5.0
Other	25.0

Source: *European Cosmetic Markets*, March 2000, p. 103.

★ 558 ★
Fragrances
SIC: 2844–ISIC: 2424–HC: 34

Top Aftershaves in the U.K.

Market shares are shown in percent.

Old Spice	17.0%
Lynx	16.0

Continued on next page.

★ 558 ★
[Continued]
Fragrances
SIC: 2844–ISIC: 2424–HC: 34

Top Aftershaves in the U.K.

Market shares are shown in percent.

Brut	7.5%
Gillette Series	7.5
Adidas	6.0
Addiction	4.0
Brut Aquatonic	3.5
Fusion	2.5
Other	36.0

Source: *European Cosmetic Markets*, March 2000, p. 105.

★ 559 ★
Fragrances
SIC: 2844–ISIC: 2424–HC: 34

Top Female Fragrance Brands in France

Market shares are shown in percent.

Eau Jeune	25.0%
Clin d'Oeil	8.0
Vanderbilt	7.0
Own label	6.5
Corine de Farme	3.5
Maroussia	3.5
Ulric de Varens	3.5
Chanson d'Eau	2.0
Kooka	2.0
Naf Naf	2.0
Other	37.0

Source: *European Cosmetic Markets*, May 2000, p. 15.

★ 560 ★
Hair Care
SIC: 2844–ISIC: 2424–HC: 34

Largest Hair Care Markets

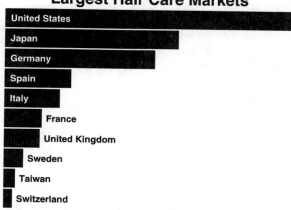

Sales are shown in millions of dollars.

	1997	1999
United States	$ 657	$ 1,038
Japan	664	628
Germany	428	543
Spain	171	238
Italy	195	197
France	121	132
United Kingdom	91	125
Sweden	53	66
Taiwan	34	37
Switzerland	17	27

Source: *Brand Strategy*, December 2000, p. 26, from Euromonitor.

★ 561 ★
Hair Care
SIC: 2844–ISIC: 2424–HC: 34

Top Hair Care Brands in France, 2000

Volume shares are shown for the year to May 2000. While shampoo and conditioners did well, the colorants category showed the greatest growth.

Elseve	15.0%
Fructis	11.5
Jacques Dessange	8.0
Ultra Doux	7.5
Dop/Petit Dop	7.0
Timotei	5.0
Jean Louis David	4.0

Continued on next page.

★ 561 ★

[Continued]
Hair Care
SIC: 2844–ISIC: 2424–HC: 34

Top Hair Care Brands in France, 2000

Volume shares are shown for the year to May 2000. While shampoo and conditioners did well, the colorants category showed the greatest growth.

Pantene Pro V 4.0%
Other 38.0

Source: *European Cosmetic Markets*, September 2000, p. 347.

★ 562 ★

Hair Care
SIC: 2844–ISIC: 2424–HC: 34

Top Hair Coloring Brands in Spain, 1999

Market shares are shown in percent.

Inedia 32.0%
Recital 13.5
Kolestint 7.0
Colorcrem 6.5
Belle Color 5.0
Colorelle 4.5
Vital Colors 4.5
Other 27.0

Source: *European Cosmetic Markets*, September 2000, p. 347.

★ 563 ★

Hair Care
SIC: 2844–ISIC: 2424–HC: 34

Top Shampoo Makers in Europe

Market shares are shown in percent.

L"Oreal 28.0%
Procter & Gamble 19.0
Unilever 12.0
Other 41.0

Source: *Forbes*, November 27, 2000, p. 174.

★ 564 ★

Hair Care
SIC: 2844–ISIC: 2424–HC: 34

Top Shampoo Makers in India

Hindustan Lever
Cavin Care ltd.
Other

Market shares are shown in percent.

Hindustan Lever 69.0%
Cavin Care ltd. 19.8
Other 11.2

Source: *Chemical Business Newsbase*, January 25, 2001, p. NA.

★ 565 ★
Hair Care
SIC: 2844–ISIC: 2424–HC: 34

Top Shampoo/Rinse Makers in Japan, 1999

Market shares are shown based on 204.8 billion yen.

Kao	19.4%
Shiseido	17.3
Nippon Lever	14.2
Kanebo	13.4
P&G	12.0
Other	23.7

Source: *Nikkei Weekly*, February 5, 2001, p. 3, from Mandom Corp. and Ministry of Economy, Trade and Industry.

★ 566 ★
Lip Care
SIC: 2844–ISIC: 2424–HC: 34

Lip Care Market in Brazil

Market shares are shown in percent.

Avon	23.0%
Natura	12.0
L'Oreal	5.0
Cotygirl Miss Sport	3.5
Marcelo Beauty	3.4
Lancome	2.8
Colorama (Revlon)	2.3
O Boticario	2.3
ColorStay (Revlon)	1.9
Helena Rubinstein	1.9
Other	41.9

Source: *Soap & Cosmetics*, March 2001, p. 67, from Euromonitor.

★ 567 ★
Lip Care
SIC: 2844–ISIC: 2424–HC: 34

Top Lip Care Makers in the U.K., 1999

Market shares are estimated based on value.

Dendron	16.2%
Smith & Nephew	14.0
Whitehall	11.0
Johnson & Johnson	5.5
Avon	4.4
Private label	13.4
Other	35.5

Source: "UK Lip Care." Retrieved January 11, 2001 from the World Wide Web: http://www.clearlybusiness.com, from Datamonitor.

★ 568 ★
Nail Care
SIC: 2844–ISIC: 2424–HC: 34

Nail Care Market in the U.K., 1999

Market shares are estimated in percent.

Coty	30.1%
Procter & Gamble	18.0
Avon	16.1
Revlon	5.2
Lancome	0.6
Private label	11.7
Others	18.3

Source: "UK Nail Make-Up." Retrieved January 12, 2001 from the World Wide Web: http://www.clearlybusiness.com, from Datamonitor.

★ 569 ★

Nail Care

SIC: 2844–ISIC: 2424–HC: 34

Nail Enamel Market in India, 1999

Urban shares are shown based on total market size reached Rs 119 crore.

Lakme	33.0%
Blue Heaven	6.3
Revlon	3.8
Maybelline	0.5
Others	56.4

Source: *Business Today*, September 21, 2000, p. 51, from ORG-MARG.

★ 570 ★

Nail Care

SIC: 2844–ISIC: 2424–HC: 34

Nail Varnish Market in France

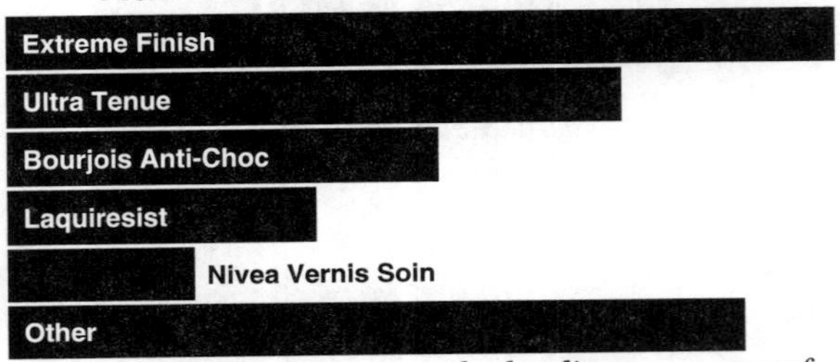

Nail and eye products were the leading segments of the cosmetics market.The mascara market was led by Volum'Express with a 22.0% share; Rouge Non Stop with a 13% share; the foundation market is lead by Non Stop Make-Up with a 21.5% share.

Extreme Finish	27.0%
Ultra Tenue	20.0
Bourjois Anti-Choc	14.0
Laquiresist	9.5
Nivea Vernis Soin	6.0
Other	23.5

Source: *European Cosmetic Markets*, November 1999, p. 439.

★ 571 ★

Oral Care

SIC: 2844–ISIC: 2424–HC: 34

Denture Care Industry in the U.K., 1999

Market shares are estimated based on value.

Polygrip & Wernets	63.0%
Fixadent	16.0
Seabond	9.0
Cushion - Grip	7.0
Steradent	1.5
Whitehall	1.2
Other	2.3

Source: ''UK Denture Care.'' Retrieved January 11, 2001 from the World Wide Web: http://www.clearlybusiness.com, from Datamonitor.

★ 572 ★

Oral Care

SIC: 2844–ISIC: 2424–HC: 34

Leading Dental Care Firms in the U.K.

Market shares are shown in percent.

Colgate Palmolive	34.0%
Smithkline Beecham	26.0
Stafford Miller	9.0
Elida Faberge	5.0
Procter & Gamble	3.0
Other	23.0

Source: ''Product Ranges.'' Retrieved May 17, 2001 from the World Wide Web: http://www.corerange.com.

★ 573 ★
Oral Care
SIC: 2844–ISIC: 2424–HC: 34

Leading Denture Care Brands in France

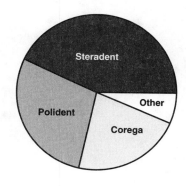

Market shares are shown in percent.

Steradent 41.3%
Polident 26.8
Corega 20.6
Other 6.1

Source: *Snapshots Industry Profile*, Annual 2000, p. NA.

★ 574 ★
Oral Care
SIC: 2844–ISIC: 2424–HC: 34

Oral Care Market in Europe, 1999

The market is shown in percent.

	France	Germany	Italy
Toothpaste	61.7%	49.3%	57.5%
Toothbrushes	21.3	19.1	15.7
Denture accessories . . .	11.2	11.8	10.7
Extra care products . . .	5.8	19.8	16.1

Source: *Brand Strategy*, February 18, 2000, p. 22, from Euromonitor.

★ 575 ★
Oral Care
SIC: 2844–ISIC: 2424–HC: 34

Toothpaste Market in the U.K.

Market shares are shown in percent.

Premium pastes 24.4%
Paste for sensitive teeth 13.7
Baking soda 5.0
Children's 4.2

Source: *Community Pharmacy*, February 13, 2001, p. 24, from Glaxo SmithKline.

★ 576 ★
Oral Care
SIC: 2844–ISIC: 2424–HC: 34

Top Dental Floss Makers in Japan, 1997

Market shares are shown based on shipments.

Kobayashi Seiyaku 35.6%
Johnson & Johnson 23.3
Lion 17.1
Sunstar 12.8
Other 11.2

Source: "DVL Market Share Library." Retrieved April 3, 2001 from the World Wide Web: http://dvl/daiwa.co.jp, from DVL Market Share Library and Marketing Data Bank.

★ 577 ★
Oral Care
SIC: 2844–ISIC: 2424–HC: 34

Top Oral Care Firms in France, 1999

Market shares are shown in percent.

Ellida Faberge	25.9%
Colgate-Palmolive	15.3
Henkel	10.0
Stafford-Miller	8.9
SmithKline Beecham	8.7
Other	31.2

Source: *CMR Focus*, May 8, 2000, p. 18, from Euromonitor.

★ 578 ★
Oral Care
SIC: 2844–ISIC: 2424–HC: 34

Top Oral Care Firms in Germany, 1999

Market shares are shown in percent.

SmithKline Beecham	26.1%
Procter & Gamble	13.1
Wybert	13.1
Colgate-Palmolive	12.0
Gillette	4.5
Other	34.5

Source: *CMR Focus*, May 8, 2000, p. 18, from Euromonitor.

★ 579 ★
Oral Care
SIC: 2844–ISIC: 2424–HC: 34

Top Oral Care Firms in Spain, 1999

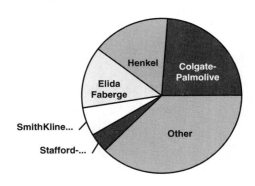

Market shares are shown in percent.

Colgate-Palmolive	23.6%
Henkel	16.0
Elida Faberge	12.8
SmithKline Beecham	5.5
Stafford-Miller	4.4
Other	37.7

Source: *CMR Focus*, May 8, 2000, p. 18, from Euromonitor.

★ 580 ★
Oral Care
SIC: 2844–ISIC: 2424–HC: 34

Top Toothpaste Brands in China

Market shares are shown in percent.

Colgate	29.9%
Zhonghua	18.1
Crest	17.2
Signal	9.4
Liangmianzhen	5.8
Heimei	3.5
Lengsuanling	2.8
Liubizhi	2.8
Kangchiling	2.5
Other	8.0

Source: ''Many Chinese Toothpaste Connoisseurs Enameled With Colgate.'' Retrieved May 10, 2001 from The World Wide Web: http://www.chinaonline.com.

Oral Care
SIC: 2844–ISIC: 2424–HC: 34

Top Toothpaste Brands in Germany, 2000

Market shares are shown for the first six months of the year.

Oral Med 3	12.5%
Blend-A-Med	11.0
Dentgard	9.0
Colgate	8.0
Signal	7.5
Elmex	7.0
Theramed	6.0
Sensodyne	3.5
Other	35.5

Source: *European Cosmetic Markets*, December 2000, p. 479, from industry estimates.

★ 582 ★
Oral Care
SIC: 2844–ISIC: 2424–HC: 34

Top Toothpaste Brands in Italy, 2000

Market shares are shown for the first six months of the year.

Mentadent	24.5%
Colgate	19.0
AZ	16.0
Aquafresh	8.5
Antica Erboristuria	6.5
Others	25.5

Source: *European Cosmetic Markets*, December 2000, p. 479, from industry estimates.

★ 583 ★
Oral Care
SIC: 2844–ISIC: 2424–HC: 34

Top Toothpaste Brands in the U.K., 1999

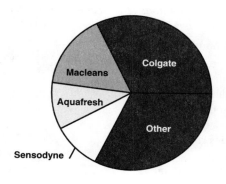

Shares are for the year ended July 11, 1999.

Colgate	33.0%
Macleans	15.5
Aquafresh	9.5
Sensodyne	9.5
Other	32.5

Source: *European Cosmetic Markets*, December 1999, p. 1.

★ 584 ★
Oral Care
SIC: 2844–ISIC: 2424–HC: 34

Top Toothpaste Makers in Brazil

Unilever

Sorriso

Other

Market shares are shown in percent.

Unilever	63.0%
Sorriso	30.0
Other	7.0

Source: *South American Business Information*, April 9, 2001, p. NA.

★ 585 ★
Personal Care Products
SIC: 2844–ISIC: 2424–HC: 34

Best-Selling Toiletry Brands in the U.K.

Sales are shown in millions of British pounds for the year ended February 1, 2000.

Lynx bodyspray	61.0
Sure 24 Hour Intensive Care deodorant	43.0
Gillette Mach 3 razor	39.5
Right Guard deodorant	28.6
Radox unisex bath liquid	27.8
Gillette Series shave preps	26.6
Dove bar soap	25.8
Soft & Gentle deodorant	22.7

Source: *Checkout*, April 1, 2000, p. 1, from Information Resources Inc.

★ 586 ★
Personal Care Products
SIC: 2844–ISIC: 2424–HC: 34

Body Care Market in Germany, 1998

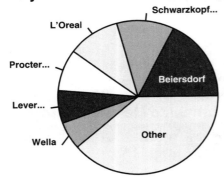

Market shares are shown in percent.

Beiersdorf	17.5%
Schwarzkopf & Henkel Cosmetics	11.5
L'Oreal	10.5
Procter & Gamble	8.5
Lever Faberge	6.5
Wella	5.5
Other	40.0

Source: *Der Spiegel*, May 15, 2000, p. 96.

★ 587 ★
Personal Care Products
SIC: 2844–ISIC: 2424–HC: 34

Cosmetics & Toiletries Industry Worldwide

Market shares are shown in percent.

Hair care	20.9%
Skin care	16.4
Color cosmetics	13.5
Fragrances	12.0
Oral care	11.5
Bath & shower products	10.4
Deodorants	5.0
Men's toiletries	4.4
Baby care	4.0
Sun care	1.9

Source: Retrieved February 29, 2000 from the World Wide Web: http://www.exposemagazine.com.

★ 588 ★
Personal Care Products
SIC: 2844–ISIC: 2424–HC: 34

Cosmetics & Toiletries Market in Asia

The market hit $39 billion last year. Its growth has been hampered by economic problems and the large percentage of rural people, who cannot afford such products. Sales are shown in millions of dollars.

	1995	1999
Skin care	$ 10,549.1	$ 9,767.0
Hair care	9,549.9	8,219.1
Bath and shower	6,092.3	6,059.0
Oral hygiene	5,411.0	5,450.9
Fragrances	1,584.0	1,403.4
Men's shaving products	1,160.3	1,110.3
Baby care	961.2	986.3
Deodorants	461.5	490.8
Sun care	299.9	275.9

Source: *Soap, Perfumery & Cosmetics*, November 2000, p. 24, from Euromonitor.

★ 589 ★
Personal Care Products
SIC: 2844–ISIC: 2424–HC: 34

Cosmetics & Toiletries Market in Eastern Europe

Sales are shown in millions of dollars.

	1995	1999
Hair care	$ 1,179.5	$ 1,588.1
Bath & shower products	1,350.1	1,339.5
Color cosmetics	1,179.5	1,255.0
Oral hygiene	1,032.1	1,093.6
Fragrances	742.8	848.3
Skin care	599.9	681.7
Deodorants	513.2	598.9
Men's shaving products	381.1	403.8
Baby care	190.1	201.3
Sun care	67.8	86.0

Source: *Soap, Perfumery & Cosmetics*, February 2000, p. 30, from Euromonitor.

★ 590 ★
Personal Care Products
SIC: 2844–ISIC: 2424–HC: 34

Cosmetics & Toiletries Market in France, 1999

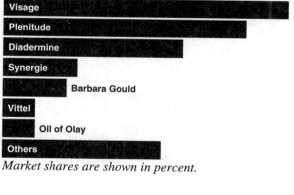

Market shares are shown in percent.

Visage	27.1%
Plenitude	22.5
Diadermine	16.7
Synergie	6.6
Barbara Gould	6.1%
Vittel	3.2
Oil of Olay	2.7
Others	15.1

Source: *Points de Vente*, February 16, 2000, p. 1, from A.C. Nielsen.

★ 591 ★
Personal Care Products
SIC: 2844–ISIC: 2424–HC: 34

Largest Body Care Markets

Sales are shown in millions of dollars.

	1997	1999
United States	$ 630	$ 859
Germany	161	217
France	105	102
Italy	100	112
Spain	46	74
United Kingdom	40	48
Japan	19	21
Switzerland	13	17
Sweden	7	8
Taiwan	5	6

Source: *Brand Strategy*, December 2000, p. 26, from Euromonitor.

★ 592 ★
Personal Care Products
SIC: 2844–ISIC: 2424–HC: 34

Men's Toiletries Market in Germany

Market is shown in percent.

Aftershave	31.0%
Fragrances	29.0
Deodorants	17.0
Shower products	11.0
Razors	9.0
Face products	3.0

Source: *Wirtschaftswoche*, April 6, 2000, p. 132, from BRE Unternehmensberatung.

★ 593 ★
Personal Care Products
SIC: 2844–ISIC: 2424–HC: 34

Men's Toiletries Market in Japan, 1999

Total shipments reached 130.4 billion yen.

Hair styling	29.2%
Scalp care	25.2
Facial care	18.4
Shampoos, rinses	6.6
Shaving products	6.5
Fragrances	6.2
Hair coloring	5.7
Deodorants	2.2

Source: *Nikkei Weekly*, February 5, 2001, p. 3, from Mandom Corp. and Ministry of Economy, Trade and Industry.

★ 594 ★
Personal Care Products
SIC: 2844–ISIC: 2424–HC: 34

Men's Toiletries Sales

The combined market for men's toiletries in the United States and Europe reached $7.3 billion. Distribution is shown for selected categories.

	Hygiene	Fragrances	Shaving
United States . .	57.1%	34.0%	51.3%
United Kingdom .	19.9	7.6	12.3
France	9.7	9.7	11.6
Germany	5.4	30.7	10.9
Italy	4.8	7.2	9.4
Spain	3.0	10.8	4.6

Source: *Chemical Market Reporter*, May 8, 2000, p. FR20, from Datamonitor.

★ 595 ★
Personal Care Products
SIC: 2844–ISIC: 2424–HC: 34

Men's Toiletries Sales by Country

Sales are shown in millions of dollars.

	2000	2001	2002
United Kingdom	$ 347.2	$ 352.8	$ 358.0
France	171.5	177.1	182.5
Germany	102.5	112.5	123.1
Italy	86.4	89.8	93.0
Spain	53.1	55.3	57.4

Source: *Global Cosmetic Industry*, March 2001, p. 66, from Datamonitor.

★ 596 ★
Personal Care Products
SIC: 2844–ISIC: 2424–HC: 34

Personal Care Industry in Europe

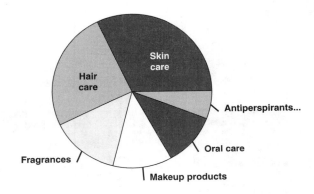

The market is valued at $28 billion. Industry specialists claim that there needs to be more consolidation. The market comprises mostly mid-sized companies, none of which holds more than a 15% share.

Skin care	32.0%
Hair care	25.0
Fragrances	14.0
Makeup products	12.0
Oral care	11.0
Antiperspirants & deodorants	6.0

Source: *Chemical Week*, December 6, 2000, p. 52, from Kline & Co.

★ 597 ★
Personal Care Products
SIC: 2844–ISIC: 2424–HC: 34

Personal Care Market in the U.K.

Sales are shown in millions of dollars. The fastest growing in the world, due in part to innovative marketing methods.

	1995	1999
Personal hygiene	$ 1,245	$ 1,446
Hair care	1,186	1,373
Skin care	991	1,239
Fragrances	981	1,100
Makeup	814	982

Source: *Global Cosmetic Industry*, October 2000, p. 56, from Datamonitor.

★ 598 ★
Personal Care Products
SIC: 2844–ISIC: 2424–HC: 34

Personal Care Products Market in France, 2000

The market is shown in percent.

Skin care	20.6%
Fragrances	19.1
Hair care	18.3
Cosmetics	13.0
Bath/shower products	7.1
Oral hygiene	6.9
Men's grooming products	5.6
Deodorants	5.3
Other	4.1

Source: *Brand Strategy*, May 2001, p. 22, from Euromonitor.

★ 599 ★
Personal Care Products
SIC: 2844–ISIC: 2424–HC: 34

Personal Care Products Market in Italy, 2000

The market is shown in percent.

Skin care	21.6%
Hair care	15.4
Cosmetics	12.9
Fragrances	12.1
Bath/shower products	10.7
Oral hygiene	10.3
Men's grooming products	6.9
Deodorants	5.5
Other	4.6

Source: *Brand Strategy*, May 2001, p. 22, from Euromonitor.

★ 600 ★
Personal Care Products
SIC: 2844–ISIC: 2424–HC: 34

Personal Care Products Market in Spain, 2000

The market is shown in percent.

Fragrances	22.3%
Hair care	16.8
Skin care	15.3
Cosmetics	12.0
Oral hygiene	8.6
Bath/shower products	6.5
Men's grooming products	6.5
Deodorants	5.0
Other	7.0

Source: *Brand Strategy*, May 2001, p. 22, from Euromonitor.

★ 601 ★
Personal Care Products
SIC: 2844–ISIC: 2424–HC: 34

Top Depilatory Brands in France, 1999

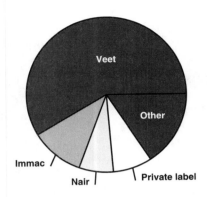

Market shares are shown in percent. Sales are at supermarkets and hypermarkets only.

Veet 58.5%
Immac 11.0
Nair 7.0
Private label 8.0
Other 15.5

Source: *European Cosmetic Markets*, June 2000, p. 227.

★ 602 ★
Personal Care Products
SIC: 2844–ISIC: 2424–HC: 34

Top Shaving Cream Makers in Japan, 1997

Market shares are shown based on shipments.

Warner Lambert 32.4%
Kao 12.0
Shiseido 10.6
Mandam 10.0
Feather Razor 9.2
Kanebo 6.8
Other 19.0

Source: "DVL Market Share Library." Retrieved April 3, 2001 from the World Wide Web: http://dvl/daiwa.co.jp, from DVL Market Share Library and Marketing Data Bank.

★ 603 ★
Skin Care
SIC: 2844–ISIC: 2424–HC: 34

Global Skin Care Market, 1998

Market shares are shown in percent.

L'Oreal 9.0%
Kanebo 8.0
Shiseido 8.0
Beiersdorf 6.0
Estee Lauder 5.0
Other 64.0

Source: *Global Cosmetic Industry*, February 1999, p. 18.

★ 604 ★
Skin Care
SIC: 2844–ISIC: 2424–HC: 34

Largest Skin Care Markets in Asia, 1998

Countries are ranked by sales in millions of dollars. Facial moisturizers led the category with sales of $765.1 million, body care had sales of $736.3 million, Facial cleansers had sales of $213.5 million and hand care had sales of $146.1 million.

	($ bil.)	Share
Hong Kong	.$ 40.52	31.44%
Japan	40.19	31.19
Taiwan	15.60	12.11
Singapore	9.16	7.11
South Korea	6.62	5.14
Malaysia	4.16	3.23
Thailand	3.85	2.99
Philippines	3.81	2.96
China	0.66	0.51
India	0.54	0.42
Other	3.75	2.91

Source: *Soap & Cosmetics*, December 2000, p. 58, from Euromonitor.

★ 605 ★
Skin Care
SIC: 2844–ISIC: 2424–HC: 34

Leading Facial Skin Care Producers in Poland

Market shares are shown in percent.

Eris	13.6%
L'Oreal	13.3
Pollena Uroda	8.5
Pollena Lechia	7.8
Soraya	7.2
Other	49.6

Source: *Soap Perfumery & Cosmetics*, November 1999, p. 49.

★ 606 ★
Skin Care
SIC: 2844–ISIC: 2424–HC: 34

Medical Skin Care Market in Germany

Market shares are shown in percent.

Sebamed	34.0%
Eucerin	30.0
Other	36.0

Source: *Lebensmittel Zeitung*, January 7, 2000, p. 1.

★ 607 ★
Skin Care
SIC: 2844–ISIC: 2424–HC: 34

Professional Skin Care Market in Europe

The effort to stay looking youthful continues to influence the skin care market. There are now roughly 250,000 beauty parlors in the United States and Europe. The professional skin care market was worth $1.4 billion in 2000. Sales are shown in millions of dollars.

	1998	1999	2000
Italy	$ 190	$ 181	$ 170
Germany	170	161	155
Spain	160	151	146
France	143	136	128
United Kingdom	124	125	131

Source: *Global Cosmetic Industry*, January 2001, p. 1, from Datamonitor.

★ 608 ★
Skin Care
SIC: 2844–ISIC: 2424–HC: 34

Skin/Body Care Sales in France

Skin care was the big segment with cleaning, wipes and the consumers wish to "trade up" to more prestige brands. As a result, the mass market is moving closer to the prestige market.

	1995	1999	Share
Facial moisturizers	$ 6,367.0	$ 7,004.8	57.80%
Cleansers	1,299.5	1,651.2	13.62
Body care	1,184.5	1,324.3	10.93
Toners	580.0	605.8	5.00
Face masks	530.0	597.9	4.93
Depilatories	458.0	687.3	5.67
Hand care	230.0	248.6	2.05

Source: *Soap Perfumery & Cosmetics*, December 2000, p. 26, from Euromonitor.

★ 609 ★
Skin Care
SIC: 2844–ISIC: 2424–HC: 34

Skin Care Sales in Germany

Data are for the first eight months.

	(mil.)	Share
Day cream	295.0	28.15%
Cleansing	265.0	25.29
Night cream	131.0	12.50
Antiaging	85.0	8.11
Toner	70.5	6.73
Wash gel/lotion	59.0	5.63
Eye care	56.0	5.34
Strips/patches	44.5	4.25
Cleansing milk	42.0	4.01

Source: *European Cosmetic Markets*, February 2001, p. 57, from industry estimates.

★ 610 ★
Skin Care
SIC: 2844–ISIC: 2424–HC: 34

Top Body Lotion/Oil Brands in Spain, 1999

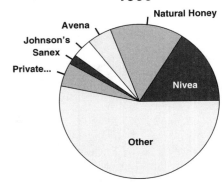

Market shares are shown in percent.

Nivea	15.5%
Natural Honey	15.0
Avena	5.0
Johnson's	4.0
Sanex	2.0
Private label	5.0
Other	53.5

Source: *European Cosmetic Markets*, June 2000, p. 227.

★ 611 ★
Skin Care
SIC: 2844–ISIC: 2424–HC: 34

Top Eye Lotion Makers in Japan, 1997

Market shares are shown based on shipments.

Rohto Pharmaceutical	44.6%
Santen Pharmaceutical	21.8
Taisho Pharmaceutical	6.0
Sanjyu Seiyaku	5.6
Lion	4.0
Other	18.0

Source: ''DVL Market Share Library.'' Retrieved April 3, 2001 from the World Wide Web: http://dvl/daiwa.co.jp, from DVL Market Share Library and Marketing Data Bank.

★ 612 ★
Skin Care
SIC: 2844–ISIC: 2424–HC: 34

Top Face Care Brands in Spain, 2000

Market shares are shown in percent for January - October 2000.

Diadermine	16.0%
Vitesse	13.0
Plenitude	11.0
Margaret Astor	8.5
Nivea	7.5
Pond's	7.5
Synergie	4.0
Other	32.5

Source: *European Cosmetic Market*, February 2001, p. 57, from industry estimates.

★ 614 ★
Skin Care
SIC: 2844–ISIC: 2424–HC: 34

Top Mass Hand/Body Care Brands in Germany, 1999

Market shares are shown in percent.

Nivea	42.0%
Bebe	5.5
Atrix	4.5
Dove	3.0
Pond's	3.0
Sebamed	3.0
CD	2.5
Penaten	2.5
Handsan	2.0
Satina	2.0
Other	30.0

Source: *European Cosmetic Markets*, June 2000, p. 227.

★ 613 ★
Skin Care
SIC: 2844–ISIC: 2424–HC: 34

Top Hand/Body Care Makers in the U.K., 1999

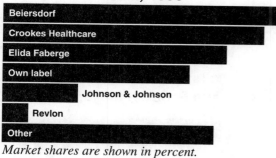

Market shares are shown in percent.

Beiersdorf	23.0%
Crookes Healthcare	20.5
Elida Faberge	17.5
Own label	15.0
Johnson & Johnson	5.5
Revlon	2.0
Other	16.5

Source: *European Cosmetic Markets*, June 2000, p. 227.

★ 615 ★
Sun Care
SIC: 2844–ISIC: 2424–HC: 34

Largest Sun Care Markets

Sales are shown in millions of dollars.

	1997	1999
United States	$ 751	$ 852
Germany	284	271
United Kingdom	252	257
France	159	162
Japan	154	161
Italy	144	156
Spain	71	92
Switzerland	35	37
South Korea	23	20
Sweden	14	15

Source: *Brand Strategy*, December 2000, p. 26, from Euromonitor.

★ 616 ★
Sun Care
SIC: 2844–ISIC: 2424–HC: 34

Largest Sun Care Markets in Western Europe, 1999

Sales are shown in millions of dollars.

	($ mil.)	Share
Germany	$ 318.5	22.38%
United Kingdom	279.7	19.65
Italy	209.8	14.74
France	201.1	14.13
Spain	100.5	7.06
Portugal	40.1	2.82
Switzerland	39.6	2.78
Greece	37.9	2.66
Other	196.1	13.78

Source: *Household and Personal Products Industry*, January 2001, p. 52, from Euromonitor.

★ 617 ★
Sun Care
SIC: 2844–ISIC: 2424–HC: 34

Sun Care Market by Segment

Figures are in millions of dollars.

	1996	2000	Share
Sun protection	$ 2,333.9	$ 2,547.9	79.82%
Aftersun	286.5	291.0	9.12
Self tanning	270.0	353.3	11.07

Source: *Soap Perfumery & Cosmetics*, March 2001, p. 19, from Euromonitor.

★ 618 ★
Sun Care
SIC: 2844–ISIC: 2424–HC: 34

Sun Care Market in Germany, 1999

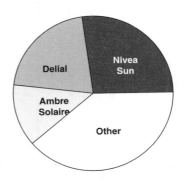

Market shares are shown in percent.

Nivea Sun	27.3%
Delial	21.0
Ambre Solaire	13.0
Other	38.7

Source: *Lebensmittel Zeitung*, May 19, 2000, p. 1, from Nielsen.

★ 619 ★
Sun Care
SIC: 2844–ISIC: 2424–HC: 34

Top Aftersun Product Makers, 1998

Market shares are shown in percent.

L'Oreal	15.6%
Beiersdorf	15.5
Johnson & Johnson	7.2
Sara Lee	5.0
Schering-Plough	4.4
Warner-Lambert	2.2
Boots	1.9
Cadey's	1.4
Tanning Research Laboratories	1.1
Other	45.7

Source: *Chemical Market Reporter*, May 8, 2000, p. 22, from Euromonitor.

★ 620 ★
Sun Care
SIC: 2844–ISIC: 2424–HC: 34

Top Self Tanning Product Makers, 1998

Market shares are shown in percent.

Estee Lauder	13.4%
Johnson & Johnson	12.8
L'Oreal	10.4
Schering-Plough	5.9
Tanning Research Laboratories	4.4
Playtex	4.3
Beiersdorf	3.2
Pfizer	2.8
Sara Lee	2.4
Other	40.4

Source: *Chemical Market Reporter*, May 8, 2000, p. 22, from Euromonitor.

★ 621 ★
Sun Care
SIC: 2844–ISIC: 2424–HC: 34

Top Sun Care Brands, 1999

Market shares are shown in percent. L'Oreal controls the market with a 11.7% share, followed by Johnson & Johnson with a 7.9% share.

Nivea	10.3%
Ambre Solaire	8.5
Coppertone	5.8
Banana Boat	4.2
Delial	3.4
Neutrogena	3.0
Piz Buin	2.3
Hawaiian Tropic	2.1
Soltan	2.1
Clinique	1.3
Other	57.0

Source: *Expose Magazine*, August 2000, p. 1.

★ 622 ★
Sun Care
SIC: 2844–ISIC: 2424–HC: 34

Top Sun Care Firms in France, 1998

Market shares are shown in percent.

L'Oreal	27.7%
Beiersdorf	11.2
Johnson & Johnson	4.8
Clarins	4.5
Other	51.8

Source: *Expose Magazine*, August 1999, p. NA, from Euromonitor Market Direction.

★ 623 ★
Sun Care
SIC: 2844–ISIC: 2424–HC: 34

Top Sun Care Firms in Spain, 1998

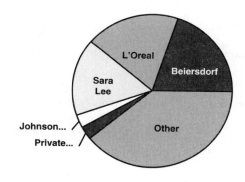

Market shares are shown in percent.

Beiersdorf	21.6%
L'Oreal	21.0
Sara Lee	18.3
Johnson & Johnson	2.7
Private label	2.7
Other	42.5

Source: ''Sun Rise, Sun Set, Sun Sales.'' Retrieved January 26, 2000 from the World Wide Web: http://www.exposemagazine.com, from Euromonitor Market Direction.

★ 624 ★
Sun Care
SIC: 2844–ISIC: 2424–HC: 34

Top Sun Care Products in Italy, 1999

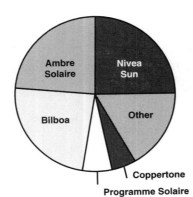

Fake tan products are experiencing a boom in sales. Sunprotection had 60% of the market, aftersun had 20% and self-tan had 10-15% share.

Nivea Sun	24.5%
Ambre Solaire	24.0
Bilboa	24.0
Programme Solaire	5.5
Coppertone	5.0
Other	17.0

Source: *European Cosmetic Markets*, April 2000, p. 139.

★ 625 ★
Sun Care
SIC: 2844–ISIC: 2424–HC: 34

Top Sun Care Products in Spain

Lotions had 70%, creams had 14% and oils had 3.5% of the market.

Nivea	21.5%
Delial	16.5
Nenuco	8.5
Ambre Soliare	7.5
Other	46.0

Source: *European Cosmetic Markets*, April 2000, p. 139.

★ 626 ★
Talcum Powder
SIC: 2844–ISIC: 2424–HC: 34

Top Talcum Powder Brands in India, 1999

Shares are for urban areas.

Pond's Dreamflower Magic	23.2%
Pond's Dreamlover	22.5
Nycil	7.8
Johnson's Baby Powder	6.2
Shower to Shower	2.5
Heaven's Garden	1.5
Other	36.3

Source: *Business Today*, June 22, 1999, p. 36, from ORG-MARG.

★ 627 ★
Paints and Coatings
SIC: 2851–ISIC: 2422–HC: 32

Powdered Coatings Market

Powder coating is the fastest growing industrial finishing method in North America. There are about 5,000 powder coating operations in North America. Market shares are shown in percent.

Europe	46.0%
North America	23.0
Far East	22.0
Other	9.0

Source: *Modern Paint and Coatings*, November 2000, p. 3.

★ 628 ★
Paints and Coatings
SIC: 2851–ISIC: 2422–HC: 32

Top Paint Brands in the U.K.

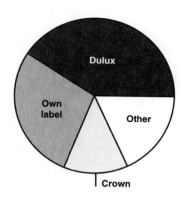

In the white emulsion sector, which is highly competitive, Crown had a 12.4% share and Dulux had a 40.6% share. Data are for the year to April 1999.

Dulux	40.8%
Own label	28.3
Crown	13.0
Other	17.9

Source: *DIY Week*, July 9, 1999, p. 6, from Gfk DIY Trak.

★ 629 ★
Paints and Coatings
SIC: 2851–ISIC: 2422–HC: 32

Top Paint/Coating Producers in the Ukraine

JSC Nord
Oxyplast
Pulver
Other

Market shares are shown in percent.

JSC Nord	60.0%
Oxyplast	15.0
Pulver	13.0
Other	12.0

Source: *Farbe & Lack*, October 2000, p. 138.

★ 630 ★
Paints and Coatings
SIC: 2851–ISIC: 2422–HC: 32

Top Paint Makers, 1999

Total demand for paint worldwide exceeded $65 billion. Market shares are shown in percent.

Akzo Nobel	11.8%
ICI	9.6
Sherwin Williams	8.8
PPG	7.0
DuPont	6.9
BASF	5.4
Kansai Paint	3.4
Nippon Paint	3.2
Total	2.9
Valspar	2.7
Others	38.3

Source: *Chemistry & Industry*, May 17, 1999, p. 381.

★ 631 ★
Paints and Coatings
SIC: 2851–ISIC: 2422–HC: 32

Top Paint Makers in India

Shares are for the decorative segment. In the industrial, GNPL has 40% and APL has 16% of the market.

Asian Paints	40.0%
GNPL	19.0
Other	41.0

Source: *The Hindu*, December 27, 2000, p. 1.

★ 632 ★
Paints and Coatings
SIC: 2851–ISIC: 2422–HC: 32

U.K. Paint and Coating Industry, 1999

The country spent 650 million British pounds on decorative paint and finishes. The country has 30 million do-it-yourself painters, with 200 million liters sold to them alone.

Retail decorative	28.0%
Trade decorative	21.5

Continued on next page.

U.K. Paint and Coating Industry, 1999

The country spent 650 million British pounds on decorative paint and finishes. The country has 30 million do-it-yourself painters, with 200 million liters sold to them alone.

Industrial exports	15.4%
General industrial	14.5
Vehicle refinish	12.1
High performance	3.5
Decorative exports	3.4
Marine	1.6

Source: *Chemistry in Britain*, September 2000, p. 31.

Brominated Flame Retardant Market, 2000

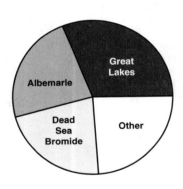

Shares are shown based on estimated sales of $900 million.

Great Lakes	31.0%
Albemarle	23.0
Dead Sea Bromide	22.0
Other	24.0

Source: *Chemical Market Reporter*, September 4, 2000, p. 15.

Flame Retardant Market

The $2.16 billion market is shown in percent.

Bromine	34.0%
Phosphorous	22.0
Antimony oxide	17.0
ATH	14.0
Chlorine	7.0
Other	5.0

Source: *Chemical Market Reporter*, May 7, 2001, p. 19, from Kline & Co. and Merrill Lynch.

Butadiene Market by End Use

Market shares are shown in percent.

Polybutadeiene	29.0%
Styrene butadiene rubber	29.0
SB	11.0
ABS	10.0
Adipinitrile	6.0
Nitrile rubber	3.0
Polychloroprene rubber	2.0
Other	10.0

Source: *Chemical Week*, February 7, 2001, p. 30.

★ 636 ★
Organic Chemicals
SIC: 2865–ISIC: 2411–HC: 29
Ethylene Market Shares

Market shares are shown in percent.

	1999	2004
North America	33.0%	31.0%
Europe	29.0	26.0
Asia/Pacific	26.0	27.0
Middle East	7.0	9.0
South America	4.0	5.0
Africa	1.0	2.0

Source: *Chemical Week*, August 9, 2000, p. 27, from CMAI.

★ 637 ★
Organic Chemicals
SIC: 2865–ISIC: 2411–HC: 29
Largest MMA Producers

MMA stands for methyl methacrylate.

Ineos Acrylics	26.0%
Rohm and Haas	15.0
Rohm	13.0
Mitsubishi Rayon	11.0
Other	35.0

Source: *Chemical Week*, December 8, 1999, p. 48, from Chem Systems.

★ 638 ★
Organic Chemicals
SIC: 2865–ISIC: 2411–HC: 29
Leading Textile Dye Makers, 1998

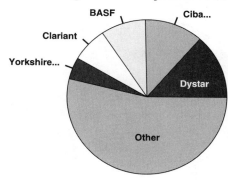

Shares are shown based on a $5.48 billion market.

Dystar	15.0%
Ciba Specialty Chemicals	13.0
BASF	10.0
Clariant	8.0
Yorkshire Group	5.0
Other	59.0

Source: *C&EN*, January 10, 2000, p. 21.

★ 639 ★
Organic Chemicals
SIC: 2865–ISIC: 2411–HC: 29
Titanium Dioxide Leaders, 2000

Total capacity reached 4.6 million metric tons.

Dupont	24.0%
Kerr-McGee	16.0
Millennium	16.0
Huntsman	13.0
Kronos	11.0
Ishihara	5.0
Kemira	2.0
Other	13.0

Source: *Chemical Week*, February 23, 2000, p. 7, from IBMA.

★ 640 ★
Organic Pigments
SIC: 2865–ISIC: 2411–HC: 29

Global Organic Pigment Market, 1998

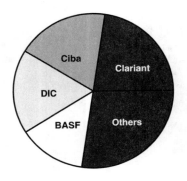

The $4.3 billion market is shown in percent.

Clariant	23.0%
Ciba	19.0
DIC	18.0
BASF	14.0
Others	28.0

Source: *Chemical Week*, June 30, 1999, p. 26, from Clariant.

★ 641 ★
Flavors & Fragrances
SIC: 2869–ISIC: 2411–HC: 29

Flavor & Fragrance Market

Market shares are shown in percent.

	1996	2000
Europe	33.1%	30.4%
North America	20.5	16.9
Japan	13.2	10.1
Other	33.1	42.5

Source: *Chemical Market Reporter*, April 23, 2001, p. 30, from Cameron & Stuart.

★ 642 ★
Flavors & Fragrances
SIC: 2869–ISIC: 2411–HC: 29

Top Flavor and Fragrance Firms, 2000

The market has been slow for the last few years but growth is expected to increase to 5% annually.

International Flavors and Fragrances	16.0%
Givaudan-Roure/Tastemaker	14.0
Quest International	12.0
H&R Florasynth	11.0
Firmenich	10.0
Other	37.0

Source: *Chemistry & Industry*, January 10, 2000, p. 28, from Consulting Resources Corporation.

★ 643 ★
Organic Chemicals
SIC: 2869–ISIC: 2411–HC: 29

Global Enzyme Market, 2000

The $1.5 billion market is shown in percent.

Novozymes	43.0%
Genecor	20.0
DSM	8.0
Other	29.0

Source: *C&EN*, February 19, 2001, p. 25, from Novozymes.

★ 644 ★
Organic Chemicals
SIC: 2869–ISIC: 2411–HC: 29
Photoresist Market Leaders, 1999

Shares are shown based on a market of $688 million.

Tokyo Ohka	31.0%
Shipley	15.0
Fuji/Arch	14.0
JSR	14.0
Sumitomo Chemical	12.0
Clariant	7.0
Others	7.0

Source: *Chemical Week*, June 28, 2000, p. 35, from The Information Network.

★ 645 ★
Agrichemicals
SIC: 2879–ISIC: 2421–HC: 31
Crop Protection Market Share Leaders, 1998

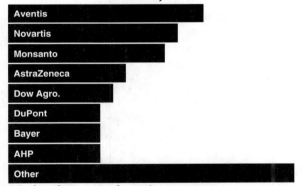

Market shares are shown in percent.

Aventis	14.6%
Novartis	13.3
Monsanto	11.5
AstraZeneca	9.1
Dow Agro.	7.5
DuPont	7.4
Bayer	7.3
AHP	7.0
Other	22.3

Source: *Wall Street Journal*, December 2, 1999, p. A3, from Wood Mackenzie.

★ 646 ★
Agrichemicals
SIC: 2879–ISIC: 2421–HC: 31
Gardening Product Sales in the U.K.

Sales are shown in millions of British pounds.

	(mil.)	Share
Growing media	180	43.69%
Lawn fertilizers	69	16.75
Weedkillers	55	13.35
Garden fertilizers	45	10.92
Insecticides & fertilizers	40	9.71
Houseplant care	10	2.43
Grass seed	8	1.94
Other	5	1.21

Source: *The Grocer*, August 26, 2000, p. 47, from Household Products Research.

★ 647 ★
Agrichemicals
SIC: 2879–ISIC: 2421–HC: 31
Leading Agrichemical Firms in Brazil

Market shares are shown in percent.

Syngenta	20.0%
Aventis	15.7
Basf	13.5
Dow Quimica	8.8
Monsanto	8.0
Milenia	7.9
Bayer	7.0
DuPont	6.8
Other	12.3

Source: *South American Business Information*, March 22, 2001, p. NA.

★ 648 ★
Fertilizers
SIC: 2879–ISIC: 2421–HC: 31

Top Fertilizer Makers in Brazil, 1999

Market shares are shown in percent. National sales reach $2.4 billion a year.

Serrana	16.0%
Manah	12.0
Cargill-Solorrico	10.0
Heringer	9.0
Fertipar	5.0
Fertibras	4.0
Fertiza	4.0
Others	40.0

Source: *Gazeta Mercantil*, April 4, 2000, p. B20.

★ 649 ★
Fertilizers
SIC: 2879–ISIC: 2421–HC: 31

Top Fertilizer Makers in the U.K., 1999

Market shares are shown based on value. In the entire garden supply market, plants lead with a 58% share, peat and compost with a 13.5% share.

Levington	36.4%
Miracle Garden Care	21.3
PBI	14.0
Arthur Bowers	3.8
Phostrogen	1.2
Other	23.3

Source: "UK Garden Supplies." Retrieved January 12, 2001 from the World Wide Web: http://www.clearlybusiness.com, from Datamonitor.

★ 650 ★
Insecticides
SIC: 2879–ISIC: 2421–HC: 31

Top Home-Use Insecticide Makers in Japan

Market shares are shown as of October 1998.

Takeda Engei	45.0%
Fumakilla	11.0
Hokko Sangyo	10.5
Sankyo Ryokuka	10.5
Nihon Nohyaku	6.6
Rainbow Yakuhin	5.8
Riken Green	5.1
Other	5.5

Source: "DVL Market Share Library." Retrieved April 3, 2001 from the World Wide Web: http://dvl/daiwa.co.jp, from DVL Market Share Library and Marketing Data Bank.

★ 651 ★
Adhesives
SIC: 2891–ISIC: 2429–HC: 39

Global Adhesives Demand

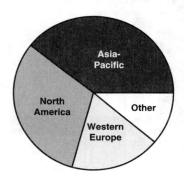

Demand is shown in millions of dollars.

	1999	2004	Share
Asia-Pacific	$ 4,886	$ 6,500	39.16%
North America	4,535	5,210	31.39
Western Europe	2,644	3,030	18.25
Other	1,450	1,860	11.20

Source: *Research Studies*, January 8, 2001, p. 1, from Freedonia Group.

★ 652 ★
Adhesives
SIC: 2891–ISIC: 2429–HC: 39
Largest Adhesive Firms

Firms are ranked by sales in millions of dollars.

Henkel	$ 2,380
3M	2,200
Avery Dennison	2,000
H.B. Fuller	1,360
National Starch and Chemical Co.	1,100

Source: *Adhesive Age*, September 2000, p. 19.

★ 653 ★
Adhesives
SIC: 2891–ISIC: 2429–HC: 39
Top Adhesives Markets in Western Europe

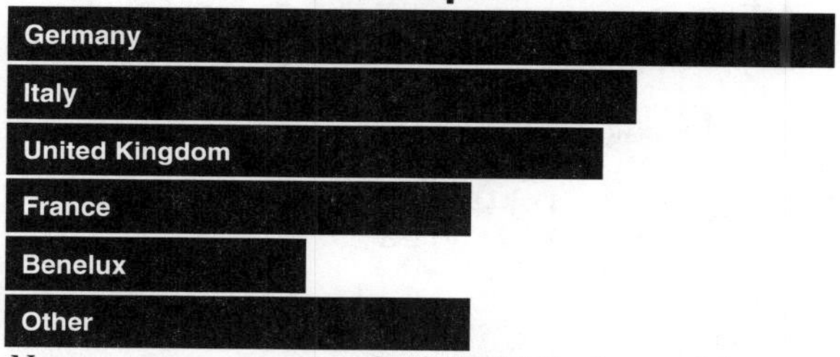

Germany	
Italy	
United Kingdom	
France	
Benelux	
Other	

Non-pressure sensitive had a 76.2% share of the market by adhesive; Packaging had the top sector with a 23% share.

Germany	24.6%
Italy	18.7
United Kingdom	18.3
France	14.3
Benelux	9.3
Other	14.3

Source: *Adhesives Age*, September 2000, p. 13, from Frost & Sullivan.

★ 654 ★
Ink
SIC: 2893–ISIC: 2429–HC: 32
Ink Market in Europe

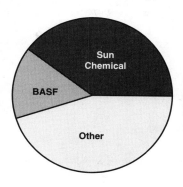

Sun's share actually exceeds 40 percent.

Sun Chemical	40.0%
BASF	15.0
Other	45.0

Source: *Ink World*, March 2000, p. 1.

★ 655 ★
Ink
SIC: 2893–ISIC: 2429–HC: 32
Printing Ink Market in Japan

The printing ink market in Asia, including Japan, is estimated at $3 to $4 billion a year.

Offset	38.0%
Gravure	33.0
Flexo	6.0
Letterpress	3.0
Other	20.0

Source: *American Ink Maker*, May 2000, p. 18.

★ 656 ★
Ink
SIC: 2893–ISIC: 2429–HC: 32

U.K. Printing Ink Sales, 1999

Market shares are shown in percent.

Packaging 36.0%
Publication 16.0
Newspaper 14.0
Overprint varnishes 11.0
Commercial 10.0
Other printing ink 9.0
Sundries 4.0

Source: *Chemistry in Britain*, September 2000, p. 31.

★ 657 ★
Ink
SIC: 2893–ISIC: 2429–HC: 39

Largest Ink Firms

Firms are ranked by ink and graphic arts sales in millions of dollars.

Dainippon Ink & Chemicals/Sun Chemical . $ 4,390
Flint Ink 1,400
Toyo Ink 950
SICPA 626
Sakata Inx 580
BASF Drucksysteme GmbH 565
Tokyo Printing Ink 541
Huber Group 410
Siegwerk Druckfarben GmbH 283
Gebr. Schmidt GmbH 260

Source: *Ink World*, November 2000, p. 41.

SIC 29 - Petroleum and Coal Products

★ 658 ★
Gasoline
SIC: 2911–ISIC: 2320–HC: 27

Top Gas Producers in Argentina

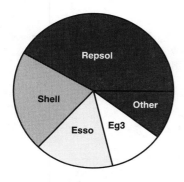

Market shares are shown in percent.

Repsol	42.0%
Shell	21.0
Esso	16.0
Eg3	11.0
Other	10.0

Source: *El Cronista*, December 1, 2000, p. 23.

★ 659 ★
Gasoline
SIC: 2911–ISIC: 2320–HC: 27

Top Gasoline Firms in Japan, 1999

Shares are shown based on domestic sales.

Nippon Mitsubishi Oil Corp.	23.3%
Idemitsu Kosan Co.	14.7
Showa Shell Sekiyu KK	12.5
Cosmo Oil Co.	11.3
Japan Energy Corp.	10.6
Other	27.6

Source: *Nikkei Weekly*, August 21, 2000, p. 9, from Nihon Keizai Shimbun.

★ 660 ★
Petroleum Refining
SIC: 2911–ISIC: 2320–HC: 27

Largest Petroleum Refiners

Companies are ranked by crude capacity, in barrels of crude per day.

ExxonMobil Corp.	5.43
Royal Dutch/Shell	3.99
BP	3.18
Sinopec	2.88
Petroleos de Venezuela SA	2.63
TotalFinaElf SA	2.50
Saudi Aramco	1.97
China National Petroleum Corp.	1.92
Petroleo Brasileiro SA	1.79
Petroleos Mexicanos	1.66

Source: *Oil & Gas Journal*, December 18, 2000, p. 57.

★ 661 ★
Petroleum Refining
SIC: 2911–ISIC: 2320–HC: 27

Largest Petroleum Refiners in Asia

Companies are ranked by crude capacity, in barrels of crude per day.

Sinopec	2.88
China National Petroleum Corp.	1.92
ExxonMobil Corp.	1.40
Royal Dutch/Shell	1.18
Nippon Mitsubishi Petroleum Rening Co. Ltd.	1.09
Pertamina	0.99
SK Corp.	0.81
Idemitsu Kosan Co. Ltd.	0.78
Chinese Petroleum Co.	0.77
Caltex Inc.	0.71

Source: *Oil & Gas Journal*, December 18, 2000, p. 57.

★ 662 ★
Petroleum Refining
SIC: 2911–ISIC: 2320–HC: 27

Largest Petroleum Refiners in Western Europe

Companies are ranked by crude capacity, in barrels of crude per day.

TotalFinaElf S.A.	2.19
ExxonMobil Corp.	1.81
Royal Dutch/Shell	1.37
BP	1.08
Agip Petroli SpA	1.00
Repsol-YPF SA	0.76
Turkish Petroleum Refineries Corp.	0.58
Compania Espanola de Petroles	0.39
Texaco Inc.	0.33
Petrogal EP	0.30

Source: *Oil & Gas Journal*, December 18, 2000, p. 57.

★ 663 ★
Engine Oil
SIC: 2992–ISIC: 2429–HC: 27

Top Engine Oil Makers in Japan, 1997

Market shares are shown based on shipments.

Toyota Motor	11.4%
Nissan Motor	8.2
Nippon Oil	6.5
Idemitsu Kosan	6.4
Honda Motor	5.7
Showa Shell Sekiyu	5.0
Cosmo Oil	4.8
Japan Energy	4.4
Other	47.6

Source: "DVL Market Share Library." Retrieved April 3, 2001 from the World Wide Web: http://dvl/daiwa.co.jp, from DVL Market Share Library and Marketing Data Bank.

★ 664 ★
Lubricants
SIC: 2992–ISIC: 2429–HC: 27

Lubricants Market in China

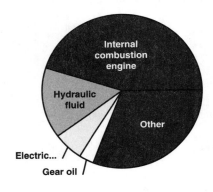

China is one of the largest producers of lube oil. Its output has reached 3 million metric tons a year. Ninteen companies control 95% of capacity. Market shares are shown in percent.

Internal combustion engine oil	45.0%
Hydraulic fluid	15.0
Electric motor oil	6.0
Gear oil	3.0
Other	31.0

Source: *China Chemical Market Newsletter*, November 1, 1999, p. NA.

★ 665 ★
Lubricants
SIC: 2992–ISIC: 2429–HC: 27

Top Lubricant Makers in India

Market shares are shown in percent.

IOC 37.0%
HPCL 22.0
Other 13.1

Source: *Business Line*, May 3, 2001, p. NA.

SIC 30 - Rubber and Misc. Plastics Products

★ 666 ★
Rubber Tracks
SIC: 3011–ISIC: 2511–HC: 40

Rubber Tracks Industry

Tracks are a growing part of the traction business, although they'll never supercede tires.

Bridgestone	75.0%
Other	25.0

Source: *Tire Business*, February 12, 2001, p. 10.

★ 667 ★
Tires
SIC: 3011–ISIC: 2511–HC: 40

Global Tire Market, 1999

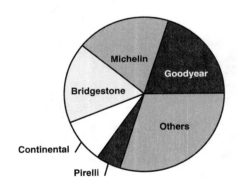

Market shares are shown in percent.

Goodyear	20.0%
Michelin	19.0
Bridgestone	17.0
Continental	9.0
Pirelli	5.0
Others	30.0

Source: *Investor's Business Daily*, April 6, 2000, p. 1.

★ 668 ★
Tires
SIC: 3011–ISIC: 2511–HC: 40

Replacement Tire Market in Poland

Market shares are shown in percent. Goodyear/ Dunlop controls 58% of the summer tire market and 37% of the winter tire market.

Goodyear/Dunlop	50.0%
Michelin	31.0
Continental	9.0
Pirelli	4.0
Other	6.0

Source: "Market for Replacement Tires." Retrieved October 27, 2000 from the World Wide Web: http://www.mac.doc.gov, from Continental Opony Polska.

★ 669 ★
Tires
SIC: 3011–ISIC: 2511–HC: 40

Replacement Tire Market in the U.K., 1999

Market shares are estimated based on volume.

Goodyear/Dunlop	23.5%
Michelin	22.0
Pirelli	10.7
Continental	10.3
Bridgestone	8.1
Other	25.4

Source: "Replacement Car Tires." Retrieved January 12, 2001 from the World Wide Web: http://www.clearlybusiness.com, from Datamonitor.

★ 670 ★
Tires
SIC: 3011–ISIC: 2511–HC: 40
Tire Market in India, 1999

Shares are of the original equipment market. Bridgestone has a commanding 27% share of the replacement market.

Bridgestone	43.0%
JK	19.0
MRF	17.0
Goodyear	14.0
Others	7.0

Source: *Business Today*, March 22, 2000, p. 36.

★ 671 ★
Tires
SIC: 3011–ISIC: 2511–HC: 40
Top Tire Makers in Indonesia

As the economy continues to recover, the market is expected to absorb about 11.2 million tires, a 40% growth. Market shares are shown in percent.

	(mil.)	Share
Gajah Tunggal	10.0	36.10%
Bridgestone Tire	7.6	27.44
Goodyear Indonesia	2.8	10.11
Mega Rubber Fac.	2.5	9.03
Intirub	1.2	4.33
Other	3.6	13.00

Source: ''Profile - Indonesia's Tire Industry.'' Retrieved October 9, 2000 from the World Wide Web: http://www.northernlight.com.

★ 672 ★
Tires
SIC: 3011–ISIC: 2511–HC: 40
Top Tire Makers in Japan, 1999

Market shares are shown based on domestic production of 1.13 million metric tons.

Bridgestone Corp.	53.7%
Yokohama Rubber Co.	16.0
Sumitomo Rubber Industries	12.6
Toyo Tire & Rubber Co.	10.4
Ohtsu Tire & Rubber Co.	5.5
Other	1.8

Source: *Nikkei Weekly*, August 14, 2000, p. 8, from Nihon Keizai Shimbun.

★ 673 ★
Athletic Footwear
SIC: 3021–ISIC: 1920–HC: 64
Sports Shoe Market in Europe

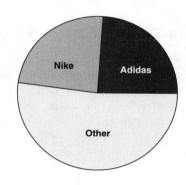

Market shares are shown in percent.

Adidas	24.0%
Nike	24.0
Other	52.0

Source: *Financial Times*, November 3, 2000, p. 18.

★ 674 ★
Athletic Footwear
SIC: 3021–ISIC: 1920–HC: 64

Sports Shoe Sales by Age in Europe

Sales are shown by age in Germany, France, Italy and Spain. Data are for the year ended September 30, 2000.

	(mil.)	Share
12-17	344	21.0%
5-11	298	18.0
25-34	237	19.0
45+	191	14.0
18-24	149	11.0
35-44	136	11.0
0-4	92	6.0

Source: *Sporting Goods Business*, December 18, 2000, p. 8, from NPD Sports Tracking Europe.

★ 675 ★
Athletic Footwear
SIC: 3021–ISIC: 1920–HC: 64

Top Sports Shoe Makers in the U.K., 1999

Total spending on sports footwear reached 1.08 billion pounds in 2000. General sports and leisure took 25% of the market, followed by running shoes with 19% of the market. Footwear's share of the entire sporting goods market was 30% in 1998 and 2000. Market shares are shown in percent.

C&J Clark	9.5%
Nike	6.0
Marks & Spencer	5.0
Reebok	5.0
Stylo	4.5
Adidas	2.0
British Shoe Corporation	2.0
Other	66.0

Source: *Marketing*, February 15, 2001, p. 19, from Euromonitor.

★ 676 ★
Athletic Footwear
SIC: 3021–ISIC: 1920–HC: 64

Top Sports Shoe Markets in Germany, 1999

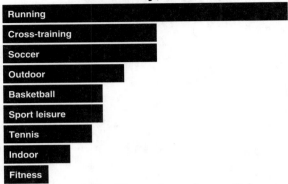

Germans buy 155 million pairs each year. Sales are shown by segment.

Running	25.6%
Cross-training	14.0
Soccer	13.6
Outdoor	11.1
Basketball	9.0
Sport leisure	8.9
Tennis	7.7
Indoor	6.0
Fitness	4.1

Source: *Market Europe*, December 2000, p. 4, from *SAZ*.

★ 677 ★
Condoms
SIC: 3069–ISIC: 2519–HC: 40

Condom Industry in Indonesia

There were about 26.8 million family planners and only 1.3% of them are regular users of condoms. Market shares are shown in percent.

	1997	1999
Sutera	1.1%	50.0%
Simplex	29.5	8.5
Other	69.4	41.5

Source: *Indonesian Commercial Newsletter*, December 5, 2000, p. 34.

★ 678 ★
Condoms
SIC: 3069–ISIC: 2519–HC: 40

Condom Market in the Czech Republic

Local condom consumption reached 2.1 million pieces.

Primeros 65.0%
Other 35.0

Source: *Hospodarske Noviny*, January 5, 2001, p. S1.

★ 679 ★
Plastic Pipe
SIC: 3084–ISIC: 2520–HC: 39

Plastic Pipe Market in Western Europe

Germany has 20% of the market, followed by Italy with 18% and France and the U.K. with 13% each.

Sewage/drainage 50.0%
Drinking water 21.0
Agriculture 9.0
Conduit pipe 8.0
Gas 5.0
Industry 4.0
Heating/plumbing 3.0

Source: *High Performance Plastics*, September 2000, p. 4.

★ 680 ★
Thermos Bottles
SIC: 3085–ISIC: 2520–HC: 39

Top Thermos Makers in Peru

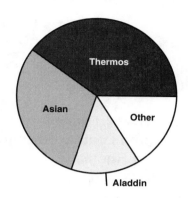

The $2.5-$3.0 million market is shown in percent.

Thermos 40.0%
Asian 30.0
Aladdin 14.0
Other 16.0

Source: *South American Business Information*, April 4, 2001, p. NA.

SIC 31 - Leather and Leather Products

★ 681 ★
Leather
SIC: 3111–ISIC: 1911–HC: 41

Largest Chrome Leather Producers in Russia

The Russian leather industry had profited from the fall of the ruble against other currencies. Imported items have become too expensive and consumers have now turned to domestically produced items. 38 factories produced leather, with most increasing production over 1998. The top 13 firms handled 90% of leather output.

TOO 'Khrom"	51.6
SP 'Rassakazovo-Invest"	35.0
AO 'Rushkon'	29.8
ZAO 'Kozha-M'	28.1
AOOT 'Kozhevnik'	16.6
AO 'Safyan'	13.8
Sterlitamak PKO	12.6
AM Venetsky Borogorodsky	12.0
Serpukhov	11.7
Kansky	10.2

Source: *Leather*, January 2000, p. 11.

★ 682 ★
Footwear
SIC: 3140–ISIC: 1920–HC: 64

Oudoor Sandal Market in Britain

Market shares are shown in percent.

Teva	60.0%
Other	40.0

Source: *In-Store Marketing*, April 1, 2000, p. 1.

★ 683 ★
Luggage
SIC: 3161–ISIC: 1912–HC: 42

Luggage Market Shares in the U.K., 1999

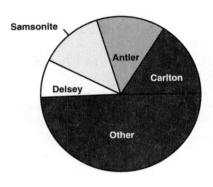

Market shares are shown based on value. Department stores had 43% of luggage sales, followed by luggage stores with 19.2% of sales.

Carlton	16.0%
Antler	14.0
Samsonite	13.0
Delsey	7.5
Other	49.5

Source: "UK Luggage." Retrieved January 12, 2001 from the World Wide Web: http://www.clearlybusiness.com, from Datamonitor.

SIC 32 - Stone, Clay, and Glass Products

★ 684 ★
Glass
SIC: 3211–ISIC: 2610–HC: 70

Lighting Glass Market

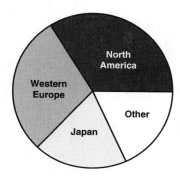

The market was estimated at $26 billion in 1997. Philips, Osram and GE are the top companies.

North America	34.0%
Western Europe	29.0
Japan	19.0
Other	18.0

Source: *Glass International*, May 2000, p. 30.

★ 685 ★
Windshields
SIC: 3231–ISIC: 2610–HC: 70

Windshield Market in the U.K.

Market shares are shown in percent.

Autoglass	35.0%
Auto Windscreen	32.0
Other	33.0

Source: *Daily Telegraph*, March 31, 2001, p. NA.

★ 686 ★
Cement
SIC: 3241–ISIC: 2694–HC: 68

Global Cement Market Shares

Shares are shown based on capacity.

Holderbank	6.0%
Lafarge	5.0
Cemex	4.0
Heidelberger	4.0
Blue Circle	3.0
Italcementi	3.0
Siam Cement	2.0
Taiheiyo Cement	2.0
Other	71.0

Source: *Financial Times*, January 8, 2001, p. 20, from *World Cement*.

★ 687 ★
Cement
SIC: 3241–ISIC: 2694–HC: 68

Top Cement Companies, 1999

Firms are ranked by estimated total controlled cement capacity. Data are in millions of tons.

Lafarge/Blue Circle	159
Holderbank	130
Heidelberger Zement	79
Cemex	71
Chicibu Onada/Nihon	60
Italcementi	53

Continued on next page.

★ 687 ★
[Continued]
Cement
SIC: 3241–ISIC: 2694–HC: 68

Top Cement Companies, 1999

Firms are ranked by estimated total controlled cement capacity. Data are in millions of tons.

Siam Cement	25
Votorantim	25
Dyckerhoff	24
Birla Group	23

Source: *Financial Times*, February 2, 2000, p. 20, from Primark Datastream, Cembureau, Deutsche Bank, and Rothschild.

★ 688 ★
Cement
SIC: 3241–ISIC: 2694–HC: 68

Top Cement Firms in Brazil

Market shares are shown in percent.

Votorantim	41.7%
Joao Santos	11.8
Cimpor	9.0
Holdercim	8.8
Lafarge	8.5
Camargo Correa	7.5
Tupi	3.6
Other	9.1

Source: *Gazeta Mercantil*, July 10, 2000, p. C3.

★ 689 ★
Cement
SIC: 3241–ISIC: 2694–HC: 68

Top Cement Firms in Chile, 2000

Shares are for the first quarter of the year.

Cemento Melon	37.0%
Cemento Polpaico	35.0
Cementos Bio Bio	27.0

Source: *Estrategia*, July 11, 2000, p. 1.

★ 690 ★
Cement
SIC: 3241–ISIC: 2694–HC: 68

Top Cement Makers in Japan, 2000

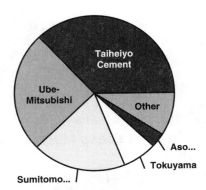

Shares are at the end of March 2000.

Taiheiyo Cement	37.3%
Ube-Mitsubishi	24.5
Sumitomo Osaka Cement	18.9
Tokuyama	6.6
Aso Cement	3.4
Other	9.3

Source: *Nikkei Weekly*, February 19, 2001, p. 10, from Nihon Keizai Shimbun.

★ 691 ★
Bricks
SIC: 3251–ISIC: 2693–HC: 68

Masonry Brick Producer Market Shares in Germany

Market shares are shown in percent.

Brick	43.5%
Calcium silicate brick (sandlime brick)	28.8
Aerated concrete (gas concrete)	15.1
Concrete and light-weight concrete	12.6

Source: *Ziegelindustrie*, April 2001, p. 9.

★ 692 ★
Tiles
SIC: 3251–ISIC: 2693–HC: 68

Top Roof Tile Makers in Japan, 1997

Market shares are shown based on shipments.

Kubota	48.8%
Matsushita Electric Works	26.0
Sekisui Chemical	14.1
Nihon Moniel	6.8
Daiken	2.0
Other	2.3

Source: ''DVL Market Share Library.'' Retrieved April 3, 2001 from the World Wide Web: http://dvl/daiwa.co.jp, from DVL Market Share Library and Marketing Data Bank.

★ 693 ★
Sanitaryware
SIC: 3261–ISIC: 2691–HC: 68

Sanitaryware Market in India

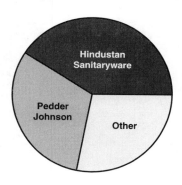

Industry turnover reached Rs 275 crore.

Hindustan Sanitaryware	41.0%
Pedder Johnson	31.0
Other	28.0

Source: *Business India*, June 26, 2000, p. 87.

★ 694 ★
Sanitaryware
SIC: 3261–ISIC: 2691–HC: 68

Top Toilet Seat Makers in Japan, 1997

Market shares are shown based on shipments.

Toto	62.8%
Inax	24.6
Janis	4.1
Asahi Eito	3.6
Other	4.9

Source: ''DVL Market Share Library.'' Retrieved April 3, 2001 from the World Wide Web: http://dvl/daiwa.co.jp, from DVL Market Share Library and Marketing Data Bank.

★ 695 ★
Artificial Marble
SIC: 3281–ISIC: 2696–HC: 68

Top Artificial Marble Makers in Japan, 1997

Market shares are shown based on shipments.

MRC DuPont	22.0%
Kuraray	9.1
Nippon Shokubai	8.8
Dainippon Ink & Chemicals	6.8
Toto	2.5
Inax	2.3
Other	48.5

Source: ''DVL Market Share Library.'' Retrieved April 3, 2001 from the World Wide Web: http://dvl/daiwa.co.jp, from DVL Market Share Library and Marketing Data Bank.

★ 696 ★
Steel Wool
SIC: 3291–ISIC: 2699–HC: 68

Steel Wool Market in Brazil

Market shares are shown in percent.

Bombril 90.0%
Other 10.0

Source: *Advertising Age International*, September 1999, p. 48.

SIC 33 - Primary Metal Industries

★ 697 ★

Steel

SIC: 3312–ISIC: 2899–HC: 72

Largest Steel Producers, 1999

Firms are ranked by production in millions of metric tons.

Pohang Iron and Steel	26.5
Nippon Steel	25.2
Arbed	22.2
Usinor	22.2
Corus	21.3
LNM Group/Ispat	20.0
Shanghai Baosteel	16.7
Thyssen Krupp Steel	16.1
Riva	14.1
NKK	12.8

Source: *Business Week*, August 28, 2000, p. 70H, from Steel Information Agency.

★ 698 ★

Steel

SIC: 3312–ISIC: 2899–HC: 72

Leading Steel Producers, 1999

Production is shown in millions of metric tons.

China	123.7
United States	97.3
Japan	94.2
Russia	51.5
Germany	42.1
Ukraine	27.5

Source: *New York Times*, November 30, 2000, p. C1, from International Iron and Steel Institute.

★ 699 ★
Steel
SIC: 3312–ISIC: 2899–HC: 72

Top Steel Makers in Japan, 1999

Market shares are shown based on domestic production of 98 million metric tons.

Nippon Steel Corp.	26.1%
NKK Corp.	12.5
Kawasaki Steel Corp.	11.1
Sumitomo Metal Industries Ltd.	9.8
Kobe Steel Ltd.	5.9
Other	34.6

Source: *Nikkei Weekly*, August 14, 2000, p. 8, from Nihon Keizai Shimbun.

★ 700 ★
Copper
SIC: 3331–ISIC: 2710–HC: 74

Leading Copper Producers

Data show share of world output.

Codelco	8.8%
Asarco	5.4
Phelps Dodge	5.4
Noranda	3.4
Cyprus Amax	3.2
KGMH Polska Miedz	3.2
LG	2.6
Norddeutsche Affinerie	2.6
Nippon Melting & Smelting	2.5
Other	62.9

Source: *Financial Times*, September 28, 1999, p. 23, from Raw Materials Data and Metal Bulletin Research.

★ 701 ★
Aluminum
SIC: 3334–ISIC: 2710–HC: 76

Global Aluminum Market, 1998

Shares are shown based on output. SBNMI stands for the State Bureau of Nonferrous Metals Industry.

Alcoa	11.3%
Alcan	6.6
SBNMI	4.5
Reynolds	4.4
Pechiney	3.9
Algroup	1.2
Others	68.1

Source: *Wall Street Journal*, August 11, 1999, p. A13, from Brook Hunt and J.P. Morgan estimates.

★ 702 ★
Aluminum
SIC: 3334–ISIC: 2710–HC: 76

Largest Aluminum Consumers

Data are in metric kilotons.

	(Kmt)	Share
Western Europe	5,325	25.98%
United States	5,055	24.66
Japan	2,335	11.39
China	1,940	9.46
Eastern Europe	900	4.39
Other	4,945	24.12

Source: *Engineering & Mining Journal*, April 2000, p. 40, from World Bureau of Metal Statistics.

★ 703 ★
Nickel
SIC: 3339–ISIC: 2710–HC: 81

Nickel Consumption by End Use

Market shares are shown in percent.

Stainless steel	65.0%
Nonferrous alloys	12.0
Plating	7.0
Alicy steels	5.0
Foundry	5.0
Batteries	4.0
Other	2.0

Source: *Engineering & Mining Journal*, April 2001, p. 30.

★ 704 ★
Aluminum
SIC: 3350–ISIC: 2720–HC: 81

Largest Aluminum Producers

Shares are shown based on total production of 22.1 metric tons.

United States	16.8%
Russia	13.6
Canada	10.7
China	9.5
Australia	7.4
Other	42.0

Source: "Summary of Mining Statistics." Retrieved June 18, 2001 from the World Wide Web: http://www.nma.org.

★ 705 ★
Wiring and Cable
SIC: 3350–ISIC: 2720–HC: 81

Wiring And Cable Sales

Data are in millions of dollars.

	1999	2004	Share
Communications and information processing	$ 26.2	$ 36.3	42.11%
Building construction	11.9	14.6	16.94
Power transmission and distribution	8.1	10.2	11.83
Other	20.3	25.1	29.12

Source: *Electronic Buyers News*, October 2, 2000, p. 44, from Freedonia Group.

★ 706 ★
Aluminum Foil
SIC: 3353–ISIC: 2720–HC: 76

Top Aluminum Foil Makers in Japan

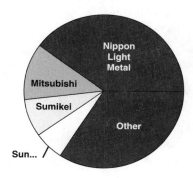

Shares are for the household foil sector.

Nippon Light Metal	40.0%
Mitsubishi	12.0
Sumikei	8.0
Sun Aluminum	6.0
Other	34.0

Source: *Metal Bulletin*, January 15, 2001, p. 5.

★ 707 ★
Aluminum Sheet
SIC: 3353–ISIC: 2720–HC: 76

Aluminum Sheet Market in South Korea, 1999

Market shares are shown in percent.

Koralu	39.5%
Alcan-Taihan	32.5
Choil	20.7
Namsun	4.9
Seoul	2.4

Source: *Metal Bulletin Monthly*, April 1, 2000, p. 1, from KMJ.

★ 708 ★
Magnesium
SIC: 3356–ISIC: 2720–HC: 80

Magnesium Market by End Use

Metal production has grown by almost 30% since 1995. Magnesium, while plentiful, has until recently had limited industrial applications.

Aluminum alloying	43.0%
Diecasting	31.0
Desulphurization	13.0
Other	13.0

Source: *Mining Magazine*, March 2000, p. 136, from Noranda and *Metals and Minerals Annual Review*.

★ 709 ★
Copper Wire
SIC: 3357–ISIC: 2720–HC: 80

Top Copper Wire Makers, 1998

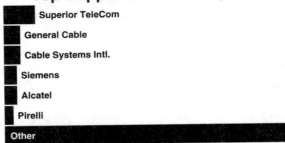

Firms are ranked by revenue in millions of dollars for the telecom sector.

	($ mil.)	Share
Superior TeleCom	$ 600	7.89%
General Cable	300	3.95
Cable Systems Intl.	275	3.62
Siemens	250	3.29
Alcatel	200	2.63
Pirelli	170	2.24
Other	5,805	76.38

Source: *Wall Street Journal*, February 16, 2000, p. B4, from CRU International.

★ 710 ★
Castings
SIC: 3360–ISIC: 2732–HC: 82

Casting Shipments in China

There are about 12,000 foundries in China, with the Eastern region holding 35% of them. Casting plants that produce less than 300 tons annually occupy 33% of the total.

	1997	1999	Share
Gray iron	6.87	7.91	63.23%
Ductile iron	1.56	2.06	16.47
Steel	1.45	1.35	10.79
Aluminum and magnesium	0.66	0.73	5.84
Malleable iron	0.35	0.35	2.80
Zinc	0.07	0.11	0.88

Source: *Modern Casting*, December 2000, p. 25.

★ 711 ★
Foundries
SIC: 3360–ISIC: 2732–HC: 82

Foundries Market Worldwide

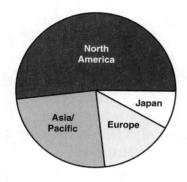

Market shares are shown in percent.

North America 52.0%
Asia/Pacific 25.0
Europe 15.0
Japan 8.0

Source: *Enews*, February 12, 2001, p. NA.

★ 712 ★
Foundries
SIC: 3360–ISIC: 2732–HC: 82

Pure-Play Foundry Market, 2000

Market shares are shown based on capacity.

TSMC 40.0%
UMC Group (Taiwan) 29.0
Chartered (Singapore) 11.0
Other 20.0

Source: *Electronic News*, February 12, 2001, p. 28, from
IC Insights and company reports.

SIC 34 - Fabricated Metal Products

★ 713 ★
Beverage Cans
SIC: 3411–ISIC: 2899–HC: 76

Largest Beverage Can Makers

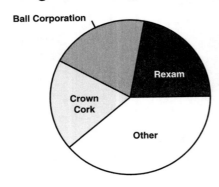

Market shares are shown in percent.

Rexam	22.0%
Ball Corporation	20.0
Crown Cork & Seal	19.0
Other	39.0

Source: *Packaging Magazine*, July 27, 2000, p. 3.

★ 714 ★
Cutlery
SIC: 3421–ISIC: 2893–HC: 82

Cutlery Market in India

The Rs 50 crore market is shown in percent.

Kishco Cutlery	40.0%
Todi/Shaheen	10.0
Other	50.0

Source: *Financial Express*, December 28, 2000, p. NA.

★ 715 ★
Razor Blades
SIC: 3421–ISIC: 2893–HC: 82

Top Razor and Blade Producers in Britain

Shares are shown for the entire razor and blade market.

Gillette	73.8%
Wilkinson Sword 3D/Protector	15.6
Own-label	8.0
Other	2.6

Source: *Sunday Times*, September 10, 2000, p. 2.

★ 716 ★
Scissors
SIC: 3421–ISIC: 2893–HC: 82

Nail Scissor Market in Saigon

Market shares are shown in percent.

Kem Nghia Co.	50.0%
Other	50.0

Source: *Saigon Times Daily*, March 20, 2001, p. NA.

★ 717 ★
Saws
SIC: 3425–ISIC: 2893–HC: 82

Jigsaw Market Shares in the U.K., 1998

Market shares are estimated based on value.

Black & Decker	52.4%
Bosch	36.7
Hitachi	5.0
Others	5.9

Source: "UK Power Tools." Retrieved January 11, 2001 from the World Wide Web: http://www.clearlybusiness.com, from Datamonitor.

★ 718 ★
Locks
SIC: 3429–ISIC: 2893–HC: 82

Top Door Lock Makers in Japan, 1997

Market shares are shown based on revenue.

Miwa Lock	33.2%
Goal	7.5
Show Lock	7.2
Nishi Seisakusho	6.0
Alpha	5.0
Kawaguchi Giken	5.0
Other	36.1

Source: "DVL Market Share Library." Retrieved April 3, 2001 from the World Wide Web: http://dvl/daiwa.co.jp, from DVL Market Share Library and Marketing Data Bank.

★ 719 ★
Bay Windows
SIC: 3442–ISIC: 2811–HC: 76

Top Bay Window Makers in Japan, 1997

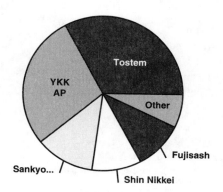

Market shares are shown based on shipments.

Tostem	32.8%
YKK AP	28.3
Sankyo Aluminum Industry	12.1
Shin Nikkei	9.8
Fujisash	9.6
Other	7.4

Source: "DVL Market Share Library." Retrieved April 3, 2001 from the World Wide Web: http://dvl/daiwa.co.jp, from DVL Market Share Library and Marketing Data Bank.

★ 720 ★
Gates
SIC: 3442–ISIC: 2811–HC: 76

Top Gate Makers in Japan, 1997

Market shares are shown based on shipments.

Toyo Exterior	36.7%
Sankyo Aluminum Industry	15.8
Shin Nikkei	14.8
YKKAp Exterior	11.7
Shikoku Chemicals	6.8
Matsushita Electric Works	5.6
Other	8.6

Source: "DVL Market Share Library." Retrieved April 3, 2001 from the World Wide Web: http://dvl.daiwa.co.jp, from DVL Market Share Library and Marketing Data Bank.

★ 721 ★
Heating Equipment
SIC: 3443–ISIC: 2811–HC: 84

Top Solar Heating Equipment Makers in Japan, 1997

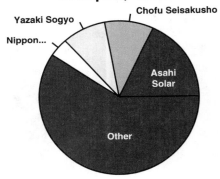

Market shares are shown based on revenue.

Asahi Solar	18.1%
Chofu Seisakusho	9.7
Yazaki Sogyo	8.5
Nippon Electric Glass	4.0
Other	59.7

Source: "DVL Market Share Library." Retrieved April 3, 2001 from the World Wide Web: http://dvl.daiwa.co.jp, from DVL Market Share Library and Marketing Data Bank.

★ 722 ★
Shackles
SIC: 3462–ISIC: 2891–HC: 73

Ship Shackle Industry in Japan

Market shares are shown in percent.

Tomo Iron & Steel	94.0%
Other	6.0

Source: "Regional Product Information." Retrieved March 29, 2001 from the World Wide Web: http://www.fukuyama.or.jp/e/productsman.html.

★ 723 ★
Bakeware
SIC: 3469–ISIC: 2891–HC: 83

Bakeware Market in the U.K., 1998

Shares are estimated. Nonstick has a 68.5% share and a stick has a 31.5% share.

Roasters	22.0%
Bun tins	15.0
Sandwich tins	15.0
Yorkshire pudding tins	12.0
Cake tins	10.0
Other	26.0

Source: *Housewares*, September 1999, p. 38.

★ 724 ★
Cookware
SIC: 3469–ISIC: 2891–HC: 83

Cookware Market in the U.K.

Saucepans have the top share, followed by frypans.

Tefal	19.0%
Swan	8.0
Prestige	4.0
Tower	4.0
Le Creuset	3.0
Meyer	3.0
Other	59.0

Source: *Housewares*, July 1996, p. 30, from *Housewares 2000*.

★ 725 ★
Stampings
SIC: 3469–ISIC: 2891–HC: 83

Finished Pressings and Stampings in the U.K., 1998

The total market was valued at 438.7 million British pounds.

	(mil.)	Share
Automotive	297.1	67.72%
Fabricated work	45.6	10.39
Refrigeration m/c	20.2	4.60
Domestic/garden appliances . . .	15.6	3.56
Industrial valves	7.8	1.78
Heating and cooling	6.6	1.50
Machine tools	1.8	0.41
Other	44.0	10.03

Source: *The Engineer*, May 14, 1999, p. 1.

★ 727 ★
Valves
SIC: 3491–ISIC: 2912–HC: 84

Valve Sales in Europe

Industrial process control valves and control elements should reach sales of $3.2 billion by 2005 from $2.89 billion in 1998.

Sliding valves and seat valves	30.6%
Hydraulic and pneumatic valves	26.0
Globe and plug valves	21.0
Other	22.4

Source: *Frankfurter Allgemeine*, November 1, 1999, p. 26, from Frost & Sullivan.

★ 726 ★
Valves
SIC: 3491–ISIC: 2912–HC: 84

Valve and Tap Market in Europe, 1999

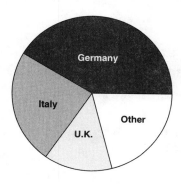

The 13 billion British pound market is shown in percent.

	(bil.)	Share
Germany	5.4	41.54%
Italy	3.1	23.85
U.K.	1.8	13.85
Other	2.7	20.77

Source: *Financial Times*, March 20, 2001, p. 23, from Anima.

SIC 35 - Industry Machinery and Equipment

★ 728 ★
Turbines
SIC: 3511–ISIC: 2911–HC: 84

All-Fossil Fuel Turbine Market, 1999

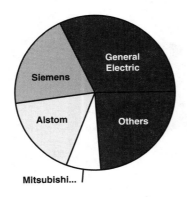

Market shares are shown in percent.

General Electric	32.0%
Siemens	20.0
Alstom	17.0
Mitsubishi Heavy Industries	7.0
Others	24.0

Source: *Financial Times*, June 20, 2000, p. 3, from Datamonitor.

★ 729 ★
Turbines
SIC: 3511–ISIC: 2911–HC: 84

Power Plant Orders, 2000

Market shares are shown in percent.

General Electric	26.0%
Siemens	13.0
Alstom	12.0
Caterpillar	12.0
Cummins	8.0
Other	29.0

Source: *Financial Times*, June 5, 2001, p. 22, from Datamonitor.

★ 730 ★
Turbines
SIC: 3511–ISIC: 2911–HC: 84

Steam Turbine Market, 1999

Market shares are shown in percent.

Alstom	24.0%
General Electric	17.0
Siemens	11.0
Mitsubishi	7.0
Others	41.0

Source: *Financial Times*, June 20, 2000, p. 3, from Datamonitor.

★ 731 ★
Turbines
SIC: 3511–ISIC: 2911–HC: 84
Wind Turbine Market, 1998

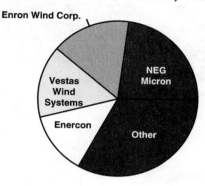

Market shares are shown in percent.

NEG Micron	23.4%
Enron Wind Corp.	16.3
Vestas Wind Systems	14.8
Enercon	12.8
Other	32.7

Source: *Reinforced Plastics*, February 2000, p. 21.

★ 732 ★
Wind Equipment
SIC: 3511–ISIC: 2911–HC: 84
Wine Energy Equipment Market in Germany

Market shares are shown in percent.

Enercon	27.5%
Vestas Germany	12.6
NEG Micron	12.3
Enron Wind	11.6
AN Windenergie	10.1
Borsig Energy	8.3
DeWind Technik	7.5
Other	9.9

Source: "Bundesverband WindEnergie." Retrieved January 24, 2001 from the World Wide Web: http://www.windenergie.de.

★ 733 ★
Farm Equipment
SIC: 3523–ISIC: 2921–HC: 84
Agricultural Equipment Sales, 1999

The market is estimated to reach $22 billion. Agco's figures does not include sales by licensees and associates.

CNH	31.0%
Deere	26.0
Agco	12.0
Other	31.0

Source: *Financial Times*, July 5, 2000, p. 17, from J.P. Morgan.

★ 734 ★
Farm Equipment
SIC: 3523–ISIC: 2921–HC: 84
Germany's Tractor Market, 1999

Germany is the second largest tractor market in Europe, with sales of 28,000 units.

AGCO	25.6%
Fendt	21.1
Deere	20.3
CNH	19.7
Case/Steyr	13.3
Same Deutz-Fahr	11.9

Source: *Farmers Weekly*, February 25, 2000, p. 1, from http://www.reedbusiness.com.

★ 735 ★
Farm Equipment
SIC: 3523–ISIC: 2921–HC: 84

Global Agricultural Machinery Demand

The market is expected to increase 4.5% a year through 2004 until reaching $60 billion. Increased industrialization in Asia and Latin America will play a major role in shaping the market. Eastern Europe's farming communities will also play a role. Demand is shown in millions of dollars.

	1999	2004	Share
Asia-Pacific	$ 14,475	$ 19,600	32.93%
Western Europe	15,470	17,675	29.69
North America	11,910	14,300	24.02
Latin America	2,340	3,250	5.46
Eastern Europe	2,000	2,675	4.49
Africa/Middle East . . .	1,550	2,025	3.40

Source: *Research Studies*, August 6, 2000, p. 1, from Freedonia Group.

★ 736 ★
Farm Equipment
SIC: 3523–ISIC: 2921–HC: 84

Harvesting Machinery Market in Brazil

Market shares are shown in percent.

SLC-John Deere	77.0%
Other	23.0

Source: *South American Business Information*, April 2, 2001, p. NA.

★ 737 ★
Farm Equipment
SIC: 3523–ISIC: 2921–HC: 84

Tractor Market in the U.K., 1998

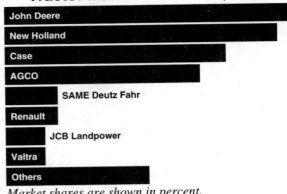

Market shares are shown in percent.

John Deere	21.6%
New Holland	21.1
Case	17.4
AGCO (MF)	15.4
SAME Deutz Fahr	4.1
Renault	3.6
JCB Landpower	3.0
Valtra	2.6
Others	11.3

Source: *Implement & Tractor*, January/February 2000, p. 9, from Equipment Manufacturers Institute.

★ 738 ★
Lawn & Garden Equipment
SIC: 3524–ISIC: 2921–HC: 84

Lawnmower Market in France

Lawnmowers are used by 38.8% of French consumers including private households and businesses.

Electric walk-behind	12.9%
Gas self-propelled	11.7
Gas walk-behind	11.2
Gas riding-type	3.3
Air cushion	2.8
Other	58.1

Source: "France: Lawnmowers." Retrieved September 19, 2000 from the World Wide Web: http://www.tradeport.org.

★ 739 ★
Construction Equipment
SIC: 3531–ISIC: 2924–HC: 84

Construction Equipment Market Shares, 1998

The $75 billion market is shown by company.

Caterpillar	18.0%
Komatsu	6.0
Case	3.0
Deere	3.0
Volvo	3.0
JCB	2.0
Liebherr	2.0
New Holland	2.0
Others	61.0

Source: *Financial Times*, May 16, 1999, p. 23.

★ 740 ★
Construction Equipment
SIC: 3531–ISIC: 2924–HC: 84

Heavy Construction Equipment Demand

World demand is expected to increase 5.9% annually to hit $93.5 billion in 2003. Fueling this growth, in part, is the recovery of Asian countries from the recent economic crisis. Many of these countries were considered high growth markets.

	1998 ($ bil.)	2003 ($ bil.)	Share
United States	$ 21.4	$ 27.4	33.13%
Western Europe	15.3	19.9	24.06
Japan	9.1	11.0	13.30
Canada/Mexico	4.3	6.0	7.26
China	4.2	6.8	8.22

	1998 ($ bil.)	2003 ($ bil.)	Share
Latin America	$ 3.4	$ 4.9	5.93%
Africa/Mideast	2.6	3.7	4.47
Eastern Europe	2.2	3.0	3.63

Source: *Pit & Quarry*, December 1999, p. 36, from Freedonia Group.

★ 741 ★
Oil and Gas Equipment
SIC: 3533–ISIC: 2924–HC: 84

Oil and Gas Equipment Market in the U.K., 1999

Market shares are estimated based on value. The market reached 25 million pounds.

Siemens	30.0%
Rockwell	28.0
Schneider	13.0
Mitsubishi	5.0
Omron	5.0
Others	19.0

Source: "UK Oil and Gas Automation." Retrieved January 12, 2001 from the World Wide Web: http://www.clearlybusiness.com, from Datamonitor.

★ 742 ★
Oil Rig Brakes
SIC: 3533–ISIC: 2924–HC: 84

Electrical Brakes on Oil Rigs

The market refers to electrical brakes used to control the drawworks for the rig - the mechanism used to raise and lower pipe in the hole.

Boots & Coots	95.0%
Other	5.0

Source: *Knight-Ridder/Tribune Business News*, August 2, 2000, p. NA.

★ 743 ★
Escalators
SIC: 3534–ISIC: 2930–HC: 84

Global Escalator Market, 1999

Companies are ranked by unit sales.

	Units	Share
Schindler	3,684	23.0%
Otis	3,380	21.0
Mitsubishi	1,850	12.0
Kone	1,630	10.0
Thyssen	1,590	10.0
Hitachi	1,290	8.0
Toshiba	590	4.0
Others	1,766	12.0

Source: *Neue Zuercher Zeitung*, April 4, 2000, p. 1.

★ 744 ★
Cranes
SIC: 3536–ISIC: 2924–HC: 84

Global All-Terrain Crane Market, 1999

Liebherr
PPM
Demag
Grove France
Tadano Faun

Shares are shown in percent.

Liebherr	29.0%
PPM	29.0
Demag	16.0
Grove France	15.0
Tadano Faun	11.0

Source: *Cranes Today*, May 1, 2000, p. 1.

★ 745 ★
Cranes
SIC: 3536–ISIC: 2924–HC: 84

Largest Truck Crane Makers in South Korea

There are 44 U.S. suppliers manufacturing 4,340 crane models in the country. They have been doing business there since 1992. U.S. suppliers hold a 60% share of the import market. Average shares are cumulative since 1992. The crane market was worth $276 million in 1997.

P&H	34.0%
Grove	15.0
Linkbelt	7.0
Lorain	4.0
Other	40.0

Source: STAT-USA, *National Trade Data Bank*, April 2000, p. NA.

★ 746 ★
Lift Trucks
SIC: 3536–ISIC: 2924–HC: 84

Top Lift Truck Makers Worldwide

The industry is expected to undergo major consolidation. The top 20 firms had sales of $15.6 billion.

Linde	15.6%
Hyster/Yale	14.1
Toyota	13.2
Other	57.1

Source: *Modern Materials Handling*, October 1, 1999, p. 1.

★ 747 ★
Powered Access Platforms
SIC: 3536–ISIC: 2924–HC: 84

U.K. Powered Access Market Shares, 1998

Shares are for December 1998. Powered access penetration is 15% of the U.K. access market compared with 45% of the U.S. and 7% of Germany.

Lavendon	16.0%
PTP (Rentokil)	11.0

Continued on next page.

★ 747 ★
[Continued]
Powered Access Platforms
SIC: 3536–ISIC: 2924–HC: 84

U.K. Powered Access Market Shares, 1998

Shares are for December 1998. Powered access penetration is 15% of the U.K. access market compared with 45% of the U.S. and 7% of Germany.

Hewden Stuart	10.0%
Ashtead	6.0
Universal	4.0
Vibroplant	3.0
SGB	2.0
Others	48.0

Source: *Financial Times*, December 6, 1999, p. 16, from Primark Database and West LB Panmure.

★ 748 ★
Industrial Haulers
SIC: 3537–ISIC: 2924–HC: 84

Atriculated Hauler Market

Market shares are shown in percent.

Volvo	54.0%
Other	46.0

Source: *World Mining Equipment*, November 2000, p. 46.

★ 749 ★
Machine Tools
SIC: 3540–ISIC: 2922–HC: 84

Largest Machine Tool Producers

Figures are in millions of dollars.

Japan	$ 7,722.7
Germany	7,481.4
Italy	3,749.6
United States	3,686.4
Switzerland	2,045.0
Taiwan	1,675.2
China	1,087.2

Spain	$ 970.9
United Kingdom	952.5
France	800.9

Source: *American Machinist*, January 2001, p. 69, from ISTAT and UCIMI.

★ 750 ★
Machine Tools
SIC: 3540–ISIC: 2923–HC: 84

Largest Machine Tool Companies

Companies are ranked by sales in millions of dollars.

Thyssen Industries	$ 1,492.5
Siemens Automation & Drive	1,400.0
Yamazaki Mazak Corp.	1,290.0
Fanuc	1,161.8
Amada	1,026.6
Okuma Machinery Works	896.4
Unova Inc.	833.3
Mori Seiki	812.9
Trumpf Seiki	812.9
Fuji Machine	769.9

Source: *Manufacturing Engineering*, February 2000, p. 18, from Association for Manufacturing Technology.

★ 751 ★
Machine Tools
SIC: 3540–ISIC: 2923–HC: 84

Machine Tool Demand

Demand is shown in billions of dollars.

	1997	1999	Share
United States	$ 7.2	$ 7.1	20.58%
Germany	4.1	5.9	17.10
Japan	3.7	2.9	8.41
China	2.9	2.2	6.38
Italy	2.6	3.0	8.70
France	1.6	1.6	4.64
Taiwan	1.3	1.2	3.48
Other	13.6	10.6	30.72

Source: *Financial Times*, May 26, 2000, p. 20.

★ 752 ★
Lathes
SIC: 3541–ISIC: 2922–HC: 84

Top NC Lathe Makers in Japan, 1999

Market shares are shown based on domestic production.

Yamazaki Mazak Corp.	29.4%
Mori Seiki Co.	22.8
Okuma Corp.	19.9
Citizen Watch Co.	11.6
Fuji Machine Mtg. Co.	6.1
Other	10.2

Source: *Nikkei Weekly*, August 14, 2000, p. 8, from Nihon Keizai Shimbun.

★ 753 ★
Files
SIC: 3545–ISIC: 2922–HC: 84

Top File Makers

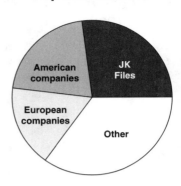

Market shares are shown in percent.

JK Files	27.0%
American companies	21.0
European companies	17.0
Other	35.0

Source: *Financial Express*, December 12, 2000, p. NA.

★ 754 ★
Power Tools
SIC: 3546–ISIC: 2922–HC: 85

Power Tool Market in Poland

Bosch
Celma
Black & Decker/Dewalts
Other

Market shares are shown in percent.

Bosch	33.0%
Celma	30.0
Black & Decker/Dewalts	8.0
Other	21.0

Source: "Power Tool Sector." Retrieved October 27, 2000 from the World Wide Web: http://www.mac.doc.gov.

★ 755 ★
Power Tools
SIC: 3546–ISIC: 2922–HC: 85

Power Tool Market in the U.K.

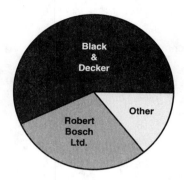

The power tool market reached retail sales of $280 million. Advertising, innovation and first-time users are the main factors driving the category right now. The main growth category is multifunction products that can operate as drills, sanders and jigsaws.

Black & Decker 57.0%
Robert Bosch Ltd. 29.0
Other 14.0

Source: "Hand and Power Tools." Retrieved November 3, 2000 from the World Wide Web: http://www.usatrade.gov.

★ 756 ★
Copper Equipment
SIC: 3547–ISIC: 2922–HC: 84

Copper Processing Equipment, 1999

Semitool	
Novellus	
Other	

Copper equipment market includes copper electroplating, CMP, barrier/seed disposition, dielectric and metal etch equipment.

Semitool 40.0%
Novellus 35.0
Other 25.0

Source: *Solid State Technology*, May 2000, p. 70.

★ 757 ★
Textile Machinery
SIC: 3552–ISIC: 2926–HC: 84

Leading Textile Machine Makers in Europe

Firms are ranked by revenues in millions of dollars.

Saurer . . . . $ 817
Rieter 660
Barmag 583
Sulzer Textile 458
Picanol 324
Dornier 174
Benninger 167
Somet 165

Source: STAT-USA, National Trade Data Bank, November 30, 1999.

★ 758 ★
Textile Machinery
SIC: 3552–ISIC: 2926–HC: 84

Leading Weaving Machine Makers, 1998

Firms are ranked by sales in millions of Swiss francs.

Sulzer Textil 747
Picanol 461
Tsudakoma 306
Dornier 260
Somet 247
Vamatex 192
Toyoda 114
Nissan 106

Source: *Textile World*, April 1999, p. 39, from Sulzer Textil.

★ 759 ★
Printing Equipment
SIC: 3554–ISIC: 2929–HC: 84

Printing Press Market, 1999

The market for printing documents, books and similar articles is estimated at $500 billion annually.

Heidelberger Druckmaschinen	20.0%
Xerox	15.0
MAN Roland	9.0
KBA	5.0
Goss	4.0
Komori	4.0
Mitsubishi	3.0
Others	40.0

Source: *Financial Times*, April 18, 2000, p. 22, from industry estimates.

★ 760 ★
Printing Equipment
SIC: 3555–ISIC: 2929–HC: 84

Superwide Printer Sales, 1998

There are more than 25,000 production screen printers worldwide. The market hit $3 billion in 1999. Shares are shown based on unit sales.

NUR	50.0%
Vutek	35.0
Scitex	8.0
Signtech	7.0

Source: *Investor's Business Daily*, February 8, 2000, p. A10, from company reports, Josephthal & Co., and CAP Ventures.

★ 761 ★
Food Equipment
SIC: 3556–ISIC: 2925–HC: 84

Who Makes Sushi Making Equipment

Data show who controls the world market.

Suzumo Machinery	75.0%
Other	25.0

Source: *Frozen and Chilled Foods*, March 1, 2000, p. 1.

★ 762 ★
Plastic Equipment
SIC: 3559–ISIC: 2929–HC: 84

Plastic Injection Molding Machine Makers in Japan, 1999

Market shares are shown based on domestic sales.

Nissei Plastic Industrial Co.	21.9%
Sumitomo Heavy Industries Ltd.	18.4
Japan Steel Works Ltd.	15.7
Toshiba Machine Co.	13.7
Fanuc Ltd.	9.9
Other	20.4

Source: *Nikkei Weekly*, August 14, 2000, p. 8, from Nihon Keizai Shimbun.

★ 763 ★
Semiconductor Equipment
SIC: 3559–ISIC: 2929–HC: 84

Largest Semiconductor Packaging/ Assembly Equipment Makers

Market shares are shown based on $4.6 billion in revenue.

Kulicke & Soffa	13.2%
Tokyo Seimitsu	9.7
ASM Pacific	9.2
ESEC	7.7
Shinkawa	7.7
Tokyo Electron	5.7

Continued on next page.

★ 763 ★
[Continued]
Semiconductor Equipment
SIC: 3559–ISIC: 2929–HC: 84

Largest Semiconductor Packaging/ Assembly Equipment Makers

Market shares are shown based on $4.6 billion in revenue.

TOWA	5.5%
Disco	4.7
Dai-Ichi	4.5
Electroglas	4.1
Other	27.8

Source: "Press Release." Retrieved May 1, 2001 from the World Wide Web: http://www.businesswire.com, from Dataquest Inc.

★ 764 ★
Semiconductor Equipment
SIC: 3559–ISIC: 2929–HC: 84

Largest Wafer Fab Equipment Makers

Market shares are shown in percent based on shipments.

Applied Materials	25.3%
Tokyo Electron Ltd.	10.0
Nikon	6.7
ASM Lithography	6.2
KLA-Tencor	4.8
Lam Research	4.1
Canon	3.5
Novellus Systems	2.9
Dai Nippon Screen	2.8
Silicon Valley Group	2.6
Other	31.1

Source: *Solid State Technology*, November 2000, p. 58, from Dataquest Inc.

★ 765 ★
Semiconductor Equipment
SIC: 3559–ISIC: 2929–HC: 84

Silicon Wafer Market, 1999

Shares are shown based on a market of $5.9 billion.

Shin-Etsu Handotai	24.0%
MEMC	17.0
Sumitomo Metal Industries	14.0
Mitsubishi Materials	11.0
Wacker	11.0
Komatsu	10.0
Toshiba	6.0
Others	7.0

Source: *Chemical Week*, June 28, 2000, p. 35, from The Information Network.

★ 766 ★
Semiconductor Equipment
SIC: 3559–ISIC: 2929–HC: 84

Top Semiconductor Equipment Firms, 2000

Firms are ranked by sales in billions of dollars.
Figures are for the first six months of the year.

Applied Materials Inc.	$ 4.90
Tokyo Electron Ltd.	2.50
Nikon Corp.	1.03
ASM Lithography Holding	0.93
KLA-Tencor Corp.	0.90
Lam Research Corp.	0.70
Novelius Systems Inc.	0.60
Canon Inc.	0.54

Continued on next page.

★ 766 ★

[Continued]
Semiconductor Equipment
SIC: 3559–ISIC: 2929–HC: 84

Top Semiconductor Equipment Firms, 2000

Firms are ranked by sales in billions of dollars.
Figures are for the first six months of the year.

Silicon Valley Group Inc. . . . . $ 0.42
ASM International 0.40

Source: *Electronic Business*, October 2000, p. 50, from
The Information Network.

★ 767 ★

Sewing Machines
SIC: 3559–ISIC: 2929–HC: 84

Industrial Sewing Machine Market in India

Market shares are shown in percent.

Juki Corporation 70.0%
Other 30.0

Source: *Textile India Progress*, January 1, 2000, p. 1.

★ 768 ★

Pumps
SIC: 3561–ISIC: 2912–HC: 84

Fluid Pump Demand

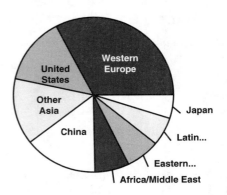

Demand is shown in millions of dollars. Developing
nations will provide the most opportunity for growth.
Centrifugal pumps are the most common.

	1999	2004	Share
Western Europe	$ 9,905	$ 12,750	32.53%
United States	4,270	5,395	13.76
Other Asia	3,695	5,440	13.88
China	3,600	5,950	15.18
Africa/Middle East . . .	1,945	2,730	6.97
Eastern Europe	1,850	2,630	6.71
Latin America	1,505	2,300	5.87
Japan	1,475	2,000	5.10

Source: *Research Studies*, August 11, 2000, p. 1, from
Freedonia Group.

★ 769 ★

Bearings
SIC: 3562–ISIC: 2913–HC: 84

Automotive Bearings Market Leaders in India

Market shares are shown in percent.

SKF Bearing 37.0%
FAG Precision 19.0
National Bearing 18.0
Needle Roller Bearing 3.0
Others 23.0

Source: *Dalal Street Journal*, April 23, 2000, p. 1.

★ 770 ★
Bearings
SIC: 3562–ISIC: 2913–HC: 84

Global Bearings Demand

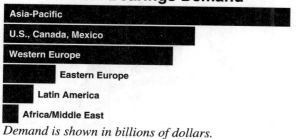

Demand is shown in billions of dollars.

	1998 ($ mil.)	2003 ($ mil.)	Share
Asia-Pacific	$ 11,015	$ 15,900	38.85%
U.S., Canada, Mexico . .	7,890	10,450	25.53
Western Europe	7,150	9,525	23.27
Eastern Europe . . .	1,950	2,750	6.72
Latin America	975	1,475	3.60
Africa/Middle East . . .	575	825	2.02

Source: *Financial Times*, August 19, 1999, p. 4, from Freedonia Group.

★ 771 ★
Bearings
SIC: 3562–ISIC: 2913–HC: 84

Spherical Roll Bearings Market Leaders in India

Market shares are shown in percent.

FAG Precision	56.0%
National Bearing	32.0
National Roll Bearing	11.0
Other	1.0

Source: *Dalal Street Journal*, April 23, 2000, p. 1.

★ 772 ★
Bearings
SIC: 3562–ISIC: 2913–HC: 84

Top Bearings Makers in Japan, 1999

Market shares are shown based on domestic sales.

NSK Ltd.	33.6%
Koyo Seiko Co.	26.5
NTN Corp.	25.9
Nachi-Fujikoshi Corp.	5.9
Minebea Co.	5.8
Other	2.3

Source: *Nikkei Weekly*, August 14, 2000, p. 8, from Nihon Keizai Shimbun.

★ 773 ★
Fasteners
SIC: 3569–ISIC: 2919–HC: 84

Industrial Fastener Demand

The market is expected to grow over six percent through 2004 to hit $43 billion. ASEAN countries have begun to recover from the recession of 1997-98. This change will be key in the industry's growth, for these countries were some of the fastest-growing markets. Demand is shown in millions of dollars.

	1999	2004	Share
United States	$ 9,245	$ 11,250	25.94%
Western Europe	8,365	11,000	25.36
China	2,050	3,700	8.53
Eastern Europe	1,875	2,650	6.11
Canada & Mexico . . .	1,825	2,300	5.30
Latin America	1,005	1,475	3.40
Other	7,945	11,000	25.36

Source: *Research Studies*, May 1, 2000, p. 1, from Freedonia Group.

★ 774 ★
Robots
SIC: 3569–ISIC: 2919–HC: 84

How Robots Are Used

Distribution is shown in percent.

Assembly	29.6%
Welding	26.7

Continued on next page.

★ 774 ★

[Continued]
Robots
SIC: 3569–ISIC: 2919–HC: 84

How Robots Are Used

Distribution is shown in percent.

Machining	9.9%
Plastic molding	8.9
Material handling	8.5
Painting, sealing, gluing	3.6
Palletizing & packaging	2.6
Measuring & testing	1.3

Source: *Wired*, May 2000, p. 107, from International Federation of Robotics.

★ 775 ★

Robots
SIC: 3569–ISIC: 2919–HC: 84

Top Industrial Robot Makers in Japan, 1999

Market shares are shown based on domestic shipments.

Matsushita Electric Industrial Co.	23.9%
Fanuc Ltd.	18.3
Yasakawa Electric Corp.	10.9
Kawasaki Heavy Industries Ltd.	5.2
Nach-Fujikoshi Corp.	3.5
Other	38.8

Source: *Nikkei Weekly*, August 14, 2000, p. 8, from Nihon Keizai Shimbun.

★ 776 ★
Computers
SIC: 3571–ISIC: 3000–HC: 84

Global Supercomputer Market

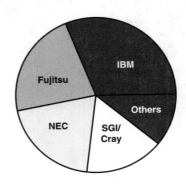

Supercomputer sales will hit $7.5 billion in 2003 from $5 billion a year ago.

IBM	31.0%
Fujitsu	22.0
NEC	20.0
SGI/Cray	16.0
Others	11.0

Source: *Investor's Business Daily*, March 23, 2000, p. A6, from International Data Corp.

★ 777 ★
Computers
SIC: 3571–ISIC: 3000–HC: 84

Handheld Device Market, 1998

Market shares are shown in percent.

Palm	42.0%
Sharp	11.2
Casio	8.8
Psion	7.5
Philips	6.0
Other	24.5

Source: *Investor's Business Daily*, December 14, 1999, p. A6, from International Data Corp.

★ 778 ★
Computers
SIC: 3571–ISIC: 3000–HC: 84

Handheld Device Market in Europe

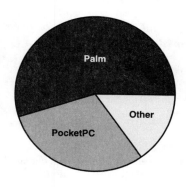

Market shares are shown in percent.

Palm	55.0%
PocketPC	30.0
Other	15.0

Source: *TechWeb*, March 15, 2001, p. NA, from Context.

★ 779 ★
Computers
SIC: 3571–ISIC: 3000–HC: 84

Rugged Mobile Computer Market

The $3.09 billion market is shown in percent.

Hand held	60.7%
Notebook	16.2
On-board/fixed vehicle	5.7
Tablet	5.3
Luggable/lunchbox	4.7
PDA	3.8
Sub-notebook	2.0
Wearable	1.6

Source: "Robust Growth Expectations." Retrieved June 7, 2001 from the World Wide Web: http://www.vdc-corp.com, from VDC Corp.

★ 780 ★
Computers
SIC: 3571–ISIC: 3000–HC: 84

Thin Client Market Shares

Thin clients are simple computer terminals that let server computers do all the application processing. Shares are shown based on revenue.

Wyse	37.0%
NCD	26.0
IBM	17.0
Boundless	4.0
Hewlett-Packard	4.0
Sun	4.0
Other	4.0

Source: *Investor's Business Daily*, February 12, 2001, p. A8, from Zona Research Inc.

★ 781 ★
Computers
SIC: 3571–ISIC: 3000–HC: 84

Top Laptop Computer Makers in China

Market shares are shown in percent.

Legend	23.16%
Toshiba	10.89
IBM	7.34
Other	55.61

Source: "Popular Computer Weekly Releases Survey Results." Retrieved October 16, 2000 from the World Wide Web: http://www.chinaonline.com, from *Popular Computer Weekly*.

★ 782 ★
Computers
SIC: 3571–ISIC: 3000–HC: 84

Top Laptop Makers in Japan, 2000

Market shares are shown in percent. Laptop PC s accounted for 48.1% of all PC sales for the year.

Sony	24.0%
NEC Corp.	22.1
Fujitsu Ltd.	13.5
Apple Computer	10.9
Sharp Corp.	7.4
Other	22.1

Source: *Japan Computer Industry Scan*, January 22, 2001, p. NA, from BCN Industry Research Group.

★ 783 ★
Computers
SIC: 3571–ISIC: 3000–HC: 84

Top Notebook Computers in Asia, 1999

Data do not include Japan.

Toshiba	17.0%
IBM	15.0
Acer	11.0
Compaq	9.0
Samsung	8.0
Other	40.0

Source: *Asiaweek*, March 17, 2000, p. 60, from International Data Corp.

★ 784 ★
Computers
SIC: 3571–ISIC: 3000–HC: 84

Top Notebook Makers in Japan

Market shares are shown in percent. Notebooks accounted for 6.66 million units of the computer market, as compared to 6.58 million desktops.

NEC Corp.	24.1%
Fujitsu Ltd.	20.4
IBM Japan Ltd.	8.8
Sony	6.9
Other	39.8

Source: *Japan Computer Industry Scan*, February 5, 2001, p. NA, from Multimedia Research Institute.

★ 785 ★
Computers
SIC: 3571–ISIC: 3000–HC: 84

Top PC Firms, 2000

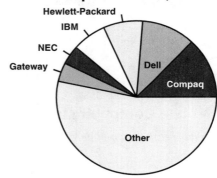

Companies are ranked by estimated shipments in millions of units.

	(mil.)	Share
Compaq	17.2	12.8%
Dell	14.5	10.8
Hewlett-Packard	10.2	7.6
IBM	9.1	6.8
NEC	5.8	4.3
Gateway	5.1	3.8
Other	72.6	53.9

Source: ''Press Release.'' Retrieved January 23, 2001 from the World Wide Web: http://www.gartner.com, from Gartner Group.

★ 786 ★
Computers
SIC: 3571–ISIC: 3000–HC: 84

Top PC Firms in Europe, 2000

Companies are ranked by third quarter shipments. The professional segment accounted for 72% of the market, or 5.8 million units. The segment grew 6.1%, compared to residential's 21.2% rate.

	(000)	Share
Compaq	1,125	14.0%
Fujitsu	821	10.2
Dell Computer	669	8.3
IBM	595	7.4
Hewlett-Packard	583	7.2
Other	4,273	53.0

Source: "Press Release." Retrieved November 9, 2000 from the World Wide Web: http://www.gartner.com, from Dataquest Inc.

★ 787 ★
Computers
SIC: 3571–ISIC: 3000–HC: 84

Top PC Firms in Finland

A total of 443,000 PCs were sold in 1998, for a market size of $1.5 billion.

Compaq	19.0%
IBM	14.0
MikroMikko (Fujitsu/ICL)	11.0
Hewlett-Packard	10.0
Other	46.0

Source: "Finland: Internet Services." Retrieved October 10, 2000 from the World Wide Web: http://www.tradeport.org.

★ 788 ★
Computers
SIC: 3571–ISIC: 3000–HC: 84

Top PC Firms in France

About 4.5 million PCs were sold in France in 1999, creating a market valued at $5.4 billion. This is a 21.7% increase in volume and 8% in value. The surge is a result of the introduction of generic brands PCs and peripherals into the marketplace. Market shares are shown in percent.

Compaq	15.0%
Packard Bell/NEC/Zenith	13.3
IBM	12.4
Dell	10.6
Hewlett-Packard	10.4
Fujitsu-Siemens	5.6
Unika	4.6
Apple	3.7
Cibox	3.3
Toshiba	3.2
Other	17.9

Source: "Printer Market." Retrieved September 7, 2000 from the World Wide Web: http://www.tradeport.org, from International Data Corp.

215

★ 789 ★
Computers
SIC: 3571–ISIC: 3000–HC: 84

Top PC Firms in India, 1999

Shares are shown based on units.

HCL	12.0%
Compaq	7.0
Zenith	7.0
Hewlett-Packard	4.0
Zenith	4.0
Others	66.0

Source: *Business India*, May 29, 2000, p. 82.

★ 790 ★
Computers
SIC: 3571–ISIC: 3000–HC: 84

Top PC Firms in Japan, 1999

Companies are ranked by unit sales.

	Units	Share
NEC	2,405	22.2%
Fujitsu	2,245	20.7
IBM Japan	1,089	10.1
Toshiba	777	7.2
Sony	736	6.8
Apple	639	5.9
Hitachi	463	4.3
Compaq	452	4.2%
Dell	405	3.7
Sotec	322	3.0
Others	1,299	12.0

Source: "Japan: PC Shipments Way Up." Retrieved September 18, 2000 from the World Wide Web: http://www.tradeport.org, from International Data Corp. and Nikkan Kogyo Shimbun.

★ 791 ★
Computers
SIC: 3571–ISIC: 3000–HC: 84

Top PC Firms in the U.K.

Market shares are shown in percent.

Dell	17.0%
Compaq	16.0
Packard Bell-NEC	8.0
Tiny	6.0
Other	53.0

Source: *Fortune*, February 21, 2000, p. 224.

★ 792 ★
Computers
SIC: 3571–ISIC: 3000–HC: 84

Top PC Firms in Turkey, 1999

Market shares are shown in percent.

Vestel	17.0%
Compaq	12.0
Hewlett-Packard	10.0
Escort	9.0
IBM	8.0
Other	44.0

Source: "IDC: Turkey PC Market Grows 23% in 1999." Retrieved April 17, 2000 from the World Wide Web: http://www.prnewswire.net, from International Data Corp.

★ 793 ★
Computers
SIC: 3571–ISIC: 3000–HC: 84

Top PC Makers in Latin America, 2000

Market shares are shown in percent.

	Units	Share
Compaq	1,459,804	21.1%
IBM	421,450	6.1
Hewlett-Packard	370,935	5.4
Acer	322,755	4.7
Dell	226,928	3.3
Alaska	218,879	3.2
Other	3,897,275	56.3

Source: "Gartner Dataquest Says Home PC Sales."
Retrieved February 5, 2001 from the World Wide Web:
http://www.businesswire.com, from Dataquest Inc.

★ 794 ★
Computers
SIC: 3571–ISIC: 3000–HC: 84

Top PC Makers in Singapore, 2000

Market shares are shown based on units.

Hewlett-Packard	14.0%
Compaq	12.0
IBM	11.7
Dell Computer	11.1
Acer	7.8
Other	44.0

Source: *Business Times (Singapore)*, February 9, 2001, p.
9, from Dataquest Inc.

★ 795 ★
Computers
SIC: 3571–ISIC: 3000–HC: 84

Top PC Makers in Switzerland, 2000

*Market shares are shown in percent. A total of 4.7
million units were installed at the edge of the year.*

Compaq	22.4%
IBM	8.7
Dell	8.5
Hewlett-Packard	8.3
Fujitsu Siemens	8.1
Other	44.0

Source: *Neue Zuercher Zeitung*, February 7, 2001, p. 11,
from Robert Weiss Consulting.

★ 796 ★
Computers
SIC: 3571–ISIC: 3000–HC: 84

Top PC Makers in the Asia/Pacific, 2000

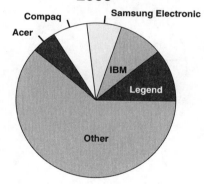

Unit shares are for the third quarter of the year.

Legend	11.1%
IBM	8.6
Samsung Electronic	7.4
Compaq	7.1
Acer	5.3
Other	60.5

Source: "Press Release." Retrieved September 27, 2000
from the World Wide Web: http://www.gartnerweb.com,
from Dataquest Inc.

★ 797 ★
Computers
SIC: 3571–ISIC: 3000–HC: 84

Top PC Makers in the Czech Republic

Market shares are shown in percent. A total of 277,900 PCs were shipped last year.

Compaq 13.7%
AutoCont 10.8
Dell 8.7
ProCa 7.3
Comfor PC Mail 5.7
Other 53.8

Source: *Prague Business Journal*, May 1, 2000, p. 1.

★ 798 ★
Workstations
SIC: 3571–ISIC: 3000–HC: 84

Leading Workstation Makers, 1999

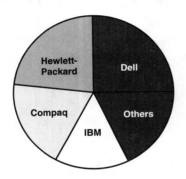

Firms are ranked by shipments.

	Units	Share
Dell	249,544	25.0%
Hewlett-Packard	230,138	23.0
Compaq	194,431	19.0
IBM	153,547	15.0
Others	179,823	18.0

Source: *Client Server News*, February 28, 2000, p. 1.

★ 799 ★
Workstations
SIC: 3571–ISIC: 3000–HC: 84

Top Unix Workstation Makers in Japan, 1999

Market shares are shown based on domestic shipments.

Nihon Sun Microsystems KK 38.5%
Hewlett-Packard Japan Ltd. 18.9
Fujitsu Ltd. 14.1
NEC Corp. 10.9
IBM Japan Ltd. 8.3
Other 9.3

Source: *Nikkei Weekly*, July 31, 2000, p. 8, from Nihon Keizai Shimbun.

★ 800 ★
Workstations
SIC: 3571–ISIC: 3000–HC: 84

Top Workstation Producers in Asia/ Pacific

Market shares are shown in percent.

Sun Microsystems 22.3%
Compaq 19.3
Hewlett-Packard 18.3
Dell 17.3
Other 22.8

Source: *Business Times*, December 18, 2000, p. NA, from Dataquest Inc.

★ 801 ★
Computer Data Storage
SIC: 3572–ISIC: 3000–HC: 84

CD-R Disc Market Shares, 1999

Shares are shown in percent.

MCC/Verbatim 9.77%
TDK 9.42
Kodak 7.22
Memtek 6.58

Continued on next page.

★ 801 ★

[Continued]
Computer Data Storage
SIC: 3572–ISIC: 3000–HC: 84

CD-R Disc Market Shares, 1999

Shares are shown in percent.

Maxell	6.44%
PDO	5.44
Princo	5.29
Sony	5.03
Imation	4.77
Samsung	4.11
Others	35.93

Source: *E-Media Professional*, August 2000, p. 12, from Santa Clara Consulting Group.

★ 802 ★

Computer Data Storage
SIC: 3572–ISIC: 3000–HC: 84

CD-ROM Drive Market in China

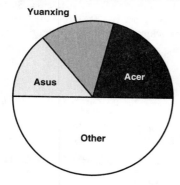

Market shares are shown in percent.

Acer	21.36%
Yuanxing	14.59
Asus	14.24
Other	49.81

Source: ''Popular Computer Weekly Releases Survey Results.'' Retrieved October 16, 2000 from the World Wide Web: http://www.chinaonline.com, from *Popular Computer Weekly*.

★ 803 ★

Computer Data Storage
SIC: 3572–ISIC: 3000–HC: 84

Disk Storage Market Shares, 2000

Shares are estimated for revenue.

	($ mil.)	Share
Compaq	$ 5.6	17.6%
EMC	5.6	17.7
IBM	3.6	11.5
Sun Microsystems	3.3	10.4
Hewlett-Packard	2.8	8.7
Dell	1.1	3.4
Hitachi	1.0	3.0
Network Appliance	0.9	2.9
Other	7.9	24.8

Source: *New York Times*, January 15, 2001, p. C4, from International Data Corp. and Dataquest Inc.

★ 804 ★

Computer Data Storage
SIC: 3572–ISIC: 3000–HC: 84

External Disk Storage System Shares

Shares are shown based on revenues.

EMC	22.7%
Compaq	14.3
IBM	10.5
Sun	8.2
Hewlett-Packard	6.6
Others	37.7

Source: *InfoWorld*, July 10, 2000, p. 8, from International Data Corp. 1999 Worldwide Disk Systems Market Forecase and Review.

★ 805 ★
Computer Data Storage
SIC: 3572–ISIC: 3000–HC: 84

Global Storage Revenue, 1999

Companies are ranked by revenue in billions of dollars.

	($ mil.)	Share
Compaq	$ 5,300	21.08%
EMC	4,100	16.31
IBM	3,500	13.92
Sun	2,600	10.34
Hewlett-Packard	1,900	7.56
Dell	1,100	4.37
Other	6,645	26.43

Source: *Computer Reseller News*, January 22, 2001, p. 20, from Dataquest Inc.

★ 806 ★
Computer Data Storage
SIC: 3572–ISIC: 3000–HC: 84

Global Writer Market Shares, 1999

Market shares are shown in percent.

Hewlett-Packard	17.03%
Philips	15.58
Yamaha	10.02
Sony	9.60
Mitsumi	8.18
Acer	5.44
TEAC	4.29
Ricoh	3.90
Plextor	3.43
Other	22.53

Source: *E Media Professional*, November 2000, p. 12, from Santa Clara Consulting Group.

★ 807 ★
Computer Data Storage
SIC: 3572–ISIC: 3000–HC: 84

Hard Drive Market in China

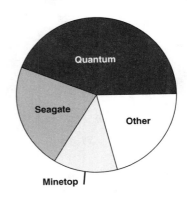

Market shares are shown in percent.

Quantum	43.85%
Seagate	22.04
Minetop	12.79
Other	21.32

Source: ''Popular Computer Weekly Releases Survey Results.'' Retrieved October 16, 2000 from the World Wide Web: http://www.chinaonline.com, from *Popular Computer Weekly*.

★ 808 ★
Computer Data Storage
SIC: 3572–ISIC: 3000–HC: 84

Storage Array Device Market

Market shares are shown in percent.

	Units	Share
Compaq	927,384	40.0%
Hewlett-Packard	240,408	10.4
Sun	217,434	9.4
IBM	193,838	8.4
Dell	175,982	7.6

Source: *Computerwoche*, February 16, 2001, p. 28.

★ 809 ★
Computer Data Storage
SIC: 3572–ISIC: 3000–HC: 84

Top Hard Disk Drive Makers, 2000

Shares are shown for the first six months of the year.

Seagate	21.0%
Quantum	17.0
Maxtor	14.0
Fujitsu	13.0
IBM	11.0
WDC	11.0
Other	13.0

Source: *Upside*, January 2001, p. 129, from International Data Corp.

★ 810 ★
Computer Hardware
SIC: 3577–ISIC: 3000–HC: 84

Largest Computer Hardware Vendors

The largest independent hardware firms are ranked by 1998 revenue in billions of dollars.

Electronic Data Systems	$ 16.89
Microsoft	14.48
Andersen Consulting	8.30
Oracle	7.14
Computer Sciences	6.60
First Data	5.11
Automatic Data Processing (ADP)	5.07
SAP	4.85
Computer Associates	4.72

Source: *Financial Times*, May 5, 1999, p. 18, from 1999 Holway Report and Datastream/ICV.

★ 811 ★
Computer Monitors
SIC: 3577–ISIC: 3000–HC: 84

Largest PC Monitor Makers

Market shares are shown in percent.

Samsung	19.6%
LG	11.2
AOC	9.7
Philips	9.5
Acer	5.5
Lite-on	5.2
Sony	5.0
Delta	4.4
Jean	4.1
Proview	4.1
Other	21.7

Source: "Envision Peripherals." Retrieved February 26, 2001 from the World Wide Web: http://www.businesswire.com.

★ 812 ★
Computer Peripherals
SIC: 3577–ISIC: 3000–HC: 84

Display Card Market in China

Market shares are shown in percent.

Leadtek	15.62%
Asus	13.36
Creative	8.49
Other	62.63

Source: "Popular Computer Weekly Releases Survey Results." Retrieved October 16, 2000 from the World Wide Web: http://www.chinaonline.com, from *Popular Computer Weekly*.

★ 813 ★
Computer Peripherals
SIC: 3577–ISIC: 3000–HC: 84

Motherboard Market in China

Market shares are shown in percent.

Micro-Star	21.81%
Asus	19.69
Gigabyte	13.80
Epox	6.78
Soyo	5.08
Other	32.84

Source: "Popular Computer Weekly Releases Survey Results." Retrieved October 16, 2000 from the World Wide Web: http://www.chinaonline.com, from *Popular Computer Weekly*.

★ 814 ★
Computer Peripherals
SIC: 3577–ISIC: 3000–HC: 84

Sound Card Market in China

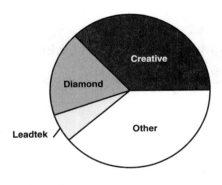

Market shares are shown in percent.

Creative	36.72%
Diamond	17.53
Leadtek	6.28
Other	39.47

Source: "Popular Computer Weekly Releases Survey Results." Retrieved October 16, 2000 from the World Wide Web: http://www.chinaonline.com, from *Popular Computer Weekly*.

★ 815 ★
Computer Printers
SIC: 3577–ISIC: 3000–HC: 84

Global Printer Market, 1999

The United States led the market with 23.8 million units, followed by Western Europe with 21.4 million unit shipments.

Hewlett-Packard	42.5%
Epson	21.9
Canon	14.2
Other	21.4

Source: "Worldwide Printer Shipments Surpass 71 Million Units." Retrieved March 24, 2000 from the World Wide Web: http://www.businesswire.com, from Dataquest Inc.

★ 816 ★
Computer Printers
SIC: 3577–ISIC: 3000–HC: 84

Inkjet Printer Market in Singapore

Market shares are shown in percent.

Hewlett-Packard	36.21%
Canon	33.12
Epson	21.10
Lexmark	8.44
Other	1.13

Source: *Business Times*, July 3, 2000, p. 2, from Dataquest.

★ 817 ★
Computer Printers
SIC: 3577–ISIC: 3000–HC: 84

Inkjet Printer Market in Southeast Asia

Market shares are shown in percent.

Canon	37.0%
Hewlett-Packard	34.0
Epson	20.0
Other	9.0

Source: *Computimes (Malaysia)*, March 19, 2001, p. NA.

★ 818 ★
Computer Printers
SIC: 3577–ISIC: 3000–HC: 84

Top Computer Printer Makers in Asia

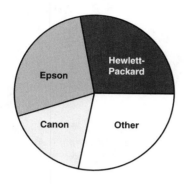

Market shares are shown in percent.

Hewlett-Packard	28.0%
Epson	27.0
Canon	17.0
Other	28.0

Source: *Straits Times*, December 14, 2000, p. 14, from Dataquest Inc.

★ 819 ★
Computer Printers
SIC: 3577–ISIC: 3000–HC: 84

Top Laser Printer Makers

Market shares are shown in percent.

	B&W	Color
HP	54.8%	41.4%
Lexmark	8.6	7.5
Brother	6.6	1.6
Canon	4.7	4.6
Epson	4.1	6.3
Xerox	2.9	19.8
QMS	0.5	6.4

Source: *Wall Street Journal*, June 5, 2001, p. A4, from International Data Corp. and Salomon Smith Barney.

★ 820 ★
Computer Printers
SIC: 3577–ISIC: 3000–HC: 84

Top Laser Printer Makers in Germany

1.13 million units were sold during 1999.

	1998	1999
Hewlett-Packard	53.7%	51.5%
Kyocerta	13.7	16.5
Lexmark	10.7	10.3
Brother	7.3	7.8
Other	14.6	13.9

Source: *Computerwoche*, March 24, 2000, p. 1.

★ 821 ★
Computer Printers
SIC: 3577–ISIC: 3000–HC: 84

Top Laser Printer Producers in Malaysia

Market shares are shown in percent.

Hewlett-Packard	70.0%
Canon	18.0
Other	12.0

Source: *The Edge*, March 19, 2001, p. NA.

★ 822 ★
Computer Printers
SIC: 3577–ISIC: 3000–HC: 84

Top Printer Producers in Australia

Market shares are shown in percent.

Canon	37.1%
Hewlett-Packard	21.1
Lexmark	17.3
Epson	15.3
Other	9.2

Source: *Newsbytes*, February 27, 2001, p. NA.

★ 823 ★
Scanners
SIC: 3577–ISIC: 3000–HC: 84

Scanner Market in China

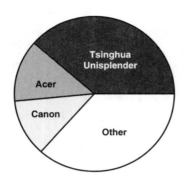

Market shares are shown in percent.

Tsinghua Unisplender 38.72%
Acer 12.72
Canon 11.92
Other 36.64

Source: ''Popular Computer Weekly Releases Survey Results.'' Retrieved October 16, 2000 from the World Wide Web: http://www.chinaonline.com, from *Popular Computer Weekly*.

★ 824 ★
Automated Teller Machines
SIC: 3578–ISIC: 3000–HC: 84

ATM Market in Europe

NCR

Siemens Nixdorf

Other

Market shares are shown in percent.

NCR 48.0%
Siemens Nixdorf 12.0
Other 40.0

Source: ''Big Ambition.'' Retrieved November 30, 1999 from the World Wide Web: http://www.atmmagzine.com.

★ 825 ★
Calculators
SIC: 3579–ISIC: 3000–HC: 84

Top Calculator Makers in Japan, 1997

Market shares are shown based on shipments.

Casio Computer 52.0%
Sharp 31.0
Canon 8.0
Citizen Watch 5.0
Other 4.0

Source: ''DVL Market Share Library.'' Retrieved April 3, 2001 from the World Wide Web: http://dvl/daiwa.co.jp, from DVL Market Share Library and Marketing Data Bank.

★ 826 ★
Office Equipment
SIC: 3579–ISIC: 3000–HC: 84

Largest Office Automation Equipment Producers

Companies are ranked by sales in millions of dollars.

Xerox . . . . $ 15.90
Canon 12.70
Ricoh 11.90
Pitney Bowes 3.30
Oce 3.00
Minolta 2.30
Brother 1.60
Eastman Kodak 1.00
Fuji Photo Film 0.78
Texas Instruments 0.47

Source: *EDN*, December 21, 2000, p. S202, from Cahners Research and *Electronic Business*.

★ 827 ★
Scanners
SIC: 3579–ISIC: 3000–HC: 84

Top Flatbed Scanner Makers in Southeast Asia

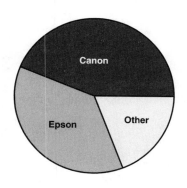

Market shares are shown in percent.

Canon	44.0%
Epson	37.0
Other	19.0

Source: *Computerworld (Malaysia)*, March 27, 2001, p. NA, from Canon Singapore.

★ 828 ★
Heating and Cooling
SIC: 3585–ISIC: 2919–HC: 84

Air Conditioner Market in China, 1999

Shares are for the second quarter of the year. The industry produces wall-type with a 61% share, cabinet-type with a 20% share and window-type with a 19% share.

MD	16.69%
Gree	15.37
Haier	11.59
Kelon/Huabao	5.74
Shanghai Sharp	5.32
Chunlan	5.07
Other	40.22

Source: *China's Foreign Trade*, November 1999, p. 41, from CHEEA.

★ 829 ★
Heating and Cooling
SIC: 3585–ISIC: 2919–HC: 84

Air Conditioning Industry in Europe

The commercial air conditioning market is worth $2.3 billion in 1999 and expected to hit $4.3 billion by 2006. Strong growth is predicted. Packaged air conditioning is expected to grow, in part, from lower installation costs. More people in Europe see air conditioning as a standard and not a luxury item.

	1999	2006
Central based	60.3%	52.5%
Packaged	39.7	47.5

Source: *Ozone Depletion Network Online Today*, July 20, 2000, p. NA, from Frost & Sullivan.

★ 830 ★
Heating and Cooling
SIC: 3585–ISIC: 2919–HC: 84

Auto Air Conditioning Market, 1999

Shares are for Western Europe.

Valeo	33.0%
Behr	28.0
Visteon	11.0
Delphi	5.0
Denso	5.0
Other	18.0

Source: *WARD's Auto World*, September 1999, p. 25.

★ 831 ★
Heating and Cooling
SIC: 3585–ISIC: 2919–HC: 84

Refrigeration Market in Russia, 1998

Market shares are shown in percent.

Stilnel	40.0%
Atlant	20.0
Outside Russia and C.I.S.	14.0
Biryusa	7.0
Nord	7.0
Other	10.0

Source: *Business in Russia*, April - May 1999, p. 78.

★ 832 ★

Heating and Cooling

SIC: 3585–ISIC: 2919–HC: 84

Top Air Conditioner Makers in India

Market shares are shown in percent.

Carrier Aircon 27.0%
Voltas 16.0
Other 57.0

Source: *Appliance*, May 2001, p. 26.

★ 833 ★

Scales

SIC: 3596–ISIC: 2919–HC: 84

Electronic Scales Market in Peru

The $10 million market is estimated.

Precision Peru 60.0%
Other 40.0

Source: *South American Business Information*, April 17, 2001, p. NA.

SIC 36 - Electronic and Other Electric Equipment

★ 834 ★
Contract Manufacturing
SIC: 3600–ISIC: 3190–HC: 85

Largest Contract Manufacturers

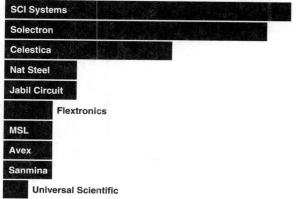

Firms are ranked by sales in millions of dollars.

	($ mil.)	Share
SCI Systems	$ 8,106	11.9%
Solectron	7,340	10.8
Celestica	4,435	6.5
Nat Steel	1,964	2.9
Jabil Circuit	1,759	2.6
Flextronics	1,513	2.2
MSL	1,205	1.8
Avex	1,066	1.6
Sanmina	1,024	1.5
Universal Scientific	797	1.2

Source: "Top 100." Retrieved February 2, 2001 from the World Wide Web: http://www.bishopinc.com.

★ 835 ★
Electronics
SIC: 3600–ISIC: 3190–HC: 85

Electronics Market in Vietnam

Total sales of electronic goods, refrigeration products, electrical household appliances and mobile phones reached $534.8 million. Market shares are shown in percent.

Electronic appliances	41.9%
Refrigeration products	29.6
Mobile phones	18.8
Other	9.8

Source: *Saigon Times Daily*, February 22, 2001, p. NA, from Gfk.

★ 836 ★
Electronics
SIC: 3600–ISIC: 3190–HC: 85

Largest Electronics Firms, 1999

Firms are ranked by electronics revenue in billions of dollars.

IBM	$ 87.5
Matsushita Electric Industrial	63.6
Fujitsu	49.5
Hewlett-Packard	45.7
NEC	40.3
Compaq	38.5
Lucent Technologies	38.0
Siemens	37.9
Sony	36.2
Motorola	33.0

Source: *EDN*, December 21, 2000, p. S180.

★ 837 ★
Electronics
SIC: 3600–ISIC: 3190–HC: 85

Largest Electronics Firms in Asia

Firms are ranked by 1999 electronics sales in billions of dollars.

Samsung Electronics	$ 22.8
LG Electronics	9.2
Hyundai Electronics	5.2
Acer	4.0
Daewoo Electronics	3.3
Samsung SDI	3.1
Tatung	2.8
Samsung Electro-Mechanics	2.6
Quanta Computer Inc.	2.4
LG Information & Communications	2.3

Source: *Electronic Business Asia*, September 2000, p. 31.

★ 838 ★
Motors
SIC: 3621–ISIC: 3110–HC: 85

Electric Motor Market in Europe

Market shares are shown in percent. Belimo's share exceeds 60%.

Belimo Holding	60.0%
Other	40.0

Source: *Neue Zuercher Zeitung*, March 13, 2001, p. 12.

★ 839 ★
Control Equipment
SIC: 3625–ISIC: 3120–HC: 85

Automation and Control Market Leaders

Data are for 1998-99.

Invensys	9.9%
Siemens	8.8
ABB	8.4
Emerson	7.5
Tyco	6.4
Schneider	5.8
General Electric	5.3
Honeywell	5.1
Rockwell	4.1
Other	38.7

Source: *Financial Times*, November 22, 1999, p. 17, from Primark Datastream.

★ 840 ★
Control Equipment
SIC: 3625–ISIC: 3120–HC: 85

Numerical Control Market

Market shares are shown in percent.

Dassault/Matra	23.0%
PTC/CV	20.0
Graphic products	12.0
Unigraphics	7.0
Hitachi Zosen	6.0
Delcam	5.0
Others	27.0

Source: *Financial Times*, August 23, 1999, p. 14, from Primark Datastream and CIMdata.

★ 841 ★
Appliances
SIC: 3630–ISIC: 2930–HC: 84

Largest Appliance Makers Worldwide, 1999

Firms are ranked by sales in billions of deutchmarks. The United States has 30% of the market, Western Europe has 26% and Southeast Asia has 20%.

Whirlpool	20.5
Electrolux	19.9
General Electric	11.0
BSH	10.7
Matsushita	9.8
Maytag	8.4
Sanyo	5.2
Miele	4.1
Sharp	3.5
Brandt	2.9

Source: *Financial Times*, December 12, 2000, p. 22, from BSH.

★ 842 ★
Appliances
SIC: 3630–ISIC: 2930–HC: 85

Household Appliance Market in Germany

Figures are in millions of deutschmarks.

	1998	1999	Share
Clothes washers	3,310	3,350	26.99%
Refrigerators	2,934	2,841	22.89
Cookers/ovens	2,415	2,270	18.29
Dishwashers	2,307	2,296	18.50
Freezers	902	884	7.12
Clothes dryers	824	772	6.22

Source: *Appliance Manufacturer*, February 2001, p. G33, from ZVEI.

★ 843 ★
Appliances
SIC: 3630–ISIC: 2930–HC: 85

Largest Appliance Makers in China

Firms are ranked by revenue in billions of rembini. Total production includes 13.4 million units for washing machines, 12.5 million units for air conditioners, 11.9 million units for refrigerators and 8.7 million units for rice cookers.

Haier Group	20.6
Kelon Group	8.2
Guangdong MD Group Co.	8.0
Chunlan Group	6.5
Jiangsu Little Swan Group Co.	5.7
Gree Electrical Appliance Co. Ltd.	5.6
Shunde Galanz Electrical Appliance Factory . .	2.9
Hefei Meiling Group	2.8
Henan Xinfei Electrical	2.2
Jinsong Group	2.2

Source: *Appliance*, October 2000, p. 50.

★ 844 ★
Appliances
SIC: 3630–ISIC: 2930–HC: 85

Largest Appliance Markets

Demand is shown and forecast in millions of units. The largest category was for cooking appliances, going from 98.1 million units in 1998 to 134.1 million units in 2008.

	1998	2003	2008
Asia/Pacific	80.1	106.4	135.1
Western Europe	64.9	69.7	73.9
North America	58.4	61.4	64.4
Eastern Europe	18.1	23.3	31.9
Latin America	18.0	21.3	25.4

Source: *Appliance Manufacturer*, February 2001, p. G13, from Freedonia Group.

★ 845 ★
Appliances
SIC: 3630–ISIC: 2930–HC: 85

Top Appliance Makers in China

Foreign manufacturers are carving out a greater share of the Chinese market, with a jump from 21% share in 1999 to 28% in 2000. Market shares are shown in percent.

Haier	30.0%
Chandsha Electrolux	13.0
Other	57.0

Source: *China Economic Review*, December 12, 2000, p. 1, from *Beijing Youth Daily* and Sino Market Research.

★ 846 ★
Appliances
SIC: 3630–ISIC: 2930–HC: 85

Top Appliance Makers in Latin America

Market shares are shown in percent.

Multibras/Consul/Brastemp	49.0%
Sharpat	40.0
Electrolux	7.0
Elgin	4.0

Source: *Appliance*, December 2000, p. 33.

★ 847 ★
Cooking Equipment
SIC: 3631–ISIC: 2930–HC: 84

Gas Cooker Market in Brazil

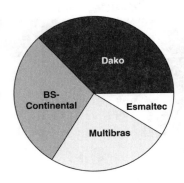

Market shares are shown in percent.

Dako	37.0%
BS-Continental	29.0
Multibras	25.0
Esmaltec	9.0

Source: *Appliance*, January 1, 2000, p. 1, from Datamark.

★ 848 ★
Cooking Equipment
SIC: 3631–ISIC: 2930–HC: 84

Top Microwave Ovens in China

Market shares are shown in percent.

Glanz	40.6%
LG	17.7
Matsushita	8.2
Haler	7.7
Samsung	6.1
Sanyo	4.8
Whirlpool	4.2
Aukema	2.6
Mitsubishi	1.6
Huibao	1.0
Other	5.5

Source: *Appliance Manufacturer*, February 2001, p. G37, from Information Center, Ministry of Internal Trade.

★ 849 ★
Refrigerators
SIC: 3632–ISIC: 2130–HC: 85

Top Refrigerator Brands in China

Shares are for December 1999.

Hai'er 28.8%
Rongsheng 15.9
Xinfei 12.6
Siemens 10.1
Meiling 9.0
Changling 5.3
Electrolux 4.8
Other 13.5

Source: *China's Home Appliance Market.'' Retrieved May 16, 2000 from the World Wide Web: http:// www.chinaonline.com, from* Beijing Youth Daily *and* China National Commercial Information Center.

★ 850 ★
Refrigerators
SIC: 3632–ISIC: 2930–HC: 84

Largest Refrigerator Makers in Japan, 1998

Market shares are shown based on domestic shipments.

Matsushita Electric Industrial Co. 21.3%
Sanyo Electric Co. 18.1
Hitachi Ltd. 13.5
Mitsubishi Electric Corp. 13.3
Toshiba Corp. 13.0
Other 22.8

Source: *Nikkei Weekly*, August 9, 1999, p. 7, from Nihon Keizai Shimbun.

★ 851 ★
Refrigerators
SIC: 3632–ISIC: 2930–HC: 84

Top Refrigerator Makers in Brazil

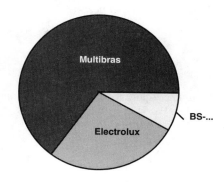

Market shares are shown in percent.

Multibras 65.0%
Electrolux 27.0
BS-Continental 8.0

Source: *Appliance*, January 1, 2000, p. 1, from Datamark.

★ 852 ★
Refrigerators
SIC: 3632–ISIC: 2930–HC: 84

Top Refrigerator Makers in India

Market shares are shown in percent.

Total 20.0%
CPL 16.0
CoolAir 13.0
Videotone 12.0
Worldpool 10.0
Kooltas 9.0
Others 20.0

Source: *Business Today*, April 7, 2000, p. 36.

★ 853 ★
Refrigerators
SIC: 3632–ISIC: 2930–HC: 84

Top Refrigerator Producers in Russia

Market shares are shown in percent.

Stinol	42.0%
Atlant	29.0
Other	13.0

Source: "Consumer Appliances." Retrieved September 19, 2000 from the World Wide Web: http://www.tradeport.org.

★ 854 ★
Laundry Equipment
SIC: 3633–ISIC: 2130–HC: 85

Top Automatic Washing Machine Brands in China

Shares are for December 1999.

Little Swan	30.0%
Haier	24.6
Rongshida Sanyo	14.2
Matsushita	7.7
Jinling	5.8
LG	4.9
Xiaoya	2.4
Hitachi	2.1
Weili	1.9
Whirlpool	1.6
Others	4.8

Source: "China's Home Appliance Market." Retrieved May 16, 2000 from the World Wide Web: http://www.chinaonline.com, from *Beijing Youth Daily* and China National Commercial Information Center.

★ 855 ★
Laundry Equipment
SIC: 3633–ISIC: 2930–HC: 84

Home Laundry Market in the U.K., 1999

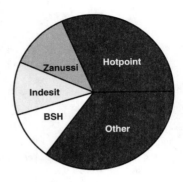

Approximately 3 million units were sold during the year. Sales of washing machines reached 2 million units; the rest were dryers.

Hotpoint	31.2%
Zanussi	12.4
Indesit	11.2
BSH	10.0
Other	35.2

Source: *Electrical & Radio Trading*, February 24, 2000, p. 1.

★ 856 ★
Laundry Equipment
SIC: 3633–ISIC: 2930–HC: 84

Largest Washing Machine Makers in Japan, 1998

Market shares are shown based on domestic shipments.

Matsushita Electric Industrial Co.	22.9%
Hitachi Ltd.	21.2
Toshiba Corp.	20.0
Sanyo Electric Co.	14.4
Sharp Corp.	14.3
Other	7.2

Source: *Nikkei Weekly*, August 9, 1999, p. 7, from Nihon Keizai Shimbun.

★ 857 ★
Laundry Equipment
SIC: 3633–ISIC: 2930–HC: 84

Top Washing Machine Brands in Beijing, China

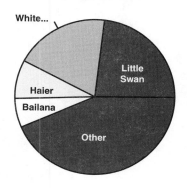

Market shares are shown in percent.

Little Swan	23.4%
White Chrysanthemum	19.3
Haier	8.2
Bailana	6.1
Other	43.0

Source: "Market Share of Washing Machines." Retrieved September 27, 2000 from the World Wide Web: http://www.office.com.

★ 858 ★
Laundry Equipment
SIC: 3633–ISIC: 2930–HC: 84

Top Washing Machine Brands in Shanghai, China

Market shares are shown in percent.

Narcissus	35.7%
Little Swan	11.6
Shenhua	10.3
Duckling	6.4
Other	36.0

Source: "Market Share of Washing Machines." Retrieved September 27, 2000 from the World Wide Web: http://www.office.com.

★ 859 ★
Laundry Equipment
SIC: 3633–ISIC: 2930–HC: 84

Top Washing Machine Brands in Xian, China

Market shares are shown in percent.

Double Gull	21.7%
Little Swan	14.0
Haier	8.1
Changfeng	7.2
Narcissus	5.7
Other	43.3

Source: "Market Share of Washing Machines." Retrieved September 27, 2000 from the World Wide Web: http://www.office.com.

★ 860 ★
Laundry Equipment
SIC: 3633–ISIC: 2930–HC: 84

Tumble Dryer Industry in the U.K., 1999

Market shares are shown in percent.

Creda	25.8%
Zanussi	15.9
Hotpoint	15.1
Other	43.2

Source: "UK Cleaning Appliances." Retrieved January 11, 2001 from the World Wide Web: http://www.clearlybusiness.com, from Datamonitor.

★ 861 ★
Air Purifiers
SIC: 3634–ISIC: 2930–HC: 85

Largest Air Purifier Makers

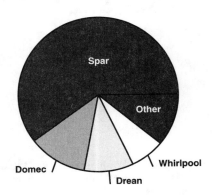

Market shares are shown in percent.

Spar	60.0%
Domec	12.0
Drean	10.0
Whirlpool	7.0
Other	11.0

Source: *South American Business Information*, April 24, 2001, p. NA.

★ 862 ★
Personal Care Appliances
SIC: 3634–ISIC: 2930–HC: 85

Men's Electric Shaver Industry in the U.K., 1999

Market shares are estimated based on value.

Philips	38.9%
Braun	25.6
Other	35.5

Source: ''UK Personal Care Appliances.'' Retrieved Janaury 11, 2001 from the World Wide Web: http://www.clearlybusiness.com, from Datamonitor.

★ 863 ★
Personal Care Appliances
SIC: 3634–ISIC: 2930–HC: 85

Top Electric Toothbrush Makers in Germany, 1999

Shares are shown based on an installed base of 13.43 million units.

Braun	46.3%
Blendax/P&G	14.6
Rowenta	8.9
AEG	4.9
Oral B	4.2
Quelle	3.2
Other	17.9

Source: *Lebensmittel Zeitung*, July 21, 2000, p. 1, from Colgate-Palmolive.

★ 864 ★
Personal Care Appliances
SIC: 3634–ISIC: 2930–HC: 85

U.K. Electric Shaver Market, 1998

The market increased from 58 million British pounds in 1997 to 60.5 million British pounds in 1998.

Philips	52.0%
Braun	23.0
Remington	12.0
Hitachi	5.0
Other	8.0

Source: *Chemist & Druggist*, July 10, 1999, p. 20.

★ 865 ★
Vacuum Cleaners
SIC: 3635–ISIC: 2930–HC: 85

Top Vacuum Cleaner Brands in China

Market shares are shown in percent.

Haier	27.2%
Sanyo	16.9
Fuda	11.1

Continued on next page.

★ 865 ★
[Continued]
Vacuum Cleaners
SIC: 3635–ISIC: 2930–HC: 85

Top Vacuum Cleaner Brands in China

Market shares are shown in percent.

Chunhua 9.8%
Philips 9.8
Kuaile 6.5
Judong 3.4
Mitsubishi 1.6
Xiaogou 1.6
Haoyunda 1.5
Other 10.6

Source: *Appliance Manufacturer*, February 2001, p. G37, from Information Center, Ministry of Internal Trade.

★ 866 ★
Vacuum Cleaners
SIC: 3635–ISIC: 2930–HC: 85

U.K. Vacuum Market

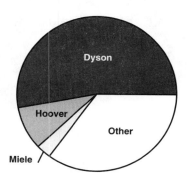

Shares are shown based on value.

Dyson 53.2%
Hoover 9.2
Miele 2.6
Other 35.0

Source: *The Guardian*, March 16, 1999, p. 7, from Gfk Leftrack.

★ 867 ★
Sewing Machines
SIC: 3639–ISIC: 2930–HC: 85

Top Sewing Machine Makers in Brazil

Market shares are shown in percent.

Singer 80.0%
Other 20.0

Source: "Brazil: Singer Launches Teens Sewing Machine." Retrieved April 10, 2001 from the World Wide Web: http://library.northernlight.com, from South American Business Information.

★ 868 ★
Lighting
SIC: 3641–ISIC: 3150–HC: 94

Solid-State Lighting Sales

Figures are in millions of dollars.

	($ mil.)	Share
Automotive	$ 350	87.5%
Traffic signals	40	10.0
Other	10	2.5

Source: *Business Week*, January 22, 2001, p. 94H, from Strategies Unlimited.

★ 869 ★
Lighting
SIC: 3647–ISIC: 3190–HC: 94

Global Headlamp Sector

Market shares are shown in percent.

Valeo 22.0%
Automotive Lighting 15.0
Other 63.0

Source: "Global Market for Automotive Lighting." Retreved May 22, 2001 from the World Wide Web: http://www.just-food.com.

★ 870 ★
Audio Equipment
SIC: 3651–ISIC: 2130–HC: 85

Audio Visual Market in Thailand

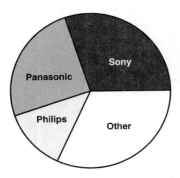

Market shares are shown in percent.

Sony 30.0%
Panasonic 25.0
Philips 13.0
Other 32.0

Source: *Bangkok Post*, February 6, 2001, p. 1.

★ 871 ★
Audio Equipment
SIC: 3651–ISIC: 2130–HC: 85

Portable Audio Market in India

Market shares are shown in percent.

Philips India 87.2%
Other 12.8

Source: *Asia Pulse*, June 4, 2001, p. NA.

★ 872 ★
Audio Equipment
SIC: 3651–ISIC: 2130–HC: 85

Top Composite/Acoustical Equipment Makers in China

Shares are for December 1999.

Aiwa 11.4%
Kenwood 11.0
Sony 9.8
Panasonic 8.1
Amoisonic 5.5
JVC 4.7
Qisheng 3.7
Other 45.8

Source: "China's Home Appliance Market." Retrieved May 16, 2000 from the World Wide Web: http://www.chinaonline.com, from *Beijing Youth Daily* and China National Commercial Information Center.

★ 873 ★
Audio Equipment
SIC: 3651–ISIC: 2130–HC: 85

Top Stereo Cassette Makers in the U.K., 1999

Market shares are estimated based on value.

Sony 12.8%
Panasonic 12.2
JVC 8.2
Other 66.8

Source: "UK Audio Equipment." Retrieved January 11, 2001 from the World Wide Web: http://www.clearlybusiness.com, from Datamonitor.

★ 874 ★
Consumer Electronics
SIC: 3651–ISIC: 2130–HC: 85

Consumer Electronics Sales in Norway, 2000

Sales are at an all-time high, roughly $2 billion.

	Sales	% of Group
Televisions	295,000	20.46%
Car radios/CD players/tape recorders	241,000	16.71
Portable radios/tape recorders/ CD players	174,000	12.07
VCRs	157,000	10.89
Portable CD players	136,000	9.43
Stereo/audio equipment . . .	133,000	9.22
Portable radios	122,000	8.46
Satellite dishes	87,000	6.03
DVD players	53,000	3.68
Video cameras	44,000	3.05

Source: "Consumer Electronics." Retrieved April 3, 2001 from the World Wide Web: http://www.usatrade.gov.

★ 875 ★
Consumer Electronics
SIC: 3651–ISIC: 2130–HC: 85

Digital TV Market in Great Britain

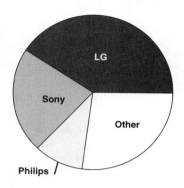

Market shares are shown in percent.

LG	41.4%
Sony	22.0
Philips	9.5
Other	27.1

Source: *Korea Times*, May 16, 2000, p. A, from GFK.

★ 876 ★
Consumer Electronics
SIC: 3651–ISIC: 2130–HC: 85

Largest VCR Makers in Japan, 1998

Market shares are shown based on domestic shipments.

Matsushita Electric Industrial Co.	23.6%
Sony Corp.	15.1
Victor Co. of Japan	13.4
Toshiba Corp.	12.5
Other	24.2

Source: *Nikkei Weekly*, August 9, 1999, p. 7, from Nihon Keizai Shimbun.

★ 877 ★
Consumer Electronics
SIC: 3651–ISIC: 2130–HC: 85

Top Audio/Video Product Makers in Germany

Market shares are shown in percent.

Sony	17.2%
Philips Deutschland	11.8
Panasonic	10.9
Grundig	10.2
Loewe	5.4
Other	44.4

Source: *Media & Marketing*, April 1, 2000, p. 1.

★ 878 ★
Consumer Electronics
SIC: 3651–ISIC: 2130–HC: 85

Top DVD Player Brands in France, 1999

Market shares are shown in percent.

Goldstar	42.0%
Panasonic	32.0
Sony	26.0

Source: *Brand Strategy*, January 2001, p. 24.

★ 879 ★
Consumer Electronics
SIC: 3651–ISIC: 2130–HC: 85

Top DVD Player Brands in Germany, 1999

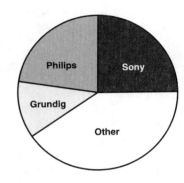

Market shares are shown in percent.

Sony	24.5%
Philips	23.0
Grundig	12.0
Other	40.5

Source: *Brand Strategy*, January 2001, p. 24.

★ 880 ★
Consumer Electronics
SIC: 3651–ISIC: 2130–HC: 85

Top DVD Player Brands in Italy, 1999

Market shares are shown in percent.

Philips	34.2%
Saba	11.4
Samsung	11.4
Other	43.0

Source: *Brand Strategy*, January 2001, p. 24.

★ 881 ★
Consumer Electronics
SIC: 3651–ISIC: 2130–HC: 85

Top DVD Player Brands in Spain, 1999

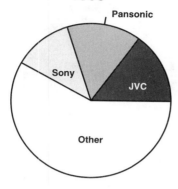

Market shares are shown in percent.

JVC	15.0%
Pansonic	15.0
Sony	12.0
Other	58.0

Source: *Brand Strategy*, January 2001, p. 24.

★ 882 ★
Consumer Electronics
SIC: 3651–ISIC: 2130–HC: 85

Top DVD Player Makers in Japan, 1999

Market shares are shown based on domestic shipments of 388,000 units.

Pioneer Corp.	38.0%
Matsushita Electric Industrial Co.	20.0
Sony Corp.	17.0
Toshiba Corp.	15.0
Sharp Corp.	8.0
Other	2.0

Source: *Nikkei Weekly*, July 31, 2000, p. 8, from Nihon Keizai Shimbun.

★ 883 ★
Consumer Electronics
SIC: 3651–ISIC: 2130–HC: 85

Top TV Brands in China

Shares are for 21-inch models for December 1999.

Konka	18.7%
Changhong	17.2
TCL	15.9
Hisense	8.9
Hai'er	8.8
Philips	7.0
Skyworth	6.5
Panda	3.0
Other	14.0

Source: "China's Home Appliance Market." Retrieved May 16, 2000 from the World Wide Web: http://www.chinaonline.com, from *Beijing Youth Daily* and China National Commercial Information Center.

★ 884 ★
Consumer Electronics
SIC: 3651–ISIC: 2130–HC: 85

Top TV Makers in Germany, 1998

Market shares are shown in percent.

Philips	18.3%
Grundig	17.0
Loewe	13.7
Sony	11.7
Panasonic	8.4
Other	30.9

Source: *Investor's Business Daily*, April 8/, 209, p. A6, from GFK Group.

★ 885 ★
Consumer Electronics
SIC: 3651–ISIC: 2130–HC: 85

Top TV Makers in India, 1999

Shares are for the first six months of the year. Data are for 21 inch TVs, which account for 43% of the market.

BPL	21.2%
Videocon	14.3
Onida	12.1
Samsung	8.0
Akai	6.4
LG	6.0
Philips	6.0
Aiwa	5.2
Sony	5.2
Others	15.6

Source: *Business Today*, September 22, 1999, p. 55, from Francis Kanoi Market Research.

★ 886 ★
Consumer Electronics
SIC: 3651–ISIC: 2130–HC: 85

Top TV Makers in Japan, 1998

Market shares are shown based on domestic shipments.

Matsushita Electric Industrial Co.	18.2%
Sony Corp.	16.5
Toshiba Corp.	12.5
Sharp Corp.	10.0
Aiwa Co.	6.8
Other	36.0

Source: *Nikkei Weekly*, August 9, 1999, p. 7, from Nihon Keizai Shimbun.

★ 887 ★
Consumer Electronics
SIC: 3651–ISIC: 2130–HC: 85

Top TV Makers in Russia

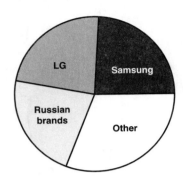

Russian brands include Rekford, Gorizont and Rubin.

Samsung	24.0%
LG	23.0
Russian brands	22.0
Other	31.0

Source: *Kommersant*, September 8, 2000, p. 8.

★ 888 ★
Recording Media
SIC: 3651–ISIC: 2130–HC: 85

Voice Recording Market

Dictaphone has lost its lead in the voice recording market, but it does control 55% of the U.S. health-care dictation market, a growing segment.

Nice Systems	20.0%
Dictaphone	19.0
Other	61.0

Source: *New York Times*, December 7, 1999, p. C3, from APS Financial Corporation and company reports.

★ 889 ★
Music
SIC: 3652–ISIC: 2213–HC: 85

Classical Music Firms in the U.K., 2000

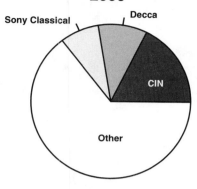

Sony Classical

Decca

CIN

Other

Shares are shown for the first quarter of the year.

CIN	17.6%
Decca	9.8
Sony Classical	7.6
Other	65.0

Source: *Music Week*, April 22, 2000, p. 1.

★ 890 ★
Music
SIC: 3652–ISIC: 2213–HC: 85

Largest Music Distributors

Market shares are shown in percent.

Universal	21.5%
Sony	14.6
Warner	12.6
EMI	12.0
BMG	9.7
Other	29.6

Source: *Advertising Age International*, December 2000, p. 15.

★ 891 ★
Music
SIC: 3652–ISIC: 2213–HC: 85

Largest Music Markets

Markets are ranked by retail sales in billions of dollars.

North America	$ 15.1
Europe	12.4
Asia	7.8
Latin America	1.9
Asia excl. Japan	1.3
Australasia	0.8
Middle East	0.4
Africa	0.2

Source: *Billboard*, April 29, 2000, p. 22.

★ 892 ★
Music
SIC: 3652–ISIC: 2213–HC: 85

Music Sales in Germany

Market shares are shown in percent.

Pop	45.7%
Rock	14.1
Classic	9.6
Folk	9.6
Dance	6.5
Jazz	1.1
Other	13.4

Source: *Wirtschaftswoche*, March 2, 2000, p. 87, from Phone Verband and GfK.

★ 893 ★
Music
SIC: 3652–ISIC: 2213–HC: 85

Top Music Firms in Australia

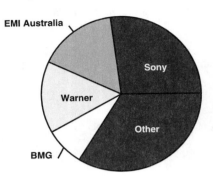

Market shares are shown in percent.

Sony	26.6%
EMI Australia	15.7
Warner	15.3
BMG	8.0
Other	34.4

Source: *Music Business international*, December 1, 1999, p. 1.

★ 894 ★
Music
SIC: 3652–ISIC: 2213–HC: 85

Top Music Firms in Colombia

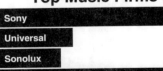

Market shares are shown in percent. The market fell from Pesos$192 billion in 1999 to Pesos$119 billion in 2000.

Sony	31.0%
Universal	11.8
Sonolux	10.2
Other	47.0

Source: *South American Business Information*, March 5, 2001, p. NA.

★ 895 ★
Music
SIC: 3652–ISIC: 2213–HC: 85

Top Music Firms in the U.K.

Market shares are shown in percent. 185 million compact discs were sold.

Universal	24.0%
Sony	15.0
EMI	13.0
Warner	10.0
Other	38.0

Source: *Marketing*, November 2, 2000, p. 1, from British Phonographic Industry.

★ 896 ★
Music
SIC: 3652–ISIC: 2213–HC: 85

U.K. Music Sales

The best-sellers included "now 45" and Moby's "Play".

	(000)	Share
CDs	38,500	91.17%
Cassettes	3,500	8.29
7-inch singles	161	0.38
Minidiscs	70	0.17

Source: *Billboard*, August 26, 2000, p. 64, from British Phonographic Industry.

★ 897 ★
Broadcasting Equipment
SIC: 3661–ISIC: 3220–HC: 85

Broadcasting Equipment Market

The 500 billion yen market is estimated in percent.

Sony Corp.	38.0%
Matsushita Electric Industrial Co.	15.0
NEC Corp.	10.0
Toshiba Corp.	6.0
Victor Co. of Japan	4.0
Other	27.0

Source: *Nikkei Weekly*, May 1, 2000, p. 1, from Nihon Keizai Shimbun.

★ 898 ★
Broadcasting Equipment
SIC: 3661–ISIC: 3220–HC: 85

Digital TV Set-Top Box Sales

Sales are shown in millions of units.

	2000	2002	2004
North America	15.3	22.6	29.7
Western Europe	8.7	14.6	24.4
Rest of world	3.5	8.9	20.4

Source: *Electronic Times*, March 5, 2001, p. 3, from Strategy Analytics.

★ 899 ★
Fax Machines
SIC: 3661–ISIC: 3220–HC: 85

Top Fax Makers in Europe, 1999

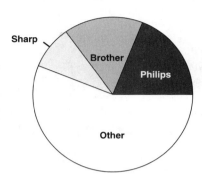

Market shares are shown in percent.

Philips	19.0%
Brother	16.0
Sharp	9.0
Other	56.0

Source: ''Press Releases.'' Retrieved November 10, 2000 from the World Wide Web: http://www.capv.com.

★ 900 ★
Fiber Optics
SIC: 3661–ISIC: 3220–HC: 85

Largest Optical Fiber Makers in Japan, 1998

Market shares are shown based on domestic shipments.

Sumitomo Electric Industries Ltd.	32.0%
Fujikara Ltd.	25.0
Furukawa Electric Co.	25.0
Hitachi Cable Ltd.	7.0
Mitsubishi Cable Industries Ltd.	4.0
Other	7.0

Source: *Nikkei Weekly*, August 9, 1999, p. 7, from Nihon Keizai Shimbun.

★ 901 ★
Fiber Optics
SIC: 3661–ISIC: 3220–HC: 85

Optical Fiber Demand, 1998

The market grew ten percent over 1997.

North America	45.0%
Western Europe	20.0
Other Asia-Pacific	15.0
Japan	10.0
Latin America and rest of world	10.0

Source: *Photonics Spectra*, April 1999, p. 78, from Corning Inc.

★ 902 ★
Fiber Optics
SIC: 3661–ISIC: 3220–HC: 85

Optical Fiber Market, 1999

Corning is the world's largest maker of fiber-optic lines and a leader in the manufacturing of optical network components. Market shares are estimated.

Corning	40.0%
Lucent	20.0
Alcatel	10.0
Japanese manufacturers	10.0
Other	20.0

Source: *Wall Street Journal*, February 3, 2000, p. 4B, from Corning, Merrill Lynch, and Baseline.

★ 903 ★
Modems
SIC: 3661–ISIC: 3220–HC: 85

Modem Market in China

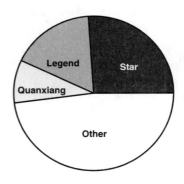

Market shares are shown in percent.

Star	26.13%
Legend	16.92
Quanxiang	9.25
Other	47.70

Source: "Popular Computer Weekly Releases Survey Results." Retrieved October 16, 2000 from the World Wide Web: http://www.chinaonline.com, from *Popular Computer Weekly*.

★ 904 ★
Modems
SIC: 3661–ISIC: 3220–HC: 85

Top Cable Modem Makers, 2000

Companeis are ranked by shipments for the second quarter.

	(000)	Share
Motorola	650	32.5%
Terayon	271	13.6
3Com	254	12.7
Com21	184	9.2
Toshiba America	150	7.5
Others	490	24.5

Source: "Press Release." Retrieved October 23, 2000 from the World Wide Web: http://www.dataquest.com, from Dataquest Inc.

★ 905 ★
Telephones
SIC: 3661–ISIC: 3220–HC: 85

Top Telephone Makers in China, 1999

The market developed quite well compared to other home appliance markets.

Qiaoxing	18.56%
BBK	14.50
TCL	8.50
Wandelai	8.33
Tianshida	4.05
Siemens	4.00
Other	45.06

Source: "Domestic Brandsd Dominate China's Telephone Market." Retrieved April 10, 2000 from the World Wide Web: http://www.prnewswire.com, from Asia Pulse.

★ 906 ★
Car Navigation Systems
SIC: 3661–ISIC: 3320–HC: 90

Top Car Navigation System Makers in Japan, 1999

Market shares are shown based on domestic shipments of 655,000 units.

Matsushita Communication Industrial Co.	21.9%
Pioneer Corp.	21.7
Alpine Electronics Inc.	15.5
Clarion Co.	15.4
Sony Corp.	6.1
Other	19.4

Source: *Nikkei Weekly*, July 31, 2000, p. 8, from Nihon Keizai Shimbun.

★ 907 ★
Cellular Phones
SIC: 3663–ISIC: 3220–HC: 85

CDMA Market Shares Worldwide

Shares are shown based on contracts or the last six months. CDMA stands for code division multiple access.

Lucent	60.2%
Motorola	20.5
Nortel	12.2
Ericsson	7.0

Source: *Dagens Industri*, February 7, 2001, p. 6.

★ 908 ★
Cellular Phones
SIC: 3663–ISIC: 3220–HC: 85

Cellular Phone Market in Brazil

There were 20 companies providing service to 18.4 million. An estimated 8.6 out of 100 Brazilians have a cell phone. Data are as of June 30, 2000.

Ericsson	38.9%
Nortel	23.4
NEC	20.8
Lucent	12.1
Motorola	4.5
Alcatel	0.3

Source: *America's Network Telecom Investor Supplement*, October 2000, p. 26.

★ 909 ★
Cellular Phones
SIC: 3663–ISIC: 3220–HC: 85

Cellular Phone Market in Korea, 1999

Market shares are shown in percent.

Nokia	39.0%
Motorola	30.0
LG Electronics	22.0
Other	9.0

Source: *Korea Herald*, November 10, 2000, p. KH.

★ 910 ★
Cellular Phones
SIC: 3663–ISIC: 3220–HC: 85

GSM Handset Market in Taiwan, 1999

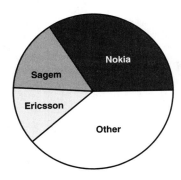

Shares are of the import market.

Nokia 34.0%
Sagem 15.0
Ericsson 12.0
Other 39.0

Source: *National Trade Data Bank*, December 1, 1999, p. NA.

★ 911 ★
Cellular Phones
SIC: 3663–ISIC: 3220–HC: 85

GSM Market Shares Worldwide, 2000

Shares are shown based on contracts or the last six months. GSM stands for global systems for mobile communications.

Ericsson 37.1%
Nokia 21.5
Motorola 15.6
Nortel 11.9
Lucent 5.9
Other 8.0

Source: *Dagens Industri*, February 7, 2001, p. 6.

★ 912 ★
Cellular Phones
SIC: 3663–ISIC: 3220–HC: 85

GSM Phone Market in Western Europe, 1998

Market shares are shown in percent. GSM stands for global system for mobile communications standard.

Nokia 28.0%
Ericsson 19.0
Motorola 16.0
Alcatel 11.0
Siemens 8.0
Panasonic 5.0
Philips 5.0
Sagem 4.0
Bosch 2.0
Others 4.0

Source: *Wall Street Journal*, December 28, 1999, p. A8, from Dataquest Inc.

★ 913 ★
Cellular Phones
SIC: 3663–ISIC: 3220–HC: 85

Mobile Phone Makers in Indonesia

Market shares are shown in percent.

Telkomsel 46.0%
Satelindo 28.8
Excelcomindo 20.9
Komselindo 2.0
Metrosel 1.7

Source: "Indonesia's Cellular Phone Sector." Retrieved March 20, 2001 from the World Wide Web: http://www.asiapulse.news.

★ 914 ★
Cellular Phones
SIC: 3663–ISIC: 3220–HC: 85

Mobile Phone Market in Australia

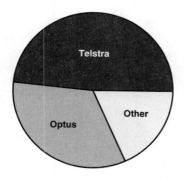

Market shares are shown in percent.

Telstra	48.2%
Optus	33.4
Other	18.4

Source: *South China Morning Post*, September 28, 2000, p. 4.

★ 915 ★
Cellular Phones
SIC: 3663–ISIC: 3220–HC: 85

Mobile Phone Market in China

Market shares are shown in percent.

Motorola	32.0%
Nokia	29.4
Ericsson	21.4
Other	17.2

Source: *South China Morning Post*, October 4, 2000, p. 5.

★ 916 ★
Cellular Phones
SIC: 3663–ISIC: 3220–HC: 85

Mobile Phone Market in Europe, 1999

Market shares are shown in percent.

Nokia	28.9%
Motorola	14.0
Siemens	12.3
Alcatel	9.7
Ericsson	9.2
Philips	6.8
Sagem	6.0
Panasonic	3.6
Samsung	3.0
Other	6.5

Source: *Wall Street Journal*, June 23, 2000, p. A16, from Dataquest Inc.

★ 917 ★
Cellular Phones
SIC: 3663–ISIC: 3220–HC: 85

Mobile Phone Market in Japan, 2000

Shares are shown based on the fiscal year ended March 2000.

Matsushita	26.0%
Mitsubishi Electric	14.0
NEC	12.0
Toshiba	8.0
Kyocera	1.0
Nokia	1.0
Other	28.0

Source: *Wall Street Journal*, June 26, 2000, p. A26, from Dataquest Inc. and Yano Research.

★ 918 ★
Cellular Phones
SIC: 3663–ISIC: 3220–HC: 85

Mobile Phone Market in Latin America, 1999

Shares are for the first half of the year.

Nokia 34.1%
Motorola 26.6
Ericsson 17.3
Philips 5.1
Qualcomm 3.4
Others 13.5

Source: "Press Releases." Retrieved March 8, 2000 from the World Wide Web: http://www,gartnerweb.com, from Dataquest Inc.

★ 919 ★
Cellular Phones
SIC: 3663–ISIC: 3220–HC: 85

Mobile Phone Market in Spain

Market shares are shown in percent.

Telefonica 59.17%
Airtel 32.72
Amena 8.10

Source: *Expansion*, March 17, 2000, p. 1.

★ 920 ★
Cellular Phones
SIC: 3663–ISIC: 3220–HC: 85

Top Cellular Phone Makers, 2000

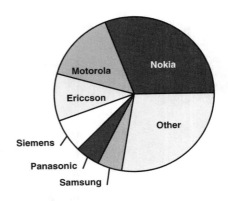

Market shares are shown in percent.

Nokia 30.6%
Motorola 14.6
Ericcson 10.0
Siemens 6.5
Panasonic 5.2
Samsung 5.0
Other 28.1

Source: *Investor's Business Daily*, February 20, 2001, p. A10, from Dataquest Inc.

★ 921 ★
Satellites
SIC: 3663–ISIC: 3220–HC: 85

GEO Satellite Market, 2000

Europe 53.0%
United States 44.0
Japan 3.0

Source: *Interavia*, December 2000, p. 45.

★ 922 ★
Bank Cards
SIC: 3669–ISIC: 3220–HC: 85

Top Bank Card Makers in Japan

Shares are for July 1998.

Mudan Card	41.1%
Long Card	27.9
Jinsui Card	13.5
Greatwall Card	11.5
Zhaoyin Card	2.7
Pacific Card	2.2
Dongfang Card	1.1

Source: "China: The Smartcard and ATM Market."
Retrieved September 19, 2000 from the World Wide Web:
http://www.tradeport.org, from *Financial News*.

★ 923 ★
Bank Cards
SIC: 3669–ISIC: 3220–HC: 85

Top Debit Card Makers in Japan

Shares are for July 1998.

Mudan Card	38.0%
Jinsui Card	22.0
Long Card	18.0
Greatwall Card	14.0
Dongfang Card	4.0
Pacific Card	2.0
Guangfa Card	1.0

Source: "China: The Smartcard and ATM Market."
Retrieved September 19, 2000 from the World Wide Web:
http://www.tradeport.org, from *Financial News*.

★ 924 ★
Information Appliances
SIC: 3669–ISIC: 3220–HC: 85

Information Appliance Sales

Sales are shown in millions of units.

	2000	2005	Share
Asia/Pacific	12.1	293.5	58.48%
North America	8.2	57.4	11.44
Europe	6.3	91.5	18.23
South/Central America	1.9	41.7	8.31
Rest of world	0.6	17.8	3.55

Source: *Infoworld*, August 14, 2000, p. 18, from ETForecasts.

★ 925 ★
Information Appliances
SIC: 3669–ISIC: 3220–HC: 85

Information Appliance Shipments Worldwide

Internet appliances are devices designed to connect the user to the Internet. Gaming devices like Sega Dreamcast and Sony Playstation 2 will take a big lead in 2002, taking more than 25 million orders. Smartphone and similar devices won't take the lead until 2004. Data are in millions of units.

	1999 (mil.)	2004 (mil.)	Share
Net TVs	6.10	17.80	20.00%
Net gaming devices	2.00	22.60	25.40
Net-smart handhelds	1.70	33.20	37.31
Net screenphones	1.10	3.60	4.05
E-mail terminals	0.10	4.60	5.17
Web terminals	0.01	6.50	7.30
Other	0.01	0.69	0.78

Source: *Industry Standard*, April 10, 2000, p. 284, from International Data Corp.

★ 926 ★
Networking Equipment
SIC: 3669–ISIC: 3220–HC: 85

ATM Switch Market, 1998

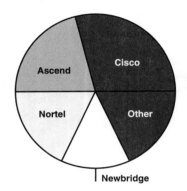

Market shares are shown based on revenues.

Cisco	28.7%
Ascend	21.1
Nortel	17.5
Newbridge	14.4
Other	18.3

Source: *Business Communications Review*, July 1999, p. 55.

★ 927 ★
Networking Equipment
SIC: 3669–ISIC: 3220–HC: 85

Cellular Infrastructure Equipment Market

Market shares are shown in percent.

Ericsson	27.0%
Lucent	14.0
Nokia	14.0
Motorola	12.0
Nortel	12.0
Other	21.0

Source: "Press Release." Retrieved August 3, 2000 from the World Wide Web: http://www.northernlight.com, from Forward Concepts.

★ 928 ★
Networking Equipment
SIC: 3669–ISIC: 3220–HC: 85

Dedicated VPN Gateway Revenue

Market shares are shown for the first half of the year.

Cisco	19.0%
Nortel	18.0
Intel	5.0
Lucent	5.0
Redcreek	5.0
3Com	2.0
VPNet	2.0
Other	44.0

Source: *Business Communications Review*, October 2000, p. 55, from Synergy Research Group Inc.

★ 929 ★
Networking Equipment
SIC: 3669–ISIC: 3220–HC: 85

DWDM Gear Market Shares

DWDM stands for dense wavelength-division multiplexing.

Nortel Networks	60.0%
Ciena	13.0
Lucent Technologies	9.0
Alcatel	5.0
Other	13.0

Source: *Wall Street Journal*, March 15, 2001, p. B12, from Dell Oro Group.

★ 930 ★
Networking Equipment
SIC: 3669–ISIC: 3220–HC: 85

Edge VOIP Gateway Market Shares

The large market segment of the Voice over-IP system industry was voice-enabled routers, with a market size of $19.4 million. Shares are shown in percent.

Voval/Tec	37.5%
Clarent	28.2
Netrix	9.0
Lucent	7.7
Linkon	7.2
Comdial/Array	3.9
Other	6.5

Source: *Business Communications Review*, April 1999, p. 13, from Synergy Research.

★ 931 ★
Networking Equipment
SIC: 3669–ISIC: 3220–HC: 85

Ethernet Market Shares

Shares are shown based on second quarter shipments.

Extreme	36.0%
Cabletron	15.0
Foundry	13.0
Nortel	10.0
Cisco	7.0
Other	19.0

Source: *Investor's Business Daily*, November 13, 2000, p. A6, from Dell'Oro Group.

★ 932 ★
Networking Equipment
SIC: 3669–ISIC: 3220–HC: 85

Frame Relay Switch Market, 1998

Market shares are shown based on revenues.

Nortel	25.7%
Ascend	25.1
Cisco	16.3
Newbridge	10.2
Other	22.5

Source: *Business Communications Review*, July 1999, p. 55.

★ 933 ★
Networking Equipment
SIC: 3669–ISIC: 3220–HC: 85

LAN Switch Port Shipments, 2000

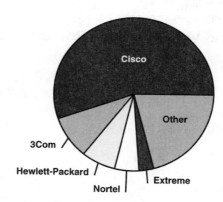

Shares are shown for the third quarter.

Cisco	56.0%
3Com	9.0
Hewlett-Packard	7.0
Nortel	5.0
Extreme	3.0
Other	21.0

Source: *Computer Reseller News*, March 5, 2001, p. 55, from International Data Corp.

★ 934 ★
Networking Equipment
SIC: 3669–ISIC: 3220–HC: 85

Layer 2-7 Ethernet Switches Market

Market shares are shown based on third quarter revenues.

Cisco	59.2%
Nortel	7.7
Cabletron	5.6
3Com	4.2
Extreme	3.6
Foundry	3.2
Others	16.5

Source: *Internet Week*, December 4, 2000, p. 34, from Dell'Oro Group.

★ 935 ★
Networking Equipment
SIC: 3669–ISIC: 3220–HC: 85

Low-End Voice Capable Routers

Shares are shown based on revenues.

Cisco	77.5%
Bay/Nortel	11.6
Motorola	3.4
3Com	2.4
Ascend	0.6
Lucent	0.6
Others	3.9

Source: *Network World*, August 14, 2000, p. 23, from Dell'Oro Group.

★ 936 ★
Networking Equipment
SIC: 3669–ISIC: 3220–HC: 85

Remote Access Market

Market shares are shown for the first three quarters of the year.

Cisco Systems	32.1%
Lucent Technologies	31.0
3Com	22.0
Nortel Networks	12.1
Other	2.9

Source: *Computer Reseller News*, February 12, 2001, p. 47.

★ 937 ★
Networking Equipment
SIC: 3669–ISIC: 3220–HC: 85

Top Leatherboard Makers, 1999

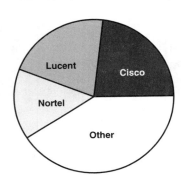

The $7.5 billion market for ATM and frame relay equipment is shown in percent.

Cisco	22.5%
Lucent	20.7
Nortel	15.4
Other	41.4

Source: "Vertical Systems Group Announces Top 3 Leatherboards." Retrieved February 24, 2000 from the World Wide Web: http://www.businesswire.com.

★ 938 ★
Networking Equipment
SIC: 3669–ISIC: 3220–HC: 85

WDM Equipment Market in Europe, 2000

The year was a milestone for Europe with 80% of the pan-Europe pure-play operators completing network build-outs. The market roughly doubled, hitting $1.7 billion. Market shares are shown in percent.

Nortel	31.0%
Lucent	19.0
Alcatel	17.0
Ciena	16.0

Source: ''RHK Study Results.'' Retrieved April 19, 2001 from the World Wide Web: http://www.businesswire.com.

★ 939 ★
Networking Equipment
SIC: 3669–ISIC: 3220–HC: 85

Wireless Market Segments

The expected size of wireless marketing building opportunities will grow to $30.5 billion by 2003. M-commerce will grow the most, hitting $12 billion.

	($ bil.)	Share
Hosting	$ 11.0	36.07%
Integration	7.0	22.95
Consulting	5.0	16.39
Operation	5.0	16.39
Security	2.0	6.56
Technology	0.5	1.64

Source: *M Business*, February 2001, p. 65, from J.P. Morgan.

★ 940 ★
Smart Cards
SIC: 3669–ISIC: 3220–HC: 85

Largest Memory Card Shippers

Companies are ranked by unit shipments.

	Units	Share
Schlumberger	397	37.56%
Gemplus	375	35.48
Giesecke & Devrient	73	6.91
Oberthur	53	5.01
Orga	39	3.69
Other	120	11.35

Source: *Card Technology*, July 2000, p. 24.

★ 941 ★
Smart Cards
SIC: 3669–ISIC: 3220–HC: 85

Leading Smart Card Vendors, 2000

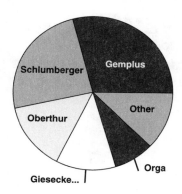

Firms are ranked by shipments in millions of units.

	(mil.)	Share
Gemplus	185	29.46%
Schlumberger (inc. Solaic)	152	24.20
Oberthur	85	13.54
Giesecke & amp; Devrient (inc. RDN)	76	12.10
Orga	53	8.44
Other	77	12.26

Source: ''Dataquest Says Worldwide Smart Card Shipments grew 45%.'' Retrieved June 29, 2001 from the World Wide Web: http://www.dataquest.com.

★ 942 ★
Smart Cards
SIC: 3669–ISIC: 3220–HC: 85

Smart Card Applications, 1999

Data show volume of cards.

	(mil.)	Share
Pay telephones	1,120	68.75%
GSM cell phones	145	8.90
Financial	110	6.75
Retail/loyalty	49	3.01
Pay TV	42	2.58
Health care	41	2.52
ID/access	39	2.39
Transportation	22	1.35
Metering/vending	21	1.29
Other	40	2.46

Source: *Solid State Technology*, March 2000, p. 55, from Orga.

★ 943 ★
Integrated Circuits
SIC: 3674–ISIC: 3210–HC: 85

Largest IC Socket Makers

Market shares are shown in percent.

Yamaichi	16.9%
AMP	13.3
Molex	9.8
Thomas & Betts	8.0
FCI	6.5
Foxconn	3.6
PCD	3.4
Elco	2.2
Methode	1.9
SMK	1.8
Other	67.4

Source: ''Top 100.'' Retrieved February 2, 2001 from the World Wide Web: http://www.bishopinc.com, from Bishop Associates.

★ 944 ★
Microprocessors
SIC: 3674–ISIC: 3210–HC: 85

32-bit Embedded Processor Market Shares, 1999

Market shares are shown in percent.

ARM	30.2%
MIPS	24.0
Motorola 68K	21.5
Hitachi SH	12.6
Other	12.2

Source: *Electronic Buyers News*, March 6, 2000, p. 1.

★ 945 ★
Microprocessors
SIC: 3674–ISIC: 3210–HC: 85

ADSL Chipset Market Shares, 1999

Alcatel

Analog Devices

GlobeSpan

STMicroelectronics

Lucent Technologies Microelectronics Group

Texas Instruments

Market shares are shown in percent. ADSL stands for asymmetric digital subscriber lines.

Alcatel	31.0%
Analog Devices	21.0
GlobeSpan	17.0
STMicroelectronics	15.0
Lucent Technologies Microelectronics Group	13.0
Texas Instruments	2.0

Source: *Electronic Buyers News*, October 23, 2000, p. 69, from Intenational Data Corp.

★ 946 ★
Microprocessors
SIC: 3674–ISIC: 3210–HC: 85

Analog Modem IC Market

Market shares are shown in percent.

	1999	2001	2003
Bundled	67.0%	77.0%	83.0%
Retail	29.0	20.0	14.0
RAS	4.0	3.0	3.0

Source: *EDN*, December 21, 2000, p. S260, from Cahners InStat.

★ 947 ★
Microprocessors
SIC: 3674–ISIC: 3210–HC: 85

Global PC Microprocessor

Shares are for the third quarter of 2000.

Intel	81.9%
AMD	17.0
Other	1.1

Source: *Wall Street Journal*, November 17, 2000, p. B5, from Mercury Research.

★ 948 ★
Microprocessors
SIC: 3674–ISIC: 3210–HC: 85

Largest DSP Producers, 1999

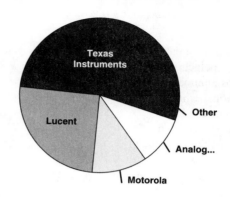

Market shares are shown in percent. DSP stands for digital signal processing.

Texas Instruments	48.0%
Lucent	25.1
Motorola	11.4
Analog Devices	10.3
Other	5.2

Source: *Business Week*, March 27, 2000, p. 102, from Forward Concepts Inc.

★ 949 ★
Microprocessors
SIC: 3674–ISIC: 3210–HC: 85

Largest IC Firms in Europe, 1999

Companies are ranked by estimated sales in billions of dollars.

	($ bil.)	Share
STMicroelectronics	$4.42	31.10%
Infineon Technologies	3.92	27.59
Philips	3.79	26.67
Ericsson	0.61	4.29
Alcatel Microelectronics	0.30	2.11
Micronas	0.20	1.41
Newport Wafer-Fab	0.15	1.06
Austria Mikro Systeme	0.09	0.63
Other	0.73	5.14

Source: *Solid State Technology*, March 2000, p. S12.

★ 950 ★
Microprocessors
SIC: 3674–ISIC: 3210–HC: 85

Leading Analog IC Producers, 1999

Shares are shown based on revenues.

Texas Instruments	13.0%
STMicroelectronics	10.0
Philips Semiconductors	9.0
Infineon Technologies	8.0
ON Semiconductor	7.0
Analog Devices Inc.	6.0
National Semiconductor	6.0
Other	41.0

Source: *E News*, November 13, 2000, p. 16.

★ 951 ★
Microprocessors
SIC: 3674–ISIC: 3210–HC: 85

Low-Voltage Logic Device Market

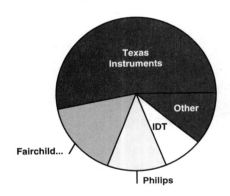

Market shares are shown in percent.

Texas Instruments	53.0%
Fairchild Semiconductor	16.0
Philips	12.0
IDT	8.0
Other	11.0

Source: *Electronic Buyers News*, January 17, 2000, p. 30, from Insight Onsite.

★ 952 ★
Microprocessors
SIC: 3674–ISIC: 3210–HC: 85

PC-Notebook 2D/3D Graphic Chip Industry

Market shares are shown in percent for fourth quarter 1999.

ATI	37.0%
NeoMagic	29.0
Trident	15.0
Other	19.0

Source: *Electronic Buyers News*, April 24, 2000, p. 5, from Mercury Research Inc.

★ 953 ★
Microprocessors
SIC: 3674–ISIC: 3210–HC: 85

Programmable-Chip Market Shares

Xilinx	35.0%
Altera	33.0
Lattice Semiconductor	16.0
Actel	7.0
Lucent Technologies	4.0
Other	5.0

Source: *Investor's Business Daily*, December 1, 2000, p. A6, from Dataquest Inc. and Altera Corp.

★ 954 ★
Microprocessors
SIC: 3674–ISIC: 3210–HC: 85

Smart Card IC Market

IC stands for integrated circuit.

Infineon Technologies	43.0%
STMicroelectronics	32.0
Hitachi	11.0
Philip Atmel	5.0
Other	9.0

Source: *Markt & Technik*, July 7, 2000, p. 1.

★ **955** ★
Microprocessors
SIC: 3674–ISIC: 3210–HC: 85

UPL Merchant Market Shares, 1999

Market shares are shown in percent.

Xilinx 35.3%
Altera 31.9
Lattice Semiconductor 15.9
Actel 6.4
Lucent Technologies 4.3
Cypress Semiconductor 1.8

Source: *EDN*, December 21, 2000, p. S221, from Cahners In-Stat.

★ **957** ★
Semiconductors
SIC: 3674–ISIC: 3210–HC: 85

FPGA Market Shares

FPGA stands for field programmable gate array.

Xilinx 57.2%
Altera 19.4
Actel 11.6
Lucent Technologies 7.8
QuickLogic 2.6

Source: *EDN*, December 21, 2000, p. S21.

★ **956** ★
Semiconductors
SIC: 3674–ISIC: 3210–HC: 85

64-Megabit DRAM Makers in Japan, 1999

Market shares are shown based on domestic sales.

Hyundai Electronics Industries Co. 23.0%
NEC Corp. 20.6
Samsung Electronics Co. 19.1
Hitachi Ltd. 13.8
Mitsubishi Electric Corp. 10.0
Other 13.6

Source: *Nikkei Weekly*, August 14, 2000, p. 8, from Nihon Keizai Shimbun.

★ **958** ★
Semiconductors
SIC: 3674–ISIC: 3210–HC: 85

Leading Automotive Semiconductor Makers, 1999

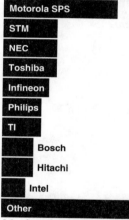

Market shares are shown in percent.

Motorola SPS 14.6%
STM 6.7
NEC 6.6
Toshiba 6.5
Infineon 6.0
Philips 5.4
TI 4.6

Continued on next page.

★ 958 ★

[Continued]
Semiconductors
SIC: 3674–ISIC: 3210–HC: 85

Leading Automotive Semiconductor Makers, 1999

Market shares are shown in percent.

Bosch	4.3%
Hitachi	4.2
Intel	3.2
Other	38.0

Source: *Autoparts Report*, September 8, 2000, p. 1, from Strategy Analytics.

★ 959 ★

Semiconductors
SIC: 3674–ISIC: 3210–HC: 85

Leading DSP Makers for Cell Phones

Market shares are shown in percent.

TI	58.0%
DSP Group	20.0
Other	22.0

Source: *Electronic Buyers News*, April 9, 2001, p. 8.

★ 960 ★

Semiconductors
SIC: 3674–ISIC: 3210–HC: 85

Semiconductor IP Market Leaders, 2000

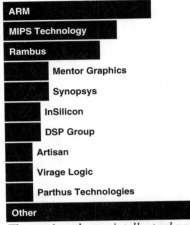

ARM
MIPS Technology
Rambus
Mentor Graphics
Synopsys
InSilicon
DSP Group
Artisan
Virage Logic
Parthus Technologies
Other

The semiconductor intellectual property market is expected to grow from $492.4 million in revenues to $689.9 million in revenues.

	1999	2000
ARM	17.9%	16.6%
MIPS Technology	17.2	13.3
Rambus	8.8	10.5
Mentor Graphics	6.5	4.9
Synopsys	4.9	4.9
InSilicon	3.9	3.8
DSP Group	3.8	3.6
Artisan	3.4	3.0
Virage Logic	2.5	3.2
Parthus Technologies	1.1	2.8
Other	29.7	33.3

Source: "Gartner Says Semiconductor IP Market Grew 40%." Retrieved June 29, 2001 from the World Wide Web: http://www.dataquest.com, from Dataquest Inc.

★ 961 ★
Semiconductors
SIC: 3674–ISIC: 3210–HC: 85

Silicon Wafer Industry

Market shares are shown in percent.

Shin-Etsu Handotai	24.0%
MEMC	17.0
Sumitomo Metal Industries	14.0
Mitsubishi Materials	11.0
Wacker	11.0
Komatsu	10.0
Toshiba	6.0
Others	7.0

Source: *Chemical Week*, October 11, 2000, p. 31, from Information Network.

★ 962 ★
Semiconductors
SIC: 3674–ISIC: 3210–HC: 85

Top Logic IC Makers in Japan, 1999

Market shares are shown based on domestic sales.

NEC Corp.	20.0%
Fujitsu Ltd.	10.1
Toshiba Corp.	9.0
Hitachi Ltd.	8.0
Matsushita Electric Industrial Co.	7.8
Other	45.1

Source: *Nikkei Weekly*, August 14, 2000, p. 8, from Nihon Keizai Shimbun.

★ 963 ★
Semiconductors
SIC: 3674–ISIC: 3210–HC: 85

Top Semiconductor Firms, 1999

Market shares are shown based on revenues. PCs and servers had 50% of the end use market. North America had the top share of 31%, followed by Asia with 25%.

Intel	15.90%
NEC	5.50
Toshiba	4.50

Samsung	4.20%
Texas Instruments	4.20
Motorola	3.88
Hitachi	3.30
Infineon	3.10
Philips	3.00
STMicroelectronics	2.00
Other	50.50

Source: *Financial Times*, November 14, 2000, p. 22, from Semiconductor Industry Alliance and Thomson Financial Datastream.

★ 964 ★
Semiconductors
SIC: 3674–ISIC: 3210–HC: 85

Top Semiconductor Makers, 2000

Market shares are shown based on revenue.

Intel	13.4%
NEC	5.0
Toshiba	5.0
Samsung	4.9
Texas Instruments	4.9
Motorola	3.6
STMicroelectronics	3.6
Hitachi	3.3
Infineon Technologies	3.0
Other	51.0

Source: "Press Release." Retrieved January 2, 2001 from the World Wide Web: http://www.businesswire.com, from Dataquest Inc.

★ 965 ★
Electronic Components
SIC: 3678–ISIC: 3210–HC: 85

Global Electronic Component Demand

The global demand for semiconductors and passive electronics is expected to increase 9.5% a year through 2004 to hit $440 billion. The growth of Internet technology and infrastructure is expected to play a key role in the sector's growth. Sales are shown in millions of dollars.

	1999	2004	Share
North America	$ 119.5	$ 175.8	39.26%
Other Asia/Pacific	65.9	118.5	26.46
Western Europe	45.0	87.4	19.52
Japan	38.3	50.2	11.21
Rest of the world	8.9	15.9	3.55

Source: *Test & Measurement World*, December 2000, p. 6, from Freedonia Group.

★ 966 ★
Electronic Components
SIC: 3678–ISIC: 3210–HC: 85

High-Speed Connector Market

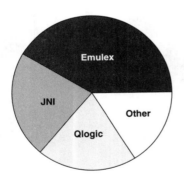

Shares exclude companies that make them for their own use.

	($ mil.)	Share
Emulex	$ 71.5	41.26%
JNI	38.5	22.22
Qlogic	35.5	20.48
Other	27.8	16.04

Source: *Investor's Business Daily*, October 20, 2000, p. A9, from International Data Corp., company reports, and First Call.

★ 967 ★
Electronic Components
SIC: 3678–ISIC: 3210–HC: 85

Top Connector Shippers, 1999

Firms are ranked by sales in millions of dollars. North America had 39.4% of sales, Europe had 27.0% of sales and Japan had 16.9% of sales.

	($ mil.)	Share
Tyco Electronics	$ 4,696.0	18.28%
FCI	1,925.0	7.49
Molex	1,906.9	7.42
Amphenol	778.5	3.03
Foxconn (Hon Hai)	755.6	2.94
3M	637.9	2.48
Yazaki	606.8	2.36
JAE	593.6	2.31
Hirose	589.1	2.29
JST	561.9	2.19
Other	12,641.4	49.20

Source: "Top 100." Retrieved February 2, 2001 from the World Wide Web: http://www.bishopinc.com.

★ 968 ★
Electronic Components
SIC: 3679–ISIC: 3210–HC: 85

Leading Audio Codec Suppliers

Market shares are shown in percent.

Cirrus	27.0%
SigmaTel	27.0
Analog Devices	19.0
EES	14.0

Source: *Electronic Engineering Times*, March 19, 2001, p. NA.

★969★
Flat Panel Displays
SIC: 3679–ISIC: 3210–HC: 85

Flat Panel Display Industry

The market is for flat panel display driver-IC suppliers.

Sharp Electronics	16.0%
Philips Electronics	15.0
Seiko Epson	15.0
NEC	10.0
Hitachi	9.0
TI	9.0
Other	26.0

Source: *Electronic Buyers News*, November 20, 2000, p. 4.

★970★
Liquid Crystal Displays
SIC: 3679–ISIC: 3210–HC: 85

Leading Liquid Crystal Display Makers

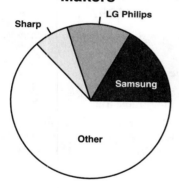

Market shares are shown in percent.

Samsung	17.0%
LG Philips	13.0
Sharp	7.0
Other	63.0

Source: *Electronic Engineering Times*, March 12, 2001, p. NA.

★971★
Liquid Crystal Displays
SIC: 3679–ISIC: 3210–HC: 85

Top Liquid Crystal Display Makers in Japan, 1999

Market shares are shown based on domestic sales.

Sharp Corp.	18.5%
Hitachi Ltd.	9.8
NEC Corp.	9.3
Toshiba Corp.	7.6
Matsushita Electric Industrial Co.	6.7
Other	48.1

Source: *Nikkei Weekly*, August 14, 2000, p. 8, from Nihon Keizai Shimbun.

★972★
Power Supply Products
SIC: 3679–ISIC: 3210–HC: 85

Largest Power Supply Providers, 1999

Firms are ranked by sales in millions of dollars. Total sales are expected to hit 33.4 billion by 2004.

Lucent	$ 1,200
Delta	850
Astec/Emerson Electric	830
Invensys/Lambda	830
Siemens	700
Ericsson	560
Artesyn Technologies	517
Marconi Com	360
Shindengen	350
Lite-On	320

Source: *Electronic Buyers News*, May 8, 2000, p. 1, from Micro-Tech Consultants.

★ 973 ★
Batteries
SIC: 3691–ISIC: 3140–HC: 85

Battery Market in India

Market shares are shown in percent. Eveready also had a 63% share of the flashlight business.

Eveready	43.0%
Indo National	26.0
Lakhanpal National	22.0
Geep	8.0
Other	1.0

Source: *Business Today*, August 22, 1999, p. 49.

★ 974 ★
Batteries
SIC: 3691–ISIC: 3140–HC: 85

Global Battery Demand

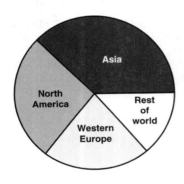

Industrialized countries wil continue to drive demand for batteries to power high-tech devices. The industry is expected to grow 8% a year through 2002.

	1997	2002	Share
Asia	$ 13.71	$ 20.52	37.52%
North America	10.47	14.57	26.64
Western Europe	8.44	11.80	21.58
Rest of world	4.89	7.80	14.26

Source: *Assembly*, May 1999, p. 11, from Freedonia Group.

★ 975 ★
Batteries
SIC: 3691–ISIC: 3140–HC: 85

Top Lithium Ion Battery Makers in Japan, 1999

Market shares are shown based on domestic production of 383.4 million units.

Sanyo Electric Co.	24.6%
Sony Corp.	24.3
Matsushita Battery Industrial Co.	20.3
AT&T Battery Corp.	13.7
GS-Melcotec Co.	8.6
Other	8.5

Source: *Nikkei Weekly*, August 14, 2000, p. 8, from Nihon Keizai Shimbun.

★ 976 ★
Batteries
SIC: 3691–ISIC: 3140–HC: 85

Top Solar Battery Makers in Japan, 1997

Market shares are shown based on shipments.

Sanyo Electric	84.5%
Saneka	9.0
Matsushita Battery Industrial	6.5

Source: "DVL Market Share Library." Retrieved April 3, 2001 from the World Wide Web: http://dvl/daiwa.co.jp, from DVL Market Share Library and Marketing Data Bank.

★ 977 ★
Batteries
SIC: 3691–ISIC: 3320–HC: 90

Battery Market by Type, 1999

The market is shown by segment.

Lithium ion 50.0%
Nickel cadmium 29.0
Nickel metal hydride 21.0
Lithium polymer 0.3

Source: *Forbes*, February 7, 2000, p. I28, from Nomura Research Institute.

★ 978 ★
Optical Disk Replication
SIC: 3695–ISIC: 2429–HC: 85

Optical Disk Replication Industry, 2000

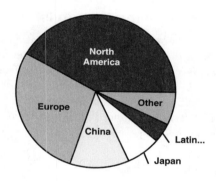

Market shares are shown in percent.

North America 42.0%
Europe 28.0
China 12.0
Japan 7.0
Latin America 4.0
Other 7.0

Source: *AV Video Multimedia Producer*, April 2001, p. 14, from International Recording Media Association.

★ 979 ★
Recording Media
SIC: 3695–ISIC: 2429–HC: 85

Top Video Tape Makers in Japan, 1997

Market shares are shown based on shipments.

TDK 18.2%
Fuji Photo Film 16.5
Hitachi Maxell 16.0
Sony 13.5
Matsushita Electric Industrial 11.8
Victor Co. of Japan 11.0
Other 13.0

Source: ''DVL Market Share Library.'' Retrieved April 3, 2001 from the World Wide Web: http://dvl/daiwa.co.jp, from DVL Market Share Library and Marketing Data Bank.

SIC 37 - Transportation Equipment

★ 980 ★
Autos
SIC: 3711–ISIC: 3410–HC: 87

Best-Selling Cars in Germany

Data show unit sales.

	Units	Share
VW Golf/Bora	316,737	9.4%
Opel Astra	157,936	4.7
BMW 3-series	147,613	4.4
Mercedes-Benz C-class	115,761	3.4
VW Passat	102,659	3.0
Ford Focus	99,400	2.9
Mercedes-Benz A-class	94,751	2.8
Opel Corsa	93,159	2.8
Mercedes-benz E-class	87,234	2.6
VW Polo	85,481	2.5

Source: "A Review of the Status of the German Automotive Industry." Retrieved March 9, 2001 from the World Wide Web: http://www.just-auto.com.

★ 981 ★
Autos
SIC: 3711–ISIC: 3410–HC: 87

Best-Selling Cars in Hungary, 2000

Data show unit sales.

Suzuki	28,072
Opel	20,559
Volkswagen	11,201
Renault	10,139
Fiat	8,463
Peugeot	7,845

Skoda	7,064
Daewoo	6,623
Toyota	5,968
Ford	5,316

Source: "Auto Sales in Hungary." Retrieved March 2, 2001 from the World Wide Web: http://www.factbook.net.

★ 982 ★
Autos
SIC: 3711–ISIC: 3410–HC: 87

Best-Selling Cars in Israel

The market has been booming, up 30% to sales of 120,0000 units in the first nine months of the year. The boom has been the result of the strong local currency and the growth of the high-tech sector, where every new programmer gets a new car. Mazda leads with a 13.8% share, followed by Hyundai with a 8.21% share.

Mazda Lantis	10,946
Hyundai Accent	4,646
Toyota Corolla	4,511
Fiat Punto	4,426
Ford Focus	3,420
Suzuki Baleno	2,969
Renault Megane	2,958
Volkswagen Golf	2,780
Daewoo Lanos	2,729
Renault Clio	2,494

Source: "The Israeli Car Market." Retrieved October 23, 2000 from the World Wide Web: http://www.just-auto.com.

★ 983 ★
Autos
SIC: 3711–ISIC: 3410–HC: 87

Best-Selling Cars in Japan, 1999

The table show unit sales.

Suzuki Wagon R	249,376
Toyota Yaris range	225,013
Toyota Corolla/Sprinter	186,384
Daihatsu Move	178,877
Honda Life	176,943
Nissan Cube/March	142,226
Mitsubishi Minica/Toppo	121,669
Nissan Sunny range	113,723
Toyota Ipsum range	113,048
Toyota Mark II range	110,198

Source: *The Economist*, June 24, 2000, p. 68, from Automotive Industry Data.

★ 984 ★
Autos
SIC: 3711–ISIC: 3410–HC: 87

Best-Selling Cars in Western Europe, 1999

The car industry has been consolidating since the DaimlerChrysler merger in 1998. Just six companies produce 75% of the 44 million vehicles expected to be sold this year. The table shows the best sellers in Western Europe.

VW Golf/Bora/Vento	795,835
Opel Astra/Zafira	770,003
Renault Megane	598,434
Ford Focus/Escort	585,676
Renault Clio	496,733
Opel Corsa	459,510
Peugeot 206/205	457,521
Fiat Punto	445,535
VW Polo	349,579
VW Passat	322,493

Source: *The Economist*, June 24, 2000, p. 68, from Automotive Industry Data.

★ 985 ★
Autos
SIC: 3711–ISIC: 3410–HC: 87

Company Car Market in Germany

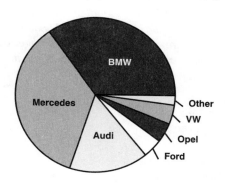

Market shares are shown in percent.

BMW	35.0%
Mercedes	35.0
Audi	16.0
Ford	4.0
Opel	4.0
VW	4.0
Other	2.0

Source: *Frankfurter Allgemeine*, March 13, 2000, p. 1, from Hay Management Consultants GmbH.

★ 986 ★
Autos
SIC: 3711–ISIC: 3410–HC: 87

Electric Vehicle Market

Global sales were estimated at more than 1 million units, valued at $24 billion in 1997. Most are battery powered, but some are hybrid and fuel cells.

Peugeot	5.4%
Fiat	5.2
General Motors	2.5
Ford	1.3
Honda	0.8
Toyota	0.8
Other	84.0

Source: *Business Economics*, October 2000, p. 6, from Freedonia Group.

★ 987 ★
Autos
SIC: 3711–ISIC: 3410–HC: 87

Global Car Sales by Segment

Data cover 94.3% of the global auto market: Western Europe, Canada, United States, Mexico, Japan and 24 other nations. They are for passenger car registrations, except for Canada, United States and Mexico, where light trucks are included.

Lower medium	21.2%
Medium	15.8
Small	13.7
Upper medium	11.4
Sport utility	10.1
Mini	6.8
Pickups	5.4
Sport	2.3
Luxury	2.2
Other	5.6

Source: *Wall Street Journal*, October 4, 2000, p. A23, from Marketing Systems and Automotive Quarterly Review.

★ 988 ★
Autos
SIC: 3711–ISIC: 3410–HC: 87

Largest Light Vehicle Markets in Europe, 2000

Data exclude most commercial vehicles.

Germany	3,382,482
Italy	2,415,600
United Kingdom	2,221,670
France	2,133,884
Spain	1,381,239
Netherlands	597,638
Belgium	515,204
Switzerland	316,435
Austria	309,929
Sweden	290,224

Source: *Automotive News*, January 22, 2001, p. 48.

★ 989 ★
Autos
SIC: 3711–ISIC: 3410–HC: 87

Leading Pickups in Thailand

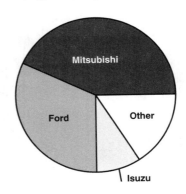

Market shares are shown in percent.

Mitsubishi	43.0%
Ford	32.0
Isuzu	9.0
Other	16.0

Source: *Nation*, September 27, 2000, p. NA.

★ 990 ★
Autos
SIC: 3711–ISIC: 3410–HC: 87

Light Vehicle Market in the Czech Republic

Skoda
Ford
Volkswagen
Other

Market shares are shown in percent.

Skoda	19.17%
Ford	16.92
Volkswagen	15.00
Other	48.91

Source: "Posititve Trends in the Czech Automotive Industry." Retrieved April 3, 2001 from the World Wide Web: http://www.usatrade.gov.

★ 991 ★
Autos
SIC: 3711–ISIC: 3410–HC: 87

Light Vehicle Sales in Eastern Europe, 2000

Market shares are shown in percent.

Volkswagen group	23.7%
Fiat group	14.8
Daewoo group	12.7
Renault group	11.3
PSA group	8.1
General Motors	7.6
Ford	4.3
Hyundai	4.0
Suzuki	3.0
Toyota group	2.8
Other	7.7

Source: *Financial Times*, February 28, 2001, p. 6.

★ 992 ★
Autos
SIC: 3711–ISIC: 3410–HC: 87

New Car Sales in New Zealand, 2000

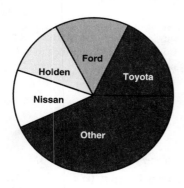

Shares are for the first three months of the year.

Toyota	18.0%
Ford	14.6
Holden	12.2
Nissan	12.0
Other	43.2

Source: *New Zealand Herald*, April 19, 2000, p. 1.

★ 993 ★
Autos
SIC: 3711–ISIC: 3410–HC: 87

Pickup Truck Market in Zambia

Market shares are shown in percent.

Delta Motor	38.0%
Nissan	23.0
Toyota	18.0
Other	21.0

Source: "Delta Leads The Way." Retrieved December 13, 1999 from the World Wide Web: http://wwww.northernlight.com.

★ 994 ★
Autos
SIC: 3711–ISIC: 3410–HC: 87

Top Auto Firms in Australia

Market shares are shown in percent.

Toyota	20.2%
Holden	19.7
Ford	14.5
Mitsubishi	9.3
Hyundai	5.8
Nissan	5.8
Honda	3.8
Mazda	3.5
Subaru	3.4
Other	14.0

Source: "Down Under Car Market." Retrieved January 9, 2001 from the World Wide Web: http://www.just-auto.com.

★ 995 ★
Autos
SIC: 3711–ISIC: 3410–HC: 87

Top Auto Firms in Austria, 2000

Companies are ranked by passenger car sales.

	Units	Share
VW Group	110,235	31.74%
GM Group	32,252	9.29

Continued on next page.

★ 995 ★
[Continued]
Autos
SIC: 3711–ISIC: 3410–HC: 87
Top Auto Firms in Austria, 2000

Companies are ranked by passenger car sales.

	Units	Share
Ford Group	28,330	8.16%
Peugeot Group	23,537	6.78
DaimlerChrysler	22,316	6.43
Fiat Group	22,214	6.40
Renault	21,787	6.27
Toyota	15,860	4.57
Other	70,761	20.38

Source: *WARD's Automotive International*, February 2001, p. 14.

★ 996 ★
Autos
SIC: 3711–ISIC: 3410–HC: 87
Top Auto Firms in Belgium/ Luxembourg, 2000

Companies are ranked by passenger car sales.

	Units	Share
VW Group	117,476	18.53%
Peugeot Group	111,384	17.57
Renault	71,043	11.21
GM Group	61,062	9.63
Ford Group	60,290	9.51
DaimlerChrysler	40,507	6.39
Fiat Group	38,149	6.02
BMW Group	26,455	4.17
Other	107,490	16.96

Source: *WARD's Automotive International*, February 2001, p. 14.

★ 997 ★
Autos
SIC: 3711–ISIC: 3410–HC: 87
Top Auto Firms in Bulgaria

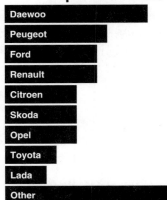

Market shares are shown in percent.

Daewoo	13.8%
Peugeot	10.4
Ford	9.3
Renault	8.7
Citroen	7.3
Skoda	6.9
Opel	6.8
Toyota	4.9
Lada	3.8
Other	28.1

Source: "Overview of the New Car Market." Retrieved March 2, 2001 from the World Wide Web: http://www.factbook.net.

★ 998 ★
Autos
SIC: 3711–ISIC: 3410–HC: 87
Top Auto Firms in Chile, 2005

Data show estimated production.

	Units	Share
Subaru	55,000	29.81%
Nissan	20,000	10.84
GM	17,000	9.21
Toyota	16,000	8.67
Hyundai	11,000	5.96
Daewoo	8,000	4.34
Franco Chilena	8,000	4.34

Continued on next page.

★ **998** ★

[Continued]

Autos

SIC: 3711–ISIC: 3410–HC: 87

Top Auto Firms in Chile, 2005

Data show estimated production.

	Units	Share
Volkswagen	6,000	3.25%
Other	43,500	23.58

Source: *Automotive Engineering International*, May 1999, p. 89.

★ **999** ★

Autos

SIC: 3711–ISIC: 3410–HC: 87

Top Auto Firms in China, 1999

Shares are shown based on 586,517 units.

SVW	39.3%
Tianjin Charade	18.0
FAW-VW Jetta	13.1
Changan Suzuki	8.6
Shenlong Citroen Fukang	7.7
Shanghai GM Buick	3.4
FAW-VW Audi	1.2
Others	8.7

Source: *Financial Times*, September 4, 2000, p. 17, from Chinese Sedan Market Association.

★ **1000** ★

Autos

SIC: 3711–ISIC: 3410–HC: 87

Top Auto Firms in France, 1999

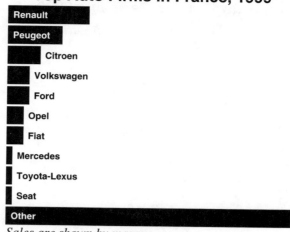

Sales are shown by marque.

	Sales	Share
Renault	602,530	14.88%
Peugeot	390,031	9.63
Citroen	235,339	5.81
Volkswagen	158,347	3.91
Ford	148,707	3.67
Opel	140,945	3.48
Fiat	103,976	2.57
Mercedes	40,918	1.01
Toyota-Lexus	40,889	1.01
Seat	38,249	0.94
Other	2,148,423	53.07

Source: "A Review of the French Passsenger Car Market." Retrieved July 28, 2000 from the World Wide Web: http://www.just-auto.com, from CCFA.

★ **1001** ★

Autos

SIC: 3711–ISIC: 3410–HC: 87

Top Auto Firms in Germany, 2000

Companies are ranked by passenger car sales.

	Units	Share
VW Group	1,061,140	28.69%
DaimlerChrysler	573,636	15.51
GM Group	428,194	11.58

Continued on next page.

★ 1001 ★
[Continued]
Autos
SIC: 3711–ISIC: 3410–HC: 87

Top Auto Firms in Germany, 2000

Companies are ranked by passenger car sales.

	Units	Share
Ford Group	317,847	8.59%
BMW Group	253,420	6.85
Renault	221,427	5.99
Fiat Group	175,328	4.74
Peugeot Group	162,124	4.38
Other	505,330	13.66

Source: *WARD's Automotive International*, February 2001, p. 14.

★ 1002 ★
Autos
SIC: 3711–ISIC: 3410–HC: 87

Top Auto Firms in Greece, 1999

The auto industry here is mainly an import and distribution business. For many years passenger cars were a source of income for the State and were heavily taxed. This situation has now changed greatly. Several auto makers have attempted to start autofacilities here, but the results have been discouraging. Shares are shown by manufacturer for the first nine months of the year.

Suzuki	10.5%
Opel	9.1
Hyundai	8.4
Fiat	7.9
Citroen	7.8
Volkswagen	7.1
Nissan	6.5
Peugeot	5.2
Renault	4.9
Other	32.6

Source: *National Trade Data Bank*, October 1999, p. 1, from Asssociation of Motor Vehicle Importers-Representatives.

★ 1003 ★
Autos
SIC: 3711–ISIC: 3410–HC: 87

Top Auto Firms in India

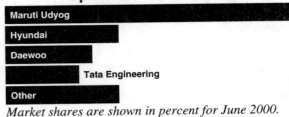

Market shares are shown in percent for June 2000.

Maruti Udyog	43.0%
Hyundai	16.6
Daewoo	12.7
Tata Engineering	11.1
Other	16.6

Source: *Financial Times*, February 23, 2001, p. 20, from Businessworld and Society of Indian Automobile Manufacturers.

★ 1004 ★
Autos
SIC: 3711–ISIC: 3410–HC: 87

Top Auto Firms in Ireland, 2000

Companies are ranked by passenger car sales.

	Units	Share
VW Group	42,433	15.33%
Ford Group	36,371	13.14
Toyota	31,103	11.24
GM Group	23,296	8.42
Fiat Group	22,526	8.14
Peugeot Group	21,113	7.63
Renault	16,801	6.07
BMW	7,347	2.65
Other	75,738	27.37

Source: *WARD's Automotive International*, February 2001, p. 14.

★ 1005 ★
Autos
SIC: 3711–ISIC: 3410–HC: 87

Top Auto Firms in Italy, 2000

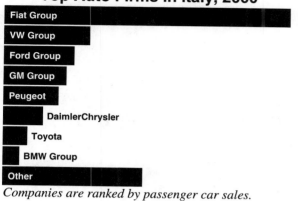

Companies are ranked by passenger car sales.

	Units	Share
Fiat Group	979,586	36.92%
VW Group	291,942	11.00
Ford Group	226,755	8.55
GM Group	214,638	8.09
Peugeot	192,365	7.25
DaimlerChrysler	121,311	4.57
Toyota	88,676	3.34
BMW Group	63,780	2.40
Other	473,875	17.86

Source: *WARD's Automotive International*, February 2001, p. 14.

★ 1006 ★
Autos
SIC: 3711–ISIC: 3410–HC: 87

Top Auto Firms in Japan, 1999

Market shares are shown in percent.

Toyota	38.0%
GM	18.0
Nissan	14.0
Honda	12.0
Mitsubishi	10.0
Ford	5.5
Other	2.5

Source: *Wall Street Journal*, January 26, 2000, p. A17, from Japan Automobile Manufacturers Association.

★ 1007 ★
Autos
SIC: 3711–ISIC: 3410–HC: 87

Top Auto Firms in the Netherlands, 2000

Companies are ranked by passenger car sales.

	Units	Share
VW Group	132,663	18.64%
GM Group	86,953	12.22
Peugeot Group	79,415	11.16
Ford Group	79,085	11.11
Renault	60,625	8.52
DaimlerChrysler	43,435	6.10
Fiat Group	42,875	6.03
Toyota	33,587	4.72
Other	152,927	21.49

Source: *WARD's Automotive International*, February 2001, p. 14.

★ 1008 ★
Autos
SIC: 3711–ISIC: 3410–HC: 87

Top Auto Firms in the Slovak Republic, 1998

The market is rather uncertain. There was a noticeable jump in new car sales in 1998, but this was because a change in import law affected the importing of used vehicles. Most cars on the road in this country are roughly 10 years old. Market shares are shown in percent.

Skoda	42.26%
Daewoo	12.32
VW	6.74
Opel	5.41
Fiat	5.19
Seat	3.67
Renault	3.63
Citroen	2.87
Peugeot	2.68
Mazda	2.17
Other	13.06

Source: "Commercial Vehicles." Retrieved November 6, 2000 from the World Wide Web: http://www.tradeport.org.

★ 1009 ★
Autos
SIC: 3711–ISIC: 3410–HC: 87

Top Auto Firms in the U.K., 2000

Companies are ranked by passenger car sales.

	Units	Share
Ford Group	540,774	21.46%
GM Group	339,199	13.46
Peugeot Group	305,140	12.11
VW Group	265,775	10.55
Renault	177,188	7.03
BMW Group	171,339	6.80
Fiat Group	126,636	5.03
DaimlerChrysler	108,449	4.30
Other	485,248	19.26

Source: *WARD's Automotive International*, February 2001, p. 14.

★ 1010 ★
Autos
SIC: 3711–ISIC: 3410–HC: 87

Top Auto Firms in Western Europe

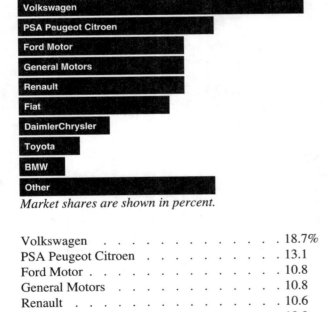

Market shares are shown in percent.

Volkswagen	18.7%
PSA Peugeot Citroen	13.1
Ford Motor	10.8
General Motors	10.8
Renault	10.6
Fiat	10.0
DaimlerChrysler	6.2
Toyota	3.7

BMW	3.4%
Other	12.7

Source: *Business Week*, February 19, 2001, p. 53, from European Car Makers Association.

★ 1011 ★
Autos
SIC: 3711–ISIC: 3410–HC: 87

Top Auto Firms Worldwide, 1999

Market shares are shown in percent.

General Motors	24.7%
Ford	13.2
Toyota	9.8
Volkswagen	9.1
DaimlerChrysler	8.6
Renault/Nissan	8.4
Other	26.2

Source: *Wall Street Journal*, March 14, 2000, p. A3, from Standard & Poor's DRI Global Automotive Group.

★ 1012 ★
Autos
SIC: 3711–ISIC: 3410–HC: 87

Top Automakers Worldwide, 1999

Sales are shown in millions of units.

General Motors	8.7
Ford Motor Co.	7.1
Toyota Motor Corp.	5.3
Renault SA	4.9
DaimlerChrysler	4.8
Volkswagen	4.8
Hyundai Motor Co.	2.6
Fiat Auto S.p.A.	2.5
PSA Peugeot Citroen	2.5
Honda Motor Co.	2.3

Source: *Automotive News Market Data Book Supplement*, May 2000, p. 14.

★ 1013 ★
Autos
SIC: 3711–ISIC: 3410–HC: 87

Top Vehicle Producers in Poland, 2000

Market shares are shown in percent.

Fiat	27.9%
Daewoo	23.0
GM-Opel	8.3
Skoda	7.3
Others	33.5

Source: *Financial Review*, November 6, 2000, p. 28, from Samar.

★ 1014 ★
Autos
SIC: 3711–ISIC: 3410–HC: 87

Vehicle Market Shares in the Philippines, 1998

Market shares are shown in percent.

Mitsubishi	24.0%
Toyota	21.2
Honda	16.5
Isuzu	7.9
Nissan	7.5
Columbian Motor Corp.	7.0
Others	15.0

Source: *Financial Times*, May 27, 1999, p. 4, from Chamber of Automobile Manufacturers of the Philippines.

★ 1015 ★
Autos
SIC: 3711–ISIC: 3410–HC: 87

Vehicle Sales in Brazil

Shares are for August 2000.

Volkswagen	27.5%
General Motors	24.3
Fiat	23.1
Ford	8.3
Other	16.8

Source: *Financial Times*, November 3, 2000, p. 21, from Adefa, Anfavea, Association of National Automobile Manufacturers, and Morgan Stanley Dean Witter.

★ 1016 ★
Trucks
SIC: 3713–ISIC: 3420–HC: 87

Largest Truck Makers

Production is for vehicles 6VW.

	2000	2003	Share
DaimlerChrysler	253,749	253,798	22.58%
Dongfeng	110,694	150,466	13.39
Navistar	137,368	140,979	12.54
Volvo-Scania	127,762	133,393	11.87
FAW	90,872	125,401	11.16
Isuzu	73,000	102,500	9.12
Paccar	95,545	95,142	8.46
RVI	68,841	65,428	5.82
Iveco	55,409	56,917	5.06

Source: *Financial Times*, December 3, 1999, p. 3, from industry sources and Economist Intelligence Unit.

★ 1017 ★
Trucks
SIC: 3713–ISIC: 3420–HC: 87

Top Heavy Truck Makers in Sweden

Market shares are shown in percent.

Scania	50.5%
Volvo	42.5
Other	7.0

Source: "Swedish Truck Market." Retrieved February 20, 2001 from the World Wide Web: http://ww.usatrade.gov.

★ 1018 ★
Trucks
SIC: 3713–ISIC: 3420–HC: 87

Top Truck Makers in Brazil

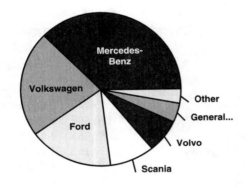

Market shares are shown in percent.

Mercedes-Benz	37.1%
Volkswagen	22.2
Ford	17.2
Scania	9.2
Volvo	6.7
General Motors	4.3
Other	3.3

Source: "Sales of Trucks Increased 27%." Retrieved January 26, 2001 from the World Wide Web: http://www.comtexnews.com.

★ 1019 ★
Trucks
SIC: 3713–ISIC: 3420–HC: 87

Top Truck Makers in Europe

Shares are shown based on 231,300 units (trucks 16 tons and greater).

Mercedes	20.8%
Volvo	15.1
Scania	14.8
MAN	13.5
Renault	12.2
Iveco	11.0
Daf	9.9
Other	2.7

Source: *Financial Times*, April 26, 2000, p. 17, from Primark Datastream.

★ 1020 ★
Trucks
SIC: 3713–ISIC: 3420–HC: 87

Top Truck Makers in Switzerland

Market shares are shown in percent.

	Units	Share
Mercedes	4,134	18.86%
VW	2,302	10.50
Toyota	2,071	9.45
Fiat	1,834	8.37
Iveco	1,816	8.29
Renault	1,246	5.69
Mitsubishi	926	4.23
Mazda	925	4.22
Ford	878	4.01
Other	5,785	26.40

Source: "Truck Market." Retrieved February 1, 2001 from the World Wide Web: http://www.usatrade.gov, from Swiss Association of Automobile Importers.

★ 1021 ★
Trucks
SIC: 3713–ISIC: 3420–HC: 87

Truck Sales by Region, 2004

Distribution is estimated.

NAFTA	28.0%
China	19.0
Western Europe	18.0
Japan	8.0
South America	6.0
India	5.0
CIS	4.0
Other	12.0

Source: *Wall Street Journal*, September 19, 2000, p. A21, from Commerzbank Global Equities.

★ 1022 ★
Auto Parts
SIC: 3714–ISIC: 3430–HC: 87

Anti-Vibration Component Sales

Sales are estimated in millions of dollars on a pro forma basis.

Trelleborg/BTR AVS	$ 800
Tokai Rubber	550
Delphi	350
CF Gomma + PSA/Rennes	300
Cooper/Standard Products	300
Hutchinson	300
Tenneco/Clevite	250

Source: *Rubber & Plastics News*, January 3, 2000, p. 1.

★ 1023 ★
Auto Parts
SIC: 3714–ISIC: 3430–HC: 87

Auto Battery Market in the U.K., 1999

Market shares are estimated based on value.

Exide	39.0%
Tungstone	13.3
Varta Bosch	11.3
Lucas Yausa	10.3
Deta	3.5
Willard	3.0
Other	19.6

Source: "Replacement Car Tires." Retrieved January 12, 2001 from the World Wide Web: http://www.clearlybusiness.com, from Datamonitor.

★ 1024 ★
Auto Parts
SIC: 3714–ISIC: 3430–HC: 87

Automotive Supercharger Market

Market shares are shown in percent.

BorgWarner Inc.	95.0%
Other	5.0

Source: *Automotive News*, August 21, 2000, p. 4.

★ 1025 ★
Auto Parts
SIC: 3714–ISIC: 3430–HC: 87

Car Brake Industry in the U.K., 1998

Market shares are estimated based on value.

Ferodo	39.0%
Mintex	21.0
AP	16.0
Lucas	10.0
Other	14.0

Source: "UK Car Brakes." Retrieved January 11, 2001 from the World Wide Web: http://www.clearlybusiness.com, from Datamonitor.

★ 1026 ★
Auto Parts
SIC: 3714–ISIC: 3430–HC: 87

Instrument Panel Market in Europe

Market shares are shown in percent.

Sommer Allibert	18.4%
Plastic Omnium	12.6
Peguform	9.8
Faurecia	9.0
Magna	7.4
Johnson Controls	6.2
Visteon	5.8
Complasud	3.5
Other	13.1

Source: *WARD's Auto World*, April 1999, p. 53, from Faurecia.

★ 1027 ★
Auto Parts
SIC: 3714–ISIC: 3430–HC: 87

Top Auto Parts Firms, 1999

Companies are ranked by sales in millions of dollars.

Delphi Automotive Systems	$ 27,259
Visteon Corp.	18,481
Robert Bosch GmbH	15,643
Denso Corp.	12,575
Lear Corp.	12,429
Johnson Controls	11,100
TRW Inc.	11,000
Dana Corp.	10,133
Magna International Inc.	9,000
Valeo SA	7,719

Source: *Automotive News*, June 19, 2000, p. 42.

★ 1028 ★
Auto Parts
SIC: 3714–ISIC: 3430–HC: 87

Top Auto Parts Firms, 2000

Firms are ranked by revenue in billions of dollars.

Delphi	$ 29.1
Bosch	20.9
Visteon	19.5
Johnson	17.2
Denso	15.8
Lear	14.1
Dana	12.2
TRW	11.0
Magna	9.8
Valeo	8.6

Source: *Financial Times*, April 10, 2001, p. 18.

★ 1029 ★
Auto Parts
SIC: 3714–ISIC: 3430–HC: 87

Top Auto Seating Makers

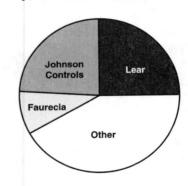

Market shares are shown in percent.

Lear	25.0%
Johnson Controls	24.0
Faurecia	9.0
Other	42.0

Source: *Urethanes Technology*, August 2000, p. 52, from Economist Intelligence Unit.

★ 1030 ★
Auto Parts
SIC: 3714–ISIC: 3430–HC: 87

Top Auto Seating Makers in Western Europe

Market shares are shown in percent.

OEM inhouse 28.0%
Fauceria 23.0
Johnson Controls 23.0
Lear 22.0
Other 4.0

Source: *Urethanes Technology*, August 2000, p. 52, from Economist Intelligence Unit.

★ 1031 ★
Telematic Equipment
SIC: 3714–ISIC: 3430–HC: 87

Vehicle Telematic Equipment Sales in Europe

Annual revenues from telematics equipment sales will be over $2.6 billion by 2006. Sales are for the top 14 markets.

	2001	2002	2003
OEM	$ 0.46	$ 1.03	$ 1.88
Aftermarket	0.31	0.52	0.78

Source: ''European Vehicle Telematics Equipment.'' Retrieved April 10, 2001 from the World Wide Web: http://www.prnewswire.com, from Strategis Group.

★ 1032 ★
Aircraft
SIC: 3721–ISIC: 3530–HC: 88

Aircraft Market by Segment

Market shares are shown in percent.

Large regional jets and single-aisle 55.0%
Intermediate size twin-aisle 21.0
Small regional jet 19.0
747s and larger 5.0

Source: *Bangkok Post*, September 26, 2000, p. 12.

★ 1033 ★
Aircraft
SIC: 3721–ISIC: 3530–HC: 88

Business Jet Market, 2000-2009

6,437 business jets worth $78.3 billion are to be shipped over the next ten years.

	($ bil.)	Share
Bombardier	20.50	26.2%
Gulfstream	16.20	20.7
Cessna	13.53	17.3
Dassault	13.38	17.1
Raytheon	10.12	12.9

Source: *Interavia*, October 2000, p. S6, from Teal Group.

★ 1034 ★
Aircraft
SIC: 3721–ISIC: 3530–HC: 88

Commercial Aircraft Market in Japan

Japan has the third largest commercial air market after United States and Canada.

Boeing 67.0%
McDonnell Douglas 17.0
Airbus 16.0

Source: *Business Week*, April 2, 2001, p. 81, from company reports.

★ 1035 ★
Aircraft
SIC: 3721–ISIC: 3530–HC: 88

Regional Small Jet Market

Market shares are shown in percent.

	Orders	Share
Boeing	2,757	40.40%
Airbus	2,046	29.98
Embraer	898	13.16
Bombardier	796	11.66
Other	327	4.79

Source: *New York Times*, December 31, 2000, p. 11.

★ 1036 ★
Helicopters
SIC: 3721–ISIC: 3530–HC: 88

Top Helicopter Makers Worldwide

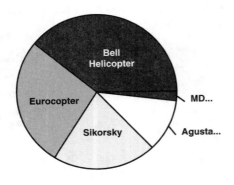

Market shares are shown in percent.

Bell Helicopter 39.0%
Eurocopter 27.0
Sikorsky 21.0
Agusta Westland 11.0
MD Helicopters 2.0
Source: *Helicopter News*, January 25, 2001, p. NA.

★ 1037 ★
Aircraft Parts
SIC: 3724–ISIC: 3530–HC: 88

Aircraft Brake Market

Shares are for the business aircraft segment.

Hydro-Aire 70.0%
Others 30.0
Source: *Aviation Week & Space Technology*, October 11, 1999, p. 60, from Crane Aerospace.

★ 1038 ★
Aircraft Parts
SIC: 3724–ISIC: 3530–HC: 88

Ejector Seat Market Worldwide

The market refers to the United States, Western Europe, the Far East and the Middle East.

Martin-Baker Aircraft Company 75.0%
Other 25.0
Source: *Financial Times*, April 23, 2001, p. 7.

★ 1039 ★
Aircraft Parts
SIC: 3724–ISIC: 3530–HC: 88

Landing Gear Market

The market is estimated at $900-1,100 million.

Messier Dowty 40.0%
BF Goodrich 25.0
Menasco 25.0
Others 10.0
Source: *Interavia*, May 1999, p. 35.

★ 1040 ★
Aircraft Parts
SIC: 3724–ISIC: 3530–HC: 88

Wheels and Brakes Market

The market is estimated at $900 million.

AlliedSignal 43.0%
BFGoodrich 29.0
ABSC 16.0
Messier Bugatti 9.0
Dunlop 3.0
Source: *Interavia*, May 1999, p. 35.

★ 1041 ★
Jet Engines
SIC: 3724–ISIC: 3530–HC: 88

777 Jet Engine Market

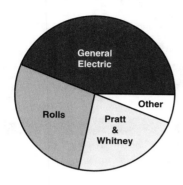

AN estimated 845 are expected to be sold through 2009.

General Electric	44.0%
Rolls	28.0
Pratt & Whitney	22.0
Other	6.0

Source: *Aviation Week & Space Technology*, March 13, 2000, p. 39, from Teal Group.

★ 1042 ★
Jet Engines
SIC: 3724–ISIC: 3530–HC: 88

Global Jet Engine Market, 1998

Market shares are shown in percent.

General Electric	54.0%
International Aero Engines	18.8
Rolls-Royce	12.4
Pratt & Whitney	8.5
BMW-Rolls Royce	4.6
AlliedSignal	1.7

Source: *Business Week*, August 9, 1999, p. 72, from Boeing Co.

★ 1043 ★
Defense Equipment
SIC: 3728–ISIC: 3530–HC: 88

Flight Surveillance Equipment Market

Market shares are shown in percent.

Aerodata GmbH	70.0%
Other	30.0

Source: "Aerodata GmbH Microelectronics." Retrieved Janaury 11, 2001 from the World Wide Web: http://www.aerodata.de.

★ 1044 ★
Boats
SIC: 3731–ISIC: 3511–HC: 89

Germany's Water Sports Industry

Used boats	21.0%
Fuel	14.0
New boats	12.0
Repair and services	11.0
Equipment and accessories	10.0
Charters	8.0
Insurance services	8.0
Marinas	8.0
Rubber dinghies	2.0
Other	8.0

Source: *Wirtschaftswoche*, June 29, 2000, p. 114, from Bundesverband Wassersportwirtschaft.

★ 1045 ★
Oil Platform Converting
SIC: 3731–ISIC: 3511–HC: 89

FPSO Terminal Market

The Floating, Production, Storage & Offloading (FPSO) terminal market is the largest market sector in which the world's specialized repair yards find conversion contracts, according to the source. There are currently 61 in operation, listed in the table below.

	No.	Share
North Sea	18	34.62%
West Africa	9	17.31
South America	7	13.46
Southeast Asia	6	11.54

Continued on next page.

★ 1045 ★
[Continued]
Oil Platform Converting
SIC: 3731–ISIC: 3511–HC: 89

FPSO Terminal Market

The Floating, Production, Storage & Offloading (FPSO) terminal market is the largest market sector in which the world's specialized repair yards find conversion contracts, according to the source. There are currently 61 in operation, listed in the table below.

	No.	Share
Australia	5	9.62%
Indonesia	3	5.77
Mediterranean	3	5.77
New Zealand	1	1.92

Source: *Marine Log*, April 2001, p. 15.

★ 1046 ★
Ship Building
SIC: 3731–ISIC: 3511–HC: 89

Leading Shipyards in China

Firms are ranked by revenue in millions of yen.

Hudong Shipbuilding Group	277.0
Jiangnan Shipbuilding Group Co. Ltd.	228.2
Dalian Shipyard	200.6
Guangzhou Shipyard International Co. Ltd.	190.9
Dalian New Shipyard	108.9
Jiangyang Shipbuilding Group	77.3
Zhonghua Shipyard	50.8
Wuchang Shipyard	50.7
Shanghai Shipyard	45.1
Bohai Shipyard	35.6

Source: "Shipbuilding Industry." Retrieved January 3, 2001 from the World Wide Web: http://www.usatrade.gov.

★ 1047 ★
Ship Building
SIC: 3731–ISIC: 3511–HC: 89

Top Shipbuilding Makers in Japan, 1999

Market shares are shown based on 11.07 million tons in gross tonnage of ships built.

Mitsubishi Heavy Industries Ltd.	12.6%
Ishikawajima Harima Industries Co.	9.6
Hitachi Zosen Corp.	6.8
Mitsui Engineering & Shipbuilding Co.	6.6
NKK Corp.	6.2
Other	58.2

Source: *Nikkei Weekly*, August 14, 2000, p. 8, from Nihon Keizai Shimbun.

★ 1048 ★
Ship Building
SIC: 3732–ISIC: 3511–HC: 89

Leading Shipbuilding Nations, 1999

Countries are ranked by order book, gross tonnage in millions.

	(mil.)	Share
South Korea	18.95	35.85%
Japan	17.44	32.99
China	2.81	5.32
Italy	2.11	3.99
Germany	1.84	3.48
Poland	1.11	2.10
Taiwan	1.05	1.99
Spain	1.03	1.95
Other	6.52	12.33

Source: *Financial Times*, November 5, 1999, p. 3, from World Shipbuilding Statistics and Lloyd's Register.

★ 1049 ★
Motorcycles
SIC: 3751–ISIC: 3591–HC: 87

Leading Motorcycle Makers in Australia

Firms are ranked by registrations at the end of 1997.

	Units	Share
Honda	89,088	28.45%
Yamaha	65,388	20.88
Suzuki	45,354	14.49
Kawasaki	43,237	13.81
Harley Davidson	31,091	9.93
BMW	13,174	4.21
Ducati	6,426	2.05
Triumph	5,997	1.92
Other	13,346	4.26

Source: "All Terrain Vehicles." Retrieved November 6, 2000 from the World Wide Web: http://www.usatrade.gov, from Australian Bureau of Statistics.

★ 1050 ★
Motorcycles
SIC: 3751–ISIC: 3591–HC: 87

Motorcycle Market in ASEAN Countries

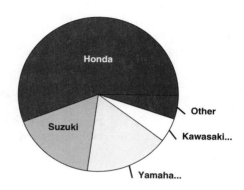

For the first seven months of the year, sales in Indonesia, Malaysia, the Philippines and Thailand climbed to 1,158,8888 units.

Honda	56.4%
Suzuki	16.8
Yamaha Motor Co.	16.6
Kawasaki Heavy Industries Ltd.	5.0
Other	5.2

Source: "Motorbike Sales in 4 ASEAN Countries up 54.3%" Retrieved October 26, 2000 from the World Wide Web: http://www.office.com, from Asian Economic News.

★ 1051 ★
Motorcycles
SIC: 3751–ISIC: 3591–HC: 87

Motorcycle Market in Europe, 1998

Shares are for 500 cc engines and larger. Data are for the first six months, annualized.

Honda	24.1%
Yamaha	22.5
Suzuki	19.1
Kawasaki	10.5

Continued on next page.

★ 1051 ★
[Continued]
Motorcycles
SIC: 3751–ISIC: 3591–HC: 87

Motorcycle Market in Europe, 1998

Shares are for 500 cc engines and larger. Data are for the first six months, annualized.

BMW	9.4%
Ducati	4.1
Harley-Davidson	3.9
Other	6.4

Source: *New York Times*, May 15, 1999, p. B1, from European Motorcycle Manufacturers Association and Motorcycle Industry Council.

★ 1052 ★
Motorcycles
SIC: 3751–ISIC: 3591–HC: 87

Top Motorcycle Firms in Switzerland

Unit sales are shown by manufacturer.

Yamaha	8,536
Honda	7,625
Piaggio	4,653
Aprilia	2,915
Suzuki	2,374
Peugeot	2,214
MBK (French sub. Of Yamaha)	2,211
Kawasaki	1,401
BMW	1,297
Malaguti	1,200

Source: *Dealernews*, August 1999, p. 42.

★ 1053 ★
Motorcycles
SIC: 3751–ISIC: 3591–HC: 87

Top Motorcycle Makers in Indonesia, 2000

Sales are for the first 11 months.

	Units	Share
Honda	433,054	54.78%
Yamaha	175,158	22.16
Suzuki	149,229	18.88
Kawasaki	28,138	3.56
Vespa	539	0.07
Other	4,345	0.55

Source: *Asiapulse News*, January 26, 2001, p. 0764.

★ 1054 ★
Motorcycles
SIC: 3751–ISIC: 3591–HC: 87

Top Motorcycle Producers in Germany

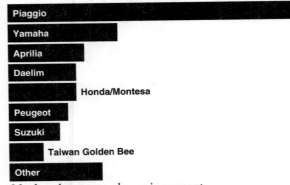

Market shares are shown in percent.

Piaggio	34.0%
Yamaha	13.0
Aprilia	9.0
Daelim	8.0
Honda/Montesa	8.0
Peugeot	7.0
Suzuki	6.0
Taiwan Golden Bee	4.0
Other	11.0

Source: *Wirtschaftswoche*, May 25, 2000, p. 130, from VFM.

★ 1055 ★
Scooters
SIC: 3751–ISIC: 3591–HC: 87

Scooter Market in India, 1999

Shares are for April - December of the year.

Bajaj Auto 56.91%
LML 23.49
TVS-Suzuki 10.15
Kinetic Honda 9.45

Source: *Business Today*, March 22, 2000, p. 55.

★ 1056 ★
Bicycle Locks
SIC: 3751–ISIC: 3592–HC: 87

Bicycle Lock Market in Korea

Market shares are shown in percent.

Jenix Co. Ltd. 60.0%
Other 40.0

Source: Retrieved March 30, 2001 from the World Wide
Web: http://expo.tpage.com/jenix.

★ 1057 ★
Bicycles
SIC: 3751–ISIC: 3592–HC: 87

Bicycle Sales in Germany

The market has been in turnaround lately. Sales are mostly in specialized stores because of the aftermarket services they offer.

Trekking bikes 23.0%
City bikes 22.0
All terrain bikes 19.0
Mountain bikes 18.0
Kid's bikes 6.0
Youth bikes 6.0
Other 27.0

Source: *Wirtschaftswoche*, March 30, 2000, p. 141.

★ 1058 ★
Bicycles
SIC: 3751–ISIC: 3592–HC: 87

Leading Bicycle Producers, 1998

Data for selected countries are in millions.

China 23.10
India 10.50
Taiwan 10.10
Japan 5.72
Germany 3.00
France 2.90
Italy 2.90
Indonesia 2.80
United States 2.50

Source: Retrieved March 1, 2001 from the World Wide
Web: http://www.bicycleretailer.news.com.

★ 1059 ★
Bicycles
SIC: 3751–ISIC: 3592–HC: 87

Top Mountain Bike Makers in Japan, 1997

Market shares are shown based on shipments.

Bridgestone Cycle	12.6%
Deki Tekkosho	10.6
Hodaka	8.0
National Bicycle Industry	5.2
Saimoto Jitensha	5.0
Ebisu Jitensha	4.8
Miyata Industry	4.8
Yokota Cycle	4.8
Other	44.2

Source: "DVL Market Share Library." Retrieved April 3, 2001 from the World Wide Web: http://dvl/daiwa.co.jp, from DVL Market Share Library and Marketing Data Bank.

★ 1060 ★
Aerospace
SIC: 3761–ISIC: 3530–HC: 88

Aerospace Industry in Europe, 1999

The 65 billion euro industry is undergoing serious consolidation. Fragmented national companies are being folded into larger ones that can challenge the presence of larger U.S. companies. Space activities have been folded into Astrium, and Augusta and Westland are on the verge of combining their helicopter business.

Aircraft final products	41.0%
Aircraft maintenance	24.2
Aircraft engines	13.9
Aircraft equipment	7.4
Space	6.5
Aerostructures	3.9
Missiles	3.0

Source: *Aviation Week & Space Technology*, July 24, 2000, p. 100.

★ 1061 ★
Aerospace
SIC: 3761–ISIC: 3530–HC: 88

Commercial Launch Market, 1998

Market shares are shown in percent.

Arianespace	29.0%
Boeing	20.0
ILS/Krunichev	18.0
ILS/Lockheed Martin	15.0
Starsem/TsSKB	8.0
China Great Wall	5.0
Other	5.0

Source: *Forbes*, July 5, 1999, p. 142, from C.E. Unterberg.

★ 1062 ★
Travel Trailers
SIC: 3792–ISIC: 3420–HC: 87

Lorry Market in Germany

Market shares are shown in percent. Total registrations were 54,353 units.

Mercedes-Benz	38.34%
MAN	29.53
Scania	9.55
Volvo	8.21
DAF	5.37
Iveco	4.94
Renault	1.92
Other	2.14

Source: *Frankfurter Allgemeine*, January 20, 2001, p. 64.

★ 1063 ★
Tanks
SIC: 3795–ISIC: 2927–HC: 87

Largest Tank Arsenals

United States	7,684
Russia	5,510
Turkey	4,206
Ukraine	4,014

Continued on next page.

★ 1063 ★
[Continued]
Tanks
SIC: 3795–ISIC: 2927–HC: 87

Largest Tank Arsenals

Germany 3,136
Greece 1,735
Poland 1,675
Italy 1,256
France 1,207

Source: *Wall Street Journal*, November 9, 1999, p. A19,
from International Institute for Strategy Studies.

★ 1064 ★
Off-Road Vehicles
SIC: 3799–ISIC: 3410–HC: 87

Off-Road Vehicle Sales in Austria

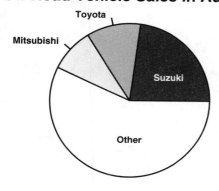

*Sales reached 14,410 units in 1999. Suzuki Grand
Vitara is the best-selling make with 1,896 units.*

	Units	Share
Suzuki	3,254	22.58%
Toyota	1,576	10.94
Mitsubishi	1,327	9.21
Other	8,253	57.27

Source: *Presse*, March 25, 2000, p. 1.

SIC 38 - Instruments and Related Products

★ 1065 ★
Meters
SIC: 3820–ISIC: 3312–HC: 90

Electricity and Water Meter Market in Germany, 1999

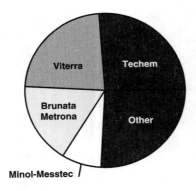

Market shares are shown in percent.

Techem	25.9%
Viterra	23.3
Brunata Metrona	16.9
Minol-Messtec	7.9
Other	26.0

Source: *Frankfurter Allgemeine*, April 19, 2000, p. 1.

★ 1066 ★
Laboratory Instruments
SIC: 3821–ISIC: 3312–HC: 90

Bech-Top Centrifuge Market, 1998

Market shares are estimated. Total sales should reach $381 million by 2000.

Beckman Coulter	28.0%
Kendro	19.0
Eppendorf	16.0
Hettich	9.0
TehrmoQuest	6.0
Other	22.0

Source: *Instrument Business Outlook*, October 15, 1999, p. 1.

★ 1067 ★
Laboratory Instruments
SIC: 3821–ISIC: 3312–HC: 90

Endoscopy Market in Brazil

Market shares are shown in percent. Brazil is the largest market in Latin America.

Karl Storz	36.8%
Smith & Nephew	20.5
Olympus	16.8
Wilson Cook	10.3
Other	15.6

Source: ''Medical Device Market Data.'' Retrieved January 2, 2001 from the World Wide Web: http://www.devicelink.com.

★ 1068 ★
Laboratory Instruments
SIC: 3821–ISIC: 3312–HC: 90

Light-Optical Microscope Market

Market shares are shown in percent.

Carl Zeiss	35.0%
Olympus	32.0
Leica	26.0
Nikon	20.0

Source: *Frankfurter Allgemeine*, September 4, 2000, p. 22.

★ 1069 ★
Process Control Equipment
SIC: 3823–ISIC: 3313–HC: 90

Distributed Control System Industry in India

DCS is the fastest growing segment of the process control instrument market. Market includes field transmitters, converters and valves. Shares are shown in percent.

Tata Honeywell	25.0%
ABB	18.0
Bharath Heavy Electricals	18.0
Yokogawa Blue Star	14.0
Foxboro	10.0
Rosemount	5.0
Siemens	5.0
Others	5.0

Source: "Industrial Process Controls." Retrieved September 19, 2000 from the World Wide Web: http://www.tradeport.org.

★ 1070 ★
Process Control Equipment
SIC: 3823–ISIC: 3313–HC: 90

Frequence Inverter Makers in Brazil

Frequence inverters are part of the main sytems of automation system components.

WEG	22.0%
Rockwell	20.0
Siemens	18.0
ABB	16.0
Yaskawa	10.0
Other	14.0

Source: *South American Business Information*, March 11, 2001, p. NA.

★ 1071 ★
Process Control Equipment
SIC: 3823–ISIC: 3313–HC: 90

Point Level Measurement Industry in the U.K., 1999

Market shares are shown in percent. Point level instruments have the largest share of the level instrument control market.

Endress & Hauser	23.0%
Vega	20.0
Meggit	10.0
Other	47.0

Source: "UK Level Measurement Instruments." Retrieved January 11, 2001 from the World Wide Web: http://www.clearlybusiness.com, from Datamonitor.

★ 1072 ★
Analytical Instruments
SIC: 3826–ISIC: 3312–HC: 90

Top Analytical Instrument Makers, 1999

The total market reached $8.0 billion.

PE Biosystems	7.2%
Thermo Electron	6.6
Agilent Tech	5.7

Continued on next page.

★ 1072 ★
[Continued]
Analytical Instruments
SIC: 3826–ISIC: 3312–HC: 90

Top Analytical Instrument Makers, 1999

The total market reached $8.0 billion.

PerkinElmer	4.6%
Waters	3.9
Shimadzu	3.7
Amersham Pharmacia	3.2
Hitachi	2.8
Other	62.3

Source: *Informations Chimie*, May 1, 2000, p. 1, from *IBO*, publication of SDI.

★ 1073 ★
Optical Instruments
SIC: 3827–ISIC: 3320–HC: 90

External Optical Modulators Market, 1999

The total market was $182 million.

North America	43.0%
Pacific Rim	28.0
Europe	27.0
Other	2.0

Source: *Lasers & Optronics*, October 2000, p. 7, from ElectroniCast.

★ 1074 ★
Sensors
SIC: 3827–ISIC: 3320–HC: 90

Automotive Sensor Market Shares in Europe

The market is being driven by increased vehicle production, higher demand for safety equipment and improved engine management. Market shares are shown in percent.

	1999	2006
Oxygen	18.1%	31.9%
Speed	25.2	20.0
Pressure	10.2	10.6
Position	7.9	10.4
Accelerometers	15.2	9.5
Temperature	7.8	5.5

Source: *Automotive Industries*, December 2000, p. 22, from Frost & Sullivan.

★ 1075 ★
First Aid Products
SIC: 3841–ISIC: 3311–HC: 90

Best-Selling First Aid Brands in the U.K.

Sales are shown in millions of British pounds for the year ended February 1, 2000.

Dettol antiseptic liquid	11.1
Savlon antiseptic cream	7.9
Elastoplast fabric	7.8
TCP antiseptic liquid	5.8

Continued on next page.

★ 1075 ★
[Continued]
First Aid Products
SIC: 3841–ISIC: 3311–HC: 90

Best-Selling First Aid Brands in the U.K.

Sales are shown in millions of British pounds for the year ended February 1, 2000.

Germolene cream	4.6
Elastoplast Airstrip	3.3
Anthisan burn string relief	2.3
Elastoplast dressing	2.1

Source: *Checkout*, April 1, 2000, p. 1, from Information Resources Inc.

★ 1076 ★
First Aid Products
SIC: 3841–ISIC: 3311–HC: 90

Top Emergency Plaster Makers in Japan, 1997

Market shares are shown based on shipments.

Johnson & Johnson	40.4%
Nichiban	5.0
Yutoku Yakuhin	4.6
Kyoritsu Yakuhin Kogyo	4.5
Riba Tape Seiyaku	4.2
Other	41.2

Source: "DVL Market Share Library." Retrieved April 3, 2001 from the World Wide Web: http://dvl/daiwa.co.jp, from DVL Market Share Library and Marketing Data Bank.

★ 1077 ★
Inhalers
SIC: 3841–ISIC: 3311–HC: 90

Asthma Inhaler Market in the U.K.

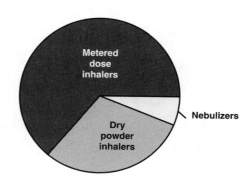

Market shares are shown in percent.

Metered dose inhalers	64.0%
Dry powder inhalers	30.0
Nebulizers	6.0

Source: *The BBI Newsletter*, November 1999, p. 243, from IMS Health.

★ 1078 ★
Medical Instruments
SIC: 3841–ISIC: 3311–HC: 90

Leading Gastroenterology Equipment Makers in France

Market shares are shown in percent.

Olympus	35.0%
Boston Scientific	19.0
Cook	14.0
CR Bard	12.0
Pentax	5.0
Storz	5.0
Other	10.0

Source: *Snapshots Industry Profile*, Annual 2000, p. NA.

★ 1079 ★

Medical Instruments

SIC: 3841–ISIC: 3311–HC: 90

Sleep Breathing Accessory Device Market

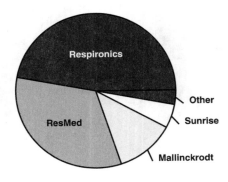

More than 20 million people suffer from sleep apnea. Global shares are shown in percent.

Respironics 47.0%
ResMed 33.0
Mallinckrodt 12.0
Sunrise 5.0
Other 3.0

Source: *Knight-Ridder/Tribune Business News*, November 22, 2000, p. ITEM0032.

★ 1080 ★

Medical Instruments

SIC: 3841–ISIC: 3311–HC: 90

Wound Management Market in the U.K.

Market shares are shown in percent. By 2005, the market should hit 42.3 million British pounds, a 13.9% growth since 2000.

Smith & Nephew 46.0%
ConvaTec 38.5
Beiersdorf 7.3
Other 8.2

Source: "Wound Management." Retrieved February 5, 2001 from the World Wide Web: http://www.clearlybusiness.com.

★ 1081 ★

Medical Supplies

SIC: 3841–ISIC: 3311–HC: 90

Disposable Medical Supply Market in Europe

Market revenue are shown in millions of dollars.

	1999	2002	Share
Infusion and related supplies	$ 7,891	$ 9,460	35.97%
Medical kits and trays . . .	7,793	9,470	36.01
Diagnostic and lab supplies	6,472	7,370	28.02

Source: *Medical & Healthcare Marketplace Guide*, 1999, p. I654.

★ 1082 ★

Medical Supplies

SIC: 3842–ISIC: 3311–HC: 90

Syringe Market Worldwide

Market shares are shown in percent.

Becton Dickinson 85.0%
Other 15.0

Source: *Health Industry Today*, January 2000, p. NA.

★ 1083 ★

Medical Supplies

SIC: 3842–ISIC: 3311–HC: 90

Top Electric Thermometer Makers in Japan, 1997

Market shares are shown based on shipments.

Terumo 48.5%
Omron 37.0
Matsushita Electric Works 4.0
Other 10.5

Source: "DVL Market Share Library." Retrieved April 3, 2001 from the World Wide Web: http://dvl/daiwa.co.jp, from DVL Market Share Library and Marketing Data Bank.

★ 1084 ★
Orthopedic Appliances
SIC: 3842–ISIC: 3311–HC: 90

Artificial Hip Market

The hip joint market was valued at $1.9 billion.

Stryker	23.0%
Johnson & Johnson	21.0
Bristol-Myers	13.0
Sulzer	12.0
Biomet	11.0
Smith & Nephew	6.0
Other	14.0

Source: *Investor's Business Daily*, August 18, 2000, p. A18, from First Union Securities Inc.

★ 1085 ★
Orthopedic Appliances
SIC: 3842–ISIC: 3311–HC: 90

Artificial Knee Market

The knee joint market was valued at $2.2 billion.

Johnson & Johnson	27.0%
Stryker	22.0
Bristol-Myers	20.0
Biomet	11.0
Sulzer	9.0
Smith & Nephew	5.0
Other	6.0

Source: *Investor's Business Daily*, August 18, 2000, p. A18, from First Union Securities Inc.

★ 1086 ★
Orthopedic Appliances
SIC: 3842–ISIC: 3311–HC: 90

Bone Cement Market in Europe, 1998

Market shares are shown based on value.

Biomet/Merck	25.9%
Schering Plough	25.2
J&J/DePuy	18.9
Stryker/Howmedica	15.6
Zimmer	2.5
Sulzer	2.4
Others	9.7

Source: "Press Releases." Retrieved Feburary 17, 2000 from the World Wide Web: http://www.datamonitor.com, from Datamonitor.

★ 1087 ★
Orthopedic Appliances
SIC: 3842–ISIC: 3311–HC: 90

Leading Cemented Hip Makers in Japan

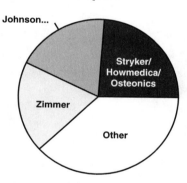

Market shares are shown in percent.

Stryker/Howmedica/Osteonics	24.0%
Johnson & Johnson/DePuy	19.0
Zimmer	19.0
Other	38.0

Source: *Health Industry Today*, June 1999, p. NA, from Datamonitor.

★ 1088 ★
Orthopedic Appliances
SIC: 3842–ISIC: 3311–HC: 90

Leading Knee Implant Makers in France

Market shares are shown in percent.

Sulzer 18.0%
Depuy 15.0
Zimmer 11.0
Howmedica 10.0
Biomet/Merck 7.0
Smith & Nephew 3.0
Other 36.0

Source: *Snapshots Industry Profile*, Annual 2000, p. NA.

★ 1089 ★
Orthopedic Appliances
SIC: 3842–ISIC: 3311–HC: 90

Leading Maxillofacial Implant Makers in France

Market shares are shown in percent.

Osteomed 69.0%
Howmedical/Leibinger 22.0
Walter Lorenz 3.0
Other 6.0

Source: *Snapshots Industry Profile*, Annual 2000, p. NA.

★ 1090 ★
Orthopedic Appliances
SIC: 3842–ISIC: 3311–HC: 90

Leading Shoulder Implant Makers in the U.K.

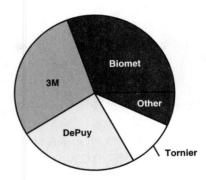

Market shares are shown in percent. The market should hit $7.7 million in 2005.

Biomet 30.2%
3M 28.2
DePuy 24.2
Tornier 10.2
Other 7.2

Source: *Snapshots Industry Profile*, Annual 2000, p. NA.

★ 1091 ★
Orthopedic Appliances
SIC: 3842–ISIC: 3311–HC: 90

Revision Knee Market in Japan, 1998

Market shares are shown based on value.

Zimmer 35.0%
Stryker 18.0
Howmedica 11.0
DePuy 9.0
Smith & Nephew 8.0
Johnson & Johnson 6.0
Sulzer 5.0
Kyocera 4.0
Other 4.0

Source: "Press Releases." Retrieved Feburary 17, 2000 from the World Wide Web: http://www.datamonitor.com, from Datamonitor.

★ 1092 ★
Surgical Appliances
SIC: 3842–ISIC: 3311–HC: 90

Prosthetics Market in Spain

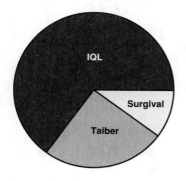

The prosthetics market in Spain divides this way: hips have 34% of the market, trauma 23%, knees 21%, spinal cords 19% and shoulders 3%. The market is growing slowly — about 2% in 1998 — in part because the country's population of 40 million is growing slowly.

IQL	65.0%
Taiber	25.0
Surgival	10.0

Source: "Spain: Prosthesis-Orthopedic Medical Equipment." Retrieved September 19, 2000 from the World Wide Web: http://www.tradeport.org.

★ 1093 ★
Surgical Implants
SIC: 3842–ISIC: 3311–HC: 90

Ear Nose and Throat Device Market, 1998

The market was worth $400 million. The entire market is growing roughly 6% a year.

Xomed	19.0%
Smith & Nephew	14.0
Karl Storz	7.0
Conmed	5.0
Stryker	4.0
Bausch & Lomb	3.0
Other	48.0

Source: *Investor's Business Daily*, August 30, 1999, p. A10, from William Blair & Co.

★ 1094 ★
Surgical Implants
SIC: 3842–ISIC: 3311–HC: 90

Europe's Spinal Implant Market, 1998

According to the source, consolidation is sweeping the industry due mostly to declining growth rates in mature orthopedic markets.

DePuy/Acromed	29.3%
Sofamor Danek	27.4
Synthes/Stratec	8.4
Stryker	6.7
Biomet	3.2
Howmedica	3.0
Aesculap	2.7
Scient'X	1.8
Other	17.5

Source: "Press Releases." Retrieved February 17, 2000 from the World Wide Web: http://www.datamonitor.com, from Datamonitor.

★ 1095 ★
Surgical Implants
SIC: 3842–ISIC: 3311–HC: 90

Global Stent Market

Stents are metal coils placed in formerly blocked arteries to keep them from becoming reoccluded. They are most commonly used in angioplasty procedures. Figures are estimated.

	1997	1999
Boston Scientific	20.0%	21.0%
Johnson & Johnson	20.0	16.0
Arterial Vascular Engineering	19.0	22.0
Medtronic	15.0	9.0
Guidant	14.0	17.0
Cook	7.0	3.0
Bard	1.0	4.0
Others	4.0	9.0

Source: *Medical & Healthcare Marketplace Guide*, 1999, pp. I-862, from Dorland Biomedical Database and other industry sources.

★ 1096 ★
Surgical Implants
SIC: 3842–ISIC: 3311–HC: 90

Precious Metal Market in the U.K., 1999

Precious metals is expected to be the largest sector of the aesthetic and prothetic market, worth 16.5 million pounds by 2005. The entire industry is expected to hit 95.6 million pounds. Market shares are estimated based on value.

Skillbond	37.0%
Metalor	18.0
Engelhard	17.0
Cookson	7.0
Cendre Metaux	6.0
Degussa	5.0
Other	10.0

Source: "Replacement Car Tires." Retrieved January 12, 2001 from the World Wide Web: http:// www.clearlybusiness.com, from Datamonitor.

★ 1097 ★
Dental Equipment
SIC: 3843–ISIC: 3311–HC: 90

Dental Equipment Market in China

The market has been growing steadily since the government started permitting private dental clinics in 1989.

Shanghai Fimet Dental Equipment Co.	25.0%
Bayer-Shangahi Dental Co.	20.0
Shuzhou Victory Co.	20.0
Southwest Medical Devices Manufactuory	15.0
Other	20.0

Source: "China Dental Equipment Market." Retrieved September 19, 2000 from the World Wide Web: http:// www.tradeport.org.

★ 1098 ★
Dental Equipment
SIC: 3843–ISIC: 3311–HC: 90

Endodontics Instrument Industry in the U.K.

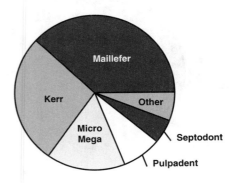

Instruments have the largest share of the endodontics market. The endodontic market has a 14.9% share of the entire dental market.

Maillefer	38.0%
Kerr	27.0
Micro Mega	16.0
Pulpadent	8.0
Septodont	5.0
Other	6.0

Source: "UK Endodontics." Retrieved January 12, 2001 from the World Wide Web: http:// www.clearlybusiness.com, from Datamonitor.

★ 1099 ★
Medical Imaging
SIC: 3844–ISIC: 3311–HC: 90

Medical Imaging Industry

Market shares are shown in percent.

X-ray	36.0%
Ultrasound	25.0
MR	22.0
CT	17.0

Source: *Password*, October 2000, p. 7, from Philips Research.

★ 1100 ★
Radiology Equipment
SIC: 3844–ISIC: 3311–HC: 90

Leading Radiology Equipment Makers in France

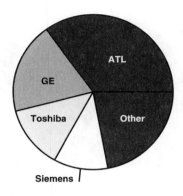

Market shares are shown in percent. The market is expected to hit $106.3 million by 2005.

ATL	35.0%
GE	19.0
Toshiba	13.0
Siemens	11.0
Other	22.0

Source: *Snapshots Industry Profile*, Annual 2000, p. NA.

★ 1101 ★
Electromedical Apparatus
SIC: 3845–ISIC: 3311–HC: 90

External Defibrillator Market

Market shares are shown in percent.

Medtronic Physio-Control	42.4%
Agilent Technologies	24.7
Zoll Medical	11.7
Other	21.2

Source: "Heart-Stopping Growth in the External Defibrillator Market." Retrieved January 31, 2001 from the World Wide Web: http://www.devicelink.com.

★ 1102 ★
Electromedical Apparatus
SIC: 3845–ISIC: 3311–HC: 90

Global Defibrillator Market

Shares are estimated.

Medtronic	50.0%
Guidant	40.0
St. Jude	6.0
Other	4.0

Source: *Star Tribune*, October 31, 2000, p. 1D, from Bancorp Piper Jaffray.

★ 1103 ★
Hearing Aids
SIC: 3845–ISIC: 3311–HC: 90

Global Hearing Aid Market

The market reached $1.94 billion.

Siemens/Rexton/A&M	21.0%
GN Resound/Beltone	18.0
Starkey	14.0
William Demant (Oticon/Bernaton)	13.0
Other	21.0

Source: *Financial Times*, November 24, 2000, p. 20, from Thomson Financial Datastream.

★ 1104 ★
Contact Lenses
SIC: 3851–ISIC: 3320–HC: 90

Contact Lens Market, 1999

The market is valued at $2.7 billion.

Johnson & Johnson	35.0%
CIBA Vision	18.0
Bausch & Lomb	17.0
Wesley Jessen	12.0
Ocular Sciences	6.0
Cooper-Vision	5.0
Other	7.0

Source: *Wall Street Journal*, May 31, 2000, p. B8, from S.G. Cowan.

★ 1105 ★
Contact Lenses
SIC: 3851–ISIC: 3320–HC: 90

Largest Contact Lens Markets, 1999

Markets are ranked by revenue in millions of dollars.

	($ mil.)	Share
United States	$ 1,130	44.19%
United Kingdom	122	4.77
France	113	4.42
Italy	81	3.17
Canada	80	3.13
Germany	74	2.89
Brazil	48	1.88
Spain	43	1.68
Other	866	33.87

Source: *Coopervision Contact Lens Market Guide*, Annual, p. 2.

★ 1106 ★
Eyewear
SIC: 3851–ISIC: 3320–HC: 90

Eyewear Market in Switzerland

The market for eyeglasses, lenses and sunglasses is valued at $460 million. There are some 1,000 shops in the market, with 80% of them being individual, independent shops.

Eyeglasses	71.0%
Contact lenses	13.0
Sunglasses	12.0
Accessories	4.0

Source: "Switzerland: Franchising and Optical Glasses." Retrieved September 19, 2000 from the World Wide Web: http://www.tradeport.org.

★ 1107 ★
Eyewear
SIC: 3851–ISIC: 3320–HC: 90

Eyewear Market Shares in Germany, 1999

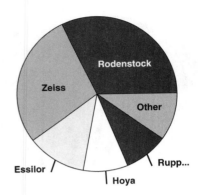

Market shares are shown in percent.

Rodenstock	32.0%
Zeiss	28.0
Essilor	12.0
Hoya	9.0
Rupp & Hubrach	9.0
Other	10.0

Source: *Wirtschaftswoche*, February 10, 2000, p. 78, from Fielmann and ZVA.

★ 1108 ★
Cameras
SIC: 3861–ISIC: 3320–HC: 90

Digital Camera Market Worldwide

Olympus
Sony
Fuji Photo
Other

Market shares are shown in percent.

Olympus	25.0%
Sony	25.0
Fuji Photo	20.0
Other	30.0

Source: *Asia Pulse News*, December 12, 2000, p. 0534.

★ 1109 ★
Cameras
SIC: 3861–ISIC: 3320–HC: 90

Digital Camera Sales by Region, 2000

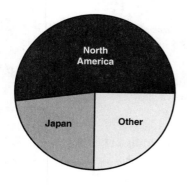

Digital camera sales now represent 13% of all camera sales worldwide. The segment is expected to grow to the point where it begins to strongly affect the film camera segment. The digital camera market is giving birth to related industries, like cableTV picture services, digital photo frames and online photofinishing. North America should have a substantial lead in the market through 2005.

North America	52.0%
Japan	23.0
Other	25.0

Source: "Digital Camera Sales Capture 13% of Worldwide Camera Market." Retrieved October 9, 2000 from the World Wide Web: http://www.businesswire.com, from InfoTrends Research Group.

★ 1110 ★
Cameras
SIC: 3861–ISIC: 3320–HC: 90

Top Compact Camera Makers in Japan, 1999

Market shares are shown based on domestic shipments of 3.35 million units.

Olympus Optical	20.1%
Canon Inc.	18.1
Fuji Photo Film Co.	18.0
Asahi Optical Co.	12.6
Konica Corp.	12.5
Other	18.7

Source: *Nikkei Weekly*, August 14, 2000, p. 8, from Nihon Keizai Shimbun.

★ 1111 ★
Cameras
SIC: 3861–ISIC: 3320–HC: 90

Top Digital Camera Makers in Japan, 1999

Market shares are shown based on domestic shipments.

Fuji Photo Film Co.	28.8%
Olympus Optical Co.	25.7
Sony Corp.	10.1
Casio Computer Co.	7.2
Seiko Epson Corp.	6.9
Other	21.3

Source: *Nikkei Weekly*, July 31, 2000, p. 8, from Nihon Keizai Shimbun.

★ 1112 ★
Copy Machines
SIC: 3861–ISIC: 3320–HC: 90

Digital Copier Market in Europe, 1998

A total of 208,150 copiers were placed during the year.

Xerox	27.9%
Ricoh	21.4
Canon	11.9
NRG	10.5
Other	28.3

Source: *Reproduire*, April 1, 1999, p. 1.

★ 1113 ★
Copy Machines
SIC: 3861–ISIC: 3320–HC: 90

Top Copy Machine Producers in Japan, 1999

Market shares are shown based on domestic shipments of 730,750 units.

Canon Inc.	30.1%
Ricoh Co.	29.9
Fuji Xerox Co.	22.4
Sharp Corp.	10.1
Konica Corp.	4.6
Other	2.9

Source: *Nikkei Weekly*, July 31, 2000, p. 8, from Nihon Keizai Shimbun.

★ 1114 ★
Photographic Film
SIC: 3861–ISIC: 3320–HC: 90

Photographic Film Market in China

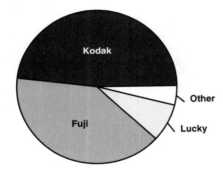

Market shares ares hown in percent for 1998.

Kodak	47.9%
Fuji	40.4
Lucky	8.1
Other	3.6

Source: *Washington Post*, June 7, 2000, p. E1.

★ 1115 ★
Photographic Film
SIC: 3861–ISIC: 3320–HC: 90

Top Photo Film Makers in Japan, 1999

Market shares are shown based on domestic shipments of 433.5 million rolls.

Fuji Photo Film Co.	67.7%
Konica Corp.	20.3
Kodak Japan Ltd.	10.5
Agfa-Gevaert Japan Ltd.	1.1
Mitsubishi Paper Mills Ltd.	0.4

Source: *Nikkei Weekly*, August 14, 2000, p. 8, from Nihon Keizai Shimbun.

★ 1116 ★
Watches
SIC: 3873–ISIC: 3330–HC: 91

India's Watch Market

Shares are estimated based on volume.

Titan	42.5%
HMT	29.1
Timex	13.3
Maxima	10.8
Others	4.3

Source: *Business Today*, July 7, 1999, p. 57.

★ 1117 ★
Watches
SIC: 3873–ISIC: 3330–HC: 91

Luxury Watch Market

The market refers to watches costing $1,500 or more.

Rolex	25.0%
Compagnie Financiere Richemont	22.0
Swatch Group	15.0
LVMH	9.0
Other	29.0

Source: *Forbes*, September 28, 2000, p. I85, from UBS Warburg.

★ 1118 ★
Watches
SIC: 3873–ISIC: 3330–HC: 91

Luxury Watch Market in Germany, 1999

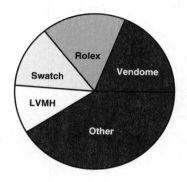

Market shares are shown in percent.

Vendome	19.0%
Rolex	17.0
Swatch	13.0
LVMH	10.0
Other	41.0

Source: *Wirtschaftswoche*, February 24, 2000, p. 98, from *Hamburger Abendblatt*, BV Jewellereee, and Un-rentachhandel.

★ 1119 ★
Watches
SIC: 3873–ISIC: 3330–HC: 91

Top Watch Makers in Japan, 1999

Market shares are shown based on domestic production.

Citizen Watch Co.	49.5%
Seiko Corp.	39.3
Ricoh Elemex Corp.	1.6
Casio Computer Co.	1.5
Orient Watch Co.	1.4
Other	6.7

Source: *Nikkei Weekly*, August 14, 2000, p. 8, from Nihon Keizai Shimbun.

SIC 39 - Miscellaneous Manufacturing Industries

★ 1120 ★

Jewelry

SIC: 3911–ISIC: 3691–HC: 71

Branded Jewelry Market

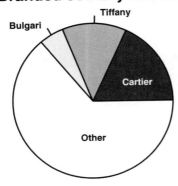

The market is valued at $3.4 billion.

Cartier	18.0%
Tiffany	13.0
Bulgari	5.0
Other	64.0

Source: *WWD*, November 13, 2000, p. 1.

★ 1121 ★

Jewelry

SIC: 3911–ISIC: 3691–HC: 71

Jewelry Sales In France

Market shares are shown in percent.

Precious jewelry	71.0%
Stones and pearls	12.0
Costume jewelry	7.0
Medals in precious metal	1.0
Other	9.0

Source: STAT-USA, *National Trade Data Bank*, November 23, 1999, p. NA.

★ 1122 ★

Musical Instruments

SIC: 3931–ISIC: 3692–HC: 92

Largest Musical Product Markets

Markets ranked by estimated sales in millions of dollars.

United States	$ 6,797.3
Japan	3,037.6
Germany	1,472.3
Canada	518.7
France	516.9
United Kingdom	502.4
Hong Kong	409.1
Italy	358.5
China	224.9
South Korea	185.0

Source: *Music Trades*, December 2000, p. 76.

★ 1123 ★
Musical Instruments
SIC: 3931–ISIC: 3692–HC: 92

Largest Musical Product Producers

Firms are ranked by estimated sales in millions of dollars. Portable keyboards were the most shipped item.

Yahama Corporation	$ 4,879.2
Kawai Musical Instrument Mfg. Ltd.	845.0
Roland Corporation	565.3
Harman Int.	433.7
Steinway Musical Instruments	304.6
Samick Corp.	285.0
Peavey Electronics	280.0
Yamano Music Company	275.0
Shure Incorporated	245.0
Young Chang Akki. Ltd.	240.4

Source: *Music Trades*, December 2000, p. 76.

★ 1124 ★
Musical Instruments
SIC: 3931–ISIC: 3692–HC: 92

Top Piano Makers in Japan, 1997

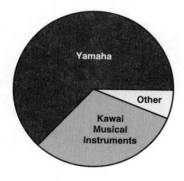

Market shares are shown based on shipments.

Yamaha	63.1%
Kawai Musical Instruments Mfg.	30.5
Other	6.4

Source: "DVL Market Share Library." Retrieved April 3, 2001 from the World Wide Web: http://dvl/daiwa.co.jp, from DVL Market Share Library and Marketing Data Bank.

★ 1125 ★
Musical Instruments
SIC: 3931–ISIC: 3692–HC: 92

Top Synthesizer Makers in Japan, 1997

Market shares are shown based on shipments.

Yamaha	46.5%
Roland	22.1
Korg	15.5
Other	15.9

Source: "DVL Market Share Library." Retrieved April 3, 2001 from the World Wide Web: http://dvl/daiwa.co.jp, from DVL Market Share Library and Marketing Data Bank.

★ 1126 ★
Toys and Games
SIC: 3944–ISIC: 3694–HC: 95

Electronic Learning Toy Market

Market shares are shown in percent.

Vtech Connect	70.0%
Other	30.0

Source: "Russell Simmons Teams Up With Vtech." Retrieved January 8, 2001 from the World Wide Web: http://www.businesswire.com.

★ 1127 ★
Toys and Games
SIC: 3944–ISIC: 3694–HC: 95

Largest Toy & Game Makers, 2000

Market shares are shown in percent.

Mattel	10.1%
Hasbro	9.3
Sony	8.6
Nintendo	7.4
Other	64.6

Source: *Brand Strategy*, June 2001, p. 28, from Euromonitor.

★ 1128 ★
Toys and Games
SIC: 3944–ISIC: 3694–HC: 95

Leading Toy Markets, 1999

Retail sales are shown in millions of dollars.

	($ mil.)	Share
North America	$ 31,291	44.01%
Asia	17,179	24.16
Europe	17,018	23.94
Latin & South America	2,755	3.88
Oceania	1,457	2.05
Middle East	1,045	1.47
Africa	350	0.49

Source: "World Toy Facts and Figures." Retrieved October 31, 2000 from the World Wide Web: http://www.toy-icti.org, from NPD Group Worldwide.

★ 1129 ★
Toys and Games
SIC: 3944–ISIC: 3694–HC: 95

Toy & Game Market by Segment, 2000

The market is shown in percent.

Console games	20.3%
Dolls/figures	13.0
Consoles	10.8
Activity/construction games	7.8
Model/wheeled games	7.6
Indoor games	7.1
Soft/plush toys	6.1
Infant/preschool toys	6.0
Outdoor games	3.6

Source: *Brand Strategy*, June 2001, p. 28, from Euromonitor.

★ 1130 ★
Toys and Games
SIC: 3944–ISIC: 3694–HC: 95

U.K. Construction Toy Market

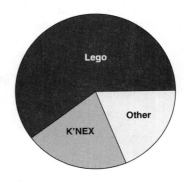

The 85 million British pound market is shown in percent.

Lego	60.0%
K'NEX	21.0
Other	19.0

Source: *Marketing*, October 8, 1998, p. 7.

★ 1131 ★
Toys and Games
SIC: 3944–ISIC: 3694–HC: 95

U.K. Toy Market, 1998

Total sales, minus video games, reached 1.67 billion British pounds. The average price of a toy was 10.2 pounds.

Activity toys	16.7%
Infant/preschool	16.1
Games & puzzles	11.6
Dolls	11.1
male action	8.2
Plush	7.7
Vehicles	7.7
Ride-ons	7.4
Other	15.1

Source: "Some Toy Facts and Figures." Retrieved September 8, 2000 from the World Wide Web: http://www.batr.co.uk.

★ 1132 ★
Video Games
SIC: 3944–ISIC: 3694–HC: 95

Best-Selling Video Games in Europe, 1998

Sales are in millions of euros.

Tomb Raider 3	68
Gran Turismo	66
Fifa 99	50
Fifa 98	48
Tomb Raider 2	39
Zelda	39
Fifa 97	37
Tekken 3	36
Colin McRae Rally	30
Resident Evil 2	29

Source: *L'Express*, February 12, 1999, p. 77.

★ 1133 ★
Video Games
SIC: 3944–ISIC: 3694–HC: 95

Global Video Game Industry

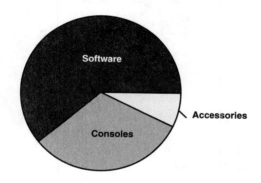

The global market for toys and games grew by almost 25% between 1994 and 1998 despite recession in key markets. Sales are shown in millions of dollars.

	1998	2000	Share
Software	$ 14,255.5	$ 21,836	61.39%
Consoles	6,276.9	11,204	31.50
Accessories	1,414.8	2,529	7.11

Source: *Brand Strategy*, March 24, 2000, p. 24, from Euromonitor.

★ 1134 ★
Video Games
SIC: 3944–ISIC: 3694–HC: 95

Global Video Game Market

Market shares are estimated in percent.

	2001	2003
Sony	58.1%	50.3%
Nintendo	23.6	25.3
Sega	14.7	9.6
Microsoft	3.6	14.8

Source: *L'Expansion*, February 14, 2001, p. 83.

★ 1135 ★
Video Games
SIC: 3944–ISIC: 3694–HC: 95

Global Video Game Sales

Sales are shown in billions of dollars.

	1998	2000	Share
Sony Playstation	$ 9.05	$ 4.74	32.71%
Nintendo 64	3.75	2.41	16.63
Game Boy	1.60	2.90	20.01
Sega Dreamcast	0.00	1.31	9.04
Sony Playstation 2	0.00	3.13	21.60

Source: *Wall Street Journal*, January 31, 2001, p. B1, from International Development Group.

★ 1136 ★
Video Games
SIC: 3944–ISIC: 3694–HC: 95

Leading Video Game Markets, 1999

Retail sales are shown in millions of dollars.

	($ mil.)	Share
North America	$ 7,174	46.46%
Asia	3,856	24.97
Europe	3,640	23.57
Oceania	294	1.90
Latin & South America	240	1.55
Middle East	213	1.38
Africa	24	0.16

Source: "World Toy Facts and Figures." Retrieved October 31, 2000 from the World Wide Web: http://www.toy-icti.org, from NPD Group Worldwide.

★ 1137 ★
Video Games
SIC: 3944–ISIC: 3694–HC: 95

Top Video Game Machine Makers in Japan, 1999

Market shares are shown based on domestic shipments of 5.44 million units.

Sony Computer Entertainment	65.3%
Sega Enterprises Ltd.	17.4
Nintendo Co.	17.2
Other	0.1

Source: *Nikkei Weekly*, July 31, 2000, p. 8, from Nihon Keizai Shimbun.

★ 1138 ★
Video Games
SIC: 3944–ISIC: 3694–HC: 95

Video Game Console Market, 2000

Shares are for the year to March 2000.

Sony Playstation	59.5%
Nintendo 64	20.9
Sega Dreamcast	15.1
Sony Playstation 2	4.5

Source: *Financial Times*, August 25, 2000, p. 19, from ING Barings.

★ 1139 ★
Video Games
SIC: 3944–ISIC: 3694–HC: 95

Video Game Market in Germany, 2000

Market shares are shown in percent.

Sony Playstation	45.0%
Nintendo Gameboy	27.0
Nintendo N64	20.0
Sega Dreamcast	8.0

Source: *Wirtschaftswoche*, December 7, 2000, p. 158, from GfK and VDU.

★ 1140 ★
Sporting Goods
SIC: 3949–ISIC: 3693–HC: 95

Alpine Ski Market in Japan

Market shares are shown in percent.

Rossignol	21.0%
Salomon	21.0
Atomic	12.0
Dynastar	7.0
Elan	7.0
Fischer	7.0
K2	7.0
Other	18.0

Source: "The Alpine Ski Market." Retrieved November 22, 2000 from the World Wide Web: http://www.csjapan.doc.gov.

★ 1141 ★
Sporting Goods
SIC: 3949–ISIC: 3693–HC: 95

Alpine Ski Market Shares in Germany

The industry grew from 220 million deutschmarks in 1993-94, fell to 200 million in 1995-96 and hit 236 million in 1998-99.

Rossignol	18.6%
Atomic	11.8
Head	11.0
Salomon	10.4
Fischer	9.3
Volki	7.5
Other	31.4

Source: *Wirtschaftswoche*, January 6, 2000, p. 58, from Kreutzer and Fischer & Partner.

★ 1142 ★
Sporting Goods
SIC: 3949–ISIC: 3693–HC: 95

Alpine Sports Market in Germany

Distribution is shown in percent.

Clothing	49.0%
Accessories	15.0
Rucksacks	11.0
Shoes	8.0
Tents	7.0
Sleeping bags	6.0
Dinghies	3.0

Source: *Wirtschaftswoche*, July 27, 2000, p. 99, from BBE.

★ 1143 ★
Sporting Goods
SIC: 3949–ISIC: 3693–HC: 95

Inline Skate Market in Germany

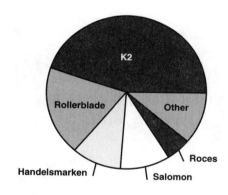

The industry was valued at 346.7 million deutschmarks.

K2	45.0%
Rollerblade	19.0
Handelsmarken	10.0
Salomon	10.0
Roces	5.0
Other	11.0

Source: *Wirtschaftswoche*, July 6, 2000, p. 80, from Industrie.

★ 1144 ★
Sporting Goods
SIC: 3949–ISIC: 3693–HC: 95

Largest Golf Equipment Importers in Argentina

Imports have $2 million of the $8 million market. The balance is from purchases abroad. There are 205 courses and 65,000 players.

Jurado Golf S.A.	21.4%
Nealon & Asociados S.R.L.	20.7
Villamily Hernandez S.A.	10.4
Wal-Mart Argentina S.A.	8.7
Sportsbrands S.A.	6.4
Monditec S.A.	3.7
D.R. Sociedad Anonima	3.6
Asociacion Argentina De Golf	2.5
Nike Argentina	2.0
Other	20.5

Source: ''Golf Equipment.'' Retrieved January 3, 2001 from the World Wide Web: http://www.usatrade.gov.

★ 1145 ★
Sporting Goods
SIC: 3949–ISIC: 3693–HC: 95

Riding Industry in Germany

Market shares are shown in percent.

Boarding	40.0%
Feed	30.0
Equipment	10.0
Breeding sales	5.0
Training/education	5.0
Other	10.0

Source: *Wirtschaftswoche*, August 17, 2000, p. 86.

★ 1146 ★
Sporting Goods
SIC: 3949–ISIC: 3693–HC: 95

Sporting Goods Industry in the U.K., 1999

Market shares are estimated based on value.

Golf	29.1%
Fitness/athletics	16.3
Fishing	9.3
Inflatable balls	4.1
Tennis rackets & balls	3.8
Skates	2.9
Other	34.5

Source: ''UK Power Tools.'' Retrieved January 11, 2001 from the World Wide Web: http://www.clearlybusiness.com, from Datamonitor.

★ 1147 ★
Sporting Goods
SIC: 3949–ISIC: 3693–HC: 95

Tennis Equipment Market in Germany

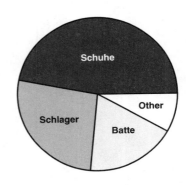

Shares are shown based on a 261 million deutschmark industry.

Schuhe	51.0%
Schlager	29.0
Batte	20.0
Other	9.0

Source: *Wirtschaftswoche*, May 11, 2000, p. 112, from Sports Tracking Europe.

★ 1148 ★
Sporting Goods
SIC: 3949–ISIC: 3693–HC: 95

Top Camping Tent Makers in Japan, 1997

Market shares are shown based on shipments.

Ogawa Tent 21.0%
Calman Japan 19.0
Kuroster 14.0
Other 46.0

Source: "DVL Market Share Library." Retrieved April 3, 2001 from the World Wide Web: http://dvl/daiwa.co.jp, from DVL Market Share Library and Marketing Data Bank.

★ 1149 ★
Sporting Goods
SIC: 3949–ISIC: 3693–HC: 95

Top Fishing Pole Makers in Japan, 1997

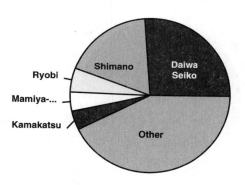

Market shares are shown based on shipments.

Daiwa Seiko 26.1%
Shimano 18.2
Ryobi 5.1
Mamiya-OP 4.3
Kamakatsu 4.1
Other 42.2

Source: "DVL Market Share Library." Retrieved April 3, 2001 from the World Wide Web: http://dvl/daiwa.co.jp, from DVL Market Share Library and Marketing Data Bank.

★ 1150 ★
Sporting Goods
SIC: 3949–ISIC: 3693–HC: 95

Top Snowboard Makers in Japan, 1999

Shares are shown based on domestic sales from winter 1999 - spring 2000.

Burton Corp. 18.6%
Salomon & Tailor Made Co. 8.4
K2 Japan Corp. 8.0
Sims Co. 7.7
Rossignol Japan Corp. 4.6
Other 52.7

Source: *Nikkei Weekly*, August 21, 2000, p. 9, from Nihon Keizai Shimbun.

★ 1151 ★
Sporting Goods
SIC: 3949–ISIC: 3693–HC: 95

Wholesale Bindings Sales

Unit sales are shown by region.

Japan 700,000
United States 514,000
Europe 481,000

Source: "Boot Figures by the Numbers." Retrieved July 17, 2000 from the World Wide Web: htttp://www.twsnow.com.

★ 1152 ★
Sporting Goods
SIC: 3949–ISIC: 3693–HC: 95

Winter Sports Equipment Sales

Sales are in millions of pairs worldwide.

Alpine skis	4.3
Alpine ski bindings	4.0
Alpine ski boots	4.0
Snowboards	1.5
Cross-country skis	1.1

Source: *Sporting Goods Business*, February 2000, p. 20, from Profile Sports Market Consultancy.

★ 1153 ★
Sporting Goods
SIC: 3949–ISIC: 3694–HC: 95

Leading Sporting Goods Firms, 1998

Firms are ranked by total business in millions of French francs.

Nike	57.4
Adidas Salomon	33.3
Reebok	19.4
Mizuno	14.8
Asics	6.9

Source: *L'Expansion*, March 18, 1999, p. 20.

★ 1154 ★
Pencils
SIC: 3951–ISIC: 3699–HC: 96

Leading Mechanical Pencil Makers in Japan

Market shares are shown for 1996.

Pentel	30.3%
Mitsubishi Enpitsu	21.5
The Pilot Pencil	15.3
Tombow Pencil	9.6
Zebra	8.5

Source: "Stationery and Office Supplies." Retrieved May 16, 2001 from the World Wide Web: http://www.tradeport.org, from Yano Economic Research.

★ 1155 ★
Pens
SIC: 3951–ISIC: 3699–HC: 96

Ballpoint Pen Market Shares in the U.K., 1999

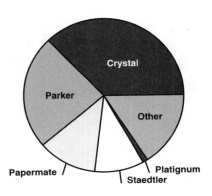

Market shares are shown based on value. The lead shares in the 260 million British pound market were Ballpoint with a 26.1% share, felt and fibre tips with a 23.4% share, fountain pens with a 16.1% share, markers with a 12.5% share.

Crystal	37.0%
Parker	24.0
Papermate	12.0
Staedtler	10.0
Platignum	1.0
Other	16.0

Source: "UK Writing Instruments." Retrieved January 12, 2001 from the World Wide Web: http://www.clearlybusiness.com, from Datamonitor.

★ 1156 ★
Pens
SIC: 3951–ISIC: 3699–HC: 96

Fountain Pen Market Shares in the U.K., 1999

Market shares are shown based on value.

Parker 24.0%
Mont Blanc 20.0
Sheaffer 14.0
Waterman 12.0
Cross 6.0
Berol 5.0
Others 19.0

Source: "UK Writing Instruments." Retrieved January 12, 2001 from the World Wide Web: http://www.clearlybusiness.com, from Datamonitor.

★ 1157 ★
Pens
SIC: 3951–ISIC: 3699–HC: 96

Luxury Pen Market

Market shares are shown in percent.

Montblanc 52.0%
Other 48.0

Source: *Jakarta Post*, November 26, 2000, p. 1.

★ 1158 ★
Pens
SIC: 3951–ISIC: 3699–HC: 96

Top Fountain Pen Makers in Japan, 1997

Market shares are shown based on shipments.

Pilot 25.0%
Platinum Fountain Pen 16.0
Mont Blanc 15.0
Sailor Pen 11.0
Parker 6.0
Other 27.0

Source: "DVL Market Share Library." Retrieved April 3, 2001 from the World Wide Web: http://dvl/daiwa.co.jp, from DVL Market Share Library and Marketing Data Bank.

★ 1159 ★
Inked Ribbon
SIC: 3955–ISIC: 3699–HC: 48

Top Inked Ribbon Makers in Japan, 1997

Market shares are shown based on shipments.

Fujicopian 30.0%
Dai Nippon Printing 25.0
General 12.0
Sony Chemicals 8.0
Ricoh 6.0
Other 19.0

Source: "DVL Market Share Library." Retrieved April 3, 2001 from the World Wide Web: http://dvl/daiwa.co.jp, from DVL Market Share Library and Marketing Data Bank.

★ 1160 ★
Brooms
SIC: 3991–ISIC: 3699–HC: 96

France's Broom Market

The 491 million French franc market is shown in
percent.

Brooms, indoor	18.5%
Mops	16.7
Brooms, flat	8.1
Brooms, outdoor	7.4
Brooms, brush	6.2
Brooms, sponge	6.0
Other	37.1

Source: *LSA Libre Service Actualities*, March 18, 1999, p.
NA.

★ 1161 ★
Brushes
SIC: 3991–ISIC: 3699–HC: 96

Top Brush Makers in Australia

Market shares are shown in percent.

E.D. Oates Pty Ltd.	65.0%
Other	35.0

Source: "The Cleaning Centre." Retrieved April 20, 2001
from the World Wide Web: http://www.yellowpages.co.nz.

★ 1162 ★
Toothbrushes
SIC: 3991–ISIC: 3699–HC: 96

Toothbrush Industry in France, 2000

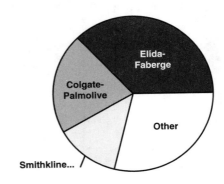

Shares are for the year ended October 22, 2000.

Elida-Faberge	36.5%
Colgate-Palmolive	21.1
Smithkline Beecham	13.2
Other	29.1

Source: *Points de Vente*, December 6, 2000, p. 44.

★ 1163 ★
Toothbrushes
SIC: 3991–ISIC: 3699–HC: 96

Toothbrush Market in the U.K., 1999

Market shares are shown based on value.

Oral B	18.0%
Reach	16.9
Aquafresh	11.4
Boots	10.8
Colgate Precision	9.2
Private label	10.0
Others	23.7

Source: "UK Toothbrushes." Retrieved January 12, 2001
from the World Wide Web: http://
www.clearlybusiness.com, from Datamonitor.

★ 1164 ★
Toothbrushes
SIC: 3991–ISIC: 3699–HC: 96

Toothbrush Market Leaders in Spain, 1999

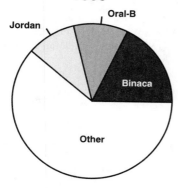

Sales are for July 1999.

Binaca	18.0%
Oral-B	11.0
Jordan	10.0
Other	61.0

Source: *European Cosmetic Markets*, December 1999, p. 1.

★ 1165 ★
Toothbrushes
SIC: 3991–ISIC: 3699–HC: 96

Top Toothbrush Brands in Germany, 2000

Market shares are shown for the first six months of the year.

Dr. Best	30.0%
Aronal	10.0
Oral-B	9.0
Blend-a-Dent	8.5
Colgate	4.5
Elmex	2.0
Signal	2.0
Other	34.0

Source: *European Cosmetic Markets*, December 2000, p. 479, from A.C. Nielsen.

★ 1166 ★
Flooring
SIC: 3996–ISIC: 3699–HC: 96

Floorcovering Market in Germany

Market shares are shown in percent.

	(mil.)	Share
Tufting	95	33.57%
Ceramic and stone tile	47	16.61
PVC	38	13.43
Laminate	32	11.31
Needle felt	27	9.54
Woven	19	6.71
Wood	16	5.65
Other	9	3.18

Source: "Textile Flooring." Retrieved May 17, 2001 from the World Wide Web: http://www.usatrade.gov, from German Federal Statistics Office.

★ 1167 ★
Flooring
SIC: 3996–ISIC: 3699–HC: 96

Hard Flooring Market in Brazil

Market shares are shown in percent.

Ceramic floor tiles	70.0%
Laminates	15.0
Other	15.0

Source: *Gazeta Mercantil*, May 2000, p. 1.

★ 1168 ★
Flooring
SIC: 3996–ISIC: 3699–HC: 96

Vinyl Floor Tile Market in Peru

The vinyl floor tile industry reached $6 million in the year 2000. PisoPak sold nearly 1.5 million square meters last year, of which 800,000 went into the domestic market. Market shares are shown in percent.

PisoPak	80.0%
Other	20.0

Source: "Peruvian Vinyl Floor Tiles." Retrieved February 12, 2001 from the World Wide Web: http://www.comtexnews.com, from PisoPak Peru.

★ 1169 ★
Artificial Playing Services
SIC: 3999–ISIC: 3699–HC: 96

Artificial Playing Surface Industry

Companies are ranked by sales in millions of dollars. Shares are shown based on an international market of $300 million.

	($ mil.)	Share
AstroTurf	$ 55	18.33%
FieldTurf	44	14.67
Sprinturf	8	2.67
Other	193	64.33

Source: *Philadelphia Inquirer*, September 25, 2000, p. C1.

Gendai Seiyaku	11.7%
Showa Kagaku	8.0
Cadog	6.9
Bombi	5.2
Other	9.0

Source: "DVL Market Share Library." Retrieved April 3, 2001 from the World Wide Web: http://dvl/daiwa.co.jp, from DVL Market Share Library and Marketing Data Bank.

★ 1170 ★
Artificial Playing Services
SIC: 3999–ISIC: 3699–HC: 96

Top Artificial Grass Makers in Japan

Market shares are shown as of October 1998.

Toray Industries	24.7%
Unitika	19.8
Asahi Chemical Industry	16.3
Kureha Chemical Industry	14.1
Sumitomo Chemical	11.7
Sekisui Chemical	7.2
Other	6.2

Source: "DVL Market Share Library." Retrieved April 3, 2001 from the World Wide Web: http://dvl/daiwa.co.jp, from DVL Market Share Library and Marketing Data Bank.

★ 1171 ★
Pet Products
SIC: 3999–ISIC: 3699–HC: 96

Top Pet Deodorizer Makers in Japan

Market shares are shown as of October 1998.

Johnson Trading	23.2%
Earth Bio Chemical	19.6
Lion Shoji	16.4

SIC 40 - Railroad Transportation

★ 1172 ★
Railroads
SIC: 4010–ISIC: 6010

Passenger Railway Market in the U.K., 1999

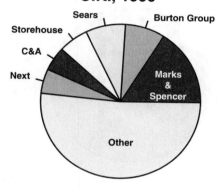

The market shrank by 5.1% to reach 1.7 billion British pounds in 1999. Market shares are shown based on value.

Marks & Spencer	16.2%
Burton Group	8.2
Sears	8.1
Storehouse	5.6
C&A	5.1
Next	4.9
Other	51.0

Source: ''UK Passenger Railways.'' Retrieved January 12, 2001 from the World Wide Web: http://www.clearlybusiness.com, from Datamonitor.

★ 1173 ★
Railroads
SIC: 4010–ISIC: 6010

Rail Freight Market in the U.K.

The market shrank by 2.2% to reach 1.7 billion British pounds in 1999. Market shares are shown based on value for 1997.

Loadhaul	38.8%
Transrail	31.1
Mainline Freight	21.1
Railfreight Distribution	9.0

Source: ''UK Rail Freight.'' Retrieved January 12, 2001 from the World Wide Web: http://www.clearlybusiness.com, from Datamonitor.

★ 1174 ★
Railroads
SIC: 4011–ISIC: 6010

World Rail Market, 1993-2002

Distribution is shown in percent.

Western Europe	29.04%
Far East & Asia	28.01
Eastern & Central Europe	18.96
U.S. & Canada	12.98
Other	11.02

Source: ''World Rail Market Outlook.'' Retrieved April 20, 2000 from the World Wide Web: http://www.transit-center.com, from METRO analysis of GEC Alsthom and European Commission data.

SIC 41 - Local and Interurban Passenger Transit

★ 1175 ★
Mass Transit
SIC: 4111–ISIC: 6021
Bus Market in the U.K.

Market shares are shown in percent.

First Group 23.1%
Stagecoach 16.4
Independents 14.6
Arriva 13.9
Management owned 6.8
National Express 6.7
Go-Ahead 6.3
Municipals 6.2
MTL 2.1
Other 4.0

Source: *The Observer*, August 15, 1999, p. 7, from TAS.

★ 1176 ★
Mass Transit
SIC: 4111–ISIC: 6021
European Rail Travel, 1999

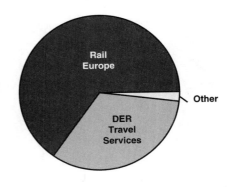

DER and Rail Europe have been competitors for some time. DER's share has nearly doubled since 1992. The majority of sales are booked through the travel agent community, major consortia or other large seller of travel.

	1992	1999
Rail Europe	80.0%	64.7%
DER Travel Services	17.9	33.0
Other	2.1	2.3

Source: *Travel Agent*, September 11, 2000, p. 8.

SIC 42 - Trucking and Warehousing

★ 1177 ★
Transportation
SIC: 4200–ISIC: 6302

Europe's Transport/Logistics Market, 1997

Deutsche Post	
Schenker/BTL	
Kuhne & Nagel	
Panalpina	
Geodis	
Ocean Group	
NFC	
THL	
Tibbet & Britten	
Others	

The 175 billion deutschmark market is shown in percent.

Deutsche Post	6.0%
Schenker/BTL (Stinnes)	6.0
Kuhne & Nagel	3.0
Panalpina	3.0
Geodis	2.0
Ocean Group	2.0
NFC	1.0
THL	1.0
Tibbet & Britten	1.0
Others	75.0

Source: *Financial Times*, May 31, 1999, p. 15, from Deutsche Post.

★ 1178 ★
Logistics
SIC: 4210–ISIC: 6023

Top Logistics Firms in Spain, 1999

Firms are ranked by sales in millions of euros.

Logistica	2,670.0
Grupo Logistico Santos	105.1
Exel Logistics	90.4
TNT Logistics Espana	48.0
Grupo Carreras	47.2
Grupo Trasaher	42.6
Serv. Logisticos Integr.	42.3
Aitena	42.0

Source: *Expansion*, April 28, 2000, p. 1, from Logistica, Transporte, and Paqueteria y Almacenjae.

★ 1179 ★
Express Delivery Services
SIC: 4215–ISIC: 6413

China-Taiwan Express Delivery Market

Market shares are shown in percent.

DHL Worldwide Express	33.4%
United Parcel Service	4.6
FedEx	3.5
Overseas Courier Service	2.3
TNT Express	1.2
Other	45.0

Source: *China Online*, March 30, 2001, p. NA.

★ 1180 ★
Express Delivery Services
SIC: 4215–ISIC: 6413

Europe's Courier/Package Delivery Market, 1997

The 55 billion deutschmark market is shown in percent.

Deutsche Post and Partners 12.7%
La Poste/DPD 10.2
DHL 6.7
TPG/TNT 6.4
UPS 6.2
Parcel Force/GP 3.6
Others 54.2

Source: *Financial Times*, May 31, 1999, p. 15, from Deutsche Post.

★ 1182 ★
Express Delivery Services
SIC: 4215–ISIC: 6413

Top Door-to-Door Delivery Firms in Japan, 1999

Shares are shown based on parcel deliveries.

Yamato Transport Co. 35.6%
Sagawa Express Co. 23.0
Nippon Express Co. 16.7
Fukuyama Transporting Co. 7.1
Seino Transportation Co. 6.4
Other 11.2

Source: *Nikkei Weekly*, August 21, 2000, p. 9, from Nihon Keizai Shimbun.

★ 1181 ★
Express Delivery Services
SIC: 4215–ISIC: 6413

Intra-Europe Express Market

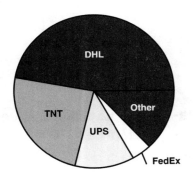

Market shares are shown in percent.

DHL 47.0%
TNT 24.0
UPS 12.0
FedEx 4.0
Other 13.0

Source: *Air Cargo World*, June 1999, p. 28, from Air Cargo Management Group.

SIC 43 - Postal Service

★ 1183 ★

Postal Services

SIC: 4311–ISIC: 6411

Europe's Letter Market, 1997

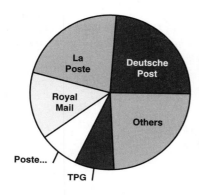

The 80 billion deutschmark market is shown in percent.

Deutsche Post	24.0%
La Poste	22.0
Royal Mail	14.0
Poste Italiane	8.0
TPG	8.0
Others	24.0

Source: *Financial Times*, May 31, 1999, p. 15, from Deutsche Post.

★ 1184 ★

Postal Services

SIC: 4311–ISIC: 6411

Leading Postal Operators, 1999

Operators are ranked by turnover in millions of British pounds.

U.S. Postal Service	59,132
UPS	25,391
Deutsche Post	22,400
La Poste	15,300
British Post Service	10,208
TPG (Netherlands)	8,536
Post Italiane	6,348

Source: *The Economist*, May 13, 2000, p. 66.

★ 1185 ★

Postal Services

SIC: 4311–ISIC: 6411

Who Handles the World's Mail

Distribution is shown in percent.

U.S. Postal Service	41.0%
Japan's postal service	6.0
Other	53.0

Source: *Wall Street Journal*, December 10, 1999, p. B1.

SIC 44 - Water Transportation

★ 1186 ★
Shipping
SIC: 4412–ISIC: 6110

Largest Shipping Companies in Japan

Companies are ranked by dead weight tonnage, in millions of tons.

China Ocean Shipping	15.87
China Shipping (Group) Co.	7.95
China Changjiang National Shipping	3.57
Shangdong Shipping	0.39
Ningbo Marine Group Co.	0.27

Source: *WWS*, October/November 2000, p. 20.

★ 1187 ★
Shipping
SIC: 4412–ISIC: 6110

Largest Shipping Lines, 2000

Companies are ranked by total imports and exports, in twenty-foot equivalent units. Figures are for the first six months of the year.

	TEUs	Share
Maersk Sealand	1,140,641	13.5%
Evergreeen Line	689,990	8.2
APL	574,878	6.8
Hanjin Shipping Co.	470,257	5.6
China Ocean Shipping . . .	461,133	5.5
Hyundai Merchant Marine . . .	370,284	4.4
P&O Nedlloyd	346,401	4.1
Orient Overseas Container Line	336,176	4.0
Yangming Maine Line	306,476	3.6
Mediterranean Shipping Co. . .	285,405	3.4

Source: *Journal of Commerce Magazine*, August 28, 2000, p. 28.

★ 1188 ★
Shipping
SIC: 4412–ISIC: 6110

U.S./Latin America Market Shares, 1999

The market shares for the U.S. Gulf to Venezuela, Trinidad, Colombia. Shares are shown based on a total of 368,778 metric tons.

Intermarine	14.0%
Graneo	13.0
P&O Nedlloyd	10.0
Signet	10.0
Sea-Land	9.0
ASCT	8.0
Columbus Line	7.0
Seaboard Marine	3.0
Other	27.0

Source: *American Shipper*, August 2000, p. 70, from PIERS and Intermarine.

★ 1189 ★
Tanker Fleets
SIC: 4412–ISIC: 6110

Deepsea Chemical Transportation, 2000

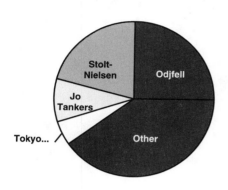

The industry is finally recovering from a slump that had cut deeply into the industry's profitability. Oversupply was caused by too many orders for new vessels and fallen demand. Shares are shown based on a total of 9 million deadweight tons.

Odjfell	25.0%
Stolt-Nielsen	21.0
Jo Tankers	9.0
Tokyo Marines	5.0
Other	40.0

Source: *Chemical Week*, May 30, 2001, p. 61, from Odfjell.

★ 1190 ★
Ferries
SIC: 4482–ISIC: 6110

Leading Greek Ferry Operators

Firms are ranked by sales for the first six months of 2000. Analysts forecast 8-10% growth yearly in the Aegan market over the next three years. More than 9 million journeys are forecast for 2000 for resorts and popular islands.

Attica Enterprises	$ 25.2
Minoan	20.7
Strintzis	11.4

Source: *Financial Times*, October 11, 2000, p. 25, from Primark Datastream.

★ 1191 ★
Ports
SIC: 4491–ISIC: 6301

Cargo Market in the Valparasio Region, Chile

Market shares are shown in percent.

Valparaiso	24.0%
Ventanas	19.0
Other	57.0

Source: "San Antonio Port Led Cargo Operations."
Retrieved January 26, 2001 from the World Wide Web:
http://www.comtexnews.com.

★ 1192 ★
Ports
SIC: 4491–ISIC: 6301

Leading Container Ports, 1998

Ports are ranked by traffic in thousands of twenty-foot equivalent units.

Singapore	15,136
Hong Kong	14,582
Kaohsiung, Taiwan	6,271
Rotterdam, Netherlands	6,004
Busan, South Korea	4,539
Long Beach	4,098
Hamburg, Germany	3,566
Los Angeles	3,378
Antwerp, Belgium	3,266

Source: *Financial Times*, May 31, 2001, p. 8, from American Association of Port Authorities.

★ 1193 ★
Ports
SIC: 4491–ISIC: 6301

Leading Ports in Latin America, 1998

Ports are ranked by number of 20 foot containers moved.

Buenos Aires	1,139,730
Colon, Panama	1,117,035
Santos, Brazil	799,476

Continued on next page.

★ 1193 ★

[Continued]

Ports

SIC: 4491–ISIC: 6301

Leading Ports in Latin America, 1998

Ports are ranked by number of 20 foot containers moved.

Kingston, Jamaica	560,219
Puerto Cabello, Venezuela	486,824
Freeport, Bahamas	470,000
Puerto Limon, Costa Rica	452,076
Veracruz, Mexico	427,487
San Antonio, Chile	415,001
Guayaquil, Ecuador	407,434

Source: *Latin Trade*, October 2000, p. 67, from American Association of Port Authorities.

SIC 45 - Transportation by Air

★ 1194 ★
Airlines
SIC: 4512–ISIC: 6210

Airline Traffic Worldwide, 1998

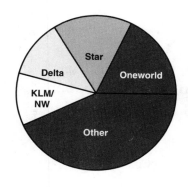

Market shares are shown in percent.

Oneworld	18.0%
Star	16.0
Delta	12.0
KLM/NW	11.0
Other	43.0

Source: *The Economist*, July 17, 1999, p. 57, from Boston Consulting Group.

★ 1195 ★
Airlines
SIC: 4512–ISIC: 6210

Business Travel in Brazil, 1999

The international business travel market generated sales of R$1.7 billion during the first eight months of the year.

Varig	40.5%
American Airlines	13.4
United Airlines	10.9

Air France	4.9%
Lufthansa	4.1
Vasp	3.6
Alitalia	2.8
Continental Airlines	2.6
Transbrasil	2.5
TAM	2.2
Other	12.6

Source: *Gazeta Mercantil*, January 13, 2000, p. A4, from Favecc and South American Business Information.

★ 1196 ★
Airlines
SIC: 4512–ISIC: 6210

Glasgow to London Air Market

Monthly shares are shown in percent.

British Airways	40.0%
British Midland	19.0
Ryannair	19.0
Easyjet	15.0
Go	7.0

Source: *Daily Record*, January 13, 2001, p. 51, from Civil Aviation Authority.

★ 1197 ★
Airlines
SIC: 4512–ISIC: 6210

Top Airlines in Brazil

Market shares are shown in percent.

TAM 29.13%
Variag 27.53
Other 43.34

Source: *South American Business Information*, May 16, 2001, p. NA, from Departmento de Aviacao Civil.

★ 1198 ★
Airlines
SIC: 4512–ISIC: 6210

Top Airlines in Colombia

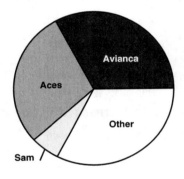

Market shares are shown in percent.

Avianca 32.7%
Aces 28.7
Sam 5.8
Other 32.8

Source: *Airline Industry Information*, January 23, 2001, p. NA.

★ 1199 ★
Airlines
SIC: 4512–ISIC: 6210

Top Airlines in Germany

Market shares are shown in percent.

Lufthansa 73.0%
Deutsche BA 19.0
Eurowings 4.0
Other 4.0

Source: *Travel Guide Gazette UK & Ireland*, October 2, 2000, p. 7.

★ 1200 ★
Airlines
SIC: 4512–ISIC: 6210

Top Airlines in Japan, 1999

Shares are shown based on passengers.

All Nippon Airways Co. 42.9%
Japan Air System Co. 22.3
Japan Airlines Co. 22.3
Air Nippon Co. 6.7
Japan TransOcean Air Co. 2.4
Other 3.4

Source: *Nikkei Weekly*, August 21, 2000, p. 9, from Nihon Keizai Shimbun.

★ 1201 ★

Airlines

SIC: 4512–ISIC: 6210

U.S. and Europe and Passenger Traffic

Market shares are shown in percent.

Oneworld	25.0%
Independent Airlines	20.6
Star Alliance	19.5
Wings	15.0
SkyTeam	13.9
Qualiflyer	6.1

Source: *Wall Street Journal*, June 12, 2001, p. A4, from Salomon Smith Barney.

★ 1202 ★

Airlines

SIC: 4512–ISIC: 6210

U.S. Far East Air Routes

Market shares are shown in percent.

Japan Airlines	23.0%
American Airlines	5.5
Cathay Pacific	5.5
Delta Airlines	3.1
Continental Airlines	1.3
Other	56.6

Source: *Air Transport Intelligence*, October 16, 2000, p. 1, from U.S. Department of Transportation.

★ 1203 ★

Air Cargo

SIC: 4513–ISIC: 6413

Air Cargo Market in Asia, 1999

Market shares are shown in percent.

Japan	29.0%
China	17.0
Taiwan	11.0
Korea	8.0
Singapore	8.0
Hong Kong	7.0%
Australia/New Zealand	6.0
Malaysia	5.0
Thailand	4.0
Other	5.0

Source: *Air Cargo World*, December 2000, p. 55, from *Boeing World Air Cargo Forecast 2000-2001*.

★ 1204 ★

Air Cargo

SIC: 4513–ISIC: 6413

Heavy-Lift Cargo Market in Russia

A large segment of work comes from the aerospace sector.

Volga-Dnepr	53.4%
Ukrai Antonov Airlines	40.1
Other	6.5

Source: *Inzhenernaia Gazeta*, April 11, 2000, p. 1.

★ 1205 ★

Air Cargo

SIC: 4513–ISIC: 6413

Largest Air Cargo Firms, 1999

Firms are ranked by billions of revenue tonne kilometers.

Federal Express	10.30
Lufthansa	6.65
United Parcel	6.01
Korean Air	5.87
Singapore	5.48
Air France	4.73
Cathay Pacific/AHK	4.57
JAL	4.49
British	4.24
KLM	3.91

Source: *South China Morning Post*, September 29, 2000, p. 16, from Boeing.

★ 1206 ★
Air Cargo
SIC: 4513–ISIC: 6413

Largest Cargo Airports in Europe, 2000

Airports are ranked by traffic for the first six months of the year.

Frankfurt	806,387
London Heathrow	689,630
Paris Charles de Gaulle	632,709
Amsterdam	618,141
Brussels	311,943

Source: *Air Cargo World*, November 2000, p. 42, from Airports Council International.

★ 1207 ★
Air Cargo
SIC: 4513–ISIC: 6413

Leading Air Freight Markets

Figures are in millions of metric tons. Data for 2000 and 2003 are forecast.

	1999	2001	2003
USA domestic	7.66	8.26	8.84
Intra-Asia	2.80	3.32	3.93
Asia/Pacific to North America	1.60	1.76	1.92
Asia/Pacific to Europe	1.40	1.56	1.74
Europe to North America	1.37	1.53	1.71
North America to Europe	1.19	1.37	1.58
Intra-Europe	1.01	1.12	1.24
North America to Asia/Pacific	0.93	1.07	1.23
Europe to Asia/Pacific	0.84	0.96	1.10

Source: *Air Cargo World*, May 2000, p. 32, from MergeGlobal Inc.

★ 1208 ★
Air Cargo
SIC: 4513–ISIC: 6413

Leading Freight Transporters in Sweden

Market shares are shown in percent.

SAS	22.6%
Lufthansa	19.1
Other	58.3

Source: *Air Cargo World*, April 2001, p. 48.

★ 1209 ★
Courier Services
SIC: 4513–ISIC: 6413

Air Courier Market in Thailand

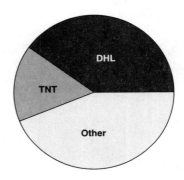

Market shares are shown in percent.

DHL	40.0%
TNT	16.0
Other	44.0

Source: *Bangkok Post*, October 15, 1999, p. B1.

★ 1210 ★
Courier Services
SIC: 4513–ISIC: 6413

Express Delivery Market in Russia

Other sources cut up the market differently: DHP controls 35% followed by UPS with 25%. EMS Garantpost believes it holds 60% of the entire delivery market, followed by DHL with 22% of the market.

DHL	55.0%
UPS	17.0
TNT	16.0
FedEx	7.0

Source: "Express Delivery Market in Russia." Retrieved January 17, 2000 from the World Wide Web: http://ww.bisnis.doc.gov, from Research International.

★ 1212 ★
Airports
SIC: 4581–ISIC: 6303

Top Cargo Airports

Airports are ranked by tons transported.

Memphis, TN	1,959,420
Los Angeles, CA	1,530,486
Miami, FL	1,490,010
Hong Kong	1,356,516
Tokyo Narita	1,342,943
New York Kennedy	1,336,500
Frankfurt, Germany	1,200,422
Chicago O'Hare	1,168,070
Seoul, Korea	1,164,427
Louisville, KY	1,154,525

Source: *Site Selection*, September 1999, p. 898, from AirConnex.

★ 1211 ★
Courier Services
SIC: 4513–ISIC: 6413

Express Shipping Market in Asia

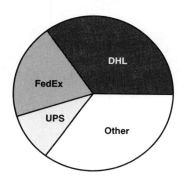

Shares are shown in percent. The express delivery market was valued at $3 billion.

DHL	35.0%
FedEx	20.0
UPS	10.0
Other	35.0

Source: *Wall Street Journal*, December 21, 1999, p. A18, from companies and industry sources.

SIC 47 - Transportation Services

★ 1213 ★
Tourism
SIC: 4720–ISIC: 6300

Most-Visited Countries by Brits, 1999

Countries are ranked by millions of U.K. visitors. There is a growing trend for most exotic locations by British vacationers. The number of vsitors to places like the Bahamas has doubled over the last five years.

France	11.94
Spain	10.37
Ireland	4.23
United States	4.05
Greece	2.44
Italy	2.11
Germany	2.10
Holland	1.94
Belgium	1.60
Portugal	1.45

Source: *Travel Trade Gazette U.K. & Ireland*, November 27, 2000, p. 5.

★ 1214 ★
Travel
SIC: 4720–ISIC: 6304

Electronic Reservation Business in Europe

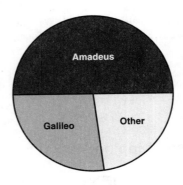

Market shares are shown in percent.

Amadeus	50.0%
Galileo	27.0
Other	23.0

Source: *Mergers & Acquisitions Report*, October 30, 2000, p. 1.

★ 1215 ★
Travel Agencies
SIC: 4724–ISIC: 6304

Largest Travel Agencies in France

Firms are ranked by total business in millions of French francs.

Havas Voyages American Express	10.7
Carlson Wagonlife Travel	8.5
Gia Manor	8.2
Selectour	7.2
Havas Voyager-C&N	6.1
Alat Voyages	5.0
Tourcom	3.5

Source: *Le Figaro*, September 18, 2000, p. 108.

★ 1216 ★
Travel Agencies
SIC: 4724–ISIC: 6304

Largest Travel Agencies in Japan, 1998

Market shares are shown based on domestic sales.

Japan Travel Bureau Inc.	14.3%
Kinki Nippon Tourist Co.	6.9
Hankyu Express International Co.	4.9
H.I.S. Co.	4.2
Nippon Travel Agency Co.	4.2
Other	65.5

Source: *Nikkei Weekly*, August 23, 1999, p. 7, from Nihon Keizai Shimbun.

★ 1217 ★
Travel Agencies
SIC: 4724–ISIC: 6304

Top Overseas Travel Firms in Japan, 1999

Shares are shown based on domestic sales.

Japan Travel Bureau Inc.	13.5%
Kinki Nippon Tourist Co.	6.5
Hankyu Express International Co.	5.8
H.I.S. Co.	4.7
Nippon Travel Agency Co.	4.1
Other	65.4

Source: *Nikkei Weekly*, August 21, 2000, p. 9, from Nihon Keizai Shimbun.

★ 1218 ★
Cruise Lines
SIC: 4725–ISIC: 6304

Cruise Line Market

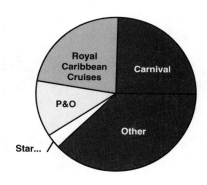

The modern cruise market began to develop in the Aegean Sea and Caribbean in the 1970s with Americans as the main customers. The top 3 companies tightened their grip on the market since the 1980s. They have bumped up the number of berths to over 2,000. Figures show millions of passenger cruise nights.

	(mil.)	Share
Carnival	13.0	25.49%
Royal Caribbean Cruises	11.6	22.75
P&O	5.9	11.57
Star Cruises	1.3	2.55
Other	19.2	37.65

Source: *Financial Times*, August 25, 1999, p. 17, from Primark Datastream and GP Wild (International).

★ 1219 ★
Cruise Lines
SIC: 4725–ISIC: 6304

World Cruise Market

The Caribbean and the Bahamas still dominate the market and are growing at 5-6% a year.

Caribbean/Bahamas	65.0%
Other	35.0

Source: *Duty-Free News International Caribbean Supplement*, February 2001, p. 3.

★ 1220 ★
Tour Operators
SIC: 4725–ISIC: 6304

Leading Tour Operators in Europe, 1999

Firms are ranked by total business in millions of French francs.

Preussag Thomson	73.8
Airtours	35.1
C&N	30.1
Accor Loisirs et Tourisme	20.0
First Choice	15.6
Kuoni	13.9
L.T.U.	13.3
Nouvelles Frontiere	10.4

Source: *Paris Match*, June 1, 2000, p. 124.

★ 1221 ★
Tour Operators
SIC: 4725–ISIC: 6304

Leading Tour Operators in Italy, 1998

Italy ranks fourth in the world's top tourism destinations. The vacation industry is alive and well for Italians, with 50.6% taking one vacation and another 22.3% taking two to four vacations. Firms are ranked by sales in billions of lira.

Alpitour SpA	1,064
Costa Crociere	834
Gruppo Francorosso	480
Viaggi del Ventaglio SpA	445
Valtur	370

Kuoni Gastaldi Spa	310
Hotelplan Italia Spa	224
MSC	173
Aeroviaggi u Jet Tours	165
Eurotravel	136

Source: *National Trade Data Bank*, August 1, 1999, p. 1.

★ 1222 ★
Tour Operators
SIC: 4725–ISIC: 6304

Packaged Tour Industry in the U.K., 1998

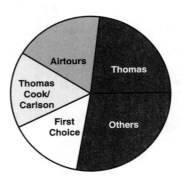

Market shares are shown in percent.

Thomas	23.0%
Airtours	18.0
Thomas Cook/Carlson	16.0
First Choice	15.0
Others	28.0

Source: *Financial Times*, September 23, 1999, p. 23, from Primark Database.

★ 1223 ★
Tour Operators
SIC: 4725–ISIC: 6304

Top Tour Brands in the U.K., 1998

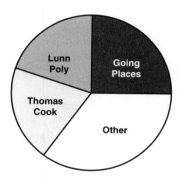

Retail brand shares are shown in percent. Going Places is by Airtours and Lunn Poly is from Thomson.

Going Places	25.0%
Lunn Poly	20.0
Thomas Cook	20.0
Other	35.0

Source: *The Observer*, May 22, 1999, p. 2.

★ 1224 ★
Freight Forwarding
SIC: 4741–ISIC: 7111

Largest Freight Forwarders, 1998

Market shares are shown in percent.

Panalpina	5.7%
Nippon Express	4.5
BAX Global	3.5
Kuehne & Nagle	3.5
Danzas	3.4
Schenker	3.2
Emery Worldwide	3.1
Kintetsu	2.7
MSAS	2.7
AEI	2.1
Other	65.6

Source: *Air Cargo World*, March 2000, p. 62, from MergeGlobal.

★ 1225 ★
Medical Assistance Services
SIC: 4780–ISIC: 6303

Medical Assistance Industry

The company was previously known as AEA International (Asia Emergency Assistance). It has 40 million members in 40 countries. Medical evacuation is a core service.

International SOS	90.0%
Other	10.0

Source: *Bangkok Post*, October 25, 1999, p. 3.

SIC 48 - Communications

★ 1226 ★
Cellular Services
SIC: 4812–ISIC: 6420

Largest Mobile Markets in Asia

Market shares are shown in percent.

	2000	2005
China	33.5%	46.7%
Japan	27.9	22.2
South Korea	14.2	8.6
Taiwan	7.6	4.1
Other	16.8	18.4

Source: *The Economist*, December 9, 2000, p. 76, from Strategic Intelligence.

★ 1227 ★
Cellular Services
SIC: 4812–ISIC: 6420

Largest Wireless Operators in Europe

Firms are ranked by millions of subscribers at the end of June 1999.

Telecom Italia Mobile	16.04
Omnitel Pronto Ialia	7.90
Mannesmann Mobilfunk	7.30
Deutsche Telekom MobilNet	7.10
France Telecom	7.02
Telefonica Moviles	6.73
Vodafone (U.K. only)	6.15
SFR	5.24
BT Cellnet	5.02
Orange	2.96

Source: *Wall Street Journal*, October 20, 1999, p. A20, from Salomon Smith Barney.

★ 1228 ★
Cellular Services
SIC: 4812–ISIC: 6420

Mobile Phone Service in France, 1999

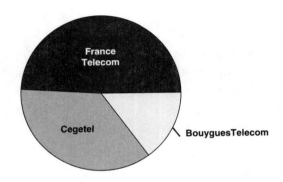

Total subscribers reached 16.2 million as of September 1999.

France Telecom	49.2%
Cegetel	36.2
BouyguesTelecom	14.6

Source: *National Trade Data Bank*, November 24, 1999.

★ 1229 ★
Cellular Services
SIC: 4812–ISIC: 6420

Top Cellular Phone Services in Japan, 1999

Market shares are shown based on subscribers.

NTT DoCoMo	57.4%
J-Phone group	16.0
DDI Cellular group	12.2
Ido Corp.	7.6
Digital-Tu-Ka group	6.8

Source: *Nikkei Weekly*, July 31, 2000, p. 8, from Nihon Keizai Shimbun.

★ 1230 ★
Cellular Services
SIC: 4812–ISIC: 6420

Top Mobile Firms in the Czech Republic

Market shares are shown in percent.

	2000	2002
Eurotel	52.4%	49.4%
Radiomobil	42.4	39.4
Cesky Mobil	5.2	11.2

Source: *Hospodarske Noviny*, December 21, 1999, p. 1, from SPT Telecom and Radiomobil.

★ 1231 ★
Cellular Services
SIC: 4812–ISIC: 6420

Top Mobile Phone Firms in Europe, 2000

Data are millions of subscribers for the first quarter.

Vodafone	39.1
Orange	20.4
TIM	19.2
Omnitel	11.5
D2 Mobilfunk	11.1
T-Mobil	10.9
Vodafone UK	8.8
SFR	8.2
BT Cellnet	7.4
Turkcell	6.2

Source: *Financial Times*, August 4, 2000, p. 21, from Morgan Stanley Dean Witter and Primark Datastream.

★ 1232 ★
Cellular Services
SIC: 4812–ISIC: 6420

Top Mobile Phone Firms in Germany

Shares are shown based on subscribers.

Mannesmann Mobilfunk	41.2%
T-Mobil	39.8
E-Plus	16.4
Viag Interkom	3.0

Source: *Financial Times*, December 10, 1999, p. 19, from FT Mobile Communications.

★ 1233 ★
Cellular Services
SIC: 4812–ISIC: 6420

Top Mobile Service Providers in Australia, 2000

Market shares are shown in percent.

Telstra	45.9%
Optus	33.3
Vodafone	19.1
Other	1.7

Source: *New York Times*, February 1, 2001, p. W1, from Goldman, Sachs.

★ 1234 ★
Cellular Services
SIC: 4812–ISIC: 6420

Top Mobile Service Providers in Brazil

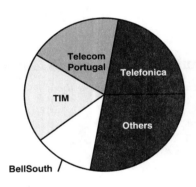

Shares are as of March 2000. Total subscribers in 2000 was estimated at 21.5 million; by 2005 that number should hit 58 million.

Telefonica	22.4%
Telecom Portugal	19.1
TIM	18.5
BellSouth	12.1
Others	27.9

Source: *Financial Times*, October 4, 2000, p. 21, from Anatel and UBS Warburg.

★ 1235 ★
Cellular Services
SIC: 4812–ISIC: 6420

Top Mobile Service Providers in Hong Kong

Market shares are shown in percent.

CSL	32.0%
Hutchinson	30.0
SmarTone	17.0
New World	9.0
Peoples	6.0
Other	6.0

Source: *IEEE Communications Magazine*, October 1999, p. 101.

★ 1236 ★
Cellular Services
SIC: 4812–ISIC: 6420

Top Mobile Service Providers in Spain

Market shares are shown in percent.

Telefoncia Moviles	55.6%
Airtel	28.3
Other	16.1

Source: *El Mundo*, May 4, 2001, p. 40.

★ 1237 ★
Cellular Services
SIC: 4812–ISIC: 6420

Top Mobile Service Providers in the U.K., 2000

Market shares are shown in percent. Shares are for the fourth quarter of the year.

Vodafone	11.7%
BT Cellnet	10.2
Orange	10.0
One2one	8.3
Other	59.8

Source: *Financial Times*, February 1, 2001, p. 25.

★ 1238 ★
Paging Services
SIC: 4812–ISIC: 6420

Largest Paging Firms in Chile

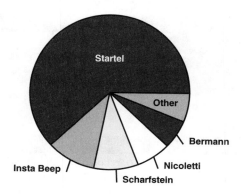

Market shares are shown in percent.

Startel 62.0%
Insta Beep 9.8
Scharfstein 9.1
Nicoletti 6.5
Bermann 6.2
Other 6.4

Source: STAT-USA, *National Trade Data Bank*, November 24, 1998, p. NA.

★ 1239 ★
Paging Services
SIC: 4812–ISIC: 6420

Largest Paging Firms in China

Five major firms are: China Motion Telecom, Sino American/AP Network, Beijing Asia Pacific First Star, Shanghai Guo Mai and Gunagzhou Gunadong GTE.

China Telecom 66.60%
Other small carriers 19.15
Five major 11.25
China Unicom 3.00

Source: *China Business Review*, July-August 1999, p. 22, from Yankee Group.

★ 1240 ★
Wireless Services
SIC: 4812–ISIC: 6420

Global Wireless Market, 2006

Market shares are shown in percent.

Western Europe 33.0%
Asia-Pacific 24.0
North America 20.0
South/Central America and Caribbean 8.0
Central Asia 7.0
Middle East and Africa 5.0
Central and Eastern Europe 3.0

Source: *M Business*, January 2001, p. 45, from Ovum.

★ 1241 ★
Wireless Services
SIC: 4812–ISIC: 6420

Largest Wireless Markets

Countries are ranked by estimated millions of subscribers.

United States 93.65
Japan 57.95
China 46.50
Italy 31.11
South Korea 27.50
United Kingdom 25.51
Germany 25.00
France 21.08
Spain 16.37
Brazil 14.43

Source: *RCR Wireless News*, December 25, 2000, p. S10.

★ 1242 ★
Wireless Services
SIC: 4812–ISIC: 6420

Largest Wireless Subscriber Firms in Asia

Firms are ranked by millions of subscribers as of June 2000. Shares are shown based on 135 million subscribers in the top 20 companies.

	(mil.)	Share
NTT DoCoMo	30.9	22.89%
China Mobile	21.6	16.00
SK Telecom	11.5	8.52
Unicom	11.1	8.22
J-Phone Group	8.7	6.44
DDI Group	6.2	4.59
KT Freetel	4.9	3.63
Telstra	4.1	3.04
Chungwa	3.9	2.89
IDO	3.9	2.89
Other	28.2	20.89

Source: *Communications International*, December 2000, p. 22, from International Telecommunications Union.

★ 1243 ★
Wireless Services
SIC: 4812–ISIC: 6420

Mobile Internet Users Worldwide

Distribution is shown in percent.

North America	41.84%
Asia Pacific	38.02
Europe	17.52
Central/South America	1.38
Australia	0.83
Russia	0.23
Africa	0.18

Source: *Business 2.0*, November 14, 2000, p. 280, from Research Portal.com.

★ 1244 ★
Wireless Services
SIC: 4812–ISIC: 6420

Voice-Over-Internet Traffic Market Shares, 1999

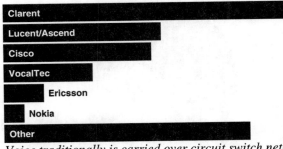

Voice traditionally is carried over circuit switch networks in analog format. Clarent's devices are designed to digitize voices, compress them and transfer them over the Internet.

Clarent	29.0%
Lucent/Ascend	16.0
Cisco	15.0
VocalTec	9.0
Ericsson	4.0
Nokia	2.0
Other	25.0

Source: *Investor's Business Daily*, February 16, 2000, p. A10, from iLocus.

★ 1245 ★
Telecommunications
SIC: 4813–ISIC: 6420

Europe's Telecom Market

Companies are ranked by revenue in billions of dollars.

	Rev. ($ bil.)	Share
Deutsche Telekom/Telcom Italia	$ 52.91	33.65%
France Telecom	21.87	13.91
British Telecom	21.67	13.78
Telefonica	13.69	8.71
Other	47.10	29.95

Source: *Wall Street Journal*, April 23, 1999, p. A11, from CIT Publications.

★ 1246 ★
Telecommunications
SIC: 4813–ISIC: 6420

Largest Telecom Firms in Europe

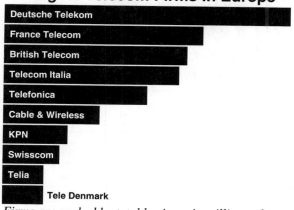

Firms are ranked by total business in millions of euros.

Deutsche Telekom	35.7
France Telecom	24.6
British Telecom	23.2
Telecom Italia	22.1
Telefonica	17.5
Cable & Wireless	12.4
KPN	8.0
Swisscom	6.5
Telia	5.3
Tele Denmark	4.8

Source: *Der Spiegel*, no. 27, 1999, p. NA.

★ 1247 ★
Telecommunications
SIC: 4813–ISIC: 6420

Public Network Service Revenues, 1999

Figures are in billions of dollars.

United States	$ 195.7
Japan	43.8
United Kingdom	31.5
Germany	30.0
China	24.5
France	21.1

Source: *Telephony*, July 24, 2000, p. 9, from Dataquest Inc.

★ 1248 ★
Telecommunications
SIC: 4813–ISIC: 6420

Telecom Market in Europe, 1998

Market shares are shown in percent.

Germany	26.3%
France	18.8
Italy	18.2
Spain	9.3
Netherlands	5.8
Switzerland	4.5
Sweden	3.9
Other	18.4

Source: *Financial Times*, March 27, 2000, p. 20.

★ 1249 ★
Telephone Services
SIC: 4813–ISIC: 6420

Largest Telephone Carriers

Firms are ranked by billions of minutes in outgoing traffic.

AT&T	10.8
WorldCom	8.2
France Telekom	4.3

Continued on next page.

★ 1249 ★

[Continued]
Telephone Services
SIC: 4813–ISIC: 6420

Largest Telephone Carriers

Firms are ranked by billions of minutes in outgoing traffic.

BT	4.0
Deutsche Telekom	3.8
Sprint	3.7
C&W Com.	3.1
Telekom Italia	2.3
Swisscom	2.2
China Tele.	1.9

Source: "Long Distance Carriers Lose Money." Retrieved October 30, 2000 from the World Wide Web: http://www.biz.yahoo.com, from TeleGeography.

★ 1250 ★

Telephone Services
SIC: 4813–ISIC: 6420

Telephone Service in Saigon

Market shares are shown in percent.

Vietnam Post and Telecommunications Corporation	98.0%
Other	2.0

Source: *Saigon Times Magazine*, February 16, 2001, p. NA.

★ 1251 ★

Telephone Services
SIC: 4813–ISIC: 6420

Top International Phone Services in Japan, 1999

KDD Corp.
Cable & Wireless IDC Inc.
Japan Telecom Co.
DDI Corp.
NTT Communications Corp.

Market shares are shown based on domestic sales.

KDD Corp.	59.7%
Cable & Wireless IDC Inc.	17.9
Japan Telecom Co.	17.6
DDI Corp.	4.0
NTT Communications Corp.	0.8

Source: *Nikkei Weekly*, July 31, 2000, p. 8, from Nihon Keizai Shimbun.

★ 1252 ★

Electronic Commerce
SIC: 4822–ISIC: 6420

E-Commerce Market, 2001

Market shares are estimated for midsize firms.

North America	68.0%
Western Europe	20.0
Asia-Pacific	10.0
Other	2.0

Source: *Investor's Business Daily*, March 22, 2001, p. A8, from AMI-Partners Inc.

Electronic Commerce
SIC: 4822–ISIC: 6420

Leading E-Commerce Markets

Sales are shown in millions of dollars.

	2001	2002	2003
United States	$ 864.1	$ 1,411.3	$ 2,817.3
Japan	64.4	146.3	363.6
Germany	46.4	102.9	211.1
United Kingdom	38.5	83.2	165.6
Canada	38.0	68.9	109.6
Italy	15.8	33.8	71.4
Korea	14.1	39.3	100.5
Auatralia	14.0	36.9	96.7
Taiwan	10.7	30.0	80.6

Source: *WWD*, June 26, 2000, p. 14, from Forrester Research.

★ 1254 ★
Electronic Commerce
SIC: 4822–ISIC: 6420

Online Auction Market in Japan

Market shares are shown in percent.

Yahoo Japan	95.0%
Other	5.0

Source: *Business Week*, June 4, 2001, p. 58.

★ 1255 ★
Electronic Commerce
SIC: 4822–ISIC: 6420

Online Purchases in China

Data are as of May 1, 2000.

	Men	Women
Books	38.0%	29.0%
Computer software	28.0	9.0
Food/groceries	20.0	26.0
Prerecorded music	16.0	9.0
Computer hardware	10.0	5.0
Entertainment (theater tickets)	8.0	13.0

	Men	Women
Travel related services	8.0%	5.0%
Prerecorded video, DVD, VCD	5.0	5.0

Source: *Far Eastern Economic Review*, August 3, 2000, p. 36.

★ 1256 ★
Electronic Commerce
SIC: 4822–ISIC: 6420

Online Travel Market in Europe

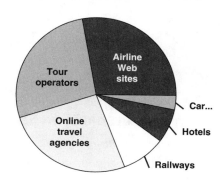

The online travel market is expected to grow from $2.9 billion in 2000 to $10.9 billion in 2002, a nearly 300% jump in two years. The jump is a result of increased use of the Internet, breakdown to e-commerce barriers (like bill payment), and increased telecom infrastructure.

Airline Web sites	28.0%
Tour operators	27.0
Online travel agencies	26.0
Railways	9.0
Hotels	7.0
Car rental companies	3.0

Source: "PhoCusWright Projects European Online Travel." Retrieved January 18, 2001 from the World Wide Web: http://www.businesswire.com, from PhoCus Wright.

★ 1257 ★
Electronic Commerce
SIC: 4822–ISIC: 6420

Top Online Purchases in Australia

Data show the most popular categories.

Books	21.0%
Groceries	17.0
Music	16.0
PC software	13.0
PC hardware	9.0

Source: *Industry Standard*, September 25, 2000, p. 183, from Taylor Nelson Sofres.

★ 1258 ★
Electronic Commerce
SIC: 4822–ISIC: 6420

Top Online Purchases in France

Data show the most popular categories.

Leisure travel	44.0%
Music	39.0
Books	17.0
Stocks/mutual funds	17.0
Toys	17.0

Source: *Industry Standard*, September 25, 2000, p. 183, from Taylor Nelson Sofres.

★ 1259 ★
Electronic Commerce
SIC: 4822–ISIC: 6420

Top Online Purchases in Germany

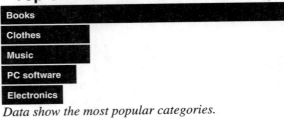

Data show the most popular categories.

Books	62.0%
Clothes	19.0
Music	19.0
PC software	16.0
Electronics	13.0

Source: *Industry Standard*, September 25, 2000, p. 183, from Taylor Nelson Sofres.

★ 1260 ★
Electronic Commerce
SIC: 4822–ISIC: 6420

Top Online Purchases in Hong Kong

Data show the most popular categories.

Groceries	32.0%
Books	29.0
Furniture	21.0
PC hardware	11.0
PC software	11.0

Source: *Industry Standard*, September 25, 2000, p. 183, from Taylor Nelson Sofres.

★ 1261 ★
Electronic Commerce
SIC: 4822–ISIC: 6420

Top Online Purchases in the Netherlands

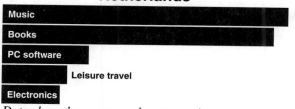

Data show the most popular categories.

Music	40.0%
Books	38.0
PC software	12.0
Leisure travel	9.0
Electronics	8.0

Source: *Industry Standard*, September 25, 2000, p. 183, from Taylor Nelson Sofres.

★ 1262 ★
Electronic Commerce
SIC: 4822–ISIC: 6420

Top Online Purchases Worldwide

Data show the most popular categories.

Books	29.0%
Music	20.0
PC software	11.0
Apparel	10.0
Food	10.0

Source: *Industry Standard*, September 25, 2000, p. 183, from Taylor Nelson Sofres.

★ 1263 ★
Electronic Learning
SIC: 4822–ISIC: 6420

Corporate E-Learning Market

The market is expected to grow from $1.78 billion in 1999 to $23.1 billion in 2004.

	1999	2004
North America	69.7%	65.2%
Japan	16.0	9.6
Western Europe	8.0	17.1
Latin America	4.1	4.4
Asia Pacific	1.5	1.8
Rest of world	0.7	1.9

Source: *Financial Times*, June 6, 2001, p. 1, from International Data Corp.

★ 1264 ★
Electronic Learning
SIC: 4822–ISIC: 6420

E-Learning in Europe

Data show projected expenditures, in millions.

	2001	2004	Share
Content	$ 409	$ 2,100	53.69%
Delivery services	165	711	18.18
Services	143	1,100	28.13

Source: *Training*, January 2001, p. 64, from International Data Corp.

★ 1265 ★
Internet
SIC: 4822–ISIC: 6420

China's Internet Market by Region

The main tasks performed online are gathering e-mail, searching and downloading software.

Beijing	21.2%
Guangdong	12.9
Shanghai	11.2
Jiangsu	5.9
Shandong	5.2
Zhejiang	4.5

Continued on next page.

★ 1265 ★
[Continued]
Internet
SIC: 4822–ISIC: 6420

China's Internet Market by Region

The main tasks performed online are gathering e-mail, searching and downloading software.

Lianoning	4.3%
Hunan	3.4
Hubei	3.3
Sichuan	3.0
Other	25.0

Source: *China Business Review*, March-April 2000, p. 24, from China Intenet Network Information Center.

★ 1266 ★
Internet
SIC: 4822–ISIC: 6420

How Russians Use The Internet

The Internet is still in its infancy with 2.5 million users (1% of the population). The lack of infrastructure and and telecom development stands in the way of this field's development.

News	13.0%
Business, finance	12.0
Humor, entertainment	12.0
Chat	10.0
Games	9.0
Music	9.0
Science	8.0
Sex	6.0
Other	18.0

Source: *Business in Russia*, October-November 2000, p. 113, from AmCham News.

★ 1267 ★
Internet
SIC: 4822–ISIC: 6420

Internet Fax Service Provider Market Shares, 1999

Shares are shown based on traffic volume.

FaxSav	28.6%
FaxNet	9.4
Cynet	8.9
AT&T	7.3
Faxaway	6.8
Other	39.0

Source: *Network World*, April 5, 1999, p. 21, from International Data Corp.

★ 1268 ★
Internet
SIC: 4822–ISIC: 6420

Internet Protocol Telephony Market in the U.K.

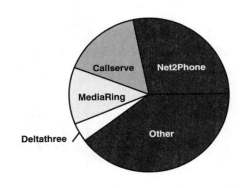

Market shares are shown in percent.

Net2Phone	28.0%
Callserve	16.0
MediaRing	12.0
Deltathree	4.0
Other	40.0

Source: ''Callserve Storms IP Telephony Market.'' Retrieved July 11, 2000 from the World Wide Web: http://www.northernlight.com, from MORI.

★ 1269 ★
Internet
SIC: 4822–ISIC: 6420

Largest Internet Users

Data are in millions.

United States	76.5
Japan	9.7
Great Britain	8.1
Germany	7.1
Canada	6.5
Australia	4.3
France	2.7
Sweden	2.5
Italy	2.1
Spain	1.9

Source: *Computer Reseller News*, September 11, 2000, p. 80, from *Computer Industry Almanac*.

★ 1271 ★
Internet
SIC: 4822–ISIC: 6420

Top Domains in the U.K., 2000

Unique visitors, in thousands, for July 2000.

MSN.com	4,121
Yahoo.com	4,058
Freeserve.com	3,618
Microsoft.com	3,410
MSN.co.uk	2,486
Passport.com	2,320
Yahoo.co.uk	2,286
Lycos.com	2,040
Demon.net	1,754
BBC.co.uk	1,641

Source: *The Guardian*, August 30, 2000, p. 20, from MMXI Europe.

★ 1270 ★
Internet
SIC: 4822–ISIC: 6420

Leading Digital Certification Makers in Japan, 1999

Shares are estimated at 3 billion yen. Digital certification systems refers to when all company employees, customers or other partners involved in an e-commerce transaction identify themselves and are issued a digital certificate of identification by a certification center. The participants use their digital IDs to make contracts and settle accounts online.

Baltimore Technologies	35.0%
VeriSign	35.0
Other	30.0

Source: *Nikkei Weekly*, March 12, 2001, p. 11.

★ 1272 ★
Internet
SIC: 4822–ISIC: 6420

Top Domains Worldwide

Total domains worldwide were 11.27 million at the end of November 1999.

	No.	Share
.com domains	6,970.4	61.82%
.net domains	1,101.8	9.77
.de domains	708.7	6.29
.org domains	682.4	6.05
.uk domains	566.8	5.03
.ar domains	124.4	1.10
.nl domains	121.2	1.07
.kr domains	104.1	0.92
.dk domains	93.1	0.83
.ch domains	91.9	0.82
Other	710.3	6.30

Source: *USA TODAY*, December 7, 1999, p. 3D, from NetNames.

★ 1273 ★
Internet
SIC: 4822–ISIC: 6420

Top Web Sites in Europe

Data show unique visitors per month. Data are in thousands.

www.yahoo.com	9,005
www.msn.com	7,307
www.aol.com	6,386
www.microsoft.com	6,312
www.t-online.de	6,078
www.lycos.com	6,014
www.altavista.com	3,257
www.freeserve.co.uk	3,109
www.netscape.com	2,845
www.real.com	2,415

Source: *Fortune*, June 12, 2000, p. 224, from MMXI Europe.

★ 1275 ★
Internet
SIC: 4822–ISIC: 6420

Websites by Country

Of the 3.6 million unique websites measured in 1999, only 2.29% were publically accessible.

United States	55.0%
Germany	6.0
Canada	5.0
United Kingdom	5.0
Japan	3.0
Australia	2.0
Brazil	2.0
France	2.0
Italy	2.0
Other	18.0

Source: *Business 2.0*, November 14, 2000, p. 278, from Online Computer Library Center.

★ 1274 ★
Internet
SIC: 4822–ISIC: 6420

Web-Hosting Revenue by Country

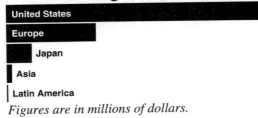

United States
Europe
Japan
Asia
Latin America

Figures are in millions of dollars.

	2000	2004	Share
United States	$ 7,700.0	$ 22,700.0	71.25%
Europe	2,200.0	6,900.0	21.66
Japan	621.0	2,000.0	6.28
Asia	41.0	248.0	0.78
Latin America	2.1	10.4	0.03

Source: *Investor's Business Daily*, March 2, 2001, p. A6, from Morgan Stanley Dean Witter.

★ 1276 ★
Online Services
SIC: 4822–ISIC: 6420

Largest ISPs in Europe

Groups are ranked by millions of users/visitors.

T-Online	4.5
America Online	3.5
Freeserve	3.1
Wanadoo	1.7
Puretec	1.3

Source: *Der Spiegel*, no. 22, 2000, p. 116.

★ 1277 ★
Online Services
SIC: 4822–ISIC: 6420

Largest ISPs in Finland

The residential market is shown in percent. Local ISPs control Finland's market with a nearly 100% market share. There are about 60 providers in the country, generating a market of $89 million. Eunet Finland Oy has less than 2% of the market, but 95% of its business is in the business market, where it has a 40% share.

Sonera (Inet)	40.0%
Helsingin Puhelin Oy (Kolumbus, Megabud)	23.0
Saunalahden Serveri (Saunalahti)	22.0
Clinet Oy	2.0
EEEUnet Finland Oy	2.0
Netti Finland Oy (Private netti)	2.0
Other	9.0

Source: "Finland: Internet Services." Retrieved October 10, 2000 from the World Wide Web: http://www.tradeport.org.

★ 1278 ★
Online Services
SIC: 4822–ISIC: 6420

Largest ISPs in France

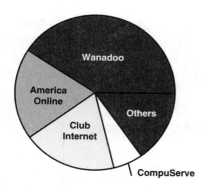

Data show subscribers.

	(000)	Share
Wanadoo	600	40.82%
America Online	280	19.05
Club Internet	280	19.05
CompuServe	90	6.12
Others	220	14.97

Source: *Wall Street Journal*, October 1, 1999, p. A12, from Fletcher Research.

★ 1279 ★
Online Services
SIC: 4822–ISIC: 6420

Largest ISPs in Italy

Data show millions of clients.

Tin.it (Telkecom Italia)	2.5
Infostrada (Vodafone-Mannesmann)	1.6
Tiscali	1.3

Source: *Wall Street Journal*, March 2, 2000, p. A21, from Il Sole/24 Ore research.

★ 1280 ★
Online Services
SIC: 4822–ISIC: 6420

Largest ISPs in Japan

Shares are shown based on subscribers.

@nifty	21.9%
BIGLOBE	17.7
OCN	6.5
So-net	5.2
Other	48.7

Source: *Japan Computer Industry Scan*, May 29, 2000, p. NA, from MultiMedia Research Insitute.

★ 1281 ★
Online Services
SIC: 4822–ISIC: 6420

Largest ISPs in Russia

Market shares are shown in percent. By 2003, the market is expected to hit $350 million.

Sistema Telekom	18.0%
Golden Telecom	14.0
Cityline	8.0
Other	60.0

Source: *Moskovskie Novosti*, January 16, 2001, p. NA, from Communications Ministry.

★ 1282 ★
Online Services
SIC: 4822–ISIC: 6420

Largest ISPs in the Czech Republic

There are 16 large Internet providers and over 300 small regional providers.

Czech On Line	37.0%
Internet On Line (Czech Telecom)	17.0
Contactel	10.0
Other	36.0

Source: "E-Commerce in the Czech Republic." Retrieved October 27, 2000 from the World Wide Web: http://www.mac.doc.gov.

★ 1283 ★
Online Services
SIC: 4822–ISIC: 6420

Popular ISPs in Argentina

Market shares are shown in percent.

Ciudad Internet	21.9%
Arnet	13.4
Advance	10.7
Sinectis	7.1
Radar	3.6
Sion	3.1
Alternativa Gratis	2.7
Infovia	2.7
Utopia	2.7
Other	10.6

Source: *AdAgeGlobal*, March 2001, p. 30, from Prince & Cooke survey.

★ 1284 ★
Radio Broadcasting
SIC: 4832–ISIC: 6420

Radio Market in Ireland

Market shares are shown in percent.

Independents	52.0%
Radio 1	27.0
2FM	20.0

Source: *Irish Times*, February 23, 2000, p. 1.

★ 1285 ★
Television Broadcasting
SIC: 4833–ISIC: 6420

Children's Television Market

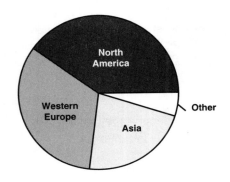

Broadcasters will spend an estimated $2.1 billion on producing. Commissioning and acquiring children's programs in 1999. Independent producers, however, are having a greater influence in the industry.

North America	40.0%
Western Europe	33.0
Asia	22.0
Other	5.0

Source: "Global Childrens Programme Worth $2.1 Billion." Retrieved September 28, 2000 from the World Wide Web: http://www.screendigest.com.

★ 1286 ★
Television Broadcasting
SIC: 4833–ISIC: 6420

Italy's TV Market, 2000

Audience shares are shown for 24 hours, Spring 2000.

RAI	22.6%
Canale 5	22.4
RAI 2	15.4
Italia 1	11.4
Retequattro	10.0
RAI 3	9.0
Telemontecarlo	2.0
Others	7.0

Source: *Financial Times*, July 26, 2000, p. 19, from Mediaset.

★ 1287 ★
Television Broadcasting
SIC: 4833–ISIC: 6420

Music Television in Poland

These are shares of the digital audience, not cable audience.

MCM	25.9%
MTV Europe	23.0
VIVA	16.0
VIVA Polska	5.8

Source: *Cable Europe*, July 4, 2000.

★ 1288 ★
Television Broadcasting
SIC: 4833–ISIC: 6420

TV Ad Leaders in Germany

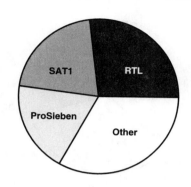

Market shares are shown in percent.

RTL	27.3%
SAT1	20.8
ProSieben	19.0
Other	32.9

Source: *Broadcasting & Cable's TV International*, February 5, 2001, p. 4, from A.C. Nielsen.

★ 1289 ★
Television Broadcasting
SIC: 4833–ISIC: 6420

TV Audience in Greece, 1998

Antenna was the first to bring news programming and daytime talk shows to Greece. This small market of just 3.2 million households has grown more competitive. The table shows audience share. Antenna also has the largest share of ad spending.

Antenna	23.8%
Mega	20.9
Skai	14.5
Star	13.7
State-owned	10.0
Other	17.1

Source: *Investor's Business Daily*, June 30, 1999, p. A10, from company reports.

★ 1290 ★
Television Broadcasting
SIC: 4833–ISIC: 6420

TV Market Leaders in Australia

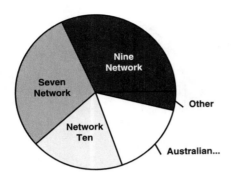

Market shares are shown in percent.

Nine Network	31.80%
Seven Network	30.01
Network Ten	18.60
Australian Broadcasting Corp.	16.00
Other	3.59

Source: *Hollywood Reporter*, April 4, 2000, pp. S-26, from A.C. Nielsen.

★ 1291 ★
Television Broadcasting
SIC: 4833–ISIC: 6420

TV Market Shares in the U.K.

Data are for December 2000.

ITV	28.8%
BBC 1	27.5
BBC 2	10.7
Channel 4/S4C	10.1
Channel 5	5.1
Other	17.8

Source: *Financial Times*, January 25, 2001, p. 23, from BARB.

★ 1292 ★
Cable Broadcasting
SIC: 4841–ISIC: 6420

Cable TV Market in Argentina

Market shares are shown in percent.

Cablevision	29.0%
Multicanal	28.0
Grupo Uno	10.0
Others	33.0

Source: *Latin Trade*, May 1999, p. 60, from CEI.

★ 1293 ★
Cable Broadcasting
SIC: 4841–ISIC: 6420

Largest Cable Nations, 1997

Data show millions of cable subscribers.

China	80.0
United States	68.0
European Union	39.7
Germany	18.9
India	18.6
Russia	14.5
Japan	14.0

Source: "China: Cable TV Programming." Retrieved September 18, 2000 from the World Wide Web: http://www.tradeport.org, from *China Economic Quarterly* and SAFRT.

★ 1294 ★
Satellite Broadcasting
SIC: 4841–ISIC: 6420

Cable/Satellite Industry in the U.K., 2000

Viewing is shown by genre.

Generalist	61.2%
Light entertainment	8.9
Children's	4.7
Sports	3.9
Movies	3.5
Documentary	2.1

Continued on next page.

★ 1294 ★
[Continued]
Satellite Broadcasting
SIC: 4841–ISIC: 6420

Cable/Satellite Industry in the U.K., 2000

Viewing is shown by genre.

Lifestyle 1.3%
Music 1.3

Source: *Screen Digest*, March 2001, p. 93, from BARB.

★ 1295 ★
Satellite Broadcasting
SIC: 4841–ISIC: 6420

Digital TV Subscribers in Italy

Market shares are shown by platform. Figures are for the second quarter of 2000.

D+/+calcio 65.7%
Stream 34.3

Source: *TV International*, August 31, 2000, p. 8.

★ 1296 ★
Satellite Broadcasting
SIC: 4841–ISIC: 6420

Digital TV Subscribers in Poland

Market shares are shown by platform. Figures are for the second quarter of 2000.

Wizja TV 50.6%
Cyfra+ 49.4

Source: *TV International*, August 31, 2000, p. 8.

★ 1297 ★
Satellite Broadcasting
SIC: 4841–ISIC: 6420

Digital TV Subscribers in Scandinavia

Market shares are shown by platform. Figures are for the second quarter of 2000.

Canal Digital 52.8%
Viasat Guild 47.2

Source: *TV International*, August 31, 2000, p. 8.

★ 1298 ★
Satellite Broadcasting
SIC: 4841–ISIC: 6420

Digital TV Subscribers in Spain

Market shares are shown by platform. Figures are for the second quarter of 2000.

Canalsatellite 62.2%
Via Digital 37.8

Source: *TV International*, August 31, 2000, p. 8.

★ 1299 ★
Satellite Broadcasting
SIC: 4841–ISIC: 6420

Global Subscriber Market, 2000

The satellite TV industry is expected to generate $46 billion in revenue.

Europe 39.0%
Asia 22.0
North America 17.0
Latin America 7.0
Middle East/Africa 7.0
Central/Eastern Europe 6.0

Source: *Investor's Business Daily*, April 16, 2001, p. A10.

★ 1300 ★
Satellite Broadcasting
SIC: 4841–ISIC: 6420
Pay TV Market in Australia

Shares are shown based on subscribers.

Foxtel 47.0%
Austar 32.0
OptusVision 21.0

Source: *Financial Times*, September 6, 1999, p. 19, from
Merrill Lynch.

SIC 49 - Electric, Gas, and Sanitary Services

★ 1301 ★
Energy
SIC: 4900–ISIC: 4000

World Energy Sources, 1999

Distribution is shown in percent.

Oil	30.0%
Coal	22.0
Renewable	19.0
Nuclear	6.0
Other	23.0

Source: *USA TODAY*, December 21, 1999, p. B1.

★ 1302 ★
Utilities
SIC: 4911–ISIC: 4010

Electricity Generation Market in Europe

Market shares are shown in percent.

EdF	17.3%
Enel	8.5
RWE/VEW	7.5
E.ON	6.9
Vattenfall	3.2
Endesa	2.8
Electrabel	2.7
British Energy	2.6
Iberdrola	2.3
Other	46.2

Source: *Financial Times*, June 16, 2000, p. 21, from Deutsche Bank Research.

★ 1303 ★
Utilities
SIC: 4911–ISIC: 4010

Electricity Market in Spain

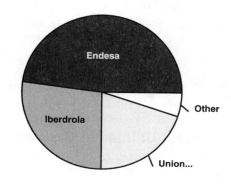

Market shares are shown in percent.

Endesa	48.0%
Iberdrola	27.0
Union Fenosa-Hidrocantabrico	20.0
Other	5.0

Source: *Electric Utility Week International*, May 29, 2000, p. 4.

★ 1304 ★
Utilities
SIC: 4911–ISIC: 4010

Largest Electric Utilities in Japan, 2000

Companies are ranked by sales in billions of yen for the first half of the year.

Tokyo Electric Power Co.	2,675
Kansai Electric Power Co.	1,348
Chubu Electric Power Co.	1,119

Continued on next page.

★ 1304 ★

[Continued]
Utilities
SIC: 4911–ISIC: 4010

Largest Electric Utilities in Japan, 2000

Companies are ranked by sales in billions of yen for the first half of the year.

Tohoku Electric Power Co.	791
Kyushu Electric Power Co.	742
Chugoku Electric Power Co.	517
Shikoku Electric Power Co.	282
Hokkaido Electric Power Co.	262

Source: *Asia Pulse News*, April 25, 2001, p. NA.

★ 1305 ★

Utilities
SIC: 4911–ISIC: 4010

Largest Utilities in Germany

Groups are ranked by power generated in billions of kilowatt hours.

RWE Energie	138
Veba	106
Viag	73
Energie Baden Wurttemberg	54
VEAG Vereingte Energiewerke	47

Source: *Wall Street Journal*, September 24, 1999, p. A10, from Association of German Electric Utilities.

★ 1306 ★

Utilities
SIC: 4911–ISIC: 4010

Largest Utilities Worldwide

The top generators have a combined capacity of 617 GW.

	GW	Share
RAO-UES of Russia	156	5.0%
EdF of France	102	3.3

Source: *Europe Energy*, April 14, 2000, p. NA.

★ 1307 ★

Water Services
SIC: 4911–ISIC: 4010

Water Service Market in Chile

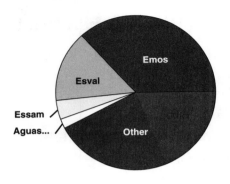

Market shares are shown in percent.

Emos	36.8%
Esval	14.7
Essam	4.0
Aguas Quinta	1.6
Other	42.9

Source: *El Diario*, December 26, 2000, p. 1.

★ 1308 ★

Dams
SIC: 4941–ISIC: 4100

Global Dam Distribution

Distribution is shown by region.

China	46.0%
United States	14.0
India	9.0
Japan	6.0
Spain	3.0
Other	23.0

Source: *Civil Engineering*, January 2001, p. 15.

SIC 50 - Wholesale Trade - Durable Goods

★ 1309 ★

Wholesale Trade - Software

SIC: 5045–ISIC: 5150–HC: 85

Software Publisher Distribution Market in France, 1998

Market shares are shown in percent. CD-ROM sales were up 54% by volume with 9.3 million units. Software products have 40% of the market, educational software has a 20% share, practical guide CD-ROMs have 16% share.

Havas Multimedia	13.0%
Ubi	11.0
Microsoft	10.0
TLC-Edusoft	10.0
Other	56.0

Source: *Points de Vente*, June 16, 1999, p. 1, from GfK.

SIC 51 - Wholesale Trade - Nondurable Goods

★ 1310 ★
Wholesale Trade
SIC: 5100–ISIC: 5139

Largest Distributors in France

Market shares are shown in percent.

Groupe Carrefour-Promodes	28.0%
Lucie	21.1
Opera	16.9
Intermarche	15.0
Groupe Auchan	12.9
Others	6.1

Source: *L'Express*, June 22, 2000, p. 69.

★ 1311 ★
Wholesale Trade
SIC: 5100–ISIC: 5139

Top Wholesalers in Denmark

Market shares are shown in percent.

FDB	38.3%
Danish Supermarket	22.3
Supervib	21.8
Dagrofa	8.8
Aldi	4.2
Chr. Kjaergaard	2.3
Other	2.3

Source: "Denmark Retail Food Sector Report Brief."
Retrieved September 1, 2000 from the World Wide Web:
http://ffas.usda.gov, from Foreign Agricultural Service and
United States Department of Agriculture.

★ 1312 ★
Wholesale Trade - Drugs
SIC: 5122–ISIC: 5139–HC: 30

Drug Wholesaling in Germany

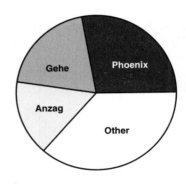

Market shares are shown in percent.

Phoenix	28.0%
Gehe	19.5
Anzag	16.0
Other	36.5

Source: *Frankfurter Allgemeine*, August 3, 2000, p. 1.

★ 1313 ★
Wholesale Trade - Drugs
SIC: 5122–ISIC: 5139–HC: 30

Drug Wholesaling Market in Poland

Market shares are shown in percent.

PGF	25.0%
Cormay	10.0
Prosper	9.0
Farmaceol	7.0
Orfe	4.0
Other	45.0

Source: *Warsaw Business Journal*, May 15, 2000, p. 1.

★ 1314 ★
Wholesale Trade - Confectionery
SIC: 5145–ISIC: 5122–HC: 17

Largest Kashi Wholesalers in Japan

Firms are ranked by sales in millions of yen.

Yamaboshi-Ya	162,500
San-Esu	157,798
Takayama	127,515
Hasegawa	56,913
Tanesei	49,176
Shikoku-ya	44,283
Tajima-ya	39,511
Shojiki-ya	39,494
Kaneko Seika-Shoten	39,000
Tanaka Seika	39,000

Source: *The Manufacturing Confectioner*, March 2000, p. 47.

SIC 52 - Building Materials and Garden Supplies

★ 1315 ★
Retailing - Home Improvement
SIC: 5211–ISIC: 5234–HC: 44

Do-It-Yourself Market in Europe, 1998

The total market size reached 99.7 billion euros.

	(bil.)	Share
Germany	35.7	35.81%
United Kingdom	16.7	16.75
France	14.4	14.44
Italy	8.5	8.53
Netherlands	3.5	3.51
Austria	3.1	3.11
Spain	2.8	2.81
Finland	2.6	2.61
Switzerland	2.6	2.61
Other	9.8	9.83

Source: "Where Wal-Mart Leads, Will Home Depot Follow." Retrieved October 17, 2000 from the World Wide Web: http://www.cior.com, from Retail Intelligence.

★ 1316 ★
Retailing - Home Improvement
SIC: 5211–ISIC: 5234–HC: 44

Top Do-It-Yourself Chains in Europe, 1998- 99

Market shares are shown in percent.

B&Q	6.8%
Obi (Tengelmann)	3.4
Praktiker (Metro)	2.8
Leroy Merlin (Auchan)	2.6
Bauhaus	1.9
Homebase (J Sainsbury)	1.9
Toom/Stinnes (Rewe)	1.5
Domaxea	1.4

Hagebau	1.4%
Marktkauf/dixi (AVA)	1.4
Other	74.9

Source: "Seeking a New Strategic Homebase." Retrieved October 17, 2000 from the World Wide Web: http://www.cior.com, from Retail Intelligence.

★ 1317 ★
Retailing - Home Improvement
SIC: 5211–ISIC: 5234–HC: 44

Top Home Improvement Firms in Benelux, 1998

Market shares are shown based on sales of $2.9 billion.

Brico	16.7%
Gamma Belgie	4.6
Bricorama	3.3
Bricoman	2.9
Hubo Belgie	2.9
Superbois	2.7
Other	66.9

Source: *National Home Center News*, June 21, 1999, p. 26.

★ 1318 ★
Retailing - Home Improvement
SIC: 5211–ISIC: 5234–HC: 44

Top Home Improvement Firms in Germany, 1998

Market shares are shown based on sales of $44.6 billion.

OBI	7.6%
Praktiker	6.8
Bauhaus	4.2
Toom	4.2
Hagebau	3.6
Other	73.7

Source: *National Home Center News*, June 21, 1999, p. 21.

★ 1319 ★
Retailing - Home Improvement
SIC: 5211–ISIC: 5234–HC: 44

Top Home Improvement Firms in Italy, 1998

Market shares are shown based on sales of $9.2 billion.

Societa Italiana Bricolage	2.76%
Obi Italia	1.73
Castorama Italia	1.36
Big Mat	0.95
Punto Legno	0.65
Self Gardino	0.39
La Centrale	0.36
Marketing Trend	0.31
Praktiker Italia	0.14
Other	91.35

Source: *National Home Center News*, June 21, 1999, p. 26.

★ 1320 ★
Retailing - Home Improvement
SIC: 5211–ISIC: 5234–HC: 44

Top Home Improvement Firms in South Africa, 1998

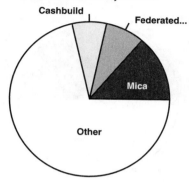

Market shares are shown based on sales of 11.9 billion rand.

Mica	13.7%
Federated Timbers	7.6
Cashbuild	6.7
Other	72.0

Source: *National Home Center News*, June 21, 1999, p. 45.

★ 1321 ★
Retailing - Home Improvement
SIC: 5211–ISIC: 5234–HC: 44

Top Home Improvement Firms in Spain, 1998

Market shares are shown based on sales of $2.7 billion.

Leroy Merlin	5.2%
AKI Bricolage	4.4
Mr. Bricolage	1.5
Bauhaus	0.7
Other	88.2

Source: *National Home Center News*, June 21, 1999, p. 21.

★ 1322 ★
Retailing - Home Improvement
SIC: 5211–ISIC: 5234–HC: 44

Top Home Improvement Firms in Switzerland, 1998

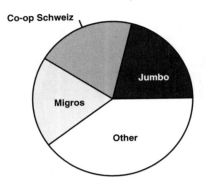

Market shares are shown based on sales of $1.64 billion.

Jumbo	21.1%
Co-op Schweiz	19.6
Migros	18.7
Other	39.9

Source: *National Home Center News*, June 21, 1999, p. 20.

★ 1323 ★
Retailing - Hardware
SIC: 5251–ISIC: 5234–HC: 82

Top DIY and Hardware Stores in the U.K., 1999

DIY stores have 68% of the market. Market shares are shown in percent.

Kingfisher	21.0%
Homebase	16.1
Do-It-All	7.5
Wicks	6.0
Great Mills	4.8
Other	44.6

Source: *Financial Times*, December 18, 2000, p. 16.

★ 1324 ★
Retailing - Hardware
SIC: 5251–ISIC: 5234–HC: 82

Top Hardware Chains in the U.K.

The table shows where regular DIY shoppers spend their money.

B&Q	49.5%
Homebase	15.3
Focus Do It All	6.8
Wickes	5.5
Great Mills	5.1
Wilkinsons	3.2
Other	14.6

Source: *Retail Week*, April 13, 2001, p. 16, from *Verdict on How Britain Shops DIY 2001*.

SIC 53 - General Merchandise Stores

★ 1325 ★
Retailing
SIC: 5300–ISIC: 5219

Largest Packaged Goods Retailers in Italy

Market shares are shown based on sales of food, drink and personal care retailers.

Coop Italia	10.5%
Conad	7.5
Vege	6.3
La Rinascente	5.3
Esselunga	5.1
Selex	4.6
Crai	4.3
CID	3.7
Despar	3.5
Standa	2.9
Other	46.3

Source: *In-Store Marketing*, April 2001, p. 25.

★ 1326 ★
Retailing
SIC: 5300–ISIC: 5219

Largest Retail Firms in Finland

Market shares are shown in percent.

Kesko	38.2%
S-Group	26.3
Tradeka/Elanto	12.2
Spar Group	10.5
Wihuri	4.7
Stockmann/Sesto	2.9
Other	5.2

Source: "Sweden Retail Food Sector." Retrieved September 1, 2000 from the World Wide Web: http://www.ffas.usda.gov.

★ 1327 ★
Retailing
SIC: 5300–ISIC: 5219

Largest Retailers in France, 1999

French retailers have always been thinking internationally; they have long been the world's most successful retailers outside their own country. Collectively, the large players generated sales 1,072.8 billion French francs in 1999 (including sales tax). Data show share of total retail sales.

New Carrefoub	10.9%
ITM Intermarche	7.5
Leclerc	7.2
Auchan/Mulliezd	6.3
Casino	4.1
Systeme Uc	2.8
PPR	2.3
Cora	2.2
Galeries Lafayette	1.7
Other	55.0

Source: "French Retailers Lead Expansion." Retrieved September 5, 2000 from the World Wide Web: http://www.just-food.com, from Retail Intelligence.

★ 1328 ★
Retailing
SIC: 5300–ISIC: 5219

Retail Establishments Worldwide, 2000

	No.	Share
Fast food outlets	136,850	20.66%
Restaurants	93,820	14.16
Service stations	93,230	14.07
Grocery stores	72,320	10.92
Grocery stores (independent)	71,100	10.73
Taverns, bars	66,360	10.02
Luncheonettes	53,730	8.11
Liquor stores	40,860	6.17
Drug stores (chain)	25,150	3.80
Discount stores	9,010	1.36

Source: *Food Institute Report*, November 13, 2000, p. 4, from Audits & Surveys Worldwide.

★ 1329 ★
Retailing
SIC: 5300–ISIC: 5219

Top Retailers in Australia, 1999

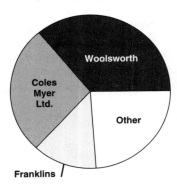

Market shares are shown in percent.

Woolsworth	36.1%
Coles Myer Ltd.	27.0
Franklins	13.2
Other	23.7

Source: *Australian Financial Review*, May 3, 2000, p. 1.

★ 1330 ★
Retailing
SIC: 5300–ISIC: 5219

Top Retailers in Central Europe, 1998

Companies are ranked by turnover in millions of deutschmarks. Central Europe refers to Slovakia, Czech Republic, Hungary and Poland.

Metro	5,550
Rewe	1,797
Tengelmann	1,654
Meinl	1,258
Jeronimo Martin	1,149
Interkontakt	1,066
Tesco	1,054
Ahold	1,032
Dohle	595
Delhaize Le Lion	480

Source: *Lebensmittel Zeitung*, December 3, 1999, p. 1.

★ 1331 ★
Retailing
SIC: 5300–ISIC: 5219

Top Retailers in Japan, 1999

Firms are ranked by fiscal year sales in billions of yen.

Mitsukoshi	$ 281.1
Seibu Department Store	276.3
Isetan	239.1
Hankyu	211.8
Takashimya (Tokyo)	200.3
Takashimya (Osaka)	176.9
Takashimya (Yokohama)	164.0
Tokyu Department Store	149.4
Matsuzakaya	145.6
Kintetsu Department Store	137.1

Source: *Nikkei Weekly*, August 21, 2000, p. 1, from Nihon Keizei Shimbun.

★ 1332 ★
Retailing
SIC: 5300–ISIC: 5219

Top Retailers in Spain

Firms are ranked by sales in billions of pesetas.

El Corte Ingles	1,088.0
Contista Continente	993.8
Grupo Eroski	639.9
Pruca	532.9
Auchan	498.0
Mercandona	453.0
Grupo Superdiplo	191.1
Caprabo	190.0
Unigro Grupo	183.0

Source: "Spanish Retail Revolution." Retrieved October 17, 2000 from the World Wide Web: http://www.cior.com, from Informe Annual Alimarket de Distribucion, Distribucion Actualisdad, and Retail Intelligence.

★ 1334 ★
Retailing
SIC: 5300–ISIC: 5219

Top Retailers in the U.K.

Firms are ranked by sales in millions of British pounds for 1998-99.

Tesco	15.8
J Sainsbury	13.1
ASDA Group	8.1
Safeway Stores	7.5
Marks & Spencer	6.6
Somerfield Stores	5.8
Kingfisher	5.4
The Boots Company	4.4
Great Universal Stores	3.6
John Lewis Partnership	3.1

Source: *Retail Week*, June 2, 2000, p. 12, from Retail Intelligence.

★ 1333 ★
Retailing
SIC: 5300–ISIC: 5219

Top Retailers in the Asia/Pacific Region

Retailers are ranked by sales in billions of dollars.

Ito-Yokado	$ 24.9
Daiei	21.3
Jusco	18.8
Mycal	14.1
Coles Myer	12.9
Woolworth's	11.9
Takashimaya	9.0
Seiyu	8.5
Uny	8.4
Mitsukoshi	7.4

Source: "Retail Food Update." Retrieved December 1, 2000 from the World Wide Web: http://ffas.usda.gov, from *Asiaweek*.

★ 1335 ★
Retailing
SIC: 5300–ISIC: 5219

Top Retailers Worldwide

Firms are ranked by retail sales in billions of dollars.

Wal-Mart	$ 163.2
Kroger	45.3
Sears	41.0
METRO AG	40.3
Carrefour	39.7
Intermarche	38.9
Home Depot	38.4
Albertson's	37.4
Kmart	35.9
Ahold	33.8
Target	33.2
J.C. Penney	31.3

Source: *Stores*, October 2000, p. G6.

★ 1336 ★
Department Stores
SIC: 5311–ISIC: 5219

Top Department Store Firms in the U.K., 1998

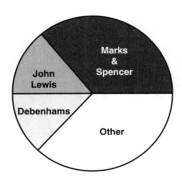

Market shares are shown in percent.

Marks & Spencer	36.0%
John Lewis	14.0
Debenhams	13.0
Other	37.0

Source: *Housewares*, September 1999, p. 1.

★ 1337 ★
Department Stores
SIC: 5311–ISIC: 5219

Top Department Stores in Japan

Retailers are ranked by sales in billions of dollars.

Takashimaya	$ 9.41
Mitsukoshi	6.12
Seibu	5.24
Marui	4.55
Daimaru	4.21
Isetan	3.74
Matsuzakaya	3.49
Hankyu	2.71
Kintetsu	2.66
Tokyu	2.64

Source: "Retail Food Update." Retrieved December 1, 2000 from the World Wide Web: http://ffas.usda.gov.

★ 1338 ★
Discount Merchandising
SIC: 5331–ISIC: 5219

Largest Discount Chains in France, 1999

There were a total of 2,533 outlets.

	Units	Share
Lidl	756	29.85%
Aldi	388	15.32
Leader Price	330	13.03
Ed Marche discount	303	11.96
CDM	234	9.24
Le Lutant	198	7.82
Ed l'Epicier	131	5.17
Norma	87	3.43
Penny	67	2.65
Other	39	1.54

Source: *LSA Libre Service Actualities*, April 26, 2000, p. 1, from A.C. Nielsen.

★ 1339 ★
Discount Merchandising
SIC: 5331–ISIC: 5219

Largest Discount Chains in Germany

Market shares are shown in percent.

Aldi	39.8%
Lidl	20.9
Penny	13.2
Plus	11.3
Netto	9.1
Norma	3.8

Source: *Lebensmittel Zeitung*, February 23, 2001, p. 4, from GfK.

SIC 54 - Food Stores

★ 1340 ★
Grocery Stores
SIC: 5411–ISIC: 5211
Largest Food Retailers in Norway

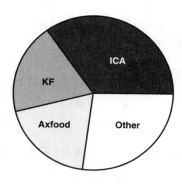

Market shares are shown in percent.

ICA 34.8%
KF 19.4
Axfood 18.6
Other 27.2

Source: ''Nordic Food Retail Market.'' Retrieved September 21, 2000 from the World Wide Web: http://www.just-food.com.

★ 1341 ★
Grocery Stores
SIC: 5411–ISIC: 5211
Organic Food Sales in France

Organic food is a small share of the French food market. However, it is growing significantly and the government is planning to stimulate both production and sales. Milk and nuts are the most popular category with some sectors like baby food, saucesand vegetarian meals have been left unexploited.

Nutrition & Sante 41.8%
Distriborg 25.0
Danone 13.5
La Vie 0.7

Source: ''Organic Food Report.'' Retrieved May 1, 2000 from the World Wide Web: http://ffas.usda.gov.

★ 1342 ★
Grocery Stores
SIC: 5411–ISIC: 5211
Top Grocery Retailers in Turkey

Market shares are shown in percent.

BIM 32.9%
Tansas 25.2
Sok 20.4
Gima 13.8
Other 7.7

Source: ''Turkish's Delight.'' Retrieved March 23, 2001 from the World Wide Web: http://www.just-food.com.

★ 1343 ★
Grocery Stores
SIC: 5411–ISIC: 5211

Top Grocery Stores in Argentina

Market shares are shown in percent.

Grupo Norte-Tia	15.9%
Disco	15.1
Carrefour	14.3
Coto	10.3
Jumbo	4.8
Wal-Mart	4.3
Patagonia	3.3
Other	32.0

Source: *Financial Times*, November 30, 1999, p. 19, from CCR and Duff & Phelps.

★ 1344 ★
Grocery Stores
SIC: 5411–ISIC: 5211

Top Grocery Stores in Australia, 2000

Market shares are shown for September 2000.

Woolworths	38.7%
Bi-Lo/Coles	32.9
Franklins	12.5
Metcash	12.0
Foodland Associated	3.7

Source: *Australian*, December 29, 2000, p. 17, from *Retail World*.

★ 1345 ★
Grocery Stores
SIC: 5411–ISIC: 5211

Top Grocery Stores in Europe

The top 12 grocery retailers account for more than 32 percent of the European food market, as well as 11.7 percent of retail sales.

Carrefour	7.2%
Tesco	3.3
Aldi	2.9
Auchan	2.9
Intermarche	2.9
Other	81.8

Source: *Retail Week*, March 2, 2001, p. 5, from Institute of Grocery Distribution.

★ 1346 ★
Grocery Stores
SIC: 5411–ISIC: 5211

Top Grocery Stores in Germany

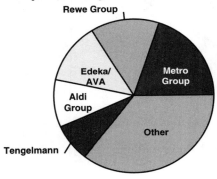

Market shares are shown in percent.

Metro Group	19.7%
Rewe Group	13.6
Edeka/AVA	12.7
Aldi Group	10.1
Tengelmann	7.6
Other	36.3

Source: *Textil-Wirtschaft*, November 18, 1999, p. 1.

★ 1347 ★
Grocery Stores
SIC: 5411–ISIC: 5211

Top Grocery Stores in Guatemala

Market shares are shown in percent.

Paiz	36.2%
Hiperpaiz	26.7
Price Smart	14.6
Despensa Familiar	14.3
La Torre	4.4
Other	3.8

Source: "Retail Food Sector." Retrieved January 1, 2001 from the World Wide Web: http://www.ffas.usda.gov.

★ 1348 ★
Grocery Stores
SIC: 5411–ISIC: 5211

Top Grocery Stores in Spain

Firms are ranked by turnover in billions of pesetas.

Grupo Eroski	639.92
Mercadona	453.00
DIASA (Espana)	356.09
Grupo Superdiplo	191.19
Caprabo	190.24
Grupo Unigro	186.00
Ahold Supermercados	120.00
Supermercados Sabeco	106.00
Supermercados El Corte Ingles	100.00

Source: *Distribucion Actualidad*, May 1, 2000, p. 1.

★ 1349 ★
Grocery Stores
SIC: 5411–ISIC: 5211

Top Grocery Stores in the U.K.

Market shares are shown in percent.

Tesco	21.8%
Sainsbury	17.1
Asda	14.1
Safeway	9.4
Morrisons	4.9

Somerfield	3.6%
Boots	3.1
Kwik Save	2.8
Other	23.2

Source: *The Grocer*, January 20, 2001, p. S5, from Taylor Nelson Sofres.

★ 1350 ★
Grocery Stores
SIC: 5411–ISIC: 5211

Top Retail Grocery Chains in France

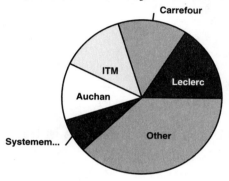

Market shares are shown in percent.

Leclerc	16.3%
Carrefour	13.9
ITM	13.2
Auchan	11.7
Systemem U	6.5
Other	38.3

Source: *LSA*, September 21, 2000, p. 38, from A.C. Nielsen.

★ 1351 ★
Grocery Stores
SIC: 5411–ISIC: 5211

Top Supermarkets in Austria

Market shares are shown in percent.

Billa	30.1%
Spar	24.1
Adeg	12.0

Continued on next page.

★ 1351 ★
[Continued]
Grocery Stores
SIC: 5411–ISIC: 5211

Top Supermarkets in Austria

Market shares are shown in percent.

Hofer	10.0%
ZEV	8.9
Ziepunkt/Loewa	4.7
Meinl	3.9
Other	6.3

Source: "Austria Retail Food Market." Retrieved November 1, 2000 from the World Wide Web: http://www.ffas.usda.gov.

★ 1352 ★
Retailing - Beverages
SIC: 5411–ISIC: 5211

Leading Juice Drink Retailers in the U.K., 2001

Shares are shown based on sales of 785 million British pound as of February 4, 2001.

Tesco	25.0%
Sainsbury	20.7
Asda	11.9
Safeway	11.3
Somerfield (inc Kwik Save)	5.8
Morrisons	4.2
Waltrose	4.1
Other	17.0

Source: *The Grocer*, April 7, 2001, p. 43, from Taylor Nelson Sofres Superpanel.

★ 1353 ★
Retailing - Food
SIC: 5411–ISIC: 5211

Largest Cereal Retailers in France

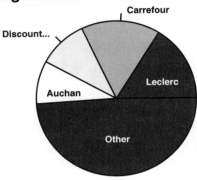

Market shares are shown in percent.

Leclerc	16.2%
Carrefour	15.8
Discount stores	9.6
Auchan	9.1
Other	49.3

Source: *LSA*, February 8, 2001, p. 56.

★ 1354 ★
Retailing - Food
SIC: 5411–ISIC: 5211

Leading Ice Cream Retailers in the U.K.

Market shares are shown in percent. Standard tubs had a 47.9% of sales for the year ended February 4, 2001, premium had a 18.5% share, chocolate snacks had a 12.8% share.

Tesco	23.7%
Sainsbury	14.9
Asda	12.0
Iceland	10.5
Safeway	10.3
Somerfield	7.1
Co-op	5.1
Morrisons	4.9
Waitrose	2.3
Other	9.3

Source: *The Grocer*, March 10, 2001, p. 37, from Taylor Nelson Sofres Superpanel.

★ 1355 ★
Retailing - Food
SIC: 5411–ISIC: 5211

Retail Food Market in Kuwait, 1998

Retail food stores reached $1.2 billion in 1998.

Consumer Coop Societies	70.0%
The Sultan Center	11.0
Wholesale market	6.0
Baqalas (mop & pop stores)	4.0
Grocery stores, class A&B	3.0
City Center	2.0
Other	4.0

Source: "Kuwait Retail Food Sector Report, 1999."
Retrieved September 1, 2000 from the World Wide Web:
http://ffas.usda.gov.

★ 1356 ★
Retailing - Food
SIC: 5411–ISIC: 5211

Top Food Retailers in Europe, 1998

Companies are ranked by sales in billions of British pounds.

Wal-Mart	$ 117.2
Metro	38.0
Carrefour	30.8
Intermarche	30.8
Rewe	29.2
Edeka	27.6
Promodes	27.6
Ahold	26.5
Tesco	25.0
Tengelmann	24.7

Source: *Financial Times*, June 23, 1999, p. 22, from
Morgan Stanley Dean Witter.

★ 1357 ★
Retailing - Fruits and Vegetables
SIC: 5431–ISIC: 5421–HC: 07

Fruit and Vegetable Market in Norway

BAMA-Gruppen	40.0%
Norgesfrukt A/S	30.0
NKL	25.0
Others	5.0

Source: "Norway Fresh Deciduous Fruit." Retrieved September 1, 2000 from the World Wide Web: http://ffas.usa.gov, from United States Department of Agriculture and Foreign Agricultural Service.

★ 1358 ★
Retailing - Bread
SIC: 5461–ISIC: 5220–HC: 19

Largest Bread Retailers, 2001

Shares are shown for the year ended April 1, 2001.

Tesco	24.0%
Sainsbury	16.0
Asda	12.0
Safeway	10.0
Morrisons	6.0
Somerfield	4.0
Iceland	3.0
Kwiksave	3.0
Waitrose	2.0
Other	20.0

Source: *The Grocer*, May 26, 2001, p. 57, from Taylor Nelson Sofres Superpanel.

SIC 55 - Automotive Dealers and Service Stations

Retailing - Auto Parts
SIC: 5531–ISIC: 5030–HC: 87

Automotive Accessory Market in France, 2000

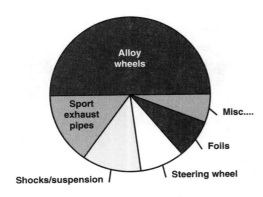

Shares are estimated based on a $170 million market.

Alloy wheels	50.0%
Sport exhaust pipes	15.0
Shocks/suspension	12.0
Steering wheel	9.0
Foils	8.0
Misc. other parts	6.0

Source: ''Automotive Accessories.'' Retrieved November 8, 2000 from the World Wide Web: http://www.usatrade.gov.

Gas Stations
SIC: 5541–ISIC: 5050–HC: 27

Service Station Market in Norway

Market shares are shown in percent.

Shell	34.3%
Statoil	26.8
Esso	22.6
Hydro Texaco	18.7

Source: *Dagens Naeringsliv*, September 15, 1999, p. 1.

Retailing - Aftermarket Products
SIC: 5541–ISIC: 5050–HC: 27

Auto Aftermarket Sales in Japan

Japan is second to the United States in number of motor vehicles on the road. The aftermarket relies on the average life of the vehicle, mileage and the quality of the new vehicle. In Japan, quality is high while demand for new products is low. Salesare shown in millions of dollars.

	($ mil.)	Share
Ordinary tires for passenger cars . .	$ 3,024	23.21%
Engine oils	2,147	16.48
Studless tires for passenger cars . .	1,528	11.73
Batteries	953	7.31
Car navigation systems	827	6.35
Compact disc players for car audios	561	4.31
Brake pads for aftermarket	458	3.51
Light-alloy wheels	440	3.38
Mini disc player for car audio . . .	432	3.32
LCD portable TVs	404	3.10

Continued on next page.

★ 1361 ★
[Continued]
Retailing - Aftermarket Products
SIC: 5541–ISIC: 5050–HC: 27
Auto Aftermarket Sales in Japan

Japan is second to the United States in number of motor vehicles on the road. The aftermarket relies on the average life of the vehicle, mileage and the quality of the new vehicle. In Japan, quality is high while demand for new products is low. Salesare shown in millions of dollars.

	($ mil.)	Share
Speakers for aftermarket	$ 400	3.07%
Air/oil filters	317	2.43
Wiper blades	214	1.64
Other	1,326	10.18

Source: ''Auto Parts and Accessories.'' Retrieved November 8, 2000 from the World Wide Web: http://www.usatrade.gov.

SIC 56 - Apparel and Accessory Stores

★ 1362 ★
Retailing - Apparel
SIC: 5611–ISIC: 5232–HC: 62

Largest Menswear Retailers in the U.K.

Shares are for the six months to September 24, 2000.

Marks & Spencer	10.2%
JJB/Sports Division	5.0
Burton	4.0
Debenhams	3.4
Next	3.3
Matalan	2.7
C&A	1.8
Asda	1.4
Bhs	1.4
House of Fraser	1.4
Other	65.4

Source: *Retail Week*, November 10, 2000, p. 1, from FashionTrak.

★ 1363 ★
Retailing - Apparel
SIC: 5621–ISIC: 5232–HC: 61

Women's Retail Apparel Market in the U.K.

Market shares are shown in percent.

Marks & Spencer	14.5%
Arcadia	11.5
Other	74.0

Source: *Wall Street Journal*, July 9, 1999, p. A8.

★ 1364 ★
Retailing - Apparel
SIC: 5632–ISIC: 5232–HC: 61

Largest Clothing Retailers in Europe, 1998

Companies are ranked by sales in millions of British pounds.

Marks & Spencer	6,215
C&A	6,091
Hennes & Mauritz	2,991
Arcadia Group	2,545
Benetton	1,911
Auchan/Mulliez	1,458
Peek & Cloppenburg	1,380
Grupo Zara	1,295
Etam Developpement	1,088

Source: "Halcyon Days Are Over for M&S." Retrieved October 17, 2000 from the World Wide Web: http://www.cior.com.

★ 1365 ★
Retailing - Apparel
SIC: 5632–ISIC: 5232–HC: 62

Lingerie Sales in France, 1999

The market divided as 48.6% for foundations, 31.9% in daywear and 19.5% share in sleepwear.

Mass retailers	26.0%
Specialty chains	22.0
Mail order	17.0
Independent stores	16.0
Department stores	8.0
Other	11.0

Source: *Body Fashions Intimate Apparel*, November 2000, p. 1.

★ 1366 ★
Retailing - Apparel
SIC: 5632–ISIC: 5232–HC: 62

U.K. Childrenswear Market, 1999

The U.K. population of kids 14 and under will continue to slide from 11.3 million now, to 10.9 million in 2005. The market is valued at 3.5 billion British pounds in 1999. Grocers had 12.1% share, department stores had a 7.6% share and home shopping a 16.2% share.

Marks & Spencer	7.0%
Woolworths	6.8
Next	5.8
Adams	5.4
Mothercare	5.1
Bhs	3.9
Etam Tommy	1.8
C&A	1.5
Primark	1.3
Other	61.2

Source: *Retail Week*, October 13, 2000, p. 13, from *Verdict on Childrenswear Retailers, 2000*.

★ 1367 ★
Retailing - Apparel
SIC: 5651–ISIC: 5232–HC: 61

U.K. Clothing Market Shares, 1998

Market shares are shown in percent.

Marks & Spencer	12.2%
Arcadia	6.3
Debenhams	3.9
Next	3.1
C&A	3.0
Sears Clothing	2.5
Bhs	2.4
Etam	2.4
John Lewis	1.3
Other	62.9

Source: *Retail Week*, April 2, 1999, p. 1, from *Verdict on Clothing Retailers, 1999*.

★ 1368 ★
Retailing - Footwear
SIC: 5661–ISIC: 5232–HC: 64

Top Footwear Retailers in the U.K.

The industry continues to go through consolidations. Market shares are shown in percent.

Clarks	9.3%
Marks & Spencer	8.1
New Look	0.7
Matalan	0.2
Other	81.7

Source: "Verdict on Footwear 2000." Retrieved September 28, 2000 from the World Wide Web: http://www.verdictonline.co.uk, from Verdict Research.

SIC 57 - Furniture and Homefurnishings Stores

★ 1369 ★
Retailing - Flooring
SIC: 5713–ISIC: 5233–HC: 63

Retail Flooring Market in the U.K.

Market shares are shown in percent.

Carpetright	14.0%
Allied Carpet	10.0
Other	76.0

Source: *The Guardian*, June 16, 1999, p. 21.

★ 1370 ★
Retailing - Homefurnishings
SIC: 5719–ISIC: 5233–HC: xx

Largest Housewares Retailers in the U.K., 1998

Market shares are shown in percent.

John Lewis	4.2%
Debenhams	3.3
Argos	3.1
Woolworths	3.0
Ikea	2.8
British Home Stores	2.2
Marks & Spencer	1.9
House of Fraser	1.7
Allders	1.5
Asda	1.5
Other	74.8

Source: *Housewares*, September 1999, p. 6.

★ 1371 ★
Retailing - Homefurnishings
SIC: 5719–ISIC: 5233–HC: xx

Largest Textile Retailers in France

Firms are ranked by 1998 turnover in millions of French francs.

Mullierz	18,235
Leclerc	14,168
Galeries Lafayette	11,479
PPR	10,823
Carrefour	10,364
3 Suisse/Otto	7,412
Decathalon	6,297
C&A	5,248
Andre	4,854
Promodes/Continent	4,441

Source: *Textil Wirtschaft*, December 9, 1999, p. 1, from CTCOE.

★ 1372 ★
Retailing - Electronics
SIC: 5722–ISIC: 5233–HC: 85

Electrical Retailing in the U.K.

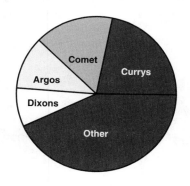

Market shares are shown in percent.

Currys	22.0%
Comet	16.0
Argos	11.0
Dixons	8.0
Other	43.0

Source: "How Britain Shops for Electricals 2000."
Retrieved September 28, 2000 from the World Wide Web:
http://www.verdictonline.co.uk.

★ 1373 ★
Retailing - Software
SIC: 5734–ISIC: 5239–HC: 85

CD-ROM Sales in Italy

The market for electronic publishing in Europe has not been growing at the same rate as in the United States. As a result, there is still a market for offline products like CD-ROMs. Italy's market grew 25 percent in 1998. Most of the market is devoted to games.

	(mil.)	Share
Computer stores	180	44.01%
Newsstand	55	13.45
Book stores	45	11.00
Educational/schools	45	11.00
Supermarkets	25	6.11
Long distance marketing	20	4.89%
Toy store	15	3.67
Direct market	9	2.20
Other	15	3.67

Source: "Electronic Publishing." Retrieved March 15, 2000 from the World Wide Web: http://www.tradeport.org.

★ 1374 ★
Retailing - Music and Video
SIC: 5735–ISIC: 5239–HC: 85

Retail Music Sales in the U.K.

Market shares are shown based on units.

HMV	17.6%
Woolworths	12.5
Virgin	10.0
Our Price/V. Shop	7.4
WH Smith	5.6
MVC	4.5
Asda	3.8
Tesco	2.5
Boots	1.8
Other	65.7

Source: *Retail Week*, February 23, 2001, p. 14, from Taylor Nelson Sofres "Audio Visual Trak Survey".

★ 1375 ★
Retailing - Music and Video
SIC: 5735–ISIC: 5239–HC: 85

Video Retail Sales in the U.K., 1999

Shares are shown in percent.

Woolworths	21.5%
Asda	6.0
Tesco	5.0
Other	47.5

Source: *The Grocer*, July 15, 2000, p. 1, from British Video Association.

SIC 58 - Eating and Drinking Places

★ 1376 ★
Foodservice
SIC: 5812–ISIC: 5220–HC: 21

Leading In-Store Restaurant Operators in Germany, 1999

Companies are ranked by turnover in millions of deutschmarks.

Dinea	450.0
Karstadt	293.2
Ikea	117.0
Le Buffet	110.7
Globus	101.3
Kaufland	61.0
Wal-Mart	60.0
Metro	49.0
toom	32.0

Source: *Lebensmittel Zeitung*, March 17, 2000, p. 1, from Foodservice/dfv.

★ 1377 ★
Foodservice
SIC: 5812–ISIC: 5220–HC: 21

Top In-Flight Meal Firms in Japan, 1997

Market shares are shown based on revenue.

TFK	43.0%
JAL Royal Catering	8.0
ANA Catering Service	4.0
Cosmo Kigyo	3.0
Kansai Shokuhin Kogyo	2.0
Other	40.0

Source: "DVL Market Share Library." Retrieved April 3, 2001 from the World Wide Web: http://dvl/daiwa.co.jp, from DVL Market Share Library and Marketing Data Bank.

★ 1378 ★
Foodservice
SIC: 5812–ISIC: 5220–HC: 21

Top Meal Delivery Service Firms in Japan, 1997

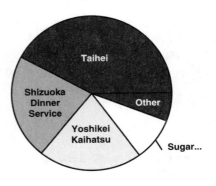

Market shares are shown based on revenue.

Taihei	42.0%
Shizuoka Dinner Service (Dinner Service Corporation)	22.0
Yoshikei Kaihatsu	21.0
Sugar Lady	9.0
Other	6.0

Source: "DVL Market Share Library." Retrieved April 3, 2001 from the World Wide Web: http://dvl/daiwa.co.jp, from DVL Market Share Library and Marketing Data Bank.

★ 1379 ★
Restaurants
SIC: 5812–ISIC: 5220–HC: 21

Hamburger Market in Hong Kong

The fast food industry has become one of the fastest growing business sectors in the country. Hamburger chains have about 34% of the fast food industry market. KFC has 75% of the chicken market and Pizza Hut has 80% of the pizza market.

McDonald's	80.0%
Hardees	9.0
Jack in the Box	4.0
Wendy's	4.0
Other	3.0

Source: "Hong Kong Fast Food Market." Retrieved October 1, 2000 from the World Wide Web: http://ffas.usda.gov.

★ 1380 ★
Restaurants
SIC: 5812–ISIC: 5220–HC: 21

Largest U.S. Chains Abroad

Chains are ranked by 1999 sales in millions of dollars.

McDonald's	$ 19,485.1
KFC	4,550.0
Burger King	2,532.9
Pizza Hut	2,500.0
Tim Hortons	1,019.0
Domino's	700.0
Wendy's	630.0
Subway	491.0
Dairy Queen	415.0
Baskin-Robbins	386.6

Source: *Restaurant Business*, November 1, 2000, p. 33.

★ 1381 ★
Restaurants
SIC: 5812–ISIC: 5220–HC: 21

Leading Casual Dining Chains in Italy, 1999

Firms are ranked by sales in millions of dollars.

Olive Garden	$ 1,519.8
Romano's Macaroni Grill	418.9
Pizzeria Uno	318.4
Carrabba's Italian Grill	170.0
Bertucci's	147.5
Maggiano's	97.8
Il Fornaio	92.3
Old Spaghetti Factory	81.0
Buca di Beppo	71.5

Source: *Chain Leader*, July 2000, p. 51, from Technomic Inc.

★ 1382 ★
Restaurants
SIC: 5812–ISIC: 5220–HC: 21

Top Chicken Restaurants in Peru, 1998

Figures are in millions of dollars.

	Sales ($ mil.)	Share
KFC	$ 14.0	29.23%
Supermarkets selfservice	14.0	29.23
Norky's	7.0	14.61
Roky's	7.0	14.61
Pardo's	3.4	7.10
Mediterraneo	2.5	5.22

Source: "Peru HRI Foodservice Sector." Retrieved September 1, 2000 from the World Wide Web: http://www.ffas.usda.gov.

★ 1383 ★
Restaurants
SIC: 5812–ISIC: 5220–HC: 21

Top Restaurant Firms in Switzerland, 1998

Firms are ranked by sales in millions of swiss francs.

Migros	682.0
McDonald's	400.2
SV-Service	372.0
Movenpick	277.8
Sair Relations	249.1
SSG	245.6
Coop	197.8
DSR	116.1
Merkur	103.7
Maus Freres	101.0

Source: ''HRI Food Service Sector.'' Retrieved December 1, 2000 from the World Wide Web: http://ffas.usda.gov.

SIC 59 - Miscellaneous Retail

★ 1384 ★
Drug Stores
SIC: 5912–ISIC: 5231–HC: 30

Drug Store Market in Chile

Market shares are shown in percent.

FASA	29.0%
Salco-Brand	29.0
Socofar	28.0
Cruz Verde	18.0

Source: *Estrategia*, August 16, 2000, p. 5.

★ 1385 ★
Retailing - Books
SIC: 5942–ISIC: 5239–HC: 49

Retail Book Market in Australia

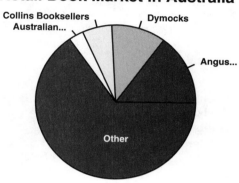

Market shares are shown in percent. Book sales reached $725 million, making it the third largest English speaking book market past the United States and the United Kingdom. Per capita book sales are $37.95.

Angus and Robertson	14.8%
Dymocks	11.1
Collins Booksellers	5.6
Australian Broadcasting Corporation	3.3
Other	65.2

Source: ''Books.'' Retrieved May 17, 2001 from the World Wide Web: http://www.usatrade.gov.

★ 1386 ★
Retailing - Books
SIC: 5942–ISIC: 5239–HC: 49

Retail Book Sales in France

The $1.9 billion market is shown by type of outlet. Book prices are regulated in France, as they are in most European countries. Television advertising of books and booksellers is prohibited. However, Amazon.com has recently launched a site there, with successful results.

Mail-order and book clubs	21.0%
Traditional bookstores	21.0
Hypermarkets	20.0
Book superstores	15.0
Newstands	10.0
Other	13.0

Source: *Wall Street Journal*, August 30, 2000, p. B12, from National Publishers Union.

★ 1387 ★
Retailing - Books
SIC: 5942–ISIC: 5239–HC: 49

U.K. Retail Book Market

Verdict Research predicts that sales volume growth in books, newsagents and stationers will be one of the slowest growing of all consumer sectors between 1998 and 2003 - roughly half a percent a year.

Waterstone's/Dillons	35.3%
WH Smith/John Menzies	32.0
Blackwell Retail	5.5
James Thin	4.0
Books Etc	3.5
Hammicks	2.9
Ottakar's	2.6
Heffer's	2.4
John Smith	2.2
Others	9.5

Source: *Financial Times*, February 15, 1999, p. 14, from MTI.

★ 1388 ★
Retailing - Toys
SIC: 5945–ISIC: 3694–HC: 95

Top Toy Retailers in the U.K., 1998

Total sales, minus video games, reached 1.67 billion British pounds.

Toy stores	27.9%
Mixed multiples	23.9
Catalog showrooms	22.0
Mail order	8.3
Supermarkets/Cash n Carry	5.7
Department stores	5.2
Other	7.1

Source: "Who Sells Toys." Retrieved September 8, 2000 from the World Wide Web: http://www.batr.co.uk, from NPD Group.

★ 1389 ★
Retailing - Toys
SIC: 5945–ISIC: 5239–HC: 95

Retail Toy Market in Argentina

Imports account for about 85% of the $300 million market. Most are from China. The areas with the highest potential for U.S. exporters are Barbie products, wheeled toys and video games.

El Mundo del Juguete	30.0%
Supermarkets/supercenters	30.0
El Pais de las Maravillas	18.0
Other	22.0

Source: "Overview of the Toy Market." Retrieved November 17, 2000 from the World Wide Web: http://www.usatrade.gov.

★ 1390 ★
Retailing - Toys
SIC: 5945–ISIC: 5239–HC: 95

Where Toys Were Sold, 1999

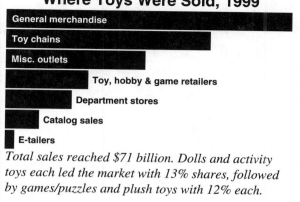

General merchandise

Toy chains

Misc. outlets

Toy, hobby & game retailers

Department stores

Catalog sales

E-tailers

Total sales reached $71 billion. Dolls and activity toys each led the market with 13% shares, followed by games/puzzles and plush toys with 12% each.

General merchandise (incl. hypers and discounters)	35.0%
Toy chains	25.0
Misc. outlets	17.0
Toy, hobby & game retailers	10.0
Department stores	8.0
Catalog sales	4.0
E-tailers	1.0

Source: "World Toy Facts and Figures." Retrieved October 31, 2000 from the World Wide Web: http://www.toy-icti.org, from NPD Group Worldwide.

★ 1391 ★
Retailing - Luggage
SIC: 5948–ISIC: 5239–HC: 42

Retail Luggage Market in the U.K., 1999

Market shares are shown based on value.

Department stores	43.0%
Luggage shops	19.2
Catalog stores	14.3
Variety stores	13.5
Mail order	2.5
Other	7.5

Source: "UK Luggage." Retrieved January 12, 2001 from the World Wide Web: http://www.clearlybusiness.com, from Datamonitor.

★ 1392 ★
Mail Order
SIC: 5961–ISIC: 5251

Largest Mail Order Firms in Europe

Germany was the largest market, generating 22.7 billion euros in sales and 40% of mail order sales.

Otto	18.0%
Quelle	13.0
GUS	7.7
Redcats	7.4
Littlewoods	4.5
Neckermann (Karstadt)	4.2
Bertelsmann	4.1
Klingel	2.8
Camif	1.9
Bruno Bader	1.6
Other	34.8

Source: "Germany Dominates Home Shopping in Europe." Retrieved October 17, 2000 from the World Wide Web: http://www.cior.com, from Retail Intelligence.

★ 1393 ★
Mail Order
SIC: 5961–ISIC: 5251

Largest TV Shopping Firms in Japan

Firms are ranked by sales in millions of yen from July 1999 - June 2000. Total sales were 107.1 billion yen, home electric appliances having the largest share with 33.9%, followed by apparel with 24.9%.

Nihon Bunka Center	21,000
JapanNet Takata	15,494
Mitsukoshi direct	13,000
Fuji Sankei Living Service	11,973
Prime	9,166
TokaDo	8,500
Jupiter Shopping Channel	8,000
Media Price	6,046
OakLawn Marketing	3,014
TV Asahi Living	3,000

Source: "TV Shopping Market." Retrieved January 3, 2001 from the World Wide Web: http://www.usatrade.gov.

★ 1394 ★
Vending Machines
SIC: 5961–ISIC: 5251

Vending Machine Sales in Europe

Data show unit sales. The switch over to the euro in January 2002 is expected to have a major influence on the industry.

	1996	1997	1998
Hot drinks	89,142	96,316	126,979
Cold drinks	47,728	68,392	89,376
Snacks/food	25,212	26,150	33,815

Source: *Automatic Merchandiser*, March 2001, p. 34, from European Vending Machine Manufacturers Association.

★ 1395 ★
Retailing - Cigars
SIC: 5993–ISIC: 5220–HC: 24

Duty-Free Cigar Industry, 1999

Cigar sales in travel-retail are expected to more than double to $658 million by 2010. Global sales should reach 12.5 billion units in 2000, 2.5% of them being sold duty-free. Airports are ranked by duty-free cigar sales.

Tel Aviv Ben Guiron Airport	$ 11.4
P&O Stena Line	8.9
London Heathrow	8.5
Amsterdam Schiphol Airport	7.9
Paris Charles de Gaulle	7.5
London Gatwick	6.8
Frankfurt am Main Airport	5.4
Hong Kong International Airport	5.2
Zurich Kloten Airport	4.5
Eurotunnel	4.2

Source: *Duty-Free News International*, March 1, 2001, p. 17, from Generation.

★ 1396 ★
Retailing - Magazines
SIC: 5994–ISIC: 5239–HC: 49

Magazine Retailing in the U.K.

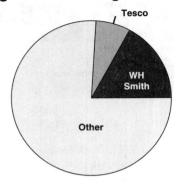

Market shares are shown in percent.

WH Smith	17.0%
Tesco	7.0
Other	76.0

Source: *Observer*, September 3, 2000, p. 1.

★ 1397 ★
Optical Goods Stores
SIC: 5995–ISIC: 5239–HC: 90

Top Optical Goods Retailers in Germany, 1998

Firms are ranked by turnover in millions of deutschmarks.

Fielmann AG	1,019
Apollo-Optik	292
Krane Optik	89
Ruhnke Optik	83
Abele Optik	74
Optiker Bode	57
Binder Optik	55
Karstadt	50
Optik Mart	47
Becker + Floge	30

Source: *Wirtschaftswoche*, February 10, 2000, p. 78, from Fielmann and ZVA.

★ 1398 ★
Optical Goods Stores
SIC: 5995–ISIC: 5239–HC: 90

Top Optical Retailers in Thailand

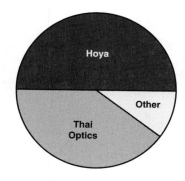

The domestic market absorbs five million lenses annually. The market is highly competitive with 2,000 outlets nationwide, half in Bangkok.

Hoya	50.0%
Thai Optics	40.0
Other	10.0

Source: *Bangkok Post*, March 27, 2001, p. NA.

★ 1399 ★
Pet Stores
SIC: 5999–ISIC: 5239–HC: xx

Top-Selling Small Animals in Pet Stores in France

France has the largest number of pets in Europe. Worldwide, it ranks second to the United States. It has 8.7 million cats and 8.1 million dogs. Cat and dog food sales reached $886.4 million.

Frogs	13.0%
Lizards	12.0
Tritons	11.0
Snakes	10.0
Turtles	10.0
Arachnids	3.0
Insects	3.0
Other	4.5

Source: ''Pet Product Market.'' Retrieved February 20, 2001 from the World Wide Web: http://www.usatrade.gov.

★ 1400 ★
Retailing - Personal Care Products
SIC: 5999–ISIC: 5239–HC: xx

Cosmetics Sales in the Netherlands

Drug stores (chain)	27.0%
Supermarkets	22.0
Drug stores (indep.)	21.0
Specialty stores (perfumery)	11.0
Other	8.0

Source: ''Cosmetics Sales In The Netherlands.'' Retrieved September 7, 2000 from the World Wide Web: http://www.tradeport.org.

★ 1401 ★
Retailing - Personal Care Products
SIC: 5999–ISIC: 5239–HC: xx

OTC Sales Market in the Netherlands, 2000

Sales of over the counter products reached $600 million.

Drug stores	77.0%
Pharmacies	17.0
Grocery retailers	6.0

Source: ''Liberalization of Dutch OTC Market.'' Retrieved April 3, 2001 from the World Wide Web: http://www.usatrade.gov.

★ 1402 ★
Retailing - Personal Care Products
SIC: 5999–ISIC: 5239–HC: xx

Personal Care Sales in the U.K.

Market shares are shown based on sales of toiletries, cosmetics and OTC medicines.

Boots	25.9%
Tesco	12.5
Superdrug	8.4
Sainsbury	7.7
Asda	6.2
Safeway	4.7
Lloydspharmacy	2.2

Continued on next page.

★ 1402 ★
[Continued]
Retailing - Personal Care Products
SIC: 5999–ISIC: 5239–HC: xx

Personal Care Sales in the U.K.

Market shares are shown based on sales of toiletries, cosmetics and OTC medicines.

Body Shop	1.9%
Holland & Barrett	1.1
Other	29.4

Source: *Chemist & Druggist*, November 4, 2000, p. 28, from Verdict Research.

SIC 60 - Depository Institutions

★ 1403 ★
Banking
SIC: 6020–ISIC: 6519

Internet Banking in Europe

Data show number of accounts, in thousands.

	(000)	Share
Nordic countries	2,075	31.79%
Germany	1,200	18.38
United Kingdom	1,200	18.38
Rest	925	14.17
Spain	580	8.88
France	500	7.66
Italy	48	0.74

Source: *European Banker*, June 30, 2000, p. 1, from Bank of Finland, company reports, HSBC Securities, and KPMG estimates.

★ 1404 ★
Banking
SIC: 6020–ISIC: 6519

Largest Banks Worldwide

Banks are ranked by assets in millions of dollars.

Mizuho Financial Corp.	$ 1,394,242
Deutsche Bank	843,761
Citigroup	716,937
BNP Paribas	701,853
Bank of Tokyo-Mitsubishi	678,244
Chase Manhattan JP Morgan	667,003
HypoVereinsbank	646,205
HSBC Holdings	638,747
Bank of America Corp.	632,574

Source: *The Banker*, November 2000, p. 20.

★ 1405 ★
Banking
SIC: 6020–ISIC: 6519

Retail Banking in Germany, 1999

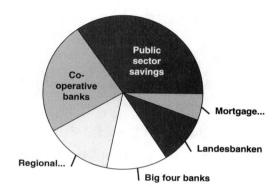

Shares are shown based on deposits.

Public sector savings bank	31.4%
Co-operative banks	21.0
Regional and other commercial banks	12.2
Big four banks	10.8
Landesbanken	9.4
Mortgage banks	5.4

Source: *Financial Times*, July 27, 2000, p. 33, from Deutsche Bundesbank, *The Banker*, and Primark Database.

★ 1406 ★
Banking
SIC: 6020–ISIC: 6519

Top Banks in Asia

Banks are ranked by assets in billions of dollars.

Bank of Tokyo-Mitsubishi	$ 680.0
Fuji Bank	550.1
Sumitomo Bank	510.8

Continued on next page.

★ 1406 ★

[Continued]
Banking
SIC: 6020–ISIC: 6519

Top Banks in Asia

Banks are ranked by assets in billions of dollars.

Dai-Ichi Kangyo Bank	$ 508.7
Sakura Bank	459.9
Sanwa Bank	444.1
Indl. & Coml. Bank of China	427.5
Industrial Bank of Japan	405.1
Bank of China	350.7
Tokai Bank	288.6

Source: *Asiaweek*, September 15, 2000, p. 80.

★ 1407 ★

Banking
SIC: 6020–ISIC: 6519

Top Banks in Central Europe

Banks are ranked by assets in millions of dollars.

PKO	$ 14,683
Bank Pekao	14,429
Komercni Banks	12,227
Ceska Sporitelna	10,143
IPB	9,879
CSOB	7,819
OTP Bank	6,955
Beogradska Banka	5,993
Bank Handlowy	4,631
PBK	4,236

Source: *Business Central Europe*, Annual 2001, p. 52.

★ 1408 ★

Banking
SIC: 6020–ISIC: 6519

Top Banks in Europe, 1999

Banks are ranked by assets in billions of yen.

Deutsche Bank	839.9
BNP Paribas	698.6
UBS	610.8

HSBC Holdings	566.5
HypoVerinsbank	503.2
ABN AMRO Bank	457.9
Credit Suisse Group	449.8
Societe Generale	406.5
Credit Agricole	401.7
Barclays Bank	396.9

Source: *Financial Times*, May 26, 2000, p. 6, from *The Banker*.

★ 1409 ★

Banking
SIC: 6020–ISIC: 6519

Top Banks in Greece, 1999

Shares are shown based on deposits.

National Bank of Greece	35.6%
Alpha Bank	16.0
Agricultural Bank of Greece	11.9
Commercial Bank of Greece	10.5
EFG Eurobank	8.4
Piraeus Bank	4.8
Other	12.8

Source: *Financial Times*, December 13, 2000, p. 3, from Bank of Greece.

★ 1410 ★
Banking
SIC: 6020–ISIC: 6519

Top Banks in Latin America

Firms are ranked by total assets in billions of dollars as of December 31, 1999.

Banco Do Brasil	$ 69.9
Caixa Economica Federal	68.4
Bradesco	31.4
Banamex	29.2
Bancomer	27.4
Banco Itau	25.0
Banca Serfin	19.0
Banco de la Nacion Argentina	17.9
Unibanco	17.4
Banespa	15.6

Source: *Latin Trade*, September 2000, p. 49.

★ 1411 ★
Banking
SIC: 6020–ISIC: 6519

Top Banks in Panama

Market shares are shown based on branches.

Itau + Banestado	31.73%
Banestado	27.72
Banco do Brasil	17.79
HSBC Bamerindus	13.38
Bradesco	9.94
Itau	4.01
Unibanco	3.21
ABN Amro	2.80

Source: *Retail Banker International*, November 10, 2000, p. 8, from *Gazeta Mercantil.*

★ 1412 ★
Banking
SIC: 6020–ISIC: 6519

Top Banks in Portugal

Shares are shown based on deposits.

Caixa Geral de Depositos	30.5%
Banco Comercial Portugues	19.1
Banco Pinto & Sotto Mayor	15.6
Banco Espirito Santo	12.0
Banco Portugues de Investimento	9.8
Other	13.0

Source: *Financial Times*, March 31, 1999, p. 12, from Portugese Banking Association.

★ 1413 ★
Banking
SIC: 6020–ISIC: 6519

Top Banks in Shanghai

Banks are ranked by assets in billions of dolalrs.

Citibank	$ 2.5
Bank of Tokyo-Mitsubishi	1.3
HSBC	1.0
Standard Chartered	1.0
Sanwa Bank	0.9

Source: *Financial Times*, May 18, 2001, p. 19.

★ 1414 ★
Banking
SIC: 6020–ISIC: 6519

Top Banks in Spain

Market shares are shown in percent.

BBVA	20.0%
BSCH	20.0
Other	60.0

Source: *Business Week*, April 23, 2001, p. 46.

★ 1415 ★
Banking
SIC: 6020–ISIC: 6519

Top Banks in Sweden

Market shares are shown based on deposits.

Swedbank	28.0%
SEB	14.0
Other	58.0

Source: *Financial Times*, February 21, 2001, p. 18.

★ 1416 ★
Banking
SIC: 6020–ISIC: 6519

Top Banks in the Philippines

Market shares are shown follwing some recent mergers.

Metropolitan Bank	13.8%
Bank of Philippine Islands	13.0
Philippine National Bank	12.1
Equitable Bank	9.5
Land Bank of the Philippines	7.0
Citibank NA	5.9
Far East Bank	5.0
PCI Bank	5.0
Other	28.7

Source: *Financial Times*, March 9, 2000, p. 17.

★ 1417 ★
Banking
SIC: 6020–ISIC: 6519

Top Banks/Investment Groups Worldwide

Groups are ranked by market value in billiosn of dollars.

Citigroup	$ 260.4
HSBC Holdings	116.3
JP Morgan Chase	95.8
Bank of America	90.9
Wells Fargo	78.4
Morgan Stanley	76.9
UBS	66.6
Royal Bank of Scotland	62.7
Merrill Lynch	58.4

Source: *Financial Times*, May 18, 2001, p. 1.

★ 1418 ★
Banking
SIC: 6081–ISIC: 6519

Cross Border Banking

Market shares are for total domestic assets in 1997.

Luxembourg	90.9%
Ireland	45.4
Belgium	28.2
United Kingdom	23.4
Greece	13.0
Portugal	9.4
Spain	8.2
Finland	7.1
Italy	5.3
Netherlands	5.3

Source: *Financial Times*, July 19, 1999, p. 13, from Primark Datastream and Salomon Smith Barney.

SIC 61 - Nondepository Institutions

★ 1419 ★
Credit Cards
SIC: 6141–ISIC: 6592

Largest Credit Card Firms in Argentina

Market shares are shown in percent.

Visa	51.0%
MasterCard	37.0
Other	12.0

Source: *South American Business Information*, February 16, 2001, p. NA.

★ 1420 ★
Credit Cards
SIC: 6141–ISIC: 6592

Largest Credit Card Issuers in Austria

Data show number of cards issued.

	Units	Share
Europay Austria	787,000	51.54%
Bank Austria	355,892	23.31
RZB	204,000	13.36
Creditanstalt	123,000	8.06
Postparkasse	57,000	3.73

Source: *Cards International*, June 28, 2000, p. 14, from company sources and Lafferty Business Research.

★ 1421 ★
Credit Cards
SIC: 6141–ISIC: 6592

Top Credit Card Firms in Japan, 1999

Shares are shown based on sales turnover.

JCB Co.	11.6%
Sumitomo Credit Service Co.	9.4
Nippon Shinpan Co.	7.5
UC Card Co.	6.9
Credit Saison Co.	6.2
Other	58.4

Source: *Nikkei Weekly*, August 21, 2000, p. 9, from Nihon Keizai Shimbun.

★ 1422 ★
Financial Services
SIC: 6150–ISIC: 6592

Consumer Finance Industry In Japan

Data are for March 1997.

Takefuji Corp.	14.0%
Acom Co.	13.0
Promise Co.	10.0
Aiful Corp.	8.0

Continued on next page.

★ 1422 ★

[Continued]
Financial Services
SIC: 6150–ISIC: 6592

Consumer Finance Industry In Japan

Data are for March 1997.

Lake Co.	7.0%
AIC Corp.	4.0
Sanyo Shinpan Finance Co.	3.0
Others	41.0

Source: *Nikkei Weekly*, November 1, 1999, p. 1, from Aiful Corp., Lehman Brothers Japan, and Ministry of Finance, Japan.

★ 1423 ★

Mortgage Loans
SIC: 6162–ISIC: 6592

Largest Local Mortgage Banks in Hong Kong

Market shares are shown in percent.

Bank of China Group	24.0%
Hang Seng Bank Group	14.5
Standard Chartered Bank Group	13.6
HSBC Group	10.9
Dao Heng Bank Group	5.3
Bank of East Asia Group	4.3
Citic-Ka Wah Bank Group	3.4
Bank of America Group	2.0
Wing Lung Bank Group	2.0
Other	20.0

Source: *Sing Tao Daily*, August 18, 2000, p. 28, from Land Registry.

★ 1424 ★

Loan Arrangers
SIC: 6163–ISIC: 6592

Loan Industry in Spain

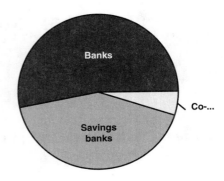

Market shares are shown for loans to the private sector.

Banks	53.0%
Savings banks	42.0
Co-operatives	5.0

Source: *Financial Times*, December 13, 2000, p. 20, from Banco de Espana, J.P. Morgan, and *The Banker*.

SIC 62 - Security and Commodity Brokers

★ 1425 ★

Investment Banking

SIC: 6211–ISIC: 6712

Foreign-Exchange Trading

London had 32% of the global market in 1999.

Deutsche Bank	12.5%
Chase Manhattan	8.3
Citigroup	8.1
UBS Warburg	5.0
HSBC	4.6
Goldman Sachs	4.4
J.P. Morgan	3.9
Merrill Lynch	3.3
Other	49.9

Source: *Wall Street Journal*, September 1, 2000, p. A8, from *Euromoney* and Thomson Financial Securities Data.

★ 1426 ★

Investment Banking

SIC: 6211–ISIC: 6712

Largest Equity-Linked Bookrunners

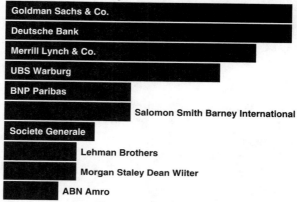

Figures are in millions of dollars.

	($ mil.)	Share
Goldman Sachs & Co.	$ 6,381.73	15.98%
Deutsche Bank	6,207.51	15.55
Merrill Lynch & Co.	5,549.10	13.90
UBS Warburg	4,884.01	12.23
BNP Paribas	2,909.45	7.29
Salomon Smith Barney International	2,722.76	6.82
Societe Generale	1,891.11	4.74
Lehman Brothers	1,787.85	4.48
Morgan Staley Dean Wiiter	1,787.49	4.48
ABN Amro	1,370.94	3.43

Source: *Euromoney*, January 2001, p. 8, from Capital Data.

★ 1427 ★

Investment Banking
SIC: 6211–ISIC: 6712

Largest Equity Underwriters in Japan, 1999

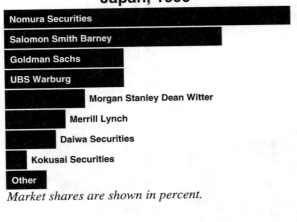

Market shares are shown in percent.

Nomura Securities	29.0%
Salomon Smith Barney	22.2
Goldman Sachs	12.3
UBS Warburg	12.1
Morgan Stanley Dean Witter	8.1
Merrill Lynch	5.9
Daiwa Securities	5.3
Kokusai Securities	1.6
Other	3.5

Source: *Wall Street Journal*, August 9, 2000, p. A16, from Thomson Financial Securities Data.

★ 1428 ★

Investment Banking
SIC: 6211–ISIC: 6712

Largest Fund Managers in New Zealand

Firms are ranked by funds managed in millions of New Zealand dollars.

Tower Group	2,111.6
AMP	1,850.1
Armstrong Jones	1,705.4
Royal & Sun	1,587.9
Westpac Trust	1,424.0
NZ Funds Management	1,403.7
BNZ	1,316.3

Axa Asia Pacific	895.6
Colonial	761.2

Source: *Australian Financial Review*, February 1, 2001, p. 15, from IPAC Securities.

★ 1429 ★

Investment Banking
SIC: 6211–ISIC: 6712

Leading Financial Groups in Portugal

Market shares are shown based on assets. BES stands for Banco Espirito Santo. BPI stands for Banco Portugues de Investimento. CGD stands for Geral de Depositos.

CGD	21.7%
BCP	21.1
BES	11.5
BSCH	10.5
BPI	7.4

Source: *Financial Times*, May 4, 2001, p. 4, from BCP.

★ 1430 ★

Investment Banking
SIC: 6211–ISIC: 6712

Leading Mutual Fund Companies in Germany

Market shares are shown in percent.

Deutsche Bank	21.9%
Sparkassen	20.2
Co-operative Banks	15.8
Dresdner Bank	13.3
Commerzbank	7.2
HypoVereinsbank	5.7
Other	15.9

Source: *Financial Times*, May 2, 2001, p. 19, from J.P. Morgan and BVI.

★ 1431 ★
Investment Banking
SIC: 6211–ISIC: 6712

Online Brokering Market in Europe, 1999

Market shares are shown in percent.

Comdirect (Commerzbank)	19.0%
Consors (Schmidt Bank)	16.0
Schwab Europe (Charles Schwab)	16.0
Deutsche Bank	11.0
Direkt Anlage Bank	11.0
Cortal (BNP-Paribas)	9.0
SE Banken	6.0
Other	12.0

Source: *Financial Times*, July 17, 2000, p. 19, from Commerzbank, J.P. Morgan, and Delbruck Research.

★ 1432 ★
Investment Banking
SIC: 6211–ISIC: 6712

Top M&A Advisers, 2000

Companies are ranked by value of announced deals in billions of dollars.

Morgan Stanley	$ 1,022
Goldman Sachs	891
CSFB	825
Salomon Smith Barney	621
Merrill Lynch	476
Chase Manhattan	378
UBS Warburg	363
JP Morgan	353
Lazard	242
Lehman Brothers	227

Source: *Financial Times*, December 29, 2000, p. 13, from Computasoft Research/CommScan.

★ 1433 ★
Investment Banking
SIC: 6231–ISIC: 6711

Largest Securities Firms, 1999

Firms are ranked by turnover in billions of U.S. dollars.

Guotai Jun'an Securities	$ 49.1
Southern Securities	40.5
Shenyin & Wanguo Securities	39.2
Haitong Securities	34.3
Huaxia Securities	31.0
Guangfa Securities	26.3
Shandong Securities	14.4
Everbright Securities	14.0
United Securities	13.0
Guangdong Securities	12.3

Source: "1999 Rankings of China's Top Brokerages." Retrieved May 16, 2000 from the World Wide Web: http://www.chinaonline.com.

★ 1434 ★
Stock Exchanges
SIC: 6231–ISIC: 6711

Largest Derivative Exchanges, 1999

Firms are ranked by volume of contracts, in millions.

Eurex	314.0
Chicago Board of Trade	254.6
Chicago Board Options Exchanges	221.3
Chicago Mercantile Exchange	200.7
Matif	188.1
London Intl. Financial Futures and Options Exchange	117.8

Continued on next page.

★ 1434 ★

[Continued]

Stock Exchanges

SIC: 6231–ISIC: 6711

Largest Derivative Exchanges, 1999

Firms are ranked by volume of contracts, in millions.

American Stock Exchange	115.2
New York Mercantile Exchange	109.5
Korea Stock Exchange	97.1
Pacific Exchange	75.8

Source: *New York Times*, August 6, 2000, p. 12, from *Futures Industry*.

★ 1435 ★

Stock Exchanges

SIC: 6231–ISIC: 6711

Largest Stock Exchanges

Markets are ranked by capitalization in billions of dollars.

New York Stock Exchange	$ 11,491
Nasdaq	5,045
Tokyo	4,296
Osaka	2,859
London	2,749
Euronext	2,174
Frankfurt	1,414
Toronto	795
Milan	705
Zurich	674

Source: *New York Times*, March 21, 2000, p. C2, from International Federation of Stock Exchanges.

★ 1436 ★

Stock Exchanges

SIC: 6231–ISIC: 6711

Online Investing Market in Japan

Market shares are shown in percent.

Matsui Securities Co.	29.4%
DLJDirect SFG Securities Inc.	12.6
Monex Inc.	9.8
Daiwa Securities Co.	8.4
Nikko Beans Inc.	6.8%
Orix Securities Co.	5.2
Nomura Securities Co.	4.7
E* Trade Securities Co.	3.5
Other	19.6

Source: *Nikkei Weekly*, April 23, 2001, p. 1, from ABN AMRO Securities Ltd.

SIC 63 - Insurance Carriers

★ 1437 ★
Insurance
SIC: 6300–ISIC: 6600

Largest Insurers in Europe, 1998

Groups are ranked by premium income in billions of British pounds.

AXA	33.2
Allianz	33.0
Generali	26.7
ZFS	25.0
CGNU	20.3
ING	14.4
CS Group	12.6
Prudential	11.4
CNP	11.1
RSA	11.1

Source: *Financial Times*, February 22, 2000, p. 13.

★ 1438 ★
Insurance
SIC: 6300–ISIC: 6600

Largest Insurers Worldwide

Companies are ranked by assets in millions of dollars at December 31, 1998.

AXA Group	$ 449,556
Allianz Group	401,406
Nippon Life	374,801
Zenkyoren & Prefectural Ins. Federations	297,477
Dai-ichi Mutual Life	261,164
American International Group	233,676

Metropolitan Life Insurance	$ 215,346
Sumitomo Life	212,200
Zurich Financial Services Group	205,963
Prudential Corp.	195,536

Source: *Wall Street Journal*, September 27, 1999, p. 27.

★ 1439 ★
Insurance
SIC: 6300–ISIC: 6600

Nonlife Insurance Market in the U.K.

Data are for the first half of the year.

Royal & Sun Alliance	14.9%
CGU	13.0
Norwich Union	10.3
AXA	9.5
Zurich Financial Services	7.6
Others	44.7

Source: *Financial Times*, December 20, 1999, p. 19, from Primark Datastream.

★ 1440 ★
Insurance
SIC: 6300–ISIC: 6600

Top Insurance Firms in Brazil, 2000

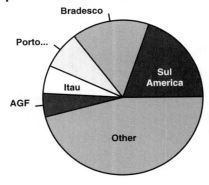

Shares are for the first two months of the year.

Sul America	20.04%
Bradesco	15.52
Porto Seguro	7.75
Itau	5.66
AGF	4.51
Other	46.52

Source: *Valor Economico*, June 2, 2000, p. 1.

★ 1441 ★
Insurance
SIC: 6300–ISIC: 6600

Top Insurance Firms in Egypt

The market is experiencing many changes as the country shifts to a market driven economy. The insurance industry will have to make itself more efficient to competer with foreign rivals. The industry consists of 12 companies and ranked 52nd in worldwide premium volume

Misr	35.0%
Al Chark	29.0
National	14.0
Mohandes	6.0
Suez	6.0
Delta	5.0
Other	5.0

Source: *Best's Review*, August 1999, p. 66, from Egyptian Insuance Supervisory Authority.

★ 1442 ★
Insurance
SIC: 6300–ISIC: 6600

Top Insurance Firms in Greece, 1999

Market shares are shown in percent.

Ethniki	22.0%
Interamerican	16.0
Aspis	12.0
Allianz	6.0
Commercial Bank	6.0
ING	6.0
Other	32.0

Source: *Financial Times*, May 30, 2001, p. 18, from Greek Insurers Association.

★ 1443 ★
Insurance
SIC: 6300–ISIC: 6600

Top Insurance Firms in Norway

Market shares are shown in percent.

Vital	24.6%
Storebrand	24.0
KLP	20.1
Gjensidige NOR	16.6
Other	14.7

Source: *Aftenposten*, May 11, 2001, p. 30, from Finansnaeringens Hovedorganisasjon.

★ 1444 ★
Insurance
SIC: 6300–ISIC: 6600

Top Insurance Firms in the Slovak Republic, 2000

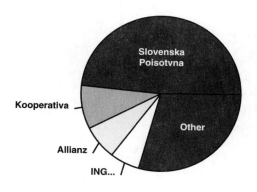

Members of the Slovak Insurers Association billed premiums of Sk27.26 billion.

Slovenska Poisotvna	48.26%
Kooperativa	9.23
Allianz	7.41
ING Nationale Nederlanden	6.03
Other	29.08

Source: *CTK Business News Wire*, February 13, 2001, p. NA, from Slovak Insurers Association.

★ 1445 ★
Insurance
SIC: 6300–ISIC: 6600

Top Insurance Firms in the U.K.

Firms are ranked by share of total gross written premiums.

CGNU	21.09%
Royal & Sun Alliance	15.77
Axa	9.31
Zurich	7.14
Cornhill	4.38
Direct Line/Privege	3.67
Winterthur	3.41

British Utd Provident Assoc Ltd.	3.34%
AIG Europe	3.21
NFU/Avon	2.05
Other	26.63

Source: *Best's Review*, February 2001, p. 42, from Best's Insight.

★ 1446 ★
Life Insurance
SIC: 6311–ISIC: 6601

Largest Life Insurers in Bulgaria

Market shares are shown in percent.

	1999	2000
DZI Life	62.43%	47.50%
Orel Life	18.58	31.35
Allianz Bulgaria Life	7.30	6.70
Vitosha Life	3.44	4.85
Bulgari Imoti Life	3.42	2.81
Bulstrad DSK Life	2.55	3.14
Other	2.28	3.65

Source: *European Banker*, March 19, 2001, p. 16, from G-mez.

★ 1447 ★
Life Insurance
SIC: 6311–ISIC: 6601

Life Insurance Market in Vietnam

Market shares are shown in percent.

Bao Viet	75.4%
Prudential	15.2
Chinfon-Manulife	7.4

Source: *Vietnam Investment Review*, March 26, 2001, p. 11.

★ 1448 ★
Life Insurance
SIC: 6311–ISIC: 6601

Top Life Insurance Firms in Hong Kong

Market shares are shown in percent.

American Int Assurance	20.1%
Manulife	13.7
AXA China Region Insurance	13.0
HSBC Life	9.7
Prudential Assurance	4.9
Pacific Century Insurance	3.9
Aetna Life Insurance	3.5
CMG Asia	3.5
Royal & Sun Alliance Int Financial Services	2.7
Royal Skandia Life Assurance	2.7

Source: *Dagens Naeringsliv*, January 13, 2001, p. 1.

★ 1449 ★
Auto Insurance
SIC: 6321–ISIC: 6603

Auto Insurance Market in Hungary, 1999

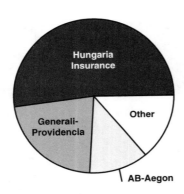

Market shares are shown in percent.

Hungaria Insurance	51.8%
Generali-Providencia	21.9
AB-Aegon	12.1
Other	14.2

Source: *Budapest Business Journal*, September 4, 2000, p. 1.

★ 1450 ★
Auto Insurance
SIC: 6321–ISIC: 6603

Auto Service Market in Britain

Market shares are shown based on members.

	(mil.)	Share
AA	9.5	46.0%
RAC	5.2	27.0
Green Flag	3.0	15.0
Britannia Rescue	0.5	3.0
Direct Line	0.3	2.0

Source: *The Guardian*, July 6, 1999, p. 22.

★ 1451 ★
Casualty Insurance
SIC: 6331–ISIC: 6603

Largest Casualty Insurers in Switzerland

Market shares are shown in percent.

Winterthur	22.1%
Zurich	18.7
Allianz	12.6
Mobiliar	11.8
Basler	8.2
Other	26.6

Source: *Neue Zuercher Zeitung*, April 10, 2001, p. 14, from Swiss Re.

★ 1452 ★
Property Insurance
SIC: 6331–ISIC: 6603

Damage/Accident Insurance Industry in Austria

Market shares are shown in percent.

Allianz Elementar	15.3%
Generali	11.9
Wiener Staditsche	11.2
Other	61.6

Source: *Presse*, July 28, 2000, p. 19.

★ 1453 ★
Pensions
SIC: 6371–ISIC: 6602

Pension Fund Market in Poland

Market shares are shown in percent.

PZU	25.0%
Bankowy	10.0
Zurich Solidarni	10.0
Orzel	9.0
AIG	8.0
Commercial Union	7.5
National Nederlanden	7.5
Other	38.0

Source: *Euromoney*, January 2000, p. 66, from Warburg Dillon Read.

SIC 64 - Insurance Agents, Brokers, and Service

Insurance Brokers
SIC: 6411–ISIC: 6720

Largest Insurance Brokers, 1999

Firms are ranked by brokerage revenue in billions of dollars.

Marsh & McLennan Cos. Inc.	$ 6,104.0
Aon Corp.	4,800.0
Willis Group Ltd.	1,239.0
Arthur J. Gallagher & Co.	586.0
Jardine Lloyd Thompson Group P.L.C.	432.0
HLF Insurance Holdings Ltd.	405.6
Acordia Inc.	337.2
Alexander Forbes Ltd.	330.0
USI Insurance Services Corp.	320.5

Source: *Business Insurance*, December 25, 2000, p. C2.

Reinsurance
SIC: 6411–ISIC: 6720

Global Reinsurance Market

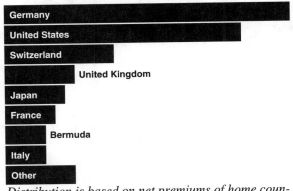

Distribution is based on net premiums of home country of insurer.

Germany	29.0%
United States	24.0
Switzerland	11.0
United Kingdom	7.0
Japan	6.0
France	5.0
Bermuda	4.0
Italy	4.0
Other	7.0

Source: *Business Insurance*, August 30, 1999, p. 4, from Standard & Poor's Corp.

★ 1456 ★
Reinsurance
SIC: 6411–ISIC: 6720

Largest Reinsurance Firms, 1999

Firms are ranked by net premiums written, in millions of dollars.

Munich Reinsurance Group	$ 13,566
Swiss Reinsurance Group	12,839
Berkshire Hathaway Reinsurance Group	9,453
Employers Reinsurance Group	6,921
Gerling Global Reinsurance Group	3,938
Lloyd's	3,799
Assicurazioni Generali Reinsurance Group	3,533
Allian AZ Reinsurance Group	3,299
SCOR Reinsurance Group	2,721
Hannover Reinsurance Group	2,564

Source: *Financial Times*, September 4, 2000, p. 1, from Standard & Poors.

★ 1457 ★
Reinsurance
SIC: 6411–ISIC: 6720

Reinsurance Industry in the Slovak Republic

Market shares are shown in percent.

Sava Re	61.9%
Triglav Re	33.6
Inter Re	4.5

Source: *Reinsurance Magazine*, October 9, 2000, p. 10, from Slovenian Insurance Association.

SIC 65 - Real Estate

Real Estate
SIC: 6531–ISIC: 7020

Factory Outlet Development in Europe

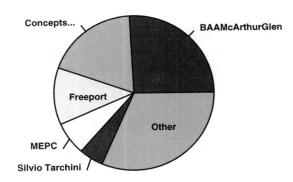

Market shares are shown in percent.

BAAMcArthurGlen	26.0%
Concepts & Distribution	18.7
Freeport	12.0
MEPC	6.6
Silvio Tarchini	4.5
Other	32.2

Source: ''Factory Outlet Centers.'' Retrieved January 11, 2001 from the World Wide Web: http://www.cior.com, from Healey & Baker.

Real Estate
SIC: 6531–ISIC: 7020

Top Real Estate Lessors in Japan, 1997

Market shares are shown based on shipments.

Able Real Estate	9.5%
Mini Mini	7.5
MDI	2.0
Daito Trust Construction	1.0
Other	80.0

Source: ''DVL Market Share Library.'' Retrieved April 3, 2001 from the World Wide Web: http://dvl/daiwa.co.jp, from DVL Market Share Library and Marketing Data Bank.

SIC 67 - Holding and Other Investment Offices

★ 1460 ★
Licensed Merchandise
SIC: 6794–ISIC: 6599

Licensed Character Market in France

The industry is shown by segment.

Character licenses	28.0%
Trading/playing cards and publishing	25.0
Toys and video games	14.0
Food	8.0
Other	25.0

Source: *Points de Vente*, March 15, 2000, p. 1.

★ 1461 ★
Patents
SIC: 6794–ISIC: 6599

Business Method Patents

Data show applications for business method patents from the European Patent Office.

United States	52.0%
Japan	10.0
France	7.0
Germany	7.0

United Kingdom	5.0%
Sweden	3.0
Australia	2.0
Canada	2.0
Finland	2.0
Netherlands	2.0
Other	6.0

Source: *Financial Times*, November 17, 2000, p. 16, from First Mover Monopoly.

★ 1462 ★
Patents
SIC: 6794–ISIC: 6599

Top Nations for Patents

United States, Germany and Japan have been the top three filers for the last decade.

	No.	Share
United States	38,171	42.0%
Germany	12,039	13.2
Japan	9,402	10.3
Great Britain	5,538	6.1
France	3,601	4.0
Sweden	3,071	3.4
Netherlands	2,587	2.8
Switzerland/Lichtenstein	1,701	1.9
Australia	1,627	1.8

Source: *Christian Science Monitor*, February 22, 2001, p. 2, from World Intellectual Property Organization.

★ 1463 ★
Franchises
SIC: 6798–ISIC: 6599

Largest Franchises Worldwide

McDonald's	
7-Eleven	
Subway	
H&R Block	
Burger King	
Jani-King	
Radio Shack	
Domino's Pizza	
Dairy Queen	
Wendy's	

Data show estimated number of units worldwide.

McDonald's	23,600
7-Eleven	18,200
Subway	13,500
H&R Block	9,000
Burger King	8,200
Jani-King	7,700
Radio Shack	7,200
Domino's Pizza	6,500
Dairy Queen	5,300
Wendy's	4,600

Source: *Christian Science Monitor*, April 24, 2000, p. 19, from International Franchise Association.

SIC 70 - Hotels and Other Lodging Places

★ 1464 ★
Hotels
SIC: 7011–ISIC: 5510

Largest Hotel Companies

Data show number of rooms.

Cendant	528,896
Bass	461,434
Marriott	328,300
Choice	305,171
Best Western	301,899
Accor	291,770
Hilton-Promus	290,000

Source: *USA TODAY*, September 8, 1999, p. 2B.

★ 1465 ★
Hotels
SIC: 7011–ISIC: 5510

Top Hotel Firms in Europe

Data show number of rooms.

Accor	161,547
Best Western	72,089
Bass Hotels & Resorts	59,249
Societe du Louvre	55,312
Sol Mella	40,336

Source: *Hotels*, February 2000, p. 6, from *The European Hotel Industry* and Travel Research Industry.

★ 1466 ★
Hotels
SIC: 7011–ISIC: 5510

Top Hotel Firms in Japan, 1999

Prince Hotels Inc.
Fujita Kanko Inc.
Hotel New Otani Co.
Imperial Hotel Ltd.
Tokyu Hotel Chain Co.
Other

Shares are shown based on domestic sales.

Prince Hotels Inc.	9.5%
Fujita Kanko Inc.	4.0
Hotel New Otani Co.	3.5
Imperial Hotel Ltd.	3.5
Tokyu Hotel Chain Co.	2.6
Other	76.9

Source: *Nikkei Weekly*, August 21, 2000, p. 9, from Nihon Keizai Shimbun.

★ 1467 ★
Time Sharing
SIC: 7011–ISIC: 5510

Time Share Industry

In 1997, there were 3,888 time share resorts and units in the top 20 countries that were members of Resort Condominums International or Interval International, the two largest time-share exchange programs. The programs allow those with time-shares toexchange weeks with other time-share owners.

	No. Projects	Share
United States	1,608	33.2%
Spain	445	9.2
Mexico	294	6.1
Italy	172	3.6
South Africa	167	3.5

Continued on next page.

★ 1467 ★
[Continued]
Time Sharing
SIC: 7011–ISIC: 5510

Time Share Industry

In 1997, there were 3,888 time share resorts and units in the top 20 countries that were members of Resort Condominums International or Interval International, the two largest time-share exchange programs. The programs allow those with time-shares toexchange weeks with other time-share owners.

	No. Projects	Share
France	153	3.2%
Argentina	124	2.6
Portugal	106	2.2
Canada	105	2.2

Source: *Detroit Free Press*, May 10, 1999, p. 7F, from American Resort Development Association.

SIC 72 - Personal Services

★ 1468 ★
Beauty Parlors
SIC: 7231–ISIC: 9302

Top Beauty Salons in Japan, 1997

Comy	
Socie World	
Fuji Beauty	
RBM	
N S Shoji	
Slim Beauty House	
The Fourubi	
Yamano Beauty Mate	
Jet Slim	
Other	

Market shares are shown based on shipments.

Comy	8.5%
Socie World	5.0
Fuji Beauty	4.0
RBM	3.8
N S Shoji	3.0
Slim Beauty House	2.5
The Fourubi	2.0
Yamano Beauty Mate	2.0
Jet Slim	1.5
Other	67.7

Source: ''DVL Market Share Library.'' Retrieved April 3, 2001 from the World Wide Web: http://dvl/daiwa.co.jp, from DVL Market Share Library and Marketing Data Bank.

SIC 73 - Business Services

Advertising
SIC: 7311–ISIC: 7430

Global Advertiser Market Shares

Market shares are shown based on total gross profits of $26 billion.

Omnicom Group	18.0%
Interpublic Group	16.0
WPP Group	16.0
Dentsu	7.0
Young & Rubicam	6.0
Grey Advertising	5.0
Havas Advertising	5.0
True North Communications	5.0
Leo Group	4.0
Others	18.0

Source: *Nikkei Weekly*, November 22, 1999, p. 3, from companies.

★ 1470 ★
Advertising
SIC: 7311–ISIC: 7430

Largest Media Spenders

Advertisers are ranked by spending outside the United States in millions of dollars.

Unilever	$ 3,110
Procter & Gamble Co.	2,988
Nestle	1,580
Coca-Cola Co.	1,178
Ford Motor Co.	1,150
General Motors Corp.	1,148

L'Oreal	$ 1,120
Volkswagen	1,009
Toyota Motor Corp.	1,007
PSA Peugeot Citroen	906

Source: *Advertising Age*, November 2000, p. 38, from A.C. Nielsen.

★ 1471 ★
Advertising
SIC: 7311–ISIC: 7430

Top Ad Firms in Australia

Firms are ranked by gross income in millions of dollars.

Clemenger Group BBDO	$ 79,856
The Comm. Group/George Patterson	61,266
Singleton Ad Agency	47,600
Y&R Australia	40,776
DDB Australia Worldwide	35,934
TMP Worldwide	30,689
McCann-Erickson Advertising	29,782
J. Walter Thompson	26,468
Leo Burnett Connaghan & May	25,624

Source: *Advertising Age*, April 24, 2000, p. S18.

★ 1472 ★
Advertising
SIC: 7311–ISIC: 7430

Top Ad Firms in Belgium

Firms are ranked by gross income in millions of dollars.

HHD O&M	$ 30,771
McCann-Erickson Co.	29,452
Euro RSCG Belgium	27,069
BBDO Belgium	24,710
Lowe Lintas & Partners	18,217
DDB Group/Belgium	15,963
Grey	15,249
TBWA/GV Group Belgium	13,629
Young & Rubicam Brussels	12,704

Source: *Advertising Age*, April 24, 2000, p. S18.

★ 1473 ★
Advertising
SIC: 7311–ISIC: 7430

Top Ad Firms in China

Firms are ranked by gross income in millions of dollars.

Ogilvy & Mather	$ 26,168
Euro RSCG China	24,738
McCann-Erickson Guangming	23,590
Saatchi & Saatchi Group	20,452
Ogilvy & Mather	18,664
FCB Hong Kong	18,208
J. Walter Thompson	17,465
DDB Worldwide/Hong Kong	17,370
Dentsu Young & Rubicam	16,089

Source: *Advertising Age*, April 24, 2000, p. S18.

★ 1474 ★
Advertising
SIC: 7311–ISIC: 7430

Top Ad Firms in Denmark

Firms are ranked by gross income in millions of dollars.

Grey Communications Group	$ 48,949
McCann-Erickson	20,692
DDB Denmark	17,580
Young & Rubicam Copenhagen	15,125
Bates Gruppen	14,686
BBDO	10,289
SCANAD Reklamebureau	8,927
Ogilvy & Mather	7,660
Leo Burnett/Copenhagen	7,155

Source: *Advertising Age*, April 24, 2000, p. S18.

★ 1475 ★
Advertising
SIC: 7311–ISIC: 7430

Top Ad Firms in Finland

Firms are ranked by gross income in millions of dollars.

AS-Grey	$ 41,260
DDB Worldwide/Finland	19,121
Hasan and Partners	17,753
Publicis Torma	8,250
Euro RSCG Finland	7,274
Lowe Lintas & Partners	7,274
Paltemaa Huttunen Santala TBWA	7,031
Viherjuuri Saatchi & Saatchi	7,012
BBDO Helsinki	4,364

Source: *Advertising Age*, April 24, 2000, p. S18.

★ 1476 ★
Advertising
SIC: 7311–ISIC: 7430

Top Ad Firms in Germany

Firms are ranked by gross income in millions of dollars.

BBDO Group Germany	$ 251,652
Grey Gruppe Deutschland	124,544
Publicis	119,393
J. Walter Thompson	88,816
Ogilvy & Mather	84,505
Young & Rubicam	78,936
Lowe Lintas & Partners	78,088
McCann-Erickson Deutschland	70,773
Springer & Jacoby	67,861

Source: *Advertising Age*, April 24, 2000, p. S18.

★ 1477 ★
Advertising
SIC: 7311–ISIC: 7430

Top Ad Firms in Greece

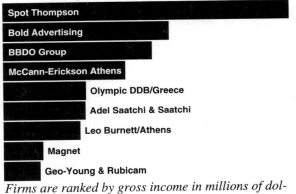

Firms are ranked by gross income in millions of dollars.

Spot Thompson	$ 44,499
Bold Advertising	25,739
BBDO Group	23,078
McCann-Erickson Athens	18,892
Olympic DDB/Greece	12,712
Adel Saatchi & Saatchi	12,624
Leo Burnett/Athens	11,795
Magnet	5,980
Geo-Young & Rubicam	5,527

Source: *Advertising Age*, April 24, 2000, p. S18.

★ 1478 ★
Advertising
SIC: 7311–ISIC: 7430

Top Ad Firms in Italy

Firms are ranked by gross income in millions of dollars.

Armando Testa Group	$ 56,247
McCann-Erickson Italiana	53,823
Young & Rubicam Italia	52,194
Barbella Gagliardi Saffiririo/DMB&B	41,801
J. Walter Thompson	38,031
Lowe Lintas Pirella Goettsche & Partners	37,388
Euro RSCG Italy	33,709
Milano & Grey	31,911
Publicis	29,922

Source: *Advertising Age*, April 24, 2000, p. S18.

★ 1479 ★
Advertising
SIC: 7311–ISIC: 7430

Top Ad Firms in Japan, 1999

Market shares are shown based on domestic billings.

Dentsu Inc.	23.0%
Hakuhodo Inc.	11.8
Asatsu-DK Inc.	5.6
Tokyu Agency Inc.	3.2
Daiko Advertising Inc.	2.7
Other	53.7

Source: *Nikkei Weekly*, July 31, 2000, p. 8, from Nihon Keizai Shimbun.

★ 1480 ★
Advertising
SIC: 7311–ISIC: 7430

Top Ad Firms in Kenya

Firms are ranked by gross income in thousands of dollars.

Scanad Marketing	$ 2,387
McCann-Erickson Kenya	2,040
Ayton Young & Rubicam	1,159

Continued on next page.

★ 1480 ★

[Continued]

Advertising

SIC: 7311–ISIC: 7430

Top Ad Firms in Kenya

Firms are ranked by gross income in thousands of dollars.

Ogilvy & Mather	$ 894
DDB-CCL	823
Century Advertising	665
MCL Saatchi & Saatchi	375
Acceff Advertising	322
Thompson Kenya Nairobi	212

Source: *Advertising Age*, April 24, 2000, p. S18.

★ 1481 ★

Advertising

SIC: 7311–ISIC: 7430

Top Ad Firms in Norway

Firms are ranked by gross income in thousands of dollars.

Leo Burnett Gruppen	$ 23,538
JBR McCann	23,005
Bates-Gruppen	17,069
Grey Communications Group	14,362
New Deal DDB/Norway	9,500
DMB&B	7,671
Ogilvy & Mather	6,321
Young & Rubicam	4,194
Publicis	3,756

Source: *Advertising Age*, April 24, 2000, p. S18.

★ 1482 ★

Advertising

SIC: 7311–ISIC: 7430

Top Ad Firms in Singapore

Firms are ranked by gross income in thousands of dollars.

Dentsu, Young & Rubicam	$ 21,206
Ogilvy & Mather	12,401
Batey Ads Singapore	$ 9,840
Saatchi & Saatchi	8,713
Euro RSCG Singapore	8,029
McCann-Erickson	7,722
DDB Singapore	7,525
Lowe Lintas & Partners	5,677
Publicis	4,560

Source: *Advertising Age*, April 24, 2000, p. S18.

★ 1483 ★

Advertising

SIC: 7311–ISIC: 7430

Top Ad Firms in Switzerland

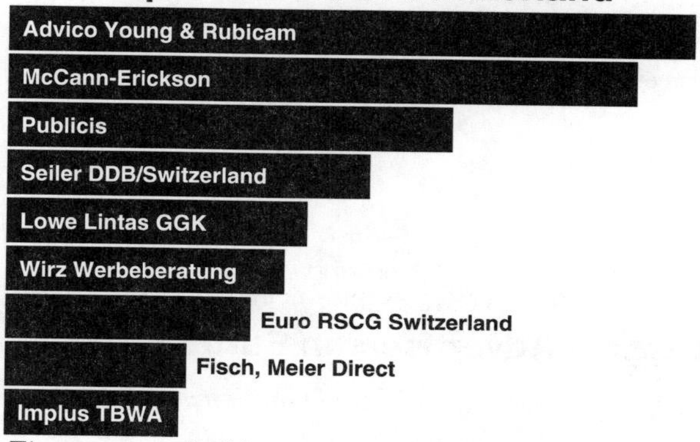

Firms are ranked by gross income in thousands of dollars.

Advico Young & Rubicam	$ 38,768
McCann-Erickson	35,489
Publicis	25,047
Seiler DDB/Switzerland	20,408
Lowe Lintas GGK	16,860
Wirz Werbeberatung	15,604
Euro RSCG Switzerland	13,707
Fisch, Meier Direct	10,107
Implus TBWA	9,700

Source: *Advertising Age*, April 24, 2000, p. S18.

★ 1484 ★
Advertising
SIC: 7319–ISIC: 7430

Largest Advertisers in Asia/Pacific, 2000

Firms are ranked by spending in millions of dollars.

Unilever	$ 838.6
Toyota Motor Corp.	607.1
Procter & Gamble Co.	527.1
Kao Corp.	425.9
Sony Corp.	387.3
Nissan Motor Co.	345.5
Nestle	341.6
Coca-Cola Co.	282.6
Honda Motor Co.	245.0

Source: *AdAgeGlobal*, November 2000, p. 36.

★ 1485 ★
Advertising
SIC: 7319–ISIC: 7430

Largest Advertisers in Europe, 2000

Firms are ranked by spending in millions of dollars.

Procter & Gamble Co.	$ 1,804.6
Unilever	1,784.7
Nestle	1,022.7
L'Oreal	1,003.5
PSA Peugeot Citroen	840.5
Ford Motor Co.	824.7
Volkswagen	796.2
Renault	766.4
Mars Inc.	732.5

Source: *AdAgeGlobal*, November 2000, p. 36.

★ 1486 ★
Advertising
SIC: 7319–ISIC: 7430

TV Advertising in Europe

Spending is shown in millions of dollars.

	1999 ($ mil.)	2003 ($ mil.)
United Kingdom	$ 5,020	$ 6,650
Germany	4,744	6,030
Italy	4,051	5,050
France	3,588	4,850
Spain	2,082	2,850
Poland	1,128	2,500
Portugal	1,128	1,450
Russia	1,010	1,230
Belgium	743	1,060
Greece	746	1,000

Source: *Electronic Media*, November 27, 2000, p. 12, from Wilkofsky Gruen Associates.

★ 1487 ★
Advertising
SIC: 7319–ISIC: 7430

Yellow Pages Advertising

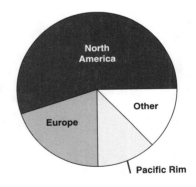

Figures are in billions of dollars.

	($ bil.)	Share
North America	$ 13.70	54.78%
Europe	5.00	19.99
Pacific Rim	3.00	12.00
Other	3.31	13.23

Source: *Yellow Pages & Directory Report*, October 25, 2000, p. NA.

★ 1488 ★
Direct Marketing
SIC: 7331–ISIC: 7499

Top Direct Mailers in the U.K.

The market continues to experience healthy growth in the face of digital media. Indeed, dot com firms have upped their spending on direct mail advertising. Firms are ranked by estimated millions of items mailed.

MBNA	120
Morgan Stanley Dean Witter	62
Barclaycard	58
Capital One	58
BCA	44
Lloyds TSB	36
Egg	33
HFC Bank	33
Littlewoods	30
Reader's Digest	29

Source: *Marketing*, December 21, 2000, p. 24.

★ 1489 ★
Cleaning Services
SIC: 7349–ISIC: 9000

Cleaning Services Market in Chile

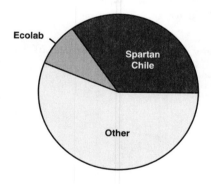

Market shares are shown in percent.

Spartan Chile	35.0%
Ecolab	9.0
Other	56.0

Source: *Estrategia*, March 10, 2000, p. 1.

★ 1490 ★
Cleaning Services
SIC: 7349–ISIC: 9000

Contract Cleaning Market in the U.K., 1999

The market is shown by region.

Southeast	36.0%
London	15.8
Southwest	14.3
Yorkshire and Humberside	7.0
West Midlands	6.5
East Midlands	6.0
West	5.1
North	4.3
Northwest	3.2
Other	1.8

Source: "UK Contract Cleaning." Retrieved January 12, 2001 from the World Wide Web: http://www.clearlybusiness.com, from Datamonitor.

★ 1491 ★
Leasing Services
SIC: 7350–ISIC: 7129

Leasing Industry in India

Market shares are shown in percent.

Nonbanking financial institutions	52.0%
Financial institutions	30.0
Scheduled commercial banks	10.0
Foreign institutional investors	6.0
Other	2.0

Source: "Leasing Industry." Retrieved September 19, 2000 from the World Wide Web: http://www.tradeport.org.

★ 1492 ★
Leasing Services
SIC: 7353–ISIC: 9302

Top Construction Machinery Lessors in Japan, 1997

Market shares are shown based on revenues.

Nikken Rental	15.0%
Actio	13.0
Nishio Rent All	10.0
Kanamato	8.0
Sakosu	4.0
Other	50.0

Source: "DVL Market Share Library." Retrieved April 3, 2001 from the World Wide Web: http://dvl/daiwa.co.jp, from DVL Market Share Library and Marketing Data Bank.

★ 1493 ★
Staffing Industry
SIC: 7363–ISIC: 7491

Largest Staffing Firms in 1999

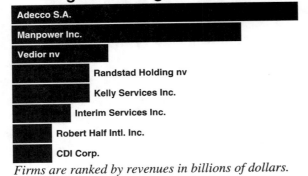

Firms are ranked by revenues in billions of dollars.

Adecco S.A.	$ 15.0
Manpower Inc.	11.5
Vedior nv	4.7
Randstad Holding nv	4.4
Kelly Services Inc.	4.3
Interim Services Inc.	3.2
Robert Half Intl. Inc.	2.1
CDI Corp.	1.6

Source: *Crain's Detroit Business*, March 27, 2000, p. 19.

★ 1494 ★
Software
SIC: 7372–ISIC: 2230–HC: 85

Antivirus Software Market

The $1.2 billion market is expected to hit $2.7 billion by 2004.

Network Associates/McAfee	39.0%
Symantec	25.0
Computer Associates Int.	13.0
Trend Micro	10.0
Sophos	2.0
F-secure	1.5

Source: *Wall Street Journal*, March 30, 2001, p. B3, from International Data Corp.

★ 1495 ★
Software
SIC: 7372–ISIC: 2230–HC: 85

Assembly Inspection Market, 1999

Total market size reached $181 million.

Robotic Vision	20.0%
ICOS	12.0
Ismeca	10.0
Laurier Inc.	5.0
STI Semiconductor	5.0
Other	48.0

Source: *Investor's Business Daily*, August 24, 2000, p. A12, from VLSI Research.

★ 1496 ★
Software
SIC: 7372–ISIC: 2230–HC: 85

CAE Software Market Shares

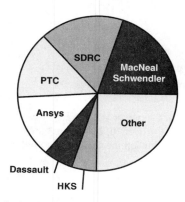

CAE stands for computer-aided engineering.

MacNeal Schwendler	20.0%
SDRC	17.0
PTC	14.0
Ansys	13.0
Dassault	6.0
HKS	5.0
Other	25.0

Source: *The Engineer*, July 23, 1999, p. 15.

★ 1497 ★
Software
SIC: 7372–ISIC: 2230–HC: 85

Call Center Software Market in Western Europe, 1998

Market shares are shown in percent.

Nortel Networks	23.0%
Lucent Technologies	18.5
Ericsson	16.9
Alcatel	11.3
Other	30.3

Source: *Wall Street Journal*, October 1, 1999, p. 1, from Dataquest Inc.

★ 1498 ★
Software
SIC: 7372–ISIC: 2230–HC: 85

Database Platform Market in China

Oracle	40.0%
Sybase	23.0
Informix	21.0
IBM	6.0
Microsoft	4.0
Others	6.0

Source: "Electronics Market in S.W. China." Retrieved September 19, 2000 from the World Wide Web: http://www.tradeport.org, from Forecast on China Electronic Industries, 1999.

★ 1499 ★
Software
SIC: 7372–ISIC: 2230–HC: 85

Desktop Operating Systems, 1999

Market shares are shown in percent.

Microsoft Windows	87.0%
Apple Macintosh	5.0
Linux	3.9
Other	4.1

Source: *Investor's Business Daily*, April 4, 2000, p. 1, from International Data Corp.

★ 1500 ★
Software
SIC: 7372–ISIC: 2230–HC: 85

Embedded OS Market Shares, 1999

Market shares are shown in percent.

Wind River Sytems	20.2%
Symbian	14.7
Palm	14.3
Microsoft	7.9
IBM	6.9
Other	36.0

Source: *Infoworld*, February 12, 2001, p. 16, from International Data Corp.

★ 1501 ★
Software
SIC: 7372–ISIC: 2230–HC: 85

Enterprise Management Systems Market in China

SSA	48.0%
SAP	7.4
QAD	5.5
Oracle	3.7
CA	2.8
JD Edwards	1.8
Other	24.7

Source: ''Electronics Market in S.W. China.'' Retrieved September 19, 2000 from the World Wide Web: http://www.tradeport.org, from Forecast on China Electronic Industries, 1999.

★ 1502 ★
Software
SIC: 7372–ISIC: 2230–HC: 85

Favorite Shareware in China

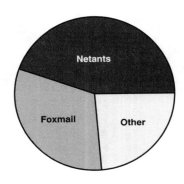

Market shares are shown in percent.

Netants	44.59%
Foxmail	31.74
Other	23.67

Source: ''Popular Computer Weekly Releases Survey Results.'' Retrieved October 16, 2000 from the World Wide Web: http://www.chinaonline.com, from Popular Computer Weekly.

★ 1503 ★
Software
SIC: 7372–ISIC: 2230–HC: 85

Foreign Language Software Market in China

Market shares are shown in percent.

Speaking English as You Please	30.03%
Kaitianpidi Memorizing Words	15.37
Other	54.60

Source: ''Popular Computer Weekly Releases Survey Results.'' Retrieved October 16, 2000 from the World Wide Web: http://www.chinaonline.com, from Popular Computer Weekly.

★ 1504 ★
Software
SIC: 7372–ISIC: 2230–HC: 85

Global Browser Market

Market shares are shown as of February 21, 2001.

Microsoft	87.71%
Netscape	12.01
Other	0.27

Source: ''Microsoft's Share of Browser Market.'' Retrieved February 27, 2001 from the World Wide Web: http://www.prnewswire.com, from StatMarket.

★ 1505 ★
Software
SIC: 7372–ISIC: 2230–HC: 85

Global Calendaring Software Market, 1998

Market shares are shown in percent.

Lotus	27.6%
Microsoft	14.1
Corporate Software & Technologies	13.4
Qualcomm	10.4
OpenText	6.7
Other	27.8

Source: *Investor's Business Daily*, September 29, 1999, p. A6, from International Data Corp.

★ 1507 ★
Software
SIC: 7372–ISIC: 2230–HC: 85

Global Media-Player Market Shares

Data show total number of users. There were 298.3 million personal computers in use in 1999, with 144.9 million connected to the Internet.

RealPlayer	90.0
Microsoft Media Player	40.0
Winamp	25.0
Sonique	5.0
Macast	0.1

Source: *Wired*, March 2000, p. 126.

★ 1506 ★
Software
SIC: 7372–ISIC: 2230–HC: 85

Global Database Market, 2000

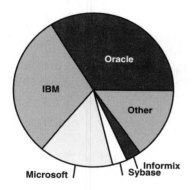

Market shares are shown in percent.

Oracle	33.8%
IBM	30.1
Microsoft	14.9
Sybase	3.2
Informix	3.0
Other	15.0

Source: "Press Release." Retrieved June 12, 2001 from the World Wide Web: http://www.gartner.com, from Dataquest Inc.

★ 1508 ★
Software
SIC: 7372–ISIC: 2230–HC: 85

Help Desk Market Worldwide, 1999

The market is forecast to grow from $1.3 billion in 2000 to $3.3 billion in 2004.

Computer Associates	40.0%
IBM	15.0
Other	45.0

Source: "Gartner's Dataquest Says E-Support Technologies." Retrieved September 14, 2000 from the World Wide Web: http://www.businesswire.com, from Dataquest Inc.

★ 1509 ★
Software
SIC: 7372–ISIC: 2230–HC: 85

Intrusion Detection Market

Company shares are shown in percent.

Axent	40.0%
ISS	24.5
Network Associates	11.7
Bindview	4.5
Cisco	4.3
Security Dynamics	3.4
Other	11.6

Source: *Investor's Business Daily*, December 14, 1999, p. A10, from International Data Corp.

★ 1510 ★
Software
SIC: 7372–ISIC: 2230–HC: 85

Largest Computer Software/Service Firms

Firms are ranked by revenue in billions of dollars.

IBM	$ 50.7
Microsoft	19.6
Electronic Data Systems	18.5
Oracle	9.3
Computer Sciences	8.6
Compaq	6.5
Hewlett-Packard	6.4
Computer Associates International	6.2
NCR	6.1
General Electric	5.3

Source: *EDN*, December 21, 2000, p. S200.

★ 1511 ★
Software
SIC: 7372–ISIC: 2230–HC: 85

Leisure Software Market

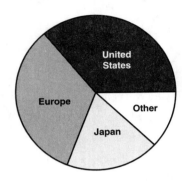

The global market for leisure software was valued at $17.7 billion. By 2002, Europe is expected to surpass the United States as the top market.

	($ bil.)	Share
United States	$ 6.3	35.59%
Europe	5.8	32.77
Japan	3.4	19.21
Other	2.2	12.43

Source: "UK Government Console Power Drives Leisure Market." Retrieved July 3, 2001 from the World Wide Web: http://www.library.northernlight.com, from European Leisure Software Publishers.

★ 1512 ★
Software
SIC: 7372–ISIC: 2230–HC: 85

Operating System Shipments, 1999

Market shares are shown in percent.

Microsoft NT Server	38.0%
Linux	25.0
Novell Netware	18.0
Unix	15.0
Other	4.0

Source: *Washington Technology*, July 3, 2000, p. 32, from International Data Corp.

★ 1513 ★
Software
SIC: 7372–ISIC: 2230–HC: 85

Packaged Software Market Worldwide, 1998

Market shares are shown in perent.

Microsoft	11.0%
IBM	9.7
Oracle	3.9
Computer Associates	3.7
SAP	2.4
Other	69.3

Source: *Infoworld*, February 8, 1999, p. 22, from International Data Corp.

★ 1514 ★
Software
SIC: 7372–ISIC: 2230–HC: 85

PC Operating System Market in China

There are over 500 software companies in the country, 60% of which are private. Local software accounts for 30% of the market.

Windows 95	60.0%
DOS 6.22/Windows 3.X	18.0
Unix	9.0
Window NT	7.0
OS/2	2.0
MAC	1.0

Source: "Electronics Market in S.W. China." Retrieved September 19, 2000 from the World Wide Web: http://www.tradeport.org, from Forecast on China Electronic Industries, 1999.

★ 1515 ★
Software
SIC: 7372–ISIC: 2230–HC: 85

Personal Tax Software in the U.K.

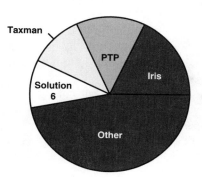

Market shares are shown in percent.

Iris	18.0%
PTP	14.0
Taxman	11.0
Solution 6	10.0
Other	47.0

Source: *Accountancy Age*, November 16, 2000, p. 13.

★ 1516 ★
Software
SIC: 7372–ISIC: 2230–HC: 85

Server Software Market Shares

Shares are for June 2000.

Apache	62.5%
Microsoft	20.4
Netscape	6.7
Rapidsite	1.7
Thttpd	1.3
Zeus	1.3
WebLogic	1.2
Other	4.9

Source: *Infoworld*, July 17, 2000, p. 24, from Netcraft.

★ 1517 ★
Software
SIC: 7372–ISIC: 2230–HC: 85

Top Software Firms, 1999

Firms are ranked by revenue in billions of dollars.

Microsoft	$ 17.4
IBM	14.9
Oracle	6.6
Computer Associates International	6.3
SAP AG	3.0
Hewlett-Packard	2.7
BMC Software	1.7
Fujitsu	1.7
Hitachi	1.5
Compuware	1.2

Source: *USA TODAY*, August 3, 2000, p. B1, from International Data Corp.

★ 1518 ★
Integrated Systems
SIC: 7373–ISIC: 7210–HC: 84

Specialist Construction Systems in the U.K.

Red Sky	53.0%
Mentor	15.0
Unisys	10.0
AS400	6.0
Coins	4.0
Foundation 2000	4.0
Mandata	4.0
Wessex	4.0

Source: *Contract Journal*, September 8, 1999, p. 15, from CIOB.

★ 1519 ★
Networks
SIC: 7373–ISIC: 7210–HC: 84

Leading Network Vendors in Australia

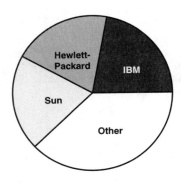

Figures are for 1999-2000.

IBM	22.0%
Hewlett-Packard	20.0
Sun	20.0
Other	38.0

Source: "Networking." Retrieved May 8, 2001 from the World Wide Web: http://www.usatrade.gov, from International Data Corp.

★ 1520 ★
Networks
SIC: 7373–ISIC: 7210–HC: 84

Leading Server Producers, 2000

Marekt shares are shown in percent.

Compaq	27.3%
IBM	16.4
Dell	14.9
Hewlett-Packard	10.9
Sun Microsystems	7.1
Other	23.4

Source: *Investor's Business Daily*, November 8, 2000, p. A6, from Dataquest Inc.

★ 1521 ★
Networks
SIC: 7373–ISIC: 7210–HC: 84

Leading Server Producers in Latin America, 2000

Shares are for the second quarter of the year.

Compaq	18.8%
IBM	14.0
Hewlett-Packard	7.0
Acer	5.6
Dell	5.2
Alaska	3.3
Sun Microsystems	2.8
Others	43.3

Source: "Press Release." Retrieved September 27, 2000 from the World Wide Web: http://www.gartnerweb.com, from Dataquest Inc.

★ 1522 ★
Networks
SIC: 7373–ISIC: 7210–HC: 84

RISC Server Market Shares, 2000

The table compares market shares for RISC entry level serrvers and high-end systems.

	Entry	High
Other	15.3%	14.9%
Sun	54.4	44.4
Compaq	6.9	16.2
IBM	16.8	15.5
Hewlett-Packard	12.6	9.0

Source: *Infoworld*, May 28, 2001, p. 26, from International Data Corp.

★ 1523 ★
Networks
SIC: 7373–ISIC: 7210–HC: 84

Top PC Server Makers in Japan, 1999

Market shares are shown based on domestic shipments.

NEC Corp.	27.3%
Fujitsu Ltd.	17.9
Compaq KK	13.9
Hitachi Ltd.	12.8
IBM Japan Ltd.	11.9
Other	16.2

Source: *Nikkei Weekly*, July 31, 2000, p. 8, from Nihon Keizai Shimbun.

★ 1524 ★
Networks
SIC: 7373–ISIC: 7210–HC: 84

Top Server Makers in China

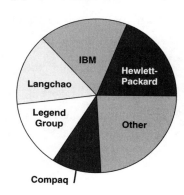

Market shares are shown in percent.

Hewlett-Packard	19.2%
IBM	17.7
Langchao	14.6
Legend Group	14.2
Compaq	10.1
Other	24.2

Source: "Chinese Server Brands Gobbling Up Market Shares." Retrieved November 14, 2000 from the World Wide Web: http://www.chinaonline.com, from CCIDnet.com.

★ 1525 ★
Information Technology
SIC: 7375–ISIC: 7240

Image Science/Information Technology Industry

Kodak describes the convergence of a image science and information technology industry as the $225 billion ''infoimaging'' industry.

	($ bil.)	Share
Photographic processing, film and papers	$ 54.6	27.37%
Photofinishing systems and networks	38.1	19.10
Health imaging	28.0	14.04
Inkjet cartridges	25.7	12.88
Document imaging	22.9	11.48
Inket printers	11.7	5.86
Inkjet papers	5.3	2.66
General-use digital cameras	3.5	1.75
Mass-market flatbed scanners	3.4	1.70
Photoprocessing equipment	3.0	1.50
Other	3.3	1.65

Source: *New York Times*, April 17, 2001, p. C1, from Kodak.

★ 1526 ★
Computer Services
SIC: 7378–ISIC: 7250–HC: 84

Leading Software Service Firms in the U.K.

Firms are ranked by software and service revenue in millions of British pounds.

EDS	1,000
IBM	630
ICL	620
SEMA Group	476
Andersen Consulting	444

Source: *Marketing*, June 4, 1998, p. 13, from *Holoway Report*.

★ 1527 ★
Computer Training
SIC: 7379–ISIC: 7290

Top Computer Training Firms, 1999

Companies are ranked by revenues in millions of dollars.

	($ mil.)	Share
IBM Global Services	$ 560	2.9%
Oracle University	480	2.5
New Horizons	435	2.2
SAP Education	394	2.0
Global Knowledge	328	1.7
KnowledgePool	293	1.5

Source: *Investor's Business Daily*, July 17, 2000, p. A12, from International Data Corp.

★ 1528 ★
Information Services
SIC: 7379–ISIC: 7290

Company, Credit & Financial Information Market

The company, credit & financial information market is a $21 billion industry. Companies are ranked by revenues in billions of dollars. Market trends include consolidation of global data sources and the creation of financial portals for content.

	($ bil.)	Share
Reuters Group PLC - Financial Information Products	$ 2.7	13.0%
Dun & Bradstreet	2.0	9.0
Equifax Inc.	1.8	8.0

Source: "Outsell Releases Landmark Report." Retrieved August 28, 2000 from the World Wide Web: http://www.businesswire.com, from Outsell Inc.

★ 1529 ★
Information Services
SIC: 7379–ISIC: 7290

News & Trade Information Market

The news & trade information market is a $92 billion industry. Companies are ranked by revenues in billions of dollars.

	($ bil.)	Share
Gannett - Newspaper Publishing	$ 4.3	4.7%
The News Corporation	4.2	4.5
Asahi Shimbun	3.5	3.8

Source: "Outsell Releases Landmark Report." Retrieved August 28, 2000 from the World Wide Web: http://www.businesswire.com, from Outsell Inc.

★ 1530 ★
Security Services
SIC: 7382–ISIC: 7492

Private Security Service Demand

Revenue are shown in millions of dollars.

	1999	2004	Share
United States	$ 27.3	$ 39.9	40.22%
Western Europe	22.6	32.1	32.36
Other world	5.8	10.5	10.58
Japan	4.2	6.1	6.15
Other Asia	4.2	7.5	7.56
Canada and Mexico	2.1	3.1	3.13

Source: *Research Studies*, December 26, 2000, p. 1, from Freedonia Group.

★ 1531 ★
Photofinishing
SIC: 7384–ISIC: 7494

Photo Development Market in the U.K.

Photo development and processing currently accounts for roughly 40% of the entire photography market, which stands at roughly 1.4 billion British pounds in the year 2000. Integrated D&P refers to Klick and Supasnaps. Standalone minilabs refer to places like Kodak Express. Market shares are estimated.

	2000	2001
High Street multiple	24.0%	24.0%
Integrated D&P	20.0	19.0
Mail order	19.0	19.0
Standalone minilabs	12.0	12.0
Pharmacies	11.0	11.0
Camera shops	7.0	6.0
Supermarkets	6.0	8.0

Source: *Chemist & Druggist*, June 9, 2001, p. 18, from Moss Pharmacy.

★ 1532 ★

Convention Space

SIC: 7389–ISIC: 7499

Largest Expo Space in Europe

Locations are ranked by size in square meters.

Hannover	446,000
Milan	372,000
Frankfurt	292,000
Cologne	275,000
Paris Expo	226,000
Dusseldorf	203,000
Paris Nord	191,000
Birmingham	190,000

Source: *The Engineer*, October 22, 1999, p. 4.

★ 1533 ★

Mergers & Acquisitions

SIC: 7389–ISIC: 7499

Largest Mergers Worldwide

Acquirers are shown in parentheses. Value of deal is shown in billions of dollars.

Time Warner (America Online)	$ 181.6
SmithKline Beecham (Glaxo Wellcome)	77.2
Nortel networks/Shareholders	61.6
VoiceStream Wireless (Deutsche Telecom)	54.7
Honeywell (General Electric)	50.1
Orange PLC (France Telecom)	45.9
Seagram (Vivendi)	42.7
SDL (JDS Uniphase)	40.9
Cable and Wireless (Pacific Century Cyberworks)	35.4

Source: *American Banker*, December 29, 2000, p. 1.

★ 1534 ★

Mergers & Acquisitions

SIC: 7389–ISIC: 7499

Top M&A Advisers in Japan

Market shares are shown in percent.

Goldman Sachs	32.0%
Merrill Lynch	29.3
Morgan Stanley Dean Witter	17.2
Nikko Salomon Smith Barney	16.8
Bank of Tokyo Mitsubishi	11.8
Lehman Brothers	11.0
Nomura	9.4
Mizuho Group	7.7
Credit Suisse First Boston	7.6

Source: *Wall Street Journal*, January 24, 2001, p. A14.

SIC 75 - Auto Repair, Services, and Parking

★ 1535 ★
Truck Rental
SIC: 7513–ISIC: 7111–HC: 87

U.K. Truck Rental Market, 1999

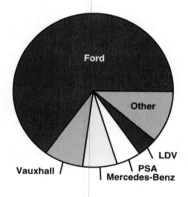

The market grew 7.5% in 1999, to reach a value of 547.7 million pounds. Shares are estimated by manufacturer.

Ford	65.0%
Vauxhall	8.0
Mercedes-Benz	7.0
PSA	5.0
LDV	4.0
Other	11.0

Source: "UK Truck Rental." Retrieved janaury 11, 2001 from the World Wide Web: http:// www.clearlybusiness.com, from Datamonitor.

★ 1536 ★
Auto Rental
SIC: 7514–ISIC: 7111–HC: 87

Top Auto Rental Firms in Argentina

Market shares are shown in percent.

Hertz Annie Millet	35.0%
Localiza	19.0
Avis	18.0
A1 Rent a Car	8.0
Dolar	8.0
Other	12.0

Source: *Buenos Aires Economico*, April 14, 2001, p. 7.

★ 1537 ★
Auto Rental
SIC: 7514–ISIC: 7111–HC: 87

Top Auto Rental Firms in Europe

Market shares are shown in percent.

Avis Europe	15.2%
Europcar	12.7
Hertz	11.1
National	9.5
Budget	5.2
Sixt	5.1
Other	41.1

Source: *Wall Street Journal*, May 24, 1999, p. B9, from Datamonitor and company reports.

★ 1538 ★
Auto Rental
SIC: 7514–ISIC: 7111–HC: 87

Top Auto Rental Firms in Japan, 1997

Market shares are shown based on shipments.

Toyota Motor	23.5%
Nippon Rent-a-Car Service	14.0
Nissan Car Lease	7.0
Mazda Rental Lease	6.5
Orix Rent-a-Car	5.5
JapaRen	2.5
Japan Rent-a-Car	1.5
Other	39.5

Source: ''DVL Market Share Library.'' Retrieved April 3, 2001 from the World Wide Web: http://dvl/daiwa.co.jp, from DVL Market Share Library and Marketing Data Bank.

★ 1539 ★
Auto Rental
SIC: 7514–ISIC: 7111–HC: 87

Top Auto Rental Firms in the U.K., 1999

Market shares are estimated based on value. Non-airport business has 82.3% of the industry.

National	18.5%
Avis	13.2
Europcar	12.1
Hertz	11.8
United Kenning	9.1
Budget	7.8
Others	27.8

Source: ''Replacement Car Tires.'' Retrieved January 12, 2001 from the World Wide Web: http://www.clearlybusiness.com, from Datamonitor.

★ 1540 ★
Auto Rental
SIC: 7514–ISIC: 7111–HC: 87

Top Auto Rental Markets in Europe, 2004

The market is set to grow from $8.14 billion 1999 to $10.8 billion in 2004. Volume is expected to increase from 202 million rental days to 2.62 million in 2004. Figures are in millions of dollars.

	($ mil.)	Share
Airport leisure	$ 2,424	22.44%
Business rental	1,730	16.02
Other	6,646	61.54

Source: *Travel Trade Gazette UK & Ireland*, September 6, 1999, p. 79.

★ 1541 ★
Auto Repair Services
SIC: 7530–ISIC: 5020–HC: 87

Vehicle Repair Sales in Italy

Shares are shown based on sales.

Independent workshops	53.6%
Car workshops approved by auto manufacturer	33.6
Spare parts dealers	2.2
Car accessory dealers	1.8
Large distributor centers	1.8
Service stations	1.8

Source: ''Italy: Garage Equipment.'' Retrieved September 19, 2000 from the World Wide Web: http://www.tradeport.org.

SIC 76 - Miscellaneous Repair Services

★ 1542 ★

Aircraft Engine Repair

SIC: 7629–ISIC: 5260–HC: 85

Largest Aircraft/Engine Maintenance Operations

| GE Engine Services |
| Lufthansa Technik |
| American Airlines |
| Delta |
| Japan Airlines |
| UAL Services |
| Pratt & Whitney |
| Rolls Royce |
| Continental |

Companies are ranked by sales in billions of dollars.

GE Engine Services	$ 5.00
Lufthansa Technik	1.71
American Airlines	1.45
Delta	1.35
Japan Airlines	1.09
UAL Services	1.04
Pratt & Whitney	1.00
Rolls Royce	1.00
Continental	0.97

Source: *Airline Business*, October 1, 1999, p. 1.

★ 1543 ★

Aircraft Maintenance Services

SIC: 7629–ISIC: 5260–HC: 85

Commercial Aviation Support Services, 1999

The market is worth $87 billion.

	($ bil.)	Share
Airport and route infrastructure services	$ 21.4	24.68%
Heavy maintenance	18.5	21.34
Airplane servicing	13.8	15.92
Airframe component repair	12.3	14.19
Engine repair (off wing)	8.4	9.69
Airframe and engine repair parts . .	8.1	9.34
Major airplane modification	1.8	2.08
Flight crew training	1.7	1.96
Used airplane remarketing	0.7	0.81

Source: *Aviation Week & Space Technology*, April 2, 2001, p. 87, from Boeing.

SIC 78 - Motion Pictures

★ 1544 ★
DVDs
SIC: 7812–ISIC: 9211–HC: 37

DVD Shipments Worldwide

Data are in millions of units.

United States	78.6
Europe	20.1
Far East	8.1
Canada	6.5
Australia	0.7

Source: *Screen Digest*, November 2000, p. 41.

★ 1545 ★
DVDs
SIC: 7812–ISIC: 9211–HC: 37

Top DVD Titles in Finland, 1999

Titles are ranked by revenues, in thousands of Finnish markkas.

The Matrix	9,934
Hajyt	2,761
Armageddon	2,211
Notting Hill	2,144
Naked Gun 4	1,923
Starship Troopers	1,920
Shakespeare in Love	1,565
Titanic	1,171
Mask of Zorro	802

Source: *Screen Digest*, June 2000, p. 179, from Suomen Elokuvatoimistojen Liitto.

★ 1546 ★
Motion Pictures
SIC: 7812–ISIC: 9211–HC: 37

France's Film Industry

Both audiences and revenue were up this year, with 166 million tickets sold (up 8.1%) and receipts hitting $789 million (up 8.5%). The increase was in part from the modernization of theaters and growth of multiplexes. The number of French-made films fell by 10 to 171.

	1999	2000
American films	53.9%	62.9%
French films	28.5	32.4

Source: *Daily Variety*, May 11, 2001, p. 22, from Centre Nationale de Cinematographie.

★ 1547 ★
Motion Pictures
SIC: 7812–ISIC: 9211–HC: 37

Global Theatrical Market Shares, 1999

Theatrical billings of the major studios reached $5.97 billion in 1999, almost 5% more than the previous year. U.S. theatrical revenue topped the foreign take for the first time since 1995.

United States	52.2%
Europe	24.7
Asia	12.7
Latin America	4.9
Canada	3.5
Middle East	0.9
Africa	0.4
Other	0.4

Source: *Hollywood Reporter*, July 11, 2000, p. 8.

★ 1548 ★
Motion Pictures
SIC: 7812–ISIC: 9211–HC: 37

Largest Film Producers in Spain

Firms are ranked by box office in millions of dollars. 35% of the population go to the movies once a week and 102 million people went to 3,155 theaters for the first nine months of the year.

Lolafilms S.A.	$ 11.2
Sociedad Gral de Cine	9.6
El Deseo	7.5
Aurum Producciones	6.9
Origen Producciones Cinematograficas	5.2
Sociedad Kino Vision	5.2
Creativos A. de Radio	4.7
Fernando Trueba P.C.	4.4
Sdad. Gral. De Decheros Audiovisuales	4.3
BocaBoca Producttiones	3.6

Source: "Films and Videos." Retrieved November 6, 2000 from the World Wide Web: http://www.usatrade.gov.

★ 1549 ★
Motion Pictures
SIC: 7812–ISIC: 9211–HC: 37

Top Films in Japan, 2000

Films are ranked by box office receipts in millions of dollars.

Mission Impossible 2	$ 62.9
The Green Mile	60.4
Pocket Monsters 3	41.9
Dinosaur	39.1
Whiteout	35.9
Toy Story 2	32.4
Perfect Storm	31.8
Doraemon	26.2

Source: *Variety*, February 19, 2001, p. 22, from A.C. Nielsen EDI/Filmsource.

★ 1550 ★
Motion Pictures
SIC: 7812–ISIC: 9211–HC: 37

Top Films in Spain, 2000

Films are ranked by box office receipts in millions of dollars.

The Sixth Sense	$ 24.3
Gladiator	17.5
American Beauty	14.8
Mission Impossible 2	12.3
Toy Story 2	11.1
What Lies Beneath	10.5
Hollow Man	9.9
Scary Movie	9.4

Source: *Variety*, February 19, 2001, p. 22, from A.C. Nielsen EDI/Filmsource.

★ 1551 ★
Motion Pictures
SIC: 7812–ISIC: 9211–HC: 37

Top Films in the U.K., 2000

Films are ranked by box office receipts in millions of dollars.

Toy Story 2	$ 63.4
Gladiator	45.1
Chicken Run	43.8
American Beauty	31.1
Stuart Little	26.0
Mission Impossible 2	25.2
Billy Elliot	24.3
X-Men	21.8

Source: *Variety*, February 19, 2001, p. 22, from A.C. Nielsen EDI/Filmsource.

★ 1552 ★
Videos
SIC: 7812–ISIC: 9211–HC: 37

Video Tape Sales in the U.K., 1999

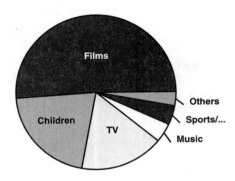

Retail video sales reached 82 million British pounds in 1999.

Films	51.0%
Children	21.0
TV	17.0
Music	4.0
Sports/fitness	4.0
Others	3.0

Source: *The Grocer*, July 15, 2000, p. 43.

★ 1553 ★
Film Distribution
SIC: 7822–ISIC: 9214

Film Distribution in Norway, 1998

231 films were released during the year. U.S. films had 55.1% of the Norwegian market.

Kommunenes Filmcentral	17.3%
Sandrew-Metronome	13.4
Egment/Columbia TriStar	11.3
Scandinavian Entertainment Group	11.3
Svensk Filmindustri	9.9
UIP	9.9
Europafilm	9.1
Other	17.8

Source: *Screen International*, August 20, 1999, p. 24.

★ 1554 ★
Film Distribution
SIC: 7822–ISIC: 9214

Leading DVD Distributors in the U.K., 2001

Shares are for the first quarter.

Universal Pictures	15.7%
Warner Home Video	14.5
Columbia TriStar Home Entertainment	12.2
Other	57.6

Source: *Billboard*, March 5, 2001, p. 87.

★ 1555 ★
Film Distribution
SIC: 7822–ISIC: 9214

Leading Film Distributors in Spain

Market shares are shown in percent.

Nexo	13.0%
Cecchi Gori	5.0
Instituto Luce	3.3
Filmauro	2.6
Key Films	2.0
Mikado Film	1.6
Lucky Red	1.3
Eagle Pictures	1.2
Other	65.0

Source: "Mifed News." Retrieved December 2, 2000 from the World Wide Web: http://www.londonmefed.com, from Cinetel and Giornale dello Spettacolo.

★ 1556 ★
Film Distribution
SIC: 7822–ISIC: 9214

Top Film Distributors in Germany, 2000

Shares are for January 3 - May 1.

Constantin	27.1%
UIP	19.8

Continued on next page.

★ 1556 ★

[Continued]
Film Distribution
SIC: 7822–ISIC: 9214

Top Film Distributors in Germany, 2000

Shares are for January 3 - May 1.

Columbia TriStar	13.6%
Warner Bros.	8.6
BVI	7.9
Fox	6.9
Kinowelt Medien	6.6
Concorde	3.0
Senator	2.5
Tobis	2.0
Other	3.7

Source: *Variety*, May 14, 2000, p. 13, from A.C. Nielsen EDI.

★ 1557 ★

Film Distribution
SIC: 7822–ISIC: 9214

Top Film Distributors in Paris

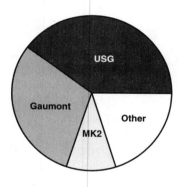

Market shares are shown in percent.

USG	40.0%
Gaumont	30.0
MK2	10.0
Other	20.0

Source: *The Guardian Unlimited*, September 18, 2000, p. 1.

★ 1558 ★

Movie Theaters
SIC: 7832–ISIC: 9212–HC: 37

Large Format Theaters Worldwide

There are about 337 large format theaters in operation, although a record number of them have been closed. Imax manufactured 90% of the 38 that were opened this year, the bulk of the m being in North America.

North America	52.5%
Asia & Far East	29.4
Europe	15.7
Africa	0.9
Latin America	0.9
Middle East	0.6

Source: *Screen Digest*, May 2001, p. 159.

★ 1559 ★

Movie Theaters
SIC: 7832–ISIC: 9212–HC: 37

Largest Cinema Chains in the U.K.

Market shares are shown in percent.

Odeon	20.6%
UCI	16.5
UGC	14.4
Warner Cinemas	14.0
Other	34.5

Source: "Rank Wraps Up Odeon Sales to Cinven."
Retrieved February 21, 2000 from the World Wide Web:
http://www.northernlight.com.

★ 1560 ★
Movie Theaters
SIC: 7832–ISIC: 9212–HC: 37

Largest Theater Chains in Belgium

Exhibitors are ranked by number of screens. Total box office reached $170 million.

Kinepolis	121
UGC	43
Carpentier	28
Carrollywood	24
Rastelli	23

Source: *Variety*, June 19, 2000, p. 52, from Federation des Cinemas de Belgique and Regie Media Belge.

★ 1561 ★
Movie Theaters
SIC: 7832–ISIC: 9212–HC: 37

Largest Theater Chains in Germany

Exhibitors are ranked by number of screens. Total box office reached $832 million.

Riech Group	311
Flebbe Group	297
Kieft & Kieft	257
UCI	166
Thiele Hoyts	78

Source: *Variety*, June 19, 2000, p. 52.

★ 1562 ★
Movie Theaters
SIC: 7832–ISIC: 9212–HC: 37

Largest Theater Chains in Greece

Exhibitors are ranked by number of screens. Total box office reached $70 million.

Village Roadshow	44
Ster Century multiplex	12
Alpha Odeon	8
Cinepolis	4

Source: *Variety*, June 19, 2000, p. 52.

★ 1563 ★
Movie Theaters
SIC: 7832–ISIC: 9212–HC: 37

Largest Theater Chains in Italy

Exhibitors are ranked by number of screens. Total box office reached $505 million.

Cecchi Gori	70
Warner Village	59
Cinema 5	46
Circuito Cinema	38
De Laurentis	32

Source: *Variety*, June 19, 2000, p. 52.

★ 1564 ★
Movie Theaters
SIC: 7832–ISIC: 9212–HC: 37

Theater Market Shares in Hungary

Market shares are shown in percent.

Hollywood Multiplex	34.0%
Ster-Kinbekor	23.0
Hollywood Multiplex	7.0
International Theaters Ltd.	4.0
Other	32.0

Source: *Budapest Business Jounral*, July 3, 2000, p. 1.

★ 1565 ★
Video Tape Rental
SIC: 7841–ISIC: 7130–HC: 37

Top Video/CD Rental Firms in Japan, 1997

Market shares are shown based on revenue.

Culture Convenience Club	40.0%
Japan AV Rental System	12.0
V Station	8.0
Geo	7.0
Saranger	6.5
Towa Enterprise	6.0
Acom	4.0
Other	16.5

Source: "DVL Market Share Library." Retrieved April 3, 2001 from the World Wide Web: http://dvl/daiwa.co.jp, from DVL Market Share Library and Marketing Data Bank.

★ 1566 ★
Video Tape Rental
SIC: 7841–ISIC: 7130–HC: 37

Top Video Chains in Poland

Market shares are shown in percent.

Beverly Hills	18.0%
Hollywood Video	4.0
Other	78.0

Source: *Screen Digest*, September 2000, p. 266.

★ 1567 ★
Video Tape Rental
SIC: 7841–ISIC: 7130–HC: 37

Video Market in Europe, 1998

Data show millions of rental transactions. Worldwide consumer spending on video software reached $35.5 billion in 1998. Distributor revenues from the sale of all video formats (VHS, laser discs, VCD, DVD) hit $17.2 billion.

Korea	88.6
Taiwan	57.4
United States	39.1
South Africa	37.7
India	33.9
Australia	31.2
Canada	29.3
Japan	22.0
Pakistan	18.8

Source: "Worldwide Video Software Markets." Retrieved October 2, 2000 from the World Wide Web: http://www.screendigest.com.

SIC 79 - Amusement and Recreation Services

★ 1568 ★
Bowling Alleys
SIC: 7933–ISIC: 9241

Bowling Alley Market in India

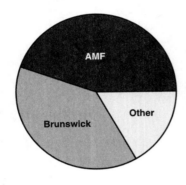

India has an estimated 200 bowling lanes. The estimated market for bowling equipment and systems is 150 - 300 lanes per year.

	Lanes	Share
AMF	90	45.0%
Brunswick	77	38.5
Other	33	16.5

Source: ''India: Amusement Games and Machines.'' Retrieved September 19, 2000 from the World Wide Web: http://www.tradeport.org.

★ 1569 ★
Opera Houses
SIC: 7941–ISIC: 9241

Largest Opera Houses

Houses are ranked by total capacity.

Metropolitan Opera (NY) 4,065
Cincinnati Opera 3,630
Lyric Opera of Chicago 3,563
San Francisco Opera 3,476
Dallas Opera 3,420
Canadian Opera Co. 3,167
Los Angeles Music Center Opera 3,098
San Diego Opera 3,076
Seattle Opera 3,017
Opera de Montreal 2,874

Source: *Christian Science Monitor*, May 9, 2000, p. 14, from *The Top 10 of Everything.*

★ 1570 ★
Stadiums
SIC: 7941–ISIC: 9241

Largest Stadiums Worldwide

Data show capacity.

Strahov Stadium (Czech Republic) 240,000
Maracana Municipa Stadium (Rio de
Janeiro) 205,000
Rungrado Stadium (North Korea) 150,000
Estadio Maghalaes Pinto (Brazil) 125,000
Estadio da Luz (Portugal) 120,000
Estadio Morumbi (Brazil) 120,000
Senayan Main Stadium (Indonesia) . . . 120,000
Yuba Bharati Krirangan (India) 120,000

Source: *Christian Science Monitor*, July 13, 1999, p. 24, from *Top 10 of Everything.*

★ 1571 ★
Gyms
SIC: 7991–ISIC: 9241

Largest Gyms in the U.K.

There are over 3,500 clubs in the country, the market is shifting towards clubs owned by specialists.

Whitbread 200,000
Cannons 125,000
Fitness First 100,000

Source: "Health Clubs." Retrieved December 14, 1999 from the World Wide Web: http://www.keynote.co.uk, from Key Note.

★ 1572 ★
Sports
SIC: 7991–ISIC: 9241

Most Valuable Sports Teams

Figures are in millions of dollars. Value was calculated using financial performance, fan loyalty, and the team's relation to competitors. See source for details.

Dallas Cowboys . . . . $ 274.3
Manchester United 258.9
Washington Redskins 210.6
New York Yankees 180.2
New York Knicks 171.1
Real Madrid 155.1
Bayem Munich 150.3
San Francisco 49ers 147.4
Los Angeles Lakers 146.6
New York Rangers 145.7

Source: *Christian Science Monitor*, February 2, 2001, p. 24, from Business Wire.

★ 1573 ★
Pinball Parlors
SIC: 7993–ISIC: 9249

Top Pinball Parlor Makers in Japan, 1997

Market shares are shown based on revenue.

Dainum 0.9%
Maruhan Corporation 0.7
Matubara Bussan 0.5
Daiichi Bussan 0.4
P Ark 0.3
Tsuzuki 0.3
Other 96.9

Source: "DVL Market Share Library." Retrieved April 3, 2001 from the World Wide Web: http://dvl/daiwa.co.jp, from DVL Market Share Library and Marketing Data Bank.

★ 1574 ★
Amusement Parks
SIC: 7996–ISIC: 9249

Amusement Park Attendance, 2000

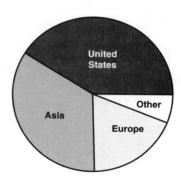

In the last decade the number of parks has risen a third to 83, the admissions have risen to 101 million and revenue to $2.2 billion.

	(mil.)	Share
United States	226	41.5%
Asia	188	34.5
Europe	101	18.5
Other	30	5.5

Source: *New York Times*, September 20, 2000, p. C1, from Economic Research Associates.

★ 1575 ★
Amusement Parks
SIC: 7996–ISIC: 9249

Most Visited Theme Parks in Europe

Data show millions of attendees.

Disneyland Paris	12.0
Blackpool (England) Pleasure Beach	6.8
Tivoli Gardens (Denmark)	3.9
Port Aventura (Spain)	3.1
Europa Park (Germany)	3.0
Liseburg (Sweden)	3.0
De Efteling (Netherlands)	2.9
Gardaland (Italy)	2.9
Bakken (Denmark)	2.5
Alton Towers (England)	2.4

Source: *Amusement Business*, December 25, 2000, p. 88.

★ 1577 ★
Amusement Parks
SIC: 7996–ISIC: 9249

Most Visited Theme Parks Worldwide

Data show millions of attendees.

Tokyo Disneyland	16.5
Magic Kingdom, Walt Disney World	15.4
Disneyland (California)	13.9
Disneyland Paris	12.0
EPCOT of Walt Disney World	10.6
Everland (South Korea)	9.1
Disney-MGM Studios Theme Park	8.9
Disney's Animal Kingdom of Walt Disney World	8.3
Universal Studios	8.1
Lotte World (South Korea)	7.2

Source: *Amusement Business*, December 25, 2000, p. 88.

★ 1576 ★
Amusement Parks
SIC: 7996–ISIC: 9249

Most Visited Theme Parks in Mexico/ South/ Central America

Data show millions of attendees.

Six Flags Mexico	2.70
Chapultapec	2.10
Hopi Hari (Brazil)	1.80
Selva Magica (Mexico)	1.80
El Salitre Magica (Columbia)	1.60
Playcenter (Brazil)	1.50
Beto Carrerro	1.10
Parque de la Costa	0.90
Parque da Monica	0.61

Source: *Amusement Business*, December 25, 2000, p. 88.

★ 1578 ★
Casinos
SIC: 7999–ISIC: 9249

Casino Market Shares in the U.K., 1999

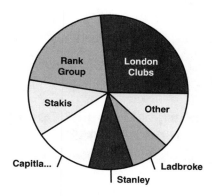

Shares are shown based on turnover.

	(mil.)	Share
London Clubs	145	27.20%
Rank Group	112	21.01
Stakis	64	12.01
Capitla Corporation	62	11.63
Stanley	46	8.63
Ladbroke	41	7.69
Other	63	11.82

Source: *Financial Times*, February 20, 1999, p. 22, from Gaming Board and Mintel.

★ 1579 ★
Tour Attractions
SIC: 7999–ISIC: 9249

Largest Tourist Attractions in France, 1999

Data show millions of visitors.

Disneyland Paris	12.5
Futuroscope	2.3
Parc Asterix	2.0
Complexe Marineland	1.2
Aqualand (5 parcs)	1.0
Walibi (3 parcs)	1.0
Aquarium et parcs Durand-Allize de Touraine .	0.9
Nausicaa	0.7
Bagatelle	0.4
Mer de sable	0.4

Source: *Le Figaro*, September 18, 2000, p. 129.

SIC 80 - Health Services

★ 1580 ★
Legal Services
SIC: 8011–ISIC: 8512
Largest Law Firms Worldwide

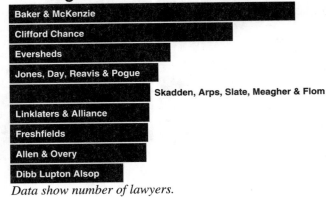

Data show number of lawyers.

Baker & McKenzie	2,300
Clifford Chance	1,795
Eversheds	1,290
Jones, Day, Reavis & Pogue	1,191
Skadden, Arps, Slate, Meagher & Flom	1,125
Linklaters & Alliance	1,116
Freshfields	1,104
Allen & Overy	1,089
Dibb Lupton Alsop	902

Source: *Financial Times*, April 29, 1999, p. 10, from *Legal Business*.

★ 1581 ★
Hospitals
SIC: 8060–ISIC: 8511
Medical/Surgical Hospital Operators in the U.K., 1999

Shares are shown based on number of beds.

	Beds	Share
General Healthcare (BMI)	2,146	20.31%
BUPA Hospitals	1,808	17.11
Nuffield Hospitals	1,617	15.31
Community Hospitals	843	7.98
PPP Columbia Healthcare	557	5.27
Others	3,594	34.02

Source: *Financial Times*, May 1, 2000, p. 18, from Laing & Buisson.

★ 1582 ★
Home Health Care
SIC: 8082–ISIC: 8519
Home Healthcare Market Worldwide

Market revenue are shown in millions of dollars.

	1998	1999	Share
Respiratory	$ 1,400	$ 1,500	39.37%
Custom rehabilitation	1,000	1,100	28.87
Patient aids and beds	650	670	17.59
Ambulatory intravenous	500	540	14.17

Source: *Medical & Healthcare Marketplace Guide*, 1999, p. I805.

★ 1583 ★
Home Health Care
SIC: 8082–ISIC: 8519

In-Home Health Care Market in Japan

Data are in billions of Yen.

	1995	2010
General assistance	133.3	594
Bathing assistance	33.4	192
Equipment rental	7.6	66
Meal and food delivery	3.7	67
Information and consultation	1.7	16

Source: *JETRO Japanese Market Report*, December 1998, p. 16, from ''Survey on In-Home Care Service Market,'' Small and Medium Enterprise Agency and Ministry of Health and Welfare.

SIC 82 - Educational Services

★ 1584 ★
Schools
SIC: 8200–ISIC: 8010

English Schools in Japan

University, high school students, misc.

Adults

Elementary schools students

Kindergarten pupils

Junior high school students

Toddlers, under 3

The market has become a 537.6 billion yen industry. According to the source, the country has always been underexposed to different languages. English can often be a difficult language to learn, which accounts for the blossoming market. Other Asian countries tend to score higher on English language proficiency tests.

	(bil.)	Share
University, high school students, misc.	313.1	58.25%
Adults	108.2	20.13
Elementary schools students	74.2	13.80
Kindergarten pupils	27.4	5.10
Junior high school students	7.5	1.40
Toddlers, under 3	7.1	1.32

Source: *Nikkei Weekly*, May 1, 2000, p. 3, from Berlitz Japan Inc. survey.

★ 1585 ★
Colleges
SIC: 8221–ISIC: 8030

Foreign Students in Japan

The number of students enrolled in higher education increased to 64,011 as of May 1, 2000. The mininstry set a goal of 100,000 in 1983.

Asia	90.5%
Europe	3.5
North America	1.9
Latin America	1.4
Africa	1.1
Middle East	0.8
Oceania	0.8

Source: *Nikkei Weekly*, February 12, 2001, p. 17, from Ministry of Education, Culture, Sports, Science and Technology.

SIC 84 - Museums, Botanical, Zoological Gardens

★ 1586 ★

Museums

SIC: 8412–ISIC: 9232–HC: 97

Largest Art Shows

Data show visitors per day. The Van Gogh exhibit was at the National Gallery; the Monet exhibit was at the Museum of Fine Arts; The Edgar Degas exhibit was at the Metropolitan Museum; the Motorcycle exhibit was at the Guggenheim Musuem; the Versace exhibit was at the Metropolitan Museum.

Van Gogh's Van Goghs	5,339
Monet in the 20th Century	5,290
The Private Collection of Edgar Degas . .	5,128
The Art of the Motorcycle	4,181
Gianni Versace	4,062

Source: *USA TODAY*, March 25, 1999, p. D1, from *The Art Newspaper*.

SIC 86 - Membership Organizations

Labor Unions
SIC: 8631–ISIC: 9120

Largest Labor Unions in Japan, 1999

Groups are ranked by membership, in thousands.

	(000)	Share
Japanese Trade Union Confederation	7,483	59.16%
National Federation of Trade Unions	1,061	8.39
Conference of Trade Unions of Japan	269	2.13
Others	3,835	30.32

Source: *Financial Times*, January 25, 2000, p. 3, from Ministry of Labor, Japan.

Labor Unions
SIC: 8631–ISIC: 9120

Organized Workers in Japan by Sector, 2000

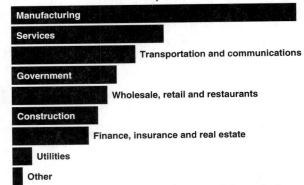

The number of organized workers as of the end of June 2000 decreased to 11.53 million. Union's share of employment fell to 21.5% low, a postwar decline.

Manufacturing	29.8%
Services	16.4
Transportation and communications	12.9
Government	11.2
Wholesale, retail and restaurants	9.6
Construction	9.2
Finance, insurance and real estate	8.2
Utilities	2.0
Other	0.7

Source: *Nikkei Weekly*, March 5, 2001, p. 17, from Ministry of Health, Labor and Welfare.

★ 1589 ★
Religious Organizations
SIC: 8661–ISIC: 9191

Largest Religions Worldwide

Data are in millions.

Christianity	1,900
Islam	1,200
Hinduism	811
Buddhism	360
Sikhism	23
Judaism	14

Source: *Christian Science Monitor*, January 25, 2001, p.
12, from *World Christian Encyclopedia*.

SIC 87 - Engineering and Management Services

★ 1590 ★
Design Services
SIC: 8710–ISIC: 7421

Largest Retail Design Firms in the U.K.

Dirms are ranked by retail design fee income in millions of British pounds.

Interbrand Newell and Sorrell	8.00
Fitch	5.20
Checkland Kindleysides	4.88
BDG McColl	4.35
Conran Design Group	3.65
20/20	3.60
Allen International	3.14
View	2.72
Hyperlink	2.64
Minale Tattersfield & Partners	2.50

Source: *Design Week*, June 2000, p. 29.

★ 1591 ★
Engineering Services
SIC: 8711–ISIC: 7421

Largest Engineering Firms in Europe

Firms are ranked by annual sales in millions of British pounds.

ABB	23,000
GKN	5,500
Sandvik	4,800
Atlas Copco	3,800
Freudenberg	3,300
Liebherr	3,300

FAG Kugelfischer	1,600
Jungheinrich	1,300
Trumpf	850
Sidel	846

Source: *Financial Times*, September 16, 1999, p. 14.

★ 1592 ★
Management Construction
SIC: 8711–ISIC: 7421

Leading Management Construction Firms in Europe

Figures are in millions of dollars.

Bovis	$ 760
John Laing	330
Carillion	270
Mace	220
John Mowlem	30
Henry Boot	16
Balfour Beatty	14
Kier	13
Amec	9
Jarvis	6

Source: *Contract Journal*, September 22, 1999, p. 10.

★ 1593 ★
Architectural Services
SIC: 8712–ISIC: 7421

Architectural Equipment/Services Market in India, 1999

Airports, roads, railroads

Civil structures

Urban planning

Commercial buildings

Ports and harbors

Other

The industry has been estimated at $3.2 billion in 1999, and is growing roughly 15% a year. Imports make up about 40% of the market, with the United States controlling 25% of that piece. The most successful firms in the field tend to be consortiums, which offer a group of partners that offer consulting, design and engineering services.

Airports, roads, railroads	40.0%
Civil structures (soil, foundation)	25.0
Urban planning	15.0
Commercial buildings	10.0
Ports and harbors	5.0
Other	5.0

Source: STAT-USA, *National Trade Data Bank*, June 2001, p. NA, from Minsitry of Industry.

★ 1594 ★
Research
SIC: 8732–ISIC: 7320

Commercial Research in Japan

Japan's research and development spending fell 0.8% to $134.5 billion. It was the first decline in five years

	Yen (trillion)	Share
Businesses	10.63	66.4%
Universities	3.21	20.0
Research institutions	2.17	13.6

Source: *Nikkei Weekly*, March 12, 2001, p. 17, from Ministry of Public Management, Home Affairs, Posts and Telecommunications.

★ 1595 ★
Research
SIC: 8732–ISIC: 7320

Largest Market Research Firms

Firms are ranked by total research revenues in millions of dollars.

A.C. Nielsen Corp.	$ 1,525.4
IMS Health Inc.	1,275.7
The Kantar Group	773.5
Taylor Nelson Sofres	601.3
Information Resources Inc.	546.3
NFO Worldwide Inc.	457.2
Nielsen Media Research	453.3
GfK Group	414.0
United Information Group Ltd.	246.3
Ipsos Group SA	245.8

Source: *Marketing News*, August 14, 2000, p. H4.

★ 1596 ★
Research
SIC: 8732–ISIC: 7320

Research Market Shares in Europe

The world total reached $13.4 billion. The Czech Republic, Hungary and Poland had strong growth rates. Indeed, it is interesting to note that wealthier countries like Greece, Ireland and Portugal had lower market research sales than Poland.

United Kingdom	28.2%
Germany	24.5
France	16.7
Italy	7.7
Spain	5.1
Netherlands	4.8
Sweden	4.3
Belgium	2.1
Austria	1.7
Denmark	1.6
Other	3.3

Source: *Market Europe*, May 2000, p. 3, from Esomar Annual Study on the Market Research Industry.

★ 1597 ★
Consulting Services
SIC: 8742–ISIC: 7414

Global Consulting Market

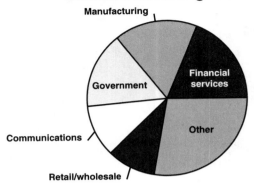

The industry is valued at $114 billion.

Financial services	19.0%
Manufacturing	16.5
Government	16.0
Communications	10.5
Retail/wholesale	10.0
Other	28.0

Source: *Investor's Business Daily*, December 21, 2000, p. A12, from www.KennedyInfo.com.

★ 1598 ★
Consulting Services
SIC: 8742–ISIC: 7414

Leading Consulting Firms, 1999

Firms are ranked by revenue in billions of dollars.

Andersen Consulting	$ 7.51
PricewaterhouseCoopers	7.17
Deloitte Consulting	5.05
Ernst & Young	4.05
CSC	3.64
KPMG Consulting	3.50
Cap Gemini	3.16
McKinsey & Company	2.90
Mercer Consulting Group	1.95
Arthur Andersen	1.40

Source: *New York Times*, August 8, 2000, p. C22, from *Consultants News* and *Public Accounting Report*.

★ 1599 ★
Design Services
SIC: 8742–ISIC: 7414

Largest Global Design Firms, 1999

Firms are ranked by international revenues in millions of dollars.

AMEC	$ 1,032.2
Bechtel Group Inc.	745.0
Foster Wheeler Corp.	741.0
Fluor Corp.	690.0
Nethconsult	659.0
Kellogg Brown & Root	634.0
ABB Lummus Global	616.2
Kvaerner PLC Group	589.0
Fugro N.V.	486.9
SNC-Lavalin International Inc.	474.5

Source: *ENR*, July 17, 2000, p. 73.

★ 1600 ★
Executive Search Industry
SIC: 8742–ISIC: 7414

Leading Executive Search Firms, 2000

Firms are ranked by revenue in millions of dollars.

Korn/Ferry Intl.	$ 576.4
Heidrick & Struggles Intl.	574.2
Spencer Stuart	345.0
Egon Zehnder Intl.	318.7
Russell Reynolds Associates	305.3
TMP Worldwide Executive Search	180.0
Ray & Berndtson	176.0
The Hever - Amrop Alliance	128.7
Whitehead Mann Group	82.5

Source: *Financial Times*, April 12, 2001, p. 11.

★ 1601 ★
Human Resource Consulting
SIC: 8742–ISIC: 7414

Largest Employee Benefit Consultants, 1999

Firms are ranked by gross consulting revenues in millions of dollars.

William M. Mercer Cos.	$ 1,320.0
Hewitt Associates L.L.C.	962.3
Towers Perrin	875.9
PricewaterhouseCoopers, Global HR Solutions	719.0
Watson Wyatt Worldwide	647.1
Aon Consulting Worldwide	576.0
Buck Consultants	360.0
Deloitte & Touche/Human Capital Advisory Services	334.7
Ernst & Young L.L.P. Human Resource Services	225.0

Source: *Business Insurance*, December 13, 1999, p. 3.

★ 1602 ★
Public Relations Services
SIC: 8743–ISIC: 7414

Largest PR Firms Worldwide

Firms are ranked by income in millions of dollars.

Burson-Marsteller	$ 274.63
Hill & Knowlton	243.30
Shandwick	240.20
Poter Novelli	214.89
Fleishmann-Hillard	213.44
Edelmann	186.03
Ketchum	149.70
BSMG	145.30
Havas/Euro RSCG	126.60
Ogilvy	125.00

Source: *PR Week*, September 25, 2000, p. 30.

SIC 92 - Justice, Public Order, and Safety

★ 1603 ★

Crime

SIC: 9220–ISIC: 7523

Software Piracy Losses

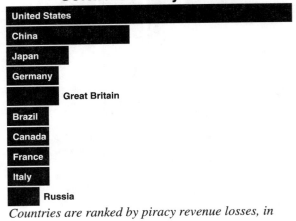

Countries are ranked by piracy revenue losses, in millions.

United States	$ 2,800
China	1,200
Japan	600
Germany	500
Great Britain	500
Brazil	400
Canada	400
France	400
Italy	400
Russia	300

Source: *Christian Science Monitor*, August 13, 1999, p. 7, from SIIA.

SIC 95 - Environmental Quality and Housing

★ 1604 ★

Land Management
SIC: 9512–ISIC: 7513

How Farmland is Used in New Zealand

New Zealand consists mainly of two islands. Forests cover about 29% of the 8.1 million hectares that make up the nation. The region underwent a high level of forest planting in the 1970s and 1980s, and that timber is now ready for use.

	North Island	South Island
Grazing, arable fodder	75.2%	86.6%
Exotic timber	15.6	5.1
Horticulture	1.1	0.1
Other	10.1	7.8

Source: STAT-USA, *National Trade Data Bank*, June 1, 2000, p. NA, from New Zealand Statistics.

SIC 97 - National Security and International Affairs

★ 1605 ★
Defense
SIC: 9711–ISIC: 7522

Largest Arms Purchasers, 1998

Data are in billions of dollars.

Saudi Arabia	$ 7.9
United Arab Emirates	2.5
Malaysia	2.1
Egypt	1.2
Algeria	0.5
Israel	0.5
Kuwait	0.5
Ethiopia	0.4
India	0.4
Saudi Arabia	0.4

Source: *Christian Science Monitor*, August 11, 1999, p. 20.

★ 1606 ★
Defense
SIC: 9711–ISIC: 7522

Largest Arms Suppliers, 1999

Countries are ranked by new weapons sales in millions of dollars.

	($ mil.)	Share
United States	$ 11,768	38.88%
Russia	4,800	15.86
Other Europe	4,600	15.20
Germany	4,000	13.22
China	1,900	6.28

	($ mil.)	Share
France	$ 900	2.97%
Great Britain	800	2.64
Italy	600	1.98
Other	900	2.97

Source: *New York Times*, August 21, 2000, p. A8, from Congressional Research Service.

★ 1607 ★
Defense
SIC: 9711–ISIC: 7522

Leading Military Exporters, 1999

Total exports reached $53.37 billlion.

United States	26.21%
United Kingdom	9.99
France	6.63
Russia	3.50
Israel	1.26
Other	5.78

Source: *Financial Times*, February 2, 2001, p. 6.

★ 1608 ★
Defense
SIC: 9711–ISIC: 7522

Military Personnel in the World

Data show personnel by country. The United States Army has 27,555 personnel in South Korea and 1,800 in Japan; The Navy has 300 in South Korea and 5,200 in Japan; the Air Force has 8,700 personnel in South Korea and 13,550 in Japan.

	Air Force	Navy	Army
Russia	1,846,000	171,500	348,000
China	420,000	230,000	2,000,000
India	140,000	55,000	980,000
North Korea	86,000	46,000	950,000
Taiwan	68,000	62,000	240,000
South Korea	63,000	67,000	560,000
Japan	45,600	43,800	150,000

Source: *Business Week*, May 28, 2001, p. 52, from International Institute for Strategic Studies, Center for Defense Information, Stockholm International Peace Research Institute, and Japan Self Defense Agency.

★ 1610 ★
Defense
SIC: 9711–ISIC: 7522

Who has the Most Military Personnel

Data show millions of personnel.

China	2.84
United States	1.43
Russia	1.20
India	1.14
North Korea	1.06

Source: *Financial Times*, February 17, 2000, p. 6, from Military Balance, 1997-98.

★ 1609 ★
Defense
SIC: 9711–ISIC: 7522

R&D on Defense in Europe

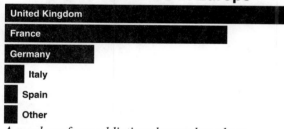

A number of consoldiations have taken place, influencing spending in a number of markets.

United Kingdom	45.0%
France	35.0
Germany	14.0
Italy	3.0
Spain	2.0
Other	2.0

Source: *Aerospace America*, August 2000, p. 36.

SOURCE INDEX

This index is divided into *primary sources* and *original sources*. Primary sources are the publications where the market shares were found. Original sources are sources cited in the primary sources. Numbers following the sources are entry numbers, arranged sequentially; the first number refers to the first appearance of the source in *World Market Share Reporter*. All told, 1112 organizations are listed.

Primary Sources

"100 Million Tonic for Scotch Whiskey." Retrieved March 3, 2000 from the World Wide Web: http://www.just-drinks.com, 268

"1999 Rankings of China's Top Brokerages." Retrieved May 16, 2000 from the World Wide Web: http://www.chinaonline.com, 1433

"The 2000-2005 World Outlook for Sugar." Retrieved June 1, 2001 from the World Wide Web: http://www.just-food.com, 202

"A Review of the French Passsenger Car Market." Retrieved July 28, 2000 from the World Wide Web: http://www.just-auto.com, 1000

"A Review of the Status of the German Automotive Industry." Retrieved March 9, 2001 from the World Wide Web: http://www.just-auto.com, 980

"About Us." Retrieved April 5, 2001 from the World Wide Web: http://www.biscol.com/about, 206

Accountancy Age, 1515

Adhesives Age, 652-653

Advertising Age, 1470-1478, 1480-1483

Advertising Age International, 279, 438-439, 696, 890, 1283, 1484-1485

"Aerodata GmbH Microelectronics." Retrieved January 11, 2001 from the World Wide Web: http://www.aerodata.de, 1043

Aerospace America, 1609

"AFBs are the Flavor of the Month." Retrieved December 5, 2000 from the World Wide Web: http://www.just-drinks.com, 260

Aftenposten, 1443

AIPM-RMBC Market Bulletin, 492

Air Cargo World, 1181, 1203, 1206-1208, 1224

Air Transport Intelligence, 1202

Airline Business, 1542

Airline Industry Information, 1198

"All Terrain Vehicles." Retrieved November 6, 2000 from the World Wide Web: http://www.usatrade.gov, 1049

"The Alpine Ski Market." Retrieved November 22, 2000 from the World Wide Web: http://www.csjapan.doc.gov, 1140

American Banker, 1533

American Ink Maker, 655

American Machinist, 749

American Metal Market, 52

American Shipper, 1188

America's Network Telecom Investor Supplement, 908

Amusement Business, 1575-1577

Appliance, 832, 843, 846-847, 851

Appliance Manufacturer, 842, 844, 848, 865

"Argentina Frozen Food Market." Retrieved September 8, 2000 from the World Wide Web: http://www.tradeport.org, 505

"Argentina: Sales of Cereal Bars Increases." Retrieved April 10, 2001 from the World Wide Web: http://library.northernlight.com, 207

Asia Pulse News, 227, 871, 1053, 1108, 1304

Asiaweek, 783, 1406

Assembly, 974

"Australia Canned Fruit." Retrieved October 1, 2000 from the World Wide Web: http://www.usda.gov, 129

"Australia Tobacco Report." Retrieved October 1, 2000 from the World Wide Web: http://ffas.usda.gov, 348

"Australia: Food Processing Sector." Retrieved September 1, 2000 from the World Wide Web: http://ffas.usda.gov, 123, 149, 166, 169, 175, 310

Australian, 1344

Australian Financial Review, 248, 278, 402, 1329, 1428

"Austria Product Brief Mayonnaise." Retrieved October 1, 2000 from the World Wide Web: http://ffas.usda.gov, 147

"Austria Retail Food Market." Retrieved November 1, 2000 from the World Wide Web: http://www.ffas.usda.gov, 1351

"Auto Parts and Accessories." Retrieved November 8, 2000 from the World Wide Web: http://

DIY Week, 628

"Domestic Brandsd Dominate China's Telephone Market." Retrieved April 10, 2000 from the World Wide Web: http://www.prnewswire.com, 905

"Down Under Car Market." Retrieved January 9, 2001 from the World Wide Web: http://www.just-auto.com, 994

Duty-Free News International, 1395

Duty-Free News International Caribbean Supplement, 1219

"DVL Market Share Library." Retrieved April 3, 2001 from the World Wide Web: http://dvl/daiwa.co.jp, 79, 85, 92, 107, 134, 140, 153, 161, 183-184, 186, 267, 332, 374-377, 383, 386, 396, 425-426, 499, 515, 539, 576, 602, 611, 650, 663, 692, 694-695, 718-721, 825, 976, 979, 1059, 1076, 1083, 1124-1125, 1148-1149, 1158-1159, 1170-1171, 1377-1378, 1459, 1468, 1492, 1538, 1565, 1573

E&MJ, 64

"E-Commerce in the Czech Republic." Retrieved October 27, 2000 from the World Wide Web: http://www.mac.doc.gov, 1282

E Media Professional, 801, 806

E News, 711, 950

Economic Times, 101

The Economist, 245, 479, 983-984, 1184, 1194, 1226

The Edge, 821

EDN, 826, 836, 946, 955, 957, 1510

Educational Marketer, 448

EFE World News Service, 89

Egg Industry, 37

Ekonom, 294

Ekonomicke Zpravodajstvi, 204

El Cronista, 17, 21, 155, 658

El Diario, 411, 508, 1307

El Mundo, 1236

Electric Utility Week International, 1303

Electrical & Radio Trading, 855

Electronic Business, 766

Electronic Business Asia, 837

Electronic Buyers News, 705, 944-945, 951-952, 959, 969, 972

Electronic Engineering Times, 968, 970

Electronic Media, 1486

Electronic News, 712

"Electronic Publishing." Retrieved March 15, 2000 from the World Wide Web: http://www.tradeport.org, 1373

Electronic Times, 898

"Electronics Market in S.W. China." Retrieved September 19, 2000 from the World Wide Web: http://www.tradeport.org, 1498, 1501, 1514

The Engineer, 725, 1496, 1532

Engineering & Mining Journal, 46, 51, 63, 702-703

ENR, 69, 1599

"Envision Peripherals." Retrieved February 26, 2001 from the World Wide Web: http://www.businesswire.com, 811

Estrategia, 42, 229, 494, 689, 1384, 1489

"Euro Ready Meals Mkt Spain." Retrieved November 16, 1999 from the World Wide Web: http://www.northernlight.com, 160

Eurofood, 120, 133, 139, 173, 189, 230, 311

Euromarketing via E-mail, 420, 553

Euromoney, 1426, 1453

Europe Energy, 1306

European Banker, 1403, 1446

European Cosmetic Markets, 513-514, 516, 519-523, 537, 541, 550, 552, 554-555, 557-559, 561-562, 570, 581-583, 601, 609-610, 612-614, 624-625, 1164-1165

European Rubber Journal, 469-470

"European Vehicle Telematics Equipment." Retrieved April 10, 2001 from the World Wide Web: http://www.prnewswire.com, 1031

"Executive Summary." Retrieved February 8, 2000 from the World Wide Web: http://www.the-list.co.uk, 338

"Experts Overview of Hot Market." Retrieved May 11, 1999 from the World Wide Web: http://www.just-drinks.com, 309

Expose Magazine, 621-622

"Express Delivery Market in Russia." Retrieved January 17, 2000 from the World Wide Web: http://ww.bisnis.doc.gov, 1210

"Factory Outlet Centers." Retrieved January 11, 2001 from the World Wide Web: http://www.cior.com, 1458

"Falcon Gains Market Share in Sweden." Retrieved June 29, 2000 from the World Wide Web: http://www.northernlight.com, 239

Far Eastern Economic Review, 1255

Farbe & Lack, 629

Farmers Weekly, 734

Feedstuffs, 82

"Films and Videos." Retrieved November 6, 2000 from the World Wide Web: http://www.usatrade.gov, 1548

Financial Express, 714, 753

Financial Review, 1013

Financial Times, 23, 30, 47, 53, 56, 66, 249, 254-255, 257-258, 265, 270, 296-297, 341, 345, 359-360, 400, 434, 442, 487-489, 673, 686-687, 700, 726, 728-730, 733, 739, 747, 751, 759, 770, 810, 839-841, 963, 991, 999, 1003, 1014-1016, 1019, 1028, 1038, 1048, 1103, 1138, 1177, 1180, 1183, 1190, 1192, 1218, 1222, 1231-1232, 1234, 1237, 1248, 1263, 1286, 1291, 1300, 1302, 1323, 1343, 1356, 1387, 1405, 1408-1409, 1412-1413, 1415-1418, 1424, 1429-1432, 1437, 1439, 1442, 1456, 1461, 1578, 1580-1581, 1587, 1591, 1600, 1607, 1610

"Finland: Internet Services." Retrieved October 10, 2000

from the World Wide Web: http://www.tradeport.org, 787, 1277

Floor Focus, 4

Food Ingredients and Analysis International, 167

Food Institute Report, 320, 1328

Food Manufacture, 327

"Food Processing and Packaging Machinery." Retrieved October 19, 2000 from the World Wide Web: http://www.tradeport.org, 84

"Foodtown's Instore Revolution." Retrieved April 11, 2001 from the World Wide Web: http://www.grocersreview.co.nz, 305

Forbes, 11, 371, 563, 977, 1061, 1117

"Foreign-brand Cigarettes Account for 25% Market Share." Retrieved October 26, 2000 from the World Wide Web: http:/www.office.com, 349

Forest Products Journal, 14

Fortune, 791, 1273

"France: Lawnmowers." Retrieved September 19, 2000 from the World Wide Web: http://www.tradeport.org, 738

Frankfurter Allgemeine, 498, 507, 727, 985, 1062, 1065, 1068, 1312

"French Retailers Lead Expansion." Retrieved September 5, 2000 from the World Wide Web: http://www.just-food.com, 1327

Frozen and Chilled Foods, 761

"Frozen Food Outperforms the Overall Food Market in 1998." Retrieved September 1, 2000 from the World Wide Web: http://www.bfff.co.uk, 98, 154, 157, 162, 201, 306-307

"Fruit and Vegetables Industry." Retrieved November 9, 1999 from the World Wide Web: http://www.just-food.com, 13

"Furniture Market Growing." Retrieved May 8, 2001 from the World Wide Web: http://www.usatrade.gov, 388

"Gartner Dataquest Says Home PC Sales.." Retrieved February 5, 2001 from the World Wide Web: http://www.businesswire.com, 793

"Gartner Says Semiconductor IP Market Grew 40%." Retrieved June 29, 2001 from the World Wide Web: http://www.dataquest.com, 960

"Gartner's Dataquest Says E-Support Technologies." Retrieved September 14, 2000 from the World Wide Web: http://www.businesswire.com, 1508

Gazeta Mercantil, 116, 194, 236, 266, 314, 367, 410, 533, 648, 688, 1167, 1195

"Germany Dominates Home Shopping in Europe." Retrieved October 17, 2000 from the World Wide Web: http://www.cior.com, 1392

Gestion, 226

Glass International, 684

"Global Brewer Handbook." Retrieved January 9, 2001 from the World Wide Web: http://www.just-drinks.com,

"Global Brewer Handbook." Retrieved January 9, 2001 from the World Wide Web: http://www.just-drinks.com, 243

"Global Childrens Programme Worth $2.1 Billion." Retrieved September 28, 2000 from the World Wide Web: http://www.screendigest.com, 1285

Global Cosmetic Industry, 542, 556, 595, 597, 603, 607

"Global Market for Automotive Lighting." Retreved May 22, 2001 from the World Wide Web: http://www.just-food.com, 869

Globe and Mail, 312

"Golf Equipment." Retrieved January 3, 2001 from the World Wide Web: http://www.usatrade.gov, 1144

"Grape Wine Market." Retrieved April 3, 2001 from the World Wide Web: http://www.usatrade.gov, 259

"Greece Tobacco Annual Report." Retrieved October 1, 2000 from the World Wide Web: http://ffas.usda.gov, 354, 356

The Grocer, 29, 80, 124, 132, 144, 146, 150-151, 174, 181, 192, 228, 301, 304, 416, 421-423, 527, 646, 1349, 1352, 1354, 1358, 1375, 1552

The Guardian, 866, 1271, 1369, 1450, 1557

"Halcyon Days Are Over for M&S." Retrieved October 17, 2000 from the World Wide Web: http://www.cior.com, 370, 1364

"Hand and Power Tools." Retrieved November 3, 2000 from the World Wide Web: http://www.usatrade.gov, 755

Hart's E&P, 61

"Hartwell Upcider is the Success Story." Retrieved May 30, 2000 from the World Wide Web: http://WWW.BUSINESSWIRE.COM, 291

"Health Clubs." Retrieved December 14, 1999 from the World Wide Web: http://www.keynote.co.uk, 1571

"Health Food Supplements." Retrieved November 3, 2000 from the World Wide Web: http://www.usatrade.gov, 335

Health Industry Today, 1082, 1087

"Heart-Stopping Growth in the External Defibrillator Market." Retrieved January 31, 2001 from the World Wide Web: http://www.devicelink.com, 1101

Helicopter News, 1036

High Performance Plastics, 679

Hindu, 275, 631

Hollywood Reporter, 1290, 1547

"Hong Hong Pet Food Market Brief." Retrieved November 1, 2000 from the World Wide Web: http://www.ffas.usda.gov, 179

"Hong Kong Bourbon and Liquor Product Brief." Retrieved October 1, 2000 from the World Wide Web: http://ffas.usda.gov, 264, 271

"Hong Kong Cakes, Cookies and Crackers Market Brief." Retrieved September 1, 2000 from the World Wide Web: http://ffas.usda.gov, 191, 200

Liquid Foods International, 346

"Long Distance Carriers Lose Money." Retrieved October 30, 2000 from the World Wide Web: http://www.biz.yahoo.com, 1249

LSA, 76, 93, 122, 193, 333, 336, 1160, 1338, 1350, 1353

M Business, 939, 1240

The Manufacturing Confectioner, 209, 212, 214, 216-220, 1314

Manufacturing Engineering, 750

"Many Chinese Toothpaste Connoisseurs Enameled With Colgate." Retrieved May 10, 2001 from The World Wide Web: http://www.chinaonline.com, 580

Marine Log, 1045

Market Europe, 9, 409, 676, 1596

"Market for Replacement Tires." Retrieved October 27, 2000 from the World Wide Web: http://www.mac.doc.gov, 668

"Market Leaders in Japan." Retrieved March 20, 2000 from the World Wide Web: http://www.just-food.com, 163

"Market Overview." Retrieved September 19, 2000 from the World Wide Web: http://www.jetro.go.jp, 33

"Market Share of Washing Machines." Retrieved September 27, 2000 from the World Wide Web: http://www.office.com, 857-859

"Market Share." Retrieved June 9, 2000 from the World Wide Web: http://www.teekanne.de/teewett2.htm, 343

"Market Size." Retrieved July 28, 2000 from the World Wide Web: http://www.invision-intech.com, 382

Marketing, 32, 440, 675, 895, 1130, 1488, 1526

Marketing Magazine, 340

Marketing News, 1595

Marketletter, 495

Markt & Technik, 954

"Marktanteile der Zigarettenhersteler." Retrieved March 12, 2001 from the World Wide Web: http://www.horizon.net, 355

Med Ad News, 1

Media & Marketing, 877

Medical & Healthcare Marketplace Guide, 1081, 1095, 1582

"Medical Device Market Data." Retrieved January 2, 2001 from the World Wide Web: http://www.devicelink.com, 1067

Mergers & Acquisitions, 446, 1214

Metal Bulletin Monthly, 706-707

"Microsoft's Share of Browser Market." Retrieved February 27, 2001 from the World Wide Web: http://www.prnewswire.com, 1504

"Mifed News." Retrieved December 2, 2000 from the World Wide Web: http://www.londonmefed.com, 1555

Mining Engineering, 45

Mining Journal, 49

Mining Magazine, 54, 708

MOCI, 115

Modern Casting, 710

Modern Materials Handling, 746

Modern Paint and Coatings, 627

Modern Plastics, 378, 463

Moskovskie Novosti, 135, 1281

"Motorbike Sales in 4 ASEAN Countries up 54.3%" Retrieved October 26, 2000 from the World Wide Web: http://www.office.com, 1050

Music Business International, 893

Music Trades, 1122-1123

Music Week, 889

Nation, 989

"National 1." Retrieved May 16, 2001 from the World Wide Web: http://www.personalinvestor.au, 428

National Home Center News, 1317-1322

National Trade Data Bank, 40, 237, 381, 389, 473, 475, 745, 757, 910, 1002, 1121, 1221, 1228, 1238, 1593, 1604

Network World, 935, 1267

"Networking." Retrieved May 8, 2001 from the World Wide Web: http://www.usatrade.gov, 1519

Neue Zuercher Zeitung, 358, 743, 795, 838, 1451

New York Times, 7, 28, 74, 313, 437, 445, 698, 803, 888, 1035, 1051, 1233, 1434-1435, 1525, 1574, 1598, 1606

New Zealand Herald, 992

Newsbytes, 822

Nikkei Weekly, 106, 159, 246, 292, 385, 433, 510, 517, 546, 565, 593, 659, 672, 690, 699, 752, 762, 772, 775, 799, 850, 856, 876, 882, 886, 897, 900, 906, 956, 962, 971, 975, 1047, 1110-1111, 1113, 1115, 1119, 1137, 1150, 1182, 1200, 1216-1217, 1229, 1251, 1270, 1331, 1421-1422, 1436, 1466, 1469, 1479, 1523, 1584-1585, 1588, 1594

"No Longer a Shoe-In in Chinese Market." Retrieved October 16, 2000 from the World Wide Web: http://www.chinaonline.com, 372

Nonwovens Industry, 363, 407, 413-415, 418

"Nordic Food Retail Market." Retrieved September 21, 2000 from the World Wide Web: http://www.just-food.com, 1340

"Norway Fresh Deciduous Fruit." Retrieved September 1, 2000 from the World Wide Web: http://ffas.usa.gov, 1357

Nutraceuticals International, 281

"Nutritional Supplements." Retrieved November 8, 2000 from the World Wide Web: http://www.usatrade.gov, 472

O Estado de Sao Paulo, 511, 524

The Observer, 121, 1175, 1223, 1396

"Office Furniture." Retrieved November 30, 2000 from the World Wide Web: http://www.csjapan.doc.gov, 395

Oil & Gas Journal, 660-662

"Organic Food Report." Retrieved May 1, 2000 from the

World Wide Web: http://ffas.usda.gov, 1341

"Outsell Releases Landmark Report." Retrieved November 1, 2000 from the World Wide Web: http://www.businesswire.com, 1528-1529

"Outsell Releases Landmark Report." Retrieved November 1, 2000 from the World Wide Web: http://www.outsellinc.com, 429-431

"Overview of the New Car Market." Retrieved March 2, 2001 from the World Wide Web: http://www.factbook.net, 997

"Overview of the Toy Market." Retrieved November 17, 2000 from the World Wide Web: http://www.usatrade.gov, 1389

Ozone Depletion Network Online Today, 829

Packaging Magazine, 713

Pais, 252

Paperboard Packaging, 397-398, 403-404, 406

Paris Match, 1220

Password, 1099

PC Magazine, 6

"Peru HRI Foodservice Sector." Retrieved September 1, 2000 from the World Wide Web: http://www.ffas.usda.gov, 1382

"Peruvian Vinyl Floor Tiles." Retrieved February 12, 2001 from the World Wide Web: http://www.comtexnews.com, 1168

"Pet Food Industry." Retrieved April 24, 2001 from the World Wide Web: http://www.bbl.co.th/mreview/200010_pet1.htm, 187

"Pet Product Market." Retrieved February 20, 2001 from the World Wide Web: http://www.usatrade.gov, 1399

"Pharmaceutical Market." Retrieved April 3, 2001 from the World Wide Web: http://www.usatrade.gov, 496

Philadelphia Inquirer, 1169

"PhoCusWright Projects European Online Travel." Retrieved January 18, 2001 from the World Wide Web: http://www.businesswire.com, 1256

Photonics Spectra, 901

PIMA's North American Papermaker, 399

Pit & Quarry, 740

"Pizza." Retrieved December 7, 1999 from the World Wide Web: http://www.just-food.com, 156

Points de Vente, 86, 90, 95, 111, 119, 128, 170, 176-177, 197, 203, 205, 316, 337, 412, 427, 590, 1162, 1309, 1460

"Poland Tobacco and Products Annual." Retrieved November 1, 2000 from the World Wide Web: http://ffas.usda.gov, 357

"Poland: Press Advertising." Retrieved October 27, 2000 from the World Wide Web: http://www.mac.doc.gov, 435

"Popcorn." Retrieved November 1, 2000 from the World Wide Web: http://www.usatrade.gov, 322

"Popular Computer Weekly Releases Survey Results." Retrieved October 16, 2000 from the World Wide Web: http://www.chinaonline.com, 781, 802, 807, 812-814, 823, 903, 1502-1503

"Posititve Trends in the Czech Automotive Industry." Retrieved April 3, 2001 from the World Wide Web: http://www.usatrade.gov, 990

"Power Tool Sector." Retrieved October 27, 2000 from the World Wide Web: http://www.mac.doc.gov, 754

PR Week, 1602

Prague Business Journal, 797

"Premium Brands Boost Instant Coffee Market." Retrieved April 11, 2001 from the World Wide Web: http://www.grocersreview.co.nz, 308

Prepared Foods, 78

"Press Release." Retrieved August 3, 2000 from the World Wide Web: http://www.northernlight.com, 927

"Press Release." Retrieved January 1, 2000 from the World Wide Web: http://www.lfra.com, 317

"Press Release." Retrieved January 2, 2001 from the World Wide Web: http://www.businesswire.com, 964

"Press Release." Retrieved January 23, 2001 from the World Wide Web: http://www.gartner.com, 785

"Press Release." Retrieved June 12, 2001 from the World Wide Web: http://www.businesswire.com, 763

"Press Release." Retrieved June 12, 2001 from the World Wide Web: http://www.dataquest.com, 904

"Press Release." Retrieved June 12, 2001 from the World Wide Web: http://www.euromonitor.com, 171

"Press Release." Retrieved June 12, 2001 from the World Wide Web: http://www.gartner.com, 786, 1506

"Press Release." Retrieved June 12, 2001 from the World Wide Web: http://www.gartnerweb.com, 796, 1521

"Press Releases." Retrieved February 17, 2000 from the World Wide Web: http://www.datamonitor.com, 60, 178, 1094

"Press Releases." Retrieved Feburary 17, 2000 from the World Wide Web: http://www.datamonitor.com, 1086, 1091

"Press Releases." Retrieved June 12, 2001 from the World Wide Web: http://www.capv.com, 899

"Press Releases." Retrieved June 12, 2001 from the World Wide Web: http://www.gartnerweb.com, 918

Presse, 1064, 1452

"Printer Market." Retrieved September 7, 2000 from the World Wide Web: http://www.tradeport.org, 788

"Private Labels Undermine Big Breakfast Brands." Retrieved June 1, 2001 from the World Wide Web: http://www.euromonitor.com, 168

"Product Ranges." Retrieved May 17, 2001 from the World Wide Web: http://www.corerange.com, 506, 529-531, 572

"Production." Retrieved June 18, 2001 from the World Wide Web: http://www.silverinstitute.org, 50

"Profile - Indonesia's Tire Industry." Retrieved October 9, 2000 from the World Wide Web: http://www.northernlight.com, 671

Publishers Weekly, 447

Quick Frozen Foods International, 188

"Rank Wraps Up Odeon Sales to Cinven." Retrieved February 21, 2000 from the World Wide Web: http://www.northernlight.com, 1559

"Rare Earths." Retrieved August 29, 2000 from the World Wide Web: http://www.buscom.com, 67

RCR Wireless News, 1241

"Regional Product Information." Retrieved March 29, 2001 from the World Wide Web: http://www.fukuyama.or.jp/e/productsman.html, 722

Reinforced Plastics, 731

Reinsurance Magazine, 1457

"Replacement Car Tires." Retrieved January 12, 2001 from the World Wide Web: http://www.clearlybusiness.com, 669, 1023, 1096, 1539

Reproduire, 1112

Research Studies, 405, 408, 651, 735, 768, 773, 1530

Restaurant Business, 1380

Retail Banker International, 1411

"Retail Food Sector." Retrieved January 1, 2001 from the World Wide Web: http://ffas.usda.gov, 1347

"Retail Food Update." Retrieved December 1, 2000 from the World Wide Web: http://ffas.usda.gov, 1333, 1337

"Retail Soups Market in Japan." Retrieved September 28, 2000 from the World Wide Web: http://www.japanscan.com, 143

Retail Week, 1324, 1334, 1345, 1362, 1366-1367, 1374

Retrieved July 6, 2000 from the World Wide Web: http://expo.tpage.com/jenix, 1056

Retrieved July 6, 2000 from the World Wide Web: http://www.bicycleretailer.news.com, 1058

Retrieved July 6, 2000 from the World Wide Web: http://www.exposemagazine.com, 587

Retrieved July 6, 2000 from the World Wide Web: http://www.just-food.com, 125

Retrieved July 6, 2000 from the World Wide Web: http://www.window.de/pr003_3.htm, 70

"RHK Study Results." Retrieved April 19, 2001 from the World Wide Web: http://www.businesswire.com, 938

"Robust Growth Expectations." Retrieved June 7, 2001 from the World Wide Web: http://www.vdc-corp.com, 779

Rubber & Plastics News, 393, 468, 1022

"Russell Simmons Teams Up With Vtech." Retrieved January 8, 2001 from the World Wide Web: http://www.businesswire.com, 1126

Saigon Times Daily, 716, 835

Saigon Times Magazine, 1250

"Sales of Trucks Increased 27%." Retrieved January 26, 2001 from the World Wide Web: http://www.comtexnews.com, 1018

"San Antonio Port Led Cargo Operations." Retrieved January 26, 2001 from the World Wide Web: http://www.comtexnews.com, 1191

"Saudia Arabia Dairy Industry." Retrieved September 8, 2000 from the World Wide Web: http://www.tradeport.org, 108

"Savory Snacks Get A Change." Retrieved March 22, 2001 from the World Wide Web: http://www.euromonitor.com, 321

Screen Digest, 1294, 1544-1545, 1553, 1558, 1566

"Seeking a New Strategic Homebase." Retrieved October 17, 2000 from the World Wide Web: http://www.cior.com, 1316

"Shipbuilding Industry." Retrieved January 3, 2001 from the World Wide Web: http://www.usatrade.gov, 1046

Sing Tao Daily, 1423

Site Selection, 1212

"Skin Care Cosmetics." Retrieved October 27, 2000 from the World Wide Web: http://www.mac.doc.gov, 549

Slovenian Business Report, 8

Snapshots Industry Profile, 480, 573, 1078, 1088-1090, 1100

Soap & Cosmetics, 501-504, 518, 526, 543, 545, 566, 588-589, 604-605, 608, 617

"Soft Drink Alert." Retrieved April 14, 2000 from the World Wide Web: http://www.just-drinks.com, 137

Solid State Technology, 457, 756, 764, 942, 949

"Solid Wood Products." Retrieved January 1, 2001 from the World Wide Web: http://www.ffas.usda.gov, 71

"Some Toy Facts and Figures." Retrieved September 8, 2000 from the World Wide Web: http://www.batr.co.uk, 1131

South American Business Information, 199, 223, 262, 283, 328, 334, 339, 342, 364, 401, 467, 485, 525, 534, 584, 647, 680, 736, 833, 861, 894, 1070, 1197, 1419

South China Morning Post, 914-915, 1205

Soybean Digest, 19-20

"Spaghetti Westerners." Retrieved April 11, 2001 from the World Wide Web: http://www.grocersreview.co.nz, 329

"Spain: Bottled Water Report." Retrieved September 1, 2000 from the World Wide Web: http://ffas.usda.gov, 276

"Spain: Prosthesis-Orthopedic Medical Equipment." Retrieved September 19, 2000 from the World Wide Web: http://www.tradeport.org, 1092

"Spain: Soft Drinks Report." Retrieved September 1, 2000 from the World Wide Web: http://ffas.usda.gov, 290

"Spanish Retail Revolution." Retrieved October 17,

2000 from the World Wide Web: http://www.cior.com, 1332

Sporting Goods Business, 674, 1152

Star Tribune, 1102

"Stationery and Office Supplies." Retrieved May 16, 2001 from the World Wide Web: http://www.tradeport.org, 1154

Stores, 1335

Straits Times, 41, 818

"Summary of Mining Statistics." Retrieved June 18, 2001 from the World Wide Web: http://www.nma.org, 43-44, 48, 55, 704

"Sun Rise, Sun Set, Sun Sales." Retrieved January 26, 2000 from the World Wide Web: http://www.exposemagazine.com, 623

Sunday Times, 715

Super Marketing, 91, 114, 509

"Sweden Retail Food Sector." Retrieved September 1, 2000 from the World Wide Web: http://www.ffas.usda.gov, 1326

"Swedish Truck Market." Retrieved February 20, 2001 from the World Wide Web: http://ww.usatrade.gov, 1017

"Swimming Pools." by STAT-USA, National Trade Data Bank, 72

"Switzerland: Franchising and Optical Glasses." Retrieved September 19, 2000 from the World Wide Web: http://www.tradeport.org, 1106

Tea & Coffee Trade Journal, 315

TechWeb, 778

Telephony, 1247

Test & Measurement World, 965

Textil-Wirtschaft, 365, 1346, 1371

Textile Asia, 24

"Textile Flooring." Retrieved May 17, 2001 from the World Wide Web: http://www.usatrade.gov, 1166

Textile India Progress, 767

Textile Industries, 366

Textile World, 368, 758

Tire Business, 666

"Tobacco Report." Retrieved December 1, 2000 from the World Wide Web: http://ffas.usda.gov, 351

Today's Refinery, 59

"Top 100." Retrieved February 2, 2001 from the World Wide Web: http://www.bishopinc.com, 834, 943, 967

Training, 1264

Travel Agent, 1176

Travel Retailer International, 3

Travel Trade Gazette U.K. & Ireland, 1199, 1213, 1540

"Truck Market." Retrieved February 1, 2001 from the World Wide Web: http://www.usatrade.gov, 1020

"Turkey: Roofing and Siding Materials." Retrieved September 19, 2000 from the World Wide Web: http://www.tradeport.org, 12

"Turkish's Delight." Retrieved March 23, 2001 from the World Wide Web: http://www.just-food.com, 1342

TV International, 1288, 1295-1298

"TV Shopping Market." Retrieved January 3, 2001 from the World Wide Web: http://www.usatrade.gov, 1393

"UK Audio Equipment." Retrieved January 11, 2001 from the World Wide Web: http://www.clearlybusiness.com, 873

"UK Bread and Rolls." Retrieved January 11, 2001 from the World Wide Web: http://www.clearlybusiness.com, 131, 195

"UK Car Brakes." Retrieved January 11, 2001 from the World Wide Web: http://www.clearlybusiness.com, 1025

"UK Cleaning Appliances." Retrieved January 11, 2001 from the World Wide Web: http://www.clearlybusiness.com, 860

"UK Contract Cleaning." Retrieved January 12, 2001 from the World Wide Web: http://www.clearlybusiness.com, 1490

"UK Denture Care." Retrieved January 11, 2001 from the World Wide Web: http://www.clearlybusiness.com, 571

"UK Dishwashing Product." Retrieved January 11, 2001 from the World Wide Web: http://www.clearlybusiness.com, 500

"UK Dog Food." Retrieved January 11, 2001 from the World Wide Web: http://www.clearlybusiness.com, 185

"UK Endodontics." Retrieved January 12, 2001 from the World Wide Web: http://www.clearlybusiness.com, 1098

"UK Furniture Polish." Retrieved January 11, 2001 from the World Wide Web: http://www.clearlybusiness.com, 535

"UK Furniture." Retrieved January 12, 2001 from the World Wide Web: http://www.clearlybusiness.com, 390

"UK Garden Supplies." Retrieved January 12, 2001 from the World Wide Web: http://www.clearlybusiness.com, 649

"UK Government Console Power Drives Leisure Market." Retrieved July 3, 2001 from the World Wide Web: http://www.library.northernlight.com, 1511

"UK Kitchen Furniture." Retrieved January 11, 2001 from the World Wide Web: http://www.clearlybusiness.com, 391, 394

"UK Level Measurement Instruments." Retrieved January 11, 2001 from the World Wide Web: http://www.clearlybusiness.com, 1071

"UK Lip Care." Retrieved January 11, 2001 from the World Wide Web: http://www.clearlybusiness.com, 567

"UK Luggage." Retrieved January 12, 2001 from the World Wide Web: http://www.clearlybusiness.com, 683, 1391

"UK Nail Make-Up." Retrieved January 12, 2001 from the World Wide Web: http://www.clearlybusiness.com,

"UK Nail Make-Up." Retrieved January 12, 2001 from the World Wide Web: http://www.clearlybusiness.com, 568

"UK Natural Cheese." Retrieved January 12, 2001 from the World Wide Web: http://www.clearlybusiness.com, 94

"UK Oil and Gas Automation." Retrieved January 12, 2001 from the World Wide Web: http://www.clearlybusiness.com, 741

"UK Passenger Railways." Retrieved January 12, 2001 from the World Wide Web: http://www.clearlybusiness.com, 1172

"UK Personal Care Appliances." Retrieved Janaury 11, 2001 from the World Wide Web: http://www.clearlybusiness.com, 862

"UK Power Tools." Retrieved January 11, 2001 from the World Wide Web: http://www.clearlybusiness.com, 717, 1146

"UK Rail Freight." Retrieved January 12, 2001 from the World Wide Web: http://www.clearlybusiness.com, 1173

"UK Scouring Products." Retrieved January 11, 2001 from the World Wide Web: http://www.clearlybusiness.com, 536

"UK Snack Nuts." Retrieved January 12, 2001 from the World Wide Web: http://www.clearlybusiness.com, 224, 319

"UK Toothbrushes." Retrieved January 12, 2001 from the World Wide Web: http://www.clearlybusiness.com, 1163

"UK Truck Rental." Retrieved janaury 11, 2001 from the World Wide Web: http://www.clearlybusiness.com, 1535

"UK Writing Instruments." Retrieved January 12, 2001 from the World Wide Web: http://www.clearlybusiness.com, 1155-1156

"UK: Europe Loses its Fizz." Retrieved October 23, 2000 from the World Wide Web: http://www.just-drinks.com, 232

"Ukraine Confections Sector." Retrieved November 3, 2000 from the World Wide Web: http://www.usatrade.gov, 211

The Unesco Courier, 15

Upside, 809

Urethanes Technology, 466, 1029-1030

USA TODAY, 16, 213, 286, 353, 443, 1272, 1301, 1464, 1517, 1586

Valor Economico, 18, 87, 97, 497, 1440

Variety, 1549-1551, 1556, 1560-1563

"Verdict on Footwear 2000." Retrieved September 28, 2000 from the World Wide Web: http://www.verdictonline.co.uk, 1368

"Vertical Systems Group Announces Top 3 Leatherboards." Retrieved February 24, 2000 from the

World Wide Web: http://www.businesswire.com, 937

Vietnam Investment Review, 1447

"Vitamins Market." Retrieved April 3, 2001 from the World Wide Web: http://www.usatrade.gov, 476

Wall Street Journal, 57, 62, 65, 81, 182, 242, 284-285, 289, 483, 645, 701, 709, 819, 902, 912, 916-917, 929, 947, 987, 1006, 1011, 1021, 1063, 1104, 1135, 1185, 1201, 1211, 1227, 1245, 1278-1279, 1305, 1363, 1386, 1425, 1427, 1438, 1494, 1497, 1534, 1537

WARD's Auto World, 830, 1026

WARD's Automotive International, 995-996, 1001, 1004-1005, 1007, 1009

Warsaw Business Journal, 103, 180, 1313

Washington Post, 1114

Washington Technology, 1512

"Where Wal-Mart Leads, Will Home Depot Follow." Retrieved October 17, 2000 from the World Wide Web: http://www.cior.com, 1315

"Who Sells Toys." Retrieved September 8, 2000 from the World Wide Web: http://www.batr.co.uk, 1388

Wired, 22, 774, 1507

Wirtschaftswoche, 261, 592, 892, 1044, 1054, 1057, 1107, 1118, 1139, 1141-1143, 1145, 1147, 1397

World Mining Equipment, 748

World Poultry, 34-36, 38

"World Rail Market Outlook." Retrieved April 20, 2000 from the World Wide Web: http://www.transit-center.com, 1174

"World Soft Drink Market." Retrieved Apriul 26, 2000 from the World Wide Web: http://www.just-drinks.com, 282

"World Toy Facts and Figures." Retrieved October 31, 2000 from the World Wide Web: http://www.toy-icti.org, 1128, 1136, 1390

"Worldwide Printer Shipments Surpass 71 Million Units." Retrieved March 24, 2000 from the World Wide Web: http://www.businesswire.com, 815

"Worldwide Video Software Markets." Retrieved October 2, 2000 from the World Wide Web: http://www.screendigest.com, 1567

"Wound Management." Retrieved February 5, 2001 from the World Wide Web: http://www.clearlybusiness.com, 1080

WWD, 548, 1120, 1253

WWS, 1186

Yellow Pages & Directory Report, 1487

Ziegelindustrie, 691

Original Sources

1999 Holway Report, 810
2000 Global State of Industry Report, 378
ABN AMRO Securities Ltd., 1436
A.C. Nielsen, 77, 91, 93, 97, 102, 114, 123, 146, 148-149,
  151, 166, 169, 173, 175, 193, 214, 263, 266, 269,
  279-280, 283-284, 301, 305, 308, 310, 329, 333-334, 339,
  345, 410, 419, 590, 1165, 1288, 1290, 1338, 1350, 1470
A.C. Nielsen EDI/Filmsource, 1549-1551, 1556
Access Asia, 118
Accordis, 471
ActivMedia Research, 6
A.D. Little, 491
Adefa, 1015
Africa News Service, 302
Agfa, 87
Agri-food and Veterinary Authority, 41
Aiful Corp., 1422
AIK/Home Living, 389, 395
Air Cargo Management Group, 1181
AirConnex, 1212
Airports Council International, 1206
Al-Bayan, 31
Alimentos Procesados, 78
Altadis, 359-360
Altera Corp., 953
AMA Research, 379
AmCham News, 1266
American Association of Port Authorities, 1192-1193
American Resort Development Association, 1467
AMI-Partners Inc., 1252
Anatel, 1234
Anfavea, 1015
Anima, 726
APS Financial Corporation, 888
Aptindo, 165
Argentine Secretariat of Agriculture, 81
ARL, 446
The Art Newspaper, 1586
Arthur Andersen, 62
Asia Pulse, 905
Asian Economic News, 1050
Asiaweek, 1333
Association for Manufacturing Technology, 750
Association of German Electric Utilities, 1305
Association of National Automobile Manufacturers, 1015
Association of the Cigarette Industry, 351
Asssociation of Motor Vehicle Importers-Representatives,
  1002
Ata Invest, 434
Audit Bureau of Circulations, 440-442

Audits & Surveys Worldwide, 1328
Australian Bureau of Statistics, 1049
Automotive Industry Data, 983-984
Automotive Quarterly Review, 987
Banc of America Securities, 484
Banco de Espana, 1424
Bancorp Piper Jaffray, 1102
Bank of Finland, 1403
Bank of Greece, 1409
The Banker, 1405, 1408, 1424
BARB, 1291, 1294
Baseline, 902
BBE, 1142
BCN Industry Research Group, 782
BCP, 1429
Bear, Stearns & Co., 62
Beijing Youth Daily, 845, 849, 854, 872, 883
Bell-Garde, 340
Berlitz Japan Inc. survey, 1584
Best's Insight, 1445
Beverage Digest, 285, 289, 296-297
Beverage Marketing Corp., 282
Bishop Associates, 943
Bloomberg Financial Markets, 7
Boeing, 1042, 1205, 1543
Boeing World Air Cargo Forecast 2000-2001, 1203
Boss Economic Information, 435
Boston Consulting Group, 1194
BP Statistical Review of World Energy, 54
BRE Unternehmensberatung, 592
British Phonographic Industry, 895-896
British Video Association, 1375
Brook Hunt, 701
BSH, 841
Bundesverband Wassersportwirtschaft, 1044
Bureau National Interprofessional du Cognac, 261
Business Communications Co., 67
Business Wire, 1572
Businessworld, 1003
BV Jewellereee, 1118
BVI, 1430
Cahners In-Stat, 946, 955
Cahners Research, 826
Cameron & Stuart, 641
Canadean, 231-232
Candean New Perspectives in Europe: The Europe Beer
  Report, 249
Canon Singapore, 827
CAP Ventures, 760
CCFA, 1000
CCIDnet.com, 1524
CCR, 247, 1343

PLACE NAMES INDEX

This index shows global regions, political entities, states and provinces, regions within countries, and cities. The numbers that follow listings are entry numbers; they are arranged sequentially so that the first mention of a place is listed first. The index shows references to more than 210 places.

PRODUCTS, SERVICES, AND ISSUES INDEX

This index shows, in alphabetical order, references to products, services, and issues covered in *World Market Share Reporter*, 5th Edition. More than 1,260 terms are included. Terms include subjects not readily categorized as products and services, including such subjects as *crime* and *welfare*. The numbers that follow each term refer to entry numbers and are arranged sequentially so that the first mention is listed first.

Products, Services, and Issues Index

Products, Services, and Issues Index

COMPANY INDEX

The more than 3,570 companies and institutions in this book are indexed here in alphabetical order. Numbers following the terms are entry numbers. They are arranged sequentially; the first entry number refers to the first mention of the company in *World Market Share Reporter*. Although most organizations appear only once, some entities are referred to under abbreviations in the sources and these have not always been expanded. Company names that begin with initials are listed in two forms: initials first and last name first. Thus *H. Bauer* appears as *H. Bauer* and also as *Bauer, H.*

Marks & Spencer, 675, 1172, 1334, 1336, 1362-1364, 1366-1367, 1370
Marktkauf/dixi (AVA), 1316
Marriott, 1464
Mars Inc., 178, 185, 208-209, 218, 1485
Marsh & McLennan Cos. Inc., 1454
Martin-Baker Aircraft Company, 1038
Martinet, 337
Marudai Food, 85
Maruha, 79
Maruha Petfood, 183
Maruhan Corporation, 1573
Marui, 1337
Marutaka Iryo, 373
Maruti Udyog, 1003
MasterCard, 1419
Masterfoods, 180, 183-184
Matalan, 1362
Matif, 1434
Matsui Securities Co., 1436
Matsushita, 841, 917
Matsushita Battery Industrial Co., 975-976
Matsushita Communication Industrial Co., 906
Matsushita Electric Industrial Co., 775, 836, 850, 856, 876, 882, 886, 897, 962, 971, 979
Matsushita Electric Works, 386, 692, 720, 1083
Matsuzakaya, 1331, 1337
Mattel, 1127
Matubara Bussan, 1573
Maus Freres, 1383
Maxell, 801
Maxima, 1116
Maxtor, 809
Maxwell House, 309
Maytag, 841
Mazda, 994, 1008, 1020
Mazda Rental Lease, 1538
MBK (French sub. Of Yamaha), 1052
MBM, 13
MBNA, 1488
MCC/Verbatim, 801
McCann-Erickson, 1472, 1474, 1482-1483
McCann-Erickson Advertising, 1471
McCann-Erickson Athens, 1477
McCann-Erickson Deutschland, 1476
McCann-Erickson Guangming, 1473
McCann-Erickson Italiana, 1478
McCann-Erickson Kenya, 1480
McDonald's, 105, 1379-1380, 1383, 1463
McDonnell Douglas, 1034
McGraw-Hill, 445
McIntosh Donald, 80
McKinsey & Company, 1598

MCL Saatchi & Saatchi, 1480
MD Foods, 88, 109
MD Helicopters, 1036
MDI, 1459
Mead, 406
Meadow Lea Foods, 149
Media Price, 1393
MediaRing, 1268
MediChem, 490
Mediterranean Shipping Co., 1187
Mediterraneo, 1382
Medtronic, 1095, 1101-1102
Mega, 1289
Mega Rubber Fac., 671
Meggit, 1071
Meias Scalina, 367
Meiji, 219
Meiji Milk Products, 92, 106-107, 112, 134
Meiji Seika Kaisha, 208
Meinl, 1330, 1351
Melitta, 532
MEMC, 765, 961
Memtek, 801
Menasco, 1039
Mentor Graphics, 960
MEPC, 1458
Mer de sable, 1579
Mercadona, 1332, 1348
Mercedes-Benz, 985, 1000, 1018-1020, 1062, 1535
Mercer Consulting Group, 1598
Merck, 486, 488
Merck KGaA, 453
Merck Sharp & Dohme, 495
Merkur, 1383
Merrill Lynch, 1417, 1425-1427, 1432, 1534
Messer, 460-461
Messier Bugatti, 1040
Messier Dowty, 1039
Metalor, 1096
Metcash, 1344
Methode, 943
Metro AG, 1330, 1335, 1346, 1356, 1376
Metropolitan Bank, 1416
Metropolitan Life Insurance, 1438
Metropolitan Museum, 1586
Metropolitan Opera, 1569
Metrosel, 913
Metsa-Serla Group, 399
Metsa-Serla Group + Modo Paper, 397-398
Meyer, 724
MFI, 390
Miami Tank, 72
MiasNebel Plant, 388

Sorriso, 584
Sotec, 790
South African Breweries, 249
Southern Securities, 1433
Southwest Medical Devices, 1097
Soyo, 813
SP 'Rassakazovo-Invest, 681
Spar Group, 861, 1326, 1351
Sparkassen, 1430
Spartan Chile, 1489
SPC, 123
Spencer Stuart, 1600
Sportsbrands S.A., 1144
Spot Thompson, 1477
Springer & Jacoby, 1476
Sprinturf, 1169
Sriboga, 165
SSG, 1383
Sta-Rite, 72
Staedtler, 1155
Stafford Miller, 577, 579
Stagecoach, 1175
Stakis, 1578
Standa, 1325
Standard Chartered Bank Group, 1413, 1423
Stanley, 1578
Star, 903, 1194, 1289
Star Alliance, 1201
Star Cruises, 1218
Starbucks, 234
Starkey, 1103
Starsem/TsSKB, 1061
Startel, 1238
State Bureau of Nonferrous Metals Industry, 701
Statoil, 1360
Steinway Musical Instruments, 1123
Ster Century multiplex, 1562
Ster-Kinbekor, 1564
Steradent, 571
Sterlitamak PKO, 681
STI Semiconductor, 1495
Stilnel, 831
Stinol, 853
STMicroelectronics, 945, 949-950, 954, 958, 963-964
Stockmann/Sesto, 1326
Stolt-Nielsen, 1189
Stone, 403
Stora Enso, 384, 398-400
Stora Enso + Consolidated Papers, 397
Storebrand, 1443
Storehouse, 1172
Storteboom, 35
Storz, 1078

Stradbroke, 348
Strahov Stadium, 1570
Stream, 1295
Strintzis, 1190
Stryker, 1084-1085, 1091, 1093-1094
Stryker/Howmedica, 1086
Stryker/Howmedica/Osteonics, 1087
Stylo, 675
Subaru, 994, 998
Subway, 1380, 1463
Suez, 1441
Sugar Lady, 1378
Sul America, 1440
Sultan Center, 1355
Sulzer, 1084-1086, 1088, 1091
Sulzer Textile, 757-758
Sumikei, 706
Sumitomo Bank, 1406
Sumitomo Chemical, 453, 455, 457, 469, 644, 1170
Sumitomo Credit Service Co., 1421
Sumitomo Electric Industries Ltd., 900
Sumitomo Heavy Industries Ltd., 762
Sumitomo Life, 1438
Sumitomo Metal Industries, 699, 765, 961
Sumitomo Osaka Cement, 690
Sumitomo Rubber Industries, 672
Sun, 780, 804-805, 808, 1519
Sun Aluminum, 706
Sun Chemical, 654
Sun Microsystems, 800, 803, 1520-1521
Sun Valley, 38
Sunipet, 386
Sunrise, 184, 1079
Sunstar, 576
Suntory, 78
Suntory Ltd., 246, 292
Supasnaps, 1531
Superbois, 1317
Superdrug, 1402
Superior TeleCom, 709
Supermercados El Corte Ingles, 1348
Supermercados Sabeco, 1348
Supervib, 1311
Surgival, 1092
Suzuki, 991, 1049-1054, 1064
Suzuki Shutter Kogyo, 383
Suzumo Machinery, 761
SV-Service, 1383
Svensk Filmindustri, 1553
Svitoch Lviv Confectionery, 211
SVW, 999
Swan, 724
Swatch Group, 1117-1118

Company Index

BRANDS INDEX

This index shows more than 990 brands—including names of periodicals, television programs, popular movies, and other "brand-equivalent" names. Each brand name is followed by one or more numerals; these are entry numbers; they are arranged sequentially, with the first mention of the brand shown first.

Brands Index

Brands Index

APPENDIX I

SIC COVERAGE

This appendix lists the Standard Industrial Classification codes (SICs) included in *World Market Share Reporter*. Page numbers are shown following each SIC category; the page shown indicates the first occurrence of an SIC. *NEC* stand for not elsewhere classified.

Appendix I - Industrial Classifications

Appendix I - Industrial Classifications

ISIC COVERAGE

This appendix lists the International Standard Industrial Classification Codes (ISICs) included in *World Market Share Reporter,* 5th Edition. Entries in the body of the book are arranged according to the Standard Industrial Classification (SIC) system of the U.S. Department of Commerce. Products may be located using either the SIC Coverage listing beginning on page 531 or the Products, Services, and Issues Index beginning on page 471.

0111	Growing of cereals and other crops nec	1542	Manufacture of sugar
0112	Growing of vegetables, horticultural specialties and nursery products	1543	Manufacture of cocoa, chocolate, and sugar confectionery
0113	Growing of fruits, nuts, beverage and spice crops	1544	Manufacture of macaroni, noodles, couscous and similar farinaceous products
0122	Other animal farming; production of animal products nec	1549	Manufacture of other food products nec
0130	Growing of crops combined with farming of animals (mixed farming)	1550	Manufacture of beverages
0150	Hunting, trapping and game propagation including related service activities	1551	Distilling, rectifying and blending of spirits; ethyl alcohol production from fermented materials
0200	Forestry, logging, and related service activities	1552	Manufacture of wines
1110	Extraction of crude petroleum and natural gas	1553	Manufacture of malt liquors and malt
1120	Service activities incidental to oil and gas extraction excluding surveying	1554	Manufacture of soft drinks; production of mineral waters
1310	Mining of iron ores	1600	Manufacture of tobacco products
1320	Mining of non-ferrous metal ores, except uranium and thorium ores	1711	Preparation and spinning of textile fibers; weaving of textiles
1429	Other mining and quarrying nec	1722	Manufacture of carpets and rugs
1511	Production, processing and preserving of meat and meat products	1723	Manufacture of cordage, rope, twine and netting
1512	Processing and preserving of fish and fish products	1729	Manufacture of other textiles nec
1514	Manufacture of vegetable and animal oils and fats	1730	Manufacture of knitted and crocheted fabrics and articles
1520	Manufacture of dairy products	1810	Manufacture of wearing apparel, except fur apparel
1531	Manufacture of grain mill products	1911	Tanning and dressing of leather
1532	Manufacture of starches and starch products	1912	Manufacture of luggage, handbags and the like, saddlery and harness
1533	Manufacture of prepared animal feeds	1920	Manufacture of footwear
1540	Manufacture of other food products	2010	Sawmilling and planning of wood
1541	Manufacture of bakery products		

2021	Manufacture of veneer sheets; manufacture of plywood, laminboard, particle board and other panels and boards
2022	Manufacture of builders' carpentry and joinery
2029	Manufacture of other products of wood; manufacture of articles of cork, straw and plaiting materials
2101	Manufacture of pulp, paper, and paperboard
2102	Manufacture of corrugated paper and paperboard and of containers of paper and paperboard
2109	Manufacture of other articles of paper and paperboard
2210	Publishing
2211	Publishing of books, brochures, musical books, and other publications
2212	Publishing of newspapers, journals, and periodicals
2213	Publishing of recorded media
2221	Printing
2230	Reproduction of recorded media
2320	Manufacturer of refined petroleum products
2411	Manufacture of basic chemicals, except fertilizers and nitrogen compounds
2413	Manufacture of plastics in primary forms and of synthetic rubber
2421	Manufacture of pesticides and other agro-chemical products
2422	Manufacture of paints, varnishes, and similar coatings, printing ink and mastics
2423	Manufacture of pharmaceuticals, medicinal chemicals, and botanical products
2424	Manufacture of soap and detergents, cleaning and polishing preparations, perfumes and toilet preparations
2429	Manufacture of other chemical products nec
2430	Manufacture of man-made fibers
2511	Manufacture of rubber tires and tubes; retreading and rebuilding of rubber tires
2519	Manufacture of other rubber products
2520	Manufacture of plastic products
2610	Manufacture of glass and glass products
2691	Manufacture of non-structural non-refractory ceramic ware
2693	Manufacture of structural non-refractory clay and ceramic products
2694	Manufacture of cement, lime and plaster
2696	Cutting, shaping, and finishing of stone
2699	Manufacture of other non-metallic mineral products nec
2710	Manufacture of basic iron and steel
2720	Manufacture of basic precious and non-ferrous metals
2732	Casting of non-ferrous metals
2811	Manufacture of structural metal products
2891	Forging, pressing, stamping and roll-forming of metal; powder metallurgy
2893	Manufacture of cutlery, hand tools, and general hardware
2899	Manufacture of other fabricated metal products nec
2911	Manufacture of engines and turbines, except aircraft, vehicle and cycle engines
2912	Manufacture of pumps, compressors, taps, and valves
2913	Manufacture of bearings, gears, gearing and driving elements
2919	Manufacture of other general purpose machinery
2921	Manufacture of agricultural and forestry machinery
2922	Manufacture of machine-tools
2923	Manufacture of machinery for metallurgy
2924	Manufacture of machinery for mining, quarrying and construction
2925	Manufacture of machinery for food, beverage, and tobacco processing
2926	Manufacture of machinery for textile, apparel and leather production
2927	Manufacture of weapons and ammunition
2929	Manufacture of other special purpose machinery
2930	Manufacture of domestic appliances nec
3000	Manufacture of office, accounting, and computing machinery
3110	Manufacture of electric motors, generators and transformers
3120	Manufacture of electricity distribution and control apparatus
3140	Manufacture of accumulators, primary cells, and primary batteries
3150	Manufacture of electric lamps and lighting equipment
3190	Manufacture of other electrical equipment nec
3210	Manufacture of electronic valves and tubes and other electronic components
3220	Manufacture of television and radio transmitters and apparatus for line telephony and line telegraphy
3311	Manufacture of medical and surgical equipment and orthopedic appliances
3312	Manufacture of instruments and appliances for measuring, checking, testing, navigating, and other purposes, except industrial process control equipment

3313	Manufacture of industrial process control equipment
3320	Manufacture of optical instruments and photographic equipment
3330	Manufacture of watches and clocks
3410	Manufacture of motor vehicles
3420	Manufacture of bodies (coachwork) for motor vehicles; manufacture of trailers and semi-trailers
3430	Manufacture of parts and accessories for motor vehicles and their engines
3511	Building and repairing of ships
3530	Manufacture of aircraft and spacecraft
3591	Manufacture of motorcycles
3592	Manufacture of bicycles and invalid carriages
3610	Manufacture of furniture
3691	Manufacture of jewelry and related articles
3692	Manufacture of musical instruments
3693	Manufacture of sports goods
3694	Manufacture of games and toys
3699	Other manufacturing nec
4010	Production, collection, and distribution of electricity
4100	Collection, purification, and distribution of water
4520	Building of complete constructions or parts thereof; civil engineering
4530	Building installation
4540	Building completion
5020	Maintenance and repair of motor vehicles
5030	Sale of motor vehicle parts and accessories
5050	Retail sale of automotive fuel
5122	Wholesale of food, beverages, and tobacco
5139	Wholesale of other household goods
5150	Wholesale of machinery, equipment, and supplies
5211	Retail sale in non-specialized stores with food, beverages, or tobacco predominating
5219	Other retail sale in non-specialized stores
5220	Retail sale of food, beverages, and tobacco in specialized stores
5231	Retail sale of pharmaceutical and medical goods, cosmetic and toilet articles
5232	Retail sale of textiles, clothing, footwear, and leather goods
5233	Retail sale of household appliances, articles, and equipment
5234	Retail sale of hardware, paints and glass
5239	Other retail sale in specialized stores
5251	Retail sale via mail-order houses
5260	Repair of personal and household goods
5510	Hotels; camping sites and other provision of short-stay accommodation
6010	Transport via railways
6021	Other scheduled passenger land transport
6023	Freight transport by road
6110	Sea and coastal water transport
6210	Scheduled air transport
6300	Supporting and auxiliary transport activities; activities of travel agencies
6301	Cargo handling
6302	Storage and warehousing
6303	Other supporting transport activities
6304	Activities of travel agencies and tour operators; tourist assistance activities nec
6411	National post activities
6420	Telecommunications
6519	Other monetary intermediation
6592	Other credit granting
6600	Insurance and pension funding, except compulsory social security
6601	Life insurance
6602	Pension funding
6603	Non-life insurance
6711	Administration of financial markets
6712	Security dealing activities
6720	Activities auxiliary to insurance and pension funding
7020	Real estate activities on a fee or contract basis
7111	Renting of land transport equipment
7129	Renting of other machinery and equipment n.e.c.
7130	Renting of personal and household goods n.e.c.
7210	Hardware consultancy
7240	Database activities
7250	Maintenance and repair of office, accounting and computing machinery
7290	Other computer related activities
7320	Research and experimental development on social sciences and humanities (SSH)
7414	Business and management consultancy activities
7421	Architectural and engineering activities and related technical consultancy
7430	Advertising
7491	Labor recruitment and provision of personnel
7492	Investigation and security activities
7494	Photographic activities
7499	Other business activities nec

Appendix I - Industrial Classifications

7513	Regulation of and contribution to more efficient operation of business	9000	Sewage and refuse disposal, sanitation, and similar activities
7522	Defense activities	9120	Activities of trade unions
7523	Public order and safety activities	9191	Activities of religious organizations
8010	Primary education	9211	Motion picture and video production and distribution
8030	Higher education	9212	Motion picture projection
8511	Hospital activities	9214	Dramatic arts, music, and other arts activities
8512	Medical and dental practice activities	9232	Museums activities and preservation of historical sites and buildings
8519	Other human health activities	9241	Sporting activities
		9249	Other recreational activities

HARMONIZED CODE COVERAGE

This appendix lists the Harmonized Code Classifications (HCs) included in *World Market Share Reporter,* 5th Edition. Entries in the body of the book are arranged according to the Standard Industrial Classification (SIC) system of the U.S. Department of Commerce. Products may be located using either the SIC Coverage listing beginning on page 531 or the Products, Services, and Issues Index beginning on page 471.

01	Live animals
02	Meat and edible meat offal
03	Fish and crustaceans, mollusks and other aquatic invertebrates
04	Dairy produce; birds' eggs; natural honey, edible products of animal origin, not elsewhere specified or included
06	Live trees and other plants; bulbs, roots, and the like; cut flowers and ornamental foliage
07	Edible vegetables and certain roots and tubers
08	Edible fruits and nuts; peel of citrus fruits or melons
09	Coffee, tea, mate, and spices
12	Oil seeds and oleaginous fruits; miscellaneous grains, seeds, and fruits; industrial or medicinal plants; straw and fodder
15	Animal or vegetable fats and oils and their cleavage products; prepared edible fats; animal or vegetable waxes
16	Preparation of meat, of fish, or of crustaceans, mollusks, or other aquatic invertebrates
17	Sugars and sugar confectionery
18	Cocoa and cocoa preparations
19	Preparations of cereals, flour, starch or milk; bakers' wares
20	Preparations of vegetables, fruits, nuts, or other parts of plants
21	Miscellaneous edible preparations
22	Beverages, spirits, and vinegar
23	Residues and waste from the food industries; prepared animal feed
24	Tobacco and manufactured tobacco substitutes
25	Salt; sulfur; earths and stone; plastering materials, lime and cement

26	Ores, slag, and ash
27	Mineral fuels, mineral oils and products of their distillation; bituminous substances; mineral waxes
28	Inorganic chemicals; organic or inorganic compounds of precious metals, of rare-earth metals, of radioactive elements, or of isotopes
29	Organic chemicals
30	Pharmaceutical products
31	Fertilizers
32	Tanning or dyeing extracts; tannins and their derivatives; dyes, pigments, and other coloring matter; paints and varnishes; putty and other mastics; inks
34	Soaps; organic surface-active agents; washing preparations; lubricating preparations; artificial waxes; prepared waxes; polishing or scouring preparations; candles and similar articles; modeling pastes; "dental waxes," and dental preparations with a basis of plaster
37	Photographic or cinematographic goods
39	Plastics and articles thereof
40	Rubber and articles thereof
41	Raw hides and skins (other than furskins) and leather
42	Articles of leather; saddlery and harness; travel goods, handbags and similar containers; articles of animal gut (other than silkworm gut)
44	Wood and articles of wood; wood charcoal
48	Paper and paperboard; articles of paper pulp, of paper, or of paperboard
49	Printed books, newspapers, pictures, and other products of the printing industry; manuscripts, typescripts, and plans
50	Silk

57	Carpets and other textile floor coverings
61	Articles of apparel and clothing accessories, knitted or crocheted
62	Articles of apparel and clothing accessories, not knitted or crocheted
63	Other made-up textile articles; needle craft sets; worn clothing and worn textile articles; rags
64	Footwear, gaiters and the like; parts of such articles
68	Articles of stone, plaster, cement, asbestos, mica. or similar materials
70	Glass and glassware
71	Natural or cultured pearls, precious or semiprecious stones, precious metals; metals clad with precious metal, and articles thereof; imitation jewelry; coin
72	Iron and steel
73	Articles of iron or steel
74	Copper and articles thereof
76	Aluminum and articles thereof
80	Tin and articles thereof
81	Other base metals; cermets; articles thereof
82	Tools, implements, cutlery, spoons and forks, of base metal; parts thereof of base metal
83	Miscellaneous articles of base metal
84	Nuclear reactors, boilers, machinery and mechanical appliances; parts thereof
85	Electrical machinery and equipment and parts thereof; sound recorders and reproducers, television image and sound recorders and reproducers, and parts and accessories of such articles
87	Vehicles, other than railway or tramway rolling stock, and parts and accessories thereof
88	Aircraft, spacecraft, and parts thereof
89	Ships, boats, and floating structures
90	Optical, photographic, cinematographic, measuring, checking, precision, medical or surgical instruments and apparatus; parts and accessories thereof
91	Clocks and watches and parts thereof
92	Musical instruments; parts and accessories of such articles
94	Furniture; bedding, mattresses, mattress supports, cushions and similar stuffed furnishings; lamps and lighting fittings, not elsewhere specified or included; illuminated signs; illuminated nameplates and the like; prefabricated buildings
95	Toys, games, and sports equipment; parts and accessories thereof
96	Miscellaneous manufactured articles
97	Works of art, collectors' pieces and antiques

APPENDIX II

ANNOTATED SOURCE LIST

The following listing provides the names, publishers, addresses, telephone and fax numbers (if available), and frequency of publications for the primary sources used in *World Market Share Reporter*.

Accountancy Age, 32-34 Broadwick Street, London W1A 2HG.

Adhesives Age, Communication Channels, 6255 Barfield Rd, Atlanta, GA 30328, *Telephone:* (404) 256-9800.

Advertising Age, Crain Communications, Inc., 220 E. 42nd St., New York, NY 10017, *Telephone:* (212) 210-0725, *Fax:* (212) 210-0111, *Published:* weekly.

Advertising Age International, Crain Communications, Inc., 220 E. 42nd St., New York, NY 10017, *Telephone:* (212) 210-0725, *Fax:* (212) 210-0111, *Published:* weekly.

Aerospace America, Advanstar Communications, Inc., 7500 Old Oak Blvd., Cleveland, OH 44130-3343, *Published*: monthly.

Aftenposten, Oslo, Norway, *Telephone*: +47 2286 3000.

Air Cargo World, Journal of Commerce, Inc., Two World Trade Center, 27th Floor, New York, NY 10048, *Telephone:* (212) 837-7000, *Fax:* (212) 837-7035.

Air Transport Intelligence, Telephone: +44 0 20 8652 3914.

Airline Business, Reed Aerospace, Quadrant House, Sutton, Surrey, SM2 5AS, U.K.

Airline Industry Information, P.O. Box 475, Coventry CV1 1ZB, U.K.

American Banker, American Banker Inc., 1 State St., New York, NY 10023, *Telephone:* (212) 408-1480, *Fax:* (212) 943-2984. *Published:* Mon.-Fri.

American Ink Maker, MacNair-Dorland Co., 445 Broadhollow Rd., Melville, NY 11747, *Telephone:* (212) 279-4456. *Published:* monthly.

American Machinist, 1300 9th St, Cleveland, OH 44114-1503, *Telephone:* (216) 696-7000, *Fax:* (216) 931-9524.

American Metal Market, Capital Cities Media Inc., 825 7th Avenue, New York, NY 10019, *Telephone:* (800) 360-7600. *Published:* daily, except Saturdays, Sundays, and holidays, *Price:* $560 per year (U.S., Canada, and Mexico).

American Shipper, Howard Publications Inc., 33 South Hogan Street, P.O. Box 4728, Jacksonville, FL 32201, *Telephone:* (904) 365-2601. *Published:* monthly, *Price:* $35 per year; $3 per single copy.

America's Network, 201 Sandepointe Ave., Suite 600, Santa Ana, CA 92707, *Telephone:* (714) 513-8602.

Amusement Business, BPI Communications Inc., Box 24970, Nashville, TN 37202, *Telephone:* (615) 321-4250, *Fax:* (615) 327-1575. *Published:* weekly.

Appliance, Dana Chase Publications Inc., 1110 Jorie Blvd., CS 9019, Ste. 203, Hinsdale, IL 60521, *Telephone:* (708) 990 - 3484, *Fax:* (708) 990 - 0078, *Published:* monthly, *Cost:* $60.

Appliance Manufacturer, Business News Publishing Co., 755 W. Big Beaver Rd., Ste. 1000, Troy, MI 48084-4900, *Telephone:* (313) 362-3700, *Fax:* (313) 244-6439. *Published:* monthly.

Asiaweek, 20th Floor, Trust Tower, 58 Johnston Road, Wanchal, Hong Kong, *Published:* weekly.

Assembly, Hitchcock Publishing Co., 191 S. Gary Ave., Carol Stream, IL 60188, *Telephone:* (708) 665 - 1000, *Fax:* (708) 462 - 2225.

Australian Financial Review, *Telephone*: (02) 9282 1815, *Fax:* (02) 9282 2484.

Automatic Merchandiser, Johnson Hill Press, 1233 Janesville Ave., Fort Atkinson, WI 53538, *Telephone:* (414) 563-6388, *Published:* monthly.

Automotive Engineering, SAE Magazines, 400 Commonwealth Drive, Warrendale, PA 15096-0001.

Automotive Industries, Capital Cities/ABC/Chilton Co., Chilton Way, Radnor PA 19089, *Telephone*: (215) 964 - 4255, *Fax:* (215) 964 - 4251.

Automotive News, Crain Communications Inc., 380 Woodbridge, Detroit, MI 48207 *Telephone:* (313) 446-6000, *Fax:* (313) 446-0347.

Autoparts Report, Intenational Trade Services, *Published:* weekly.

AV Multimedia Producer, 701 Westchester Ave, White Plains NY, 10604, *Published*: monthly.

Aviation Week & Space Technology, McGraw-Hill, Inc., 1221 Avenue of the Americas, New York, NY 10020, *Telephone:* (212) 512-2294, *Fax:* (212) 869-7799. *Published:* weekly.

Bangkok Post, Post Publishing Company Ltd., Bankok Post Building, 136 Na Ranong Road, Office Kosa Road, Klong Toei, Bangkok, Thailand 10110, *Published:* daily.

The Banker, Greystoke Place, Feteer Lane, London, England EC4A IND, *Telephone:* (071) 405-6969, *Published:* monthly.

The BBI Newsletter, AHC, P.O. Box 740058, Atlanta, GA 30374.

Best's Review, A.M. Best Co. Inc., Ambest Rd., Oldwick, NJ 08858, *Telephone:* (908) 439-2200, *Fax:* (908) 439-3363. *Published:* monthly.

Beverage Industry, Advanstar Communications, Inc., 7500 Oald Oak Blvd., Cleveland OH 44130, *Telephone:* (216) 243-8100, *Fax:* (216) 891-2651. *Published:* monthly, *Price:* $40 per year.

Beverage World, Keller International, 150 Great Neck Rd., Great Neck, NY 11021.

Billboard, BPI Communications, 1515Broadway, 14th Floor, New York, NY 10036, *Telephone*: (212) 764-7300, *Fax:* (212) 536-5358.

Body Fashions Intimate Apparel, Advanstar Communications, 7500 Old Oak Blvd., Cleveland, OH 44130, *Telephone:* (212) 826-2839.

Boersen, P.O. Box 11 09 32, 60044 Frankfort am Main, Dusseldorf Strabe 16, 60329.

Brand Strategy, *Telephone*: +44 (0)20 7943 8173, *Published:* monthly.

Broadcasting & Cable TV Intl., Cahners Publishing, 1705 DeSales Street NW, Washington D.C. 20036, *Telephone:* (800) 554-5729.

Budapest Business Journal, Szent Istvan Korut III en, 1055 Budapest Hungary.

Business 2.0, Thomas Mellon, Suite 305, San Francisco, CA 94134.

Business Central Europe, The Economist Bldg, 111 W. 57th St., New York, NY 10019, *Telephone:* (212) 541-5730, *Fax:* (212) 541-9378

Business Communications Review, BCR Enterprises, Inc., 950 York Rd., Hinsdale, IL 60521, *Telephone:* (800) 227-1324. *Published:* monthly.

Business Economics, 1233 20th Street, NW, Ste. 505, Washington D.C. 20036, *Telephone:* (202) 463-6223.

Business in Russia, UI Profsoyuznaya 73, Moscow 117342, *Telephone:* (7-095) 330-15-68, *Telex*: 4-4 741.

Business India, Living Media India, Connaught Place, New Delhi, India 11001, *Published:* weekly.

Business Insurance, Crain Communications, Inc., 740 N. Rush St., Chicago IL 60611, *Published:* monthly.

Business Times, Times House, 7 Bahadurshah Zafar Marg., New Delhi 110 002, India.

Business Today, Living Media India Ltd., Connaught Place, New Delhi 11001, *Telephone:* 3315801-4, *Fax:* 3313180.

Business Week, McGraw-Hill Inc., 1221 Avenue of the Americas, New York, NY 10020. *Published:* weekly, *Price:* U.S.: $46.95 per year; Canada: $69 CDN per year.

BusinessWorld, BusinessWorld Publishing Corp., 95 Balete Drive Extension, New Manila, Quezon City, *Telephone:* 727-0091 to 97, 411-0268 to 85, *Published:* weekdays.

C&EN, Amercan Chemical Society, Dept. L-0011, Columbus OH 43210, *Telephone:* (800) 333-9511, *Fax:* (614) 447-3776.

Cable Europe, Phillips Business Information, *Published*: biweekly.

Campaign, 22 Lancaster Gate, London W2, UK, *Telephone:* 081-943 5000, *Published*: weekly.

Candy Industry, Advanstar Communications, 7500 Old Oak Blvd, Cleveland OH 44130.

Cards International, Faulkner & Grey, 11 Penn Plaza, 17th Fl, New York, NY 10001.

Cards Technology, Faulkner & Grey, 11 Penn Plaza, 17th Fl, New York, NY 10001.

Carpets & Floorcovering Review, PPA, Queens House, 28 Kingsway, London WC2B 6JR, *Telephone*: 020 7400 7540.

Ceramic Industry, Business News Publishing Co., 5900 Harper Road, Suite 109, Solon, OH 44139, *Telephone:* (216) 498-9214, *Fax:* (216) 498-9121. *Published:* monthly, *Price:* U.S.: $53 per year; Mexico: $63; Canada: $66.71 (includes postage & GST).

Chain Leader, Reader Services, 1350 E. Touhy Ave. P.O. Box 5080, Des Plaines, IL 60017-5080.

Checkout, 1-3 Dungar Terrace, Dun Laoghaire, company Dublin.

Chemical Business, McGraw-Hill Inc., 1221 Avenue of the Americas, New York, NY 10020, *Telephone:* (212) 512-2000. *Published:* monthly.

Chemical Market Reporter, Schnell Publishing Co., Inc., 80 Broad St., New York, NY 1004-2203, *Telephone:* (212) 248-4177, *Fax:* (212) 248-4903, *Published:* weekly.

Chemical Week, Chemical Week Associates, P.O. Box 7721, Riverton, NJ 08077-7721, *Telephone:* (609) 786-0401, *Published:* weekly, except four combination issues (total of 49 issues), *Price:* U.S.: $99 per year; Canada: $129 per year. Single copies $8 in U.S. and $10 elsewhere.

Chemist & Druggist, Pharmacy UK, *Telephone:* 00 377-97704175.

Appendix II - Annotated Source List

Chemistry & Industry, 15 Belgrave Square, London SW1X 8PS, U.K., *Telephone:* 0171 235 3681, *Fax*: 0171 235 9140.

Chemistry in Britain, 15 Belgrave Square, London SW1X 8PS, U.K., *Telephone:* 0171 235 3681, *Fax*: 0171 235 9140.

Chicago Tribune, 435 N. Michigan Ave., Chicago, IL 60611, *Telephone:* (312) 222-3232. *Published:* daily.

China Business Review, China Business Forum, 1818 N St., NW Ste 500, Washington D.C. 20036, *Telephone:* (202) 429-0340, *Fax:* (202) 775-2476, *Published:* 6x/yr.

China Chemical Industry News, Telephone: 86-10-62389210/62002059.

China Chemical Market Newsletter, Telephone: 86-10-62389210/62002059.

China Economic Review, Alain Charles Publishing, Alain Charles House, Wilfred Street, London SW1E 6PR, U.K.

China's Foreign Trade, 28 Donghouxiang, Anwai, Dongcheng District, 100710, Beijing, Chian, Telephone: (010) 64246856/64216661-1101.

The Christian Science Monitor, Christian Science Publishing Society, One Norway St., Boston, MA 02115, *Telephone:* (800) 456-2220, *Published:* daily, except weekends and holidays.

Civil Engineering, ASCE, 1801 Alexander Bell Dr., Restoin, VA 20191.

Client Server News, G2 Computer Intelligence, 323 Glen Cove, Sea Cliff, NY 11579, *Telephone:* (516) 759-7025.

CMR Focus, Schnell Publishing Co., Inc., 80 Broad St., New York, NY 1004-2203, *Telephone:* (212) 248-4177, *Fax:* (212) 248-4903, *Published:* weekly.

Communications International, Nelson Publishing, 2504 N Tamiami Tr, Nelson Bldg., Nokomis, FL 34275, Telephone: (813) 966-9521, Fax: (813) 966-2590, Published: monthly.

Community Pharmacy, Pharmacy UK, *Telephone:* 00 377-97704175.

Computer Reseller News, CMP Media Inc., One Jericho Plaza, Jericho, New York 11753, *Published:* $199; Canada $224

Computerwoche, Brabanter Str. 4, 80805 Munchen, *Telephone:* (089) 36086-175 (-170), *Fax:* (089) 36086-175 (-170).

Computerworld, P.O. Box 2043, Marion, OH 43305-2403, *Telephone:* (800) 669-1002, *Published*: weekly.

Computimes, Balai Berita 31, Jalan Riong 59100, Kuala Lumpur, Malaysia.

Contract Journal, Quadrant House, Sutton, Surrey, SM2 5AS.

Control Engineering, 1350 E. Touhy Ave., P.O. Box 5080, Des Plaines, IL 60017-5080, *Telephone:* (847) 635-8800, *Fax*: (847) 390-2744, *Published*: monthly.

*Converting Magazine,*Delta Communications Inc., 455 N. Cityfront Plaza Drive, Chicago, IL 60614, *Telephone*: (312) 222-2000, *Fax:* (312) 222-2026, *Published*: monthly, *Cost*: $25.

Crain's Detroit Business, Crain Communications, 1400 Woodbridge, Detroit, MI 48207-3187, *Telephone:* (313) 446-6000, *Published:* weekly.

Cranes Today, Telephone: +44 (0) 1322-394519, *Fax:* +44 (0) 1322 276487.

Dagens Naeringslivr, Gjorwellsgatan 30, Stockholm, Sweden, *Publsihed:* daily.

Daily Record, 1 Central Quay, Glasgow G3 8DA.

The Daily Telegraph, 1 Canada Aquare, Canary Wharf, London E14 5AR, *Published:* daily.

Dairy Foods, Gorman Publishing Co., 8750 W. Bryn Mawr Ave., Chicago, IL 60062, *Telephone:* (312) 693-3200. *Published:* monthly, except semimonthly in Aug.

Dairy Markets Weekly, Agra Europe Ltd, 80 Calverley Road, Tunbridge Wells, Kent, TN1 2UN, England, *Telephone*: +44 1892-533813.

Dalel Street Journal, Lawrence & Mayo House, 2nd Fl, 276, BN Road, Fort, Bombay 400001.

Dealernews, Advanstar Communications, 1700 E Dyer Rd. Ste 250, Santa Ana, CA 92705.

Der Spiegel, Brandstwiete 19, 20457 Hamburg.

Design Week, Centaur Comm., 50 Poland Street, London W1V 4AX, U.K.

Detroit Free Press, Knight-Ridder, Inc., 1 Herald Plaza, Miami, FL 33132, *Telephone:* (305) 376-3800, *Published:* daily.

Detroit News, 615 West Lafayette, Detroit, MI, *Telephone:* (313) 222-2283.

Distribucion Actualidad, Ip Mark, *Telephone:* 913 159845.

DIY Week, Morgan Grampian, U.K., *Published:* monthly.

Duty Free News International, Euromoney, Nestor House, Playhouse Yard, London EC4V 5EX, UK.

E&MJ, Maclean Hunter Publishing Co., 29 Wacker Dr., Chicago, IL 60606, *Fax:* (312) 726-2574, *Published:* monthly.

E-Media Professional, Online Inc., 462 Danbury Road, Wilton, CT 06897-2126, *Published:* monthly, *Cost:* $55; $98 corporate.

Economic Times, Times House, 7 Bahadurshah Zafar Marg., New Delhi 110 002, India.

The Economist, The Economist Bldg, 111 W. 57th St., New York, NY 10019, *Telephone:* (212) 541-5730, *Fax:* (212) 541-9378, *Published:* weekly, *Cost:* $110; $3.50 per single issue.

EDN, Cahners Business, 275 Washington, Newton, MA 02458.

Educational Marketer, Simba Information, P.O. Box 4234, 11 River Bend Drive South, Stanford, CT 06907-0234.

Egg Industry, Watt Publishing Co., 122 S. Wesley Ave., Mount Morris, IL 61054-1497, *Telephone:* (815) 734-4171, *Fax:* (815) 734-4201, *Published:* bimonthly.

Ekonom, Dobrovskeho 25, 170 55 Praha 7, Ceska Republika.

Ekonomicke Zpravodajstvi, Telephone: (02) 2410 2206.

El Cronista, Laprida 5054 Planta Baja A, Santa Fe, Argentina,*Telephone*: 0342 - 4521906.

El Diario, Calle Loayza, number 118, *Telephone:* (591) (2) 332233.

El Mercurio, Cassilla 13-D Stigo, Madrid.

El Mundo, Calle Pradillo, 42 28002, Madrid, *Telephone:* (34) 91586 4800.

Electrical & Radio Trading, dmg Business Media, Queensway, Redhill Surrey, England RH1 1QS.

Electronic Business, CMP Publications Inc., 8773 South Ridgeline Blvd., Highlands Ranch, CO, 80126-2329, *Telephone:* (516) 562-5000, *Fax:* (516) 562-5409, *Published:* monthly.

Electronic Business Asia, CMP Publications Inc., 8773 South Ridgeline Blvd., Highlands Ranch, CO, 80126-2329, *Telephone:* (516) 562-5000, *Fax:* (516) 562-5409, *Published:* monthly.

Electronic Buyers News, CMP Media, 600 Community Drive, Manhasset, NY 11030.

Electronic Engineering Times, CMP Media 600 Community Drive, Manhasset, NY 11030.

Electronic Media, 488 Madison Ave., New York, NY 10022.

Electronic News, Electronic News Publishing Corp., 488 Madison Ave., New York, NY 10022, *Telephone:* (212) 909-5924, *Published:* weekly, except last week of Dec.

Electronic Times, CMP Media, 600 Community Drive, Manhasset, NY 11030.

The Engineer, Quadrant House, Sutton, Surrey, SM2 5AS.

ENR, McGraw-Hill Inc., Fulfillment Manager, ENR, P.O. Box 518, Highstown, NJ 08520, *Telephone:* (609) 426-7070 or (212) 512-3549, *Fax:* (212) 512-3150, *Published:* weekly, *Price:* U.S.: $89 per year; Canada: $75 per year. Single copies $5 in U.S.

Estrategia, Luis Carrera 1289, Vitacura, Santiago, Chile, *Fax:* +56+2+6556125.

Euromoney, Euromoney Publications PLC, Nestor House, Playhouse Yard, London EC4V 5EX UK, *Published:* monthly.

Europe Energy, European Information Service, *Published:* weekly.

The European, P.O. Box 14, Harold Hill, Romford RM3 8EQ, England, *Published:* weekly, *Cost:* $135 yr.

European Banker, Lafferty Publications, *Published:*weekly.

European Cosmetic Markets, Wilmington Publishing, 6-14 Underwood St, London N1 7JQ, U.K., *Telephone:* +44 (0) 20 7549-8626, *Fax:* +44 (0) 20 7549-8622.

European Report, European Information Service, *Published:* weekly.

European Rubber Journal, Crain Communications Ltd., 20-22 Bedford Row, London WC1R 4EW, UK *Telephone:* (071) 831-9511, *Fax:* (071) 430-2176, *Published:* monthly, except August.

Far Eastern Economic Review, 181-185 Gloucester Road, Centre Point, Hong Kong, *Published:* weekly.

Farbe & Lack, Vincentz Verlag, P.O. Box 62 47, D-30062, Hannover, *Fax:* +49 (511) 9910-299.

Feedstuffs, Miller Publishing Co., 191 S. Gary Ave., Carol Stream Il 60188, *Published:* weekly, *Cost:* $109 yr.

Financial Express, C-6 Qutab Institutional Area, New Delhi, 110 016, India.

Financial Times, FT Publications Inc., 14 East 60th Street, New York, NY 21002, *Telephone:* (212) 752-4500, *Fax:* (212) 319-0704, *Published:* daily, except for Sundays and holidays, *Cost:* $425.

Floor Focus, 28 Old Stone Hill, Pound Ridge, NY 10576, *Telephone:* (914) 764-0556.

Food Ingredients and Analysis International, Leatherhead Foods, Randalls Rd, Leatherhood KT22 7RY, UK.

Food Institute Report, Food Institit, Elwood Park, New Jersey.

Food Manufacture, Miller Freeman, U.K., *Published*: monthly.

Food Technology, Institute of Food Technologists, 221 N LaSalle St., Ste. 300, Chicago IL 60601, *Telephone:* (312) 782-8424, *Fax:* (312) 782-8348.

Forbes, Forbes, Inc., P.O. Box 10048, Des Moines, IA 50340-0048, *Telephone:* (800) 888-9896, *Published:* 27 issues per year, *Price:* U.S.: $54 per year; Canada: $95 per year (includes GST).

Forest Products Journal, Forest Products Society, 2801 Marshall Ct, Madison, WI 53705-2295.

Fortune, Time Inc., Time & Life Building, Rockefeller Center, New York, NY 10020-1393, *Published:* twice monthly, except two issues combined into a single issue at year-end, *Price:* U.S.: $57 per year; Canada: $65 per year.

Frankfurter Allgemeine, D-60267, Frankfurt, Germany.

Frozen and Chilled Foods, DMG Business Media, *Published:* monthly.

Gazeta Mercantil, Rua Engenheiro Francisco Pitta Brito, 125, CEP 04753-080, Sao Paulo, Brasil.

Glass International, DMG World Media, Equitable house, Lyon Road, Harrow HA1 2EW.

Global Cosmetic Industry, Advanstar Communications, 270 Madison Ave., New York, NY 10016.

Globe and Mail, 444 Front St. W., Toronto, ON, Canada M5V 2S9, *Telephone:* (416) 585-5000, *Fax:* (416) 585-5085, *Published:* Mon.-Sat. (Morn.).

The Grocer, The Mews, Eden Road, Dun Laoghaire, Dublin.

The Guardian, Guardian Newspapers Ltd., 119 Farrington Road, London EC1R, *Telephone:* 0171-278-2332, *Published:* daily.

Hart's E&P, Hart Publications, 4545 Post aka Place, Suite 210, Houston, TX 77027.

Health Industry Today, Business World, 5330 S. Roslyn, Ste 400, Englewood. CO 80111.

Helicopter News, P&A House, Alma Road, CHESHAM, Bucks, HP 5 3HB, U.K.

The Hindu, 859-860 Anna Salai, Channai, 600002, India, *Telephone*: 91-044-8413344.

Hollywood Reporter, 5055 Wilshire Blvd., 6th Fl, Los Angeles, CA 90036, *Telephone:* (213) 525-2000.

Horizont, B2B On-Line GmbH, Mainzer Landstr. 251, D-60326 Frankfurt, Main.

Hospodarske Noviny, Drenova 34, 821 02 Bratislava, *Telephone*: (07) 4342 5451, *Fax:* (07) 4342-5452.

Hotels, Cahners Publishing Co., 1350 Touhy Ave., P.O. Box 5080, Des Plaines, IL 60017-5080, *Telephone:* (708) 635-8800, *Fax:* (708) 635-6856.

Household and Personal Products Industry, Rodman Publishing, 17 S. Franklin Turnpike, Box 555, Ramsey, NJ 07446, *Telephone:* (201) 825-2552, *Fax:* (201) 825-0553, *Published:* monthly.

Housewares, Faversham House, 232a Addington Road, South Croydon, Surrey CR2 *LE.

IEEE Magazine, 345 E 47th Str, New York, NY 10017.

Implement & Tractor, Farm Press Publications, P.O. Box 1420, Clarksdale, MS 38614.

In-Store Marketing, Centaur Communications, 50 Poland Street, London W1V 4AX, U.K.

Indonesian Commercial Newslatter, PT Data Consult, Divisi EDP, *Telephone:* (021) 3904711-3901880.

Industrial Ceramics, Cahners Publishing Company, 275 Washington Street, Newton, MA 02158, *Telephone:* (617) 964-3030, *Published:* monthly.

The Industry Standard, Internet Industry Publishing, 315 Pacific Ave., San Francisco, CA 94111-1701, *Telephone:* (415) 733-5400, *Fax:* (415) 733-5401, *Published:* weekly.

Info Chimie, SETE, 4 rue de Seze, 75009 Paris, France.

Infoworld, Infoworld Publishing Co., 155 Bovet Rd., Ste. 800, San Mateo, CA 94402, *Telephone:* (415) 572-7341, *Published:* weekly.

Ink World, 70 Hilltop Road, Ramsey NJ 07446.

Instrument Business Outlook, Strategic Directions, 6242 Westchester Pkway, Suite, 100, Los Anglees, CA 90045, *Telephone:* (310) 641-4982.

Interavia, Swissair Centre, 31 Route de l'Aeroport, P.O. Box 437, 1215 Geneva 15, Switzerland, Switzerland, *Telephone:* (902) 788-2788, *Published:* monthly, Price: $128 per year.

International Herald Tribune, 850 Third Avenue, 10th, New York, NY 10022, *Telephone:* (212) 752-3890, *Fax:* (212) 755-8785.

Internet Week, CMP Media Inc., 600 Community Drive, Manhasset, NY 11030, *Published:* weekly, *Cost:* free to qualified companies.

Investor's Business Daily, P.O. Box 661750, Los Angeles, CA 90066-8950, *Published:* daily, except weekends and holidays, *Cost:* $128 per year.

Inzhenernaia Gazeta, Redaksiia Gazety, *Published:* weekly.

Irish Times, 11-15 D'Olier, Dublin, Ireland, *Published:* daily.

Jakarta Post, Gedung Kompas Fl 4, Jl. Gajahmada 110, Jakarta 11140, *Telephone:* (62-21) 260-1777.

Japanscan Food Industry Bulletin, Upper Quinton, Stratford-on-Avon, CV37 8SX, England, *Telephone:* +44 1789-720395.

JETRO Newsletter, Japan External Trade Organization, Toranomon 2-chrome, Minato-ku, Tokyo, 105 Japan.

Journal of Commerce, Journal of Commerce, Inc., Two World Trade Center, 27th Floor, New York, NY 10048, *Telephone:* (212) 837-7000, *Fax:* (212) 837-7035.

Kommersant, East View Publications, 3020 Harbor Lane, Minneapolis, MN 55447.

Korea Herald, 1-12 3-ga Hoehyon-dong, Jung-gu Seoul, CPO Box 6479, Postal Code 100-771

Korea Times, Telephone: (02) 724-2711-1.

Lasers & Optronics, Cahners, 301 Gibraltar Drive, Morris Plains, NJ 07950.

Latin Trade, Freedom Communications Inc., 200 South Bicauyne Blvd., Suite 1150, Miami, FL 33131, *Published:* monthly.

Le Figaro, SA-33 rue Traverrsiere, 92100 Boulogne-Billancourt, Paris, *Published:* daily.

Leather, Polygon Media, Tubs Hill House, Sevenoaks TN13 1BY, England.

Lebensmittel Zeitung, Mainzer Landstr. 251, D-60326 Frankfurt/Main.

Les Echos, 46 Street Boetie, 75381 Paris Cedex, *Telephone:* 01-49-53-6565.

L'Expansion, 482 F Grupe Expansion, 25 Rue Leblanc, F-75842, Paris Cedex 15.

L'Express, 67 Ave. De Wagram, 75017 Paris, Telephone: (1) 47 631211.

Liquid Foods International, Church Hill, Dartford DA2, Great Britain, 7EF.

LSA, 12-14 Rue Mederic, 7509 Paris Cedex 17, *Telephone*: 01-5679-4100.

M Business, CMP Media, 600 Harrison St., San Francisco, CA 94107, *Telephone:* (415) 905-2200.

The Manufacturing Confectioner, The Manufacturing Confectioner Publishing Company, 175 Rock Rd., Glen Rock, NJ 07452, *Telephone:* (201) 652-2655, *Fax:* (201) 652-3419, *Published:* 12 times per year, *Price:* $25 per year, single copies $10 each, except $25 for April and July issues.

Manufacturing Engineering, Society of Manufacturting Engineers, 1 SMA Drive, P.O. Box 930, Dearborn, MI 48121, *Telephone:* (313) 271-1500, *Fax:* (313) 271-2861, *Published:* monthly.

Marine Log, Simmons-Boardman, 345 Hudson St, New York, NY 10014, *Telephone:* (212) 620-7200.

Marketing, Centaur Communications, 50 Poland Street, London W1V 4AX, U.K.

Marketing Magazine, Maclean Hunter Canadian Publishing, P.O. Box 4541, Buffalo, NY 1420-4541, *Telephone:* (800) 567-0444.

Marketing News, American Marketing Assn., 250 S. Wacker Dr., Ste. 200, Chicago, IL 60606-5819, *Telephone:* (312) 993-9517, *Fax:* (312) 993-7540, *Published:* biweekly.

Marketletter, 54-55 Wilton Rd., London 5W1V 1DE, U.K., *Telephone:* +44 (0) 20 7828-7272.

Markt & Technik, Martin-Keller, Str. 10-12, 81829, Munchen.

Med Ad News, Engel Communications, 820 Bear Tavern Ste. 302, West Trenton, NJ 08628, *Telephone:* (609) 530-0044.

Medcal Marketing & Media, CPS Communications, 7200 West Camino, Ste 215, Boca Raton, FL 33433.

Mergers & Acquisitions, Securities Data Publishing, 40 West 57th Street, New York, NY 10019.

Metal Bulletin Monthly, 220 5th Ave., New York, NY 10001, *Telephone:* (212) 213-6202.

Mining Engineering, Society for Mining, Metallurgy and Exploration Inc., 8307 Shafer Parkway, P.O. Box 625002, Littleton, CO 80127, *Telephone:* (303) 973-9550, *Fax:* (303) 973-3845.

Mining Journal, 60 Worship St., London EC2A 2HD U.K., *Telephone:* +44 (0) 20 7216 6060.

Mining Magazine, 220 5th Ave., 19th Fl, New York, NY 10001.

MOCI, LP 2010-75761, Paris Cedex 16, *Telephone:* 01 40 73 33 18.

Modern Casting, American Foundry Society, 505 State St., Des Plaines, IL 60016, *Telephone:* (847) 824-0181.

Modern Materials Handling, 275 Washington St., Newton MA 02458.

Modern Paint & Coatings, Communication Channels Inc., 6255 Barfield Rd., Atlanta GA 30328, *Telephone:* (404) 256-9800, *Fax:* (404) 256-3116, *Published:* monthly.

Modern Plastics, McGraw-Hill, Inc., Attn. Fulfillment Manager, P.O. Box 481, Highstown, NJ 08520, *Telephone:* (800) 525-5003, *Published:* monthly, *Price:* U.S.: $41.75 per year, $62.70 for 2 years, $83.50 for 3 years; Canada:$CDN 53 per year, $CDN 80 for 2 years, $CDN 106 for 3 years.

Moskovskie Novosti, East View Publications, 3020 Harbor Lane, Minneapolis, MN 55447.

Music Business International, 460 Park Ave, 9th Floor, New York, NY 10016, *Telephone:* (212) 378-0482.

Music Trades, P.O. Box 432, 80 West Blvd., Englewood, NJ 07631, *Telephone:* (201) 871-1965, *Fax:* (201) 871-0455, *Published:* monthly.

The Nation, Nation Company, 33 Irving Place, New York, NY 10003, *Telephone:* (212) 209-5400.

National Home Center News, Lebhar-Friedman Inc., 425 Park Ave., New York, NY 10022, *Telephone:* (212) 756-5151.

National Trade Data Bank, STAT-USA, U.S. Department of Commerce, Washington D.C., 20230, *Telephone:* (202) 482-1986, *Fax:* (202) 482-2164.

National Underwriter, The National Underwriter Co., 505 Gest St., Cincinnati, OH 45203, *Telephone:* (800) 543-0874, *Fax:* (800) 874-1916, *Published:* weekly, except last week in December, *Price:* U.S.: $77 per year, $130 for 2 years; Canada: $112 per year, $130 for 2 years.

Network World, Network World Inc., 161 Worcester Rd., Framingham, MA 01701-9172, *Telephone:* (508) 875-6400, *Published:* weekly.

Neu Zuercher Zeitung, Falkenstr. 11, 8021 Zurich, Switzerland, *Telephone:* +41 1 258 1111, *Fax:* +41 1 252 1329.

New Zealand Herald, P.O. Box 32, Auckland, New Zealand, *Telephone:* (09) 379-5050.

New Straits Times, Balai Berita 31, Jalan Riong 59100, Kuala Lumpur, Malaysia.

New York Times, New York Times Co., 229 W. 43rd St., New York, NY 10036, *Telephone:* (212) 556-1234. *Published:* daily.

Newsweek, The Newsweek Building, Livingston, NJ 07039-1666, *Telephone:* (800) 631-1040, *Published:* weekly, *Price:* U.S.: $41.08 per year; Canada: $61.88 per year (send to P.O. Box 4012, Postal Station A, Toronto, ON M5W 2K1).

Nikkei Weekly, 1-9-5 Otemachi, Chiyoda-ku, Tokyo 100-66 Japan.

Nonwovens Industry, 70 Hilltop Road, Third Floor, Ramsey, NJ 07446, *Telephone:* (201) 825-2552, *Fax:* (201) 825-0553.

Nutraceuticals World, 70 Hilltop Road, Ramsey, NJ 07446, Telephone: (201) 825-2552.

The Observer, Guardian Newspapers Ltd., 119 Farrington Road, London ECR1R ER, *Telephone:* (0171) 278-2332, Published: sundays.

Oil & Gas Journal, PennWell Publishing Co., P.O. Box 2002, Tulsa OK 74101, *Telephone:* (800) 633-1656, *Published:* weekly.

Packaging Magazine, 245 W. 17th St., New York, NY 10011.

Paperboard Packaging, Advanstar Communications Inc., 131 West First Street, Duluth, MN 55802, *Telephone:* (218) 723-9477, *Fax:* (218) 723-9437, *Published:* monthly, *Price:* U.S.: $39 per year, $58 for 2 years; Canada: $59 per year, $88 for 2 years.

Pais, Miguel Yeste 40, 28037 Madrid, *Telephone:* (91) 337 8200.

Paris Match, BP 01, 77115 Blandy-les-Tours.

Password, Koninklijke Philipe Electronics, *Published:* monthly.

PC Magazine, 28 E 28th Street, New York, NY 10016-7930, *Telephone:* (212) 503-5255, *Published:* weekly.

PC Week, Ziff-Davis Publishing Company L.P., Customer Service Dept., PC WEEK, P.O. Box 1770,

Riverton, NJ 08077-7370, *Telephone:* (609) 461-210, *Published:* weekly, except combined issue at year-end, *Price:* U.S.: $160 per year; Canada/Mexico: $200 per year.

Philadelphia Inquirer, Philadelphia Newspapers Inc., 400 N. Broad St., Box 8263, Philadelphia, PA 19101, *Telephone:* (215) 854-2000, *Published:* daily.

Photonics Spectra, Laurin Publishing Company Inc., Berkshire Common, P.O. Box 4949, Pittsfield, MA 01202, *Telephone*: (413) 499-0514.

PIMA's Papermaker, 2400 East Oakston Street, Arlington Heights, IL 60005.

Pit & Quarry, Edgell Communications, 7500 Old Oak Bld, Cleveland, OH 44130.

Points de Vente, 84 databases of Sebastopol, 75003 Paris.

PR Week, PR Publications, 220 Fifth Ave., New York, NY 10001, *Telephone*: (212) 532-9200, *Fax:* (212) 532-9200.

Prague Business Journal, Sokolska 120 00 Prague, Czech Republic.

Prepared Foods, Cahners Publishing Company, 44 Cook St., Denver, CO 80217-3377, *Telephone:* (303) 388-4511, Published: monthly, except semimonthly in April, *Price:* qualified manufacturers - $41 per year; all others in U.S. - $84 per year.

Presse, A-1015 Wien, Parkring 12a, *Telephone*: +43 (1 514 140)

Publishers Weekly, Cahners Publishing Company, ESP Computer Services, 19110 Van Ness Ave., Torrance, CA 90501-1170, *Telephone:* (800) 278-2991, *Published:* weekly, *Price:* U.S.: $129 per year; Canada: $177 per year (includes GST).

Quick Frozen Foods International, E.W. Williams Publications Co., 2125 Center Ave., Ste. 305, Fort Lee, NJ 07024, *Telephone:* (201) 592-7007, *Fax:* (201) 592-7171, *Published:* quarterly.

RCR, RCR Publications, 777 East Speer Blvd., Denver CO 80203.

Reinforced Plastics, International Newsletters, P.O. Box 133, Witney, Oxon OX29 6ZH, U.K.

Reproduire, Case postal 41072, Levis, Quebec G6W 7N1.

Research Studies, BCC Inc., 25 Van Zant, Norwalk, CT 06855-1781.

Research Studies, Freedonia Group, 767 Beta Drive, Cleveland, OH 44143, Telephone: (440) 684-9600.

Restaurant Business, Penton Publishing, 1100 Superior Ave, Cleveland, OH 44114, *Telephone:* (216) 696-7000.

Retail Banker International, P&A House, Alma Road, CHESHAM, Bucks, HP 5 3HB, U.K., *Telephone:* +44 (1494) 771930.

Retail Week, P&A House, Alma Road, CHESHAM, Bucks, HP 5 3HB, U.K., *Telephone:* +44 (1494) 771930.

Rubber & Plastics News, Crain Communications, 1725 Merriman Road, Ste. 300, Akron, OH 44313, *Telephone:* (330) 836-9180, *Fax:* (33) 836-1005, *Published:* weekly.

Rubber World, 1867 W. Market St., PO Box 5485, Akron, OH 44313, *Telephone:* (216) 864-2122, *Fax:* (216) 836-1005.

Screen Digest International, EMAP Media Ltd., 33-39 Bowling Green Lane, London EC1R ODA, *Telephone*: 44 (0)171 505 8056/8060, *Published*: weekly.

Site Selection, Conway Data, 40 Technology Park, Norcross, GA 30092-9990.

Slovenian Business Report, GV, Dunajska 5, Ljublijana, Slovenia, *Telephone:* 386 61 13212 30, *Fax:* 386 61 1321 012.

Snapshots Industry Profile, 5 Dryden Street, London UK WC2E 9NB,Telephone: +44 (020) 7829 8408.

Soap & Cosmetics, 455 Broad Hollow Road, Melville, NY 11747-4722, *Published:* monthly.

Solid State Technology, PennWell Publishing Company, 1421 S. Sheridan Road, Tulsa, OK 74112, *Telephone:* (603) 891-0123.

South China Morning Post, Morning Post Bldg., Tong Chong St., P.O. Box 47, Quarry Bay, Hong Kong, *Telephone:* (5) 620161.

Soybean Digest, American Soybean Association, 540 Maryville Centre Drive, P.O. Box 411007, Saint Louis, MO 63141-1007, *Telephone:* (314) 576-2788, *Fax:* (314) 576-2786.

Sporting Goods Business, Gralla Publications, Inc., 1515 Broadway, New York, NY 10036, *Telephone:* (212) 869-1300.

Star Tribune, 425 Portland Ave., Minneapolis, MN 55488, *Telephone:* (612) 673-4000.

Spray Technology & Marketing, Industry Publications, Inc., 389 Passaic Ave., Fairfield, NJ 07004, *Telephone:* (201) 227-5151, *Fax:* (201) 227-921, *Published:* monthly.

Stores, NRF Enterprises Inc., 100 West 31st St., New York, NY 10001, *Published:* monthly, *Price:* U.S./Canada: $49 per year, $80 for 2 years, $120 for 3 years.

The Sunday Times, Times Newspapers, P.O. Box 495, Virginia Street, London E19XY.

Super Marketing, Reed Elsevier Business Publishing, *Published:* biweekly.

Tea & Coffee Trade Journal, Lockwood Trade Journal Co., 130 W. 42nd St., Ste. 2200, New York, NY 10036-7802, *Telephone:* (212) 391-2060, *Fax:* (212) 827-0945, *Published:* monthly, *Price:* $29 per year.

Telephony, Intersec Publishing Corp., 9800 Metcalf, Overland Park, KS 66282-2960, *Published:* monthly.

Test & Measurement World, 275 Washington Street, Newton, MA 02458-1630, *Telephone:* (617) 558-4671.

Textil-Wirschaft, Niederureseler Alleee, 8-10, P.O. Box 6105, 65735 Eschborn, HRB 7518 Frankfurt, *Telephone:* 06196-405-0.

Textile Asia, Tak Yan Commercial Bldg., 11th Fl., 30-32 D'Aguilar St., Hong Kong, *Telephone:* (5) 247467, *Published:* monthly.

Textile India Progress, *Telephone:* 91-22-407 2913, *Fax:* 91-22-407 7875.

Textile Industries, Billian Publishing, 2100 Powers Ferry Rd, Atlanta, GA 30339, *Published:* monthly.

Textile World, Maclean Hunter Publishing Co., Circulation Dept., 29 N. Wacker Dr., Chicago, IL 60606, *Price:* U.S./Canada: $45 per year, $75 for 2 years, $105 for 3 years.

Tire Business, Crain Commincations, Inc., 1725 Merriman Rd., Ste. 300, Akron, OH 44313-5251, *Telephone:* (216) 836-9180, *Fax:* (216) 836-1005.

Today's Refinery, Chemical Week Assocaites, 110 William St., New York, NY 10138, *Telephone:* (212) 621-4900.

Traffic World, Journal of Commerce Inc., 2 World Trade Center, 27th Floor, New York, NY 10048, *Telephone:* (212) 837-7000, *Fax:* (212) 837-7035.

Training, American Society for Training and Development, 1640 King Street, P.O. Box 1443, Alexandria, VA 22313-2043, *Telephone:* (703) 683-8100.

Travel Agent, One Park Avenue, New York, NY 10016, *Telephone:* (212) 951-6600, *Fax*: (917) 326-6360.

Travel Retailer International, P&A House, Alma Road, CHESHAM, Bucks, HP5 3HB, U.K.

Travel Trade Gazette U.K. And Ireland, Genesys, Clarendon House, 125 Shenley Road, Borehamwood, Herts WD6 1AG.

The Unesco Courier, UNESCO, 4611-F Assembly Drive, Lanham MD, 07706-4391, *Telephone:* (301) 459-7666, *Published:* monthly.

Upside, Upside Media Inc., 2015 Pioneer Court, San Mateo, CA 94403, *Telephone:* (650) 377-0950, *Fax:* (650) 377-1962, *Published*: monthly.

Urethane Technology, Crain Communications Inc., 1725 Merriman Rd., Ste. 300, Akron, OH 44313-5251, *Telephone:* (216) 836-9180, *Fax:* (216) 836-1005, *Published:* 6x/yr, Price: $83.

USA TODAY, Gannett Co., Inc., 1000 Wilson Blvd., Arlington, VA 22229, *Telephone:* (703) 276-3400, *Published*: weekdays.

Valor Economico, Brazil, *Published:* daily.

VAR Business, CMP Media Inc., 1 Jericho Plaza A, Jericho NY 11753, *Telephone:* (516) 733-6700, *Published:* weekly.

Variety, 475 Park Ave., South, New York, NY 10016, *Telephone:* (212) 779-1100, *Fax:* (212) 779-0026. *Published:* weekly.

Vietnam Investment Review, 175 Nguyen Thai Hoc St., Hanoi, *Telephone:* (844) 8450537.

Wall Street Journal, Dow Jones & Co. Inc., 200 Liberty St., New York, NY 10281, *Telephone:* (212) 416-2000. *Published:* Mon.-Fri.

WARD's Auto World, Ward's Communications, 28 W. Adams, Detroit, MI 48226, *Telephone:* (313) 962-4456. *Published:* monthly.

WARD's Automotive International, Ward's Communications, 28 W. Adams, Detroit, MI 48226, *Telephone:* (313) 962-4456. *Published:* monthly.

The Warsaw Business Journal, ul Stoneczna 29, 00-789 Warsaw Poland, *Telephone*: (48-22) 646-0575, *Fax*: (48-22) 646-0576.

The Washington Post, The Washington Post, 1150 15th St., N.W., Washington, DC 20071, *Published:* weekly, *Price:* $48 per year.

Washington Technology, Tech News Inc., 1953 Gallows Road, Ste. 130, Vienna, VA 22182.

Wired, 520 3rd St., 4th Fl., San Francisco, CA 94107-1815, Telephone: (415) 276-5000, *Published*: monthly, *Price:* $39.95; Corporate: $80.

Wirtschaftswoche, 4045 Dusseldorf, Postfach 1054, 65 Kasermanstrabe, Germany 67 40213.

World Mining Equipment, 220 5th Ave., 19th Fl, New York, NY 10001.

World Poultry, Misset International, P.O. Box 4, 7000 BA, Doetinchem, the Netherlands, *Telephone:* 31 8340-49562, *Fax:* 31 8340-40515, *Price:* U.S.: $79 per year, $123 for 2 years, $155 for 3 years.

WWD , Fairchild Publications, 7 E. 12th St., New York, NY 10003, *Telephone:* (212) 741-4000, *Fax:* (212) 337-3225. *Published:* weekly.

WWS, World Wide Shipping Guide Inc., 77 Moehring Drive, Blauvelt, NY 10913-2093.

Yellow Pages & Directory Report, Simba Information, P.O. Box 4234, 11 River Bend Drive South, Stanford, CT 06907-0234.

Ziegelindustrie, Bauverlag GmbH, D-65173 Wiesbaden, Germany, Telephone: (0 61 23) 7 00-0.